Routledge International Handbook of Children's Rights Studies

Since the adoption of the UN Convention on the Rights of the Child (1989) children's rights have assumed a central position in a wide variety of disciplines and policies. This handbook offers an engaging overview of the contemporary research landscape for those people involved in the theory and practice of children's rights.

The volume offers a multidisciplinary approach to children's rights, as well as key thematic issues in children's rights at the intersection of global and local concerns. The main approaches and topics within the volume are:

- Law, social work and the sociology of childhood and anthropology
- Geography, childhood studies, gender studies and citizenship studies
- Participation, education and health
- Juvenile justice and alternative care
- Violence against children and female genital mutilation
- Child labour, working children and child poverty
- Migration, indigenous children and resource exploitation

The specially commissioned chapters have been written by renowned scholars and researchers and come together to provide a critical and invaluable guide to the challenges and dilemmas currently facing children's rights.

Wouter Vandenhole holds the UNICEF Chair in Children's Rights – a joint venture of the University of Antwerp and UNICEF Belgium – at the Faculty of Law of the University of Antwerp (Belgium). He is the spokesperson of the Law and Development Research Group and chairs the European Research Networking Programme GLOTHRO. He has published widely on economic, social and cultural rights, children's rights and transnational human rights obligations and is a founding member of the Flemish Children's Rights Knowledge Centre and co-convener of the international interdisciplinary course on children's rights.

Ellen Desmet is a Postdoctoral Fellow at the Law and Development Research Group of the University of Antwerp and the Human Rights Centre of Ghent University (Belgium). Before, she was a research and policy staff member at the Children's Rights Knowledge Centre, and taught anthropology of law at the University of Leuven.

Didier Reynaert is a lecturer in social work at the Faculty of Education Health and Social work of the University College Ghent. He is involved in several research projects in the field of child and youth policy and children's rights. He is member of the board of the Flemish Children's Rights Knowledge Centre. Previously, he worked for the Flemish Children's Rights Coalition, the Child Legal Centre and as a civil servant at the Ministry of the Flemish Community on youth protection.

Sara Lembrechts is full-time staff member at the Children's Rights Knowledge Centre (KeKi), where she is responsible for the collection and dissemination of children's rights research, as well as for policy advice to the Flemish government.

Routledge International Handbook of Children's Rights Studies

*Edited by Wouter Vandenhole, Ellen Desmet,
Didier Reynaert and Sara Lembrechts*

LONDON AND NEW YORK

First published 2015
by Routledge

2 Park Square, Milton Park, Abingdon, Oxon OX14 4RN
711 Third Avenue, New York, NY 10017, USA

First issued in paperback 2017

Routledge is an imprint of the Taylor & Francis Group, an informa business

Copyright © 2015 selection of editorial material, Wouter Vandenhole, Ellen Desmet, Didier Reynaert and Sara Lembrechts; individual chapters, the contributors

The right of Wouter Vandenhole, Ellen Desmet, Didier Reynaert and Sara Lembrechts to be identified as editors of this work has been asserted by them in accordance with sections 77 and 78 of the Copyright, Designs and Patents Act 1988.

All rights reserved. No part of this book may be reprinted or reproduced or utilised in any form or by any electronic, mechanical, or other means, now known or hereafter invented, including photocopying and recording, or in any information storage or retrieval system, without permission in writing from the publishers.

Notice:
Product or corporate names may be trademarks or registered trademarks, and are used only for identification and explanation without intent to infringe.

British Library Cataloguing in Publication Data
A catalogue record for this book is available from the British Library

Library of Congress Cataloging-in-Publication Data
Routledge international handbook of children's rights studies / Edited by Wouter Vandenhole, Ellen Desmet, Dider Reynaert, and Sara Lembrechts.
p. cm.
ISBN 978-1-138-02370-3 (hardback) -- ISBN 978-1-315-76953-0 (ebk)
1. Children's rights. 2. Children--Legal status, laws, etc. I. Vandenhole, Wouter, editor. II. Title: International handbook of children's rights studies.
K639.R68 2015
323.3'52--dc23
2014037888

ISBN: 978-1-138-02370-3 (hbk)
ISBN: 978-1-138-08449-0 (pbk)

Typeset in Bembo
by FiSH Books Ltd, Enfield

Contents

	Contributors	*viii*
	Preface	*xv*
1	Introduction: A critical approach to children's rights *Didier Reynaert, Ellen Desmet, Sara Lembrechts and Wouter Vandenhole*	1

PART I
Disciplinary perspectives   25

2	Children's rights from a legal perspective: Children's rights law *Wouter Vandenhole*	27
3	The Convention on the Rights of the Child: Reflections from a historical, social policy and educational perspective *Eugeen Verhellen*	43
4	Children's rights and childhood studies: From living apart together towards a happy marriage *Bruno Vanobbergen*	60
5	The sociology of childhood and children's rights *Berry Mayall*	77
6	Children's rights from a social work perspective: Towards a lifeworld orientation *Didier Reynaert and Rudi Roose*	94
7	Anthropologists, ethnographers and children's rights: Critiques, resistance and powers *Geraldine André*	112

8   Children's rights: A critical geographic perspective   131
    Stuart C. Aitken

9   Children's rights from a gender studies perspective: Gender,
    intersectionality and the ethics of care   147
    Katrien De Graeve

10 Children's rights and citizenship studies: Re-theorising child citizenship
    through transdisciplinarity from the local to the global   164
    Richard Mitchell

PART II
Selected themes at the intersection of the global and the local   183

11 Children and young people's participation: A critical consideration of
    Article 12   185
    E. Kay M. Tisdall

12 Education and children's rights   201
    Ann Quennerstedt

13 Health and children's rights   216
    Ursula Kilkelly

14 Juvenile justice from an international children's rights perspective   234
    Ton Liefaard

15 The human rights of children in the context of formal alternative care 257
    Nigel Cantwell

16 Violence against children   276
    Gertrud Lenzer

17 Female genital mutilation in Europe from a children's rights perspective 295
    Els Leye and Annemarie Middelburg

18 Child labour, working children and children's rights   316
    Karl Hanson, Diana Volonakis and Mohammed Al-Rozzi

19 The human rights of children in the context of international migration 331
    Pablo Ceriani Cernadas

20 Child poverty in the context of global social development   357
    Francine Mestrum

21 Indigenous children's rights: Opportunities in appropriation and
    transformation   371
    Natasha Blanchet-Cohen

22 Natural resource exploitation and children's rights   387
    Ellen Desmet and José Aylwin

23 Conclusions: Towards a field of critical children's rights studies 412
    Ellen Desmet, Sara Lembrechts, Didier Reynaert and Wouter Vandenhole

    Index   *430*

Contributors

Stuart C. Aitken is Professor of Geography and June Burnett Chair at San Diego State University. He directs the Center for Interdisciplinary Studies of Young People and Space (ISYS). Dr. Aitken's research interests include critical social theory, qualitative methods, children, young people, families and communities. His recent books include *The Ethnopoetics of Space and Transformation: Young People's Engagement, Activism and Aesthetics* (Ashgate 2014), *The Fight to Stay Put* (Verlag 2013), *Young People: Border Spaces and Revolutionary Imaginations* (Routledge 2011), *Qualitative Geographies* (Sage 2010) and *The Awkward Spaces of Fathering* (Ashgate 2009). Stuart has published over 200 papers in academic journals and edited book collections. He is a past editor of *The Professional Geographer* and *Children's Geographies: Advancing Interdisciplinary Understanding of Younger People's Lives*. Stuart has worked for the United Nations on issues of children's rights, qualitative methods, migration and dislocation.

Mohammed Al-Rozzi is a PhD student at the University of Fribourg, Switzerland. Before commencing his doctoral studies, Mohammed completed his undergraduate studies at Bethlehem University, where he earned a BSc in Occupational Therapy. In 2011, he completed his Master's degree in Childhood Studies at the University of Edinburgh, UK. Mohammed has worked with many international non-governmental organizations and UN agencies, including Mercy Corps, Terre des Hommes, the Norwegian Refugee Council, World Vision and UNICEF. Through his work experience, Mohammed has developed extensive multidisciplinary expertise in child protection and participation issues, education in post-conflict settings and psychosocial wellbeing at times of crisis. He is particularly interested in researching children in the Majority World. His research interests include child labour, juvenile justice and education policy.

Géraldine André is a Postdoctoral Researcher for the National Fund for Scientific Researcher in Belgium. She is currently visiting fellow at LSE, and in Belgium, she is affiliated to Pôle Sud and the Lasc at the University of Liège. Her PhD on working class youth and vocational education was published in 2012 (PUF, 2012). Her postdoctoral research focuses on the case of African child workers in small-scale artisanal mining. She seeks to analyse the effects on the legislation of children's rights on the evolution of processes of socialization in Sub-Saharan Africa.

José Aylwin is a Lawyer specialized in human rights in Latin America, with special focus on indigenous peoples' rights. With studies at the Faculty of Law of the University of Chile in Santiago (1981) and at the School of Law of the University of British Columbia (Canada), where he obtained a Master in Laws degree (1999), he has researched and published for different academic and human rights institutions internationally. He acted as Director of the Instituto de Estudios Indígenas of the Universidad de la Frontera in Temuco, Chile (1994–1997). He currently acts as Co-director of the Observatorio Ciudadano (Citizens'Watch), an NGO aimed at documenting, promoting and protecting human rights in Chile. He is part of the board of directors of the North-South Institute in Canada and of the National Council of the National Institute for Human Rights of Chile. He teaches Indigenous Peoples' Rights at the School of Law of the Universidad Austral de Chile, in Valdivia, Chile.

Natasha Blanchet-Cohen is an Associate Professor in the Department of Applied Human Sciences at Concordia University, Montreal. Her research centres on community youth development with a focus on rights-based approaches to programmes and services, culture, and eco-citizenship, particularly as it relates to immigrant and indigenous young people. She is interested in the opportunities and limitations for immigrant and indigenous young people in being change agents in their schools, homes, and communities, as well as the perspectives of youth in providing for rights-based and culturally-responsive services and programmes. She is also interested in developmental evaluation as a way of creating space to engage young people and communities to assess their own realities and use this knowledge to inform future action. As an interdisciplinary and engaged scholar, her participation in national and international initiatives have contributed to building the capacity of human ecologies to positively support the quality of young peoples' lives.

Nigel Cantwell is a Geneva-based international consultant on child protection policies who has been working in the field of the human rights of children for over 30 years. He coordinated the inputs of international NGOs throughout the drafting of the Convention on the Rights of the Child. Having founded and worked for Defence for Children International for 16 years, he joined UNICEF in 1994, initially as a consultant and then as head of the "Implementation of International Standards" unit at UNICEF's Innocenti Research Centre in Florence until 2003. He played a key role in the development of the 2009 UN Guidelines for the Alternative Care of Children and co-authored the "Moving Forward" handbook supporting their implementation (CELCIS, 2012). His current work focuses especially on safeguarding children's rights in relation to intercountry adoption and alternative care.

Pablo Ceriani Cernadas is the Coordinator of the Migration and Asylum Program, Center of Justice and Human Rights of the National University of Lanús, Argentina (UNLA). He is Member of the United Nations Committee for the Protection of the Rights of Migrant Workers and Their Families (2014–2017). He is Professor on Migration and Human Rights (University of Buenos Aires Law School; Master on International Migration Policies – University Tres de Febrero; Master on Human Rights and Democratization – University of San Martin; and Master on Human Rights – UNLA). He is also a PhD candidate at the University of Valencia, Spain. At Lanús University, he coordinates a research team that carries out a number of projects on migration and human rights, mainly focused on the rights of children in the context of migration, both at global, regional and national level. He has been a consultant of UNICEF, UNFPA and ILO, on migration and human rights issues. From 2002 to 2006, he coordinated the *Legal Clinic for Immigrants and Refugee's Rights* (UBA-CELS-CAREF).

Katrien De Graeve is a Postdoctoral Research Fellow of the Research Foundation Flanders, affiliated to the Department of Languages and Cultures of Ghent University, Belgium. In 2013–2014, she worked as a fellow of the Helsinki Collegium for Advanced Studies, Finland. She holds a PhD in Comparative Sciences of Culture from Ghent University and her doctoral thesis examined parenting practices and belonging in Belgian-Ethiopian adoption. Her research interests are situated at the intersection of critical care, kinship and family studies, and the anthropology of migration and postcoloniality, with transnational adoption, foster care and guardianships of refugee minors as a specific empirical focus. She has published in various journals, including *Bioethics*; *Citizenship Studies*; the *European Journal of Cultural Studies*; *Ethnos*; *Culture, Health and Sexuality*; and *Social and Cultural Geography*.

Ellen Desmet is a Postdoctoral Fellow at the Law and Development Research Group of the University of Antwerp and the Human Rights Centre of Ghent University (Belgium). Before, she was a research and policy staff member at the Children's Rights Knowledge Centre, and taught anthropology of law at the University of Leuven. She complemented her law studies with a master's in Cultures and Development Studies and a master's in Development Cooperation, and holds a PhD in Law from the University of Leuven. Her research interests include human rights (with a focus on children's rights and indigenous peoples' rights), legal anthropology and research methodology.

Karl Hanson is Professor of Public Law at the Centre for Children's Rights Studies (CCRS) at the University of Geneva, Switzerland. He received his PhD in Law from Ghent University, Belgium, where he worked as a Researcher at the Children's Rights Centre and as a Senior Researcher at the Human Rights Centre. His publications and main research interests are in the emerging field of interdisciplinary children's rights studies and include international children's rights advocacy, child labour and working children, juvenile justice and the role of independent national children's rights institutions. He teaches at the University of Geneva in the *Master interdisciplinaire en droits de l'enfant* (MIDE). He is also the Programme Director of the *Master of Advanced Studies in Children's Rights* (MCR) and a member of the Directive Committee of the European Network of Masters in Children's Rights (ENMCR). He is an editor of *Childhood. A Journal of Global Child Research* (Sage).

Ursula Kilkelly is a Professor of Law at the School of Law, University College, Cork, Ireland. She has been researching children's rights for nearly 20 years and has published several books on children's rights including the first book on the subject of *The Child and the ECHR* (1999). She has undertaken multiple research projects in the area of healthcare and children's rights and has been a consultant to the Council of Europe in this and other areas.

Sara Lembrechts is a full-time staff member at the Children's Rights Knowledge Centre (KeKi), where she is responsible for the collection and dissemination of children's rights research, policy advice to the Flemish government and the organization of the International Training Programme Human Rights for Development. She has a MA in Childhood Studies and Children's Rights from the Free University of Berlin (Germany), as well as an LLM in International and European Law and a BA in European Studies, both from the University of Maastricht (Netherlands). Sara worked as an intern with Amnesty International in New Zealand, with UNICEF in Geneva and with the Belgian National Commission on Children's Rights (NCRK). In addition, she has regularly assisted KeKi with projects and events since 2010.

Gertrud Lenzer is Professor of Sociology and Children's Studies at Brooklyn College and the Graduate Center of the City University of New York. In 1991 she was both the Founding Chair of the Sociology of Children Section of the American Sociological Association and the co-founder of the interdisciplinary field of Children's Studies. She held the position as the Founding Director of the Children and Youth Studies Program until 2013 and has served as the Founding Director of the Children's Studies Center for Research, Policy and Public Service since its inception in 1997. The human rights of children represent the overarching framework of both the Program and Center.

Els Leye is a Professor of Global Health/Gender Related Practices at the International Centre for Reproductive Health of the Ghent University in Belgium, where she coordinates the Programme on Harmful Cultural Practices. The main topics of research of this programme include female genital mutilation, honour related violence, forced marriages, hymen reconstructions, cosmetic genital surgeries. She is also postdoctoral researcher at and coordinator of the Centre for Gender, Diversity and Intersectionality of the Vrije Universiteit Brussel. Els Leye holds a master's in Socio-Cultural Sciences and a PhD in Comparative Sciences of Culture. She has been and is actively involved in policy development on female genital mutilation in Belgium and Europe, among others in collaboration with the European Institute for Gender Equality, European Parliament, Belgian senate and the Flemish Forum Child Abuse. She is author of various peer reviewed papers and book chapters, and is a founding member of the European Network for the Prevention of FGM and La Palabre vzw.

Ton Liefaard is Professor of Children's Rights (UNICEF Chair) at Leiden University, Leiden Law School, in the Netherlands. He holds a PhD in Law from the VU University Amsterdam. His research focuses on the meaning of international children's rights for the (legal) position of children at the domestic level, with particular attention for children in conflict with the law, children in need of alternative care, children deprived of their liberty and children's participation. He teaches students and professionals on various children's rights themes and coordinates the Leiden Summer School on International Children's Rights. He regularly works as a consultant for international and national organizations (e.g. Council of Europe, UNICEF, Dutch Children's Ombudsperson) and governments. Liefaard is a deputy juvenile judge at the Criminal Court of Amsterdam and member of the State Commission advising the Dutch Government on the position of children in changing parental relationships.

Berry Mayall is Professor of Childhood Studies at the University of London. Over the last 40 years she has carried out over 20 research projects, mostly focused on the lives and experiences of children and their parents. She has helped to develop the sociology of childhood, over the last 30 years, and has written many books and papers on the subject.

Francine Mestrum has a PhD in social sciences from the Université Libre de Bruxelles. She is a researcher, international consultant and activist and works mainly on poverty and inequality, social development and globalization. She is chairwoman of "Global Social Justice" (www.globalsocialjustice.eu), an association working on the promotion of transformative universal social protection and the Common Good of Humanity. She represents Imodev (Institut du Monde et du Développement – Paris) in Belgium and is a member for CETRI (Centre Tricontinental, Louvain-la-Neuve) of the International Council of the World Social Forum. She published various books in Dutch, French and English on development and development cooperation, poverty and international taxes.

Annemarie Middelburg is a PhD researcher at the International Victimology Institute Tilburg (INTERVICT) at Tilburg University in the Netherlands. She holds a bachelor degree in

Contributors

International and European Law and an LLM in Public International Law and Human Rights and an LLM in the Research Master in Law. Her PhD research focuses on compliance with the international human rights framework with regard to Female Genital Mutilation/Cutting (FGM/C) in Senegal. As part of her PhD research, she conducted a four-month field study in Senegal where she interviewed over 50 experts working in the field of FGM/C. She was a research consultant for the UNFPA in New York, and interned at the Netherlands Embassy in Israel. She is a board member of the Mukomeze Foundation, which aims to improve the lives of women, and girls who survived sexual violence during the genocide in Rwanda. Her interest lies in international law, human rights and harmful cultural practices.

Richard C. Mitchell is a Professor of Child and Youth Studies at Brock University in Ontario, Canada, and obtained his doctorate in Sociology and Social Policy from Scotland's University of Stirling in 2006. The focus of his research, teaching, service and consultancies has been upon local, international and transdisciplinary approaches to implementing the human rights of young people within institutional and community-based settings. In a previous career, Mitchell worked as a child and youth counsellor within British Columbia education, youth justice, mental health, and specialized foster-care sites for two decades. Most importantly, he is a doting father to nine-year-old Finn and six-year-old Siobhán, and a loving life partner with Dr Shannon A. Moore.

Ann Quennerstedt is Associate Professor in Education at Örebro University, Sweden. She has researched value issues in education for 15 years, and has for some time taken a special interest in what children's human rights mean in education. She is one of Sweden's leading children's rights researchers, and has led several research projects studying education as a site for children's rights and the role and responsibility of education for rights. She has published widely on the topic. Quennerstedt is engaged in international networking in her field, and is co-convenor for the European network 'Research in Children's Rights in Education'. She is also a member of the editorial advisory board for the peer-reviewed academic journal *International Journal of Children's Rights*.

Didier Reynaert holds a bachelor in pediatric nursing and a master's in educational sciences (special education/orthopedagogics). In 2012 he obtained his PhD in Social Work at Ghent University with a dissertation on children's rights education and the role of the children's rights movement in implementing the UN Convention on the Rights of the Child. As a lecturer in social work at the University College Ghent, he is a member of the research group on "Social Work and Human Rights" of the Department of Social Work. His main focus is the study of child and youth policy in relation to human rights (of children). He is a founding member of the Flemish Children's Rights Knowledge Centre, current president of the board and co-convener of the International Training Programme Human Rights for Development (HR4DEV). Previously, he worked for the Flemish Children's Rights Coalition, the Child Legal Centre and as a civil servant at the Ministry of the Flemish Community on youth protection.

Rudi Roose holds a master's in Psychological and Educational Sciences and a master in Criminology at Ghent University, Belgium. In 2006 he obtained his PhD in Educational Sciences at Ghent University with a dissertation on the educational perspective in child welfare and child protection work. He is Professor in social work at the Department of Social Welfare Studies at Ghent University, where he teaches, among other things, youth criminology and juvenile justice and social work theories. He is a founding member of the Flemish Children's Rights Knowledge Centre.

E. Kay M. Tisdall is Professor of Childhood Policy at the University of Edinburgh. She established the MSc in Childhood Studies (www.sps.ed.ac.uk/pgtcs) and is Co-Director of the Centre for Research on Families and relationships (www.crfr.ac.uk). She has worked practically on promoting children and young people's participation in legislation and policy, as well as developing a related research programme. Recent publications from this programme include an article in *Global Studies of Childhood* (2013) and the edited books *Children and Young People's Participation and Its Transformative Potential: Lessons from across Countries* (Palgrave, 2014) and the forthcoming *Sage Handbook for Early Childhood Research* (Sage, 2015).

Wouter Vandenhole teaches human rights and holds the UNICEF Chair in Children's Rights – a joint venture of the University of Antwerp and UNICEF Belgium – at the Faculty of Law of the University of Antwerp, Belgium. He is the spokesperson of the Law and Development Research Group and chairs the European Research Networking Programme GLOTHRO. He has published widely on economic, social and cultural rights, children's rights and transnational human rights obligations. Vandenhole is a founding member of the Flemish Children's Rights Knowledge Centre and Co-Convener of the International Advanced Summer Course Human Rights for Development (HR4DEV).

Bruno Vanobbergen received his PhD in Educational Sciences at Ghent University (Belgium). He published several national and international articles in journals and chapters in books on the history of childhood, focusing on processes of commodification, medicalization and educationalization. Bruno Vanobbergen was lecturer at Groningen University (The Netherlands) and visiting fellow at the Department of Childhood Studies of Rutgers University (USA). He is member of the editorial board of *Paedagogica Historica*. Since June 2009, Vanobbergen is the Flemish Children's Rights Commissioner. He is also guest Professor of Childhood Studies at Ghent University.

Eugeen Verhellen is Emeritus Professor of Juvenile Justice Law and Children's Rights at Ghent University, Belgium, where he was the founding director of the Children's Rights Centre (awarded the Human Rights Award of the League for Human Rights, 1995). He was the Co-ordinator of the European Erasmus/Socrates programme on Children's Rights and of the UNESCO-programme CRUN (Children's Rights Universities Network), and the organiser of an annual International Interdisciplinary Course on Children's Rights. Professor Verhellen has been a consultant on children's rights to the Council of Europe and the United Nations and to international non-governmental organisations. He still lectures on children's rights and juvenile justice at different universities. He is co-founder and member of the editorial board of *The International Journal of Children's Rights* (Martinus Nijhoff) and of *A commentary on the United Nations Convention on the Rights of the Child* (Martinus Nijhoff). He has published widely in Dutch, French and English on children's rights issues.

Diana Volonakis is teaching and research assistant at the Centre for Children's Rights Studies (CCRS) and PhD student at the University of Geneva, Switzerland. She holds a Bachelor's degree in History and English Literature from Lausanne University, Switzerland, and an Interdisciplinary Master's degree in Children's Rights from the Kurt Bösch University Institute in Sion, Switzerland. Her research interests include the history of education, child labour and children's rights in the USA. She is currently researching her doctoral thesis on the history of apprenticeship and child work in the 19th-century watch-making industry in Western Switzerland.

Preface

Although a lot has been written about children's rights, there is as yet no multidisciplinary, accessible handbook on children's rights, let alone one informed by a critical approach. Even more so, there is hardly a tradition in the (academic) field of children's rights of critically analysing children's rights without rejecting them. With this handbook, we have the ambition to fill this gap.

The idea for this handbook originated from two developments. The first one is the organization of an international interdisciplinary course on children's rights, *Children's Rights in a Globalised World: Critical Perspectives*. This course takes place biannually as a joint initiative of Flemish universities and university colleges, in close cooperation with the Children's Rights Knowledge Centre (KeKi; as of 2012, the course has been embedded in the International Advanced Summer Course Human Rights for Development [HR4DEV], see www.hr4dev.be). Targeting 'leaders of the future' in children's rights practice, policy and academia, past editions equipped participants from all over the world to engage in a critical and strategic reflection on the integration of children's rights in their professional activities, and stimulated them to pass on the knowledge and skills gained during the course in their own context. In the course of subsequent editions in 2008, 2010 and 2012, it became clear that a solid handbook on children's rights was needed, and that the course had the potential to produce such a handbook.

The second reason for this handbook results from the observation that 'something seems to be going on' in children's rights scholarship. Several scholars have recently proposed new conceptualizations of children's rights that reflect a shift from a top-down understanding towards a bottom-up approach of children's rights. What unites these perspectives is their 'contextual orientation' that criticizes dominant paradigms in children's rights research.

This volume is distinctive in combining the breadth of disciplines and topics with a critical approach, and in its format as an accessible handbook. It offers different disciplinary perspectives and covers a wide range of themes of global interest. This is done from a critical perspective, by zooming in on tensions and the potential and limits of children's rights. We hope that this handbook will be of use to many and diverse constituencies of students of children's rights, but even more, that it will help to build a field of critical children's rights studies.

The editors
Ghent/Antwerp, September 2014

1

Introduction

A critical approach to children's rights

Didier Reynaert, Ellen Desmet, Sara Lembrechts and Wouter Vandenhole

Over the last few decades, children's rights have assumed a central position in a wide variety of disciplines and policies. More than 25 years after the adoption of the UN Convention on the Rights of the Child (CRC) in 1989, it is time to take stock of the achievements and challenges.

The volume consists of two parts, a disciplinary and a thematic one. Taken together, both parts seek to further children's rights realization, not by downplaying key challenges, but by addressing them. The first part provides an insight into various (inter)disciplinary approaches to children's rights, with contributions from law, history, social policy, educational sciences, childhood studies, sociology, social work, anthropology, geography, gender studies and citizenship studies. The second part takes a thematic entry point, disentangling a selection of children's rights issues that are of particular relevance from a global perspective. Here, participation, education, health, juvenile justice, alternative care, violence, female genital mutilation, child labour and working children, migration, poverty, indigenous children and natural resource exploitation are addressed. A detailed introduction to each chapter is offered in the final section of this introduction.

This dual entry point of disciplinary approaches and thematic analyses helps to deepen the understanding of children's rights. Both parts mutually enrich and reinforce each other: they are interconnected and complementary. The common thread ensuring coherence throughout the two parts and their respective chapters is the *critical* approach that is adopted. This critical approach, aspects of which are elaborated on hereinafter and revisited and consolidated in the conclusion, will help children's rights scholarship to mature into critical children's rights *studies* (see concluding Chapter 23), and to take a distance from children's rights activism when needed.

The Handbook takes issue with the observation that 'something seems to be going on' in children's rights scholarship. Several scholars have recently proposed new conceptualizations of children's rights that reflect a shift from a top-down understanding towards a bottom-up approach of children's rights, in parallel with a similar evolution in general human rights scholarship (Merry, 2010; De Feyter, 2007, 2011; de Gaay Fortman, 2011). Reflections on children's rights in terms of 'children's rights from below' (Liebel, 2012), 'living rights' (Hanson and Nieuwenhuys, 2013), 'localizing children's rights' (Vandenhole, 2012) or a 'lifeworld approach in children's rights' (Reynaert *et al.*, 2011) are all grounded in a bottom-up approach

1

to children's rights. What unites these perspectives is their 'contextual orientation' that criticizes dominant paradigms in children's rights research. These dominant paradigms understand children's rights as an objective set of goals applicable for any context, and take the CRC as the key point of reference. Not only is such an approach blind to the social, economic and historical contexts in which children grow up, it also does not sufficiently take account of the diversity of interpretations and meanings that children's rights can have. Nevertheless, the context-oriented approaches raise new questions and dilemmas, while simultaneously re-challenging 'old' ones. How far can a context-specific interpretation of the CRC go without violating children's rights? How can different interpretations of children's rights coexist, and how do they relate to more 'traditional' ideas of social justice and human dignity? And in what sense can the CRC be considered as an instrument for social change to address imbalanced power-relations, both locally and globally?

In what follows, we address four analytical puzzles that are at the core of this Handbook: definitions and understandings of children, childhood and children's rights; a context-specific approach; disciplinary interactions; and an approach of critique. Next, we briefly introduce each chapter by summarizing its key contents and by flagging how it engages with the analytical puzzles developed below.

1. Understanding children's rights

There are no universally accepted definitions of the concepts of children, childhood and children's rights. In what follows, we explain how these notions have been defined by the editors for the purposes of this volume.

1.1. Children

The notion of 'children' is used to refer to a particular group in society, which is distinguished on the basis of its age. Who is considered a 'child' is not a given; it varies with social, economic and cultural circumstances. Article 1 of the CRC states: 'For the purposes of the present Convention, a child means every human being below the age of eighteen years unless under the law applicable to the child, majority is attained earlier.' The provision explains how the term 'child' is to be understood *for the purposes of that treaty*. It does not state that every person below 18 years equals a child *as such*. This is nonetheless how the concept of 'children' has become commonly defined, namely as all persons below eighteen, leading to an invisibility and even 'infantilisation of adolescents' (Abramson, 1996, p. 397; Cantwell, 2011).[1] It therefore seems more appropriate to talk about 'children and young people' when referring to the persons who come within the scope of the CRC. The application of the CRC to 'young people' or adolescents is moreover challenging. The *text* of the CRC is not always adapted to the needs and interest of adolescents, and there has been a lack of attention in the *implementation* of the CRC to this age group as well (Desmet, 2012).

Both the beginning and the end of childhood are contested terrain. Regarding the beginning of childhood, there is a debate on the extent to which children's rights are or should be applicable to the unborn child (Joseph, 2009; Cornock and Montgomery, 2011). As concerns the end of childhood, neuroimaging research has found that the brain is only fully developed

---

1   Moreover, the concept of age is in this way reduced to 'chronological age', not paying attention to other and broader conceptions of age, such as 'social age' (Clark-Kazak, 2009). For practical and implementation purposes, however, an age limit seems defendable.

at the age of 25 (Johnson, Blum and Giedd, 2009). Although neuroscientists warn against drawing causal conclusions on the relation between neuromaturational processes and real-world behaviour (Johnson, Blum and Giedd, 2009, p. 216), this finding of longer brain immaturity has led to claims to extend the protection of children's rights to the age group of 18- to 25-year-olds (Veerman, 2010). Moreover, the societal context seems characterized by two opposite evolutions: on the one hand, the transition to adulthood is being further postponed, often until far above the age of 18 (Elchardus and Roggemans, 2010); on the other, the age at which one ventures into certain domains is decreasing. For instance, the confrontation with multiple sources of information occurs at an ever lower age, among others through internet and social media (Boonaert and Siongers, 2010).

Within the age group of 0–18, discussions on capacity and (the necessity to establish) age limits abound. When is a child 'capable of forming his or her own views', so that her or his views are to be given due weight 'in accordance with the age and maturity of the child' (Art. 12 CRC)? The answer to this question is of crucial importance – at least in mainstream thinking – for the participation of children in matters affecting them, such as divorce proceedings or alternative care settings. Another example concerns the minimum age of criminal responsibility (Cipriani, 2009). The recognition of 'children' as fully-fledged persons, as promoted by the children's rights movement, may be – unduly – used as an argument in favour of (further) lowering the minimum age of criminal responsibility.

1.2. Child images and childhood

The observation that defining the notion of 'the child' or 'children' is not so straightforward builds on the understanding that the way we look at children is determined by the social and cultural context and practices in which children grow up. Because different social and cultural contexts coexist, both within as well as across societies, different understandings are possible on what 'the child' is. This idea is captured in the notion of 'child image'. 'Child image' refers to the way we look at children, i.e. the often implicit assumptions such as biological or psychological traits that co-design the way we deal with children.

For instance, the most dominant impact on the way we perceive children comes from developmental psychology. The 'invention' in the seventeenth century – at least in the global North – of different developmental phases in childhood linked to 'sensitive periods' in a person's lifetime, is a way to look at children that is still prominently present in child rearing today. In this view, children are considered as objects in need of protection because of their vulnerability. What characterizes them is their position of 'adults in waiting' or their 'not yet' status, i.e. 'not-yet-fully-developed'. In terms of children's rights, the focus then is on protection rights of children. Another child image, which has been common in many societies around the world but only gained ground more recently in the global North, is that of the 'autonomous child' (Reynaert et al., 2009). It considers children as active agents and autonomous and independent human beings. The interdisciplinary field of childhood studies has contributed to developing this new child image by recognizing the social and political significance of children's meaning making and ideas. The key thought of this paradigm is the recognition that children are competent human beings. The children's rights movement carried out these ideas in practice and policy by advocating for the recognition of the participation rights of children.

'Childhood' refers to the historical and socio-cultural structuring of children and child images in our society. A key characteristic of this structuring is the separation of children from adults based on child-specific traits such as biological and psychological determinants. This structuring has been labelled the 'youth moratorium' or the 'institutionalized youth land'

(Verhellen, 2000; Zinnecker, 2000). The notion of 'youth land' or 'youth moratorium' refers to the institutionalization of childhood into '… preparatory arenas that implement a principle of integration by means of separation'. (Honig, 2008, p. 201). It can be considered as the result of a historical process in which children are gradually separated from the adult world with the aim to prepare them for adult life (Reynaert and Roose, 2014).

With the rise of the children's rights movement and the academic field of childhood studies, questions were raised in relation to an exaggerated institutional paternalism when dealing with children. This stemmed from the critique that children are not merely 'passive receivers of society's messages' (James and James, 2012). Children's actions and processes of appropriation were recognized to equally contribute to transforming the historical and socio-cultural structuring of childhood in our society (James, 2009). The institutionalized youth land was contested and both the social and legal position of children were challenged. Children, it was said, are not only the future generation; childhood should likewise be considered as an actual part of current society (James and James, 2004). The cover of this Handbook, picturing a girl 'inflating the globe', represents such an image of children as agents, who give meaning and co-shape the world.

Important to notice is the fact that throughout time, different child images and different social constructions of childhood, coexist. 'Old' child images are not fully replaced by new ones. They continue to exist as part of society's view on childhood. As James and Prout (1997) argue, the way we look at children and childhood is anchored in the past and reshaped in the present. Likewise, until today, the institutionalized youth land remains the horizon against which childhood in the Western world is shaped, although the 'nature' of this youth land has changed over time (Reynaert and Roose, 2014).

This coexistence of different child images and constructions of childhood creates confusion and tensions. Different societal actors may emphasize different characteristics of the same social phenomena, often resulting in the paradox of 'the child in danger' versus the 'dangerous child'. In the public sphere for instance, no age group has so much expertise about social media as children and young people have. These so-called 'digital natives' are characterized by the integration of digital technology in their daily lives. However, popular discourses on social media and children often focus on phenomena such as cyberbullying or cyberstalking, portraying children as *dangerous*. At the same time, however, these discourses point at the harms the internet can cause to young people, resulting in the development of new technologies to *protect* children. Similar observations can be made in relation to the presence of children in the public sphere. Children can participate in public life, as long as they behave. Initiatives such as a curfew or mosquitos[2] are meant to protect society against the anti-social behaviour of 'dangerous' children. At the same time, public participation of children is limited due to the risks that go along with, for instance, traffic. Here, children are considered to be 'in danger', resulting in 'child-friendly' public spaces where children can play and meet. However, these places are often isolated from the broader public life, resulting in a further 'islandization' of childhood. These diverging views on childhood are all entrenched in the CRC, with the recognition of both protection as well as participation rights.

---

2 'Mosquitos' are devices that produce a very unpleasant buzzing sound with such a high ultrasonic frequency that only young people can hear it. It has been used in the Netherlands and the UK to 'chase' loitering youths away from public places.

1.3. Children's rights

The CRC (1989) is the key legal instrument on children's rights. This Convention and its three optional protocols codify the human rights of children in international, legally binding instruments. With almost all states in the world being parties to the treaty,[3] the CRC offers a set of minimum standards on children's rights for which states can be held accountable. Guided by what has gradually come to be seen as the four underlying general principles – i.e. of (i) non-discrimination, (ii) best interests of the child, (iii) right to life, survival and development, and (iv) participation (Committee on the Rights of the Child, 2003, § 12) – the CRC grants children protection, provision and participation rights. For the first time, civil and political as well as economic, social and cultural rights were put together in a human rights treaty. Holistically addressing children as fully-fledged persons, these rights are inextricably related, with no intrinsic hierarchy between them (KeKi, 2012, pp. 11–12).

Even though the CRC is an essential component in the legal embedding of the rights of children in the wider human rights framework, this Handbook does not confine children's rights to that Convention. From a legal perspective, it is important to acknowledge that children's rights are also enshrined in other international human rights instruments at the universal, regional and domestic level. But more importantly, in our understanding children's rights include the wider societal context in which rights are given meaning. The reality of children's rights is much richer than a legal instrument and its implementation. Children's rights are not only about rules, but also about structures, relationships and processes (Morrow and Pells, 2012).

1.4. Children's rights as human rights

For the purposes of this Handbook, children's rights are understood as fundamental claims for the realization of social justice and human dignity for children. Children's rights are *fundamental*: not all norms relating to or relevant for children (e.g. on social security or education) can or should be characterized as 'children's rights'. Just like human rights more generally, children's rights originate from the quest for human dignity and social justice. However, the concrete meaning of these notions will be different for different people. For some, human dignity is about maximum agency and self-determination. For others, it is about protection of core values, in particular of vulnerable groups, and if necessary even against their own will. Also, children's rights are not synonyms or code for human dignity: they carry more specific meaning, and while they cannot and should not be equated with legally recognized rights, they do quite often have a degree of legal back-up.

The CRC can be seen as the historic culmination point of a long struggle for recognition of children as fully-fledged human beings – as subjects of rights (Verhellen, 2004, pp. 17–20), fully in line with similar struggles for recognition of humanity of women, people with disabilities, migrant workers, or elderly people.[4] The legal codification of children's rights at the global level in the CRC is considered to be one of the nine core human rights treaties, which confirms the human rights nature of children's rights. The drafting history of the CRC is telling about the extent to which children's rights are politically and legally part of the human rights framework (Alston, 1994, p. 6). The submission of a draft convention on children's rights

---

3   Only the United States of America and South Sudan have not ratified the CRC.
4   In 2012, an initiative was taken to start the codification of the rights of the older persons.

by Poland (a socialist state at the time) to the UN Commission on Human Rights in 1978, was meant to make clear that human rights initiatives were not a monopoly of Western states, and in particular of the then president of the United States Jimmy Carter (Lopatka, 2007, p. xxxviii). Because of ideological obstruction from the Western camp, progress on the CRC initially depended on progress on the Convention against Torture, which was of importance to some Western states (Cantwell, 1992, p. 23). When in a later stage the United States gave up their obstruction and sought to insert civil and political rights, they were less motivated by a desire to accord civil and political rights to children, but rather concerned how they could make the CRC less appealing for Poland and its allies (Lopatka, 2007, p. xxxviii).

However, the relationship between human rights in general and children's rights in particular is also ridden with tension, and confusion about the nature of children's rights is often rampant. This had led to a growing apart of human rights and children's rights, conceptually and in practice. Tension between children's rights and other human rights often originates from human rights competition with other so-called vulnerable groups, such as women or adult migrants, for children tend to be considered more vulnerable, and are therefore believed to deserve better or privileged treatment. More generally, tensions may arise between children's rights and the human rights of adults, the latter quite often being their parents. This tension is particularly apparent with regard to placement into care of children, where their best interests tend to trump the right to protection of family life.

Conceptually, children's rights have grown apart from human rights. This has sometimes led to conceptual impoverishment on both sides. For example, the dominant categorization among children's rights proponents and CRC commentators is the three Ps: rights to protection, provision and participation. This categorization may have been of considerable importance to explain in a couple of words what the CRC is about. The downsides of this categorization should not be overlooked, though. First, it departs from the main categorization that human rights actors are familiar with, i.e. that of civil and political rights on the one hand, and economic, social and cultural rights on the other.[5] Second and more importantly, the term 'provision rights', which refers to e.g. rights to education, health and social security, tends to confirm the outdated misunderstanding or misrepresentation that economic and social rights are exclusively about provision. It has meanwhile been widely accepted that the obligations relating to economic, social and cultural rights (ESC rights) are to be understood as obligations to respect, to protect and to fulfil, and that the latter obligation consists of sub-obligations to facilitate, to promote and to provide. Only the sub-obligation to fulfil-provide requires considerable mobilization of resources. So, while in general human rights law the understanding of ESC rights has matured over more than two decades of conceptual scholarship and practice, the children's rights community tends to gloss over these developments, thereby conceptually weakening children's rights, and potentially, human rights more generally. On the other hand, general human rights scholarship and practice may benefit from conceptual developments in children's rights – one could think of the notion of best interests, the emphasis on participation, or the use of general principles.

In practice too, children's rights and human rights movements have more often than not taken separate paths. Typically, the human rights movement does not engage very strongly with children from a children's rights perspective, and vice versa. Although a division of labour is inevitable and to be welcomed in principle, what seems to happen in reality is that children's

---

5   This is not to say that that categorization is beyond criticism, or even preferable. The point we want to make is that children's rights use categorizations of rights that are different from those used in the broader human rights community.

rights organizations frequently have no sense of belonging to the broader human rights community: they tend to be oblivious of the human rights of other groups, and seem to be sometimes willing to push through children's rights even at the expense of the human rights of others (probably more often than not simply unaware about the human rights effects for other individuals or groups).

In sum, children's rights are part and parcel of human rights. Whereas they do not simply coincide with general human rights, they do share a common origin in human dignity, and should be conceptually analysed in conformity with general human rights whenever possible. In practice as well, children's rights should be part of the larger human rights agenda.[6]

2. A context-specific approach

In recent years, human rights research has increasingly addressed the interaction 'between the global and the local' (Goodale and Merry, 2007). Global initiatives shape local contexts, but local evolutions equally lie at the basis of and feed into global developments. Moreover, '[t]he local appropriates and transforms the global for its own needs' (Merry, 2000, p. 129). The attention paid to the interaction between the global and the local is also of key importance to children's rights scholarship, since children are not a homogeneous group. There is a large diversity within children, who moreover grow up in contexts that may be socially, culturally, politically, economically and geographically very different (Reynolds, Nieuwenhuys and Hanson, 2006). Children's rights should take this variety of contexts into account, leaving space for a context-specific approach.[7] This means that children's rights, depending on the context, may be interpreted and realized in a different, 'localized' way (De Feyter, 2007, 2011; Vandenhole, 2012). Such context-sensitivity also (partly) meets the objection that the formulation and implementation of children's rights has been too Western or Eurocentric (Nieuwenhuys, 1998). Contextualization does not imply, however, that individual preferences can trump societal norms 'just like that'. Neither can it be equated to a relativistic approach; nor does it indicate an 'anything goes'-attitude.

The thematic contributions of this book are situated within this interaction between the global and the local. They address issues that take on a global dimension, but pay attention to local appropriation and transformation as well as to changes coming from below. The weight given to global and local perspectives differs between the various chapters. Whereas, for instance, the contributions on migration and child poverty pay more heed to dynamics at the global level, the ones on alternative care, female genital mutilation and natural resource exploitation point to the importance of a localized approach.

3. At the crossroads of disciplines

The relationship between reality and academic research seems characterized by a perpetual ambivalence. The living realities of children and young people cannot be compartmentalized

---

6   As has been pointed out above, saying that children's rights are a fundamental part of human rights is not to say that the specific historical development and characteristics of the human rights of *children* are denied or rejected.
7   The terms 'contextualization', 'context-sensitive approach' and 'context-specific approach' are used interchangeably.

to neatly fit academic disciplines and university structures (Brewer, 1999). Disciplines imply a particular 'way of looking', comparable to viewing a research object each time through differently coloured glasses. A comprehensive understanding of children's rights thus implies combining various disciplinary perspectives. At the same time, increased disciplinary specialization has considerably deepened our understanding of particular aspects of (the rights of) children and young people. Through specialization in disciplines, knowledge has been advanced in a way that would probably not have been possible otherwise. This duality – the need to combine disciplines to arrive at a holistic understanding, on the one hand, and the value of specialized knowledge building, on the other – has sparked an intensive debate on how disciplines (should) relate to and interact with each other.

This debate is characterized by the three notions of multi-, inter- and transdisciplinarity. Although there are no universally accepted definitions of these concepts, and these prefixes may be interpreted differently by different researchers, a certain consensus seems to be emerging to understand these concepts as referring to different degrees of engagement between disciplines along a continuum. Multidisciplinarity is then understood as referring to 'the juxtaposition of disciplines', without real interaction (Klein, 1990, p. 56), thus in an 'additive' way (Mitchell, Chapter 10, referring to Choi and Pak, 2006; see also Vick, 2004, p. 165). Interdisciplinary research implies 'the appropriate combination of knowledge from many different specialities – especially as a means to shed new light on an actual problem' (Brewer, 1999, p. 328). It involves 'integrating and organizing traditional forms of knowledge, skills and experience in a new and original fashion' (Banakar and Travers, 2005, p. 6); the key adjective being 'interactive' (Mitchell, Chapter 10, referring to Choi and Pak, 2006). Klein (1990) distinguishes four basic types of 'interdisciplinary interaction': (i) borrowing, where analytic tools, methods or concepts from another discipline are used; (ii) the interaction between disciplines with the aim of solving a specific problem 'with no intention of achieving a conceptual unification of knowledge'; (iii) the 'increased consistency of subject matters and methods', leading to an 'overlapping area' between two disciplines; and (iv) the development of a new interdiscipline. A transdisciplinary approach goes even further: here, disciplines become irrelevant to the larger framework (Klein, 1990, p. 66); they are 'integrated to the point beyond demarcations' (Dalrymple and Miller, 2006, p. 30), and result in a 'holistic' approach (Mitchell, Chapter 10, referring to Choi and Pak, 2006).

The overall approach of this Handbook is largely a multidisciplinary one. Each chapter of the first part reviews the main features of a certain disciplinary or sometimes interdisciplinary perspective on children's rights and critically evaluates the state of the art of this (inter)discipline in relation to children's rights. Also in the second, thematic part of this Handbook, various authors predominantly write from a particular disciplinary viewpoint.[8] However, within the confines of each chapter, there is often an engagement with other (inter)disciplinary perspectives, particularly when assessing the merits and drawbacks of a particular (disciplinary) approach to children's rights. Within these chapters, there is thus a greater or lesser degree of 'interdisciplinary interaction' (Klein, 1990). This makes the overall qualification of this Handbook a mixed one, somewhere on the continuum between multi- and interdisciplinarity, with some peaks in either direction.[9]

The first part of this volume offers a rich analysis of how children's rights are understood and researched from a variety of disciplinary windows. Some of these approaches are

---

8 But see, e.g. Hanson, Volonakis and Al-Rozzi, Chapter 18, for a more sustained interdisciplinary approach.
9 See, e.g. Mitchell on transdisciplinarity, Chapter 10.

'traditional' mono-disciplinary ones, such as law, sociology, social work, anthropology and geography. Others, namely childhood studies, gender studies and citizenship studies, are by their nature interdisciplinary, as they resulted from a sustained interaction between various disciplinary perspectives, which led to the establishment and development of a distinct and independent (inter)discipline.[10] Arguably, children's rights may or could also be a topic of interest in many other disciplines, such as criminology, media studies, medical sciences, philosophy and psychology – to only name a few. The disciplines included in this Handbook were selected on the basis of their track record regarding children's rights, namely whether the discipline has engaged with children's rights in a systematic way, which has led to a certain degree of theory formation. So, while not exhaustive, the diversity of disciplinary perspectives that have been included ensures sufficient breadth and depth.

For the disciplines incorporated in this edited volume too, the degree and nature of the interaction with children's rights varies. Both historically and in the present day, legal scholars have been particularly active in the domain of children's rights. Although logical to a certain extent (given the intimate relation between children's rights and law), the predominance of *legal* children's rights research entails the risk that children's rights are narrowed down to or enclosed within children's rights *law* (see further Vandenhole, Chapter 2). Therefore, this Handbook purposively pays equal attention to other disciplinary perspectives. The proportionally larger involvement of legal scholarship with children's rights generally speaking is reflected in the disciplinary backgrounds of the editors (the majority of them are lawyers) and the authors of the thematic part of this Handbook. Nevertheless, although a number of thematic chapters have a legal entry point, in keeping with the critical ambitions of this Handbook, they provide a broader analysis of children's rights than what can usually be found in traditional legal scholarship, as they adopt as a minimum a contextual approach and incorporate insights from other disciplines.

4. An approach of critique

A distinctive starting point for this book is its critical perspective on children's rights. In the societal as well as academic discussion of children's rights, it often seems as if children's rights are first and foremost considered as a *solution* for social problems. From this point of view, the primary question is *how* children's rights can be used to overcome difficulties in children's lives. For example, the adoption of a law prohibiting corporal punishment – a long-standing demand of the children's rights movement – is considered to be a comprehensive answer to deal with violence within the family. Likewise, pupil councils in schools are assumed to enhance the participation of children at school. The solution for social problems is thus sought in the development or strengthening of the legal position of minors or in the creation of well-defined educational methods. No matter how sincere these initiatives are, they ignore a concern that should precede them, i.e. *which social problems* become visible when looking at children's lives from a children's rights perspective and *how these social problems are defined*. This question requires an ethical stance rather than a technical position, and that is what a critical perspective on children's rights is about.

A 'critical perspective' on children's rights can (probably) be understood in different ways. It is therefore important to distinguish 'critique', as the main activity in a critical perspective,

---

10 To enhance readability, the reference to 'disciplines' in the remainder of this Handbook should be understood as including these interdisciplinary perspectives.

from 'criticism' (Evans, 2005). The latter refers to *judging* something', either positively or negatively, e.g. it is *bad* to use violence when trying to achieve an educational goal or it is *good* to involve children in shaping school policy. Regardless of how appropriate these evaluations are, they often leave out a thicker analysis of the problem at stake. This is where 'critique' comes in, which should be understood as an on-going exercise of questioning assumptions, knowledge and acts as well as the associated norms and values that shape the social, educational or legal practices that rely on the children's rights framework. These assumptions mostly remain implicit within these practices. Critical reflection (critique) renders these implicit assumptions explicit. In the case of a legal ban on corporal punishment, critique can show for instance that a particular group of children and parents may be singled out by that legal ban, i.e. children (and their parents) growing up in difficult circumstances such as poverty. This insight gives the debate on corporal punishment and children's rights a different twist, as the focus shifts from the 'problematic' behaviour of parents (who slap their children) to the difficult living conditions in which these parents raise their children. In a similar manner, a critical perspective on pupils' councils can shift attention to the question as to who participates in these forums and who does not. It can show that these kinds of participation structures are more suitable for a certain group of children, i.e. those raised in a household where negotiation and verbal competencies are highly valued. This finding compels us to think about what participation really means in a school context and how it can be conceived differently than in a merely formal way.

What is at stake in these examples, and thus in a critical perspective on children's rights, are at least two distinctive issues. The first issue is the *deliberative character* of children's rights practices. Critique makes implicit knowledge underlying children's rights practices explicit and therefore subject of debate. A critical approach of children's rights means that we do not consider the basic assumptions underlying children's rights as 'truths', i.e. objective knowledge that must be understood in a univocal way. On the contrary, it means that our understanding of children's rights is essentially an interactive process between all stakeholders involved: children, parents, adults, civil society, the government etc. Throughout this dialectic process, we attempt to understand and interpret the lifeworlds of children by using the framework of children's rights as a 'sensitizing concept'; a frame of reference that appeals to fundamental principles of human dignity. Different interpretations of these lifeworlds can coexist, together with different ideas on what children's rights are and how human dignity can be understood and realized (Reynaert *et al.*, 2012).

Moreover, the lifeworlds of children cannot be considered apart from the broader societal order in which ideas are embedded that co-construct these lifeworlds. For instance, the way we understand childhood, how rights are comprehended and function in our current societies, ideas on agency and responsibility, etc., all these and other presumptions are not unique to the particular lifeworld of children. They are part of the structure of society itself and constructed through social, educational and legal practices. Unravelling these presumptions and trying to understand them is key to a critical perspective on children's rights. At the same time, being aware of how norms and values influence the way we construct children's rights allows us to reconceptualize the way we deal with and experience children, and it opens up the possibility for changing our practices.

The latter shows the second issue at stake in a critical perspective, i.e. the *transformative character* of a critical perspective. A critical perspective creates space for alternative ideas on children's rights. The awareness that children's rights are shaped in a particular way and governed by certain logics that are human-made, eliminates an essentialist understanding of children's rights, i.e. an understanding of children's rights as determinate, unchangeable entities with consistent characteristics. A critical perspective on the other hand has an *emancipatory* objective: it considers children's rights as a framework for social action and a lever to change societal conditions towards greater respect for the human dignity of children.

The authors that have contributed to this volume all engage with the critical approach, albeit to different degrees. Some clearly were more familiar and/or feel more comfortable with such an approach, whereas for others this was their first exposure or they may be more sceptical/reluctant to adopt a critical approach in all its dimensions. What unites all contributions though, is the dissatisfaction with dogmatic children's rights activism and the desire to move beyond the intellectual poverty of children's rights research that focuses exclusively on the implementation gap as the one and only challenge for children's rights.

In the concluding chapter, we further flesh out the approach of critique to children's rights, and try to deepen our understanding of its diagnostic, deliberative and emancipatory dimension.

5. Towards a field of children's rights studies

To unsettle dominant discourses, patterns, interpretations and representations and to discuss, analyse and reflect upon children's rights-based practices using social imagination are fundamental components of a critical perspective on children's rights. However, as Alanen (2011) properly observes: (academic) debate today on children's rights lacks critique. Children's rights indeed are barely a 'contested terrain'. There is hardly a tradition in the (academic) field of children's rights that critically analyses children's rights without at the same time forswearing the framework of children's rights (Reynaert *et al.*, 2012), some exceptions notwithstanding (see e.g. Holland and Scourfield, 2004; Kjorholt, 2002; Pupavac, 2001; Quennerstedt, 2010; Such and Walker, 2005; Hanson and Nieuwenhuys, 2013). Much more insight is needed in the underlying norms, values and logics that shape children's rights practices today and the way in which these are understood.

Exactly in the mission of making these norms, values and logics explicit, lies the fundamental goal of what can be considered as a 'new' academic field of 'children's rights studies'. The knowledge that this academic field should produce can make a fundamental contribution to obtaining insights in children's rights-based practices and can give ground for further dialogue on these practices, with the aim to change these practices in the direction of a greater respect for the human dignity of children. Hence, it is only by making these underlying processes explicit, that they become 'arguable'. When these norms, values and logics remain unknown, and research and practice in the field of children's rights lock themselves up in their own beliefs, the children's rights framework tends to be an ideology rather than a socio-political frame of reference (Reynaert *et al.*, 2012). In the conclusion, we will tentatively set a research agenda for this field of critical children's rights studies.

6. Introduction to the structure and chapters of the book

This edited volume consists of two parts. The first part offers a multiplicity of disciplinary perspectives. The second covers a wide range of themes at the intersection of the local and the global. This is done from a critical perspective, by zooming in on tensions and the potential and limits of children's rights. Each author has been invited to offer the state-of-the-art, to reference key literature, to engage with the ideas in the draft introduction, and to end with questions for discussion and debate. The latter is meant to increase the practicality of this Handbook. At the end, the editors draw extensive conclusions on the approach adopted in this Handbook, and on the way forward to a field of critical children's rights studies.

Authors were not expected, and do not, toe the same doctrinal line. A clear-cut example is the way in which the agency-vulnerability, protection-participation dichotomy is addressed: whereas some authors overtly subscribe to a vulnerability paradigm (e.g. Lenzer, Chapter 16), others lean towards the agency paradigm (e.g. Tisdall, Chapter 11, but she warns for reification). So the critical approach is really more a matter of perspective on children's rights, than a uniform straightjacket on substantive issues.

We have deliberately invited scholars who come from different traditions, regional or professional backgrounds and schools of thought, so as to expose readers to the diversity of the thinking. Some contributions are therefore more grounded in theoretical work, while others are more practice-based. Some contributions have a stronger emphasis on a technical analysis within their discipline, while others include more of a meta-reflection on their discipline. Some have an explicit emancipatory or activist agenda, whereas others less explicitly pursue a certain agenda. All these categorizations are characterized by fluid demarcations, though. Moreover, a contribution that draws on practice is not necessarily activist; it can be 'critical', whereas an academic piece that remains purely technical may miss a critical dimension.

6.1. Part 1 – Disciplinary perspectives

Wouter Vandenhole opens this Handbook with a chapter on *Children's rights from a legal perspective: Children's rights law.* Seeking to familiarize the reader with the global and regional legal frameworks on children's rights, the chapter starts with a description of key legal instruments, monitoring bodies and procedures on the supra-national level. Second, legal reasoning on children's rights is introduced, drawing primarily on the codification of children's human rights in the CRC. Third, case law, mainly by the European Court of Human Rights, makes the legal reasoning concrete for three substantive themes (juvenile justice, family matters and education). In a fourth and final part, the author questions to what extent children's rights law – and standard setting through legislation and litigation in particular – can contribute to social change. Being cautious not to overestimate the transformative potential of a legal approach to children's rights, Vandenhole concludes with a plea for critical legal scholarship to increase insight in the complex ways in which children's rights law and social realities interact.

In doing so, Vandenhole offers a number of building blocks for a critical approach to children's rights. As the legal discipline has appropriated a substantial part of children's rights scholarship, highlighting some of the challenges inherent to a legal perspective is vital to keeping the children's rights debate alive, both within this discipline and beyond. In addition, the chapter puts to discussion a common assumption (among lawyers and others) that relevant standards exist for each children's rights issue, that the meaning of these standards is clear and that these standards are able to satisfactorily address every issue at stake. The author not only asks the fundamental question whether these standards indeed suffice, but also pleas for legal scholarship to engage more systematically with legally defining and re-defining the meaning of children's rights (law) beyond the implementation of these standards.

The chapter by **Eugeen Verhellen**, *The Convention on the Rights of the Child: Reflections from a historical, social policy and educational perspective*, explores children's rights from the perspective of the CRC. It starts by explaining where the growing interest in children's rights originated. Verhellen locates the onset of children's rights at the intersection of two macro-social developments. The first one concerns a changing child-image recognizing children as subjects instead of objects; the second one is about the development of a global human rights project since World War II. Verhellen considers the CRC as a framework to structure the debate on children's rights. He gives an overview of the main characteristics of the Convention and examines the consequences of the adoption of the CRC for social policy. In his conclusion, Verhellen makes a case for considering the CRC as a *geopolitical social contract*.

Verhellen's chapter points at important difficulties and tensions for states and other actors to implement the CRC in social policy. One of the tensions he highlights is how to deal with the simultaneous importance of both dependence and autonomy for children. Verhellen takes a nuanced stance in relation to participation rights by emphasizing the 'pragmatic trend' in children's rights: i.e. to assume that children are competent unless it can be proven that they are not. This would help to ensure that children can acquire a prominent place in society.

The chapter by **Bruno Vanobbergen**, *Children's rights and childhood studies: From living apart together towards a happy marriage*, examines the relationship between children's rights and childhood studies. First, the main themes of the paradigm of the childhood studies are critically analysed. Vanobbergen looks at both childhood as a structural form and at children's agency, and this from different schools within childhood studies, with a particular focus on representatives of the sociology of childhood. In the second part of his contribution, Vanobbergen translates the insights from childhood studies to the field of children's rights with the ambition to deepen children's rights as a concept. The main line of argumentation in this part is informed by a critique on the attempt to try to fit children into an adult-based political construction. As an alternative, Vanobbergen makes a case for the recognition of the uniqueness of children, arguing that only then will children obtain a fully-fledged place as a social citizen in our societies.

The contribution of Vanobbergen to the field of children's rights is important in several ways. First, he brings together two fields – childhood studies and children's rights – that are very closely related but nevertheless often separated. From the perspective of children's rights, this exercise is extremely valuable because the theoretical substantiation in the field of childhood studies is much more elaborated than in the field of children's rights. Second, Vanobbergen's contribution critically engages in the discussion on the 'adultification' of children's rights. For Vanobbergen, children's rights should not be considered in an adultocentric way, i.e. understanding children's rights in the same way as the rights granted to adults. As an alternative, he argues in favour of recognizing the difference between children and adults. Childhood studies can contribute to the development of such a perspective in children's rights.

In her chapter, *The sociology of childhood and children's rights*, **Berry Mayall** outlines the key ideas that have been developed in the sociology of childhood. On the one hand, sociologists have been developing structural approaches to childhood, considering children as members of society and childhood as a social category in society. On the other hand, sociology was concerned with relational processes, focusing on the way childhood and adulthood relate at both macro and micro levels, and how each level of these relational processes affects the other. Mayall further elaborates these ideas in relation to children's rights and analyses why there is a need for a separate category of children' rights. Subsequently, she examines some recent sociological studies in order to provide a critical look at the assumptions, norms and values that shape practices based on the idea that children have rights. In the conclusion, the author points out the necessity for sociology to think about local understandings of what childhood is, and how childhood relates to adulthood, within socio-economic and political contexts.

It is exactly this latter insight that offers a significant potential for critical engagement with children's rights from a sociological perspective. Mayall shows how attention to the large-scale is essential to understanding childhoods and whether and how children's rights are respected. Through the case of the ambiguous consequences of globalization on childhood and children's rights, Mayall argues that competing ideas about childhood can exist and be debated both in local and international contexts. This also holds for the discussion on responsibility, where local understandings of children's rights are linked to interdependent family relations across generations and to the idea of community.

In their chapter on *Children's rights from a social work perspective: Towards a lifeworld orientation*, **Didier Reynaert and Rudi Roose** reflect on ways in which social work can contribute to a deliberative critical dialogue on the interpretation of children's rights principles. First, the fragmented identity of social work is explained, both as a human rights profession and as an academic discipline. Using examples from Western Europe that transcend the particular social work terrains, the chapter continues with a critical discussion on the implications for social work of, on the one hand, a shifting image of childhood, and, on the other, the institutionalization of childhood into separate 'youth lands'. The authors submit that in both of these tendencies, the complex interplay between the child's social, economic, political, cultural and historical context and his or her personal meaning-making have been largely overlooked. In response, the authors suggest a 'lifeworld orientation' as a way in which power relations could be changed in order to achieve greater respect for the human dignity of children.

This chapter contributes to a critical field of children's rights studies by questioning a number of fundamental assumptions. First of all, a contextualized lifeworld orientation focuses on the way 'rights are made, constructed and shaped through numerous social practices' (Grunwald and Thiersch, 2009, p. 108). As such, it clearly challenges the dominant children's rights paradigm in which children's rights are seen as solutions to social problems, to be implemented and imposed from above. Second, the authors draw the attention to the pitfalls of uncritically taking over the children's rights movement's new image of the autonomous child. Dominant interpretations of autonomy, which overlook interdependency between individuals, underestimate differences between children and overestimate the ability of legal instruments to change social realities, are questioned. The authors finish their analysis by pointing out a number of limitations of the discipline of social work for researching children's rights. As such, they contribute not only to the critical reflection on children's rights as part of the ethical foundations of the social work profession, but also to the increasing recognition of social work as an academic discipline in its own right.

The chapter *Anthropologists, ethnographers and children's rights: Critiques, resistance and powers* by **Geraldine André** reviews anthropological and ethnographic approaches to children's rights, paying special attention to the relations between anthropology and children's rights since the adoption of the CRC. André starts her analysis with what she calls 'a strange paradox'. On the one hand, she highlights anthropologists' resistance against and critique of global children's rights law, and the CRC in particular, in the wake of cultural relativism. On the other hand, she notes how the CRC inspired a renewed interest in children's rights amongst anthropologists, and how this interest transformed both the anthropological theory and methodology so as to better grasp children's experiences. Here, the author distinguishes between bottom-up anthropological approaches that study children's rights from below, and anthropological perspectives that conceptualize children's rights as (linked to) structures of power, including global capitalism and child protection, that affect children's rights, lifeworlds and subjectivities.

André's analysis highlights a number of tensions that go beyond the children's rights debate in anthropology, carrying strong ties with other disciplines including legal sciences, sociology, psychology and educational science. Moreover, the anthropological discipline in general – and this chapter in particular – not only presents an excellent opportunity to raise critical questions on the dominant children's rights discourses, but also to make explicit how childhood images, children and young people's capacity for action, as well as the constraints, social structures and power relations they face in exercising this capacity, vary throughout societies.

Stuart Aitken's contribution on *Children's rights: A critical geographic perspective* introduces the relationship between children's rights, space and place. The chapter starts off with the question why space matters for children's rights. Afterwards, Aitken draws on Marxist- and feminist-inspired geographical scholarship to point out adults' and children's collective right to be part of the politics that shape, create, produce and reproduce space between the local and the global. Reproduction remains an important theme further on, when children's rights in the variegated contexts of global space or *heteretopias* are discussed. Finally, Aitken considers critiques of the CRC, specifically with relation to children's rights in place and rights to space in a globalized world.

Aitken begins and concludes his chapter with two examples – one from Slovenia and one from Chile – in which he illustrates his fourfold starting point for a critical geographic perspective on children's rights. In particular, he argues that childhood is a geographically diverse phenomenon; that children's rights and societal wholes are geographically variable; that children have the potential to interrogate the core of geo-economic restructuring and neoliberal statehood; and that understanding the ways in which young people interact with space is crucial for understanding children's rights. As such, he contests universal children's rights and global discourses that fix individual categories of existence and identity (e.g. in terms of the object/subject dualism inherent in the CRC), in favour of an interpretation of rights that takes into account spatial variability, personal flexibility and the role of children in co-creating their rights.

In *Children's rights from a gender studies perspective: Gender, intersectionality and the ethics of care*, **Katrien De Graeve** reviews a selection of literature and discussions that have emerged at the interface of gender and childhood studies. Using the feminist concepts of 'intersectionality' and 'ethics of care', she explores what a gender studies perspective can contribute to the theory and practice of a contextualized, bottom-up approach to children and their rights. Her two-fold analysis shows how both concepts can provide theoretical tools for enriching the analysis of children's experiences and rights, not only by providing insight into the contexts and relations in which children are embedded, but also by highlighting the plurality of their identity, as well as the vectors of power and subordination that operate in their lives.

Starting from the assumption that sex and gender profoundly shape and limit children's experiences, De Graeve holds up a critical mirror to those children's rights paradigms, discourses and policies that start from a universal understanding of childhood. Against the backdrop of a gender-sensitive, intersectional approach, her analysis invites a re-balancing of priorities in policy and research. In particular, she suggests counteracting the interlocking inequalities, adult-dominance, gender-bias and other forms of discrimination, with the ultimate aim of revaluing difference (e.g. in terms of age, gender and other axes of social signification) and interdependency (e.g. in meaningful (care) relations) alongside and in relation to individual rights. At the same time, the chapter takes an honest self-critical look at her own discipline, being blind neither to a number of challenges that remain for the integration of intersectional theory and ethics of care within the children's rights framework, nor to the prevailing critiques on the feminist concepts used.

Richard Mitchell's chapter on *Children's rights and citizenship studies: Re-theorising child citizenship through transdisciplinarity from the local to the global* problematizes previous theoretical notions of how children's citizenship rights are constituted and applied: citizenship can no longer be analysed within the binaries of state or statelessness, citizenship or rights. He proposes a re-theorizing of child citizenship, i.e. one that is being crafted on human rights principles rather than on nation-states. Second, he argues that a transdisciplinary re-theorizing of adult-centric citizenship concepts through application of the CRC opens up new opportunities from local to global scales.

Mitchell engages with some of the key elements of the critical approach adopted in this Handbook. He considers researching, teaching and engaging with children neither as a uni-disciplinary nor a uni-directional knowledge exchange, but as a co-constructed and reflexive experience of citizenship for both adults and young people alike. He also pleads for a problem-centred rather than a disciplined-centred approach, which he calls transdisciplinary. His account of children's rights though remains firmly within the confines of children's rights law, and more in particular of the CRC.

6.2. Part 2 – Selected themes at the intersection of the global and the local

Part 2 discusses a number of key themes within children's rights scholarship, offering a representative, but certainly not exhaustive review. These themes are situated at the crossroads of the local and the global.

Kay Tisdall's chapter on *Children and young people's participation: A critical consideration of Article 12* deals with a widely discussed topic in children's rights, i.e. that of child participation. The chapter first explores definitions and typologies of children and young people's participation, in light of the CRC and the children's rights literature. Next, Tisdall analyses two Scottish cases of children and young people's participation. The first case discusses children's participation from an individual perspective in the context of family law proceedings. The second case considers children and young people's participation collectively, in school councils. In the final section, the author evaluates the limitations as well as the potential of the concept and practices of participation.

Tisdall makes a strong case for considering practices of participation as discursive and ambiguous practices. In critically analysing the current debate, she points out some important tensions and discussions in relation to children and young people's participation. One is the pitfall of participation becoming an instrumental practice, integrating children and young people into the existing dominant order, rather than supporting transformative agendas. A second tension concerns the observation that practices of participation tend to separate out children from adults, reifying distinctions between childhood and adulthood rather than mainstreaming children and young people's participation. To overcome some of these problems, Tisdall holds a strong plea for recognizing children and young people's informal ways of participation in their 'everyday' lives rather than seeking to drag them into adult, invited spaces.

In *Education and children's rights,* **Ann Quennerstedt** examines the relationship between education and children's rights from an educational perspective. Starting from the distinction between the right *to* education and rights *in* education, she identifies three aspects of the relation between children's rights and education to accommodate increased complexity: *access* to education, *content* of education and *relations* in education. Analysing the right *to* education in terms of access and content, she discusses in particular the tension between children's and parents' rights, educational segregation and the rights of non-citizen children to education. Looking at rights *in* education from the perspective of content and relations, she points to the importance of educational *processes* (such as experience-based learning and participation) next to topics, and seeks to understand the resistance in education to children's rights-oriented change.

Reflecting on the state of research on children's rights issues in educational sciences, Quennerstedt argues that more research is needed on the meaning of the right to education, the significance of educational content (topics and processes) and the significance of relations in education for learning. She also pleads for more theory-driven and Convention-critical research. Finally, children's rights research should be more grounded in the particular

Introduction: Critical approach

knowledge interest of a certain discipline. This implies a shift in perspective: from a children's rights perspective on education to an educational perspective on children's rights.

Ursulla Kilkelly zooms in on *Health and children's rights*. She outlines the right of the child to health by analysing key CRC provisions as well as the interpretative work of the Committee on the Rights of the Child. Second, the chapter considers some of the silences in the legal children's rights framework, in particular on consent, sexual health, and health promotion. A section on children's rights in healthcare in practice pays attention to the right of the child to participate in healthcare decision-making, which is considered 'a key barometer of child's rights compliant healthcare' (Kilkelly, Chapter 13, p. 217). Key issues include the preference for age rather than maturity, the lack of access to information, and relational attitudes of health professionals. Participation in policy making, service design and delivery has equally proven challenging.

Kilkelly sees a major challenge in the approach of children in health care as a homogenous group, while they are not: they differ in age and levels of maturity but also in socio-economic background. She criticizes the legal instruments and interpretative work on children's rights, i.e. the CRC and the Committee, on their silence with regard to dilemmas and controversies like consent, sexual health and health promotion. Implicitly, Kilkelly seems to favour a multi-disciplinary approach, as her own empirical work on participation also reflects. She remains more reluctant, however, to engage with the approach of critique, in particular in its deliberative dimension.

The chapter by **Ton Liefaard**, *Juvenile justice from an international children's rights perspective*, deals with the complex area of juvenile justice. Mainly from a legal perspective, Liefaard raises the question to what extent children's rights provide authoritative guidance on how to approach the (legal) position of children in conflict with the law. Three key issues in juvenile justice are elaborated. The first one is about the question whether a specific and specialized justice system for children in conflict with the law is required. The second issue concerns the right to a fair trial for children, and the broader and more recent notion of child-friendly justice. Finally, Liefaard deals with the issue of alternative sentences, extreme sentences and deprivation of liberty.

In his chapter, Liefaard shows the difficulty of implementing (inter)national human rights standards applicable to children in conflict with the law and the administration of juvenile justice in practice. This is caused by the complexity of this particular area and its inherent tensions, ambiguities and controversies. One such important tension relates to the often conflicting objectives of juvenile justice. A juvenile justice system aims at protecting society against violent and dangerous offenders and at the same time makes special re-educating interventions in trying to reintegrate child offenders in society. On top of that, cases of juvenile offences are highly sensitive in public media and often result in moral panic and a call for being tough on crime. The author acknowledges this complexity of juvenile justice and offers a nuanced insight into how the framework of children's rights can be used as authoritative guidance.

In his contribution *The human rights of children in the context of formal alternative care*, **Nigel Cantwell** analyses children's rights in relation to children who are not looked after by their parents, or who are at risk of being so. After a historical overview of children's rights instruments addressing (the prevention of) formal alternative care, he discusses the principles of necessity and suitability, to which placements in formal alternative care settings must conform today. Three key areas are explored more in depth. First, Cantwell points to (the increasing recognition of) the importance of informal kinship care in avoiding formal alternative care, and the difficulties in pinpointing state obligations in that respect. Second, he analyses the limits of formal family-based alternative care, among others because of entrenched societal resistance towards taking up 'stranger children' in one's family. Third, challenges surrounding (strategies for) deinstitutionalization are disentangled, again paying explicit attention to the different ways in which these institutions have been set up across the globe.

Providing a nuanced account, Cantwell deeply engages with a critical approach. He particularly emphasizes the crucial importance of a context-specific interpretation and application of children's rights in relation to alternative care, given the highly diverse ways in which societies have informally responded to children without parental care, the large variety in formal alternative care systems, and the multiple child images underlying these approaches. He also demonstrates how considerations other than purely children's rights questions (such as financial considerations) may influence how alternative care is provided – and he argues that they should therefore be taken into account. Finally, he adopts an attitude of critique towards children's rights, regretting the tendency towards 'human rights inflation' and dismissing the 'right to a family' language employed against institutional care. A 'purist' view of children's rights may moreover generate simplistic representations, that may be directed towards the wrong actors or imply assumptions that are not supported by reality.

The main focus of **Gertrud Lenzer**'s chapter on *Violence against children* is the emergence of the concept of violence against children, its history, and related topics. In Lenzer's view, the comprehensive notion of violence against children represents a paradigm shift in the discussion of children's rights, in that it focuses on the protection of children. She then looks in particular into corporal punishment as a major form of violence against children. These more conceptual sections are followed by a case study of the prevalence of violence against children in the United States. In a second part, Lenzer vehemently rejects the bottom-up approach to children's rights in the context of violence against children: 'No matter how desirable it would be for children to participate in their own liberation, the hard social, economic and legal realities are an iron cage that makes such participation impossible.' (Lenzer, Chapter 16, p. 289). In her view, this 'down- or out-sourcing of adult responsibilities to the children themselves' would make children an unprotected social class (Lenzer, Chapter 16, p. 289). This argument is corroborated by biological findings from the neurosciences and epigenetic research about the health and social effects of child maltreatment both for the life course of children and trans-generationally.

Lenzer emphatically pleads for an interdisciplinary approach in the field of children's studies, which should be guided by the CRC. She also puts such an approach into practice, by drawing on empirical work to demonstrate the scope of violence against children in the US, and the impact of maltreatment on children. While she subscribes to the emancipatory agenda and seems to use the concept of violence against children also as a diagnostic device to show the amplitude and devastating impact of maltreatment and the like, she categorically rejects openness to diversity in meaning-giving and interpretation. To the contrary, she warns that a liberationist approach is harmful to children, as it renders them *de facto* unprotected.

In the chapter *Female Genital Mutilation in Europe from a children's rights perspective*, **Els Leye and Annemarie Middelburg** analyse how the practice of female genital mutilation (FGM) can be qualified as a violation of general human rights law as well as children's rights law, and review the state duties flowing from the international legal framework. A case study evaluates how European Union Member States have tackled FGM. Among others, the authors warn against overestimating the importance of prosecutions when evaluating the implementation of a law: an absence of legal cases may indicate the effectiveness of prevention strategies. They conclude that tackling FGM requires a comprehensive, multidisciplinary and context-specific approach: protecting children and young women, prosecuting those responsible, providing psychological, health-related and other services and establishing partnerships between all stakeholders.

Leye and Middelburg flag various challenges and tensions in dealing with FGM. For instance, professionals working with girls at risk must seek an appropriate balance between prevention (which implies collaboration with the family) and prosecution (which may jeopardize an otherwise well-functioning family). A tension also emerges between mandatory medical screening and freedom rights. Moreover, the chapter raises the question of how to deal with cultural arguments. Finally, health professionals who favour harm reduction strategies – through medically performing a 'light' form of FGM – above a ban are criticized for adopting only a health perspective while ignoring the human rights dimension.

Karl Hanson, Diana Volonakis and Mohammed Al-Rozzi discuss the multi-faceted dimensions of child labour in their chapter on *Child labour, working children and children's rights*. They critically engage with dominant perspectives on child labour upheld by the majority of actors, i.e. that child labour is in violation of children's rights. They challenge the dominant abolitionist approach of child work, and contrast it with the recognition of working children's right to work in dignity. After a historical and anthropological account, they discuss the notions of 'child labour', 'child work', 'child employment' and 'working children' and their underlying conceptions. The authors then move on to identify four different stances in reaction to child labour: 'laissez-faire', 'abolitionism', 'regulation' and 'empowerment'.

In this chapter, a critical and emancipatory perspective is taken on working children. The authors take an empowerment approach to working children, to which the views of children are central. They reject an abolitionist approach as the 'sole path towards social justice' (Hanson, Volonakis and Al-Rozzi, Chapter 18, p. 326), in light also of a contextual analysis of the phenomenon. Hanson, Volonakis and Al-Rozzi build on a variety of disciplinary entry points to working children in order to analyse the underlying socio-economic issues.

In his contribution *The human rights of children in the context of international migration*, **Pablo Ceriani Cernadas** explains what we empirically know about children in migration, identifying categories of children affected by migration and reflecting on some of the root causes of migration. He then moves into an analysis of legal standards; he mainly develops a *de lege ferenda* argument, i.e. how children's rights law *should* be applied to migration of children. As regards migration control policies, the principles of non-deportation and non-detention of child migrants are discussed, as well as the due process of law guarantees that should apply when repatriation or deportation measures are envisaged. Other issues reviewed include parents' detention and deportation, the right to a family life, social rights and the duties of countries of origin. The chapter acknowledges that diverging legal interpretations of human rights norms may result in either a protective or restrictive impact on rights, depending on the kind of interpretation that is given. The strong reliance on the general principles as developed by the Committee on the Rights of the Child seems to suggest that more concrete standards and norms are lacking or that they are unsatisfactory.

At first sight, the chapter may come across as a more traditional implementation gap analysis. However, it pictures a rather radical shift in migration policies and in the way children's rights should govern them, in order for children's rights to realize the transformative potential they may have. At least implicitly, an argument is made for drastic changes in migration control policies, including regularization procedures. Ceriani submits that children can never be held responsible for irregular migration; parents' legal status should be determined by the interests and rights of their children. He concludes that introducing a childrights-based approach in migration policies would (and should) lead to a paradigm shift.

Francine Mestrum discusses *Child poverty in the context of global social development*. Whereas she welcomes specific actions against child poverty, she argues that these should be framed within a broader context that looks beyond poverty and beyond age-determined groups. She analyses the poverty creating economic policies under inequality globalization, and discusses the semantic confusion around 'poverty' and the ideology of poverty. She welcomes the recent attention paid to social protection instead of poverty reduction as an approach more in line with the alter-globalization that she adheres to.

Mestrum explicitly pleads for a contextualization of child poverty and children's rights within general poverty and human rights. She also urges to take into account the societal context in which children are living. Mestrum points out the political and ideological dimensions of the (child) poverty debate, and argues that 'empowering people in a disempowering political context can only lead to frustration' (Mestrum, Chapter 20, p. 362). Whereas she does not challenge children's rights law, she does plead for sufficient attention to be paid also to collective rights.

In her chapter *Indigenous children's rights: Opportunities in appropriation and transformation*, **Natasha Blanchet-Cohen** demonstrates how indigenous peoples have addressed the challenges of implementing the CRC, by interpreting and giving new meaning to its provisions. This process of 'appropriation and transformation' is illustrated in three areas: defining the concept of indigenous; grasping the meaning and implications of the right to 'enjoy his or her own culture', and identifying duty-bearers. Other examples are drawn from the fields of education and child protection. The author concludes that the CRC holds real potential for improving indigenous children's lives – and as such can realize its emancipatory objective – if indigenous children and communities gain ownership of the Convention and are actively involved in its implementation.

In contrast to the general 'growing apart' of human rights and children's rights mentioned earlier in this introduction, Blanchet-Cohen notes a positive spill-over from human rights of indigenous peoples to children's rights of indigenous peoples. She also emphasizes the importance of a contextual approach: indigenous understandings of 'best interests' may differ from dominant conceptions, and children's participation in indigenous communities is often more indirect than what is envisaged by the CRC. Adopting a critical perspective, she invites children's rights to embrace tensions instead of ignoring them.

Ellen Desmet and José Aylwin explore in their chapter *Natural resource exploitation and children's rights* the relevance of children's rights (law) in the context of natural resource exploitation, with a focus on Latin America. They discuss the experiences of children and young people with natural resource industries, review relevant human and children's rights legal standards and zoom in on two fields of tension, i.e. child-specificity and incorporating insights from other disciplines. Similar to Mestrum with regard to poverty, Desmet and Aylwin argue that whereas child-specific approaches may be beneficial, a more general take on the matter is needed. They also point out how the incorporation of insights from other disciplines in legal analysis may have empowering or disempowering effects, depending on how these insights are used. The chapter ends with three future-oriented themes: the need for effective remedies and change at the domestic level, the importance of an intercultural and context-specific approach, and the proposal to shift focus in future research towards a more inclusive approach on how we engage with – rather than exploit – natural resources.

Desmet and Aylwin engage with all aspects of a critical approach. They conclude that the image of a vulnerable child is predominant, although recognition of children's and young people's agency is on the increase. They highlight the ambivalence of a separate 'domain' of children's rights in analysing a transversal issue like resource exploitation, and argue that the current legal conceptualization of children's and human rights runs up against its limits. They equally emphasize the need to understand children's rights in a holistic, intercultural and context-specific way, and draw on insights from other disciplines, in particular anthropology.

Acknowledgment

This research has been funded by the Interuniversity Attraction Poles Programme (IAP) initiated by the Belgian Science Policy Office, more specifically the IAP 'The Global Challenge of Human Rights Integration: Towards a Users' Perspective' (www.hrintegration.be).

References

Abramson, B. (1996). The invisibility of children and adolescents: The need to monitor our rhetoric and our attitudes. In E. Verhellen (ed.), *Monitoring Children's Rights* (pp. 393–402). Martinus Nijhoff.

Alanen, L. (2011). Critical childhood studies? *Childhood: a Global Journal of Child Research*, 18(2), 147–150.

Alston, P. (1994). The Best Interests Principle: Towards a Reconciliation of Culture and Human Rights, *International Journal of Law and the Family*, 8: 1–25.

Banakar, R., and Travers, M. (2005). Law, Sociology and Method. In R. Banakar and M. Travers (eds), *Theory and Method in Socio-Legal Research* (pp. 1–25). Oxford: Hart.

Boonaert, T., and Siongers, J. (2010). Jongeren en media: van mediavreemden tot hybride meerwaardezoekers [Young people and media: from media strangers to hybrid value seekers]. In N. Vettenburg, J. Deklerck and J. Siongers (eds), *Jongeren in cijfers en letters. Bevindingen uit de JOP-monitor 2* [Young people in numbers and letters. Findings from the JOP-monitor 2] (pp. 135–159). Acco.

Brewer, G.D. (1999). The challenges of interdisciplinarity. *Policy Sciences*, 32(4), 327–337.

Cantwell, N. (1992). The origins, development and significance of the United Nations Convention on the Rights of the Child. In S. Detrick (ed.), *The United Nations Convention on the Rights of the Child: A Guide to the 'Travaux Préparatoires'*. Martinus Nijhoff, 19–30.

Cantwell, N. (2011). Are children's rights still human? In A. Invernizzi and J. Williams (eds), *The human rights of children : from visions to implementation* (37–59). Aldershot, UK: Ashgate.

Choi, B., and Pak, A. (2006). Multidisciplinary, interdisciplinary and transdisciplinarity in health research, services, education and policy: 1. Definitions, objectives, and evidence of effectiveness. *Clinical Investigation and Medicine*, 29(6), 351–364.

Cipriani, D. (2009). *Children's Rights and the Minimum Age of Criminal Responsibility: A Global Perspective*. Aldershot, UK: Ashgate.

Clark-Kazak, C.R. (2009). Towards a Working Definition and Application of Social Age in International Development Studies. *Journal of Development Studies*, 45(8), 1307–1324.

Cornock, M., and Montgomery, H. (2011). Children's rights in and out of the womb. *The International Journal of Children's Rights*, 19(1), 3–19.

(CRC) Committee on the Rights of the Child (2003, 27 November), General Comment No. 5, *General Measures of Implementation of the Convention on the Rights of the Child (arts. 4, 42 and 44, para. 6)*, UN Doc. CRC/GC/2003/5.

Dalrymple, J., and Miller, W. (2006). Interdisciplinarity: A key for real-world learning. *Planet*, 17, 29–31.

De Feyter, K. (2007). Localising human rights. In W. Benedek, K. d. De Feyter and F. Marrella (eds), *Economic Globalisation and Human Rights* (pp. 11–40). Cambridge: Cambridge University Press.

De Feyter, K. (2011). Sites of rights resistance. In K. De Feyter, S. Parmentier, C. Timmerman and G. Ulrich (eds), *The Local Relevance of Human Rights* (pp. 11–39). Cambridge: Cambridge University Press.

de Gaay Fortman, B. (2011). *Political Economy of Human Rights. Rights, Realities and Realization*. Routledge.

Desmet, E. (2012). Implementing the Convention on the Rights of the Child for 'Youth': Who and How? *The International Journal Of Children's Rights*, 20(1), 3–23.

Elchardus, M., and Roggemans, L. (2010). De ideale levensloop van jongeren [The ideal life course of young people]. In N. Vettenburg, J. Deklerck and J. Siongers (eds), *Jongeren in cijfers en letters. Bevindingen uit de JOP-monitor 2* [Young people in numbers and letters. Findings from the JOP-monitor 2]. (pp. 161–180). Acco.

Evans, T. (2005). International human rights law as power/knowledge, *Human Rights Quarterly*, 27(3), 1046–1068.

Goodale, M., and Merry, S.E. (2007). *The Practice of Human Rights: Tracking Law between the Global and the Local*. Cambridge: Cambridge University Press.

Grunwald, K., and Thiersch, H. (2009). The concept of the 'lifeworld orientation' for social work and social care. *Journal of Social Work Practice*, 23(2), 131–146.

Hanson, K., and Nieuwenhuys, O. (eds) (2013). *Reconceptualizing Children's Rights in International Development: Living Rights, Social Justice, Translations.* Oxford: Oxford University Press.

Holland, S., and Scourfield, J. (2004). Liberty and respect in child protection, *British Journal of Social Work*, 34(1): 21–36.

Honig, M.-S. (2008). Work and care: Reconstructing childhood through childcare policy in Germany. In A. James and A.L. James (eds), *European Childhoods: Cultures, politics and childhoods in Europe* (pp. 198–215). Basingstoke, UK: Palgrave Macmillan.

James, A. (2009). Agency. In J. Qvortrup, W.A. Corsaro and M.-S. Honig (eds), *The Palgrave Handbook of Childhood Studies* (pp. 34–45). Basingstoke, UK: Palgrave Macmillan.

James, A., and James A.L. (2012). *Key Concepts in Childhood Studies* (2nd ed.). London: Sage.

James, A., and James A. L. (2004). *Constructing Childhood: Theory, policy and social practice.* Basingstoke, UK: Palgrave Macmillan.

James, A. and Prout, A. (eds) (1997). *Constructing and Reconstructing Childhood: Contemporary issues in the sociological study of childhood* (2nd ed.). London: Falmer Press.

Johnson, S.B., Blum, R.W., and Giedd, J.N. (2009). Adolescent maturity and the brain: The promise and pitfalls of neuroscience research in adolescent health policy. *Journal of Adolescent Health*, 45, 216–221.

Joseph, R. (2009). *Human Rights and the Unborn Child.* Leiden: Martinus Nijhoff.

KeKi (Kenniscentrum Kinderrechten vzw) (2012). *Kinderrechten: Reflectietekst van het Kenniscentrum Kinderrechten*, Ghent: Kenniscentrum Kinderrechten.

Kjorholt, A.T. (2002). Small is powerful: Discourses on 'children and participation' in Norway, *Childhood*, 9(1), 63–82.

Klein, J.T. (1990). *Interdisciplinarity: History, Theory, and Practice.* Detroit, MI: Wayne State University Press.

Liebel, M. (2012). *Children's Rights from Below: Cross-Cultural Perspectives.* Basingstoke, UK: Palgrave Macmillan.

Lopatka, A. (2007). Introduction in OHCHR, *Legislative History of the Convention on the Rights of the Child.* Geneva: United Nations.

Merry, S.E. (2000). Crossing Boundaries: Ethnography in the Twenty-First Century. *PoLAR Political and Legal Anthropology Review*, 23(2), 127–133.

Merry, S.E., Levitt, P., Rosen, M. Ş., and Yoon, D.H. (2010). Law from below: Women's human rights and social movements in New York City. *Law and Society Review*, 44(1), 101–128.

Morrow, V., and Pells, K. (2012). Integrating children's human rights and child poverty debates: examples from young lives in Ethiopia and India, *Sociology*, 46(5): 906–920.

Nieuwenhuys, O. (1998). Global Childhood and the Politics of Contempt. *Alternatives*, 23, 267–289.

Pupavac, V. (2001). Misanthropy without borders: The international children's rights regime. *Disasters* 25(2), 95–112.

Quennerstedt, A. (2010). Children, but not really humans? Critical reflections on the hampering effect of the "3 p's", *International Journal of Children's Rights*, 18(4), 619–635.

Reynaert, D., Bouverne-De Bie, M., and Vandevelde, S. (2009). A review of children's rights literature since the adoption of the United Nations Convention on the Rights of the Child. *Childhood*, 16(4), 518–534.

Reynaert, D., Roose, R., Vandenhole, W. and Vlieghe, K. (eds) (2011). *Kinderrechten: Springplank of Struikelblok? Naar Een Kritische Benadering Van Kinderrechten* [Children's rights: Steppingstone or stumbling block? Towards a critical approach of children's rights]. Antwerpen: Intersentia.

Reynaert, D., De Bie, M., and Vandevelde, S. (2012). Between 'believers' and 'opponents': critical discussions on children's rights. *The International Journal of Children's Rights*, 20(1), 1–15.

Reynaert, D., and Roose, R. (2014). Children's rights and the capability approach: Discussing children's agency against the horizon of the institutionalised youth land. In *Children's Rights and the Capability Approach* (pp. 175–193). Springer Netherlands.

Reynolds, P., Nieuwenhuys, O., and Hanson, K. (2006). Refractions of children's rights in development practice: A view from anthropology—Introduction. *Childhood*, 13(3), 291–302.

Such, E., and Walker, R. (2005). Young citizens or policy objects? Children in the 'rights and responsibilities debate'. *Journal of Social Policy*, 34: 39–57.

Vandenhole, W. (2012). Localising the human rights of children. In M. Liebel (ed.), *Children's rights from below: cross-cultural perspectives* (pp. 80–93). Basingstoke, UK: Palgrave Macmillan.

Veerman, P.E. (2010). The Ageing of the UN Convention on the Rights of the Child. *The International Journal of Children's Rights*, 18(4), 585–618.

Verhellen, E. (2000). *Convention on the rights of the child. Background, motivation, strategies, main themes.* Antwerp: Garant.

Verhellen, E. (2004). The Convention on the Rights of the Child. In A. Weyts (ed.), *Understanding Children's Rights. Collected Papers Presented at the Seventh International Interdisciplinary Course on Children's Rights, Ghent, November-December 2004,* Children's Rights Centre, 17–34.

Vick, D.W. (2004). Interdisciplinarity and the Discipline of Law. *Journal of Law and Society, 31*(2), 163–193.

Zinnecker, J. (2000). Childhood and Adolescence as Pedagogic Moratoria. *Zeitschrift fürPädagogik,* 46(2): 36–68.

Part I
Disciplinary perspectives

2
Children's rights from a legal perspective
Children's rights law

Wouter Vandenhole

It may be fair to say that the legal discipline has appropriated a substantial part of children's rights scholarship. Legal literature is mostly thematic, i.e. addressing a certain issue or right, although some general works exist (see in particular Van Bueren, 1998; Detrick, 1992; Hodgkin and Newell, 2007). Legal scholarship ranges from (sub-)national (Williams, 2013) to regional (Van Bueren, 2007; Kilkelly, 1999) and global publications (Apodaca, 2010; Drumbl, 2012).

Some terminological clarification is needed from the start, as there is substantial confusion about children's rights in the language used on the subject, in particular by non-lawyers. Children's rights law differs from child law and children's rights. Child law is arguably the broadest legal category, encompassing all law concerning children and childhood: this may be domestic law on e.g. adoption, education or affiliation, or international law on e.g. parental abduction. Children's rights law is a narrower legal category that refers to the fundamental rights of children, i.e. the human rights of children (Morrow and Pells, 2012, p. 909). Children's rights law is about the fundamental rights of children that have been legally recognized in national constitutions and/or in international law (and in particular in treaty law). A legal instrument belonging to the latter category is e.g. the UN Convention on the Rights of the Child (CRC). Children's rights refers also to the fundamental or human rights of children, but is not (necessarily) a legal category. It may be argued, for example, that there is a children's right to work, based on notions of self-determination or human dignity, but such a right has not been legally recognized so far. To add to the confusion, "children's rights" tends to be used as a shorthand for children's rights law too. This chapter deals with children's rights law, i.e. the legal codification of human rights of children, and will draw on international law at the global and regional level in particular, to the exclusion of national (constitutional) law.

A considerable part of the legal literature deals with the so-called implementation gap (see introduction). Lawyers (and others) tend to see outstanding children's rights issues mainly as a problem of lack of implementation of the existing legal standards. They thereby seem to assume that relevant standards exist for each children's rights issue, that the meaning of these standards is clear, and that these standards are able to satisfactorily address the issue at stake. The standards themselves are therefore seldom called into question. Whereas in litigation it may be important at times not to re-open the discussion on the (beneficial) meaning of legal guarantees in a specific case, but to have them "simply" applied and implemented, legal scholarship should engage not only with questions of implementation, but also with legally defining and re-defining the meaning of children's rights. There is an emerging school of interdisciplinary thinking that takes up the challenge of critical reflection on children's rights in their legal codification (Hanson and Nieuwenhuys, 2013; Liebel et al., 2012), but that approach is far from being mainstreamed.

The objective of this chapter is threefold. First of all, it seeks to familiarize readers with the international legal frameworks on children's rights. Second, legal reasoning on children's rights will be introduced, in particular by clarifying the general obligations incumbent on States, the general principles guiding the interpretation of children's rights law, as well as by introducing some of the case-law. Third, the chapter wants to offer some building blocks for a critical assessment of the legal approach to children's rights, highlighting some of its strengths and weaknesses.

In what follows, key legal instruments, monitoring bodies and procedures at the global and regional level will first be introduced. Second, general obligations and general principles as key parameters for children's rights law will be fleshed out, followed by the exploration of case-law on three topics: juvenile justice, family matters and education. Before concluding, some moot points of social change through children's rights law will be discussed. At the very end, some questions for reflection and discussion are flagged.

1. Legal frameworks at global and regional level

International law has three sources of binding law: treaties, custom, and general principles. In the field of human rights law (including children's rights law), the most important source is treaty law. Treaty law is only binding on the parties, usually States, that have ratified or acceded to the treaty.

At the global level, there are meanwhile nine core UN human rights treaties,[1] which are all of relevance to children – for children are human beings that are equally entitled to all human rights as adults are. Among these UN human rights treaties, the Convention on the Rights of the Child (CRC, 1989) is without doubt the landmark legal instrument on the human rights of children. The CRC currently counts 195 States parties, and is the most widely ratified human rights treaty. In 2000, two substantive optional protocols were adopted, one on the Involvement of Children in Armed Conflict (hereafter OPAC) and one on the Sale of Children, Child Prostitution and Child Pornography (hereafter OPSC). More recently, in 2011, a third optional protocol was adopted on a communications procedure (hereafter OPIC). The latter entered into force on 14 April 2014.

The CRC consists of three parts. Part I offers a definition of the child, contains general principles and obligations and a detailed list of specific rights and obligations. The CRC is very comprehensive in scope, and covers civil, political, economic, social and cultural rights. A popular categorization among children's rights proponents and CRC commentators is the three Ps: rights to protection, provision and participation (for a critical assessment, see Quennerstedt, 2010). Part II deals with the CRC's monitoring body, the Committee on the Rights of the Child. Part III holds some final provisions on ratification, amendments, reservations, denunciation, etc.

The Committee on the Rights of the Child, composed of 18 experts elected by the States Parties, meets three times a year. It monitors State compliance with the CRC and its protocols

---

1   Available at www.ohchr.org/EN/ProfessionalInterest/Pages/CoreInstruments.aspx (last accessed 8 July 2013).

through the reporting procedure. Initial reports are to be submitted two years after the coming into effect of the CRC for the State. Periodic reports are to be submitted every five years (Art. 44 CRC). States that are equally parties to the CRC and the (substantive) optional protocols are to submit a separate initial report under the substantive optional protocols, but can thereafter include information on the implementation of the protocols in their periodic reports on the implementation of the CRC (Art. 8 OPAC and Art. 12 OPSC). With the entry into force of OPIC, the Committee is also able to receive individual complaints and inter-state complaints, and to engage in an inquiry procedure for grave or systematic violations (provided that the State concerned has opted in for the inter-state complaints, and not opted out of the inquiry procedure).

Since the Committee started its practice of issuing general comments in 2001, it has adopted 17 general comments, on issues as diverse as (in order of adoption) the aims of education; the role of independent national human rights institutions; HIV/AIDS; adolescent health and development; general measures of implementation; the treatment of unaccompanied and separated children outside their country of origin; early childhood; corporal punishment and other cruel or degrading forms of punishment; disability; juvenile justice; indigenous children; the right to be heard; violence; the best interests of the child; the right to health; the business sector; and the right to leisure and play.[2] General comments are meant to promote further implementation of the Convention and its Protocols, and to assist States parties in fulfilling their reporting obligations (Rule 73 Rules of Procedure) by offering a deeper understanding of the content and implications of the Convention. Strictly speaking, they have not the same legal force as the CRC or its Optional Protocols. They are authoritative interpretations of the treaties' monitoring body.

It is important to recall that other UN core human rights treaties too contain child-relevant and child-specific provisions. Child-relevant, for a child is a human being, and a human right recognized to belong to "every person" therefore also belongs to every child. For example, provisions on the right to education will be of particular relevance for children too (see Art. 12 International Covenant on Economic, Social and Cultural Rights (ICESCR); Art. 24 Convention on the Rights of Persons with Disabilities (CRPD); Art. 30 and 45 Convention on the Protection of the Human Rights of All Migrant Workers and Members of their Families (CMW). Child-specific, for children are explicitly accorded some rights under these treaties: e.g., Art. 10 (3) ICESCR provides for special measures of protection and assistance for all children and young persons; Art. 6 (5) International Covenant on Civil and Political Rights (ICCPR) does not allow for the imposition of the death penalty on minors; Art. 14 (1) and (4) ICCPR pays particular attention to "juvenile persons" in the context of fair trial guarantees, and Art. 24 ICCPR ensures the right to protection, name and nationality to every child (similarly, Art. 29 CMW guarantees the right to a name, to birth registration and a nationality). Art. 7 CRPD is dedicated to children with disabilities, and Art. 25 International Convention for the Protection of All Persons from Enforced Disappearance (ICED) deals with children who have been affected directly or indirectly by enforced disappearance.

At the regional level, three continents have developed their own human rights framework and machinery. Within the Organization of American States, there is no children's rights specific instrument, but the American Convention on Human Rights (1969) contains an

---

2   The full titles and text of these general comments can be found on http://tbinternet.ohchr.org/_layouts/treatybodyexternal/TBSearch.aspx?Lang=enandTreatyID=5andDocTypeID=11 (last accessed 5 March 2014).

explicit provision on children (Art. 19 on the right to protection), and also guarantees the rights of the family (Art. 17) and the right to a name (Art. 18) and nationality (Art. 20). The Additional Protocol to the American Convention on Human Rights in the Area of Economic, Social and Cultural Rights (Protocol of San Salvador) similarly contains rights that are highly relevant to children (e.g. Art. 13 on the right to education; Art. 15 on the formation and protection of families), as well as a child-specific provision (Art. 16 deals with protection, non-separation from the mother and education). Both the Inter-American Commission and the Inter-American Court monitor the treaty, also under an individual complaints mechanism.[3] The African Union has its African Charter on the Rights and Welfare of the Child (1990), which is monitored by the African Committee of Experts on the Rights and Welfare of the Child. The latter has become active in recent times, and has dealt with a couple of complaints.[4] In addition, the African Charter on Human and Peoples' Rights, in its Art. 18, ensures the protection of children's rights "as stipulated in international declarations and conventions".

Within the Council of Europe, the general human rights treaty on civil and political rights, the Convention for the Protection of Human Rights and Fundamental Freedoms (ECHR, 1950), does not explicitly reference children's rights, but its monitoring body, the European Court of Human Rights, has developed an impressive body of case-law on the topic.[5] We will highlight some of these cases in the sections that follow. The Revised European Social Charter (RESC, 1996) contains two explicit provisions on children's rights, Art. 7(10) on the right to protection (particularly in the context of work) and Art. 17 on the right to social, legal and economic protection. The latter was inspired by the CRC. Other relevant Council of Europe treaties include the European Convention on the Exercise of Children's Rights (1996), the Convention on the Protection of Children against Sexual Exploitation and Sexual Abuse (2007) and the European Convention on the Adoption of Children (Revised) (2008). Mention should also be made of the European Union Charter of Fundamental Rights of 2007, which contains a general children's rights provision (Art. 24) in addition to one that prohibits child labour and offers protection at work (Art. 32). This Charter is now binding on the EU and its member states, and the Court of Justice of the European Union increasingly relies on the Charter in its case-law.

The fact that treaties are internationally binding on States that have ratified them does not automatically mean that they can be invoked in the domestic legal orders. In dualist systems, the treaty needs to be incorporated into domestic law. In monist systems, the treaty is directly applicable in the domestic legal order (no incorporation is needed), but that does not mean that it can also be directly invoked by individuals in legal proceedings. Often, additional requirements must be fulfilled in order to grant treaty provisions direct effect, e.g. that the provision has a clear and unequivocal meaning. In addition, the findings of monitoring bodies, with the exception of those of courts, are not legally binding.[6] All this means that, notwithstanding the existence of a mainly impressive legal framework and monitoring system, the human rights of children as laid down in international (treaty) law often lack strong legal implementation and proper realization in domestic legal orders.

---

3   For an overview of children's rights case-law. Available at www.oas.org/en/iachr/children/ (last accessed 5 March 2014).
4   Available at http://caselaw.ihrda.org/acerwc/ (last accessed 5 March 2014).
5   That case-law can be found in a separate database, Theseus, available at www.coe.int/t/dg3/children/WCD/ simpleSearch_en.asp (last accessed 5 March 2014).
6   For a dismissal of the binding–non-binding dichotomy, see Schabas (2011).

2. General obligations and principles

In what follows, we will mainly focus on the CRC in order to clarify the general obligations incumbent on States parties, as well as to highlight the general principles informing children's rights law. Much of this is by and large applicable to other treaty regimes too.

The general obligation incumbent on States, as defined in Art. 4 CRC, is to take "all appropriate" measures, legislative, administrative and other (Rishmawi, 2006). In addition, Art. 42 and 44.6 CRC impose obligations of children's rights education for children and adults, and of wide dissemination of the state report. What these appropriate measures may mean in practice has been spelt out in the CRC Committee's General Comment No. 5. The second paragraph of art. 4 CRC makes clear that the general obligation is not the same for all rights. This differentiated general obligation means in practice that States have much more leeway in the implementation of economic, social and cultural rights. For the latter, the State is required to take all appropriate measures to "the maximum extent of their available resources" only (Alston, 1994, p. 7; Cantwell, 1992, p. 27). In the CRC Committee's view, "[t]he second sentence of article 4 reflects a realistic acceptance that lack of resources – financial and other resources – can hamper the full implementation of economic, social and cultural rights in some States; this introduces the concept of 'progressive realization' of such rights." (CRC, 2003, p. para. 7).

So, whereas the CRC is very comprehensive in scope, and covers civil, political, economic, social and cultural rights, it is relatively weak in the protection of economic, social and cultural rights. The practical consequences of this differentiation should not be overstated though. Interpretative work of monitoring bodies, and in particular of the Committee on Economic, Social and Cultural Rights, as well as scholarly analysis have meanwhile clarified the meaning of progressive realization. First of all, the obligation of progressive realization does not mean that a State can endlessly postpone realization: it is under an obligation to take immediate steps towards full realization. Moreover, there is a strong presumption that retrogressive measures are not permitted. Finally, minimum core obligations need to be realized immediately (Committee on Economic, 1990; Vandenhole, 2003). Interestingly, the available resources not only include domestic resources, but also those that are available through international cooperation. Whether there is a legal obligation to cooperate for development is highly contested though (Vandenhole, 2009a).

Whereas the CRC itself does not make reference to general principles, the CRC Committee has identified in its Reporting Guidelines four over-arching general principles,[7] which are reflected in CRC provisions: the right to equality and non-discrimination (Art. 2 CRC); the best interests of the child (Art. 3 CRC); the right to life, survival and development (Art. 6 CRC); and respect for the views of the child, sometimes also referred to as the right to participation (Art. 12 CRC). The best interests principle in particular is believed to have a scope of application beyond the CRC, but all or some of these general principles have meanwhile been introduced in children's rights provisions in other treaties. However, some scholars have questioned the conceptual underpinning for these general principles, and challenged their vagueness and versatile meaning (Tobin, 2011).

Compared to non-discrimination clauses in other (older) human rights treaties, the CRC's non-discrimination provision is broader in that it also offers protection against discrimination on the basis of status, activities, expressed opinions, or beliefs of a child's parents, legal guardians or family members. Moreover, it explicitly lists the parent's or legal guardian's race, and the

---

7   Available at file:///H:/G9118171.pdf (last accessed 5 March 2014).

children's ethnic origin and disability as prohibited grounds (CRC, 2006). In line with general human rights law, the prohibition of discrimination in the field of economic, social and cultural rights can be argued not to be limited by article 4 CRC, and to be of immediate effect.[8]

The best interests of the child was introduced to international law as a new interpretation principle by the CRC (Freeman, 2007, p. 1). Its meaning and application remain challenging, notwithstanding attempts to clarify them, most recently by the CRC Committee itself (CRC, 2013). The interests of the child can be understood in different ways: as basic interest, developmental interest or autonomy interest (Eekelaar, 1992), or also in light of children's needs, potential harm to children or their wishes and feelings (Freeman, 2007, p. 31). In light of the interdependence and interaction between the different rights in the CRC, the best interests of the child are to be understood in light of all other rights and general principles, so that children themselves should have a say in defining what is in their interest (Archard and Skivenes, 2009). It is noteworthy that in Art. 3 CRC, the best interests of the child are only "*a* primary consideration", not *the* primary or paramount consideration. The best interests of the child are therefore often to be balanced with other interests (Freeman, 2007, p. 60). In other CRC provisions, in the African Charter on the Rights and Welfare of the Child (Art. 4) and in the approach of European instruments, the best interests of the child are often considered *the* primary consideration; they therefore seem to prevail over the interests of others.

The right to life, survival and development in Art. 6 CRC is unique in its formulation. Other core human rights treaties protect the right to life only, without mentioning survival and development. The reference to survival was intended to emphasize the positive obligations incumbent on states parties to prolong children's lives. Survival is closely related to a healthy development of children, and thereby introduces obligations of fulfilment (Nowak, 2005, pp. 12–14 and 36–37). The development of children is to be understood holistically (CRC, 2003, para. 10), and is closely related to the concept of human development as advocated in the 1980s by the World Health Organization and UNICEF (Nowak, 2005, p. 7 and 14).

Finally, the right to participation is a cluster of rights, with at its core the right to express one's view and the right to have that view being taken into account (Archard, 2006, p. v; CRC, 2009). The right to express one's views is limited to children who are capable of forming their views, and extends only to matters that affect them. The right to have the views expressed taken into account is qualified by references to age and maturity (Ang *et al.*, 2006, p. 14). Quite often, the right to participation is balanced with or pitched against the best interests of the child (Ang *et al.*, 2006, p. 18). Whereas the Committee suggests a harmonious coexistence of both general principles (CRC, 2009, 2013), in reality, an adult's defined best interests principle tends to prevail in e.g. family or migration matters.

3. Some themes

In what follows, we discuss some substantive themes in the area of children's rights: juvenile justice; family and alternative care; and education. The selection of these themes is pragmatic: for these topics, a fair amount of case-law is available. The availability of international case-law may be indicative of the importance of these themes. The ambition is not to offer a comprehensive legal analysis, but rather to illustrate what a legal approach of children's rights looks like. We mainly draw on the case-law of the European Court of Human Rights (ECtHR).

---

8   Contra: (Besson, 2005, p. 455).

3.1. Juvenile justice[9]

Juvenile justice questions have been the subject of extensive soft law standard-setting, often prior to, and outside the realm of children's rights law (see in particular the Beijing Rules, Riadh Guidelines, Havana Rules and Vienna Guidelines).[10] Some basic principles have been codified in the CRC, and further elaborated upon in the CRC Committee's General Comment on children's rights in juvenile justice (CRC, 2010). Art. 37 CRC deals with the prohibition of torture and the right to freedom. Deprivation of liberty is a measure of last resort and shall be used for the shortest *appropriate* period of time. Art. 40 CRC offers fair trial guarantees in case of infringement of penal law. This provision is characterized by an inherent tension: whereas it "seeks to establish a child centred criminal justice system focusing on the child's welfare which is not necessarily one safeguarded by lawyers […]", it also "recognizes that traditional juvenile justice is dependant [sic] upon lawyers." (Van Bueren, 2006, p. 8).[11] Given the focus of Art. 40 on child-centred criminal justice, some due process guarantees found in general human rights law were not repeated in the CRC. On the other hand, reintegration, rather than rehabilitation "as an undesirable form of social control", is the stated aim of child-centred criminal justice (Van Bueren, 2006, p. 12). Reintegration does not attribute responsibility solely with the individual, but takes also the social environment into account (Van Bueren, 2006, p. 12). The approach to juvenile justice in the CRC may be indicative of the possibility in principle to include contextual factors in a legal rights approach, and may help to dismiss claims that legal rights framing inevitably entails individuation of social problems.

In the case-law of the European Court of Human Rights, several questions of juvenile justice have arisen. As to deprivation of liberty by keeping minors in pre-trial detention, the Court has expressed "its misgivings about the practice of detaining children in pre-trial detention" (Güveç v. Turkey, 2009, para. 109). It acknowledged that in light of international standards, deprivation of liberty must be a measure of last resort and that alternative methods must be considered first. As to the conditions of detention, the Court held that the compounded effect of the applicant's age (a minor), the length of his detention in prison together with adults, the failure of the authorities to provide adequate medical care for his psychological problems, and the failure to take steps with a view to preventing his repeated attempts to commit suicide, amounted to inhuman and degrading treatment (Güveç v. Turkey, 2009, para. 98).

On the difficult question of the minimum age of criminal responsibility, the European Court of Human Rights has been far less leading. Admittedly, the CRC offers no other guidance than that States parties have to establish a minimum age of criminal responsibility. It remains silent on the *appropriate* age for setting that minimum. The CRC Committee has suggested that twelve is the absolute minimum (CRC, 2010), but the 2010 Council of Europe Guidelines on Child-Friendly Justice only suggest that it should not be too low (Europe, 2010). The Court held in 1999 that the attribution of criminal responsibility to a 10-year-old was not in itself in violation of article 3 ECHR (T. v. UK, 1999). It is a matter of debate whether the Court would find differently had it to assess the question nowadays (Van Bueren, 2006, p. 27). Whereas the Court did not reject criminal responsibility of a young teenager as such (from the

---

9   For a thorough and extensive analysis, see Schabas and Sax (2006); Van Bueren (2006); Liefaard (2008, Chapter 14 in this Handbook).
10 Available at www.unodc.org/unodc/en/justice-and-prison-reform/childrensvictimswomens issues.html (last accessed 5 March 2014).
11 It should be noted that the reference here to a welfare approach does not correspond necessarily with the welfare school of thought as defined by Hanson (2012, pp. 75–77)

perspective neither of the prohibition of inhuman or degrading treatment, nor of the right to a fair trial), it did require additional fair trial guarantees: it considers it essential that a child charged with an offence is dealt with in a manner which takes full account of his age, level of maturity and intellectual and emotional capacities, and that steps are taken to promote his ability to understand and participate in the proceedings (T. v. UK, 1999). Effective participation in one's own trial was also at stake in more recent cases. In the Salduz-case, the Court has highlighted the importance of access to a lawyer in pre-trial proceedings, and emphasized "the fundamental importance of providing access to a lawyer where the person in custody is a minor" (Salduz v. Turkey, 2008, para. 60).

Finally, the Court has adopted a reintegration and child-oriented, welfarist criminal justice approach on the question of expulsion of a foreign juvenile offender. In balancing the right to respect for private and family life with public interest considerations of crime prevention and control, it argued that a State has to take into account its obligation to facilitate reintegration of juvenile offenders into society. That duty stems from the best interests principle, and makes severing of family and social ties through expulsion a measure of last resort. In case of non-violent crimes, the obligation to facilitate reintegration makes it extremely difficult to justify expulsion of juvenile offenders who have been living in the country since their childhood (Maslov v. Austria, 2008, paras. 83–84).

In sum, no radical child welfare approach has been taken to juvenile offenders in children's rights law, with the notable exception of expulsion of foreign offenders who are settled migrants. Instead, additional or stronger procedural guarantees have been devised, and the exceptional character of deprivation of liberty has been emphasized.

3.2. Family and alternative care[12]

The CRC recognizes children's right to respect of family life (Art. 16), and protects them against separation from their parents against the latter's will (Art. 9). It gives parents the primary responsibility for the upbringing and development of the child (Art. 18), including with regard to the conditions of living (Art. 27). At the same time, the CRC imposes an obligation on States to take all appropriate measures to protect children from all forms of violence, abuse or neglect while in the care of parents (Art. 19). It is therefore acknowledged that separation from parents may be necessary for the best interests of the child (Art. 9 CRC). In 2009, the UN Guidelines on Alternative Care were adopted, which provide detailed guidance on alternative care (UN General Assembly, 2010).

The delicate balance between protection against violence, abuse or neglect, and respect for family life, has also been at stake in the case-law of the European Court of Human Rights. The State is under a positive obligation to provide children protection (X., Y. and Z. v. United Kingdom, 1997), but must show restraint in taking children into care outside the family. As the mutual enjoyment by parent and child of each other's company is considered a fundamental element of family life, placement into care is a measure of last resort, and a temporary measure that is to be discontinued as soon as circumstances permit, with the ultimate aim of family reunion. A State enjoys a large margin of appreciation with regard to the necessity of taking a child into care – in particular in emergency situations – but has less policy space in case of further limitations to family life, e.g. by restricting parental rights of access (H.K. v. Finland, 2006). Procedurally, parents and (older) children are entitled to information and involvement

---

12   See also Cantwell, Chapter 15 in this Handbook.

in the decision-making process (H.K. v. Finland, 2006; Saviny v. Ukraine, 2008). The European Committee of Social Rights' approach to placement is very much in line with the Court's one (CRC, 2009, p. 6). This strong preference for the preservation of natural family life is fully understandable in light of horrendous practices whereby "unworthy" parents were and are deprived of their children because of poverty or ethnic origin. There is also evidence that the lack of *a* family life is particularly harmful to young children, and that institutional care is therefore not beneficial for them: "More than 50 years of research provides convincing evidence that institutional care is detrimental to the cognitive, behavioural, emotional, and social development of young children". (Kilkelly, 1999). But beyond these elements, the strong preference for biological family life may need further justification.

Importantly, no placement is justifiable exclusively on the basis of material deprivation. The mere possibility of a more beneficial environment does not on its own justify removal from the parents; such a precarious situation needs to be addressed by less radical means (Saviny v. Ukraine, 2008, para. 50). Whether the promotion of family life creates an entitlement to a particular standard of living at public expense is unsettled in the Court's case-law (Saviny v. Ukraine, 2008, para. 57), although some support for such an entitlement – under circumscribed circumstances of inability and financial incapacity – could be found in a combined reading of Art. 9 (no separation of children from parents) and 27 CRC. The latter provides that States must take appropriate measures to assist parents to implement the right of the child to an adequate standard of living, and must "in case of need provide material assistance and support programmes, particularly with regard to nutrition, clothing and housing".

A challenging issue in the context of family life (and beyond) is whether parents are entitled to slap or smack their children (corporal punishment). In recent years, the language and legal qualification of "violence against children" has become dominant. The children's rights law position on violence against children is generally straightforward and condemnatory. The CRC Committee has clarified the meaning of Art. 19 CRC – which prohibits all forms of violence against children – with regard to corporal punishment and other cruel or degrading forms of punishment in 2007, and more generally in 2011 (CRC, 2011). The degrading nature of punishment seems to be the decisive element, and underlying it, the human dignity and physical integrity of the child (CRC, 2007, paras. 11, 16 and 26). Whereas the Committee seems to favour criminal law *prohibition*, it does not plead primarily for *prosecution* of parents, nor for the separation of children from parents: "the aim should be to stop parents from using violent or other cruel or degrading punishments through supportive and educational, not punitive, interventions". (CRC, 2007, para. 40). The European Committee of Social Rights (ECSR), for its part, has consistently interpreted Art. 17 RESC as prohibiting any form of violence against children, regardless of place, perpetrator (parents, teachers, …), or purpose (punitive, educational, …). The prohibition of all forms of violence must have a legislative basis. Adequate, proportionate and dissuasive sanctions are required. Several states have been held not to be in conformity with Art. 17 RESC for lack of an explicit legal prohibition of all forms of violence against children, including for educational purposes, thus not offering sufficient guidance to parents and others to model their conduct on the prohibition in Art. 17 RESC (World Organisation against Torture (OMCT) v. Belgium, 2004, paras. 39, 46 and 48).

The ECtHR has struggled somewhat with the legal qualification of the issue, as the ECHR does not contain any prohibition on violence. Its entry point has been Art. 3 ECHR (prohibition of torture, inhuman or degrading treatment or punishment), which requires however a minimum threshold of severity in order to be applicable. The modalities and severity of corporal punishment, rather than a blanket ban, took therefore a prominent place in some of the older cases on corporal punishment in the penal system and schools. In 1998, in a case of severe beating of a nine-year-old boy by his stepfather (so, within the family), the Court found the UK in violation of article3 ECHR for failure to provide adequate protection. In the circumstances of the case, the stepfather had been acquitted on defence of reasonable chastisement (A. v. UK, 1998).

In sum, corporal punishment in the family has received much attention in children's rights law. The strong calls for adequate protection through legal prohibition (criminally or otherwise) and dissuasive sanctions have been accompanied sometimes with softer calls for educational and supportive measures towards the parents. This brings us to the heart of the matter: what are the effects of principled and legitimate calls for the prohibition of corporal punishment on children and parents? Do they lead to the demonization of parents? Do they undermine practices of positive discipline? Do they work inhibitively towards physical intervention or use of force when a child is in danger, or forms a real danger for others? How to respond to corporal punishment, punitively or supportively? And what comes first: legislation or change in public attitudes towards corporal punishment as an educational method?[13]

Other issues that have received considerable attention in human rights litigation are adoption (Todorova v. Italy, 2009) and parental abduction (Shuruk and Neulinger v. Switzerland, 2010). They raise difficult questions on the protection of family life, consent and best interests of the child.

3.3. Education[14]

The right to education is guaranteed and protected in general human rights treaties (see, e.g., Art. 13 ICESCR) as well as in the CRC (Art. 28). As a right that is generally considered to belong to the category of economic, social and cultural rights,[15] it is subject to the general obligation of progressive realization. Nonetheless, the UN Committee on Economic, Social and Cultural Rights (CESCR) has argued that the right to *primary* education has to be realized immediately, inter alia on the basis of the stronger wording of Art. 13 (2) ICESCR (CESCR, 1999, para. 51). Unfortunately, Art. 28 CRC contains regressive language on this point; it explicitly submits the right to primary education to the progressive realization obligation too. Whereas that is legally speaking not problematic for states that are a party to both treaties, as the most conducive provision to the realization of children's rights prevails (see Art. 41 CRC), it has undoubtedly negative consequences for states that are only a party to the CRC, and it risks weakening the public and political perception.

European litigation on the right to education concerns inter alia educational freedom of parents, which we will not discuss further, and questions of inclusive education and accessibility of education for undocumented children. Inclusive education, which is at the intersection of the right to education and non-discrimination, has been discussed with regard to two groups in particular, i.e. children with disabilities and Roma children. With regard to children with disabilities, integration into mainstream schools should be the norm, and teaching in specialized schools the exception (Art. 24 CRPD; Art. 15 RESC) (Autism Europe v. France, 2003, paras. 48–49; European Action of the Disabled (AEH) v. France, 2013). This is a matter of

---

13 Evidence on the effects of a legal ban on physical punishment in Sweden suggests that there is no demonstrable effect of law reform on public attitudes (Roberts, 2000).
14 Basic literature on the right to education includes Verheyde, 2006; Beiter, 2006; Quennerstedt, Chapter 12 in this Handbook.
15 Albeit that it also contains clear aspects of a civil rights nature, i.e. the right to educational freedom of parents.

availability and accessibility of education. Of course, in many cases children with disabilities will have special needs that need to be accommodated; this is a question of adaptability of education. In this regard, the CRPD refers to reasonable accommodation, whereas the ECSR has argued that real (substantive) equality requires that appropriate measures be taken to take account of existing differences (Mental Disability Advocacy Center (MDAC) v. Bulgaria, 2008, para. 51). This was concluded to mean that in case of justified special education for children with disabilities, "the children concerned must be given sufficient instruction and training and complete their schooling in equivalent proportions to those of children in mainstream schools" (Mental Disability Advocacy Center (MDAC) v. Bulgaria, 2008, para. 36). Whereas inclusive education and mainstreaming strongly reflects the approach of children with disabilities as full members of society, and as human beings of equal worth, it does meet with resistance and does not always seem wanted by children with disabilities in the first place (for some of the conceptual and practical challenges, see inter alia Barton, 1997; Evans and Lunt, 2002).

The question of segregation versus integration of Roma children in schools has been adjudicated upon in various concrete contexts, ranging from explicit policies for special schools for Roma children, to concrete practices of separate premises for Roma children or special classes for pupils with language deficiencies. The Court has consistently labelled differentiation on the ground of ethnic origin suspect, given its affiliation with racial discrimination. This means that differential treatment that is exclusively or decisively based on ethnic origin will not be objectively justifiable (D.H. v. Czech Republic, 2007; Sampanis v. Greece, 2008). The organization of special classes to address language deficiencies required the most sophisticated analysis. The Court held that temporary placement in separate classes due to lack of adequate command of language does not automatically amount to discrimination. However, when a measure disproportionately affects members of a specific ethnic group, appropriate safeguards need to be in place. These relate to the initial placement in these language classes (are there specifically designed tests; is the insufficient language command immediately addressed?), the curriculum offered (is it specifically designed to address the language deficiencies; are special language lessons offered?), and the transfer and monitoring procedure (what is the time-frame to move on to the "ordinary" classes?). The Court also emphasized the need to structurally involve social services in order to take positive measures that encourage school attendance and prevent dropout, as well as the importance of involving the parents. Most recently, the Court held that maintaining a situation in which a school is exclusively attended by Roma children and refraining from taking effective anti-segregation measures, cannot be objectively justified and is in violation of the right to education in combination with the prohibition of discrimination (Lavida v. Greece, 2013). In these cases, difficult questions arise with how to deal with the hostile attitudes of non-Roma parents, and with the acceptance of the situation by Roma parents. As to the latter, the Court has held that given the public interest at stake, a waiver of the prohibition of discrimination is not possible. One may wonder, of course, whether and to what extent a judicial decision can change realities on the ground, whether the Court is realistic in its approach, and whether there are other and better ways of integrating Roma pupils in mainstream education. Or even, whether that is for them the best option. What happens, e.g., when they are in mainstream schools, but do not receive appropriate attention and support within and outside school?

As to the availability and accessibility of education for undocumented migrants, the CMW guarantees to each child of a migrant worker, regardless of legal status, the "basic right of access to education on the basis of equality of treatment with the nationals of the State concerned". (Art. 30 CMW). However, at least partly because of the rights guaranteed to all migrant workers, regardless of legal status, this human rights treaty has not been ratified by any of the

Western states of employment of migrant workers. The CESCR confirmed in the late 1990s that "the principle of non-discrimination extends to all persons of school age residing in the territory of a State party, including non-nationals, and irrespective of their legal status" (CESCR, 1999, para. 34). Likewise, the ECSR has argued that states are required to ensure "that children unlawfully present in their territory have effective access to education as any other child" (ESCR, 2012, p. 6). The CRC Committee too has held that every child, "irrespective of status, should have full access to education […] in line with articles 28, 29(1), 30 and 32 of the Convention and the general principles developed by the Committee" (CRC, 2003). The European Court of Human Rights had to decide whether a state can charge fees for secondary education to undocumented migrants, while that education is free to nationals and legally residing foreigners. The Court took a careful approach, and made clear that what was at stake was not whether and to what extent states can charge fees for education, but rather whether states may deny free education to a distinct group of people. It acknowledged that states may have legitimate reasons for curtailing the use of resource-hungry public services like education by short-term and illegal immigrants, who do not contribute to their funding. However, it argued that the right to education is a very particular type of public service, which benefits those using it but also serves broader societal functions. Second, because of the increasing importance of secondary education in a knowledge society, it did not grant a very wide margin of appreciation to the state in order to assess the proportionality between the differential treatment and the aim pursued. It concluded that the prohibition of discrimination in conjunction with the right to education had been violated, not without emphasizing the "very specific circumstances of this case", i.e. the fact that the authorities had no substantive objection to the pupils' presence on their territory, so that considerations relating to the need to stem or reverse a flow of illegal immigration were not applicable, and the fact that the pupils had not tried to abuse the educational system (Anatoliy and Vitaliy Ponomaryov v. Bulgaria, 2011, paras. 59–63). Whereas there is undeniably a strong and consistent tendency in human rights law to guarantee the right to education regardless of legal status,[16] the careful and highly qualified approach of the Court shows that migration control policies cannot be excluded from the equation. Moreover, access to education alone will not be sufficient for undocumented children: as important is the kind of education that is offered, and there is also the reality that education is decisively influenced by other factors, such as housing but also the very status of irregularity itself (Vandenhole et al., 2011).

4. Social change through children's rights law?

What does the above tell us about the importance of children's rights law in practice? How effective is standard-setting through legislation and litigation to change social realities? How relevant are current standards for realities on the ground? And is it tenable under children's rights law to only assign legal obligations to the domestic state?

This chapter attempts to move beyond the "implementation gap approach" that many legal scholars adopt, by pointing out challenges related to the legal framing of children's rights as well as to the naïve way social change through children's rights law is approached sometimes. What I mean with the "implementation gap approach" refers to the understanding of many practitioners and scholars that the main challenge for children's rights is implementation. The

---

16 On the tendency to consider irregularity rather than nationality a justified ground of differentiation, see Vandenhole (2013).

standards and norms are presumed to be clear, appropriate and beyond doubt, the remaining challenge is to implement them properly. What can be criticized is the lack of implementation, the gap between the ideal norms and the realities, not the norms themselves. I do not want to question the often enormous implementation gap that exists. However, I believe that children's rights scholarship should move beyond the "implementation gap approach", by looking more into the way children's rights have been (and could be) legally framed, and into the role of children's rights law in social change.

The process of norm-setting, i.e. the creation of children's rights legal standards, tends to be top-down and adult-driven. This approach has been challenged in emerging scholarship on "Children's Rights from Below" (Liebel et al., 2012). In the latter approach, children's rights are social practices that emerge from daily realities, in different social and cultural contexts; there is therefore a need to contextualize and to localize their meaning (Liebel et al., 2012, p. 2), and arguably also the way they are legally framed. This approach requires a new methodology, and close cooperation among sociologists, anthropologists and lawyers. Only in this way, the claims children make in their lived experience, their life-world – which have been called "living rights" (Hanson and Nieuwenhuys, 2013) – may be appropriately captured and legally articulated. This approach has mainly been explored in the area of child labour (Hanson and Vandaele, 2013; Liebel, 2013), but also to some extent with regard to child soldiering (Hanson, 2011) and harmful traditional practices (Vandenhole, 2012).

Another important challenge for legal scholarship on children's rights is to develop a more sophisticated understanding of the role of law in social change. Commonly held assumptions by lawyers and others about impact and change through legal reform may not hold true, as e.g. borne out by evidence on the legal ban on corporal punishment in Sweden: legal reform did not affect public attitudes, nor did it accelerate decline in support for corporal punishment (Roberts, 2000). As a minimum, the limitations of law reform for implementing children's rights need to be acknowledged (Goonesekere, 2008, p. 3).

The more general literature on human rights, litigation and social change offers important insights, that also apply to children's rights law. I argued elsewhere that human rights law and litigation cannot be an autonomous vector of structural societal change, but that they rather need to be embedded in a broader strategy. In addition, human rights law faces intrinsic and ideological limits (Vandenhole, 2009b). For some, scepticism about the transformative nature of human rights law prevails (Koskenniemi, 2010). Empirically, it has become clear that the effectiveness of litigation in bringing about change needs to be contextualized, qualified and linked to broader policy provisions. In particular with regard to socio-economic rights of children, Nolan found that there are limits to judicial intervention, although its efficacy should not be dismissed too easily. Nonetheless, she admits that more empirical work needs to be done before any firm conclusions can be drawn (Nolan, 2011, pp. 187–188 and 258–259).

A final point relates to the exclusive focus under children's rights law (as under human rights law) on the domestic state as the duty-bearer. Legal technically, children's rights obligations apply to states only, and more in particular to the state that exercises jurisdiction over a child. Typically, that is the state the territory of which a child is on. Globalization, and in particular economic globalization, as a process of dispersion of power, has made it increasingly difficult to understand and tackle social challenges at a local or national level alone. These developments challenge the legal concept of children's rights as entitlements towards the territorial state, and necessitate the widening of the duty-bearer side of children's rights if they are to function as a leverage for social change (Vandenhole et al., 2014).

5. Conclusions

This chapter sought to familiarize readers with the international legal frameworks on children's rights, by clarifying the general obligations incumbent on states and the general principles guiding the interpretation of children's rights law, as well as by introducing some of the case-law on juvenile justice, family matters and education. It cautioned not to overestimate the transformative potential of a legal approach to children's rights, be it through litigation or otherwise, and urged legal scholarship to move beyond an implementation gap understanding.

Undoubtedly, the legal codification of children's rights, as reflected in the fairly impressive legal architectures globally and regionally, has its merits. That is commonly understood and accepted. What this chapter and the whole book teaches us, is that children's rights should not be reduced to their legal codification. Moreover, critical legal scholarship should pay more attention to the limits and drawbacks of legal provisions and a legal approach, and increase insight in the complex ways in which children's rights law and social realities interact.

Questions for debate and discussion

- What are the strengths and weaknesses, opportunities and threats of a legal approach to children's rights?
- On which issues/questions could children's rights law usefully learn from/draw on the insights in other disciplines?
- Which weaknesses can be identified in the legal framing of juvenile justice/placement into care/inclusive education?
- Can you think of other areas where the legal understanding of children's rights is confronted with fundamental limits/inherent weaknesses?

References

A. v. UK (ECHR 1998).
Alston, P. (1994). The Best Interests Principle: Towards a Reconciliation of Culture and Human Rights. *International Journal of Law and the Family*, 8, 1–25.
Anatoliy and Vitaliy Ponomaryov v. Bulgaria (ECHR 2011).
Ang, F., Berghmans, E., Cattrijsse, L., *et al.* (2006). Participation Rights in the UN Convention on the Rights of the Child. In F. Ang, E. Berghmans, L. Cattrijsse *et al.* (eds), *Participation Rights of Children* (pp. 9–26). Antwerp: Intersentia.
Apodaca, C. (2010). *Child Hunger and Human Rights: International Governance*. Abingdon, UK: Routledge.
Archard, D. (2006). Preface. In F. Ang, E. Berghmans, L. Cattrijsse, *et al.* (eds), *Participation Rights of Children*. Antwerp: Intersentia.
Archard, D., and Skivenes, M. (2009). Balancing a Child's Best Interests and a Child's Views. *The International Journal of Children's Rights*, 17(1), 1–21.
Autism Europe v. France (ECSR 2003).
Barton, L. (1997). Inclusive Education: Romantic, Subversive or Realistic? *International Journal of Inclusive Education*, 1(3), 231–242.
Beiter, K. D. (2006). *The Protection of the Right to Education by International Law* (Vol. 82). Leiden: Martinus Nijhoff.
Besson, S. (2005). The Principle of Non-Discrimination in the Convention on the Rights of the Child. *The International Journal of Children's Rights*, 13(4), 433–461.
Cantwell, N. (1992). The Origins, Development and Significance of the United Nations Convention on the Rights of the Child. In S. Detrick (ed.), *The United Nations Convention on the Rights of the Child: A Guide to the "Travaux Préparatoires"* (pp. 19–30). Dordrecht: Martinus Nijhoff.
CESCR (1990). General Comment No. 3 – The nature of States parties obligations (Art. 2, par. 1).
CESCR (1999). General Comment No. 13 – The right to education (Article 13 of the Covenant).

Council of Europe (2010). *Guidelines of the Committee of Ministers of the Council of Europe on child-friendly justice*.
CRC (2003). General Comment No. 5 – General measures of implementation.
CRC (2006). General comment No. 9 – The rights of children with disabilities.
CRC (2007). General Comment No. 8 (2006) – The right of the child to protection from corporal punishment and other cruel or degrading forms of punishment (arts; 19, 28, para. 2; and 37, inter alia).
CRC (2009). General Comment No. 9 – The right of the child to be heard.
CRC (2010). General Comment No. 10 – Children's rights in juvenile justice.
CRC (2011). General comment No. 13 (2011) – The right of the child to freedom from all forms of violence.
CRC (2013). General comment No. 14 (2013) – The right of the child to have his or her best interests taken as a primary consideration (art. 3, para. 1).
D.H. v. Czech Republic (ECHR 2007).
Detrick, S. (1992). *The United Nations Convention on the Rights of the Child: A Guide to the "Travaux Préparatoires"*. Dordrecht: Martinus Nijhoff.
Drumbl, M. A. (2012). *Reimagining Child Soldiers in International Law and Policy*: Oxford: Oxford University Press.
Eekelaar, J. (1992). The Importance of Thinking That Children Have Rights. *International Journal of Law and the Family*, 6(1), 221–235.
ESCR (2012). Conclusions 2011 – General Introduction: Council of Europe. Strasbourg: Council of Europe.
European Action of the Disabled (AEH) v. France (ECSR 2013).
Evans, J., and Lunt, I. (2002). Inclusive Education: Are There Limits? *European Journal of Special Needs Education*, 17(1), 1–14.
Freeman, M. (2007). *Article 3: The Best Interests of the Child*. Leiden: Martinus Nijhoff.
Goonesekere, S. (2008). Introduction and Overview: Protecting the World's Children: Impact of the Convention on the Rights of the Child in Diverse Legal Systems. In UNICEF (ed.), *Protecting the World's Children: Impact of the Convention on the Rights of the Child in Diverse Legal Systems* (pp. 1–33). Cambridge: Cambridge University Press.
Güveç v. Turkey (ECHR 2009).
Hanson, K. (2011). International Children's Rights and Armed Conflict. *Human Rights and International Legal Discourse*, 5, 40–62.
Hanson, K. (2012). Schools of Thought in Children's Rights. In M. Liebel (ed.), *Children's Rights from Below. Cross-Cultural Perspectives* (pp. 63–69). Basingstoke, UK: Palgrave Macmillan.
Hanson, K., and Nieuwenhuys, O. (2013). *Reconceptualizing Children's Rights in International Development: Living Rights, Social Justice, Translations*. Cambridge: Cambridge University Press.
Hanson, K., and Vandaele, A. (2013). Translating Working Children's Rights into International Labour Law. In K. Hanson and O. Nieuwenhuys (eds), *Reconceptualizing Children's Rights in International Development: Living Rights, Social Justice, Translations* (pp. 250–272). Cambridge: Cambridge University Press.
H.K. v. Finland (ECHR 2006).
Hodgkin, R., and Newell, P. (2007). *Implemention Handbook for the Convention on the Rights of the Child* (3rd ed.). Geneva: UNICEF.
Kilkelly, U. (1999). *The Child and the European Convention on Human Rights*. Aldershot, UK: Ashgate.
Koskenniemi, M. (2010). Human Rights Mainstreaming as a Strategy for Institutional Power. *Humanity: An International Journal of Human Rights, Humanitarianism, and Development*, 1(1), 47–58.
Lavida v. Greece (ECHR 2013).
Liebel, M. (2013). Do Children Have a Right to Work? Working Children's Movements in the Struggle for Social Justice. In K. Hanson and A. Vandaele (eds), *Reconceptualizing Children's Rights in International Development: Living Rights, Social Justice, Translations* (pp. 225–249). Cambridge: Cambridge University Press.
Liebel, M., Hanson, K., Saadi, I., and Vandenhole, W. (2012). *Children's Rights from Below: Cross-cultural Perspectives*. Basingstoke, UK: Palgrave Macmillan.
Liefaard, T. (2008). *Deprivation of Liberty of Children in Light of International Human Rights Law and Standards*. Antwerp: Intersentia
Maslov v. Austria (ECHR 2008).
Mental Disability Advocacy Center (MDAC) v. Bulgaria (ECSR 2008).
Morrow, V., and Pells, K. (2012). Integrating Children's Human Rights and Child Poverty Debates: Examples from *Young Lives* in Ethiopia and India. *Sociology*, 46(5), 906–920.

Nolan, A. (2011). *Children's Socio-Economic Rights, Democracy and the Courts* (Vol. 16). Oxford: Hart.
Nowak, M. (2005). *Article 6: the Right to Life, Survival and Development*. Leiden: Martinus Nijhoff.
Quennerstedt, A. (2010) Children, But Not Really Humans? Critical Reflections on the Hampering Effect of the "3 p's". *International Journal of Children's Rights*, 18, 619–635.
Rishmawi, M. (2006). *Article 4: the nature of states parties' obligations* (Vol. 4). Leiden: Martinus Nijhoff.
Roberts, J.V. (2000). Changing Public Attitudes Towards Corporal Punishment: The Effects of Statutory Reform in Sweden. *Child Abuse and Neglect*, 24(8), 1027–1035.
Salduz v. Turkey (ECHR 2008).
Sampanis v. Greece (ECHR 2008).
Saviny v. Ukraine (ECHR 2008).
Schabas, W. A. (2011). On the Binding Nature of the Findings of the Treaty Bodies. In M. C. Bassiouni and W. A. Schabas (eds), *New Challenges for the UN Human Rights Machinery. What Future for the UN Treaty Body System and the Human Rights Council Procedures?* (pp. 97–106). Cambridge: Intersentia.
Schabas, W. A., and Sax, H. (2006). *Article 37. Prohibition of Torture, Death Penalty, Life Imprisonment and Deprivation of Liberty* (Vol. 37). Leiden: Martinus Nijhoff.
Shuruk and Neulinger v. Switzerland (ECHR 2010).
T. v. UK (ECHR 1999).
Tobin, J. (2011). Understanding a Human Rights Based Approach to Matters Involving Children: Conceptual Foundations and Strategic Considerations. In A. Invernizzi and J. Williams (eds), *The Human Rights of Children. From Visions to Implementation* (pp. 61–98). Farnham, UK: Ashgate.
Todorova v. Italy (ECHR 2009).
UN General Assembly (2010). *Guidelines for the Alternative Care of Children: Resolution adopted by the General Assembly*, 18 December 2009, A/RES/64/142. Available at www.refworld.org/docid/4c3acd162.html
Van Bueren, G. (1998). *The International Law on the Rights of the Child*. The Hague: Martinus Nijhoff.
Van Bueren, G. (2006). *Child Criminal Justice*. Leiden: Martinus Nijhoff.
Van Bueren, G. (2007). *Child rights in Europe*. Strasbourg: Council of Europe Publishing.
Vandenhole, W. (2003). Completing the UN Complaint Mechanisms for Human Rights Violations Step by Step: Towards a Complaints Procedure to the International Covenant on Economic, Social and Cultural Rights. *Netherlands Quarterly of Human Rights*, 21, 423–462.
Vandenhole, W. (2009a). Economic, Social and Cultural Rights in the CRC: Is There a Legal Obligation to Cooperate Internationally for Development? *International Journal of Children's Rights*, 17, 23–63.
Vandenhole, W. (2009b). The Limits of Human Rights Law in Human Development. In E. Claes, W. Devroe and B. Keirsbilck (eds), *Facing the Limits of the Law* (pp. 355–374). Berlin: Springer.
Vandenhole, W. (2012). Localising the Human Rights of Children. In M. Liebel, K. Hanson, I. Saadi and W. Vandenhole (eds), *Children's Rights from Below: Cross-cultural Perspectives* (pp. 80–93). Basingtoke, UK: Palgrave Macmillan.
Vandenhole, W. (2013). Discrimination and Migration. In V. Chetail and C. Bauloz (eds), *Research Handbook on International Law and Migration*. Cheltenham, UK: Edward Elgar.
Vandenhole, W., de Wiart, E. C., De Clerck, H. M.-L., Mahieu, P., Ryngaert, J., Timmerman, C., and Verhoeven, M. (2011). Undocumented Children and the Right to Education: Illusory Right or Empowering Lever? *The International Journal of Children's Rights*, 19(4), 613–639.
Vandenhole, W., Türkelli, G. E., and Hammonds, R. (2014). New Human Rights Duty-bearers: Towards a Re-conceptualisation of the Human Rights Duty-bearer Dimension. In A. Mihr and M. Gibney (eds), *Handbook of Human Rights*. London: Sage.
Verheyde, M. (2006). Article 28. The Right to Education. In A. Alen, J.V. Lanotte, E. Verhellen, F. Ang, E. Berghmans and M. Verheyde (eds), *A Commentary on the United Nations Convention on the Rights of the Child* (Vol. 28). Leiden: Martinus Nijhoff.
Williams, J. (2013). *The United Nations Convention on the Rights of the Child in Wales*. Cardiff: University of Wales Press.
World Organisation against Torture (OMCT) v. Belgium, No. 21/2003 (ECSR 2004).
X., Y. and Z. v. United Kingdom (ECtHR 1997).

3

The Convention on the Rights of the Child

Reflections from a historical, social policy and educational perspective

Eugeen Verhellen[1]

1. Introduction

Even though scholarship about the human rights of children is scattered in a variety of paradigms, research tracks, disciplines and schools of thought (Hanson, 2012; Op de Beeck *et al.*, 2013, p. 8), the framework used most frequently to structure children's rights discussions and debates remains that of the Convention on the Rights of the Child (1989, hereafter *the CRC* or *the Convention*). By now, more than 25 years after its adoption, the Convention is regarded as a historical milestone. On the one hand, it is the culmination of a difficult power struggle over decades, aiming at improving children's position in society by introducing a set of minimum performance standards against which States can be held accountable. On the other hand, it is the beginning of a new pedagogical practice of how to deal with children, not only for States, but for every member of society.

The CRC was adopted without a vote by the United Nations General Assembly on 20 November 1989 (A/RES/44/25). It entered into force less than one year later, on 2 September 1990. The Convention complemented and anchored the moral obligations with regard to children, already enshrined in the 1924 Geneva Declaration and the 1959 Declaration on the Rights of the Child, in a legally binding international human rights document. Meanwhile, the CRC has been complemented by three optional protocols. Two of these, one relating to the involvement of children in armed conflict and another to the sale of children, child prostitution and child pornography, were adopted on 25 May 2000 (A/RES/54/263) and entered into force in 2002. The third optional protocol providing a communications procedure was adopted on 19 December 2011 (A/RES/66/138) and entered into force on April 14th, 2014. Today, the CRC has been ratified or acceded to by 195 States parties, which makes it the most widely

---

[1] Emeritus Professor Ghent University. The author is grateful to Sara Lembrechts for her helpful and precious assistance in updating the text in line with the aims of this Handbook. The chapter can be read as a compilation of the author's earlier work, and in particular as an update of Verhellen (1992).

ratified international human rights treaty in the world. With only South Sudan and the USA lacking in the list, the CRC asserts a quasi-universal definition of children's rights.

The CRC did not appear out of the blue, however. In order to explain where the growing interest in children's rights came from, this chapter starts by discussing two macro-social developments leading to the adoption of the CRC: (1) a changing child-image and (2) the development of a global human rights project since World War II (see also Verhellen, 2006). Second, the CRC framework of children's rights is described, so as to provide a starting – rather than an ending – point of quality requirements about how to deal with children in law, social policy and education. The conclusion will bring the analysis to a close, focusing on the educational consequences of the CRC's children's rights framework.

2. A growing interest in children's rights: Historical background

2.1. Changing childhood images up to 1989

Child-images capture the way in which children and childhood can be understood in a diversity of cultures, contexts, discourses and perspectives. As has been pointed out in the introduction to this Handbook, the way we look at and deal with children is determined not only by biological factors, but also by the social and cultural contexts and practices in which children grow up. As such, the child-image is subject to change over time and space. Indeed, historians, sociologists and anthropologists, while differing in their views, point to various significantly different approaches to the way in which adults and children interact (Verhellen, 1992; Montgomery, 2009; Liebel, 2012).

These changes are consequences not so much of individual, psychological changes in the child, but rather of changes on the macro-level of society (*sociogenesis*) (Elias, 2000). This macro-social evolution gradually causes individuals' expectations of others to change. A gradual change in behaviour generated by the dominant expectations will also affect the individual personality (*psychogenesis*). In other words, changing expectations of certain groups of people, such as children, play a crucial role in the way we deal with them and thus also influence child-images. It is therefore important to understand that our image of children is a *social construct*, thus *man-made*, flowing from our expectations, and that children are not just children *by nature* (Ariès, 1979 [1962]).

In fact, regarding children as a *separate social category* is a rather recent phenomenon in the global North.[2] In essence, one can roughly say that until about the end of the Middle Ages, there was little or no awareness of children as a "social group". Given the very high mortality rate for children under six or seven, their main task was to try to survive. After this age, they disappeared into the world of adults. This was reflected in the law: children simply did not exist as a separate social category, and where they did, they were regarded as their father's private property and treated like any other "goods" (Dasberg, 1986).

---

2   Insight into the social construction of child-images is profoundly influenced by historical research in the global North, notably by Philippe Ariès (1979[1962]). However, the disciplines of sociology and anthropology of childhood have highlighted different ways of behaving towards children in a variety of (native) cultures of the global South. As Montgomery (2009, p. 55) illustrates, "[t]he idea that childhood is a specific stage of life, separated from adulthood, does not hold true in many places", for example where stages of social immaturity "last well beyond puberty and even marriage" (Montgomery, 2009, p. 55) or, to the contrary, where children of five or six years old carry out "jobs that a child in the West would not be considered capable of doing for many years" (Montgomery, 2009, p. 56).

It was not until the Enlightenment (eighteenth century), with its belief in the supremacy of Reason, that children were discovered as a social group. Gradually, children became to be considered as *"future citizens"*, as the *"future performers"* of the Enlightened Society. They became *"tomorrow's prosperity"*. This enduring stress on "the future" and "progress" turned children slowly into *"not-yet" human beings*. This status of not-yet knowing, not-yet capable, not-yet adults created a *separate social category* of social immaturity in comparison to the ideal of the fully-knowing, capable adult.

Gradually, "specific" laws and "specific" institutions were invented to force the new enlightened moral tasks on children and those responsible for them (parents, teachers …). Indeed, around the turn of the nineteenth century, practically simultaneously in almost all Western countries, so-called "child protection laws" and "compulsory education" were introduced, systematically separating adults/parents and children into different regimes of social control and socialisation.

The far-reaching macro-social definition of children as *not-yet*s was long taken for granted. This had numerous consequences. For example, these specific laws and institutions simultaneously *excluded* children from the adult world and *included* them in a world of their own. Children ended up in a kind of *limbo*, where they had to wait, learn and prepare themselves for "real" life. This macro-social process turned children into *objects* designed to achieve the ideal society of the future. It is with this child-image that the Global North enters the twentieth century. In fact, this limbo has not disappeared until today. To the contrary, in many aspects of children's lives, their *not-yet* status has been reinforced (see also Reynaert and Roose, Chapter 6) or prolonged, even beyond the legal age of majority. National legislation reflects this status of the *child as an object*, also found in international rules.[3]

However, from then on (and still today), the image of childhood as an exclusively future-oriented view on children has been increasingly criticised. At the beginning of the twentieth century, for example, the Polish-Jewish paediatrician Janusz Korczak ([1919] in Berding, 2008) has highlighted that because of this dictate of the "future", children gradually lose their "right to the present". Subsequently, in 1962, when H. Kempe launched the notion of the battered child syndrome (Kempe *et al.*, 1962; Camper Soman, 1974), the status of not-yet-being was challenged for a variety of reasons by different people from various sectors and levels of society. This became clear during the first international congress on children's ombudswork (Verhellen and Spiesschaert, 1989). The main aim of this school of thought, which became known as the "Children's Rights Movement", was to have children considered as fully-fledged citizens. They argued for children to be regarded as individuals with their own human rights, and as competent to exercise these rights independently. As will be elaborated in part two of this chapter, this new image of childhood became one of the foundations of the CRC.

2.2. The human rights project

As the introduction to this Handbook points out, children's rights are understood as the human rights of children, i.e. fundamental claims for the realisation of social justice and human dignity for children. The right to participate in democratic decision-making, to autonomy and to exercise rights independently are important aspects of how to realise these claims. The ontological view behind the children's rights movement and the changing child image that accompanies

---

3 The 1924 Geneva Declaration particularly, and, to a lesser extent, also the 1959 Declaration on the Rights of the Child, see the child not as subject but as object. This is clearly demonstrated by the terminology used:*"The child must be given…"*.

it, is that children are human *beings*. Therefore, children are entitled to all human rights. Children do not need to be *given* rights, they *have* them. We, adults, only have to *recognise* that they are bearers of rights and ensure that the necessary tools to *enforce* them are available to all children. Human rights have therefore become a point of reference in the debate on children's situation in society. From this point of view, recognising that children are bearers of rights forms part of much wider changes that began to take effect internationally especially after World War II. Some characteristics of this human rights project are discussed below.

3. Generations of human rights

Modern ideas on human rights gradually evolved as of the end of the eighteenth century. The *first generation* of civil and political human rights came about mainly through the American (1776) and French (1789) revolutions – most notably in the French Declaration of the Rights of Man and of the Citizen (1789), which contained traditional rights such as the right to freedom of opinion, freedom of the press, the right of assembly, the right to life, etc. They could be described as the first *defensive* weapons against sovereign rulers. The State has to abstain from interference in the (private) life of its citizens.

The *second generation* of human rights displays a far more *offensive* attitude to the State. Abstention from exaggerated interference (first generation) is now complemented by an urgent appeal to a sense of social responsibility on the part of the State. Recognising *economic, social and cultural human rights*, such as the right to a minimum income, to work, to health care, to education, to leisure, etc. means the State has to act. This second generation, dealing in essence with *social justice*, was enshrined in legally binding texts for the first time in the Russian Constitution (1918) right after the Russian revolution (1917).

In the last few decades, there has been more and more talk of *peoples' rights*, a *third generation* of human rights. These are the so-called *solidarity rights*, such as the right to peace, a healthy environment, cultural integrity, self-government, sustainable development etc. The official international starting point was the 1992 Rio UN World Conference on the Environment and Development (UNCED), resulting, inter alia, in international texts containing rules on the third generation of human rights: the Declaration of Rio and the action programme Agenda 21.[4] Debate about the actual shape and content of these new rights is still going on.[5] Taking the example of the right to a healthy environment, an increasing global recognition is to be noted with ever more new constitutions incorporating this right, ranging from Kenya, the Dominican Republic (2010), Jamaica, Morocco and South Sudan (2011), to Iceland and Zambia (pending). In addition, in 2012, the UN Human Rights Council appointed an independent expert to report on the universal right to a healthy environment (Boyd, 2012).[6]

4. Internationalisation and regionalisation: From declarations to legally binding instruments

At first, human rights were found in the legislation and constitutions of most (Western) countries. Although the ideas had gained international acceptance, human rights remained a matter

---

4   A/CONF. 151/26 (VOL I), 12 August 1992.
5   A/RES/64/236, 31 March 2010, Implementation of Agenda 21, the Programme for the Further Implementation of Agenda 21 and the outcomes of the World Summit on Sustainable Development.
6   A/HRC/19/L.8/Rev.1.

for national concern. The League of Nations (1920) was the first real attempt at internationalisation. Its major concern, avoiding the recurrence of war, is characteristic of a mainly *re-active* (*defensive*) approach: avoiding human rights abuses (for children this is exemplified by the Geneva Declaration adopted by the League of Nations in 1924). It would take until after the Second World War for the internationalisation of the human rights project really to take off, with the setting up of the United Nations (1945). This also involved a change of course, since as of now a *pro-active* (*offensive*) approach predominated.

In fact, the UN Charter (the international community's constitution) not only mentions human rights explicitly, but also emphasises that respect for human rights is the best guarantee for peace and democracy. This means not only fighting human rights abuses, but also making efforts to improve people's living conditions, to promote human dignity. In this way, for the first time human rights were tackled pro-actively and received an international legal basis in the Universal Declaration of Human Rights (UDHR), approved on 10 December 1948 (A/RES/217A (III)). In 1966, in the context of the Cold War, the Universal Declaration was further elaborated in two separate, legally binding treaties: the International Covenant on Economic, Social and Cultural Rights (hereafter ICESCR) and the International Covenant on Civil and Political Rights (hereafter ICCPR) (A/RES/ 2200 A (XXI)). Together, these three instruments (the Universal Declaration and the two Covenants) are called *The International Bill of Rights*. Subsequently, more and more declarations and treaties have been adopted which refer on the one hand to *specific groups* (children, women, refugees, the stateless, workers, persons with disabilities ...) and on the other to *specific problems* of international concern (genocide, war crimes, torture, racial discrimination...).

Besides instruments with a global scope, one can also identify *regional human rights instruments*. They are adopted by and on behalf of regional structures (Europe, Africa, Americas and increasingly in Asia as well) where there is, theoretically at least, a greater degree of shared cultural identity. In fact, the ambition of achieving universal human rights, assuming this to be possible, often leads to vague and imprecise wording (in order to achieve consensus), making it difficult to turn these rules into precisely defined positive rules for the purposes of legislation.

The best-known and most influential regional human rights instrument is the 1950 European Convention for the Protection of Human Rights and Fundamental Freedoms (ECHR).[7] The ECHR is the first international treaty with a binding enforcement mechanism. It was adopted on 4 November 1950 in Rome and entered into force in 1953. All 47 member States of the Council of Europe have ratified or acceded to it. In case of an alleged violation of any of the rights contained in the European Convention, proceedings can be instituted before the ECHR's monitoring body, the European Court of Human Rights in Strasbourg, provided that all national legal avenues have been exhausted. The judgements or rulings of the Court are binding on the Member States. The ECHR deals mainly with first generation civil and political rights, as contained in the 1948 UDHR. Its second generation counterpart at the European level, the *European Social Charter* (ESC, adopted in 1961 and revised in 1996), contains economic and social rights.[8]

Although in principle the civil, cultural, economic, political and social rights specified in the ECHR, the ESC and the UN Covenants also apply to children, in 1989 the international community decided to adopt a *separate* Convention on the Rights of the Child alongside the existing Treaties and Conventions, treating children explicitly as a category of *rights holders*.

---

7   CETS, N°: 005 (1950–1953)
8   CETS N°: 163 (1996–1999).

There was, and still is, discussion whether or not a separate convention is cutting off children from the general human rights treaties.[9] The idea behind the adoption of a separate Convention stems from the fact that explicit measures were deemed necessary to ensure that children could enjoy their human rights on an equal basis with other human beings (De Graaf, 1989). Wording like *human dignity* to be respected, appears several times directly and indirectly in the substantive articles of the CRC and in the concluding observations of the Committee.[10]

However, the debate on children's (legal) competence to exercise these rights independently is not yet over and questions often rose as to the usefulness and/or the necessity of a separate convention on children's rights (De Graaf, 1989, pp. 14–24). At the time, in 1989, the practical application of the existing treaties to children had only just begun and was not yet, as it is increasingly today, part of a general human rights-based approach within the work of the various Committees and Courts, both at UN and regional level (see, among others, Kilkelly, 2004).

5. The UN Convention on the Rights of the Child: Implications for social policy

As mentioned, the CRC evolved from a Declaration (1924) made up of a small preamble and five points, to a Declaration (1959) with a preamble and 10 principles, to a Convention (1989) with an extensive preamble (13 paragraphs) and no less than 54 articles. The articles can be subdivided into three main parts: Art. 1–41: the substantive articles, defining the rights of the child and the obligations on states parties; Art. 42–45: procedures for monitoring the implementation of the Convention; and Art. 46–54: formal provisions governing the entry into force of the Convention.

5.1. Preamble

A preamble explains the background to, and the reasons for, the Convention. Hence the preamble does not contain binding principles, but gives a frame of reference, in the light of which the articles are to be interpreted. Among other provisions, the preamble refers to the notion that children should grow up in an atmosphere of happiness, love and understanding (§6), and that the child should be brought up in the spirit of the ideals proclaimed in the UN Charter, and in particular in the spirit of peace, dignity, tolerance, freedom, equality and solidarity (§ 7).

5.2. Characteristics of the Convention

Articles 1 to 41 cover the rights guaranteed by the CRC. Here we find all those articles dealing with the rights of children or others' obligations to them. Considering each article separately in this contribution would be too much and has been done elsewhere.[11] Therefore, hereafter some general characteristics of the CRC are discussed, notably its comprehensiveness, including the holistic image of childhood it represents, and its legally binding nature.

---

9   For a quick overview of this discussion see Hanson (2014).
10 CRC/GBR/CO/ 20 October 2008.
11 For an article by article commentary on the CRC, see Alen *et al.* (2005–2012).

5.2.1. Comprehensiveness

5.2.1.1. First and second generation of human rights together in one single document

The CRC is the first human rights treaty that combines the two generations of human rights in one single text, by which it explicitly emphasises the *indivisibility* of human rights.[12] By bringing civil, political, economic, social and cultural rights together, the CRC broke through the traditional subdivision of human rights as represented in the Bill of Rights. This subdivision is harmful, as it hampers a fully fledged respect for human dignity, for example when these two categories are really separated and/or seen in a hierarchical structure. It can even lead to paradoxical situations. South Africa, for example, has signed but not ratified the ICESCR, which means that legally speaking, children have been attributed more rights than adults in this State. Similarly, children in South Africa, which signed but did not yet ratify the ICESCR, will lose rights upon reaching majority age.

The spirit of the CRC implies that there should be neither distinction, nor priority between different groups of rights. On the contrary, by bringing them together in one single instrument, it is the aim to indicate that they are of equal importance and – what is more – they are interdependent and inextricably related. This has consequences for social policy and practice in the implementation phase of the Convention. Connecting both generations of rights forces States parties to conduct an integrated policy that intentionally moves beyond the borders of different ministries. This new kind of policy causes a lot of difficulties for the States parties and their (legal) experts, since it is rather habitual to read a treaty "article-by-article". Moreover, the very different nature of these generations causes "technical" problems, for instance the problem of the *self-executing force* of treaty-provisions (infra).

5.2.1.2. Three Ps and four basic principles

The Committee on the Rights of the Child (2003, §12; hereafter referred to as *the Committee*), the treaty-based monitoring body of the CRC (see below at 5.2.2), identified *four basic principles* which are to be read by States parties as *horizontal* implementation and interpretation principles throughout all the provisions of the CRC (CRC/C/5, §§13–14; CRC/C/58, §§25–47). Guided by these principles, i.e. of non-discrimination (Art. 2) (Besson, 2005; Abramson, 2008), the best interests of the child (Art. 3) (Freeman, 2007; Op de Beeck *et al.*, 2014), survival and development (Art. 6) (Nowak, 2005) and respect for the views of the child (Art. 12) (Ang *et al.*, 2006), the CRC grants children with "rightful entitlements" (Lundy and McEvoy, 2012, p. 77) relating to protection (e.g. against violence), provision (e.g. of an adequate standard of living) and participation (e.g. to express one's opinion freely); or, in short, the "three *Ps*" – another commonly used typology to group the different articles together (Heiliö *et al.*, 1993).

Rather than separating rights into different categories, which would be in breach of the comprehensive and holistic spirit of the CRC,[13] this scheme is deemed useful to gain a better

---

12 In 2006, the Convention on the Rights of Persons with Disabilities (CRPD) followed a similar holistic framework incorporating both first and second generations of human rights.
13 This holistic approach is also mentioned in the reporting guidelines of the Committee on the Rights of the Child. CRC/C/58, 1996, Para. 9. General Comment n° 5 (2003), General measures of implementation of the Convention on the Rights of the Child. CRC/GC/2003/5. This opinion was already mentioned during the World Conference on Human Rights. A/CONF.157/23, 12 July 1993, Para. 5.

insight into the scope of children's rights as stipulated in the Convention. Hence, the three *P*s have to be interpreted as *interdependent and indivisible* in the same way as the Convention itself: no protection without provisions and participation, no provisions without protection and participation, no participation without provisions and protection.

Protection: Careful reading of the CRC reveals that the former principles of the 1959 Declaration on the Rights of the Child are repeated and extended and now made legally binding. These principles are better defined in order to monitor them more stringently. These rights are specific for children, addressing their special needs and especially their vulnerability in comparison to adults. Protection rights aim to shield children from the consequences of harmful decisions of others. Besides the right to life, survival and development (Art. 6), we find specific rights to be protected from certain activities: maltreatment and neglect (Art. 19 and Art. 39, see also Lenzer, Chapter 16 in this Handbook), child labour (Art. 32, see also Hanson, Volonakis and Al-Rozzi, Chapter 18 in this Handbook), other forms of exploitation (Art. 36), torture and deprivation of liberty (Art. 37), sexual exploitation (Art. 34), sale, trafficking and abduction (Art. 35).

Provision: Provision rights are about creating and guaranteeing access to certain goods and services in order to ensure children's healthy development, not only physically, but also emotionally and spiritually. These include the right to education (Arts. 28 and 29, see also Quennerstedt, Chapter 12 in this Handbook), the right to health care (Art. 24, see also Kilkelly, Chapter 13 in this Handbook), the right to social security (Art. 26), the right to an adequate standard of living (Art. 27) and the right to rest, leisure, recreation and cultural activities (Art. 31). As they appear also in other instruments, these rights are not new (with the exception of the aims of education in Art. 29). However, the CRC reinforces the recognition of these rights as specific *children's* rights (Verhellen, 2008).

Participation: Participation rights are about rights to act and to participate in society. Within this cluster, one can identify the right to express an opinion, either personally or through a representative, and have due weight attributed to that opinion (Art. 12, see also Tisdall, Chapter 11 in this Handbook), freedom of expression (Art. 13), freedom of thought, conscience and religion (Art. 14), freedom of association (Art. 15), protection of privacy (Art. 16), access to information (Art. 17). In Art. 9§2, stipulating the right of the child not to be separated from his/her parents, the right to speak and be heard is even taken further, recognising the child as a "*party*" to the proceedings, having the opportunity to fully participate and make his/her views known.

5.2.1.3. The holistic childhood image in the CRC

As we have seen, prior to the drafting of the Convention, the image of childhood was mainly based on paternalistic perceptions. There was little or no attention for children's individual personality, let alone for any specific human rights related to that (Price Cohen, 1991, p. 60). Instead, children were merely viewed as incomplete human beings, whose only remedy was "to grow up" ([O'Neill, 1988], quoted in Freeman, 2007, p. 10). As has been described above, the CRC countered this view, but did not make it disappear entirely. At its adoption in 1989, the Convention included the dominant currents of what had by then grown out to become the international children's rights movement, proclaiming the *simultaneous importance of both dependency and autonomy* for children (Verhellen, 2006; Reynaert et al., 2011, p. 2).

Hence, holistically addressing children as persons in their entirety, the CRC demonstrates that there has been a growing consensus about the fact that children should not only be considered as passive objects of protection, but should also be regarded as active bearers of rights.

Replacing the old "the child must be given..." by "the child has the right to..." is a new phrasing, referring directly to the child as *subject*. Especially Art. 12 is key in this changing image.[14] Via paragraph 1 of this article, the CRC is recognising the fact that the child already has an opinion and no longer a "not-yet"-opinion. Fundamentally, this (legal) standard is reflecting the recognition of every child as a *meaning-maker* and as such he/she has *the right to speak*, irrespective of their age (provided that the child has a certain level of *maturity*) or the topic at hand (provided that it concerns a *matter affecting the child*). Also notice that via the wording "... *being given due weight* ...", this right to speak is referring to at least the *duty to* listen to this opinion and to take it into account. This implies that children are seen as competent, unless it is proven that they are not, in which case adults and the State have the obligation to guide them towards this competence.

There is, however, still a lot of controversy about the (legal) capacity of children to exercise these rights independently. The most fundamental, recurring argument against autonomous rights for children is their supposed incompetence to take well-founded decisions. According to this view, children are physically, intellectually and emotionally not sufficiently mature and lack the necessary experience to make a rational judgement on what is and is not in their best interests. In the debate on children's rights, a central role is played by this – often emotionally loaded – *(in)competence argument*. The validity, soundness and relevance of the incompetence argument are, however, disputed, for example in the view of children as "resilient" in situations of extreme hardship (Boyden and Mann, 2005).

However, even among advocates of increased competence for children, different schools of thought can be distinguished. First of all, there is a reformist trend that regards the arguments in favour of incompetence as valid (*presumption of incompetence*), but is of the opinion that our society seriously underestimates children's capacity to take well-founded, rational decisions. The supporters of this view feel that children acquire this capacity much younger than is generally assumed, and that this capacity is gradually acquired. Hence, they argue in favour of lowering the age of majority and of the gradual acquisition of rights by children.[15]

Second, the so-called children's liberationists, a radical trend in the discussion on children's competence, dispute the validity of the incompetence arguments on moral grounds; their basic principle (the highest moral standard) is equality of all people. Any form of discrimination, including therefore discrimination on the basis of age, is considered morally wrong. To them, granting children all human rights – and the capacity to exercise these – is the only solution.[16]

A third trend, the pragmatic or emancipatory trend, is of increasing importance. Supporters add a pragmatic or emancipatory view to the liberationalists' perspective by wondering why it would not be possible, in practice, to grant children all rights. This would include the right to exercise these rights autonomously (*presumption of competence*), unless it can be proven that children are incompetent (*juris tantum* principle) to exercise certain rights, and there is general

---

14　Article 12: (1) States Parties shall assure to the child who is capable of forming his or her own views the right to express those views freely in all matters affecting the child, the views of the child being given due weight in accordance with the age and maturity of the child. (2) For this purpose, the child shall in particular be provided the opportunity to be heard in any judicial and administrative proceedings affecting the child, either directly, or through a representative or an appropriate body, in a manner consistent with the procedural rules of national law.

15　See e.g. Resolution 72 (29) on the lowering of the age of full legal capacity, adopted by the Committee of Ministers of the Council of Europe (1972) on 19 September 1972.

16　This approach is found mainly in the Anglo-Saxon countries and within a few decades a remarkable amount of publications appeared (see, among others, Adams *et al.*, 1971; Cohen, 1980; Farson, 1974; Goodman, 1960; Gottlieb, 1973; Gross and Gross, 1977; Holt, 1975).

agreement on this ("children have all rights unless…") (De Wilde, 2007; Hanson, 2012, p. 77). Experience with adults shows this is perfectly possible. The main advantage compared to the present situation would be that the onus of proof is reversed. Indeed, at the moment children are in a much weaker position because the burden of proof lies with them. They have to demonstrate they are competent ("children have no rights unless…").

The outcome of this competence debate ought to be that it is essential that the child's competence be recognised *in order to* make her/him more competent and not the other way around: that her/his competence be (gradually) recognised because (step by step) she/he gained more competence. Therefore, the present situation has become somewhat confused and, at times, even paradoxical. Indeed our relationship with children is still based on the established dominant child-image of children as objects, while, simultaneously, a new one, of children as subject, is gaining ground.

This discussion highlights that reading the CRC as a combination of protection, provision and participation rights will confront States parties with serious problems. Because of the historically developed and still-dominant child image emphasising the need to *protect* children, the recognition and the realisation of participation rights is obviously not yet acquired. Repeatedly, the cause is not about the "attitude towards participation", but rather the way we (still) look at children as not-yet-capable "human becomings".

5.2.1.4. "Existing" standards

Additionally, article 41 CRC has to be mentioned here as an important qualification for the rights in the Convention. It states that if any standards set in national law or other applicable international instruments are higher than those of the CRC, it is the higher standard that applies. This article demonstrates that the CRC contains only minimum standards that can always be improved. In fact, the Convention is calling on States parties to do better than the obligations imposed by the CRC. By "other applicable instruments", one could think about instruments from international organisations like The Hague Conference for Private International Law, ILO, the Council of Europe, the EU…

5.2.2. Monitoring and enforcement obligations of a legally binding Convention

All too often, both in spirit and in practice, the CRC is still considered as a kind of (soft) "declaration of love". Therefore, it should be repeated that the CRC is a Convention. Conventions are so-called "hard law", in other words legally binding. Indeed when a State joins a Convention (i.e. ratifies it or accedes to it), it enters into an international agreement with the other States parties. Along with the others, it has to become and stay politically conscious that it has accepted the obligation to put into practice the provisions of that Convention and translate these principles systematically into its national legal system. The legal principle *pacta sunt servanda* therefore also applies to international treaties between States. A problem arising here, as in other areas of international law, is monitoring and enforcement. Each Convention is only as effective as its *monitoring system*, in combination with the *enforcement mechanisms* provided in the national legal systems.

5.2.2.1. At the international level

The CRC provides its own system to monitor the implementation by States parties (Verhellen, 1996; Verhellen and Spiesschaert, 1994). This task is taken up by the treaty body, the *Committee on the Rights of the Child*. The Committee is composed of 18 independent experts[17] and was established in Articles 43–45 of the CRC. Among other tasks, the Committee is to monitor progress made by States parties in accomplishing their children's rights obligations under the Convention (Verheyde and Goedertier, 2006). For this purpose, within two years after ratification (and thereafter every five years), States parties have to report their achievements and remaining challenges to the Committee (Art. 44§1). Next to the official State reports, the Committee also receives shadow reports by agencies, NGOs or other experts who are familiar with the children's rights situation in the country under scrutiny (Art. 45, a). Even children have in the past addressed the Committee directly, for example in UNICEF Belgium's *What do you think* project (2013). Based on all these different sources of information, the Committee enters into a public "constructive dialogue" with the State. It formulates concluding observations – to be seen as *sui generis* jurisprudence (Price Cohen, 2005), which constitute, in their turn, the starting point for the next State report and discussion.

As such, ratifying the CRC implies the obligation for States parties to engage in a sustainable process of public scrutiny. This reporting process is in itself *non-judicial*. Indeed, the drafters of the CRC opted for advice and assistance in the format of non-binding recommendations to support implementation, in order to achieve one of their main objectives: bringing about a *"positive" monitoring climate*. The involvement of non-State actors turns reporting into an active means, also via mutual assistance and cooperation (Art. 4), of improving children's situation rather than just a passive means of monitoring implementation. Also other activities of the Committee point in the same direction, e.g. to undertake urgent actions in serious situations,[18] to initiate research studies (Art. 45,c), to hold regular days of general discussion[19] and to formulate general comments (Art. 45,d).[20]

In addition to the States parties' *duty to report* (Art. 44§1) the sustainable process of public scrutiny also implies the important *duty to inform* (Art. 44§6). This means that States must widely disseminate the reports, summary records and concluding observations adopted by the Committee.[21] In fact, this obligation is a direct result of Art. 42, a unique provision that emphasises States parties' duty to "*make the principles and provisions of the Convention widely known, by appropriate and active means, to adults and children alike.*" As such, the CRC not only seeks to clarify whether children's rights are infringed, it also indicates that widespread knowledge of the rights of the child in public opinion is the best protection against such infringements. The absence of such systematic campaigns remains a weakness in most, if not all, States parties to the Convention.

In addition to the reporting process described above, since April 14th, 2014, the CRC also has an *optional protocol* providing a *communications procedure* (Lembrechts, 2012; Verhellen, 2013). Following the Protocol, children and their representatives may submit complaints of violations

---

17 Art. 43§2 CRC speaks about 10 members. In 1995, Costa Rica proposed an amendment to article 43§2 in order to extend the number of members from 10 to 18 (A/RES/50/155). After reaching the two-thirds majority States parties at their meeting of 23 February 2003 indeed elected the members of the extended Committee. At their 33rd session (19 May–6 June 2003) the Committee first met with 18 members. The Committee, by (provisionally) meeting in parallel chambers, can handle now 48 reports instead of 27. The proposal to meet in parallel chambers was adopted on 23 December 2004 (A/RES/59/261).
18 CRC/C/10, 1992, para. 54–58.
19 CRC/C/4, 1991, rule. 75.
20 CRC/C/4, 1991, rules. 71–73. At the time of writing, the CRC Committee has interpreted the content of the Convention in 17 thematic general comments.
21 CRC/C/58, 1996, para. 23.

of rights recognised by the Convention and the first two Optional Protocols to the Committee, if they cannot find solutions in their country and if their State has ratified this Protocol. The Protocol not only provides children with a mechanism to address violations of their rights, it also strengthens their status as rights holders. As such, it ensures compliance by duty bearers to the CRC standards.

Finally, since the creation in 2006 of the *Universal Periodic Review* (UPR), children's rights got an additional important monitoring mechanism.[22] The UPR is an inter-governmental review mechanism under which the Human Rights Council examines the overall human rights situation, including child rights issues,[23] in every member State of the UN. Each State is examined every four and a half years.[24] Since the process is State-driven, and thus not initiated by a group of independent experts like the Committee, it is highly political, resulting in often vague and general recommendations that make follow-up extremely difficult (Abebe, 2009, p. 34). However, the results of the UPR-process are integrated in the constructive dialogue before the Committee where relevant, as the latter takes the child-rights-related recommendations from the UPR-report into consideration during its own review process.

5.2.2.2. At the national level

The mutual duties between States parties also have consequences on the domestic legal order. On the one hand, *indirectly*, States parties have the obligation to implement the CRC within their own jurisdiction. Therefore, they "shall undertake all appropriate legislative, administrative, and other measures" (Art. 4) (Rishmawi, 2006). In fact, this is the duty to bring national legislation and practice into full conformity with the principles and provisions of the CRC. To this end, the Committee has given detailed information on how States should act (CRC/GC/2003/5). It must be clear that, by doing this, special attention should be given to the comprehensiveness of the CRC. Last but not least, new proposed laws or amended existing laws affecting children should follow a child rights approach and not lower the (minimum) standards of the CRC.

On the other hand, there are *direct* consequences as well. The Committee stressed that new or amended domestic law(s) should mean that the provisions of the CRC could be directly invoked before the courts (CRC/GC/2003/5). Here we touch on the *self-executing force* of international treaties. After ratification of a Convention, (some of) its provisions are directly included in the national legal order, others need to be (indirectly) transposed into national legislation. This is only the case if the State party has recognised the principle of direct applicability of international treaties in its domestic legislation. In addition, if a Convention such as the CRC is to be directly applicable, its content must meet a number of conditions (Alen and Pas, 1996): The individual wishing to claim or enforce the right must fall within the jurisdiction of the State; the Article he or she wishes to rely on must be recognised as a right by the State party (i.e. the State cannot have submitted a reservation to qualify the content of a certain right); and the content of the provision must be precise and specific enough to be applied by a national authority without any further act of the State (Cremer, 2011). Finally, it is up to the national courts to decide which provisions have or do not have direct effect. The self-executing force of some CRC-rights is recognised by domestic courts in several States parties (Vandaele

---

22 A/RES/60/251, 5(e)
23 A/HRC/7/L.34, 26 March 2008, 7.
24 Available at www.ohchr.org/EN/HRBodies/UPR/Pages/UPRMain.aspx.

and Pas, 2004). It must be clear that much depends on the willingness and creativity of lawyers and magistrates in making the CRC directly capable of being invoked by individuals.

6. Conclusion: Educational consequences of the CRC framework

This chapter described how the CRC is unique in being the most widely ratified international human rights treaty. No less than 195 States have committed themselves to respect, promote and protect the rights of children through the implementation of the standards and principles enshrined in it. With its universal appeal, the indivisibility of its provisions, the repeatedly (e.g. Art. 4, Art. 23(4), Art. 24(4), Art. 28(3), art. 45 (d)) strong plea for international cooperation, its comprehensiveness and its legally binding character, the CRC is challenging us with a never-before-seen *geo-political social contract*. Since its entry into force in 1990, legal, legislative and policy reforms have produced positive results both at a national, regional and international level (UNICEF, 2007).

However, over the same period of time, it has become all too clear that this promising development does not mean that children's rights enjoy universal respect in practice. Despite the continuous effort to monitor and enforce the Convention, violations of children's rights continue to persist in all layers of society in all corners of the world. This means that our task as academics, policy makers or practitioners aiming to realise a balanced society in which social justice and human dignity for children are fully realised, remains an open-ended challenge.

In providing a new framework on how to relate to children as moral *and* legal rights holders, the legal content of the CRC provides guidance on how this challenge can be taken up in law and social policy. At the same time, however, the CRC reflects a significant educational agenda. Educational science, teaching us how to deal with children, and children's rights as stipulated in the Convention, are inextricably linked.

Whereas earlier instruments had focused on protection claims for children, the CRC codified a new discourse of children as "rights holders". Inspired by the CRC – and the social movements that preceded its adoption – a new child image gains in strength: children are no longer regarded as beings who are "not-yet" (adults), but as fully-fledged individuals with their own meaning-making capacity, competent to exercise their human rights, if necessary with some support, independently (Verhellen, 2006). Enshrining these rights in positive law (standard setting) is, however, not the end of the matter. Implementation, monitoring, enforcement and translation of these legal principles to the pedagogical practice, i.e. the way we deal with children, are continuing challenges.

The notion *bearers* or *subjects of human rights* includes that children are seen as meaning-makers and competent to exercise their rights. This competence approach is reflected in the CRC and is indeed quite new. It is of importance, then, to experience that the more their competencies are recognised and realised, the more children will gain a prominent space and place in society, and the more they will ultimately be able to challenge the dominant child image that still does not see them as capable human beings on their own. This so-called pragmatic trend is growing: presupposing (*juris tantum*) that the child is competent unless it can be proven that she/he is not. In the end, children will not only become more visible, but above all they will become visible in a different way (as meaning-makers). The emerging child image will not only influence this relationship on the micro level, but also, the macro structural level will undergo substantial changes. The legally binding characteristics of the CRC will lead to new laws and new structures. The processes of sociogenesis and psychogenesis (discussed above) are working here too. The new way of dealing with children will become more and more horizontal: mutual respect will enter everyday reality.

However, the CRC is still rather young, and therefore it is not the end but rather a new starting point. In other words, standard setting is still going on today. Even more so, the existing standards continue to be challenged, e.g. by bottom-up approaches that may lead to other or reverse forms of standard setting (Liebel, 2012; Hanson and Nieuwenhuys, 2013). In light of these parallel developments, also implementation and monitoring need urgent and serious attention. For instance, most countries still suffer while trying to implement genuine participation rights. Mostly there is not a difficulty with a view to participation, but rather with a view to perceiving children still as not-yet competent. This may explain why so many participation projects are seen as preparing children to be able to participate later on, which is an "instrumental" conceptualisation of children's participation. Again, children *are* meaning makers and as such they already participate. Recognising this capacity seems to be a difficult learning process. It is thus not so surprising that a lot of youth and/or educational policy documents reflect that this learning process is going at snail's pace.[25]

Finally, it is of the utmost importance to keep alive the consciousness, and to strengthen the professionalisation, among other things, through an intentional and systematic human/children's rights education policy and keep the courage and (political) will to continue the complex implementation process. Therefore, the powerful continuation of the already existing critical discussion to which this Handbook aims to contribute, is a *sine qua non*. For, human/children's rights are not gifts, but are more like *verbs* to conjugate in the present and the future – and this by means of *all* personal pronouns.

Questions for debate and discussion

- What are the challenges for research, policy and practice in the way in which the CRC – and children's rights more broadly – unite law, social policy and education?
- What are the implications of the dual childhood image the CRC contains, i.e. an image that attributes simultaneous importance to both dependency and autonomy?
- How can contextualised, bottom-up approaches complement the CRC framework in our way of dealing with children?
- What are arguments in favour or against a separate Convention for children alongside the other UN human rights conventions, and how does this relate to the stance that children should be seen as human beings on equal footing with adults?

References

Abebe, A.M. (2009). Of shaming and bargaining: African states and the universal periodic review of the United Nations Human Rights Council. *Human Rights Law Review*, 9(1), 1–35.

Abramson, B. (2008). Article 2. The right of non-discrimination. In A. Alen *et al.* (eds), *A Commentary on the United Nations Convention on the Rights of the Child*. Leiden, the Netherlands: Martinus Nijhoff.

Adams, P., Berg, L., Berger, N., Duane, M., Neill, A.S. and Ollendorf, R. (1971). *Children's Rights. Towards the Liberation of the Child*. New York: Praeger.

Alen, A. and Pas, W. (1996). The UN Convention on the rights of the child's self-executing force character. In E. Verhellen (ed.), *Monitoring Children's Rights*. The Hague: Martinus Nijhoff, pp. 165–186.

---

25 This is illustrated, for example, by the slow pace at which the legal status and participation of children at school (in Flemish *Leerlingenstatuut*) got translated into a binding decree in Flanders. Recommendations from the Children's Rights Commissioner have focused on the necessity of strengthening the position of pupils since 1999 already (Kinderrechtencommissariaat, 2014, p. 2).

Alen, A., Vande Lanotte, J., Verhellen, E., Ang, F., Berghmans E. and Verheyde, M. (eds) (2005–2012). *A Commentary on the United Nations Convention on the Rights of the Child*. Leiden, the Netherlands: Martinus Nijhoff.
Ang, F., Berghmans, E., Cattrijsse, L., Delens-Ravier, I., Delplace, M., Staelens, V., Vandewiele, T., Vandresse, C. and Verheyde, M. (eds) (2006). *Participation Rights of Children*. Antwerpen, Belgium: Intersentia.
Ariès, P. (1979[1962]). *Centuries of childhood: A Social History of Family Life*. London: Penguin.
Besson, S. (2005). The principle of non-discrimination in the convention on the rights of the child. *The International Journal of Children's Rights*, 39(4), 433–461.
Berding, J.W.A. (2008). Janusz Korczak: An introduction. In Th. Cappon and J. Tchikhatcheva (eds). *Dutch International Janusz Korczak Youth Conference*. [Report]. Amsterdam: Janusz Korczak Association in the Netherlands, pp. 80–88.
Boyd, D.R. (2012). *The Constitutional Right to a Healthy Environment*. Available at www.environmentmagazine.org/Archives/Back%20Issues/2012/July-August%202012/constitutional-rights-full.html (last accessed 28 May 2014).
Boyden, J. and Mann, G. (2005). Children's risk, resilience, and coping in extreme situations. In M. Ungar (ed.), *Handbook for Working with Children and Youth: Pathways to Resilience Across Cultures and Contexts*, Thousand Oaks, CA: Sage, pp. 3–25.
Camper Soman, S. (1974). *Let's Stop Destroying Our Children*. New York: Hawthorn.
Cohen, H. (1980). *Equal rights for children*. Towata: NJ: Littlefield-Adams and Co.
Committee of Ministers of the Council of Europe (1972). Resolution 72(29) on the lowering of the age of full legal capacity, adopted on 19 September 1972.
Committee on the Rights of the Child (2003). *General Comment n° 5 on general measures of implementation of the Convention on the Rights of the Child*. CRC/GC/2003/5.
Cremer, H. (2011). *Die UN-Kinderrechts-konvention – Geltung und Anwendbarkeit in Deutschland nach der Rücknahme der Vorbehalte* [The UN Convention on the Rights of the Child: Validity and Applicability in Germany after the withdrawal of the Reservations]. Berlin: German Institute for Human Rights. Available at www.institut-fuer-menschenrechte.de/uploads/tx_commerce/die_un_kinderrechtskonvention.pdf (last accessed 28 May 2014).
Dasberg, L. (1986). *Grootbrengen door kleinhouden als historisch verschijnsel* ['Bringing up by keeping small' as a historical phenomenon]. Boom, Belgium: Meppel.
De Graaf, J.H. (1989). De betekenis van de ontwerpconventie inzake de rechten van het kind [The meaning of the draft Convention on the Rights of the Child]. In M. De Langen, J.H. De Graaf and F.B.M. Kunneman (eds), *Kinderen en recht*. Arnhem, the Netherlands: Quint, pp. 14–24.
De Wilde, C. (2007). *Integrated Youth Care in Flanders: Basis for an Inclusive Policy Regarding Youth Care*. Paper presented at the conference 'Barriers to access: Paths of inclusiveness, conference presentation', Scotland, 5–8 June 2007.
Elias, N. (2000). *The Civilizing Process: Sociogenetic and Psychogenetic Investigations*. Oxford: Blackwell.
Farson, R. (1974). *Birth Rights*. Harmondsworth, UK: Penguin.
Freeman, M. (2007). Article 3. The best interests of the child. In A. Alen *et al.* (eds), *A Commentary on the United Nations Convention on the Rights of the Child*. Leiden, the Netherlands: Martinus Nijhoff.
Goodman, P. (1960). *Growing up Absurd*. New York: Random House.
Gottlieb, D. (ed.) (1973). *Children's Liberation*. Englewood Cliffs, NJ: Prentice Hall.
Gross, B. and Gross, R. (eds) (1977). *The Children's Rights Movement*. New York: Anchor Press.
Hanson, K. (2012). Schools of thought in children's rights. In M. Liebel (ed.), *Children's Rights From Below: Cross-cultural Perspectives*. Basingstoke, UK: Palgrave Macmillan, 63–79.
Hanson, K. (2014). Separate childhood laws and the future of society. *Law, Culture and the Humanities*, 1743872114529502. doi:10.1177/1743872114529502 [e-pub ahead of print].
Hanson, K. and Nieuwenhuys, O. (eds) (2013). *Reconceptualizing Children's Rights in International Development: Living Rights, Social Justice, Translations*. Cambridge: Cambridge University Press.
Heiliö, P., Lauronen, E. and Bardy, M. (eds) (1993). *Politics of Childhood and Children at Risk: Provision, Protection, Participation*. [Eurosocial Report 45]. Vienna: European Centre for Social Welfare Policy and Research.
Holt, J. (1975). *Escape from Childhood*. Harmondsworth, UK: Penguin.
Kempe, C., Silverman, F., Steele, B., Droegemueller, W. and Silver, H. (1962). The battered child syndrome. *Journal of the American Medical Association*, 181(1), 17–24.
Kilkelly, U. (2004). Children's rights: A European perspective. *Judicial Studies Institute Journal*, 4(2), 68–95.

Kinderrechtencommissariaat (2014). *Rechtspositie leerlingen in basis- en secundair onderwijs en partcipatie op school* [The legal status of school children in primary and secondary education and participation at school]. Advies 2013–2014/10 aan de Commissie voor Onderwijs en Gelijke Kansen, 26 February 2014. Available at www.kinderrechtencommissariaat.be/sites/default/files/bestanden/2013_2014_10_rechtspositie_onderwijs.pdf (last accessed 3 March 2014).

Lembrechts, S. (2012). Wiens klachtenrecht? het kind-concept in het derde Facultatief Protocol bij het Verdrag inzake de Rechten van het Kind betreffende de instelling van een communicatieprocedure [Whose right to complain? The image of the child in the Third Optional Protocol to the Convention on the Rights of the Child]. *in Tijdschrift voor Jeugd en Kinderrechten*, 2, 96–113.

Liebel, M. (ed.) (2012). *Children's Rights from Below: Cross-cultural Perspectives*. New York: Palgrave Macmillan.

Lundy, L. and McEvoy (Emerson), L. (2012). Childhood, the United Nations Convention on the Rights of the Child and research: what constitutes a rights-based approach. In M. Freeman (ed.), *Law and Childhood*. Oxford: Oxford University Press, pp. 75–91.

Montgomery, H. (2009). *An Introduction to Childhood: Anthropological Perspectives on Children's Lives*. Oxford: Wiley-Blackwell.

Nowak, M. (2005). Article 6. The right to life, survival and development. In A. Alen *et al.* (eds), *A Commentary on the United Nations Convention on the Rights of the Child*. Leiden, the Netherlands: Martinus Nijhoff.

Op de Beeck, H., Put, J. and Lembrechts, S. (2013). *Zwaartepunten in het Vlaams kinderrechtenonderzoek vanaf 2004. Een thematische analyse op basis van de KeKi onderzoeksdatabank* [Focal points in Flemish children's rights research as from 2004. A thematic analysis based on the KeKi children's rights research database]. Ghent, Belgium: Kenniscentrum Kinderrechten vzw.

Op de Beeck, H., Herbots, K., Lembrechts, S. and Willems, N. (2014). *Children's Best Interests between Theory and Practice: A Discussion of Commonly Encountered Tensions and Possible Solutions Based on International Best Practices and Policy Strategies since 2004*. Ghent, Belgium: Kenniscentrum Kinderrechten vzw.

Price Cohen, C. (1991). United Nations Convention on the Rights of the Child: Individual rights concepts and their significance for social scientists. *American Psychologist*, 46(1), 60–65.

Price Cohen, C. (ed.) (2005). *Jurisprudence on the Rights of the Child*. Ardsley, NY: Transnational.

Reynaert, D., Roose, R., Vandenhole, W. and Vlieghe, K. (eds) (2011). *Kinderrechten: Springplank of Struikelblok? Naar Een Kritische Benadering Van Kinderrechten* [Children's rights: Steppingstone or stumbling block? Towards a critical approach of children's rights]. Antwerpen: Intersentia.

Rishmawi, M. (2006). Article 4: The nature of States parties' obligations. In A. Alen *et al.* (eds), *A Commentary on the United Nations Convention on the Rights of the Child*. Leiden, the Netherlands: Martinus Nijhoff.

UNICEF (2007). *Law Reform and Implementation of the Convention on the Rights of the Child*. Florence: Innocenti Research Centre. Available at www.unicef-irc.org/publications/pdf/law_reform_crc_imp.pdf (last accessed 28 May 2014).

Vandaele, A. and Pas, W. (2004). International human rights treaties and their relation with national law: Monism, dualism and the self-executing character of human rights. In E. Verhellen and A. Weyts (eds), *Understanding Children's Rights*. [Ghent papers on children's rights, N° 7]. Ghent, Belgium: Children's Rights Centre, Ghent University, pp. 375–393.

Verhellen, E. (1992). Changes in the images of the child. In M. Freeman and P. Veerman (eds), *The Ideologies of Children's Rights*. Dordrecht, the Netherlands: Martinus Nijhoff, pp. 79–94.

Verhelllen, E. (ed.) (1996). *Monitoring Children's Rights*. The Hague: Martinus Nijhoff.

Verhellen, E. (2006). *Convention on the Rights of the Child. Background, Motivation, Strategies, Main Themes*. Antwerpen, Belgium: Garant.

Verhellen, E. (2008). Citizenship and participation of children: In search of a framework and some thoughts. In D. Ferring, K. Hanson, M. Majerus, Ch. Schmitt and J. Zermatten (eds), *Les droits de l'enfant : Citoyenneté et participation*. Luxembourg: Université du Luxembourg, pp. 14–32.

Verhellen, E. (2013). Le 3 ème protocole à la CIDE. Des opportunités manquées et des défis [The third optional protocol to the CRC: Missed opportunities and challenges]. *Journal du droit des Jeunes [Journal of Youth Law]*, 328, 19–25.

Verhellen, E. and Spiesschaert, F. (eds) (1989). *Ombudswork for Children. A Way of Improving the Position of Children in Society*. Leuven, Belgium: Acco.

Verhellen, E. and Spiesschaert, F. (eds) (1994). *Children's Rights: Monitoring Issues*. Ghent, Belgium: Mys and Breesch.

Verheyde, M. and Goedertier, G. (2006). Articles 43–45: The UN Committee on the rights of the child. In: Alen, A. *et al.* (eds), *A commentary on the United Nations Convention on the Rights of the Child*. Leiden, the Netherlands: Martinus Nijhoff.

4

Children's rights and childhood studies

From living apart together towards a happy marriage

Bruno Vanobbergen

1. The revolutionary nature of the Convention on the Rights of the Child and the origins of childhood studies as an interdisciplinary approach of children and childhood

Children's rights have received a higher profile by means of the International Convention on the Rights of the Child (CRC). The CRC, adopted by the UN General Assembly on 20 November 1989, was a long time in the making. It therefore has a long history, not only politically, but also from a theoretical-paradigmatic standpoint. With regard to the latter, we could say that the CRC ascribes to a (pedagogical) tradition in which Rousseau and Montaigne, for example, played a key role. But the role of a figure such as Janusz Korczak who, in the 1920s, drafted a 'Charter for the protection of children' was also crucial. This Charter exerted an important influence on the development of the various international children's rights instruments as we know them today, and of which the 1989 CRC can be considered the apotheosis. At that time, the 1959 Declaration of the Rights of the Child became a convention. Henceforth, the demand for attention to the rights of children no longer rested on a mere statement of intention (a declaration), but on a text that must be seen as a framework of reference for all legislation in those countries that have ratified the Convention.

It is important to keep in mind that the CRC is first of all a text that arises from indignation concerning an existing state of affairs and that very explicitly strives to change this situation (Meirieu, 2002). Children were invisible for a long time, and where they were visible, there was very often little importance given to what children experienced and what they had to say. An illustration of this is the recent investigation by the Samson Committee in the Netherlands into the prevention of sexual abuse in institutions. The investigation demonstrates very clearly, for instance, how children who were the victim of sexual abuse prior to 1980 were absolutely not taken seriously when they told others about the sexual abuse. 'They were mocked, ridiculed, not believed, and in many instances were even punished for their supposed lies, "filthy talk" and improper thoughts' (Samson Committee Report, 2012, p. 69). Attention to the rights of children appeared in this light as a protest against the continual failure to appreciate children.

This protest served as the impetus for the long struggle for the recognition of the 'here and now' of children. Childhood is indeed much more than mere preparation for adult life. As Korczak (2007, 171) very clearly formulates it:

> Children are future adults – so they say. They are only in the process of becoming, they actually do not yet entirely exist, they do not yet belong. ... What does this mean? We children: are we not yet alive, do we not feel, do we not suffer – just like adults? And childhood: is it not a part of real life – of everyone? Why do they wish to make us wait – and for what?

Accepting that there is also a 'here and now' for children means that we, as adults, pay attention to the meanings that children and youth attach to what is happening in their present lives. 'Children are the future', as is often said. But the present is just as important as this future perspective. It therefore means that what children perceive as important plays a role in the decisions that we take in and about the lives of these children and youth.

In addition to the attention to the 'here and now', the CRC also very clearly offers opportunities to revisit the traditional model of the adult–child relationship. Traditionally, the adult appears as the finished, the complete, while the child appears as 'the not-yet'. The child is developing; the adult is developed. This has important consequences for the manner in which we view children. Let us take the example of the long-term sick child. When children are sick for a long time, one of the elements that initially surprises adults is the resilience that children and youth possess. The image of the strong, sick child contradicts the way that we currently think about granting the right to decide to children concerning their own treatment. In practice, we often notice that this right is linked to a number of conditions (Hemrica, 2004). The most notable of which is the question whether children indeed have sufficient skills to think with us about their illness and its treatment – a question which is not, or only exceptionally, asked of adults. The applicable rule for children is that they must prove that they meet a certain norm. For adults, on the contrary, it is assumed to be self-evident that they meet this norm. Furthermore, this norm is very cognitively coloured. It then has to do with, for instance, the understanding of the nature and seriousness of the illness, or the understanding of the advantages and disadvantages of various possibilities of treatment. The significance of social and emotional skills seems hardly relevant. This seems to suggest that taking the 'right' decision is not only rational, but apparently is also taken alone and independent of others. Just like adults, the child is determined by his feelings and intelligence. The child is a serious being and therefore always deserves to be taken seriously. It is not about ascribing to children the same interests and values as adults (Mortier, 2002). It rather concerns ascribing equal value to divergent interests and values.

Attention to children's here and now, recognizing children in their specificity, having an eye for children and childhood as a separate social group, the development of a new child policy (and in connection with this, an alternative image of the adult)... these are all themes that have played a role in childhood studies in the last few decades. Today, childhood studies can be defined as the study of childhood from an interdisciplinary perspective. Several disciplines such as geography, ethics, history, consumer studies, and sociology for example have played a central role in establishing this interdisciplinary approach of childhood. In this, childhood studies are different from the sociology of childhood as the latter need to be seen as the study of childhood from the discipline of sociology. However, the sociology of childhood has been very important in elaborating an alternative paradigm on childhood, a paradigm that has been influential for the other disciplines within the childhood studies.

The start of this alternative thinking on childhood can be situated in the work of Gertrud Lenzer, Professor of Sociology at Brooklyn College (Lenzer, 1991; see also Lenzer, Chapter 16 in this Handbook). Lenzer criticized the lack of attention on children within the social sciences. She thought it strange, for instance, that children received a great deal of attention from the advertising industry, but did not constitute a systematic subject of scientific research as an important group in society. Lenzer's thoughts were heard, as the American Sociological Association (ASA) decided in 1992 to create a new division, the Sociology of Children. The ASA initiative soon inspired other associations. For instance, the Deutschen Gesellschaft fur Soziologie (DGS) created a *Working Group*, 'Soziologie der Kindheit' (Sociology of Childhood) (Honig, Leu and Nissen, 1996). And in the same period, we witnessed the generation of interest in a 'Sociologie de l'enfance' in France (Sirota, 1998, 12). It would signify the start of a new discipline, which we today summarize under the broad term 'childhood studies', but which previously and currently is equally called child studies or children's studies. A number of issues were notable from the beginning. For instance, the pioneers heavily emphasized the importance of an interdisciplinary approach. This includes, for example, attention on the history of beliefs about childhood, for the growth of scientific approaches to studying children, for the significance of gender, and for debates around children's rights. Unilateral perspectives on children and childhood sell children short. A holistic approach to children and childhood is important. At the same time, it is notable how the emphasis on diversity among children receives greater attention. From the very start, it turned the childhood studies story into a place where highly divergent forms of childhood are addressed (Nieuwenhuys, 2010).

In this contribution, we want to take a closer look at the relationship between, on the one hand, the paradigm shift that childhood studies as a discipline represents, and on the other hand, children's rights as a concept by which to fully comprehend the social and pedagogical position of children. In accordance with the intent of this Handbook, to this end we will rely heavily on what is considered as the basic literature within childhood studies. The investigation of the interrelation between children's rights and childhood studies is not evident. Already in 1998, Freeman (1998) wrote how remarkable it was that two disciplines, which have so much in common, have so little dialogue with one another. One really can say that both disciplines were living apart together. Since then, the theme of children's rights has received greater attention within childhood studies (e.g. Mayall, 2000; Kaufman and Rizzini, 2009; Alanen, 2010). The current status of childhood studies furthermore increases the difficulty of the exercise. Childhood studies are a field of study that may indeed have a common denominator, but with many different faces. James (2010) therefore uses the interesting metaphor of 'the fabric of childhood studies'. 'We can focus on the entire piece of cloth and recognize from its shape and dimensions the separateness of children from adults, as well as admiring the complexity of the patterns that are created by the weaving together of the different elements of the warp and weft' (James, 2010, 496).

In what follows we take three steps. With the first step we examine the breakthrough of the new paradigm of childhood. We briefly outline the context in which the new paradigm has developed and, to this end, we also focus on, among others, the criticisms formulated about the concept of development in relation to children and childhood. With the second step, the main themes of the paradigm of the childhood studies take centre stage: (1) childhood as a structural form and (2) children's agency. Both ideas are made explicit and illustrated with regard to the work of the most important authors within the field of childhood studies, with a specific focus on those representing the sociology of childhood. Finally, with the last step we formulate a few ambitions with regard to the continued translation and deepening of children's rights as a concept. The starting point in this regard is that to this day, children's rights are still considered too much from an adult perspective.

2. Searching for an alternative to the unilateral developmental-psychological perspective on children

2.1. Development and socialization as the leading concepts for thinking about children

And still we want it to move quickly. And this is why we lift the little plant up with our impatient fingers, though in so doing we pull out the thin root fibres, and the little plant shrinks. Or we place it in a hothouse, and it quickly grows big, yet is unsuitable for the cold soil. Growing occurs slowly. And whoever does not believe that should just go look at a plant for a few hours. Then he will see that he sees nothing. And yet the plant has grown in those few hours.

Thus writes Jan Ligthart in his 'Verzamelde Opstellen' (Collected Articles) from 1917. Ligthart was one of the educators who considered the development of children as a growing process that follows a natural course. Views about the child and her development were repeatedly borrowed from the way that people deal with nature. Children themselves determined the pace of their development to a significant extent; the most important task of the educator was simply to follow. In the literature providing pedagogical advice, we also see comparisons between children and the laws of nature appearing until the late sixties.

In the meantime, a new science of the child emerged at the end of the nineteenth century. References to natural processes made way for experimental research into developmental phenomena. The new approach began to make waves under a variety of names such as developmental psychology, child psychiatry, child studies and pedagogical pathology (Depaepe, 1993). From this point on, knowledge about the child was scientific knowledge – so concluded the enthusiastic followers of the new science. The desire for education, the need of the educator to intervene in the environment of the child in this way received a scientific foundation (Dekker, 2010). The new science of the child went hand-in-hand with medical science in its pursuit of mapping out child defects in order to in this way promote the image of the normal child. The enthusiastic belief in the new science led to the need for greater monitoring of the child and education, which was justified by referring to the interest of the child. Max Weber used the term *Entzauberung der Welt/Disenchantment of the World* to describe this process (Dassen, 1999). Whereas romantics took the disenchantment of the world as an indication of the world becoming increasingly less attractive, with Weber it appeared as a challenge that people should dare to face head on. Applied to children, youth and their education, this implied that at the start of the twentieth century, there was a conviction that at some point it would be possible to fully know and fathom the child in her totality (Turmel, 2008). It was therefore no more than a matter of time until all the secrets of children and childhood would be thoroughly and clearly mapped out.

'Development', an essentially temporal notion, is the primary metaphor through which childhood is made intelligible, both in the everyday world and also within the specialist vocabularies of the sciences and agencies which lay claim to an understanding and servicing of that state of being.

(Jenks, 2005, 36)

In this way Jenks refers to the crucial role that Piaget played in the realization of this notion of development, and at the same time shows how Piaget's psychological theory and Parsons's sociological theory opposed one another in a symbiotic relationship. For Parsons, the child symbolized the other, and consequently it constitutes a threat to order in the social world. The social activities of the child therefore must be situated entirely within the discourse of socialization. Or as Corsaro (1997, 9–10) states it:

> In Parsons' view the child is a threat to society; he must be appropriated and shaped to fit in. Parsons envisioned a society as an intricate network of interdependent and interpenetrating roles and consensual values. The entry of the child into this system is problematic because although she has the potential to be useful to the continued functioning of the system, she is also a threat until she is socialized.

Mayall (2002, 23) describes Parsons and Piaget as 'the twin towers of sociology and psychology who provide the interlocked and complementary framework for commonplace notions of childhood'.

More or less the same idea of the child lies at the basis of the developmental psychology of Piaget, as well as the functionalist socialization model of Parsons. The child appears here as a *not yet* being that willingly passes through the stages of its development or easily adapts to the existing social systems. Childhood or the stage of being a child is not considered valuable as such, but is always seen from the perspective of adulthood. In this sense, the child stage is nothing more than a transitional phase. It is interesting how Jenks (2005) nevertheless links two different images of normal childhood to one another. First of all there is the Dionysian image of the child. The child, burdened from birth by original sin, appears here as a small demon that must be cast into the proper form with all means available. The child is wild and primitive, a Pippi Longstocking *avant la lettre*. The task of education consists of taming the wild child and civilizing her. The Apollonian child, on the contrary, is presented as intrinsically good. The child displays the characteristics of a noble savage or a naive genius who, with his poetic worldview, is very close to the divine origin of things. Both of these images of the child result in education as social control, even if this education assumes a different form in each situation. The model of education in line with the Dionysian image of the child is characterized by strong control and an explicit use of power. The Apollonian image of the child rather results in controlling children by means of 'child-centred approaches' (Jenks, 2005, 66). Smith (2011) claims that Jenks's distinction between the two images of the child is not so much about the difference between innocence and evil but rather about the distinction between innate innocence and acquired innocence. And thus we find ourselves back with Piaget and Parsons.

> The Dionysian notion of acquired innocence resonates with modes of socialization in which virtuous habits must be inculcated through external discipline. The innate innocence symbolized by the Apollonian child indicates an alternative form of socialization, grounded in subtler modes of manipulation, by which children are allowed to develop 'naturally'.
>
> *(Smith, 2011, 27)*

2.2. Breakthrough of an alternative paradigm

'What Foucault's work allows us to understand is that the truths of Piaget's and other claims about development are not timeless and universal scientific verities but are produced at a specific historical moment as an effect of power' (Walkerdine, 2009, 116). Walkerdine indicates that, within a developmental-psychological perspective, children's thought is considered as a way of thinking that gradually moves in the direction of mature thought. Children's thought is therefore described as fundamentally different from that of adults. And the difference described appears in terms of a lack or shortcoming of the child. This natural lack disappears as children grow up. Within this perspective, children are 'human becomings' rather than 'human beings', according to Walkerdine (2009, 117).

'Development' as the leading concept from which to think about children and childhood – certainly in the early stages of childhood studies – is an object of severe criticism. It would be too static, by which is meant that children's own contribution and activity is thoroughly neglected. Furthermore, it would borrow too much from statistics. With this, people take issue with the notion that for a long time, developmental psychology was primarily the study of similarities, the common, the averages and the norms, and much less the study of variation and diversity. It is simply assumed that all people grow and develop according to a previously established plan, which entails that someone who diverges from this plan is very quickly perceived as 'different' and is thus considered to be a problem. In connection with this, Popkewitz (1999) points out the danger of the dominance of the concept of time over, for instance, the spatial concept, which plays into the hand of thinking in universal terms. 'From the use of Piaget's conception of "stages" to Vygotsky's "zones of proximal development", research emphasized time dimensions that "tell" the researcher whether some intervention is significant or not' (Popkewitz, 1999, 23). The dominance of the concept of time goes together with a firm belief in the continual progress of humanity, the belief that not only groups of people, but also individuals continually develop toward a higher condition. Development is placed on the same line as ideas such as growth and progress, which contributes to the establishment of a competitive ethics in which mental and manual skills are subjected to a hierarchical evaluation (i.e. 'When did your child start walking?' 'My child was speaking by the time he was 13 months old').

Children's behaviour is not only normalized, but also decontextualized. People prefer to view individual children or mother–child dyads without taking into consideration their social and economic or cultural context. By focusing on the individual child as a social unit, differences in gender, social class and cultural knowledge are hardly taken into account. As a result, people do not demonstrate the least diffidence when formulating universal claims concerning the development of children. 'These sciences have produced a mass of literature using "children" from the western world that have psychologized and biologized younger human beings, creating the universal condition of childhood' (Cannella, 1999, 37). By presenting children and childhood in this way, an image of the child is formed which is fundamentally different from that of the adult.

> They are the ultimate 'Other' than the adult – those who must have their decisions made for them because they are not yet mature – those who must gain knowledge that has been legitimized by those who are older and wiser – those whose ways of being in the world can be uncovered through the experimental and observational methods of science – those who can be labelled as gifted, slow, intelligent, or special.
>
> *(Cannella, 1999, 36)*

It is clear that, certainly in the 1990s, the wide interest in the development of children – opponents summarize this under the denominator of 'developmentalism' – came heavily under attack. These criticisms lessened at the start of the twenty-first century (Woodhead, 2009). The battle with the most rigid versions of developmental psychology appears to have been waged. Authors do emphasize though that a number of concepts and tools that attempt to grasp the dependence and vulnerability of children cannot be avoided. For instance, Vygotsky's zone of proximal development is referred to, among others. Woodhead (2009, 57) summarizes this shift eloquently: 'In short, a strong research agenda on change and transitions in children's growth, learning and well-being is essential for Childhood Studies, even if we choose no longer to describe this agenda as about "child development"'.

Meanwhile, resistance and criticism had already led to the creation of a new paradigm. The fundamental principles of this new paradigm are thereby formulated in stark contrast to the notions of development and socialization. According to Jenks (2005) and James and Prout (1997), the fundamental assumptions of the new paradigm are as follows: (1) Childhood is understood as a social construction and thus provides a framework for the interpretation of the first years of life, (2) childhood cannot possibly be considered as a natural or universal characteristic among a group of people, but rather appears as a specific structural and cultural component within diverse societies, (3) children's social relations and cultures are worth studying in themselves, independent of the perspective and concerns of adults, and (4) children are active in determining their social life, the life of those they live together with and the society in which they reside, and are consequently not the passive subjects of social structures and processes.

In 2009, with the publication of the *Palgrave Handbook of Childhood Studies*, the following five characteristics of the new childhood paradigm were advanced (Qvortrup *et al.*, 2009): (1) the focus on the 'normal' child instead of the child who deviates from the norm, (2) the emphasis on the 'here and now' of children instead of on their coming adulthood, (3) the appreciation of children's agency and participation instead of only viewing them in terms of receivers of knowledge, (4) the analysis of the structural conditions under which childhood takes shape within a specific society, and (5) the scientific study of children and childhood is conducted in the same way as other groups in society are studied. From the initial chapters of the 2009 handbook, it also seems that childhood studies are in fact based upon two main perspectives (Wintersberger, 2012). There is the perspective introduced by Jens Qvortrup in which childhood is considered as a structural category or as a permanent segment of every society. The emphasis is thus on childhood as a generational unity, comparable with unities such as adulthood or seniors. Additionally there is Allison James's perspective. Here the focus is on children as actors. Children are efficacious actors in creating their lives, the lives of those close to them and the society in which they live. We will examine this in greater depth in the following section.

3. The sociology of childhood: Child of many fathers and mothers

The role of the sociology of childhood has been essential in the growth of childhood studies into a fully-fledged academic discipline. While we could say that in the early 1990s the two largely coincided, the sociology of childhood today forms part of a broader field in which, for instance, the history of childhood and an ethics of childhood have claimed a place (Kehily, 2009; Wall, 2010). Given the importance of the sociology of childhood, in what follows we take a more extensive look at the various elements it contains.

While the various researchers within the *Sociology of Childhood* present themselves as forming part of one single paradigm, notable differences can in fact be identified in the way in which the attempt is made to map out an alternative to the functionalist socialization model of Parsons. In the paragraphs that follow, we attempt to clarify these (subtle) differences by referring to the research of a few leading (and widely cited) researchers within the *Sociology of Childhood* paradigm.

3.1. Corsaro's 'interpretive reproduction'

Corsaro (1997), as opposed to most proponents of the *Sociology of Childhood* paradigm, situates the origin of his alternative model with Piaget, and more specifically with his constructivist approach to child development. Second, Corsaro also considers Vygotsky's theory about the zone of proximal development as a key element in the development of his constructivist-inspired model of socialization. From a social perspective, in the zone of proximal development, children can indeed participate in social activities in which they otherwise could never participate in on their own. While he is not blind to the shortcomings in the theories of Piaget and Vygotsky – for instance, he adheres to the criticism of the exaggerated focus on the individual development of children – Corsaro strongly believes in linking constructivist ideas to a form of socialization that places the collective and the social at the heart of children's activities.

At the very least, Corsaro's position with regard to socialization can be called ambiguous. On the one hand, he wants to continue to hold onto this concept in his thinking about the relationship between the child and society, but on the other hand, he also realizes its problematic character. 'It has an individualistic and forward-looking connotation that is inescapable. One hears the term and the idea of training and preparing the individual child for the future keeps coming right back to mind' (Corsaro, 1997, 18). Corsaro attempts to resolve this ambiguity by introducing the notion of 'interpretive reproduction'. The 'interpretive' component refers to the innovative and creative aspects in the social participation of children. The 'reproduction' component includes the idea that children do not simply internalize social and cultural norms, but actively contribute to cultural production and social change. The term simultaneously means that children, in their social participation, experience the limitations that coincide with the existing social structures. Children do not escape the influence of the society and culture of which they are a part. At the same time children do not simply imitate the world around them. 'They strive to interpret or make sense of their culture and to participate in it. In attempting to make sense of the adult world, children come to collectively produce their own peer worlds and cultures' (Corsaro, 1997, 24). Children are introduced into the culture by their family from the time they are born, after which they rather quickly explore other cultural contexts with other children and adults. According to Corsaro, childhood is thus a period in the course of an individual's life in which that individual enters a certain culture (with its subcultures) and then participates in it, and in this way helps (re)produce her proximal future.

To this point, Corsaro's *Sociology of Childhood* is thus situated only at the micro level: the social world is produced and reproduced by inter-human interaction (Alanen, 2000). However, Corsaro introduces a second element in his conceptualization – this time at the macro level – which confirms that through 'interpretive reproduction', children not only contribute to their proximal culture, but also to the cultural reproduction and change of the society in which they live. To this end, his theory requires a conceptual link between the level at which the cultural activities of children take place and the level of the social structures in which social reproduction and change can occur. Corsaro finds this link in the structural perspective that was mainly developed by Qvortrup (Qvortrup, 1990). The notion of childhood as a period within the lifetime of an individual is coupled to a second notion of childhood as being a permanent structural category in society (and in this way is comparable with concepts such as social class). In summary, 'interpretive reproduction' covers three types of common activities: (1) the creativity with which children assimilate information and knowledge from the adult world, (2) the participation of children in a series of *peer cultures* and (3) children's contribution to the reproduction and expansion of adult culture.

Despite his attention to the structural perspective, it is clear that Corsaro bases and sees the foundation of his *Sociology of Childhood* in ethnographic research of and with children. The *peer cultures* collectively produced by children form the starting point of his alternative to a unilateral, development-oriented approach, and it is from this that he attempts to further conceptualize his sociological theory. A *Sociology of Childhood* as presented here is characterized by a strong orientation to the subject and environment. Honig *et al.* (1996, 21) in this context talk about 'akteursbezogene Kinderforschung' (actor-related child research), in which the greatest attention is paid to the experiences of children in their daily life. The counterpart to the 'akteursbezogene Kinderforschung' is the 'strukturbezogene Kindheitsforschung' (structure-related child research), in which the work of James, Jenks and Prout can be considered as groundbreaking.

3.2. Breakthrough of 'the sociological child'

> Die Kindheitsforschung faßt 'Kind' als ein Konstrukt auf, das sozial und kulturell variabel ist. 'Kindheit' ist insofern nicht nur die Bezeichnung für eine Lebensphase individueller Sozialisationsprozesse, sie geht diesen Prozessen als ein historisch-spezifisches soziokulturelles Muster auch immer schon voraus.
>
> [Childhood studies look at the child as a construct that varies in different social and cultural spaces. Childhood refers therefore not only to an individual phase in life, but also to a specific historical and socio-cultural idea.]
>
> *(Honig et al., 1996, 21)*

In other words, childhood appears here as a discursive (culturally constructed) phenomenon and therefore always depends on the context. In their book, *Theorizing Childhood* (1998), James, Jenks and Prout formulate the ambition of mapping out the various (pre)sociological models of childhood and weighing them against one another. To this end they work chronologically and within this chronology identify a clear transition to thinking about children in terms of *agency*. Their most important distinction in this is the one between the traditional image of the socially developing child – James, Jenks and Prout (1998, 23) talk in this regard about a 'transitional theorizing about the child' in which the central concept is the socialization process – and a fourfold classification of *new* approaches to childhood in which *being* rather than *becoming* is the leitmotif. The child is thereby conceived as a person, as a status, as a set of needs, rights and differences.

A first image of the child within the new childhood studies is the 'social structural child'. Children constitute a structural category; they form part of social life and consequently must be understood as forming part of any social system. In this approach, the child is summarized as an analysis-unit *sui generis* that is comparable with any other analysis-unit in society. 'Discourses centred around the social structural child claim childhood as a generalizable category, an enduring (though changing) feature of the social structure of any society and one which is universal, global and in possession of a recognizable identity' (James *et al.*, 1998, 210).

The second image of the child is the 'minority group child', described as the political version of the 'social structural child'. This approach emphasizes the fact that children in society are often discriminated against structurally by all sorts of institutionalized forms of power. Just as with the first image of the child, this form of childhood is perceived as a universal experience. All children, albeit to different degrees, are short-changed regarding their human rights. This approach often establishes the link with the women's movement, the difference being that it is no longer *gender* but *age* that forms the object of the struggle.

The discourse on childhood of the third approach describes the child as the 'socially constructed child'. With this, a radically relativist position is assumed by not accepting the existence of the child in itself, but by always seeing it as the result of constitutive practices. 'Childhood is always structured, in either a strong or weak fashion but it is none the less temporal and susceptible to change' (James et al., 1998, 214). The 'socially constructed child' is rather a place than a global phenomenon, and we hereby obtain a very particular conceptualization of childhood.

The final discourse about childhood – heavily inspired by anthropology – ultimately refers to the child as a 'tribal child', in its turn, the political version of the 'socially constructed child'. Here childhood is mainly defined in terms of being separate from other cultures within a society. This separation is not the result of a natural process, but should be seen as the result of the autonomy of children, which points to a clear victory of *agency* over *structure*. 'Tribal children's culture is to be regarded as the self-maintaining system of signs, symbols and rituals that prescribes the whole way of life of children within a particular socio-historical setting' (James et al., 1998, 215). Such a conceptualization of childhood includes a great deal of critical potential. It indeed offers numerous possibilities for resistance against, for example, the normalizing effects of age hierarchies, socialization theories and education practices.

According to James et al. (1998), these four sociological images of the child should be situated within a framework of a series of conceptual dualisms, of which the *agency–structure* dichotomy is the most prominent and determinative. A second important dualism is formed by a more particular versus a more universalistic interpretation of childhood. The result of this is that the 'socially constructed child' belongs in the *structure/particularism* cell, the 'minority group child' in the *agency/universalism* cell, the 'tribal child' in the *agency/particularism* cell and the 'social structural child' in the *structure/universalism* cell.

The great merit of the approach of James et al. (1998) is clearly ordering the various *new* sociological discourses about childhood, and presenting them in such a way that the differences in nuance between these discourses are brought more sharply into focus. At the same time, however, there is something problematic about this endeavour. For instance, it is unclear why the political version of a certain image of the child immediately belongs in a different cell. James et al. (1998, 207) indeed acknowledge the problematic character of their classification when they claim, 'we shall emphasize the overlaps and areas of agreement between the four discourses rather than attempt to demarcate their differences and begin an arid process of rigid and permanent separation'.

The most significant criticism of the models distinguished by James et al. (1998), however, is found in the assumption that the unit most referred to in the sociological study of childhood should be children either as individuals in all their particularity – such as, for instance, the 'socially constructed child' – or as a group or cohorts – such as, for instance, the 'minority group child' (Alanen, 2000). Opposed to this thinking in terms of categorizing children, various authors take a relational approach to childhood. In this relational approach to sociological forms, relationships between people rather than people as individuals are the unit of analysis. 'Relational thinking is both structural and processual, and agential without confining agency exclusively to the level of individual actors' (Alanen, 2000, 500). In this way a different interpretation of *agency* appears as the central concept within the theory of the *Sociology of Childhood*. We currently rediscover this interpretation with representatives of the German as well as the Anglo-Saxon tradition of the *Sociology of Childhood*. We will elaborate this in the next paragraph.

3.3. On 'generationing processes' and 'generationelle Ordnung' (generational order)

By 'generationing', Mayall (2002, 27) means, 'the relational processes whereby people come to be known as children, and whereby children and childhood acquire certain characteristics, linked to local contexts, and changing as the factors brought to bear change'. In their relationship with adults, children are confronted with knowledge and experiences that have their origin in an earlier time. Adults, in turn, perceive that children understand the social world in a different way than themselves because the learning of these children is bound to their membership in a different generation. Alanen (2000, 14) formulates it as follows: '"generationing" refers to processes through which some individuals become ("are constructed as") "children" while others become ("are constructed as") "adults", having consequences for the activities and identities of inhabitants of each category as well as for their interrelationships'. In this way, generation becomes a key concept for the study of childhood. Mayall and Alanen are in this regard heavily inspired by the generation concept as developed by Mannheim (Mayall, 2002; Alanen, 2009). According to Mannheim, people can undergo the same socio-historical processes at the same place and time, but differ significantly in their capabilities and limitations in dealing with these processes. Whereas Mannheim mainly applies this idea to various social classes in a society, Mayall sees possibilities for applying this to children. 'If we accept that children are a distinct social group exploited by adults at school, then it is a short step to thinking of children as being specifically *located*, and having specific experiences of social developments' (Mayall, 2002, 160–161). According to Mayall, this conceptualization of 'generationing' displays significant parallels with 'gendering' as the process by which *being a woman* is defined from *not being a man*.

Alanen (2000) couples to this attention to 'generationing processes' an appeal for a strongly imposed constructionist research methodology. According to her, most Childhood Studies – despite their assumption that childhood is a social and historical construction – demonstrate an unacceptable constructionist deficit by the fact that 'the condition of being a child is simply assumed as a starting point without giving attention to the complexity of material, social and discursive processes and their interplay through which childhood is daily reproduced as a specifically generational condition' (Alanen, 1999, 14). In this perspective, *agency* cannot remain limited to constructionism at a micro level that only emphasizes the child as a social actor. It rather refers to the power and capabilities of those who are placed in a position of a child in order to help influence, control and organize the activities that take place in their everyday lives. To this end, *agency* should be directly studied in relation to the generational structures in which children move, 'the source of their agency as "children" is to be found in the social organization of generational relations' (Alanen, 2000, 15).

The author who to this point has succeeded in demonstrating the greatest ability for synthesis within the shaping of *agency* is undoubtedly Michael-Sebastian Honig. Honig (1999) demonstrates that there is indeed room for developmental thinking within the conceptual framework of the *Sociology of Childhood*. This developmental thinking cannot just be oriented toward an image of the future, and as a result cannot only refer to developmental and socialization processes. 'Entwicklung ist definitiv kein teleologisches Konzept mehr. Dem Individuum kommt als 'Konstrukteur' seiner Biographie eine zentrale Stellung zu' [Development can no longer be seen as a teleological concept as the individual appears as the one who constructs his own biography] (Honig, 1999, 73). As opposed to growth and development, the course of life comes to be a key concept, such that childhood can be considered as one stage in the life of humankind, a stage that can only be seen in relationship to other stages of life.

Childhood as a relational construct is also partly interpreted from the perspective of development and partly from a generational perspective. From a developmental perspective, it refers to the difference between child and adult and their mutual relationship within a historical-biographical context. From a generational perspective it refers to family links within a broader social context. Within the context of late modernity, childhood is characterized by an interrelation of both aspects. In this way, childhood is not an arbitrary discursive product, but refers to a discursive practice or a set of practices. Analysis of these generational practices should make it possible to obtain a view of what childhood means today. The study of childhood thus demands multiple perspectives, whereby the objective of childhood research is situated in the mapping out of the cultural grammar that structures the relationships between children and adults in a society.

4. The ambitions of an approach to children's rights from a perspective of childhood studies

There is clearly a strong bond between children's rights as a concept and the most important themes in childhood studies. When we follow Wintersberger (2012) in his suggestion that in fact two perspectives play a role in childhood studies, then we see how both perspectives – childhood as a social category and the child as actor – have clearly played a role in the last decade concerning the further translation and implementation of the CRC.

Childhood as a separate structural segment in our society has become readily apparent. For instance, we note that more and more research takes the child as the unit of analysis instead of the family. The result is that the impact on and the perspective of the children involved in discussions concerning housing, poverty or divorce can be delineated much more clearly. In many European countries e.g. there is an increasing attention on child poverty, defined as a violation of children's rights. Additionally, we also see it in the increasing application of the label 'child-friendly'. Cultural centres, hospitals, legal institutions… attempt to organize themselves in such a way that they can realize greater openness and accessibility with regard to children. In this, the provision rights of children are given form from a children's perspective. Also inside the Council of Europe, people have picked up the thread by, among other things, formulating new guidelines for more child-friendly health care and more child-friendly justice (see also Liefaard, Chapter 14 in this Handbook). Finally, the attention on children as a social group also has a retroactive nature. Thus, we are currently seeing within the history of childhood a great deal of research into the position and the experience of children within the various types of institutions that have been established specifically for them since the middle of the nineteenth century (see e.g. Bakker, 2007; Prochner et al., 2009; Frijhoff, 2012). Frijhoff (2012, 16–17) refers in this respect to an interesting field of tension:

> In the eyes of a historian of childhood, the Convention on the Rights of the Child, adopted on 20 November 1989 by the United Nations, is, therefore, fraught with some ambiguity. Recognising the full rights of childhood, it also keeps children confined into their childhood and the interpretation given to this stage of life in the different parts of the world, streamlining their personality ever more into a standard child, distrustful with regard to autonomous growth, and rejecting the right to adventure. Scholars may freely experience a Eureka feeling, but children must fight harder and more often for their own right to discovery.

We also rediscover the field of tension described by Frijhoff in the whole discussion about children as social actors. Being described by international treaties and standards as a 'subject with rights' does not mean that people are also immediately recognized as such. Furthermore, participating in society entails much more than simply possessing rights of participation. It is impossible to explain the different positions with regard to children as social actors in the scope of this contribution. Hanson (2012) presents an up-to-date and interesting overview. In so doing he distinguishes four different currents. The first current is characterized by the traditional view of children: they are 'becomings', not 'beings'. The second approach, 'the welfare approach', allows the balance to shift more in the direction of the right to protection rather than the right to participation (Hanson, 2012, 76). Within the third, more emancipatory approach, children are considered competent as long as the contrary is not demonstrated. And in the libertarian current, people ultimately talk about children as independent citizens who can make autonomous decisions. The problem with all these approaches is that they remain caught up in the question of what the child is rather than asking the question about the potential of the child of the child (Honig, 2009). In other words, it truly seems that, in our search for the meaning of children's rights, we remain bound by our view on children as non-adults. In their analysis of the scientific literature about children's rights, Reynaert et al. (2009) demonstrate that three themes have dominated since the 1989 International Convention on the Rights of the Child. First of all, there is attention to autonomy and participation rights as the new norm in practice and policy. Second, research also deals with the field of tension between children's rights and the rights of parents. And finally there is the rise of the 'global children's rights industry'. The first two themes are very clearly related. The stress on participation and autonomy too often gets bogged down in a discussion in which children and adults come to be diametrically opposed to one another. The cause of this is found in the concept of agency itself, which has very clear roots in a conceptual framework in which the image of the autonomously thinking adult takes centre stage. The dominant thinking of agency and participation thus actually tries to fit children within an adult model rather than questioning the model itself (Wall, 2012).

It is important to notice that in the debate on the rights of the child up until now the emphasis is on the rights that children have. Masschelein and Quaghebeur (2005), for example, show in their analysis of the discourse on the right of the child to participate, how the child will be more and more defined as a participatory subject. The child has been described in terms of 'being able to express herself', as 'making active choices', as 'self-responsible' or as 'negotiating meanings'. Defining the child in terms of a participatory subject constitutes an individualizing principle, challenging the child to transform herself into a certain kind of individual with her own self-determined identity. Several authors point out risks of a rights tradition emphasizing individuality and autonomy. Such and Walker (2005) show how the responsibility for realizing rights from the state to the individual may result in a policy by which children can enjoy their rights as long as they behave as responsible citizens. According to Mortier (2002), the emphasis on people as autonomous individuals ignores the fact that they often do not act autonomously. Roose and De Bie (2007) illustrate how the concept of the autonomous individual sharpens the contrast between the 'citizen' and the 'non-citizen'. The standard of the autonomous individual creates a structural residue of 'not yet' citizens (children, for example), 'no longer' citizens (elderly people, for example) or 'not entirely' citizens (such as people with a disability). This group of people who cannot sufficiently participate is growing all the time, as society is becoming more and more complex and the calls for participation are becoming ever stronger. As a result, the problem of children at risk increased both *qualitatively*, with new child risks and new parental risks, and *quantitatively*, with even more parts of the population at risk. Jeroen Dekker (2009) concludes that, paradoxically, the CRC can be considered as an important multiplier of the phenomenon of the child at risk. According to Dekker (2009), the Century of the Child turned into the Century of the Child at Risk.

This conclusion requires us to move beyond modernity's morally autonomous individual. As long as rights are grounded in free, equal, or autonomous individuality, children will be pushed to the outer edges of the social circle. As John Wall (2010) indicates, human rights need to be imagined as more than mere expressions of individual liberties or entitlements. Human rights ultimately derive their meaning and purpose from their capacity to expand the diversity and inclusiveness of human relations. A good example of this can be found in the discussion about giving the right to vote to children and young people. Recently some countries such as Brazil and Nicaragua decided to give minors from sixteen years old the right to vote (see also Mitchell, Chapter 10 in this Handbook). This decision connects with a broader social movement to look at children and youngsters as active citizens. Children do not become citizens; they are citizens from the early beginning. In its turn this connects with the attention on the participation rights as one of the central pillars of the CRC, although the right to vote is not mentioned within the CRC. Discussing the lowering of the age to vote is interesting, but up until now this discussion gets stuck in a rather conservative thinking on democracy. We are giving the right to vote to those about whom we are convinced they can act and think as we adults do. Thus, what we are doing is trying to fit children in an adult-based political construction. Minors get the right to vote once the difference with adults is reduced to a minimum. However, what we need today is a kind of democracy in which the difference between children and adults is fully awarded. In this democracy one could think e.g. about giving the right to vote to all children and young people.

In this interpretation, children's rights and human rights are rights that are to be shaped in a participative way, a process during which parents and children themselves participate in the definition and the content of these rights (Roose and De Bie, 2007). Rights then function as a starting point for dialogue. Children must be accepted as co-actors in dialogue about their best interests. This implies that in every context, children and educators, such as parents, must look at how children's rights are given full play. The rights of children must be placed in their broader social context. It is not so much that people are or are not citizens, but rather that citizenship is actualized in diverse activities and relationships.

> Children are thus not expected to become citizens by seeking to attain a given norm, supported by the rights they can rely on, but to achieve citizenship through their various relationships and actions, a citizenship that can assume different shapes. This orientation also influences the position of the pedagogue, who is not expected to guide the child towards fully-fledged citizenship, but to act rather as an adult who enters into a dialogue with the child.
>
> *(Roose and De Bie, 2007, 439)*

The ultimate aim of every educational intervention then lies in the accomplishment of and the support for opportunities for responsible action. In this approach, responsibility relies on the awareness that one has to learn to deal with situations in society where choices have to be made and where those choices raise the issue of how individual and social responsibility relate to each other. The opposite of the image of democracy as a project to be realized is the image of democracy as a fact. It concerns a type of coexistence where all citizens have the opportunity to develop an opinion and where there is no decisive criterion regarding political issues. In such a case, democracy and citizenship, just like community building, are a consequence of the experience people gain. Then, upbringing and education should not be regarded as a reconstructing activity, but rather as a constructing and creative activity.

5. Conclusion

At the heart of childhood studies research today is the question: 'What allows us to be able to talk about children and childhood?' The traditional answer to this question is that children are people in the process of becoming and in so doing make the transition from 'nature' to 'reason'. Childhood considered from this perspective still retains the promise of a better future. It is clear that the circumstances in which the various forms of childhood currently take shape have changed. When we only describe childhood in terms of learning and development, we sell the child short. Today, a sort of a-pedagogical approach to the organization between generations is taking place, which reduces the value of the traditional adult–child relations.

Anyone who considers children's rights to be important is hereby faced with a huge challenge. The fact that the promise inherent to children's rights must still largely be realized has much to do with the mainly adult interpretation of children's rights. Children form a third of the world population, but to this point we have not succeeded in including their perspectives and experiences in our thinking about human rights. Consequently, what we need is a transition from a view of children as those who have the same rights as adults, to a view of children that contributes to shaping our understanding of human rights. Societies indeed do not only take shape based upon concepts such as equality, freedom and rationality; today they are perhaps much more influenced by the notions of diversity and difference. Only when we can consider and give specific form to children's rights in this way will children obtain a fully-fledged place as a social citizen in our societies.

This happy marriage between childhood studies and children's rights can result in a stronger understanding of the richness of children's rights. In this, especially the history of childhood probably plays a crucial role. We may not forget that children's rights already was a central idea within social anarchist theories of the mid-nineteenth century. These theories were far more radical than e.g. recent pupil voice work as it visualizes an education without schools as most people would recognize it. It would be interesting e.g. to contrast the CRC with some of the anarchists view of young people having a voice which is not dependent on adult consultation. What will appear is young people's capacity to critique, re-imagine and reconstruct the communities they belong to. However, contemporary neo-liberalism seems to have marginalized alternative traditions of thought and action. The marriage between childhood studies and children's rights therefore also offers us the privilege of an alternative. It is an alternative we would do well to value and emulate wherever and whenever we can. The age demands it.

Questions for debate and discussion

- How can we construct and understand a history of children's rights that is much more than only a series of activities and ideas that ended up with the CRC?
- How can we rethink and reconstruct children's rights within today's neo-liberal discourse (in which citizens more and more are considered as clients and in which rights often appear as something you consume)?
- How do we map the dynamic interplay between children, parents and the state from a 'rights as responsibilities' approach?
- What active roles can children play in shaping our (re)thinking about human rights?

References

Alanen, L. (2000). Visions of a social theory of childhood. *Childhood,* 7(4), 493–505.
Alanen, L. (2009). Generational order. In J. Qvortrup, W.A. Corsaro, and M.-S. Honig (eds), *The Palgrave Handbook of Childhood Studies.* Basingstoke, UK: Palgrave Macmillan, pp. 159–174.
Alanen, L. (2010). Taking children's rights seriously, *Childhood,* 17(1), 5–8.
Bakker, N. (2007). Sunshine as medicine: Health colonies and the medicalization of childhood in the Netherlands (1900–1960). *History of Education,* 36(6), 659–679.
Burman, E. (2008). *Deconstructing Developmental Psychology* (2nd rev. ed.). London: Routledge.
Cannella, G. (1999). The scientific discourse of education: Predetermining the lives of others – Foucault, education, and children. *Contemporary Issues in Early Childhood,* 1(1), 36–44.
Corsaro, W.A. (1997). *The Sociology of Childhood.* Thousand Oaks, CA: Pine Forge Press.
Dassen, P. (1999). *De onttovering van de wereld. Max Weber en het probleem van de moderniteit in Duitsland 1890–1920* [The disenchantment of the world: Max Weber and the problem of modernity in Germany 1890–1920]. Amsterdam: Uitgeverij G.A. van Oorschot.
Dekker, J. (2009). Children at risk in history: A story of expansion, *Paedagogica Historica,* 45(1–2), 17–36.
Dekker, J. (2010). *Educational Ambitions in History. Childhood and Education in an Expanding Educational Space from the Seventeenth to the Twentieth Century,* Frankfurt am Main: Peter Lang.
Depaepe, M. (1993). *Zum Wohl des Kindes? Pädologie, pädagogische Psychologie und experimentelle Pädagogik in Europa und den USA, 1890–1940* [Serving children's well-being? Paedalogy, psycho-pedagogy and experimental pedagogy in Europe and the USA 1890–1940], Leuven: Leuven University Press.
Freeman, M. (1998). The sociology of childhood and children's rights. *International Journal of Children's Rights,* 6(4), 433–444.
Frijhoff, W. (2012). Historian's discovery of childhood. *Paedagogica Historica,* 48(1), 11–29.
Hanson, K. (2012). Schools of thought in children's rights. In M. Liebel *et al.* (eds), *Children's Rights from Below: Cross-Cultural Perspectives.* Basingstoke, UK: Palgrave MacMillan, pp. 63–79.
Hemrica, J.C. (2004). *Kind-zijn tussen opvoeding en recht. Een grondslagenonderzoek naar kindbeeldenin discussies op het grensvlak van opvoeding en recht* [Childhood between education and justice: Analyzing childhood images in discussions on the border between education and justice], Leuven: Garant.
Honig, M.-S. (1999). *Entwurf einer Theorie der Kindheit* [A plan for a theory about childhood]. Frankfurt am Main: Suhrkamp.
Honig, M-S. (2009). How is the child constituted in childhood studies? In J. Qvortrup, W.A Corsaro, and M.-S. Honig (eds), *The Palgrave Handbook of Childhood Studies.* New York: Palgrave Macmillan, pp. 62–77.
Honig, M.-S., Leu H.R. and Nissen, U. (1996). Kindheit als Sozialisationsphase und als kulturelles Muster [Childhood as a period of socialization and as a cultural model]. In M-S. Honig, H.R. Leu and U. Nissen (eds), *Kinder und Kindheit. Soziokulturelle Muster – sozialisationstheoretische Perspektiven* [Children and Childhood: Sociocultural models – Socializationtheoretical perspectives] (pp. 9–29). Weinheim: Juventa Verlag.
James, A. and Prout, A. (eds) (1997). *Constructing and Reconstructing Childhood: Contemporary Issues in the Sociological Study of Childhood* (2nd ed.). London: Falmer Press.
James, A., Jenks, C. and Prout, A. (1998). *Theorising Childhood.* Cambridge: Cambridge University Press.
James, A.L. (2010). Competition or integration? The next step in childhood studies? *Childhood,* 17(4), 485–499.
Jenks, C. (2005). *Childhood* (2nd ed.). London and New York: Routledge.
Kaufman, N.H. and Rizzini, I. (2009). Closing the gap between rights and the realities of children's lives. In J. Qvortrup, W.A. Corsaro, and M.-S. Honig (Eds), *The Palgrave Handbook of Childhood Studies.* New York: Palgrave Macmillan, pp. 422–434.
Kehily, M.J. (2009). Understanding childhood: An introduction to some key themes and issues. In M.J. Kehily (ed.), *An Introduction to Childhood Studies* (2nd ed.). Maidenhead, UK: Open University Press, pp. 1–21.
Korczak, J. (2007). *Het recht van het kind op respect* [The child and its right to respect], Amsterdam: Uitgeverij SWP.
Lenzer, G. (1991). Is there sufficient interest to establish a sociology of children? *Footnotes,* 19(6), p. 8.
Ligthart, J. (1917). *Verzamelde Opstellen* [Collected Essays]. Groningen: Wolters.
Masschelein, J. and Quaghebeur, K. (2005). Participation for better or for worse? *Journal of Philosophy of Education,* 39 (1), 51–65.

Mayall, B. (2000). The sociology of childhood in relation to children's rights. *International Journal of Children's Rights*, 8(3), 243–259.
Mayall, B. (2002). *Towards a Sociology for Childhood: Thinking from Children's Lives*. Maidenhead, UK: Open University Press.
Meirieu, P. (2002). *Le pédagogue et les droits de l'enfant* [The pedagogue and the rights of the child], Paris: Tricorne.
Mortier, F. (2002). We zijn allemaal kinderen: bruggen tussen rechten voor kinderen en rechten voor volwassenen [We are all children: Bridges between the rights of children and the rights of adults]. *Tijdschrift voor Jeugdrecht en Kinderrechten*, 3(extra editie), 10–17.
Nieuwenhuys, O. (2010). Keep asking: Why childhood? Why children? Why global? *Childhood*, 17(3), 291–296.
Popkewitz, T.S. (1999). A social epistemology of educational research. In T.S. Popkewitz and L. Fendler (eds), *Critical Theories in Education: Changing Terrains of Knowledge and Politics*. New York: Routledge, pp. 17–42.
Prochner, L., May, H. and B. Kaur (2009). 'The blessings of civilisation': Nineteenth-century missionary infant schools for young native children in three colonial settings – India, Canada and New Zealand 1820s–1840s. *Paedagogica Historica*, 45(1–2), 83–102.
Qvortrup, J. (1990). Childhood as a social phenomenon: An introduction to a series of national reports. *Eurosocial Report*, 36. Vienna: European Centre for Social Welfare Policy and Research.
Qvortrup, J., Corsaro, W.A. and Honig, M.-S. (eds) (2009). *The Palgrave Handbook of Childhood Studies*. New York: Palgrave Macmillan.
Reynaert, D., De Bie, M. and Vandevelde, S. (2009). A review of children's rights literature since the adoption of the United Nations Convention on the Rights of the Child. *Childhood*, 16(4), 518–534.
Roose, R. and De Bie, M. (2007). Do children have rights or do their rights have to be realised? *Journal of Philosophy of Education*, 41(3), 431–443.
Samson Committee Report (2012). *Omringd door zorg, toch niet veilig. Seksueel misbruik van door de overheid uit huis geplaatste kinderen, 1945 tot heden* [Surrounded by care, although not safe: Sexual abuse of children in residential care, 1945–present]. Amsterdam: Boom.
Sirota, R. (1998). L'emergence d'une sociologie de l'enfance: evolution de l'objet, evolution du regard [The rise of a Sociology of Childhood: The evolution of the object, the evolution of our views on children]. *Education et Societes. Revue Internationale de Sociologie de l'Education*, 1(2), 9–33.
Smith, K. (2011). Producing governable subjects: Images of childhood old and new. *Childhood*, 19(1), 24–37.
Such, E. and Walker, R. (2005). Young citizens or policy objects? Children in the 'rights and responsibilities' debate. *Journal of Social Policy*, 34, 39–57.
Turmel, A. (2008). *A Historical Sociology of Childhood: Developmental Thinking, Categorization and Graphic Visualization*. Cambridge: Cambridge University Press.
Walkerdine, V. (2009). Developmental psychology and the study of childhood. In M.J. Kehily (ed.), *An Introduction to Childhood Studies* (2nd ed.). Maidenhead, UK: Open University Press, pp. 112–123.
Wall, J. (2010). *Ethics in Light of Childhood*. Washington, DC: Georgetown University Press.
Wall, J. (2012). Can democracy represent children? Toward a politics of difference. *Childhood*, 19(1), 86–100.
Wintersberger, H. (2012). [Book review: Jens Qvortrup, William A. Corsaro and Michael-Sebastian Honig (eds) (2009) *The Palgrave Handbook of Childhood Studies*.] *Childhood*, 19(2), 283–287.
Woodhead, M. (2009). Child development and the development of childhood. In J. Qvortrup, W.A. Corsaro, and M.-S. Honig (eds), *The Palgrave Handbook of Childhood Studies*. New York: Palgrave Macmillan, pp. 46–61.

5
The sociology of childhood and children's rights

Berry Mayall

1. Introduction

In 1967 secondary school students (aged 11 to 18) in England were asked (via an invitation set out in a national newspaper) what kind of school they would like. The resulting book (Blishen 1969), is studded with students' contributions, and records an indictment of school as they experienced it. Students argued that school entailed being treated as passive recipients by teachers who assumed they knew best and also imposed pointless, trivial rules; but school should offer opportunities for children to take part in decisions about what to learn, to discover, to delight in, in the context of more democratic relations with teachers. Blishen comments that the children felt imprisoned; for adults imprisoned children's courage and curiosity. In 2001 a similar project was carried out, this time including school-age children aged from 5 to18 (Burke and Grosvenor 2003). Children were invited, as individuals or as groups, to present their ideas in any form (written, pictorial, via videos) and thousands responded, from across the country and from a variety of schools. It is worth quoting a summary of the main findings from the 2001 project, which echoes Blishen's findings.

> 'Respect' was the word that occurred most; it was what the children wanted, but felt they didn't get. They were forced to do work they weren't interested in, in buildings that were falling down around their ears. They were expected to fit into a structure and a curriculum that seemed to have been created without the first reference to what they might enjoy or respond to. Most of all, they were sick of not being listened to. Sick of being treated like kids.
>
> *(Burke and Grosvenor, 2003, Foreword, pp. ix–x)*

This summary leads towards a number of considerations and questions. First, we may ask why it is that English children's experiential knowledge teaches them that at school they are not treated as human beings, as people, in accordance with their human rights. For indeed the United Nations Convention on the Rights of the Child (CRC) has to be understood as a human rights convention, with specific points, which were hammered out through negotiation, in relation to children's structural positioning in a range of societies. We may also note on this, that though the UK ratified the CRC in 1991, these two studies indicate that ten years later the government had not altered the education system, in accordance with its provisions. Why is that? Second, therefore, we may wish to consider the argument that long-established traditions, policies and practices, operate not only at macro-level, but also as factors affecting the day-to-day negotiations that children engage in at school. On the essential matter of respect for their membership of human society, it would seem that the English children at school in the 2000s were having much the same experiences as those in school thirty or more years earlier.

This chapter aims to draw attention to the usefulness of keeping our attention focused on the large-scale and its intersections with the small-scale, on the inter-relations of the macro with the micro, on inter-relations between structure and agency. In respect of children and their experiences, it insists on the importance of what the sociologists' sociologist, C. Wright Mills (1967) pointed to – the critical and central importance of seeing connections between private troubles and public issues. Thus it is useful to consider children's experiences and activities in the light of large-scale social structures. Sociology comprises a key assemblage of concepts, valuable in understanding why, for instance, English children at school are not respected, not accorded dignity as human beings. Furthermore, I argue that sociology is useful (and even essential?) for understanding why we need a separate rights convention for children; and further, why it is so difficult for adults to operationalise the articles of the Convention and for children to challenge their ascribed subordinate status. Or to put it another way, sociology points the finger at the problem social group – adults – and shows why many of them are reluctant to respect the Convention.

In making the above assertions, I am aligning myself with those who adopt a critical approach to sociological work (see e.g. Layder 1994). That is, the sociological aim is to provide – or in the case of this chapter to draw on – analyses of how a social organisation or a society is organised and to make suggestions arising about the implications of the character of that organisation for the experience of individuals or social groups. This is the approach made by, for instance, Margaret Stacey (1988) in her feminist study of the health care system; she documents how traditional 'malestream' studies focused on the paid health care workers (doctors and nurses) and neglected the unpaid, the people who look after their own health and the women who care for men and children, at home. By including women's unpaid health work, she not only widens the territory for investigation but she shows how women's work has been devalued. Similarly, Bourdieu, having carried out a detailed study of the French education system, saw it as appropriate to offer a critique of the class-based character of the system and suggestions for improvement (e.g. Bourdieu and Passeron 1977; Bourdieu 1986).

In order to explore the above points, this chapter starts by outlining some key ideas that have been developed in the last thirty or more years, in what has been called the 'sociology of childhood'. Then I go on to consider the relevance of these ideas for understanding why we need the CRC. I then discuss some studies carried out in a range of countries, which help us to understand the Convention as an aspirational rather than prescriptive document; and which point to how established traditions and understandings underpin and shape local interpretations of children's rights.

2. Sociological approaches to childhood

2.1. Structural approaches

As the example given at the outset suggests, children's experiences and their acquired experiential knowledge are fundamentally influenced by large-scale policies, by long-established traditions sedimented into practice, by assumptions driving policy, which are based on sometimes outdated understandings. English children today experience childhoods under the weight of ideas about children and childhood, dating back at least one hundred years.

Though the history of the study of childhood is outside the scope of this paper, some initial points have to be made, as introduction (these draw on my history of the sociology of childhood [Mayall, 2013]). And in this section, I am giving further discussion of points made about definitions of childhood in the Introduction to this Handbook. Thus, it is fair to say that since the mid-to-late nineteenth century, theoretical approaches to childhood in minority world countries have been dominated by developmental psychology (for a brief history and balanced view, see Woodhead 2009). It can be said that it is the *idea* of development towards adulthood, rather than the detail of varying theories, that has permeated the consciousness of people in minority world societies. Probably most people there take a commonsense view that what children mainly do during childhood is develop towards adulthood. Furthermore, the basic idea of developmentalism permeates policy-making and practice. Thus when children become the objects of attention by the law, the police, the education system, it is to experts in the shape of psychologists that these professions turn. At home, parents are offered advice grounded in developmentalism on how to 'rear' or 'socialise' their children. Perhaps one of the most influential ideas stemming from developmental psychology is that children are above all to be protected and provided for in order that they may develop well, in a conceptual space regarded as a-political. Childhood should take place in a private arena, in a garden, until children are ready to enter the public domain and engage with adult life. Ideas associated with children's unreadiness are inadequacies such as incompetence, instability, credulity, unreliability; and these lend credibility to adults' understanding that children are not (yet) fully human.

However, the last thirty or so years have seen challenges to the attractive vision of the garden of childhood. It is not by accident that the work towards the CRC took place in the same years that ideas and assumptions about children and childhood were being challenged. Sociological and psychological studies about how childhoods differed across time and place provided one strand in this thinking (Kessen 1965, 1975; Bronfenbrenner 1971; Bettelheim 1971); another strand was theories that noted how people's experiences and their self-image could be powerfully affected by the identifications imposed on them, for instance in schools, asylums and prisons (Goffman, e.g. 1961) and by the diffusion of power through the policies and practices of institutions (e.g. Foucault 1977). As regards children in particular, Holt (e.g. 1975), among others, argued that the character of schooling and of societal norms more generally oppressed children.

It has been said that a basic sociological step forward is to move children and childhood out of 'a conceptual space that has been declared a-political' (Elshtain 1981: Chapter 6; see also Elshtain 1996). This entails recognising that political decisions (on, for instance, health, welfare and education) do indeed affect children's experiences; that is, that these experiences are structured by large-scale policies and by social traditions and assumptions. It also entails recognising that children are members of society, are active agents in society and, importantly, that they contribute to it, although children's agency is itself socially structured (James 2009). This is where the important, central arguments of Jens Qvortrup and his colleagues come in. Qvortrup argues that children should be conceptualised as a social group, in the sense that they share commonalities, especially in relation to the economic system; these can be identified at local, inter-personal levels and in the specific ways in which macro-structures, policies and practices influence their lives (e.g. Qvortrup *et al.*, 1994, 2009). For detailed examination of these influences, see Wintersberger (1994) and Sgritta (1994), who investigate the division of national resources as between various groups in society; and argue that children are discriminated against economically by national policies and practices. These points about children as a social group are also discussed by Reynaert, Bouverne-de Bie and Vandevelde (2012) in section 4 of their paper, where they argue that children's rights have been largely interpreted as individual rights, whereas it may also be useful to think about them as 'collective rights', and thus to take account of power relations that children experience and work with, and to analyse these power relations in order to work towards more respectful relations between adults and children.

Qvortrup argued in his first paper on childhood as a structural form (1985) that historical analysis showed the direct economic contributions children made – to their households and to the societal economy – during most of recorded history. Nowadays, he argues, children's contributions in minority world societies are through the work children do in school, acquiring the knowledge and skills appropriate for that society. To put it more grandly, his analysis identifies children's contributions to the division of labour. This contribution to thinking about children as workers in minority world countries has been taken up in later studies, where the idea that minority world children have stopped directly contributing to economic welfare has been challenged; for studies have documented children's paid work and their unpaid work for households, including caring for family members (e.g. Morrow 1994; Mizen et al., 2001; Zelizer 2002, 2005). It is interesting that when English children themselves are asked whether what they do in school constitutes work, they give mixed responses; compared to what adults do, they say no; but as preparation for adulthood, some say yes (Mayall 2002: Chapter 5). It seems that some present-day children have absorbed the argument that they are not economic contributors to society.

Some of the arguments about children as contributors to the division of labour derive from feminist analyses. Male sociologists had conceptualised society into public and private domains, into the economic and the cultural. Women identified the need to tackle male assumptions that what they did at home was a natural part of emotional relationships; that men out there in the public sphere worked and that women at home in the private sphere did not. Instead, from the early 1970s onwards, women in the United States of America and across Europe argued that what they did at home should be conceptualised as work: washing, cleaning, cooking, caring for and caring about family members; indeed producing and caring for the next generation can be thought of as work without which society could not continue (e.g. Mitchell 1971; Oakley 1972). Similarly it can be argued – and has been documented – that children too carry out household tasks and that they too engage in caring work, forming and maintaining relations within the family (e.g. Alanen 1992; Mayall 2002: Chapter 5). These arguments about children's contributions to the division of labour have, of course, particular resonance once we look at the wider world beyond minority world societies; and as will be discussed later on, the division of children's labour between immediately productive work and school work, and local understandings of this division, perhaps have important lessons for minority world societies.

Consideration of children as members of society, contributing to its welfare, yet also having claims to be protected and provided for by adults, raises questions about children as a social group. Thus it has been argued that childhood is necessarily subordinated to adulthood and children to adults just because young children have to rely on adults to keep them alive, and to provide them with the means to grow healthily (Shamgar-Handelman 1994). Thence follow the cultural traditions whereby children must obey adults and be socialised by adults; and in particular the traditions of patriarchal power and rights (Therborn 1993; see also Hood-Williams 1990; Bardy 1994). Thence often also follows the argument that children are best off living with parents, since they should be regarded as responsible for their children and are best placed to protect and to provide. However, the CRC contributes an important point here, by arguing (Article 5) for the responsibilities, rights and duties not only of parents, but of 'the members of the extended family or community, as provided for by local custom'. It can be argued that, to the extent that societies neglect the rights of the social group children to a fair allocation of national resources, and to the extent that children are discriminated against, by those in power and by the power structures in a society, children can be understood as a minority social group (e.g. Sgritta 1994).

Göran Therborn's (1993) argument is relevant here. He argues that the extent to which children's rights are respected can be linked to or interpreted through consideration of large-scale influences in any given society, notably religion and law. Thus, through study of (mainly) European societies, he argues that some countries, including some southern societies, have strong Catholic traditions whereas others, including many northern societies, have Protestant traditions; and he argues that Catholicism has a stronger hold over citizens' beliefs and practices than Protestantism, and relatively more fixed, long-established ideologies. Further, he argues, some societies, including many southern European societies have 'civil law' traditions, often based on Roman law, which include both 'positive laws' to suit men's needs and 'natural laws', that is ideal laws; these laws may be further solidified by being coded, as in the Napoleonic Code. Other societies, including many northern societies, rely on legal systems (including common law), which are developed over time, through consideration of judicial precedents and through changing legislation. Again, he argues, civil law is more prescriptive and fixed than these developing systems. In both cases, religion and the law, the more prescriptive version relies heavily on and endorses patriarchy. Therborn concludes that the likelihood of a society respecting children's rights will vary according to how fixed and unresponsive its religion and legal system are. And he argues that Nordic countries have gone further in respecting children's rights than southern European ones. This argument provides an important instance of how sociological analysis can help us understand the circumstances in which children's rights are or are not respected, and of how those rights are likely to be interpreted in accordance with the religious and legal traditions of the society. However, more work needs to be done on the extent to which children's rights are indeed respected, both in law and in practice, in countries across Europe – and beyond.

At this point, it may be useful to take account of the analysis by Galant and Parlevliet (2005) of ways of understanding rights. Their four-part presentation provides a way into understanding sociological approaches to rights. Thus the authors argue that there are four dimensions to rights: rights as rules, rights as structures, rights as relationships and rights as processes. In brief, rights as rules refers to agreements, including legislation, and including also what is agreed in a society through custom or norms. Second, rights can also be understood as implemented through the structures of a society, through its institutions (such as education, welfare and health services) and policies designed to advance certain behaviours. Third, human rights fundamentally involve relations at all levels, between the individual and the state, between social groups, and between people in their everyday lives. And finally, the implementation of rights requires processes, through which participation in negotiations, in compromises, allows people to reach agreement. The authors note that there must be coherence between all four of these rights, so that people can rely on the clarity and integrity proposed by the four-part framework. The sociological approach to children's rights (outlined in this chapter) can be understood as resting on this framework, with its emphasis on maintaining dialogue between the small-scale and the large-scale; and on relational processes through which change, including improvement, can be made. These points lead us on to the second section of this exploration of sociological ideas.

2.2. Studying relational processes

Here, we are concerned with how childhood and adulthood relate, at both macro and micro levels, and how each level of these relational processes affects the other. Indeed at this point we have to consider the argument that generation is a fundamental concept structuring how we are to think about childhood (Qvortrup 2009; Alanen 2009). For it can be said that essentially childhood and adulthood are not age-related; instead they are characterised in opposition to each other, that is, relationally. The status of child is arrived at by considering what it is not, that is the status of adulthood. For the status of adulthood includes the idea that the people inhabiting it do valuable things; and as briefly set out above, women have had to fight to get acceptance that what they do too is socially valuable. Indeed it has been proposed that one key reason why minority world children have been denied valuable status is that they have not been understood as doing socially valuable things (La Fontaine 1998). This point is recognised in the habit indulged in by colonial masters, of calling their servants 'boys'; and, we may add, in the practice of some men in referring to women as 'girls', thus in both cases denying them the status of adult, that is of a valuable person. These points provide a commentary on the age-related definitions of the CRC (see for discussion, Chapter 1 in this Handbook, page 2).

It is also clear (and the above examples point to this) that in many societies, including minority world societies, the status 'child' is assigned to those who occupy positions of dependency vis-à-vis adults. As Judith Ennew (1994) explains, '… modern childhood constructs children *out* of society, mutes their voices, denies their personhood, limits their potential.' The young people of minority world societies experience restrictions, conventions, assumptions, which emphasise what they must do and must not do, as well as what they cannot do. We have to recognise that social structures surrounding children generally emphasise chronological age as a marker of childhood, and indeed the CRC itself suggests under-18s are generally included in childhood, while recognising that societies may mark transition to adulthood at other ages or on the basis of concepts such as maturity or puberty. But alongside this common assumption that chronological age defines the limits of childhood, it is relevant to focus on this social ordering of childhood, this assignment to children of particular social locations and institutions, from which positions they participate in social life, and in particular participate in relations with those inhabiting the other major social location, adulthood (Alanen 2009). Alanen argues that just as gender has been a useful concept for deconstructing relations between the sexes, so when we are thinking about the childhood social group and the adult social group, we are concerned with relations between the generations.

One way of considering generational relations is to build on the work of Mannheim (1952/1928). He proposed that people born at a particular time are influenced by the traditions, policies, practices that are current at the time. Mannheim argued that some groups of people actively constitute themselves as a generational group, working together to construct new ideas that modify or challenge existing ideas. The French impressionists provide an example – a small group of young men (and a few women), who lived in Paris from the 1860s, met, talked, collaborated, exchanged notes, and through their paintings challenged contemporary 'academic' painting traditions and changed the character of pictorial art in France. Another example, making a slightly different point, is provided by 'the 1968 generation'. In the 1960s, in revolt against post-war attempts to re-impose patriarchal and other traditional practices, people began to challenge these attempts and to propose more democratically organised societies. In that case, it can be suggested, it is not so much when these people were born, as the extent to which they identified with the new ideas. So the 1960s generation could be mixed in age-composition. This idea about generation was, perhaps for the first time, taken up in

Germany by sociologists interested in childhood; they compared their own childhoods at around the time of the Second World War, with 1960s and 1970s childhoods, and related the on-the-ground character of these two sorts of childhoods to the large-scale changes and events taking place (see Zeiher, 2003, for a description of the study).

When we are thinking about relations between those assigned to childhood and those assigned to adulthood, we can go beyond chronological age as marker of these two groups, and instead think about the social structures, norms and practices that influence how people called children or adults are expected to live their lives. Then we can better understand what factors help to structure the relational processes that children and adults engage in. Currently in England, for example, government policies are requiring people up to the age of 18 to remain in education or training (including apprenticeships); in a sense, this means politicians are raising the age of entering adulthood from 16 (the former school-leaving age) to 18. The negotiations some of these young people are now having with teachers and parents are likely to reflect young people's challenge to this enforced prolonging of the dependencies of childhood, for they might prefer to participate more directly in the social and economic activities of society – to be out at work, taking on some financial independence and contributing to the economic welfare of their household and of the society more generally. Indeed they may wish to participate more effectively in decision-making about how they spend their time, in accordance with Article 12 of the CRC.

At a macro level, we can study how local traditions, established policies and institutional norms provide bases for structuring services such as education, health and welfare. We can then consider how people, on the ground, respond to the character of these services: by acceptance, challenge or revolt. We can also consider the inter-personal relations of (as above) children and teachers, or parents and health professionals, in the light of the macro-structures organising their relations. An interesting take on these negotiations is provided by Bourdieu. He proposes that at inter-personal levels, a person negotiates his or her status vis-à-vis that of another person, by bringing to bear their 'habitus', that is, their assumptions, acquired knowledge, understanding of their place in the social system (Bourdieu and Wacquant 1992: 94–130). Though he does not deal directly with childhood (but see Bourdieu 1995), an example could be the negotiations children have with their parents, for instance about what clothes they could or should wear, how much attention they should give or wish to give to school work, what importance they may and should give to friendships; for again, children's participation rights are at issue here. The two generations bring differing knowledge and assumptions (habitus), as well as varying amounts and varying types of economic, social and cultural capital, to bear to these negotiations, based on their differing experience deriving from the traditions, customs, policies and practices of social worlds thirty or forty years apart.

Relational sociology offers a conceptual space for consideration of children's own experiential knowledge and in recent years there has been a huge number of empirical studies that have explored that knowledge, by enlisting children to talk about their experiences (for discussion see James 2009). For one way of linking the small-scale with the large-scale is by situating children's own accounts of their childhoods within the context of larger-scale factors that affect those childhoods (Alanen 2001); children's agency can then be located within consideration of social structures. Feminism again offers a way into making sense of what children say and in doing so provides a fuller account of what their knowledge means and implies. Thus it has been argued that listening to women's accounts means taking seriously the voices of those who are outsiders to the male-dominated social order; and through listening and analysing we move towards standpoint: gaining a fuller understanding of how the social order is experienced by an important social group (Smith 1988). The same point can be made about children: as a minority social group they have important points to make about their experiences of childhood within the context of child–adult relations, and about how far they perceive that their rights are respected (Waksler 1996; Hutchby and Moran-Ellis 1998; Mayall 2002: Chapter 9). Of course it can be argued that for women to listen to women and then to analyse and discuss the wider social order in relation to women's accounts, is different, perhaps more likely to be successful, than for adults to engage with children's experiences. On the other hand, we adults have all been children and perhaps retain some empathy with their social status. Perhaps as time goes on more space (and funds) will be granted to children to carry out their own research, and to reflect on what they find. We should note too that the explosion of empirical studies with and for children has led on to work both on methods of working with children to elicit their perspectives (e.g. Greene and Hogan 2005; Christensen and James 2008) and on the ethics of research with children (e.g. Alderson and Morrow 2011).

3. The sociology of childhood in relation to children's rights

The above brief account of some major features of the sociology of childhood allows us to consider why we need a separate convention for children and for childhood; and also why it is so hard for its articles to be cemented into the laws and practices of societies. If we think of children's rights as human rights, then sociology allows us to compare the character of childhoods with the character of adulthoods, and to consider differences and how these point to the need for a convention specifically aimed at improving childhoods. We may take three kinds of difference to make the point.

First, child–adult relations are characterised through adult understandings at a specific time in a specific society of what childhood consists of. When children are thought of as incomplete, as lacking the crucial abilities adults associate with themselves, with children regarded as embarked on a socialisation journey towards the gold standard of adulthood, it is an easy response for adults to relate to children through authoritarian behaviour, through oppression, through the imposition of norms for childhood that may be experienced by children themselves as inappropriate. Alongside such behaviours, adults may focus on protecting and providing for children, not only when children are young and lacking the physical competence to provide for themselves, but when children manifestly can do so. As Gerison Lansdown (1994) argued, adults tend to confuse biological vulnerabilities with social constructed ones. Adult assumptions and behaviours can then be found incorporated into customs, religions, norms and practices, governing what children may and may not do. However, it is an important feature of the CRC (though itself devised by adults) that it helps to alter the balance of power by focusing on the concept of participation rights whereby children may work towards changing adult–child relations.

Second, of particular concern for those who have listened to children talking about how adults behave to them is the point outlined at the start of this chapter: that children experience adult unwillingness to believe that they are morally competent. Evidence from minority world children indicates that they find they are routinely not believed, and not thought capable of judging rationally; they talk of being falsely blamed. At root is their experience that they are not taken seriously as members of the human species (Waksler 1996; Mayall 2002: Chapter 5). I do not know how far this experience is common across societies and the topic would merit investigation.

Third, in minority world societies, children are not regarded as contributing to the division of labour. Instead, childhood is conceptualised as preparation, outside the political sphere. Contributions to the division of labour are restricted to adults. At its most problematic, this perceived absence means that children and their activities are not valued; their value is seen as entirely in the future, as economic contributors in adulthood. It is one of the merits of the globalisation of childhood research that it is forcing minority world people to take account in their thinking of the economic contributions to household and national economies made by children across the majority world; and to reconsider the division of children's time and effort between schooling and more direct economic contributions across both majority and minority world societies.

All in all, study of childhood in relation to adulthood clearly points to the need for a convention that takes account of the specific differences between childhood and adulthood, which may differ across societies, but which will be found in any society. That is, that children, especially in early childhood, are weaker and less experienced than adults. In this context, it is clear that a convention is required in order to encourage adults to respect children as human. The CRC has fulfilled this need, in the sense that it recognises that in all societies young children do require adults to protect them and provide for them, alongside the recognition that children must be enabled to take part in decision-making in matters that affect them. This entails adult respect for children as moral agents, and recognition of and respect for children's developing physical capacities, which will enable them to take part in productive activities.

However, sociological investigation also clearly points to the power of established beliefs, customs, norms and practices in shaping how people live their lives. It is the power of these beliefs, customs, norms and practices as operationalised by adults that inhibit adults from implementing children's rights. And sociology points to how these beliefs and so on become formalised into institutions and laws, so that people live out their lives on the basis of unconsidered assumptions. In commentaries on the drafting processes towards the CRC, it has been noted how international negotiations had to be carefully undertaken and compromises made in order that countries would be willing to sign up to the Convention (e.g. Johnson 1992; Freeman 2000; Cantwell 2011). In the next section of this chapter, I consider some reports on recent research studies, relating to children's rights, in order to examine in more detail how the macro and micro have been found to inter-relate and what the consequent character of childhood turns out to be. I try to show how study of relational processes across the generations contribute to understanding, and to changes in the status and character of childhood – and of adulthood. And in addition the aim is to explore how local beliefs and practices shape understandings of children's rights.

4. Lessons from research studies

Here, I consider some recent research studies in order to provide a critical look at the assumptions, norms and values that shape practices based on the idea that children have rights. For, the simple appeal to articles of the Convention as a basis for practice is not adequate in the task of uncovering understandings that lie deep and may be unquestioned. All the studies chosen here relate local practice and experience to large-scale features of the society, and thus can be understood as broadly sociological in approach. Consideration of these studies provides a commentary on the points made in the Introduction to the Handbook about the importance of approaching children's rights through a critical perspective, taking account of local circumstances and of interactive processes between stakeholders. Quennerstedt (2013) gives further discussion of these points.

A paper by Lucia Rabello de Castro (2012) describes a study of how students (aged 12 to 21) at private and municipal schools in Rio de Janeiro, Brazil, defined participation in the school setting. She conducted open-ended interviews with students and with school staff in order to investigate this topic. She found that both students and staff, in the main, worked according to a 'conservative' understanding of participation; that is, students said that participation comprised conformity to school norms: 'an individual endeavour to act out the students' role adequately, that is to attend classes, to be attentive during classes, to study and do the homework'. This vision was endorsed by the staff, who explained that the students were immature and needed guidance, for otherwise they would act unwisely; furthermore, students, and especially those elected to stand on school councils, should also help the staff with the smooth running of the school. A minority of students argued in favour of some form of individual or collective resistance to the norms of the school. Rabello de Castro, discussing the findings, notes that staff feared losing control over students' behaviour, and she emphasises how the prevailing norms of student behaviour reflected developmental assumptions about children's incompetence and immaturity. She argues, in conclusion, that it will be necessary for the education system in Brazil to take what she defines as political steps, towards democratising the schools. This conclusion points to the intersection of the articles in the CRC; in order to work within its spirit, it is not enough to conform to just one or a selection of articles (in this case the right to schooling); the character of schooling has to be thought of in relation not only to the articles referring to participation but to the spirit that underpins the CRC as a whole. Again, I refer to the initial example in this chapter, where it appears that providing a free comprehensive and compulsory school system in England has not altered the assumptions of policy-makers and teachers about the proper relations of adults to children. As Rabello de Castro concludes, what is required is a politicising of child–adult relations. For a further interesting discussion of the politics of respecting children's rights, see also Helle Rydstrøm's (2006) paper on problematic inter-relations between deep-seated ideas about rearing boys in rural Vietnam and respect for children's rights.

Just how complex a matter it is to respect children's rights adequately is demonstrated in a paper exploring how far children are consulted when they are within the asylum-seeking system in Norway (Lidén and Rusten 2007). Norway is one the few countries that has deliberately incorporated the CRC into its domestic law (in 2003) and it is therefore an interesting country to consider in respect of implementation. When asylum-seeking children and parents arrive in Norway it is customary for officials to interview both adults and children, in order to establish their stories and their reasons for seeking asylum. Various issues arise. It will be important that the adults who do the interviews know how best to talk with children. And though, according to the Norwegian regulations, children must be accompanied to the interview by a parent, the presence of this parent may be inhibiting to the child and may influence what he or she says. And then there is the question of what weight is to be given to the respective views and reported experiences of the adults and of the children who are seeking asylum.

This paper points up the complexities that have to be faced in a thorough-going approach to implementation of the CRC. It appears that aiming for good practice, in accordance with children's rights has presented Norway with as yet unsolved problems. The researchers argue that there is a need in the asylum system for better understanding about child-specific forms of persecution and suffering, as well as a more systematic approach to the use of human rights standards in the analysis of claims, including cross-referencing of CRC articles. Here they note in particular the intersecting relevance of Articles 2, 3, 6 and 12. They also argue for better training for case-workers who interview children and parents so that they may elicit more appropriate data. And they argue that lawyers should be given a mandate to include children in the family's asylum proceedings, so that children's participation rights and their best interests come together.

A number of studies have highlighted the importance of sociological understanding of norms and values in any society where people, either its citizens or others visiting the society with the aim of helping, are concerned with implementing the CRC. For instance, a paper by Henderson (2006) focuses on the importance of analysing a specific topic in relation to local understandings of family and community. She carried out a detailed study over three years focusing on children in South Africa whose parents had died of AIDS. She found that a minority world assumption that these children should be defined as 'vulnerable victims' and as 'orphans' did not fit with how the children and local adults responded after these parental deaths. For, commonly, the children had wider kin connections and came to live with relatives in the extended family, whose members regarded themselves as responsible for the children, or they were taken into the households of other members of the local community. And though the children themselves had suffered and still suffered from their bereavement, they were active in reconfiguring a sense of place for themselves, drawing on networks of kin and local opportunities for agency. In so doing they were taking part in the economic and cultural activities of the community. So this study raised questions about what kind of help incomers to the society can most usefully give; if any.

Another example of how those seeking to promote children's rights must take account of cultural beliefs and practices and how these intersect with structural factors, if they are to make any headway, is provided in a study of a small community in northern Tanzania. Marida Hollos (2002) examined adult ideas about childhood, and about inter-relations between adults and children. She found that large-scale economic factors had brought about local change in these ideas. Traditionally, adults had made their living through agriculture (in an area of poor fertility), within a patrilineal system of responsibility and dependency. In these 'lineage societies', children were understood and valued as responsible participants in the work of their family and were cared for in the family on the basis that they took part in economic activity (see also Punch 2001). But over several generations, the custom of parcelling out the very limited arable land available to sons (usually at marriage) and the consequent inability of people to make a living from the unfertile and overworked land area, has forced young men to find other work, in some cases far from home. Young men may establish a wife and children in their home area, and visit when they can. Following these changes, there has then been a move among some people in the area to focus their resources more on the nuclear family; and arising out of this change, has come a change in adult valuations of children; children are described as having emotional value, bringing joy to their parents. Hollos gives a summary of how these changes work out: in lineage families children 'work a lot, play little, and rest and study even less'; in nuclear families, children 'work little, play a lot, rest quite a bit, and study'. Hollos' study demonstrates in detail how changing economic conditions feed into changes in how children are valued: what children and childhood are for. Anyone wishing to promote children's rights would have to work with these varying and changing valuations of childhood.

A final example of how a sociological approach is key to understanding human rights at local level is provided by Virginia Morrow and Kirrily Pells (2012). For this paper, they draw on the Young Lives programme of longitudinal research into the lives of young people growing up in poverty in Andra Pradesh (India) and Ethiopia. They note that debates and programmes concerned with poverty in the twenty-first century have seldom connected up with discussions and actions relating to children's rights; and they argue by contrast that it is essential to consider how economic deprivation affects children directly, and to focus on the political and economic processes, and the structures that create, or fail to reduce, poverty. Poverty structures local understandings of rights and responsibilities. For this paper they draw mainly on interviews and discussions with young people. Young people (aged 15 to 16) in

Andra Pradesh found that work was hard, and it was difficult to combine work with school, but it was essential for them to contribute to the family's economic survival. Further, as in other studies, they said that work teaches you valuable skills and it is fundamental to relations with others in the community. Another sub-study, in Ethiopia, focused on orphans (defined by intervening agencies as orphans and vulnerable children) and again, through interviews with children aged 9 to 16, the researchers found that poverty underlay many of the children's concerns; it was necessary to work in order to help the household they lived in. Morrow and Pells argue that the common minority world assumption that these children are above all 'vulnerable' (as also documented by Henderson 2006) does not reflect the children's own perspectives and experiences, which are locked into their relations with those they live with, and have to be understood through engagement with the structures and processes of poverty within which these children exercise agency and live out their childhoods.

5. Further comments

The points made earlier about how sociology can help us understand the social positioning of children and the relational processes that they engage in, have been explored in relation to some examples. The research studies emerging from the minority and majority worlds are pointing to the key importance of studying how children relate to the economic and political contexts they live in; and how adult ideas about childhood locally and internationally shape those childhoods, but are challenged by children themselves. The study of children's rights, if and how they are respected, shows it is necessary to think about local understandings of what childhood is, and how childhood relates to adulthood, within socio-economic and political contexts.

Thus, for instance, let us consider ideas about children's relations with family. Studies, such as those for the Young Lives programme, show that children's engagement with family may comprise the responsibility of all members to contribute to the economic, as well as social, welfare of the family, as soon as they are physically able. But other studies show another set of ideas, which we may regard as complementary rather than competing. An example of how family and dependency may be differently envisaged comes from a study in Bangladesh, where women and children are regarded as dependents, and a crucial social system involves guardianship, whereby a male, usually but not always related, is responsible for the behaviour and development of women and children (White 2007). This does not mean that women and children are not economically active, but it does mean that their agency is under the control of the guardian. This example resonates with commonly held views in the UK, where children are commonly regarded as dependents (and traditionally as under patriarchal power); and parents are held responsible for their children's behaviour (see Therborn 1996). White argues that an adequate approach to children's rights is to regard them as human rights but to think about them in a given society in relation to the customs, history and norms of that society. Through this analysis one would aim to find the conceptual spaces that may allow for progress to be made on children's rights. However, here it will be crucial for local people, rather than incomers, to take the lead in considering avenues of change. In the UK, for example, as in many minority world societies, responsibility for initiating and implementing change will depend on what division of responsibility for children is in force, as between parents and the state; for in the UK we may argue that responsibility for children's provision and protection rights rests ultimately with government and can thus be best pursued through political processes; whereas when it comes to participation, some researchers aim to demonstrate children's competence, through study of their agency and active engagement with social problems (e.g. Percy-Smith and Thomas 2009). However, it is crucial, if progress is to be made, that adults who work with and for children at all levels of society (parents, paid workers in the law, education and social work, civil servants, politicians) be educated about children's rights.

The globalising world brings with it both disadvantages and advantages (as the Introduction points out). Thus Morrow and Pells (2012) argue that globalisation, organised or influenced by international agencies, brings with it undue emphasis on 'modernisation', and on 'outcomes', conceived of in mainly economic terms. As regards children, these goals carry dangers, since the aim may be to change childhoods in line with minority world childhoods, without due attention to local understandings and conditions. Alongside that problem, is the perennial challenge: how to tackle the task of improving childhoods, given local socio-economic conditions (Rizzini and Bush 2002). A case in point is schooling. In order that children may 'compete' in the globalised world, it may be proposed that childhood everywhere should be fully scholarised, and that children's productive work be abolished. This would require a re-ordering of state and family responsibility for children, in the direction of the provision of free schooling. Yet globalisation has upsides; it improves our understanding. Thus we learn from children who do paid work – in both the minority and majority worlds – that apart from its directly economic benefits, work confers dignity, self-worth, connection to the local community, as well as useful skills (Mizen *et al.*, 2001; see also Hanson, Volonakis and Al-Rozzi, Chapter 18 in this Handbook); and we also learn from our scholarised children that they do not feel valued, as moral agents or as contributors to the local or more general good. Globalisation is also allowing for a range of sometimes competing ideas about childhood to circulate, to be debated and to be considered in local and international contexts. Olga Nieuwenhuys (2005) has provided a useful discussion of the ILO's and World Bank's endorsement of children's rights to a protected scholarised childhood, and she offers a more nuanced view of the intergenerational reciprocities and responsibilities observable in majority – but also in minority – world societies. Empirical research studies in both majority and minority world societies are forcing us in the minority world to rethink childhood, especially as regards children as economic contributors; and more generally to reconsider the status of childhood in our societies. For instance a series of seminars brought together researchers from a range of societies to discuss their projects and their ideas about childhood, across societies (Tisdall and Punch 2012).

This chapter has woven together a macro approach to childhood with an emphasis on relationality. It has shown how attention to the large-scale is essential to understanding childhoods and to understanding whether and how children's rights are respected. An important theme in these considerations is the inter-relations between responsibility, family and community. Freeman (2009) noted that during the negotiations towards the CRC, the notion of intergenerational responsibility in families was debated and it was concluded that children's responsibilities towards older generations in their family could not be included in the CRC, since they could not be enforced and/or might lead to children becoming economic slaves of their parents. However, several African countries did argue for the inclusion of inter-generational responsibilities, and the African Charter on the Rights and Welfare of the Child (1990) included Article 31 stressing these. And a theme running through many of the empirical studies with children (in many societies) is their understanding that they do have responsibilities up the generations, notably to help maintain the economic welfare of the family. It has been an important aim of research with children to explore these understandings in majority world societies (e.g. Liebel 2012) and also in minority world societies (e.g. Mizen *et al.*, 2001). Further, the notion that as people we are interdependent members of communities (however defined, and with whatever scope and range), as discussed, for instance by John O'Neill (1994), is an important consideration that seems to hover at the edges of debates about rights, and about responsibilities. Young people themselves tend to discuss their increasing independence in the context of their continuing interdependence within their families and peer relations (Gillies, Ribbens McCarthy and Holland 2001; for more general discussion, see also Morrow 2003). Furthermore, in the examples discussed above, respect for rights seems to be linked into high evaluation of inter-dependent family relations across the generations and of the idea of community. Thus the Brazilian students and staff looked for a well-functioning school community (Rabello de Castro 2012), the Norwegians were working towards including asylum-seekers into their community (Lidén and Rusten 2007), the 'AIDS orphans' in South Africa were welcomed into the homes of community members (Henderson 2006); the Andra Pradesh young people valued their work in part because it gave them a stake in their community (Morrow and Pells 2012); and the life or death of a Tanzanian community was interlinked with how children's responsibilities to family were conceptualised (Hollos 2002). It would seem therefore that there is room for in-depth studies of how children's rights in a given society link in with understandings of both responsibilities and community.

Questions for debate and discussion

- What are the limits of children's agency?
- What contributions do children make to the division of labour, in varying societies?
- How useful is it to think of childhood as social status (rather than as defined by age)?
- How can children and adults collaborate towards greater respect for children's rights?
- In what respects is it useful to think in terms of children's collective rights (rather than, or as well as, their individual rights)?
- What is the importance of concepts of community and inter-generational responsibilities for understandings of children's contributions to societal well-being?

References

Alanen, L. (1992). *Modern Childhood: Exploring the 'child question' in sociology*. Research Report 50. Finland: University of Jyväskylä.
Alanen, L. (2001). Explorations in generational analysis. In L. Alanen and B. Mayall (eds), *Conceptualising Child-adult Relations*. London: RoutledgeFalmer.
Alanen, L. (2009). Generational order. In J. Qvortrup, W.A. Corsaro, M.-S. and Honig (eds), *The Palgrave Handbook of Childhood Studies*. London: Palgrave Macmillan.
Alderson, P. and Morrow, V. (2011). *The Ethics of Research with Children and Young People: A Practical Handbook* (3rd ed.). London: Sage.
Bardy, M. (1994). The manuscript of the 100-years project: Towards a revision. In J. Qvortrup, M. Bardy, G. Sgritta and H. Wintersberger (eds), *Childhood Matters: Social theory, practice and politics*. Aldershot, UK: Avebury Press.
Bettelheim, B. (1971). *Children of the Dream*. London: Paladin Books.
Blishen, E. (1969). *The School that I'd Like*. Harmondsworth, UK: Penguin Books
Bourdieu, P. (1986). The forms of capital. In J. G. Richardson (ed.), *Handbook of Theory and Research for the Sociology of Education*. London: Greenwood Press.
Bourdieu, P. (1995). 'Youth' is just a word. In P. Bourdieu (ed.), *Sociology in Question* (pp 94–102). London: Sage.
Bourdieu, P. and Passeron J.-C. (1977). *Reproduction in Education, Society and Culture*. London: Sage
Bourdieu, P. and Wacquant, L. (1992). *Invitation to Reflexive Sociology*. Cambridge: Polity Press.
Bronfenbrenner, U. (1971). *Two Worlds of Childhood: USA and Russia*. New York: Pocket Books.
Burke, C. and Grosvenor, I. (2003). *The School I'd Like*. London: RoutledgeFalmer.
Cantwell, N. (2011). Are children's rights still human? In A. Invernizzi and J. Williams (eds), *The Human Rights of Children*. Farnham, UK: Ashgate.
Christensen, P. and James, A. (eds) (2008). *Research with Children: Perspectives and practices*. Second edition. London: Falmer Press.

Elshtain, J. B. (1981). *Public Man, Private Woman: Women in social and political thought*. Princeton NJ: Princeton University Press.
Elshtain, J. B. (1996). Commentary: political children. *Childhood*, 3, 1: 11–28.
Ennew, J. (1994). Time for children or time for adults? In J. Qvortrup, M. Bardy, G. Sgritta and H. Wintersberger (eds), *Childhood Matters: Social Theory, Practice and Politics*. Aldershot, UK: Avebury Press.
Foucault, M. (1977). *Discipline and Punish*. Harmondsworth: Penguin Books.
Freeman, M. (2000). The future of children's rights. *Childhood and Society* 14, 4: 277–94.
Freeman, M. (2009). Children's rights as human rights: Reading the UNCRC. In J. Qvortrup, W.A. Corsaro, M.-S. and Honig (eds), *The Palgrave Handbook of Childhood Studies*. London: Palgrave Macmillan.
Galant, G. and Parlevliet, M. (2005). Using rights to address conflict: A valuable synergy. In P. Gready and J. Ensor (eds), *Reinventing Development: Translating Rights-based Approaches from Theory into Practice*. London: Zed Books.
Gillies, V., Ribbens McCarthy, J. and Holland, J. (2001 *Pulling Together, Pulling Apart: The Family Lives of Young People*. London: Joseph Rowntree Foundation/Policy Studies Centre.
Goffman, E. (1961). *Asylums*. Harmondsworth, UK: Penguin Books.
Greene, S. and Hogan, D. (eds) (2005). *Researching Children's Experience: Approaches and Methods*. London: Sage.
Henderson, P. C. (2006) South African AIDS orphans: Examining assumptions around vulnerability from the perspective of rural children and youth. *Childhood*, 13, 3: 303–28.
Hollos, M. (2002). The cultural construction of childhood: changing conceptions among the Pare of northern Tanzania. *Childhood*, 9, 2: 167–89.
Holt, J. (1975). *Escape from Childhood: The Needs and Rights of Children*. Harmondsworth, UK: Penguin Books.
Hood-Williams, J. (1990). Patriarchy for children: On the stability of power relations in children's lives. In L. Chisholm, P. Büchner, H.-H. Krüger and P. Brown (eds), *Childhood, Youth and Social Change: A Comparative Perspective*. London: Falmer Press.
Hutchby, I. and Moran-Ellis, J. (eds) (1998). *Children and Social Competence*. London: Falmer Press.
James, A. (2009 Agency. In J. Qvortrup, W.A. Corsaro, M.-S. and Honig (eds), *The Palgrave Handbook of Childhood Studies*. London: Palgrave Macmillan.
Johnson, D. (1992). *Cultural and Regional Pluralism in the Drafting of the UN Convention of the Rights of the Child*. In M. Freeman and P. Veerman (eds), *The Ideologies of Children's Rights* (pp. 95–114). Dordrecht: Martinus Nijhoff.
Kessen, W. (1965). *The Child*. New York: John Wiley.
Kessen, W. (1975). *Childhood in China*. New Haven: Yale University Press.
La Fontaine, J. (1998). Are children people? In J. La Fontaine and H. Rydstrøm (eds), *The Invisibility of Children*. Papers presented at an international conference on anthropology and children, May 1997. Department of Child Studies, Linköping University, Sweden.
Lansdown, G. (1994). Children's rights. In B. Mayall (ed.), *Children's Childhoods: Observed and Experienced*. London: Falmer Press.
Layder, D. (1994). *Understanding Social Theory*. London: Sage.
Lidén, H. and Rusten, H. (2007). Asylum, participation and the best interests of the child: New lessons from Norway. *Children and Society*, 21, 4: 273–83.
Liebel, M. (2012). *Children's Rights from Below: Cross-cultural Perspectives*. London: Palgrave Macmillan.
Mannheim, K. (1952). The problem of generations. In K. Mannheim (ed.), *Essays on the Sociology of Knowledge*. (First published 1928. London: Routledge and Kegan Paul.)
Mayall, B. (2002). *Towards a Sociology for Childhood: Thinking from Children's Lives*. Maidenhead, UK: Open University Press.
Mayall, B. (2013). *A History of the Sociology of Childhood*. London: Institute of Education Press.
Mills, C. W. (1967). *The Sociological Imagination*. Oxford: Oxford University Press.
Mitchell, J. (1971). *Woman's Estate*. Harmondsworth, UK: Penguin Books.
Mizen, P., Pole, C. and Bolton, A. (eds) (2001). *Hidden Hands: International Perspectives on Children's Work and Labour*. London: RoutledgeFalmer.
Morrow, V. (1994). Responsible children? Aspects of children's work and employment outside school in contemporary UK. In B. Mayall (ed.), *Children's Childhoods: Observed and Experienced*. London: Falmer Press.
Morrow, V. (2003). Moving out of Childhood. In J. Maybin and M. Woodhead (eds), *Childhoods in Context*. Chichester, UK: John Wiley in association with the Open University Press.

Morrow, V. and Pells, K. (2012). Integrating children's human rights and child poverty debates: Examples from young lives in Ethiopia and India. *Sociology*, 45, 5: 906–20.
Nieuwenhuys, O. (2005). The wealth of children. In J. Qvortrup (ed.), *Studies in Modern Childhood: Society, Agency, Culture*. London: Palgrave Macmillan.
Oakley, A. (1972). *Sex, Gender and Society*. London: Temple Smith.
O'Neill, J. (1994). *The Missing Child in Liberal Theory*. Toronto: University of Toronto Press.
Percy-Smith, B. and Thomas, N. (2009). *A Handbook of Children and Young People's Participation: Perspectives from Theory and Practice*. Abingdon, UK: Routledge.
Punch, S. (2001). Negotiating autonomy: childhoods in rural Bolivia. In L. Alanen and B. Mayall (eds), *Conceptualizing Child-adult Relations*. London: RoutledgeFalmer.
Quennerstedt, A. (2013). Children's rights research moving into the future: Challenges on the way forward. *International Journal of Children's Rights*, 21: 233–47.
Qvortrup, J. (1985). Placing children in the division of labour. In P. Close and R. Collins (eds), *Family and Economy in Modern Society*. London: Macmillan.
Qvortrup, J. (2008). Macroanalysis of childhood. In P. Christensen and A. James (eds), *Research with Children: Perspectives and Practices* (2nd ed.). London: Routledge.
Qvortrup, J. (2009). Introduction. In J. Qvortrup, W.A. Corsaro, M.-S. and Honig (eds), *The Palgrave Handbook of Childhood Studies*. London: Palgrave Macmillan.
Qvortrup, J., Bardy, M., Sgritta, G. and Wintersberger, H. (eds) (1994). *Childhood Matters: Social Theory, Practice and Politics*. Aldershot, UK: Avebury Press.
Qvortrup, J., Corsaro, W. A. and Honig, M.-S. (eds) (2009). *The Palgrave Handbook of Childhood Studies*. London: Palgrave Macmillan.
Rabello de Castro, L. (2012). The 'good-enough society', the 'good-enough citizen and the 'good-enough student'. Where is children's participation moving to in Brazil? *Childhood*, 19, 1: 52–68.
Reynaert, D., Bouverne-de Bie, M. and Vandevelde, S. (2012). Between 'believers' and 'opponents': Critical discussions on children's rights. *International Journal of Children's Rights*, 20: 155–68.
Rizzini, I. and Bush, M. (2002). Editorial. *Childhood*, 9, 4: 371–4.
Rydstrøm, H. (2006). Masculinity and punishment; Men's upbringing of boys in rural Vietnam. *Childhood*, 13, 3: 329–48.
Sgritta, G. (1994). The generational division of welfare: Equity and conflict. In J. Qvortrup, M. Bardy, G. Sgritta and H. Wintersberger (eds), *Childhood Matters: Social Theory, Practice and Politics*. Aldershot, UK: Avebury Press.
Shamgar-Handelman, L. (1994). To whom does childhood belong? In J. Qvortrup, M. Bardy, G. Sgritta and H. Wintersberger (eds), *Childhood Matters: Social Theory, Practice and Politics*. Aldershot, UK: Avebury Press.
Smith, D. (1988). *The Everyday World as Problematic: Towards a Feminist Sociology*. Milton Keynes, UK: Open University Press.
Stacey, M. (1988). *The Sociology of Health and Healing*. London: Routledge.
Therborn, G. (1993). Children's rights since the constitution of modern childhood: A comparative study of western nations. In J. Qvortrup (ed.), *Childhood as a Social Phenomenon: Lessons from an International Project*. Papers from an international conference, held at Billund, Denmark, September 1992. Eurosocial Report 47/1993. Vienna: European Centre.
Therborn, G. (1996). Child politics: dimensions and perspectives. *Childhood*, 3, 1: 29–44.
Tisdall, E. K. M. and Punch, S. (2012). Not so 'new'? Looking critically at childhood studies. *Children's Geographies: Playing, Living, Learning*, 10, 3: 249–64.
Waksler, F. C. (1996). *The Little Trials of Childhood and Children's Strategies for Dealing with Them*. London: Falmer Press.
White, S. C. (2007). Children's rights and the imagination of community in Bangladesh. *Childhood*, 14, 4: 505–20.
Wintersberger, H. (1994). Costs and benefits: The economics of childhood. In J. Qvortrup, M. Bardy, G. Sgritta and H. Wintersberger (eds), *Childhood Matters: Social theory, Practice and Politics*. Aldershot, UK: Avebury Press.
Woodhead, M. (2009). Child development and the development of childhood. In J. Qvortrup, W.A. Corsaro, M.-S. and Honig (eds), *The Palgrave Handbook of Childhood Studies*. London: Palgrave Macmillan.
Zeiher, H. (2003). Intergenerational relations and social change in childhood: Examples from West Germany. In B. Mayall and H. Zeiher (eds), *Childhood in Generational Perspective*. London: Institute of Education Press.

Zelizer, V. (2002). Kids and commerce. *Childhood*, 8,4: 375–96.
Zelizer, V. (2005). The priceless child revisited. In J. Qvortrup (ed.), *Studies in Modern Childhood: Society, Agency, Culture*. London: Palgrave Macmillan.

6
Children's rights from a social work perspective
Towards a lifeworld orientation

Didier Reynaert and Rudi Roose

1. Introduction

At the beginning of the 21st century, UK social work expert Nigel Parton stated that:

> While the emergence of modern social work occurred in the nineteenth century at a similar time to many of the mainstream social sciences such as sociology, psychology, criminology and so on, social work is still seen as 'newer', 'younger', 'less developed'.
> *(Parton, 2000: 450)*

Social work is indeed mainly appreciated as a *profession*, a vocation that requires certain skills and qualifications, rather than as an *academic discipline*. Slowly, this reality is changing. Social work is increasingly regarded as a proper domain of knowledge with a particular object, distinct theories and theoretical concepts and specific research methods, institutionalized at universities in separate research departments or academic degrees. The recently revised international definition of social work gives evidence of this progress:

> Social work is a practice-based profession and an academic discipline that promotes social change and development, social cohesion, and the empowerment and liberation of people. Principles of social justice, human rights, collective responsibility and respect for diversities are central to social work. Underpinned by theories of social work, social sciences, humanities and indigenous knowledge, social work engages people and structures to address life challenges and enhance wellbeing.
>
> The above definition may be amplified at national and/or regional levels.
> *(International Federation of Social Workers, 2014)*

Walter Lorenz (2008), an authority in the field of European social work, amongst others (see e.g. Sharland, 2012; Göppner and Hämäläinen, 2007), notes that social work acquired a distinct identity as an academic discipline. One vital characteristic of this identity is the framework of human rights and social justice (Healy and Link, 2012; Lundy, 2011; Ife, 2010a, 2010b, 2001;

Borowski, 2007; Reichert, 2007), as mentioned in the international definition. The international definition not only considers human rights as the core values for the discipline of social work but also for the profession, to the extent that social work can be regarded, as both Healy (2008) and Hare (2004) acknowledge, as a 'human rights profession'. Following the assumptions of the introductory chapter, we consider children's rights as a particularization of human rights. Therefore, children's rights belong to both the ethical and theoretical foundations of social work.

In this chapter, we explore the framework of children's rights from the discipline of social work. We do this from a generic point of view, meaning that we discuss issues that transcend particular terrains in social work such as child protection, child care, youth work, child psychiatry, etc. Instead, two interrelated key concerns that are fundamental in the debate on children's rights from a social work perspective will be explored. First, we will go into the implications of the shift in 'child image' for social work. Second, we will examine how these new ideas on the way we look at children are institutionalized in society through conceptions of 'childhood' and what this means for social work. In analysing these issues, we will make use of concrete examples coming from a variety of domains in social work. In both cases, we will subject these evolutions to critical reflection. What these reflections unify is their critical approach to the understanding of children's rights 'from above'. In trying to deal with these critiques in social work, we will subsequently present some alternative ideas in how children's rights can be understood. We present these ideas under the notion of a 'lifeworld orientation' of children's rights, an alternative paradigmatic stance that seeks to understand children's rights 'from below'. However, we begin this chapter by explaining the complex identity of social work. Because social work emerged as part of the development of (Western) nation states, it is important to acknowledge that social work encompasses different 'architectures', depending on the historical, cultural, political and socio-economic context of a particular nation state. Consequently, the way children's rights are understood from a social work perspective logically rests on the social work tradition in which it is shaped. Since social work derives its architecture from its contextual embedment in a particular reality, very different traditions of social work exist throughout the world (for a further elaboration of this issue, see e.g. Gray *et al.*, 2012; Gray, 2005; Gray and Fook, 2004). Gray *et al.* (2012) for instance refer to 'indigenous social work' as an alternative for Euro-American social work approaches. They explain that indigenous social work is culturally relevant social work 'responsive to local and national contexts worldwide' (Gray *et al.*, 2012: xxvi). Furthermore, they argue that, although indigenous social work is rooted in local contexts and traditions, it is at the same time 'consistent with the larger purpose of professional values and ethics' (Gray *et al.*, 2012: 5). Payne (2005) too references alternatives to Western social work theory like for instance Gandhian social work in India or perspectives from China and Africa. In the remainder of this chapter, we further explore the discipline of social work from a 'Western perspective' as both the authors are from the West and do their research in a Western context. However, as Shardlow (2007) explains with reference to the practice of family group conferences in New Zealand, even Western traditions of social work nowadays are highly influenced by non-Western traditions. What he is saying is that social work practice and theory is mutually influenced across national and cultural boundaries.

2. The fragmented identity of social work

As the international definition of social work demonstrates, current ideas of social work have a universal orientation with the recognition of human rights and social justice as key assumptions. Notwithstanding this universal orientation, Penna *et al.* (2000) point out the 'dual configuration' of social work: linked to an international agenda with global concerns (i.e. human rights and social justice) on the one hand, strongly embedded in the nation state (see also Ife, 2001) on the other hand. Especially this latter feature, according to Lorenz (2008), presents social work as a 'picture of disunity'. He states that:

> The most striking feature of social work's current identity is the fragmentation of the profession and discipline, not just in an international context, where it presents a bewildering variety of professional titles and intellectual discourses, but also at national level, where in every country several professional profiles exist in parallel, sometimes contesting each other's territories.
>
> *(Lorenz, 2009: 145)*

Reasons for this, still following Lorenz (2008), are to be found in linguistic division, a variety of academic discourses with different analytical and conceptual fields, diverse social policy contexts and different histories of practice. While generally, this fragmentation is considered as a weakness of the discipline, mainly because as a result social works lacks a clear identity, Lorenz argues that exactly this division is a strength of social work. This is so because it emphasizes the *social* dimension of social work, i.e. being based in and linked to the way in which society defines well-being, integration, solidarity, etc. This is evident from the way social work progressed from a 'charitable practice' towards a 'human rights-based practice'.

Originally, social work emerged as a project of the modern nation state at the end of the nineteenth century, where it operated in the 'social sphere', the hybrid space between the private sphere of the household and the public sphere of the state (Jordan and Parton, 2004). It formed part of a political agenda that aimed at realizing social pacification and cohesion (Payne and Campling, 2005; Parton, 2000). Social work had to deal with the consequences of industrialization, in particular with social problems such as proletarianization and impoverishment, defined by French historian Jacques Donzelot (1979) as the 'social question'. The social work mandate was to maintain social order by social integration. As such, social work was part of a process of 'civilization', characterized by its disciplining nature and mainly executed through private initiatives in the sphere of the church and philanthropy (Payne and Campling, 2005).

A paradigm shift in social work occurred after World War II. Besides law enforcement and regulation of the labour market, the post-war nation state was commissioned to warrant greater social equality. This was due to the devastating consequences of the World War and inspired by the Universal Declaration of Human Rights of 1948. The focus on social equality acknowledged the recognition of fundamental rights for all citizens. This meant a reorientation of the socio-political goals of the nation state. Governments became increasingly responsible for guaranteeing a right to live a life in human dignity for all (Maeseele, 2012; Witkin, 1998). The ideological foundations of human rights, on which the post-war nation state was built, required also a reorientation of social work. Social work transformed from a charitable and philanthropic practice to a human rights-based practice (Maeseele, 2012). As a result, social work was no longer merely an instrument of social control in the hands of private organizations. It grew into a relatively autonomous actor within the welfare state aiming at emancipation and social equality. As such, the distinction between the social sphere and the public sphere faded as social work became part of public social policy.

It is important to notice that, notwithstanding this paradigm shift, social work did not shake off its old cloak of social control. The controlling character remained a fundamental trait in the new configuration of social work, where it came into tension with the more emancipating and liberating feature of social work. This 'double character', according to Roose et al. (2010), typifies social work: at the same time controlling and emancipating; disciplining and empowering; adjusting and liberating (see also Jordan and Parton, 2004).

The development of social work based on the foundations of human rights was equally noticeable in the field of child and family social work. In 1959, the Declaration on the Rights of the Child was adopted, building upon the 1924 Declaration of Geneva. Although strongly oriented towards the *protection* of children, the child in the 1959 Declaration became more and more portrayed as a *subject*, rather than an *object* of rights. As such, a changing childhood image increasingly recognizing the agency of children was expressed as a manifestation of the striving towards a greater social equality between children and adults. A more definite translation of a human rights approach for children followed in 1989 with the adoption of the United Nations Convention on the Rights of the Child (CRC). At least two elements are of importance in this development. First, a convention adds a legally binding character to the moral value of a declaration. This created the possibility for a movement towards stronger legal protection of children. Second, the CRC recognized protection, provision, as well as participation rights. These rights have to be considered in interdependence and comprehensiveness (for a thorough description of the value of the CRC: see Chapter 3 of Verhellen in this Handbook). The recognition of participation rights, especially, is indicated as an important milestone (Archard, 2004). It implied the acknowledgement of children as co-citizens in our society. The CRC subsequently became an important instrument in the expansion of a social policy directed at children and young people (Therborn, 1996). It became an important instrument for social work through the development of practices that are based on the framework of children's rights, thereby – as stated in the international definition of social work – striving for social justice.

So, depending on the social, cultural, historical and political context, both social policies and socio-political goals differ; and consequently also social work and the way in which social work deals with social control and emancipation will emanate in different ways. With regard to Europe, two different traditions of social work can be discerned, often described as an *Anglo-Saxon tradition* and a *continental tradition* (see e.g. Crimmens, 2006; Hämäläinen, 2003). However, these labels seem to oversimplify both history and current reality, as these demographic connotations do not correspond with the diversity of approaches within one defined socio-cultural region. Therefore, we prefer to make a distinction between relational social work on the one hand and structural social work on the other hand, as both these conceptual traits can be recognized within regions, in and outside Europe.

Within the tradition of *relational social work*, social work is considered to satisfy needs, shortcomings, deficits, etc. of service-users in a variety of problem situations. Social work is thus an answer to social problems, in particular problems associated with people living in vulnerable situations such as poverty. This answer is dominantly individual-oriented with social work operating at a relational level. It aims at creating a (therapeutic) relationship of trust between clients and social work in order to support people in developing the abilities to deal with social problems and to realize their rights (van Ewijk, 2010). Because this kind of social work does not engage with social structures and society as a whole, but contrary falls back on individual relations with people, it is argued that this approach is characterized by social integration, understood as individual participation in social life (Roose et al., 2010; Lorenz, 2005). From a positive viewpoint, the role of social work then is considered to support people in their endeavour to connect with the conventional values and norms in society, in accordance with a societal consensus on what 'good citizenship' is about. From a more negative viewpoint, the activating and controlling character of social work is highlighted. Social work from this latter point of view is an instrument in function of goals that do not primarily aim at enhancing social welfare but rather pursue economic or security objectives like participation in the labour market or prevention of crime (e.g. Bradt and Bouverne-De Bie, 2009; Lorenz, 2005).

In the *structural tradition* of social work, both community and society are fundamental concepts. Structural social work is characterized by its orientation on the socialization of people in the community and society. Practices in the tradition of structural social work support people in their learning process to become part of a community. By thematizing the community and/or society, structural social work aims at being an answer to the strongly individual approach in relational social work. It aims at contributing to participation and citizenship in society (Hämäläinen, 2003) by providing the social conditions in order for people to realize their rights. The main aim thus is not to integrate people in a pre-structured social order. In the *structural tradition* of social work, the structure of the social order itself is questioned, including the way citizens (can) relate to this order (Coussée et al., 2010). Although these different traditions in social work can be conceptually differentiated, the distinction is of course not absolute. In reality, elements of both traditions and discussions are intertwined. Hämäläinen (2003) argues that in the past years both traditions have increasingly converged or even integrated. When we will discuss children's rights from the perspective of social work further on in this chapter, elements of both traditions will be combined.

3. Social work, children's rights and images of the child

Interventions of social work are never neutral. They are driven by presumptions of different kinds: ideas on human beings, (un)wellbeing, the role of the state, empowerment, etc. In the case of social work with children and young people, presuppositions on what the 'child' or 'childhood' consist of is of paramount importance. A key notion in this area is the 'agency' of children (Stoecklin, 2012; Valentine, 2011: James, 2009). In social work, debate on the notion of agency originated largely from the field of child protection and youth care (see e.g. Bolin, 2014). This is not a coincidence, as exactly in these fields, the use of power from social workers or parents is present in a very explicit way, often neglecting the agency of children. It was exactly against the absence of a consciousness that children are also active human beings, with individual capacities to make choices and to express their own ideas, that the children's rights movement arose. The children's rights movement, as an amalgam of (organized) initiatives in- and outside social work, criticized the *social status* of children common in youth care. They labelled the status of children as 'the incompetent child', an image of children emphasizing them as objects in need of protection because of their vulnerability (Reynaert et al., 2009). Verhellen explains that from this understanding of children, the child is regarded as 'not-yet-being' (Verhellen, 2000: 16). In the same line, Matthews and Limb (1998: 67) describe children as 'adults in waiting', lacking adult competencies and undergoing their status in a passive way. Consequently, the incompetent child was not accorded any responsibility (Such and Walker, 2005). Furthermore, the children's rights movement questioned the *legal status* of children. Especially, youth care was criticized for its poor legal nature, resulting in an unlimited possibility to intervene in the lives of children, ignoring the most fundamental principles of fair trial (Muncie, 2002).

In its ambition to express an alternative child-image, the children's rights movement considered children as social actors, as independent meaning-makers, active agents and autonomous human beings, constructing their lives in their own right (Reynaert et al., 2009). Complementing the plea for an alternative child-image, the children's rights movement sought for the recognition of a legal status for children. The agenda-setting of the children's rights movement, containing both these claims, was primarily realized in the fields of child protection and youth care. Large-scale social institutions of youth care were condemned as they make children 'disappear in the organization'. Even so, the geographic separation of youth care institutions – often isolated from the daily life in communities – was criticized for creating a rupture with everyday life and contacts with the outside world, thereby further isolating children from society. Opposing that was a raft of initiatives to grant social care to children within a tendency towards de-institutionalization (for an elaboration of the issue of alternative care for children: see Cantwell, Chapter 15 in this Handbook). The (legal) recognition of the agency of children was likewise part of a broader ambition for the acknowledgement of participation rights of children in child and family social work. It resulted in a striking growth of new initiatives that put children's participation rights at centre stage (Thomas, 2007; Cavet and Sloper, 2004). This tendency can likely be observed at the larger level of social policy. Melton (2005), amongst others, observes that children's rights offer a (judicial) framework to rethink child-oriented policies in the direction of ensuring children's dignity. Significant for social work is the importance that Davis and Powell (2003), together with other authors (e.g. Kabasinskaite and Bak, 2006; Woll, 2001), evoke when they point at two important aspects of implementing the CRC in child-oriented policies. First, state parties should take steps to provide child services and child care facilities (*access* to child services). Second, state parties should ensure that child services and child care facilities meet certain standards (*quality* of child care) (Reynaert et al., 2009).

Scholarly work on children's rights (in social work) seems to have been preoccupied with the shift in childhood image from the incompetent child towards the autonomous child.

> The image of the autonomous child is considered as an evolution to a more human dealing with children in both practice and policy. It is without doubt to the merit of the children's rights movement that it has grasped the concept of individualization … and brought to the fore a group in society that has for a long time been invisible and discriminated against on the base of age …, thereby opening the discussion on the position of children in our society … .
>
> *(Reynaert et al., 2009, 522–523)*

However, caution remains in relation to this new image of childhood. The children's rights agenda is indeed not free from 'critique'. We will subsequently engage in three issues of discussion in relation to the new childhood image of the autonomous child.

A first issue concerns the essence of the new childhood image of the autonomous child itself. Certain (dominant) interpretations of children's agency regard children as independent, autonomous human beings that have to be granted the same rights as those recognized for adults. The presumption is that human beings, including children, are capable of rational reasoning when facing choices and skilled to act appropriately, based upon rational reasoning. It is a position that starts from an egalitarian doctrine, emphasizing equal treatment, freedom and rights to self-determination (Reynaert and Roose, 2014). The expectation is that children know their own needs, interests, societal expectations, etc. and can deal with these in a socially suitable way. However, it is questionable whether the interpretation of autonomy as an outcome of rational reasoning corresponds with reality. Ethicist Freddy Mortier (2002) argues that the idea of the autonomous, rational human being is likely to be a *myth* that, neither for children nor for adults, corresponds with the way people in general act in daily life. To demonstrate this statement, Mortier discusses the issue of granting the right to vote to young people from the age of 16, a proposal of several (children's rights) organizations across Europe. Based on the argument that children are incompetent, this right is currently not assigned to minors. However, Mortier argues that competence is not a condition for adults to be granted the right to vote, while the ability of adults to understand complex political decisions is probably as limited as that of young people. What Mortier illustrates is that the misconception of the idea of rational reasoning and corresponding acting neither for children, nor for adults is consistent with the real acting of children and adults in daily practice. Generally, people, children and adults, act in interdependency with others (Dean, 2009) or act very irrationally or contextually. This observation brings Mortier to the understanding that it might be much more acceptable that 'we are all children' rather than that we are all adults (Mortier, 2002).

A second issue recounts the way the idea of the autonomous child often operates in practice. Social work practices increasingly view children (and their parents) as 'entrepreneurial citizens' (Muncie, 2006; Vandenbroeck and Bouverne-De Bie, 2006; Masschelein and Quaghebeur, 2005), assuming that they can, as a consequence of rational reasoning, independently realize, advocate and enforce their rights. As such, a norm (i.e. being able to act autonomously) is imposed upon a group of children without taking into account the great diversity that exists with children in terms of for instance socio-economic or cultural background. Nor is there any consideration on the diversity of child-rearing contexts in which children grow up. The underlying dynamic is that of 'homogenization': this new childhood image of the autonomous child is generalized to the whole group of children and accordingly presented as a new norm in education. The problem with this dynamic is that it starts to function as a standard against which a certain situation is weighed. Such a yardstick includes a certain group in society – those children who conform to the standard of being autonomous – but, at the same time, excludes a group of children from society (Reynaert et al., 2010). This is what legal philosopher Koen Raes (2001) calls the 'paradox of equality': applying an equal norm in unequal situations creates inequality. Practices in the social work of parenting support give evidence of this dynamic. Parenting support using the framework of children's rights acknowledges the participation rights of children. The idea of family education that is (implicitly) promoted throughout these practices is that of the 'negotiation household', an education model that replaced the 'old' model of the 'command household' (Vanobbergen et al., 2006). Hence, negotiating in family education is, from a children's rights perspective, considered as the desirable way of child-rearing. However, negotiating requires certain skills and capacities that are not present or desired in all family contexts. Vandenbroeck and Bouverne-De Bie (2006) point at the fact that negotiation might favour certain groups of children and parents, i.e. those who are familiar with negotiating rationalities. Consequently, this means that at the same time, families who do not comply with the new norm of the negotiating household risk of becoming labelled as 'bad parents'. The question then arises what to do with these families. In such cases, Roose and De Bie (2008) warn for social work practices that operate as 'disciplinary action', where children and parents are expected to behave in a particular way and act as active and accountable citizens, as this can result in subjecting children and parents to further marginalization and exclusion (Roose et al., 2013). Such a dynamic links up with the controlling character of social work where social work, although aiming at empowerment and emancipation, ends up as a new instrument of 'civilization'.

A final issue relates to the legal translation of this new child-image of the autonomous child, where underlying values such as self-determination or freedom are defined in legal rules or a legal status. It suggests that legal instruments can have the ability to arrange social relationships and interactions between people, for instance between children and their parents or between children and social workers. However, especially in the context of social work, that is often involved in complex and ambiguous educational settings, translating these relationships and interactions in legal terms risks reinforcing conflictual relations between people, strengthening dichotomies between children and parents or between children and social workers (Roose and De-Bie, 2008; Huntington, 2006; Cockburn, 2005). Likewise, it also risks separating certain (problematic) situations from the parties involved and turning them over to so-called 'neutral others', for instance a mediator or a judge. This can result in an alienated experience of the stakeholders, resulting in a loss of power over the situation (Raes, 2001) and eventually creating 'winners' and 'losers' (Holland and Scourfield, 2004; Pupavac, 2001). Such a legal approach conceives rights as an end of dialogue rather than as a starting point for a communal search for a solution (Roose and De Bie, 2008; Huntington, 2006). The discussion on the claim of children's rights organizations worldwide to legally ban corporal punishment can illustrate this point (see also Reynaert et al., 2010). The prohibition of corporal punishment by means of a law starts from the assumption that a legal instrument can resolve – or at least can contribute to a solution of – a problem in education, i.e. the use of violence. However, this presumption ignores the complexity of child-rearing contexts and the different meanings that are given to corporal punishment by children, parents and social workers.

> By referring to legal principles, the debate on the ban of corporal punishment then is positioned on the abstract level of what, according to social acceptable norms, is regarded as a 'good education'. It also creates dichotomies between good parents, for whom prohibition is already a reality, and other parents, who still use corporal punishment in raising their child … . For the latter, a legal prohibition of corporal punishment can result in being labelled a 'bad parent' and possibly being criminalized.
>
> *(Reynaert et al., 2010: 64)*

What we criticise here is not law in itself, but the way law is often used in practice. Braye and Preston-Shoot (2006) detect three guiding assumptions about the relationship between law and social work practice: i) The belief that law provides a clear map for welfare practice; ii) The belief that the legal map is the only one practitioners need; iii) The belief that if the map is accurate enough (i.e. that the law is sound), it will lead safely to the destination. These presumptions consider legal frameworks in social work as an end of dialogue. A legal ban on corporal punishment could be justifiable if we consider it a starting point for a dialogue on the actual behaviour in education. Law is then considered as a frame of reference or an instrument that makes it possible to question educational interactions, given the complex and pluralistic educational contexts and, if necessary, to shape these interactions in a different way (Reynaert et al., 2010).

4. Social work, children's rights and the institutionalization of childhood

An important debate in the tradition of structural social work in relation to children's rights is the social and cultural structuring of the way we perceive children and childhood in our society, i.e. the debate on the institutionalization of childhood. Because of the assumption in the 'old' child-image of the incompetent child that children are vulnerable and therefore in need of protection, children were excluded from the adult world. Instead, a separate 'world' for children was created in which they were prepared for adulthood. This 'youthland' (Smith, 2007; Verhellen, 2000) or 'youth moratorium' (Zinnecker, 2000) is defined by Honig (2008: 201) as '… preparatory arenas that implement a principle of integration by means of separation'. Generally, childhood was considered as a period of socialization in or preparation for adulthood or a growth towards autonomy (e.g. Such and Walker, 2005). Therefore, institutions such as the school, youth work, youth care and so on were established at the end of the nineteenth century through the first children's laws (Benporath, 2003). This institutionalized youth land is still today the 'architecture' or 'grammar' of childhood, at least in Western societies. Marc Depaepe (1998), professor in history of education, terms this process of progressive institutionalization of childhood as 'educationalization' ('Pädagogisierung'). Educationalization refers to the increased attention that is being given to the pedagogical aspects of the daily life of children as it is apparent from the establishment of various child-centred institutions.

In a context of a broader social contestation at the end of the 1960s, the historically developed youth land was likewise questioned. It was argued, inter alia by the children's rights movement, that the new child-image of the autonomous child raised questions in relation to the legitimization of a separate world for children. Breaking through the moratorium became the central claim of the children's rights movement under the radical slogan 'bring children back into society' (Verhellen, 1998: 486). Children were not merely seen as the future generation. Their current presence in society is equally meaningful and should therefore be considered as such (James and James, 2004).

The discussion on the institutionalized youth land has an important topicality, also for social work. Current developments in social work give us an antagonistic illustration of the meaning of the institutionalized youth land. On the one hand there is a process of 'blurring boundaries' with interventions from social work breaching the borders of the institutionalized youth land. In the case of child offending for instance, we can observe an increasing tendency towards the recognition of the criminal responsibility of children, at least from a certain age (for an elaboration of this issue: see Liefaard on juvenile justice, Chapter 14 in this Handbook). This principle breaks with the long-recognized principle of the neutralization of the criminal responsibility of children as it was introduced at the end of the nineteenth century under the protection model of juvenile justice. The starting point was the recognition that children could not be held responsible when committing an offense as a consequence of their status as a minor. Accordingly, in case a minor committed an offence, he was not punished, as it is the case in the criminal justice system for adults, but instead re-educated (Put and Walgrave, 2006). The reintroduction of the recognition of the criminal responsibility of children in current debates on juvenile justice and children's rights again links up closely with the traditional model of criminal justice that is common for adults (Muncie, 2008). Simultaneously with the blurring of boundaries, an opposing development of 'strengthened boundaries' takes place. The breaching of the borders of the institutionalized youth land is indeed not that radical that it results in an equalization of children and adults. The particularity of children remains recognized, and what happens, according to Mortier (2002), is that children as a group acquire similar instruments of power as adults to defend their specific interests. Returning to the case of juvenile justice, models that acknowledge the criminal responsibility of children, inspired by the framework of children's rights, do not aim at introducing a retributive treatment, which characterizes the criminal justice model for adults. Instead, they hold on to the educative character of a protection model and aim at re-educating child offenders to respect the offended rule; and this in a specialized and/or separated system for minors. At the same time, re-education should take place in a system that acknowledges the principles of fair trial for minors (Goldson and Muncie, 2006).

This twin process of antagonistic developments with regard to the institutionalized youth land is often very confusing in understanding current issues in relation to children. It is likewise confusing to understand how social work influences these antagonistic developments and whether its impact is going in the desired direction, i.e. results in more social justice for children. We will subsequently discuss two issues that are important to face from a children's rights perspective when discussing the institutionalized youth land. Both issues are related to the question of redistribution of social resources by social work.

The first issue is a critique related to fair redistribution of social resources *within* the institutionalized youth land. The children's rights movement defined a group in society based on age that became the target group for whom more equal power relations is pursued. This is done, at least with regard to the provision rights of children, by holding on to the institutionalized youth land. Recalling the example of child offending, we explained that ideas to reform systems that deal with child offending from a children's rights perspective attempt to adopt specialized or separated systems for children. As such, children are separated from adults. However, what is often overlooked is that this separation has a dissimilar impact on children. Social institutions for children such as schools, welfare organization, sport clubs, cultural organizations, etc. often operate in a very selective way vis-à-vis children in at least two directions. On the one hand, some children profit more from the same provisions than others, who consequently profit less. This is what has been called the 'Matthew effect', a redistribution dynamic in social policy that shows that people from higher income groups benefit relatively more from social services than people from lower income groups. As such, people from higher income groups appeal to more public expenditures (Ghysels and Van Lancker, 2010). In relation to children, this dynamic has been shown in several domains of social work and education. On the other hand, children from socially vulnerable groups, when coming into contact with social institutions, experience the controlling and sanctioning aspects of these institutions relatively more than the supporting ones. This idea is elaborated in the theory of social vulnerability as it was developed, amongst others, by Vettenburg (see e.g. Vettenburg *et al.*, 2013; Berten *et al.*, 2013). These observations demonstrate that other dimensions in the life of children might be much more important in striving for more equality than the child–adult (age) dimension. The impact of, for instance, the socio-economic dimension or the cultural dimension can hardly be overestimated. Consequently, extending the institutionalized youth land by the realization of provision rights for children should similarly provoke the question as to how this institutionalized youth land impacts on children and how a negative impact can be avoided. Buelens and Mortier (1989) remind us that if the recognition of provision rights for children is not tied with efforts for (socio-economic) redistribution, this will not stop one from participating in an unequal distribution of social goods. This is an important topic of attention in relation to for instance the issue of poverty. For children growing up in poverty, often additional provisions are made available. However, when these provisions are not embedded in a broader social, economic and political context, making use of these additional provisions does not make one less poor in a socio-economic sense (Roose *et al.*, 2014).

A second critique concerns an issue of fair redistribution of social resources *outside* the institutionalized youth land. This matter concerns a subject of intergenerational solidarity. As we argued before, claims of children for the realization of a particular right can come into conflict with claims of adults for other rights. This can become problematic when the question of intergenerational justice and solidarity, i.e. the question how the institutionalized youth land relates to the adult world, is avoided and children's rights are cut loose from human rights. The case of the use of public space can illustrate this. In Flanders, several cases emerged where children playing in public places (kindergartens, playgrounds, etc.) caused disturbances in the neighbourhood. Residents living in the neighbourhood of kindergartens and playgrounds complained about the intensity of the noise that children made. They saw this as a violation of their right to rest and privacy. As a counteraction, children and their sympathizers united and claimed their right to play. This case shows that problems related to the condition of 'living together' cannot be translated as adversarial interests, certainly not at the individual level. These matters call for a certain kind of collectiveness and solidarity between children and adults (De Visscher and Bouverne-De Bie, 2006) and raise the question of fair and equal redistribution of social resources across all members of society. Children's rights organizations too often seem to ignore these issues and focus merely on the interests of children.

These critiques on the institutionalized youth land do not mean that we are in favour of abolishing the separate world for children and young people. This would be both a-historical and naïve. It does mean, however, that the (scholarly) debate on children's rights often remains too silent on the diversity of contexts within which children make use of resources situated in the institutionalized youth land or how these resources relate to resources in the broader society. We will further deal with these critiques in our final part.

5. Social work and children's rights: A 'lifeworld orientation'

What the critiques as discussed throughout this chapter have in common is that they all oppose a certain epistemological foundation of the world and of humanity, one that emanates from scientific objectivism. In this philosophical position, it is assumed that reality can exist objectively. Consequently, only one correct description of this reality can be thought about as 'truth'. So, children's rights need to be understood as a set of objective norms presented in the form of legal rules. Children's rights-based social work from this point of view comes down to choosing the 'right' technique that can contribute to the implementation of children's rights in the lives of children. Social work practices of this type are supposed to be neutral and power-free (Reynaert et al., 2009). However, this point of view denies the discursive character of children's rights-based social work practices. As we have illustrated with several examples, children's rights are shaped out of a process of meaning-making that occurs in the lifeworld of people.

The concept of 'lifeworld' arises from the work of the German philosopher Edmund Husserl, who introduced it as the central notion of his phenomenological theory (Husserl, 1970). Husserl defined the lifeworld as the 'horizon' against which observations and actions acquire meaning. It is the social, political, cultural and historical background that constitutes subjective human experience. The lifeworld in Husserl's conceptualization is both subject-relative and generally structured. Each person has its own subjective lifeworld but at the same time, through intersubjective experience, people constitute their common lifeworld consisting of prevailing structures. The concept of lifeworld was further developed by Jürgen Habermas (1987) in his theory of communicative action in which he distinguished the practical rationality of the 'lifeworld' from the instrumental rationality of the 'system'. He argued that in modern societies, the lifeworld has been 'colonized' by instrumental rationality, by which people become means for political and economic ends. In the field of social work, the notion of lifeworld was applied by Klaus Grunwald and Hans Thiersch (2009). They explain that a lifeworld orientation 'uses the issues, crises and experiences within service users' lifeworld situations as reference points' (Grunwald and Thiersch, 2009: 133). It is a contextual orientation in social work that starts from the daily life experiences of people in pursuing human dignity and social justice (Roets et al., 2013). In the words of Australian Emeritus Professor and human rights expert in social work, Jim Ife (2004), it is about 'ordinary people constructing and reconstructing ideas of human rights in their day-to-day lives'. Important for social work is the recognition that in a lifeworld orientation personal meaning-making of an individual needs to be understood in the complex interplay with social, political, cultural and historical traits of a context. These include, amongst other things, provisions and resources presented by social work. As Roets et al. (2013) state, it is about the '… dynamic and interpretable ways in which material, social and cultural resources as well as discourses are viewed as constraints, opportunities and limitations for children to practise their agency, constituting their lived experiences and indicating the state of children's welfare.' Social work practices of children's rights are considered as experience-based learning practices of children with parents, social workers and other stakeholders constructing rights in their intersubjectivity with each other (Todd, 2007) and in confrontation with the arrangements present in the lifeworld. In the next part, we further elaborate this lifeworld orientation in children's rights-based social work, distinguishing three main features of this approach: i) a 'resourcist view' on children's rights, ii) children's rights as capabilities, and iii) children's rights as an individual and collective learning process.

5.1. A 'resourcist view' on children's rights

Agency, as a fundamental notion in the framework of children's rights is, as we have argued throughout this chapter, often understood in both a very individualistic and essentialist way. We showed a number of risks associated with such an interpretation of agency. However, when we consider agency, or in a broader sense participation rights, in interdependence and comprehensiveness with provision and protection rights, then agency is not to be seen merely as an individual competence that someone has or has not and that distinguishes children from adults. This division ignores the important differences that exist between children or between adults or the difference that exists in the living conditions of children and adults. In contrast, a 'resourcist view' (Mortier, 2002) understands agency as the capacity to exercise a positive freedom – the freedom to do those things that one considers to be important – and which only can be realized under the condition of having access to basic resources. These resources are situated in the inter-relational dimension of children's rights-based social work practices, i.e. in the inter-relation with others. These resources are equally situated in the structural dimension of children's rights-based social work practices, i.e. in the existence of collective provisions addressing and supporting children in their capability to act. Seen from a resourcist view, the difference between children and adults is not that special (Dixon and Nussbaum, 2012), as both children and adults need resources to realize their agency.

5.2. Children's rights as capabilities

A resourcist-view brings about the awareness that the way in which we put into practice children's rights differs not much from the realization of human rights. Next to that, the recognition that the interests of children cannot be understood without associating them with the interests of others in society, strengthens our belief that children's rights need essentially be considered in relation to human rights. Nevertheless, as Nussbaum (1997) argues, there is a large difference in the subjective needs for social resources that people need in order to realize their agency. Furthermore, there is an inequality in the access to resources that people need to support them in realizing their rights.

> An approach focusing on resources does not go deep enough to diagnose obstacles that can be present even when resources seem to be adequately spread around, causing individuals to fail to avail themselves of opportunities that they in some sense have, such as free public education, the right to vote, or the right to work.
>
> *(Nussbaum, 1997: 284)*

From this critique, connection is sought with the actual lifeworld of people, raising the question not only with regard to the extent that social resources are present, but equally, in how far these social resources enable people to function in a fully human way. Human rights (of children) from this perspective are seen as 'capabilities', i.e. people's real opportunities for functioning and choice (Dixon and Nussbaum, 2012: 557). The capabilities approach presents important elements to situate human and children's rights in the lifeworld of people themselves (Stoecklin and Bonvin, 2014).

5.3. Children's rights as an individual and collective learning process

Referring to social work practices of children's rights as an *individual learning process* means that children, in interaction and interrelation with others, seek at understanding and interpreting their lifeworld, including the understanding of their social relationships with others. Children's rights can be considered as a sensitizing frame of reference that supports children in this process of interpretation. By defining children's rights-based social work practices as a learning process, we argue that children's rights cannot be understood without the interaction with others and without the horizon of the lifeworld. The *learning dimension* of the social work practices of children's rightslies exactly in its contextual orientation. This presupposes an open learning process that is not directed at a pre-structured or pre-defined social norm in society. On the contrary, learning entails dealing with uncertainty and unpredictability, with learning process outcomes that can be very diverse. We accept that there is a plurality of interests and entitlements in contemporary society and that this plurality refers to a diversity of socio-historical, economic and cultural contexts in which children grow up. In our understanding this also means that we have to recognize that different understandings of human dignity may exist, depending on these contexts, and that consequently also different understandings of children's rights can occur. Inspired by Mouffe, we can call this a 'mestiza conception' of children's rights. This contains a context-specific interpretation of children's rights, thus leaving space for different meanings, depending on these contexts (Mouffe, 2005).

The reference to the *collective* dimension of the learning process implies that social work practices of children's rights are not only directed at the daily experiences of children and their surroundings. It necessarily presupposes the recognition that learning also relates to culture and to structuring and restructuring this culture. An understanding of human dignity is equally shaped from what German social pedagogue Klaus Mollenhauer (1993) calls the 'heritage of the social structure', i.e. the structure of our forms of life or our cultural contents containing our social regulations. Practices of children's rights can only be relevant if they recognize that both the individual level and the structural level are interrelated (Flathman, 1976), and that this interrelation is latently present in these practices itself. Social work practices of children's rights should make these hidden processes explicit. Social work practices of children's rights should reveal these 'social rules' so that children, parents, social workers, etc. can learn to know these rules, position themselves in relation to these rules and even learn to change these rules (Mollenhauer, 1993). So, children's rights-based social work '… should be approached in a fashion that includes the analysis, understanding and reading of power relations and social forces so as to enable a struggle to change those power relations that impede the full realization of human rights' (CEDAL, 1996). A similar approach to social work practices of children's rights 'from below' (Baxi, 1997; Ife, 2001, 2010a; Ife and Fiske, 2006; Stammers, 2009) requires existing power relations, that co-shape the lifeworlds of children, to be questioned, with the aim of changing these power relations towards greater respect for the human dignity of children. Implementing children's rights is not a neutral, value-free or power-free practice of applying the right technique, but basically entails a political character aimed at abolishing the exclusion of children from society.

6. Epilogue: Limitations of the discipline of social work for researching children's rights

We conclude this chapter with some critical reflections regarding the 'shortcomings' or 'risks' that are relative to researching children's rights from the discipline of social work.

A first issue that needs further understanding is how a relational tradition in social work can go together with a structural tradition. Trying to be engaged in both and connect them together in an integrated theory risks resulting in the neglect of one dimension or the other. Hence it is important for social work to also keep the interrelational in view, as social work that focuses solely on the structural would also be invalid, as it risks neglecting the personal grievances of individual clients. By extension, structural social work is often weak in offering practical guidelines, besides raising awareness of the complexity of current social problems in society. However, it is argued that a critical analysis of society and societal conditions under which people have to live their lives and realizing human/children's rights has a practical finality in itself, for instance in involving clients in critical analysis by giving them voice (Payne, 2005).

A second issue that necessarily requires further theoretical deepening in social work theory is how to deal with the danger of social relativism that could go together with a lifeworld orientation. When it is acknowledged that both an individual and collective learning process is of fundamental importance in a lifeworld orientation, and that the outcome of this learning process can be very diverse, than this might suggest that we can lapse into some kind of social relativism where 'anything goes'. Belgian political theorist Chantal Mouffe acknowledges that learning processes such as the ones at stake here are fundamentally shaped in a field of tension that she calls 'conflictual consensus'. This means that there should be a (temporary) consensus on the ethical and political values like, for instance, freedom and equality, but dissensus on the interpretations of these values. Applied to children's rights-based social work practices, this means that the principles of children's rights included in the CRC, or translations in specific laws are (temporary) not under discussion but, at the same time, the interpretation of these principles should be the subject of deliberative dialogue. Children's rights-based social work, both practice and theory, is precisely about bringing these diverse interpretations into 'conflict'.

Questions for debate and discussion

- What are the strengths and weaknesses, opportunities and threats of a lifeworld orientation in social work regarding children's rights?
- What are the opportunities and challenges for the recognition of agency for children both at the interrelational and the structural level?
- How can we understand children's rights from 'non-Western' traditions in social work and how are they related to a lifeworld orientation?
- How can we construct children's rights starting from a lifeworld perspective and at the same time acknowledge the formal framework of the CRC, without relapsing into legal translations of rights?
- How can we avoid social relativism with regard to social practices of children's rights if a lifeworld orientation is adopted in social work?

References

Archard, D. (2004). *Children: Rights and Childhood* (2nd ed.). London: Routledge.

Baxi, U. (1997). Human rights education: The promise of the third millennium? In G. Andreopoulous and R.P. Claude (eds), *Human Rights Education for the Twenty-First Century*. Philadelphia, PA: University of Pennsylvania Press.

Benporath, S.R. (2003). Autonomy and vulnerability: On just relations between adults and children. *Journal of Philosophy of Education*, 37(1), 127–45.

Berten, H., Cardoen, D., Van Rossem, R., Brondeel, R., and Vettenburg, N. (2013). Alcohol use among young adolescents in Belgium, the Netherlands, Germany and Austria: The effects of type of education. *Young*, 21(4), 363–385.

Bolin, A. (2014). Children's agency in interprofessional collaborative meetings in child welfare work. *Child and Family Social Work*. doi: 10.1111/cfs.12167 [e-pub ahead of print.]

Borowski, A. (2007). On human dignity and social work, *International Social Work*, 50(6), 723–726.

Bradt, L., and Bouverne-De Bie, M. (2009). Victim-offender mediation as a social work practice. *International Social Work*, 52(2), 181–193.

Braye, S., and Preston-Shoot, M. (2006). The role of law in welfare reform: Critical perspectives on the relationship between law and social work practice. *International Journal of Social Welfare*, 15(1), 19–26.

Buelens, J. and Mortier, F. (1989). Het competentieargument in het kinderrechten debat [The argument of competence in the children's rights debate]. In E. Verhellen, F. Spiesschaert and L. Cattrijsse (eds), *Rechten van kinderen. Een tekstbundel van de Rijksuniversiteit Gent naar aanleiding van de UNO-Conventie voor de rechten vanhet kind* [Children's rights. A reader of the Ghent University on the occasion of the UN-Convention on the Rights of the Child]. Antwerpen: Kluwer.

Cavet, J., and Sloper, P. (2004). The participation of children and young people in decisions about UK service development. *Child: Care, Health and Development*, 30(6), 613–621.

Cockburn, T. (2005). Children and the feminist ethic of care. *Childhood*, 12(1), 71–89.

Coussée, F., Bradt, L., Roose, R., and Bouverne-De Bie, M. (2010). The emerging social pedagogical paradigm in UK child and youth care: Deus ex machina or walking the beaten path?. *British Journal of Social Work*, 40(3), 789–805.

Crimmens, D. (2006). Editorial. *European Journal of Social Work*, 9(4), 403–405.

Davis, M.F., and Powell, R. (2003). The International Convention on the Rights of the Child: A catalyst for innovative childcare policies. *Human Rights Quarterly*, 25(3), 689–719.

Dean, H. (2009). Critiquing capabilities: The distractions of a beguiling concept. *Critical Social Policy*, 29(2), 261–278.

Depaepe, M. (1998). Educationalisation: A key concept in understanding the basic processes in the history of Western education. *History of Education Review*, 27(1), 16–28.

De Visscher, S., and Bouverne-De Bie, M. (2006). De Lauwe gekte. Een gemist debat? [The madness of Lauwe. A missed debate?] *Krax*, 6(1), 28–32.

Dixon, R., and Nussbaum, M. (2011–2012). Children's rights and a capability approach: The question of special priority. *Cornell Law Review*, 97(2011–2012), 549–593.

Donzelot, J. (1979). *The Policing of Families*. New York: Pantheon Books.

Flathman, R.E. (1976). *The Practice of Rights*. New York: Cambridge University Press.

Ghysels, J., and Van Lancker, W. (2010). De terugkeer van het mattheuseffect? De casus van de kinderopvang in Vlaanderen. *Tijdschrift voor sociologie*, 31(2), 151–163.

Goldson, B., and Muncie, J. (2006). Rethinking youth justice: Comparative analysis, international human rights and research evidence. *Youth Justice*, 6(2), 91–106.

Göppner, H.-J., and Hämäläinen, J. (2007). Developing a science of social work. *Journal of Social Work*, 7(3), 269–287.

Gray, M., and Fook, J. (2004). The quest for a universal social work: Some issues and implications. *Social Work Education*, 23(5), 625–644.

Gray, M. (2005). Dilemmas of international social work: Paradoxical processes in indigenisation, universalism and imperialism. *International Journal of Social Welfare*, 14(3), 231–238.

Gray, M., Coates, J., and Bird, M. Y. (eds). (2012). *Indigenous Social Work Around the World: Towards Culturally Relevant Education and Practice*. Aldershot, UK: Ashgate.

Grunwald, K., and Thiersch, H. (2009). The concept of the 'lifeworld orientation' for social work and social care. *Journal of Social Work Practice*, 23(2), 131–146.

Habermas, J. (1987). *The Theory of Communicative Action* (Vol. 2). Boston, MA: Beacon.

Hämäläinen, J. (2003). The concept of social pedagogy in the field of social work. *Journal of Social Work*, 3(1), 69–80.

Hare, I. (2004). Defining Social Work for the 21st Century. The International Federation of Social Workers' Revised Definition of Social Work. *International Social Work*, 47(3), 407–24.

Healy, L.M. and Link, R.J. (2012). *Handbook of International Social Work: Human Rights, Development, and the Global Profession*. Oxford: Oxford University Press.

Healy, L. M. (2008). Exploring the history of social work as a human rights profession. *International Social Work*, 51(6), 735–748.

Holland, S., and Scourfield, J. (2004). Liberty and respect in child protection, *British Journal of Social Work*, 34(1), 21–36.

Honig, M.-S. (2008). Work and care: Reconstructing childhood through childcare policy in Germany. In A. James and A.L. James (eds), *European childhoods: Cultures, Politics and Childhoods in Europe* (pp. 198–215). Basingstoke, UK: Palgrave Macmillan.

Huntington, C. (2006). Rights myopia in child welfare. *UCLA Law Review*, 53(3), 637–699.

Husserl, E. (1970). *The Crisis of European Sciences and Transcendental Phenomenology: An Introduction to Phenomenological Philosophy*. Northwestern University Press.

Ife, J. (2010a). *Human Rights from Below: Achieving Rights Through Community Development*. Cambridge: Cambridge University Press.

Ife, J. (2010b). Local and global practice: Relocating social work as a human rights profession in the new global order. *European Journal of Social Work*, 4(1), 5–15.

Ife, J. (2004) *Evaluating Human Rights Education*. Paper presented at 'Living and learning together: The role of human rights education in strengthening communities in New Zealand and the Pacific' conference, Auckland, New Zealand, 11–13 July.

Ife, J. (2001). *Human Rights and Social Work. Towards Rights-Based Practice*. Cambridge: Cambridge University Press.

Ife, J. and L. Fiske (2006) Human rights and community work: Complementary theories and practices. *International Social Work*, 49(3), 297–308.

International Federation of Social Workers (2014). *Global Definition of Social Work*. [Definition approved by the IFSW General Meeting and the IASSW General Assembly in July 2014]. Available at http://ifsw.org/get-involved/global-definition-of-social-work/

James, A. (2009). Agency. In J. Qvortrup, W.A. Corsaro, and M.-S. Honig (eds), *The Palgrave Handbook of Childhood Studies* (pp. 34–45). Basingstoke, UK: Palgrave Macmillan.

James, A., and James, A.L. (2004). *Constructing Childhood: Theory, Policy and Social Practice*. Basingstoke, UK: Palgrave Macmillan.

Jordan, B., and Parton, N. (2004). Social work, the public sphere and civil society. In R. Lovelock, K. Lyons and J. Powell (eds), *Reflecting on Social Work: Discipline and Profession* (pp. 20–36). Aldershot, UK: Ashgate.

Kabasinskaite, D., and Bak, M. (2006). Lithuania's children's policy in the period of transition. *International Journal of Social Welfare*, 15, 247–256.

Lorenz, W. (2009). Research as an element in the social work's ongoing search for identity. In R. Lovelock, K. Lyons and J. Powell (eds), *Reflecting on Social Work: Discipline and Profession* (pp. 20–36). Aldershot, UK: Ashgate.

Lorenz, W. (2008). Paradigms and politics: Understanding methods paradigms in an historical context: the case of social pedagogy. *British Journal of Social Work*, 38(4), 625–644.

Lorenz, W. (2005). Social work and a new social order: Challenging neo-liberalism's erosion of solidarity. *Social Work and Society*, 3(1), 93–101.

Lundy, C. (2011). *Social Work, Social Justice, and Human Rights: A Structural Approach to Practice*. Toronto: University of Toronto Press.

Maeseele, T. (2012). *From Charity to welfare rights? A study of Social Care Practices* (Doctoral dissertation, Ghent University, Belgium).

Masschelein, J., and Quaghebeur, K. (2005). Participation for better or for worse? *Journal of Philosophy of Education*, 39(1), 51–65.

Matthews, H., and Limb, M. (1998). The right to say: The development of youth councils/forums in the UK. *Area*, 30(1), 66–78.

Melton, G.B. (2005). Treating children like people: A framework for research and advocacy. *Journal of Clinical Child and Adolescent Psychology*, 34, 646–657.

Mollenhauer, K. (1993). *Vergeten samenhang. Over cultuur en opvoeding* [Forgotten connections. On culture and education] (2nd ed.). Amsterdam: Boom.

Mortier, F. (2002). We zijn allemaal kinderen: bruggen tussen rechten voor kinderen en rechten voor volwassenen [We are all children: bridges between rights for children and rights for adults]. *Tijdschrift voor Jeugdrecht en Kinderrechten [Journal for Youth Law and Children's Rights]*, 3(extra editie): 10–17.

Mouffe, C. (2005). *On the Political*. London: Routledge

Muncie, J. (2008). The 'punitive turn' in juvenlie justice: Cultures of control and rights compliance in Western Europe and the USA. *Youth Justice*, 8(2), 107–121.

Muncie, J. (2006). Governing young people: Coherence and contradiction in contemporary youth justice. *Critical Social Policy*, 26(4), 770–793.

Muncie, J. (2002). Children's rights and youth justice. In B. Franklin (ed.), *The New Handbook of Children's Rights: Comparative Policy and Practice* (pp. 81–96). London: Routledge.

Nussbaum, M.C. (1997). Capabilities and human rights. *Fordham Law Review*, 66, 273.

Parton, N. (2000). Some thoughts on the relationship between theory and practice in and for social work. *British Journal of Social Work*, 30(4), 449–463.

Payne, M. (2005). *Modern Social Work Theory*. Basingstoke, UK: Palgrave Macmillan.

Payne, M., and Campling, J. (2005). *The Origins of Social Work: Continuity and Change*. Basingstoke, UK: Palgrave Macmillan.

Penna, S., Paylor, I., and Washington, J. (2000). Globalization, social exclusion and the possibilities for global social work and welfare. *European Journal of Social Work*, 3(2), 109–122.

Pupavac, V. (2001). Misanthropy without borders: The international children's rights regime. *Disasters*, 25(2), 95–112.

Put, J., and Walgrave, L. (2006). Belgium: From protection towards accountability? In J. Muncie and B. Goldson (eds), *Comparative Youth Justice*. London: Sage.

Raes, K. (2001). *Controversiële rechtsfiguren: rechtsfilosofische excursies over de relaties tussen ethiek en recht* [Controversial legal forms: legal philosophical excursions on the relationship between ethics and law]. Academia Press.

Reichert, E. (2007). *Challenges in Human Rights: A Social Work Perspective*. Thousand Oaks, CA: Sage.

Reynaert, D., and Roose, R. (2014). Children's rights and the capability approach: Discussing Children's agency against the horizon of the institutionalised youth land. In D. Stoecklin and J. M. Bonvin (eds), *Children's Rights and the Capability Approach* (pp. 175–193). Amsterdam, The Netherlands: Springer.

Reynaert, D., Bouverne-De Bie, M., and Vandevelde, S. (2010). Children, rights and social work: Rethinking children's rights education. *Social Work and Society*, 8(1), 60–69.

Reynaert, D., Bouverne-De Bie, M. and Vandevelde, S. (2009). A review of children's rights literature since the adoption of the United Nations Convention on the Rights of the Child. *Childhood*, 16(4), 518–534.

Roets, G., Roose, R., and Bouverne-De Bie, M. (2013). Researching child poverty: Towards a lifeworld orientation. *Childhood*, 20(4), 535–549.

Roose, R., and De Bie, M. (2008). Children's rights: A challenge for social work. *International Social Work*, 51(1), 37–46.

Roose, R., Roets, G., and Schiettecat, T. (2014). Implementing a strengths perspective in child welfare and protection: A challenge not to be taken lightly. *European Journal of Social Work*, 17(1), 3–17.

Roose, R., Roets, G., Van Houte, S., Vandenhole, W., and Reynaert, D. (2013). From parental engagement to the engagement of social work services: Discussing reductionist and democratic forms of partnership with families. *Child and Family Social Work*, 18(4), 449–457.

Roose, R., Coussée, F., and Bradt, L. (2010). Going beyond the bounds of possibility: Questioning the delimitation of the social in social work. *Social Work and Society*, 8(1), 1–5.

Sharland, E. (2012). All together now? Building disciplinary and inter-disciplinary research capacity in social work and social care. *British Journal of Social Work*, 42(2), 208–226.

Shardlow, S.M. (2007). Social work in an international context. In M. Lymbery and K. Postle (eds), *Social Work: A Companion to Learning*. Thousand Oaks, CA: Sage.

Smith, A. (2007). Children and young people's participation rights in education. *International Journal of Children's Rights*, 15, 147–164.

Stammers, N. (2009). *Human Rights and Social Movements*. London: Pluto Press.

Stoecklin, D., and Bonvin, J. M. (2014). *Children's Rights and the Capability Approach*. Amsterdam, The Netherlands: Springer.

Stoecklin, D. (2012). Theories of action in the field of child participation: In search of explicit frameworks. *Childhood*, 20(4), 443–457.

Such, E., and Walker, R. (2005). Young citizens or policy objects? Children in the 'rights and responsibilities debate'. *Journal of Social Policy*, 34, 39–57.

Therborn, G. (1996). Child politics: Dimensions and perspectives. *Childhood*, 3(1), 29–44.
Thomas, N. (2007). Towards a theory of children's participation. *International Journal of Children's Rights*, 15, 199–218.
Todd, S. (2007). Promoting a just education: Dilemmas of rights, freedom and justice. *Educational Philosophy and Theory*, 39(6), 592–603.
Van Ewijk, H. (2010). Positioning social work in a socially sensitive society. *Social Work and Society*, 8(1), 1–10.
Valentine, K. (2011). Accounting for agency. *Children and Society*, 25(5), 347–358.
Vandenbroeck, M., and Bouverne-De Bie, M. (2006) Children's agency and educational norms: A tensed negotiation. *Childhood*, 13(1), 127–143.
Vanobbergen, B., Vandenbroeck, M., Roose, R., and Bie, B. D. (2006). 'We are one big, happy family': Beyond negotiation and compulsory happiness. *Educational Theory*, 56(4), 423–437.
Verhellen, E. (2000). *Convention on the Rights of the Child: Background, Motivation, Strategies, Main Themes.* Leuven, Belgium: Garant Publishers.
Verhellen, E. (1998). *Jeugdbeschermingsrecht* [Youth Protection Law]. Ghent: Mys and Breesch.
Vettenburg, N., Brondeel, R., Gavray, C., and Pauwels, L. J. (2013). Societal vulnerability and adolescent offending: The role of violent values, self-control and troublesome youth group involvement. *European Journal of Criminology*, 10(4), 444–461.
Witkin, S. L. (1998). Human rights and social work. *Social Work*, 43(3), 197–201.
Woll, L. (2001). Organizational responses to the convention on the rights of the child: International lessons for child welfare organizations. *Child Welfare*, 130(5), 668–679.
Zinnecker, J. (2000). Childhood and adolescence as pedagogic moratoria. *Zeitschrift für Pädagogik*, 46(2), 36–68.

7
Anthropologists, ethnographers and children's rights
Critiques, resistance and powers

Géraldine André[1]

Since its foundation, anthropology has been particularly motivated to allow the voices of subaltern and marginal groups to be heard. Ethnography and participant observation, by which researchers aim to grasp the perspectives of actors, are the central methodological approaches of the discipline, which allow anthropologists to play a key role in political and ethical processes of recognition of the "others." At this level of analysis, children constitute a social group with an especially marginal status at the economic, social and legal levels (Scheper-Hugues and Sargent 1998: 1). The renewed interest in childhood and children in anthropology since the end of the 1980s accompanies a strong will to make visible the "lifeworlds" of children (Nieuwenhuys 1994), the strategies that children and young people deploy for managing their own survival (Reynolds 1991; Hecht 1998), and their own perspectives regarding social life (Montgomery 2001, 2009). In short, anthropology asks to what extent children are active agents working in and for the shaping of social, political and economic processes (Honwana and De Boeck 2005).

While anthropologists of childhood are determined to take seriously the points of view of children and young people, this does not mean that they deny their potential vulnerability and the numerous social structures that constrain their capacity for action. On the contrary, anthropologists interested in children's rights are especially conscious of the threefold domination that children must face, especially those from Southern societies and dominated social groups with whom anthropologists have been mostly concerned. First, located in a generational structure, children and young people are typically dominated by adults: their capacity for action and their autonomy are not recognized on the public scene (Elson 1982; Nieuwenhuys 1994; Montgomery 2001; Cheney 2007), and their symbolic creativity is constrained by the viewpoints of their elders. Second, especially those children and young people belonging to the rural masses or to the lower classes of urban areas, are frequently positioned at the bottom of the social hierarchy.[2] Finally, many children and young people are

---

1   The author is postdoctoral researcher at F.R.S.-FNRS Pôle Sud and Lasc-University of Liège.
2   Since its foundations and beyond the so-called primitive societies, anthropology has been very concerned with the minority and dominated social groups, the subalterns. This is especially visible for the most leading anthropologists that have done their research with children (Nieuwenhuys 1994, 2001; Montgomery 2001).

members of societies considered to be poor nations, or still perceived and labelled as "developing countries" with a history of colonial domination and subordination, whose symbolic references and institutions take place in a network of power relations with dominant nations. This last dimension is especially important in the case of childhood, which, since the end of the Cold War, has been progressively globalized through international human rights law and instruments such as the Convention on the Rights of the Child (CRC), but also through powerful international institutions and NGOs involved in the shaping and in the monitoring of childhood all over the world.

Consequently, anthropologists who tackle children's rights – particularly in Southern societies – face two fundamental moral tensions with epistemological and methodological implications. In the wake of cultural relativism, which historically constitutes a crucial epistemological position of the discipline (Hatch 1997; Nagengast 1997), anthropologists seek to describe how children experience their rights according to the common norms and representations of childhood and parenthood that are present in their own society. But anthropologists who focus on human rights, and on children's rights in particular, are aware of how previously more remote societies have been progressively penetrated by external dimensions and global systems of values and monitored by global institutions that have integrated them into global power relations (Cowan et al. 2001: 5). As a result, for anthropologists, describing how children's rights law is challenged by cultural diversity all over the world is nowadays far from sufficient; even though globalization processes have not smoothed down the numerous and diverse ways in which childhood is locally perceived and lived across the globe. This opposition between relativism and universalism, progressively replaced by the tension between the local and the global, is related to another opposition: the capacity of children for action, which varies throughout societies, on the one hand, and the very constraints, social structures, and power relations that limit the autonomy of children and young people, on the other.

These tensions convey two epistemological pitfalls that anthropologists continuously try to leave behind: "populism" and "miserabilism" (Grignon and Passeron 1989). With populism, social science researchers focus on the capacity of children to make sense of their life, but without taking into account the dominations and power relations that shape it. Miserabilism, in its turn, looks at young lives in Southern societies through their domination, and also through the globalized and legitimate child images, for example, through the image of the child protected by the "loving bonds" of the nuclear family. In order to avoid these pitfalls, anthropologists and ethnographers who study children's rights juggle bottom-up and top-down approaches.

These dimensions will help to present and structure this review of anthropological approaches to children's rights, with special attention to the relations between anthropology and children's rights since the adoption of the Convention on the Rights of the Child. The first part analyses a strange paradox: while the CRC has contributed to a renewed interest in children among anthropologists, as well as to deep theoretical and methodological transformations in the discipline for grasping children's experiences, anthropologists have strongly criticized global children's rights law. After examining different forms of critiques that anthropologists have addressed to children's rights law and their interest for the latters, the second part of the chapter will focus on bottom-up approaches, which aim at understanding rights as they are experienced by children, in particular in non-Western societies. The last section will analyse the anthropological trends that look at children's rights as structures of power, or as being linked to structures of power that affect children's lives. Consequently, this chapter, which reviews the anthropological works on children's rights, tackles children's rights defined in a variety of ways.

The majority of the work reviewed here was conducted by anthropologists; but many of these scholars, including the representatives of the main trends, have carried out their work in building strong ties with researchers from other disciplines (legal science, sociology, psychology and educational sciences). On the other hand, many social science researchers who claim to be affiliated with "childhood studies", or who have theoretical affinities with this scholarship, have used ethnography or other qualitative research in order to tackle children's rights "from below." For these two reasons, this paper will refer to these researchers and "ethnographers" as well.

1. Children's rights law and anthropologists: Interest and critiques

1.1. The resurgence of interest in childhood in anthropology

Since the beginning of the 1990s and alongside the adoption of the Convention of the Rights of the Child in 1989, there has been a renewed interest in social sciences for the study of children with works claiming to adhere to "Childhood Studies" or the "Anthropology of Childhoods" (Bluebond-Langner and Korbin 2007: 241). The sociology of childhood came to life with the decline of "grand narratives"[3] (Lyotard, 1979) and with the questioning of theories of socialization (Sirota 2006). Anthropologists, however, had started focusing on childhood earlier. But in the light of concepts such as "cultural transmission", children were conceived as mere recipients of parental culture and upbringing (Schwartzman 2001; Hirschfeld 2003; LeVine 2007). Studies sought to grasp many aspects of the child's passage to adulthood in its interaction with group culture and within relations of filiation and kinship (Mead 1928a, 1928b, 1930; Benedict 1935; Middleton 1970; Spindler 1997; Whiting and Whiting 1975), rather than in how children behave as children as autonomous participants in society (Montgomery 2001: 17; Razy et al. 2012). For example, in the case of child work, the anthropological tradition highlighted the nesting of productive activities performed by children in subsistence societies in a reciprocal nexus of duties, gifts, responsibilities and compliance towards elders (Richards 1939; Raum 1940; Fortes 1978; Schildkrout 1978), or at the heart of exchange relations in the context of kinship (Goody 1981; Lallemand 1993, 2002). Perceived as important producers and working for the reproduction of the group, children, by means of their activities, were socialized to the rules of a society in which they gradually would define their place (Katz 1996). In African societies, children and their work have also been studied as resources (productive force) at the root of conflicts between families and communities, even generations (Katz 1996). Since the late 1980s and early 1990s, anthropological studies have either seen the role of adults as knowledge transmitters or construed culture as an item that needed assimilation (LeVine 2007). As Montgomery remarks (2001: 15), "the beginning and end of childhood" have been analysed, but "the nature of childhood itself" and the social construction of childhood as well as its cultural variations have remained under-researched for several decades.

Beginning in the 1990s, in the social sciences, analyses of childhood saw a renewed interest that would give rise to important theoretical and methodological shifts: researchers sought to grasp the experiences and particular perspectives of children, conceiving them more generally as agents with a capacity for action or even experts (James et al. 1998; Gaskins 2000; De Boeck and Honwana 2000). To go further, some authors have begun to devise new tools for collecting data on children and to construct a new dominant paradigm in relation to childhood. Danic et

---

3   The "grand narratives" are great explanations that aim at highlighting history, by establishing connections between events through key notions, for example the concept of class struggle within Marxism. Postmodernism refers to this age of the end of the belief in such great explanations.

al. (2006: 52) argue that there are different studies, nowadays, which provide a new orientation to these issues. They are based on a particular methodology, one that places the child at the centre and views it as an interlocutor in the inquiry. These studies also set a new direction, since they construct their object around the viewpoint of the child (Danic *et al.* 2006: 52). The United Nations General Assembly's adoption of the Convention on the Rights of the Child in 1989, coupled with the ability of NGOs to mobilize opinion and resources at massive scales, seem directly linked to the resurgence of interest in children among anthropologists and other social scientists. The CRC has contributed to giving rise to a global field of childhood; this field is structured by global agents, international agencies and global NGOs, and is animated by numerous child welfare practitioners working all over the world to resolve different kinds of problems that affect children. In addition, over the past two decades, images of child labourers, children suffering from starvation or from HIV/AIDS, and child soldiers have been abundantly displayed in popular media (Denov 2010). This global field, aided by the media, has helped make children more visible on the international scene and drawn the attention of anthropologists and other researchers. Indeed, as Sirota (2006) expressed concerning Latin America (in a way applicable to other societies as well), what is catching the attention now is the protection of the poor child, especially by means of social and educational policies, backed by prominent international organizations such as the World Bank, UNICEF and ILO. But most importantly, this sector and the worldwide media determine the so-called universal and legitimate outlines of childhood (Boyden 1990; Ruddick 2003; Rosen 2007) in a way that stigmatizes other ways of being a child. As we will see, many anthropological approaches to children's rights have emerged in reaction against the emphasis on misery and suffering in international rhetoric on children's rights.

On the other hand, this revived interest is not a mere fashion. The renewed focus on children also reflects processes, evolutions and transformations of childhood and youth in developing countries. For example, de Boeck (2000) pointed out how the phenomenon of child witches in the Democratic Republic of the Congo (DRC) has to be understood according to deep and intense transformations of "the categories of maternity, gerontocracy, authority and more generally of family itself" in the country (and more broadly throughout the continent). In the same vein, while young people in Africa needed to go through a long process of initiation "for becoming a fully realized human being", the process of disarmament of youth soldiers is traversed by other discourses on young people, such as the ones who are under 18 years old, discourses that assimilate young people with children (Hoffman 2003). This polyphony in discourses of childhood and youth in developing countries is especially related to the field of aid and international development, and the multiple programmes that promote patterns of childhood in conformity with international children's rights instruments such as the CRC. Guillermet (2010) shows how the status of an orphan in Niger is constructed and negotiated between local and global conceptions of childhood and parenthood. In this context, a diversity of competing discourses about childhood and youth gives rise to conflicts between generations (Archambault 2011).

While children's rights have thus contributed to the resurgence of interest amongst anthropologists in children, the next part will show that, immediately after the adoption of the CRC, many anthropologists hurried to express their reservations and uncertainties regarding universal legal frameworks for protecting the rights of the child.

1.2. Anthropologists' reservations regarding children's rights

The attitude of scepticism of anthropologists towards child rights law and instruments such as the CRC was not surprising, as children's rights are partly, as it has been said in the introduction of the book, human rights. Actually, since the adoption of the Universal Declaration of Human Rights (UDHR) in response to the horrors of the Second World War, anthropologists have been relatively disengaged concerning human rights issues (Goodale 2006). After briefly locating the origin of the initial detachment of anthropologists vis-à-vis human rights, this section of the chapter will describe the main critiques of children's rights formulated by anthropologists.

The early disengagement of anthropologists regarding human rights lay in the concept of cultural relativism, initially developed by scholars such as Benedict and Herskovits, in order to ask respect for cultural difference (Nagengast 1997; Hatch 1997). According to cultural relativism, all cultures have to be recognized as having an "equal value" and should consequently be grasped in their own logics (Nieuwenhuys 2008: 5). Actually, in 1947, the American Anthropological Association, through the figure of Herskovits, had strongly refused to take part in the shaping of human rights instruments, in part because of cultural diversity, but also, and more specifically, because of the normative nature of the UDHR, which anthropologists refused to support (Goodale 2006; Brems 2013). This rejection occurred when many Southern societies were still colonized and consequently at a time when anthropologists were afraid of the shadow of "a moral imperialism" behind the statement of universal human rights (Hernandez-Truyol, quoted by Goodale 2006). This initial rejection in this specific context did not encourage anthropologists to consider human rights as a worthwhile topic for anthropological inquiry or analysis; one had to wait until the end of the 1980s for a focus on human rights as an anthropological or ethnographic subject of research (Turner 1997; Goodale 2006).

Thus, the link between human rights and culture was at first formulated as an irreducible dichotomy (Cowan *et al.* 2001: 4). And yet, cultural relativism in its opposition to the so-called universality of human rights, involves many other dichotomies, such as public and private spheres, individual and collective rights, civil/political and social/economic rights (Nagengast 1997, 353). For example, anthropologists, for whom human individuals are especially the product of networks of social relationships, consider that many legislations and policies of human rights problematically refer to a Western conceptualization of the human which is the "property of the individual", "inhabiting an individual body", overlooking the collectives in which human beings are inscribed (Turner 1997: 275).

But anthropologists have gradually distanced themselves from cultural relativism to the point that it is now more condemned than strongly accepted (Hatch 1997: 371). The problem of this concept is that it can be used strategically to justify and tolerate a distinct treatment of dominated social groups such as women, indigenous groups or children (Nagengast 1997: 352). Another difficulty with cultural relativism is that it essentializes cultural difference. Indeed, according to cultural relativism, social phenomena are only understandable when they are related to the logics of the cultures within which they occur (Nieuwenhuys 2008: 5). The ethical consequence of this epistemological position is that social phenomena such as "genital mutilation" cannot be universally condemned in the name of human rights because they vary according to the cultural setting in which they are inscribed (Nieuwenhuys 2008). The problem of such a position, according to Nieuwenhuys (2008: 6) is that, while universalism as contained in human rights regimes leads to the essentialization of childhood, cultural relativism essentializes and makes permanent cultural features. Yet, with societal transformations in the wake of various processes of globalization, the majority of anthropologists have come to agree that cultures are not homogenous, but an evolving set of unstable, conflicting and contested meanings (Turner 1997; Nagengast 1997; Cowan *et al.* 2001; Merry 2006; Nieuwenhuys 2008). But while anthropologists have moved beyond the use of such concepts as tradition or culture – at least, if these are understood as a fixed set of meanings – theorists of children's rights and development agents very frequently use terms such as "tradition", "culture", "victimhood," and "collective rights" (Archambault 2011). In doing so, they essentialize social practices such as early marriage or child domestic work, which are generated more by structural factors, such as social position, social class relations or dynamics of capitalism, than cultural ancestral dynamics (Archambault 2011; Jacquemin 2009). Thus, children can be victims of these essentialized constructions of their tradition or culture, which restrain their active participation in the world (Stephens 1995: 32).

Therefore, if cultural relativism is still influencing current anthropological approaches of human rights, it is not through a coherent theoretical position but rather with specific epistemological lenses by which moral judgements are suspended for a better understanding of other cultures (Turner 1997: 275). Nevertheless, the first relation between anthropology and children's rights was not based on a similar initial rejection. Messer (1993: 234) notices that since the beginning, anthropologists took an active role in educational matters or in the question of child labour policies. This active participation of anthropologists in the field of children's rights, whether through critical involvement or through research responding to policy agendas stimulated by the CRC (Ennew 1986, 2000; Bonnet et al. 2006; Boyden and de Berry 2004; Boyden and Bourdillon 2012) is growing nowadays. The sector of international development, which has made children one of its main targets, now offers anthropologists professional openings or resources (de Waal and Argenti 2002; Massart 2007, 2009; Thorsen 2012a, 2012b, 2012c).

Through this involvement and in other ways, anthropologists interested in children's rights are sceptical regarding the establishment of moral standards to monitor and regulate childhood all over the globe. On the one hand, their criticism is grounded in the perception of the diversity of childhood across the world: children are indeed perceived by anthropologists as especially "dependent on local meaning and practices" (Stephens 1995; Scheper-Hughes and Sargent, 1998: 8). Childhood differs from one country to another (Boyden 1990), from one specific society to another. This "relativist caution" can strongly underlie the work of anthropologists when they study children's rights issues. Montgomery's classic study on child prostitutes in Thailand, for example, analyses how the trajectories that lead children towards prostitution in Thailand are underpinned by a very different conception of sexuality (Montgomery 2001) and a very different representation of children from the one conveyed by the CRC: indeed, children have more duties and respect towards their mothers than their mothers have an obligation to protect their offspring. In this perspective, child prostitution "was a job which brought in relatively large amounts of money which could be used by the children as a way of fulfilling their perceived obligations" (Montgomery 2001: 89). On the other hand, anthropologists' scepticism concerns rights talks, discourses and practices that are intertwined with cultural values that are neither neutral nor universal. More precisely, their critiques question the specific context in which children's rights law has emerged. In 1990, Boyden pointed out that the CRC failed to take into account the "evidence that the conception of rights is intimately tied up with cultural values and the outlook of any given society" (Boyden 1990: 203). Indeed, the Children's Rights Movement, which progressively led to the adoption of the CRC by the United Nations, suggests that the notion of children's rights is connected to the "social question"[4] in nineteenth-century Western societies (Hawes 1991). The foundation of the school as a public institution and the institution of compulsory education are indeed the solutions that were enforced so as to control and direct "the political energies of the

---

4 By social question, we refer here to the questioning of politicians and elite regarding the harsh conditions of the labour class in nineteenth-century Europe: political solutions were needed for counteracting the threat of insurrection of the "dangerous class".

working-class" in Europe (Clarke, quoted by James *et al.* 1998: 49). This original context is very different from the current situation of Southern societies. In the latter case, the foundation of the school was a key political strategy of the colonial authorities. Nevertheless, and as Boyden (1990) has argued, the first attempts made at the state regulation of childhood in the South occurred under colonial ruling and were influenced by what had happened in Western societies during the nineteenth century. For example, as Nieuwenhuys (1994) has shown, the legal approach to child labour from nineteenth-century Europe aimed at managing the problems linked to the employment of children in factories. This legislation built a dichotomy between child labour in the factories and other activities such as housekeeping, child care, etc., then considered as training, help or socialization (Nieuwenhuys, 1994). "The welfare priorities devised at that time continue to shape the structures and forms of provision in the present" (Boyden, 1990: 200).

The other main critique formulated by anthropologists regarding children's rights law concerns the philosophical thought that underlies current formal human rights discourses. The specificity of the CRC is that it brings an additional dimension to the status of children, in that it recognizes them as subjects who have rights, and not simply as beneficiaries of adult protection (Landsown 2001). For many anthropologists (Stephens 1995; Scheper-Hughes and Sargent 1998), however, this acknowledgment is related to the neoliberal philosophy of the self-governing individual, which is far from corresponding to the "ethos" which continuously informs the lives of children and young people in rural African societies for example, even if these have been evolving according to the "new challenges of new situations and contexts brought by education, urbanization and evangelism" (Droz 2006: 115–116). As Turner (1997) indicated, there is a deep ambiguity in the contribution of Enlightenment Liberalism to current thought about human rights (and children's rights) (Turner 1997: 279). While the universalistic ambition of human rights thinking led to the removal of any reference to class relations, ethnic differences, or social and historical specificities, it has been "formulated from the standpoint of the dominant class position of the bourgeoisie" (Turner 1997: 279). In this vein, many anthropologists critically emphasize how the representations of childhood and parenthood diffused by child rights discourses, talks and law promote the dominant urban nuclear middle-class family of the centres against the rural and working-class families of the peripheries[5] (Boyden 1990; Stephens 1995; Scheper-Hughes and Sargent 1998). In addition, these discourses convey a rather passive image of children and youth. Anthropologists generally take a critical position with regard to the emphasis on misery and suffering in international rhetoric on children's rights: Cheney, for example, criticizes the discourse of children's rights as it relates to Africa's orphans because it has few empowering virtues; rather it disempowers vulnerable children (Cheney 2012).

In the next section we will see that these critiques have led many anthropologists to recall the variety of conceptions of childhood, but especially to transmit children's own views and to insist on the importance of their rights and capacity for action. These approaches on children's rights are based especially on ethnographic approaches in developing countries, where the gap between international law and rights as they are experienced by children is particularly significant, and challenges the relationships between dominant and dominated nations (Hanson and Nieuwenhuys, 2013).

---

5 By the opposition between "centres" and "peripheries", we refer here to the opposition between dominant and dominated nations, opposition that comprises different oppositions. For instance, between Northern and Southern societies, between Western and non-Western societies, between developed and developing countries, and between former colonial empires and their colonies.

2. Children's rights from below

If the debate between cultural relativism and universalism has reached an impasse in the discipline because, among other reasons, anthropologists have distanced themselves from concepts such as tradition or culture as stable, shared sets of meanings and values, anthropologists remain deeply focused on realities as they are lived at the local level. In fact, anthropological perspectives that go along with "bottom-up approaches" of children's rights deal not so much with culture as with daily lives and ordinary experiences which continuously influence the ways in which processes of globalization take place. This section will focus on anthropological approaches that pay attention to the daily life of children and their communities as they shape the ways in which rights discourses are implemented, challenged and altered (Cowan *et al.* 2001: 1). In this sense, they join one of the two main current trends[6] in the anthropology of human rights – namely, the ethnographic trend – in order to describe how human rights work as a social practice (Goodale 2006).

Like scholars from other disciplines, including political and social scientists, lawyers and developmental psychologists (e.g. Liebel 2012; Hanson and Nieuwenhuys, 2013), anthropologists consider that top-down approaches to human rights are far from being sufficient (Nieuwenhuys 1994; Montgomery 2001; Cheney 2007; Hanson and Nieuwenhuys 2013; Cowan *et al.* 2001). Not surprisingly, anthropologists challenge issues of human rights implementation by analysing these processes from below. In the field of children's rights, their line of reasoning firstly concerns the social abilities for which children are given credit. While these scholars – like their counterparts in other disciplines – would neither reject the notion that the subjectivities of children are shaped by global discourses and law, nor would they claim that children's agency is equal to the skills of adults, they see young people as social actors able to form their own ideas concerning their rights (Montgomery 2001; Cheney 2007). Far from justifying forms of child abuse, such as child prostitution, or the behaviour of adults who take part in these processes of child mistreatment, for these researchers young people are "taken seriously as both research subjects and as analysts of their own lives and circumstances" (Montgomery 2001: 3; Lundy *et al.* 2011). It is at the methodological level that one can at first locate this child-centred dimension: anthropologists and ethnographers analyse the discourses of children and young people about their rights. Pells, for example, has shown that children and youth in Rwanda perceive their rights as they are formulated in official discourses as "everything that they don't have" (Pells 2012).

Most importantly, and beyond words and discourses about rights as they are formulated in official documents, anthropologists analyse how children's rights are experienced and lived by children, their families and their communities. In this vein, the social anthropologist Nieuwenhuys and the legal scientist Hanson (Hanson and Nieuwenhuys 2013) have recently systematized a very challenging approach where children's rights are a living practice. Even though within their conceptual framework, "the translation from principles to practice is never solely either a top-down or a bottom-up activity" (Hanson and Nieuwenhuys 2013: 19), they emphasize the fact that the rights of the child are far from being only the result of processes of legal deliberations and negotiations. Beyond the viewpoint according to which rights have been formalized within international institutions and legislation, they depict children and their

---

6 According to Goodale (2006), there are two approaches developed by anthropologists when they started to re-engage with human rights: an anthropology of human rights that aims at contributing to "emancipatory cultural politics" and an anthropology that tackles human rights as a question that has to be analysed empirically.

families continually making and recreating their own rights as they are facing and struggling with the daily concerns of their life. Many anthropological studies of children's strategies and capacity for action to secure their own life can be included in this trend that identifies children's rights as a living practice. For example, in African agricultural societies, Reynolds (1991) has explored how children develop their own strategies for survival, support, and nurture in the web of relationships that they construct with different kinsmen (Reynolds 1991: 138). Young people in Southern societies are in such material conditions that anthropologists and ethnographers portray them as fighting for securing their livelihood. Indeed, strategies for survival are deployed by the young in harsh conditions and contexts with limited choices and possibilities. For example, in South Africa, in a context of widespread HIV/AIDS and consecutive deaths in the family network, Henderson (2013) has shown that girls prefer contracting "an informal marriage" and thus overcoming the shrinkage of kinship relationships, rather than realizing their right to education as it is promoted by development agents with their gender agenda. Generally, these children's ideas and practices concerning their rights clash with the rights discourses and programmes as they are practised in the field of development. While international law on children's rights deems child mining activities as one of the worst forms of child labour, the ethnographer Okyere has shown how these activities are important strategies by which young people try to pursue the achievement of their basic needs and rights such as eating and going to school (Okyere 2012).[7] The strategies for survival that children develop are not always opposed to the categories expressed by rights discourses as they are practised by development agents. Children can use them strategically in order to secure their basic needs. Cheney has shown that the "orphan identification with victimhood" is used by children and adults when they are pursuing the goal of survival (Cheney 2012: 153).

These strategies for survival are not deployed just for achieving individualistic projects and goals. Anthropologists pay attention to the broader networks of relations and ties of interdependence in which children and young people are involved; these groups also take part in different forms of collective organizations and resistance related to a specific "ethic of subsistence" (Scott 1976) in which norms and values of reciprocity, mutual benefit through inter-generational exchanges, and kinship relationships enable local communities to survive (Hanson and Nieuwenhuys 2013: 11; see also Droz 2006). As Hanson and Nieuwenhuys (2013: 12) have argued, the capacity of children and young people for survival and sense of justice are consubstantial with what anthropologists have conceptualized as the "moral economy".[8] In her seminal ethnography on child labour in India, Nieuwenhuys (1994) has shown how the many work activities carried out by children and young people – such as young boys foraging' habits in fishermen societies or girls cleaning coir in the production of coir yarn – although undefined, non-formalized and almost invisible, play a central role in the livelihood of their families (Nieuwenhuys 1994). What is depicted through their ethnographies is a very different portrait

---

7   In some way, his ethnographic approach is very similar to the one of political scientist Saadi (2012) about the case of working children's organizations that shows how children have specific views on childhood and labour.
8   The concept of moral economy was first described by Thompson (1993/1963), who noted the subjective orientations of the poor in late eighteenth-century England regarding their living conditions. Other scholars such as Scott (1976) developed the concept further by relating it to peasant rebellions in the South. In Scott's work, the moral economy refers to the "notion of economic justice" and the "working definition of exploitation" of the peasants, which is related to an ethic of subsistence. This ethic of subsistence is a non-capitalist ethic determined rather by the need of securing subsistence than by making profit. This ethic resorts to interdependence relations and the principle of mutuality within the group (household, community).

of youth. These young people are not autonomous individuals pursuing the achievement of their rights as they are formulated by international institutions, but rather considered as social beings who have incorporated schemes of behaviours, perceptions, and representations depending on social situations and specific networks of social relations in which they are inscribed. This is especially visible in the work of Montgomery – also referred to above – on Thai children who, in a context of restricted work possibilities and poverty, prostitute themselves in support of their parents to whom they are obliged (Montgomery 2001: 82). This perspective of interdependency appears especially relevant for grasping the agency of poor African children who, in the context of an absent welfare state, are "interdependent beings whose daily livelihoods are intricately entwined with and are inseparable from that of the family collective" (Abebe 2013:72). André and Godin (2013) have shown that, in the DRC, in a context of very low public investment in primary education, in which parents' financial participation in their children's schooling has become more and more significant (Poncelet *et al.* 2010; De Herdt 2011: 115–156), children have decided to work in small-scale artisanal mining in order to help their elders – their parents or the community. While mining is labelled as one of the worst forms of child labour, children have been led to perform such activities because of their dispositions of respect and duties toward their elders that they actively pursue in the artisanal mining sector. This "collective dimension", in which children's strategies and abilities are inscribed, need not be romanticized, as it was in the past in some anthropological accounts of production activities in rural subsistence societies (Nieuwenhuys 2006). It has also been analysed through the perspective of local dominations and power relations from which rural communities or other dominated social groups are not exempted, such as the seniority system, through which the autonomy of children and young people is not recognized on the public stage (Elson 1982; Nieuwenhuys 1994).

This ability for action and resistance is not limited to the material level; it also refers to the ability to give meaning to one's own life (Willis 1977), that is, to the levels of symbolic representation and identity, as young people "[negotiate] their identities as individuals and as social selves" (Cheney 2007: 15). At the symbolic level, anthropologists analyse children's capacity for resistance towards, for example, the ideals of the nuclear family and residential permanency conveyed by development projects or school programmes (Archambault 2010). Or, while child migrations are perceived as child trafficking in anti-child-trafficking policy in Benin, Howard (2012) has shown that young people leave their homes to pursue such ambitions as acquiring skills that the school and local sphere could not provide. At this cultural level, the symbolic input of the young is quite important in the neoliberal age. Comaroff and Comaroff (2000) have analysed the paradoxical effects of the current exclusion of the young by neoliberal capitalism: while it marginalizes young people from the labour force and other networks of power, it makes possible the creation of their own culture. In the interstices of their exclusion, which are governed by a horizontal organization rather than vertical relations (de Suremain 2006), children and young people can develop a specific sense of justice and freedom which challenges those of adults (O'Neill 2012). Indeed, in the case of child labour in Nepal, O'Neill (2012) depicts the resistance of young carpet weavers against the domination of their capitalist employers in factories: while learning weaving skills, they also acquire in the same time a sense of their own liberty. Finally, the contribution of children and young people also concerns the shaping of political processes. The demobilization and reintegration programmes addressed to former child-soldiers generally do not take into account the fact that these children and young people wanted to take arms in order to contribute to changing the political system (Hoffman 2003: 304).

All these anthropologists studying children's rights from the perspective of children are very engaged in contributing to "emancipatory cultural politics" (Turner 1997). In this sense, even if they are not quite standard-bearers for applied anthropology, their basic perspectives of research are closely intertwined with moral considerations or political recommendations (Montgomery 2001; Reynolds et al. 2006; Hanson and Nieuwenhuys 2013). This commitment appears in a field that is very sensitive, as it contains very emotionally charged issues such as child prostitution, child labour, or child soldiers, which especially call into question the "neutrality" of the "participant observer" (Montgomery 2001). Their first contribution lies in the critiques that they address to the very miserabilist overtones of the discourses of children's rights advocates. Anthropologists do not necessarily disagree with such discourses; they even recognize and celebrate the assiduity of development agents in defending children's rights (see e.g. Montgomery 2001: 2), but they insist on the necessity of grasping categories by which children formulate and live their experience (Montgomery 2001) in order to improve the ways in which rights discourses can really improve the lives of children. On the other hand, their contribution is formulated regarding the gap between two kinds of rights, children's rights law and children's practical ability for justice, in other words through a "critical analysis" that enriches the critical perspectives defined in the introduction of the book. The gap between what is formalized in children's rights law and children's real lives can be so significant that children ignore the former, because its relevance and meaning do not appear in social spaces of severe marginality (Snodgrass 1999). This aspect of their work is especially carried out and made possible through close collaborations with scholars from other disciplines that lead to challenging interdisciplinary concepts, for instance, the metaphor of "refraction" (Reynolds et al. 2006, Hanson and Nieuwenhuys 2013). By this notion, anthropologists Reynolds and Nieuwenhuys, in association with Hanson, their legal science counterpart, explain how children's rights law "change[s] the direction of children's experiences" when they make "conscious choices" in response to the terrible circumstances of their lives (Reynolds et al. 2006: 12–13). They warn against the fact that many "positive aspects of children's lives" can be wasted when children's rights are brandished (Reynolds et al. 2006: 13). As such, if anthropologists interested in children's rights are especially critical of children's rights discourses, their criticisms are directly linked to their commitment to "social justice" (Hanson and Nieuwenhuys 2013) and, even indirectly, to the improvement of the formulation and the implementation of rights.

This section has analysed an anthropological trend which accounts for children's rights by putting more emphasis on their bottom-up dynamics than their top-down forces, while not denying that children's rights are developing both from above and from below (Cheney 2007, Hanson et al. 2006, Hanson and Nieuwenhuys 2013). The next section will attend to anthropological approaches that have put their focus on the top-down strengths contained in children's rights law.

3. Children's rights and global powers

While many anthropologists who focus on children's rights are especially interested in the dynamics that come from below, they do not perceive the bottom-up processes as if they were totally disconnected from top-down dynamics and constraints. Although childhood is often perceived as an apolitical realm, it is one of the primary fields of existence concerned with many different kinds of power relations and controls. The category of childhood is shaped by numerous projections and political projects that pursue the maintenance of social cohesion (Rose 1989; Stephens 1995; Scheper-Hughes 1998 and Sargent; Cheney 2007). These projects impel an increasing surveillance of children by means of "the constructed boundaries of childhood as a particular stage of innocence and dependency" (Cheney 2007: 14). In this section, I will show how anthropologists of children's rights also analyse national and global politics as well as continuous forces that seek to control the lives and bodies of children and young people.

3.1. Children's rights and global capitalism

In the 1990s, anthropologists as Stephens (1995); Scheper-Hughes and Sargent (1998) were worried by the ways in which "the treatment and place" of children were affected by the flows and activities of global capitalism, especially the growing dominance of neoliberal economic policies that started disturbing the economies of the developing countries from the 1980s on: the latter have been bombarded by pressures from international institutions such as the World Bank and the IMF to adopt structural adjustment programmes (see also Mestrum, Chapter 20 in this Handbook). These changes have had numerous devastating consequences for Third World populations, especially women and children, as these adjustments programmes involve severe economic restrictions in social-welfare programmes and give rise to harsh disorders in local social and work-related networks (Stephens 1995; Scheper-Hughes and Sargent 1998). That is why some anthropologists perceived the expansion of the human rights movement since then as "a reaction to political alienation in contemporary states under conditions imposed by global capitalism, and in particular the effects of neoliberal policies" (Turner 1997: 283). This was particularly the case for the development of children's rights according to Scheper-Hughes and Sargent (1998: 3). In the early 1980s, UNICEF expressed its concerns regarding the rapid economic evolution and changes motivated by neoliberal global economics and launched many campaigns in favour of children and women who had been relegated to the lowest priorities of world capitalism (Scheper-Hughes and Sargent 1998: 4). Texts and expressions from international institutions such as UNICEF's "World's children" or "The State of the World's Children" reflect this increasing global preoccupation for children. The answers of UNICEF to the hostile effects of global capitalism on child survival has been critically analysed by anthropologists such as Scheper-Hughes (1987).

While the spread of children's rights and human rights movements has been seen as a response to these broader economic changes, anthropologists as Scheper-Hughes and Stephens started to analyse how the representations and the values that underlie children's rights law must themselves be grasped in a complex entanglement with processes of capitalist globalization (Stephens 1995; Scheper-Hughes and Sargent 1998). The global, late-capitalist society promotes workers who are liberated from any attachment such as residence, family obligations, and kinship duties, and who are fully dedicated to making profit and taking individual initiative (Scheper-Hughes and Sargent 1998: 7; see also Stephens 1995). In this perspective, rights rhetoric is proposed to be interpreted as "a screen for the transfer of Western values and economic practices dependent on a neoliberal conception of independent and rights-bearing *individuals* as opposed to ideas of social personhood embedded in, and subordinate to, larger social units, including extended families, lineages, clans, and village (or ethnic) communities" (Scheper-Hughes and Sargent 1998: 7). In an ambitious theoretical programme that her abruptly interrupted life did not allow her to achieve (Malkki 2003), Stephens (1995) analyses children's rights, especially the rights of the child to culture, in the wake of the global politics of culture, which are strongly related to late capitalism. She analyses historical and social constructions of childhood in their entanglement with the interconnected structures of modernity: namely "capital", the nation-state, urban life, and the diverse cultural forms and subjective orientations characterizing modern Western capitalist society (Stephens 1995). Following the seminal work of the geographer Harvey, she conceptualizes the restructuring of childhood as a movement from state forms of capitalism to a period of globalized structures of capital. In this perspective, Stephens (1995: 37) argued that the culture "to which the child has primary rights is the international culture of modernity". Consequently, if in the CRC children's rights to culture refer to identity, this identity is more individual (and in some ways familial and national), rather than based on collective belongings, and the promotion of indigenous cultures is very limited (Stephens 1995). In the field of education, one can observe serious changes affecting educational systems intended to prepare children and young people to take part in a flexible society directed to the interests of profit (Stephens 1995). Within this theoretical orientation, Field (1995) shows how Japanese children are being assaulted in mind and body by continuous logics of production in the goal of taking their place in the market (Field 1995). In the same vein, André and Godin (2014) have shown that in DRC, the child labour law is implemented in the wake of the liberalization of the mining sector. As such, development programmes that try to put an end to child labour in artisanal mines, diffuse children's and parents' images in favour of a capitalist exploitation of the mines headed by transnational corporations.

3.2. Child protection, state control, and international development

Projects concerning young lives are related to state issues as well. When ratifying the CRC, numerous national governments in the South promulgated their own laws on child protection. The social anthropologist Cheney (2007) explores how international institutions such as UNICEF have mobilized, with child rights discourses, the attention of African governments and led them to direct their national development campaigns towards children as a key step in the growth of the nation. She shows how the discourse of children's rights has become a crucial aspect of the construction of child citizenship in African countries such as Uganda, to the point that even children perceive the fulfilment of their citizenship through the lens of their own rights (Cheney 2007: 44).

Beyond formal texts and political measures, childhood appears to be a public concern in many developing countries; public in the sense that issues linked to children are present on the radio, on television, and in other media through awareness-raising activities and local debates concerning issues such as child labour; the rights of the child have also become a topic of the programmes of public schools (Cheney 2007). Whereas for a long time public policies of childhood especially targeted the formal education of children, the context has now changed. Public policies are interested in children, not only while at school, but also outside school, as children categorized as "street children", "child labourers", "child soldiers, etc. These categorizations reflect the increasing fears for children and young people in society, especially "children out of place" (Connolly and Ennew 1996: 132) who, outside adult supervision, have a degree of autonomy never seen before: marginalized from the normative world of work and wages, they are "independent players" (De Boeck and Honwana 2000, Comaroff and Comaroff 2000). In such a way, the child then appears as a social concern or as a public problem. More broadly, by means of the category of childhood and in the name of the child's best interest, state power can monitor and police troubled and troubling families of different sorts within their private domain (Donzelot 1977). In such a perspective, Droz (2006) has shown how Kenyan government policy strategically refers to the language of children's rights, but in a locally adapted version, in order to control the most precarious sections of the population in ways that favour the local business class.[9]

---

9   The government has been developing "rehabilitation projects" for street families that convey the Kibaki's ethnic group ethic, which is very individualistic, comprising values of individual accountability, work and self-discipline. In doing so, these projects strategically refer to children's rights and target street children rather than street families, focusing on individuals and denying the sociological cause of the problem (Droz 2006: 359).

Anthropologists show that the development field is also involved in this powerful network of discourses about the child. Indeed, there are many actions devoted to children and many NGOs dedicated to childhood specifically. After the issue of gender, children have become the target population of many development projects in many areas: education, health and labour, to name just a few. Children and youth represent "the possibility of either an exit from Africa's current predicament or an intensification of that predicament" (Argenti and de Waal 2002: 8–9). These projects also concern different categories of children. As Boyden (1997) outlined, the Convention has become one of the main frames of reference for NGOs and international organizations linked to childhood.[10] Some anthropologists refer to the work of Foucault to analyse children's rights policies as a set of interconnected discourses spreading through all the social world, that is to say a technique of governmentality, which gives rise to "self-governing individuals" (Howard 2012: 559). With this perspective, Howard (2012) gives a very critical appraisal of anti-child-trafficking policy in Benin because it would aim to control poor children and their communities by spreading discourses on the responsibility of poor parents to keep their children at home and in school. In the same vein, Godin and André show that development programmes that aim at putting an end to child labour in artisanal mines, position and task family members in relation to the principles and representations of "responsible parenthood" (André and Godin 2014).

4. Conclusion

Anthropologists, in studying the rights of the child, are so sceptical and critical that one can legitimately pose a question similar to Hirschfeld's (2003) regarding children and anthropology: do anthropologists not like the rights of the child? As it has been argued throughout this chapter, children are so structurally dominated that their perspectives have only been recently recognized in anthropology as a worthy topic of enquiry. The renewed interest in children in anthropology is especially motivated by the desire to document and analyse their lifeworlds, the ways in which they perceive social life, as well as their ability for resistance and symbolic creativity. An initial disbelief in human rights was also shared by anthropologists who did not consider human rights as a noble subject for anthropological enquiry until societal evolutions, including globalization, shook up economies and cultures all over the world. These scepticisms bring tensions amongst anthropologists when they deal with children's rights. On the one hand, they have reservations on the images of child victims that children's rights law or development programmes can convey; on the other, they cast doubt on the relevance of children's rights law when it is based on images of autonomous children. To surmount the diverse tensions that traverse their perspective on children's rights, they tackle children's rights both from above and from below.

---

10 This may be understood within the frame of postcolonial relations. While colonial policies on childhood focused on education primarily, children, nevertheless, were far more important targets in the colonial context. Indeed, children were used by the colonial authorities as purveyors of the impulse of social change, in the interest of the colonization. In the French and Belgian colonies, the foundation of schools and the education of children were two of the key political strategies of the colonial governments. They have had considerable effect on the functioning of the African states and the formation of the political elites. Whether it is assimilationism, as adopted by France, or the politics of indigenism, understood as the Belgian version of "indirect government", the education of children was a key piece of the colonial project.

Without conceding to a strict cultural relativism which is nowadays more condemned than promoted in anthropology as in other disciplines, anthropologists go beyond the position that rights of the child are only the result of processes of official deliberations and legal negotiations: children's rights in Southern societies are also produced through strategies of survival that children, as profoundly interdependent beings, deploy in a network of social relationships, in response to sometimes very difficult circumstances. They do not deny the need for top-down structures, they even recognize the values of top-down interventions. But their empirical research shows that social justice results not only from processes in which children are protected from above, but also through the energies of children and young people from below. The political contribution of anthropologists is in this sense important: the descriptive data can help to improve the implementation of children's rights, especially for reshaping and redirecting them when their formulations are against the positive aspects of children's life. At this stage, collaborations with scholars from other disciplines are of great consequence and give rise to challenging interdisciplinary perspectives (Hanson and Nieuwenhuys 2013; Boyden and Bourdillon 2012). Anthropologists also see children as being located at a crossroads of many cultural and political projects. These are the result of the violence and risks that children have had to face in contexts shaped by neoliberal politics from the late 1980s on. At the same time, these multiple projects, including children's rights law, correspond to violence and an increasing expansion of global capitalism. These projects concerning young lives are also related to governments' attempts to control children and adults and to the field of international development.

In sum, anthropologists have been developing critical analyses of children's rights from both below and above. Emphasizing the diverse conceptions of justice and numerous powers that shape children's life, anthropologists might play a key role in the improvement of politics of children's rights that would pursue social justice. But as the scepticism of anthropologists regarding top-down interventions, structures and the agents involved in these processes remains, one can legitimately ask: in which ways is anthropology able to improve children's rights law?

Questions for debate and discussion

- What are the tensions that anthropologists have to face when they tackle children's rights?
- What are the epistemological and methodological challenges to which anthropologists have to rise while developing analyses of children's rights?
- In which ways do anthropologists tackle children's rights both from below and from above?
- How can they go beyond their suspicion and engage with other disciplines for improving children's rights law?

References

Abebe T. (2013), "Interdependent rights and agency: the role of children in collective livelihood strategies in rural Ethiopia", in Hanson K and Nieuwenhuys O. (eds), *Reconceptualizing Children's Rights in International Development: Living Rights, Social Justice, Translations*. Cambridge: Cambridge University Press: 71–92.

André G. and Godin M. (2014), "Children's rights in the DRC and neoliberal reforms: the case of mines in the province of Katanga", in Twum-Danso A. I. and Ansell N (eds), *Children's Lives in an Era of Children's Rights: The Progress of the Convention on the Rights of the Child in Africa*, London: Routledge.

André G. and Godin M. (2013), "Child labour, agency and family dynamics: The case of mining in Katanga (DRC)", *Childhood* (First published online before print).

Archambault C. (2011), "Ethnographic Empathy and the Social Contexts of Rights: *Rescuing* Maasai Girls from Early Marriage", *American Anthropologist*, 113(4): 632–643.

Archambault C. (2010), "Fixing families of mobile children: Recreating kinship and belonging among Maasai adoptees in Kenya", *Childhood,* 17(2): 229–242.

Benedict R. (1935), *Patterns of Culture,* London: Routledge and Kegan Paul.

Bluebond-Langner M. and Korbin J. E. (2007), "Challenges and Opportunities in the Anthropology of childhoods: Introduction to *In Focus* Section on Children, Childhoods and Childhood Studies", *American Anthropologist*, 109(2): 241–246.

Bonnet M., Hanson K., Lange M.-F., Nieuwenhuys O. and Schlemmer B. (2006), *Enfants travailleurs. Repenser l'enfance,* Lausanne: Page Deux.

Boyden J. (1997), Childhood and the policy makers: A comparative perspective on the globalization of childhood. In James A. and Prout A. (eds), *Constructing and Reconstructing Childhood: Contemporary Issues in the Sociological Study of Childhood,* London: Falmer Press.

Boyden J. and Bourdillon M. (2012), *Childhood Poverty: Multidisciplinary Approaches.* Basingstoke, UK: Palgrave Macmillan.

Boyden J. and de Berry J. (2004), *Children and Youth on the Front Line. Ethnography, armed conflict and Displacement,* New York: Berghahn Books.

Brems E. (2013), "Inclusive universality and the child-caretaker dynamic", Hanson K. and Nieuwenhuys O., *Reconceptualizing Children's Rights in International Development. Living Rights, Social Justice, Translations,* Cambridge: Cambridge University Press.

Cheney K. E. (2012), "Killing them softly? Using children's rights to empower Africa's orphans and vulnerable children", *International Social Work*, 56(1): 92–102.

Cheney K. E. (2007), *Pillars of the Nation: Child Citizens and Ugandan National Development*, Chicago: University Chicago Press.

Comaroff J. and Comaroff J. (2000), "Réflexions sur la jeunesse. Du passé à la postcolonie", *Politique africaine,* 80 : 90–110.

Connolly M. and Ennew J. (1996), "Introduction. Children Out of Place", *Childhood,* 3(2): 131–145.

Cowan J. K., Dembourg M.-B. and Wilson R. A. (2001), *Culture and Rights: Anthropological Perspectives,* Cambridge: Cambridge University Press.

Danic I., Delalande J. and Rayou P. (2006), *Enquêter auprès d'enfants et de jeunes : objets, méthodes et terrains de recherche en sciences sociales.* Rennes: Presses universitaires de Rennes.

De Boeck F. (2000), "Le 'deuxième monde' et les 'enfants-sorciers' en république démocratique du Congo", *Politique Africaine,* 80(4): 32–57.

De Boeck F. and Honwana A. (2000), Enfants, jeunes et politique, *Politique africaine,* 80.

De Herdt T. (2011), *À la recherche de l'État en RD Congo: acteurs et enjeux d'une reconstruction post-conflit*. Paris: l'Harmattan.

Denov M. (2010), *Child Soldiers: Sierra Leone's Revolutionary United Front.* Cambridge: Cambridge University Press.

De Suremain Ch.-E. (2006), "Affinité horizontale et stratégies de survie parmi les *enfants de la rue.* La bande Solitarios à La Paz (Bolivie)", *Tiers Monde*, 185(1): 113–132.

De Waal A. and Argenti N. (eds) (2002), *Young Africa: Realizing the Rights of Children and Youth,* Trenton, NJ: Africa World Press.

Donzelot J. (1977), *La police des familles,* Paris: Editions de Minuit.

Droz Y. (2006), "Street children and the ethic of work: New policy for an old morale, Nairobi", *Childhood,* 13(3): 349–363.

Edelman M. and Haugerud A. (2005), *The Anthropology of Development and Globalization. From Classical Political Economy to Contemporary Neoliberalism,* Malden, MA: Blackwell.

Elson D. (1982), "The differentiation of children's labour in the capitalist labour market", *Development and Change,* 13(4): 479–97.

Ennew J. (2000), *Street and Working Children: A Guide to Planning,* London: Save the Children.

Ennew J. (1986), "The sexual exploitation of children", Basingstoke, UK: Palgrave Macmillan.

Field N. (1995), "The child as laborer and consumer: The disappearance of childhood in contemporary Japan", in Stephens, S. (ed.), *Children and the Politics of Culture.* Princeton, NJ: Princeton University Press: 51–76.

Fortes M. (1978), "Family, marriage and fertility in West Africa", in Oppong C. (ed.), *Marriage, Fertility, and Parenthood in West Africa,* Canberra: Australian National University Press: 17–54.

Gaskins S. (2000), "Children daily activities in a Mayan Village: A culturally grounded description", *Cross-Cultural Research*, 34: 375–389.
Goodale M. (2006), "Introduction to *Anthropology and Human Rights in a New Key*", *American Anthropologist*, 108(1): 1–8.
Goody E. (1981), *Parenthood and Social Reproduction. Fostering and Occupational Roles in West Africa*, Cambridge: Cambridge University Press.
Grignon C. and Passeron J.-C. (1989), *Le Savant et le Populaire. Misérabilisme et populisme en sociologie et en littérature*, Paris: Seuil.
Guillermet E. (2010), *Constructions de l'orphelin au Niger. Anthropologie d'une enfance globalisée*, Saarbrücken, Germany: Editions Universitaires Européennes.
Hanson K. and Nieuwenhuys O. (eds) (2013), *Reconceptualizing Children's Rights in International Development: Living Rights, Social Justice, Translations*. Cambridge: Cambridge University Press.
Hatch E. (1997), "The good side of relativism", *Journal of Anthropological Research*, 53(3): 371–381.
Hawes J. M. (1991), *The Children's Rights Movement: A History of Advocacy and Protection*, Boston, MA: Twayne Publishers.
Hecht T. (1998), *At Home in the Street: Street Children of Northeast Brazil*; New York: Cambridge University Press.
Henderson P. C. (2013), "*Ukugana* : 'Informal marriage' and children's rights discourse among rural 'AIDS-orphans' in KwaZulu-Natal, South Africa", in Hanson K. and Nieuwenhuys O. (eds), *Reconceptualizing Children's Rights in International Development. Living Rights, Social Justice, Translations*. Cambridge: Cambridge University Press: 29–47.
Hirschfeld L. A. (2003), "Pourquoi les anthropologues n'aiment-ils pas les enfants?", *Enfant et apprentissage, Terrain*, 40: 21–48.
Hoffman D. (2003), "Like beasts in the bush: Synonyms of childhood and youth in Sierra Leone", *Postcolonial Studies*, 6(3): 295–308.
Honwana A. and De Boeck F. (2005), *Makers and Breakers. Children and Youth in Postcolonial Africa*, Oxford, Trenton and Dakar: James Currey, Africa World Press and Codesria.
Howard N. P. (2012), "A critical appraisal of anti-child trafficking discourse and policy in Southern Benin", *Childhood*, 19(4): 554–568.
Jacquemin M. (2009), *Petites nièces et petites bonnes à Abidjan. Les mutations de la domesticité juvénile. Travail, genre et sociétés*, 22.
James A., Jenks C. and Prout A. (1998), *Theorizing Childhood*, Cambridge, UK: Polity Press.
Katz C. (1996), "On the back of children: Children and work in Africa", *Anthropology of Work Review*, 17(1): 3–8.
Lallemand S. (2002), "Esquisse de la courte histoire de l'anthropologie de l'enfance. Ainsi que de certains de ses thèmes électifs", *Journal des Africanistes*, 71(1): 9–18.
Lallemand S. (1993), *Circulation des enfants en société traditionnelle. Prêt, don, échange*. Paris: L'Harmattan.
Lansdown G. (2001), "Promouvoir la participation des enfants au processus décisionnel démocratique", UNICEF, Insight Inocenti, Italie.
Le Vine R. A. (2007), "Ethnographic studies of childhood: A historical overview", *American Anthropologist*, 109(2): 247–260.
Liebel M. (ed.) (2012), *Children's Rights from Below: Cross-Cultural Perspectives*. New York: Palgrave Macmillan.
Lundy L., McEvoy L. and Byrne B. (2011), "Working with young children as co-researchers: An approach informed by the United Nations Convention on the Rights of the Child", *Early Education and Development*, 22(5): 714–736.
Lyotard J.-F. (1979), *La Condition postmoderne : rapport sur le savoir*, Paris: Minuit.
Malkki L. (2003), "Children and the gendered politics of globalization: In remembrance of Sharon Stephens", *American Ethnologist*, 30(2): 216–224.
Massart G. (2009), Les pratiques de mobilité des enfants et des jeunes en Afrique de l'Ouest. Analyses de leurs motivations et expériences. Available at http://masscabas.net/pdf/article%20mobilite%20Massart.pdf.
Massart G. (2007), *Violence Against Girls: Their Experience and Protection in West Africa*, Plan International.
Mead M. (1928a), *Coming of Age in Samoa*, New York: William Morrow.
Mead M. (1928b), "Samoan children at work and play", *Natural History*, 28: 626–636.
Mead M. (1930), *Growing up in New Guinea*, New York: William Morrow.
Merry S. E. (2006), *Human Rights and Gender Violence: Translating International Law into local Justice*, Chicago and London: The University of Chicago Press.

Messer E. (1993), "Anthropology and human rights", *Annual Review Anthropology*, 22: 221–249.
Middleton J. (ed.) (1970), *From Child to Adult: Studies in the Anthropology of Education*, New York: Natural History Press.
Montgomery H. (2009), *An Introduction to Childhood: Anthropological Perspectives on Children's Lives*, Malden, MA: Wiley-Blackwell.
Montgomery H. (2001), *Modern Babylon. Prostituting Children in Thailand*, New York and Oxford: Berghahn Books.
Nagengast C. (1997), "Women, minorities, and indigenous peoples: Universalism and cultural relativity", *Journal of Anthropological Research*, 53, 349–369.
Nieuwenhuys O. (2008), "Editorial. The ethics of children's rights", *Childhood*, 15(1): 4–11.
Nieuwenhuys O. (2001), "By the sweat of their brow? 'Street children', NGOs and children's rights in Addis Ababa. *Africa*, 71(4): 539–557.
Nieuwenhuys O. (1994), *Children's Lifeworlds: Gender, Welfare, and Labour in the Developing World*, London and New York: Routledge.
Okyere S. (2012), *Understanding child labour: The case of children working in artisanal gold mining at Kenyasi, Ghana*, Thesis submitted to the University of Nottingham for the degree of Doctor of Philosophy, University of Nottingham.
O'Neill T. (2013), "Young carpet weavers on the rights threshold: Protection or practical self-determination?", in Hanson K. and Nieuwenhuys O. (eds), *Reconceptualizing Children's Rights in International Development*, Cambridge: Cambridge University Press: 93–112.
Pells K. (2012), "Rights are everything we don't have: Clashing conceptions of vulnerability and agency in the daily lives of Rwandan children and youth", *Children's Geographies*, 10(4): 427–440.
Poncelet M., André G. and De Herdt T. (2010), La survie de l'école primaire congolaise (RDC) : héritage colonial, hybridité et résilience, *Autrepart*, 54(2): 23–41.
Raum O. (1940), *Chaga Childhood*, London: Oxford University Press.
Razy E., de Suremain C.-E., and Pache Huber V. (2012), Introduction, 'Les anthropologies de l'enfance et des enfants à travers le monde. In Elodie Razy, Charles-Edouard de Suremain, Véronique Pache Huber (éds), *AnthropoChildren. Ethnographic Issues on Children and Childhood* 1. Available at http://popups.ulg.ac.be/AnthropoChildren/sommaire.php?id=121.
Reynolds P, Nieuwenhuys O and Hanson K. (2006), "Refractions of children's rights in development practice: a view from anthropology", *Childhood*, 13(3): 291–303.
Reynolds P. (1991), *Dance Civet Cat: Child Labour in the Zambezi Valley*, Harare: Baobab Books.
Richards A. (1939), *Land, Labour, and Diet in Northern Rhodesia: An Economic Study of the Bemba Tribe*, London: Oxford University Press.
Rose N. (1989), *Governing the Soul: The Shaping of the Private Self*, London: Routledge.
Rosen D. M. (2007), "Child soldiers, international humanitarian law and the globalization of childhood", *American Anthropologist*, 109(2): 296–306.
Ruddick S. (2003), "The politics of aging: Globalization and the restructuring of youth and childhood", *Antipode*, 35: 334–362.
Saadi I. (2012), "Children's rights as 'work in progress': The conceptual and practical contributions of working children's movements", in Liebel M. (ed.), *Children's Rights from Below: Cross-Cultural Perspectives*. New York: Palgrave Macmillan: 143–160.
Scheper-Hughes N. and Sargent C. (1998), "Introduction: The cultural politics of childhood", in Scheper-Hughes N. and Sargent C. (eds), *Small Wars: The Cultural Politics of Childhood*, Berkeley, Los Angeles and London: University of California Press.
Scheper-Hughes N. (1987), *Child Survival: Anthropological Perspectives on the Treatment and Maltreatment of Children*. Boston, MA: Reidel.
Scheper-Hughes N. (1992), *Death without Weaping: The Violence of Everyday Life in Brazil*. Berkeley, CA: Uniersity of California Press.
Schildkrout E. (1978), "Age and gender in Hausa society: Socioeconomic roles of children in urban Kano", LaFontaine J. S. (ed.), *Sex and Age as Principles of Social Stratification*, New York: Academic Press: 69–86.
Schwartzman H. B. (2001), *Children and Anthropology: Perspectives for the 21st Century*, Westport: Bergin and Garvey.
Scott J. (1976), *The Moral Economy of the Peasant: Rebellion and Subsistence in Southeast Asia*, New Haven, CT: Yale University Press.
Sirota R., 2006, *Eléments pour une sociologie de l'enfance*, Presse universitaire de Rennes.

Snodgrass G. A. (1999), "Our right is the right to be killed: Making rights real on the streets of Guatemala City", *Childhood*, 6(4), 423–442.
Spindler G. (1997), *Education and Cultural Process: Anthropological Approaches*. Prospect Heights, IL: Waveland Press (First Edition: 1975).
Stephens S. (1995), *Children and the Politics of Culture*, Princeton, NJ: Princeton University Press.
Thompson E. P. (1993), *The Making of the English Working Class,* London: Penguin. (First published 1963.)
Thorsen D. (2012), *Child Domestic Workers: Evidence from West and Central Africa*. Discussion Paper, Dakar: UNICEF WCAR.
Thorsen D. (2012), *Children Begging for Qur'ānic School Masters: Evidence from West and Central Africa*. Discussion Paper, Dakar: UNICEF WCAR.
Thorsen D. (2012), *Children Working in Commercial Agriculture: Evidence from West and Central Africa*. Discussion Paper, Dakar: UNICEF WCAR.
Turner T. (1997), "Human rights, human difference: Anthropology's contribution to an emancipatory cultural politics", *Journal of Anthropological Research*, 53: 273–290.
UNICEF, *The State of the World's Children 1980–81*. Available at www.unicef.org/sowc/archive/ENGLISH/The State of the World%27sChildren1980-81.pdf
Willis P. (1977), *Learning to Labour: How Working-Class Kids Get Working-Class Jobs*, Farnborough: Saxon House.
Whiting B. B. and Whiting J. W. M. (1975), *Children of Six Cultures: A Psycho-cultural Analysis,* Cambridge, MA: Harvard University Press.

8
Children's rights
A critical geographic perspective

Stuart C. Aitken

> ... [C]hildhood *is* a geographically diverse phenomenon. In the real world, universal childhood or youth do not exist. Young individuals lead very different kinds of lives depending on their socio-cultural context, geo-economic position, the politico-legal system of their society and other determinants that render them particular.
>
> *(Kallio and Häkli 2013, 1)*

Two relatively recent struggles highlight the importance of understanding that young people's rights are geographically variable. In the early 2000s, as Slovenia prepared for accession to the European Union, a series of rights abuses came to light. These violations involved the official "erasure" of over 25,671 people (mostly ethnic Serbs, Croats, Bosnians, and some Roma) from Slovenia's permanent residential register in 1991, thereby denying them legal status and an opportunity for citizenship. Official statistics enumerate 5,360 of the erased as under 18 years of age (Kogovšek 2010, 133). *Izbrisani* ("erased") infants were entered into the Slovenian register of births as citizens of another Yugoslav republic, but often the republics in question were not informed of the birth. In that *jus sanguinis* was used to grant citizenship, it did not matter that these children were born in and lived their whole life in Slovenia. Not only were they denied rights and legal status in Slovenia, they were not claimed by any other former Yugoslavian states. Erasure led to stateless children. For years, these young people were literally locked-in-place with few rights and considerable privations. The direct consequences of losing status during the erasure process included loss of health insurance, no state-funded schooling beyond primary level, little likelihood of attaining legal employment and no possibility of legally driving a car or getting married. Other aspects of erasure included daily exposure to the sometimes arbitrary conduct of police officers and bureaucrats, thereby limiting free movement and access to information. The contexts of erasure sometimes showed up as strictures and rebukes, as detention and expulsions, or as denial of access in processes that seemed capricious and at the whim of bureaucrats. In a subtle form of state violence, during the 1990s and early 2000s, erased young people were isolated one from another, and blame for their misery was placed squarely on their and their family's shoulders. The situation was sufficiently dire for erased resident Aleksander Todorović that he began a hunger strike at Ljubljana Zoo in February 2002 and, by so doing, brought the plight of the *Izbrisani* to the attention of the media. From this action the *Association of the Erased Residents* was created, which not only provided a political focus for the group, it also created a forum for the collection of erasure stories (cf. Zorn and Lipovec Čebron 2008). A series of hunger strikes in 2005 began at the Croatian border and then moved to the UNICEF headquarters in Ljubljana to publicize the children who were part of the erasure. In 2006 a group of *Izbrisani* (including young people), activists and lawyers drove to the European Court on Human Rights in Strasbourg in what was dubbed "The Caravan of the Erased" to highlight, among other things, the plight of erased children.[1]

The second example of the geographic variability of child rights violations arises at about the same time as the *Izbrisani* were beginning to get media and legal attention in Europe. In Spring 2006, students in Chile took to the streets and occupied high schools to protest the neoliberal privatization of education that began with the Pinochet administration in the 1980s and continued through the 1990s to accelerate disparities between rich and poor students. Within a few weeks the protests grew from a single march in Santiago to a nationwide campaign that placed half of the schools in Chile on strike or under occupation by students. The marches peaked on May 30 2006 when 800,000 students took to the streets. The protests and occupations became known as the Penguin Revolution because of the black and white uniforms (and sometimes school desks) that filled the streets, and it is often referred to as the first social media revolution because of young people using mobile phones and texting to organize quickly and in advance of government reactions. The *Pingüinos* received coverage on the websites of international non-governmental organizations (NGO), and they gained support from labor organizations and from students in affluent private schools who came out onto the streets in support. The United Nations (in particular, UNICEF) contacted the Chilean government to voice concerns on behalf of children's rights. By taking over the streets in their school uniforms – by being, literally, out-of-place[2] – the *Pingüinos* created a new space that caught the attention of the world. The movement simultaneously occupied virtual space through social media and the Internet.

I begin with these two examples because they not only question the quirky geographic contexts of mobility, citizenship, and education, and raise the potency of children's presence and young people's voices to interrogate the core of geo-economic restructuring and neoliberal statehood, but they demand, in different ways, an understanding of the relations between children's rights and space. *Izbrisani* children were locked-in-place and deprived of basic human rights to protection and civic identity; with school uniforms and desks, *Pingüino* children were out-of-place to highlight their right to a fair and just education system. Together, these examples suggest children's rights in place and rights to space. The idea of place that I focus on in this chapter is less about a phenomenological sense-of-place and belonging wherein people emotionally experience their place in the world (although it is that too), and more about the political use of places to define those who have access and rights and those who are excluded.

---

1   The European Court of Human Rights (Third Section), the case of Kurić and others v. Slovenia (application No. 26828/06), initiated in 2006, judgment in favor of plaintiffs in 2012.
2   This is a somewhat different context from the "out-of-place" elaborated by Mark Connolly and Judith Ennew (1996, 132), which focused on street children's "dislocation from the places that are commonly referred to as "normal" for western, modern middle-class children – family homes schools and clubs organized by adults," because the *Pingüinos'* actions were not about dislocation but about a willful, politically-motivated relocation that aligned in part with Henri LeFebvre's (1991, 1996) call for the right to urban space as a common right to renewed access and transformation (of space and of ourselves).

Ironically, the *Izbrisani* children were locked-in-place by forces of exclusivity, which made clear that they did not have rights or belong, but they could not leave for fear of being unable to return to the place they knew as home. Space as I use the term in this chapter is less about a surface upon which we are placed, and more about the way spaces are created and produced (LeFebvre 1991; Massey 2005). Most often, space is taken for granted and the ways it is created and produced are left un-thought. But there are inherent politics to that creation and production, and we – adults and children alike – have a collective right to be part of those politics, and hence the production of space. The *Pingüinos'* case highlights the power of young people wilfully occupying spaces (schools) and taking over streets to push for a fair and just education system; the *Izbrisani* case highlights the ways a group of people collected around the power of young stories and took political action to win rights in place. As David Harvey (2008: 23) points out "[t]he freedom to make and remake our cities [read spaces] and ourselves is ... one of the most precious yet most neglected of our human rights".

In what follows I begin by sketching a critical perspective on why space matters to children's rights. I follow this with a brief discussion of the early work on children's rights by Marxist geographer Bill Bunge before moving, in the third part of the chapter, through some feminist-inspired work by geographers that focuses on sites of reproduction. Understanding reproduction is a critical expansion of Marx's production/consumption dialectic, and feminist geographers have taken pains to show the ways that this dialectic lands in local places to impact the lives of women and children (Katz 2004) and how, in turn, the work of women and children is crucial for the global political economy (Gibson-Graham 1996, 2006). I expand on reproduction in the fourth section with a consideration of children's rights in the variegated contexts of global space; what geographers call *heteretopias*. In the fifth section I consider critiques of the 1989 United Nations Convention on the Rights of the Child (CRC) in advance of problematizing children's rights in a globalized world and, specifically, their rights in place and their rights to space. In the last twenty-five years a growing concern with post-structural and relational perspectives raises questions about what, specifically, children's rights do. What are their affects? I argue in this penultimate section for a consideration of what rights do spatially and, concomitantly, for the importance of spatial rights. In the conclusion I return briefly to the ongoing *Izbrisani* and *Pingüino* struggles and offer questions for future consideration.

1. Space matters

In 1994, Jens Qvortrup and his colleagues published *Childhood Matters,* an anthology of papers emphasizing new critical theories and interpretations of children in modern society. The enduring focus of the papers was that children mattered in and of themselves, and in terms of their relations with families and communities, and the state. The volume was in part responsible for what became known as the new sociology of childhood, which emphasized young people's agency and autonomy (James *et al.* 1998). Qvortrup and his colleagues argued that children are important in their own right not only for themselves but also for the role they play in society, and it is not appropriate to think of young people as merely developing and integrating into larger societal wholes (Qvortrup *et al.* 1994). With this chapter I argue that societal wholes are always geographically variable, and that studying the ways young people imagine, create, inhabit and produce spaces is crucial for understanding children's rights.

A critical geographical perspective on children's rights is founded on a *post-structural relationality* that positions space as something more than a mere container of young people's activities. *Post-structuralism* requires that we understand space as imagined, created, produced and dynamic rather than as a static three-dimensional structure within and through which life is played out. In her classic admonition to not neglect the importance of space, Doreen Massey (2005, 17) argues that the concept has "... the implacable force of the patently obvious" and, she notes forcefully, "that is the trouble" with space. Concepts of space, place and scale are much too important to suggest a simple mechanistic Cartesian association or an apolitical phenomenological embeddedness.[3] Massey (2005, 19) suggests that when space is used in ways that relate to banal connections, it comes to be associated with habituation that disassociates it from a "full insertion into the political." A contemporary geographical perspective on children's rights reinforces the perspective that space is produced, is palpable and is fully political.

Relationality embraces the diverse contexts of young people's lives with an understanding that their social world is imagined and produced through spatial processes and, concomitantly, that their spatial world is imagined and produced through social processes. Geographers call this interleaving of social processes shaping the spatial and spatial processes shaping the social *spatiality*. Places are not simply sites that help understand a particular context of young people's lives, they are actively created by young people and their relations with the world (including other young people, adults, communities, institutions and environments). Interlocked with and woven throughout these socio-spatial complexities are the contexts of scale and how it is produced. At its most abstract, scale is conceived as the relations between the local and the global, and within those relations are embedded powerful family, community, city, regional, national and state forces. Scale conceived in this way problematically suggests a nested, hierarchical structure through which young people come to understand the world, but it is altogether reasonable to think of the world as ontologically flat wherein scale is seen as simply another network of relations (cf. Marston *et al.*, 2005). Within these assemblages, young people occupy and move through a range of relations: some are intense, others banal; some are exploitative, others coddling; some are about exposure and tokenism, others about erasure; some are about dependencies, others are about political will.

A common misuse of the so-called spatial turn in the sciences, social sciences and humanities is to uncritically add the physicality of space to the mix and stir. Space is much more nuanced than its tangibility suggests, but an enduring research and policy legacy from the Enlightenment onwards is to work through human relations, including rights perspectives, with the assumption that location is a self-referential system of unquestionable materialism (Harvey 2014). If noted at all in public policy discussions focusing on children's rights, space is seen as a container in the sense of distinctions between private and public abuses, the location of the next crisis, or discussions about where intervention is possible. From this diminished perspective, space is distinguished simply as a site of disaster, exploitation and abuse or as an area traversed.

The metaphor of space as an unwavering coordinate system resonates with a static and universal rights-based approach to children's well-being, which fixes young people in particular subject positions from where they are allowed to move only into limited and prescribed adulthoods. A critical rights-based approach to children's geographies not only creates participation, provision and protection as prescribed by the CRC, but also flexibility and

---

3   Cartesian associations are exemplified in the two- and three-dimensional spaces of maps and plans. They are guided and grounded by abstract frameworks such as x/y/z coordinate systems, degrees of latitude and longitude, or local cadastral systems. Apolitical phenomenological embeddedness is represented by ideas that focus exclusively on concepts like sense-of-place, *genius loci*, or belonging, without consideration of the forces that produce these spaces and attempt to keep them for particular people and/or events. Often we give little thought to the ways spaces are produced and created.

opportunities for children and young people simultaneously to *be* as politically recognized and engaged participants in the world (even, simply, by their presence) and to *become-other* in the sense that their "development" (and the world's) is not simply towards something prescribed by adults (and the "developed" Global North). Thus, for example, provision is not just about sending in aid packages as a humanitarian gesture in times of need, it is about unpacking corporate and state power structures to uncover the processes behind the spatial inequalities that harm children. Protection, then, is about understanding why, for example, some neighborhoods are safe for young people while others are not, while participation is about understanding the political implications of children's presence in a particular place, and not simply their token input into policies that affect them. Creating flexibility and opportunities for children moves us away from a problematic cause/effect rationale for protection, provision and participation and enables young people to *become* something other than what is prescribed by the adult world (and chose to take on parts of the world that fit and discard that which does not necessarily work): it creates a space for dislocation and surprise so that things do not necessarily remain the same. To suggest a critical perspective that enables young people to make and remake spaces and themselves as a collective right suggests a change of global proportions that is not unrealistic: it resonates with an interconnected world where schoolchildren take over public streets in Chile to overturn aspects of an unjust education policy, and where the destitution of Slovenian erased children erupts into a constitutional crisis.

2. Geographical expeditions

Bill Bunge was one of the first geographers to focus on children's rights by suggesting that the plight of poor children is the touchstone upon which the ills of society reside; that children are the "canaries in the coalmine" (Bunge and Bordessa 1975, 7). In his "geographical expeditions" in Detroit and Toronto in the 1970s, Bunge highlighted the plight of poor children to make visible socio-spatial problems and he argued for a focus on children's rights as a solution to those problems (Bunge 1971, 1973; Bunge and Bordessa 1975). His famous map of Detroit with infant mortality rates from the Global South superimposed on US census tracks suggests the nearness of seemingly distant issues; that the so-called Third World resides in Detroit. His "fly cover baby regions" map was created from field observations of whether houses had screens on windows and doors. Bunge's focus on spatial "immediacy" wrecks the idea of static research that is out of touch with what children need now: He describes encounters with African-American women who

> hated my concern about the three dimensionality of the species ... filled with hatred against me because I did not notice the children being murdered by automobiles in front of their homes or children starving in front of abundant food. "Immediacy" was their cry, "To Hell with the World!"
>
> *(Bunge 1971, 170)*

Bunge was a scientist and a Marxist, and his intent was to stir a revolution that was as obvious to him as if it were part of Darwin's theories of species evolution (cf. Bunge 1973).

Beginning with a concern for children's rights and well-being, Bunge moved through extensive fieldwork to produce knowledge that enabled the creation of new kinds of maps. Donna Haraway (1991, 191) calls these "maps of consciousness" for people, who by virtue of their age, class, ethnicity or sex are marginalized through masculinist, racist and colonialist domination. Haraway raised concerns about the ways we, as researchers, situated ourselves vis-à-vis our so-called research subjects. For Bunge, in the 1970s, there were no social theories of situatedness. Nonetheless, he saw the ways that spatial and economic models of the time masked important social and political contexts, because they missed sites of reproduction where certain groups – especially children, but also injured workers, retired workers, unemployed workers and sexually, racially, ethnically and religiously discriminated-against workers – constituted marginalized groups even during periods of national economic well-being (Bunge 1971, 61). To offset this problem he reworked the standard spatial models of the day, such as those of the Chicago School of Urban Ecology, to emphasize oppression and rights (cf. Aitken 2010, 53–56).

The pioneering work of Bunge and others propelled a spatial revolution in academia through the 1970s and 1980s that led to geography as a discipline gaining credibility as a science with the development, amongst other spatial technologies, of Geographic Information Science (GIS) and Global Positioning Systems (GPS). During the 1990s, strands of this work focused on young people's map-making abilities and their apprehension of places and environments (e.g. Matthews 1992), and by the 2000s GIS was used to highlight children's activities and health (e.g. Wridt 2010), and their relations to planning and policy-making (e.g. Berglund and Nordin 2007). Unfortunately, Bunge's critical spatiality and his focus on children's rights were mostly lost to the technological mandates of spatial science. An enduring rights-based approach that encompassed young people emerged from elsewhere in the discipline, as feminist geographers focused on sites of reproduction.

3. Sites of reproduction

In 1982, Jan Monk and Sue Hanson published a landmark paper that heralded the beginnings of feminist geography. In making an argument for not excluding half of the human in human geography, they put forward the case for looking at women's rights and issues in a discipline that was at the time focused on the politics, economics and cultures of men. In addition to opening geography to the work and lives of women, feminism raised the importance of reproductive spheres and the rights of those who resided within them; these spheres became known as sites of reproduction. Kim England (1993), for example, highlighted the "pink-collar ghettoes" of mid- to late-twentieth-century suburban areas as sites of reproduction that sequestered women, the elderly and children in spaces deprived of adequate economic and political opportunities. Monk and Katz (1993) brought together the work of geographers, anthropologists and sociologists in an edited collection that focused on the spaces through which young girls are raised to women, and the spatial processes that are woven through intergenerational and embedded community relations. A clarion call to also focus on young people's rights in and through space was made to the extent that by the early 2000s, Robert Vanderbeck and Cheryl Dunkley were able to claim that

> (t)he very coalescence of children's geographies into a recognizable subfield has … been predicated on (the) exclusion … of young people's lives and experiences from mainstream human geography, mirroring broader patterns of social relations which peripheralize young people's experiences and perspectives.
>
> *(Vanderbeck and Dunkley 2004, 178)*

Perhaps more than any other geographer, Cindi Katz (1991, 2004, 2011, and also Mitchell *et al.* 2004) situates the work, lives and rights of children and young people within this evolving critical feminist perspective on social reproduction. She notes the ways that young people's rights to education and economic opportunities are undervalued by a global neoliberal system that is based upon uneven spatial distributions of wealth. Young people who were part of her empirical work in Sudan and New York, Katz argues, are fodder for an unjust global system, and their rights to education are sorely distorted in favor of creating specific kinds of labor. In rural Sudan, economic restructuring through the 1980s and 1990s moved development money into large-scale irrigation projects that attracted young men away from villages, which then became dependent on remittances and the on-site labor of women and children. By comparison, in New York City (NYC) the education system failed a generation of young people who were trained for jobs that no longer existed. In both these cases, Katz argues, larger neoliberal economic forces reworked capital through particular endeavors (e.g. banking, tied aid) and sites (e.g. housing, large scale development projects) while a state-based welfare safety net that bolstered basic rights to food, health-care and housing was stripped of resources at the same time that the political clout of organized labor diminished. The enduring result in both Sudan and NYC, argues Katz, was the creation of an army of de-skilled and desperate young people without adequate rights to work, health-care or housing.

At around the same time that Katz was raising awareness of children's rights in the context of social reproduction and globalization, feminist sensitivities to difference, diversity and political activism at the local scale focused discussion on children's agency (Aitken 1994, 2001; Holloway and Valentine 2000), and adolescents as unique social and political actors (Skelton and Valentine 1998). In addition, the notion of what constitutes a "normal childhood" (e.g. innocent, playful, carefree and focused on education) in "normal spaces" (e.g. nuclear and extended families in caring communities and states) was challenged by geographic work that confronted normalcy, contextualized children's rights in different ways and looked at young people's competencies in a variety of adult spaces where they might be thought of as out-of-place (Connolly and Ennew 1996) and/or doing unchildlike things (Aitken 2001).

Bosco and his colleagues (2011), for example, use Moosa-Mitha's (2005) difference-centered approach to argue the rights of young children to translate for their non-English speaking parents in immigrant communities at a time when California was considering making such practices illegal. Other work challenges assumptions that childhood should be a time devoted to play and education. Researchers raise concerns about children's right to play and education as an enduring focus of institutions such as the International Labor Organization (ILO). Alternatively, and particularly in the global South, studies show the importance of children as part of the productive sphere through paid labor (Aitken *et al.* 2006; Nieuwenhuys 2008). In addition, Elsbeth Robson and Nicola Ansell's (Robson 2010; Ansell *et al.* 2011) studies of young people in sub-Saharan African home-based health care suggest a growing sense of self-esteem fostered by taking on adult responsibilities. Studies from the global North note young people's independence through video gaming or on email and their rights to the Internet, social media and other virtual spaces (Valentine and Holloway 2002), while others focus on specific spaces of the political including young people's civic rights in relation to communities, society and the state (Bosco *et al.* 2011, Kallio and Häkli 2011, 2013). In addition, and developing from the right-to-the-city movement (Mitchell 2003), geographers focused on young people's rights to protest and take back public space (Staeheli and Mitchell 2008; Staeheli *et al.*, 2013; see also Mitchell, Chapter 10 in this Handbook), and their rights to engage politically at a variety of scales (Azmi *et al.*, 2013; Aitken 2014). Empirical studies that challenge the normalcy of childhood and the banality of space developed in combination with theoretical discussions and policy debates on what precisely constitutes the place of children in cities and in a rapidly globalizing world governed by increasingly neoliberal social, economic and political structures.

3.1. Children's rights through global heterotopias and local places

In terms of current neoliberal agendas, the rights of children to participate freely in society are ascertainable only within specific socio-historic and geographic contexts. Mehmoona Moosa-Mitha (2005) is particularly concerned about Enlightenment ideas that espouse individuation, communitarianism and cosmopolitanism, and offers instead a difference-centered approach to rights and citizenship that focuses on two axes of recognition. Her first axis establishes the notion of the citizen as an active self, and the second defines the citizen self as a relational, dialogical self, who gains a sense of identity through relationships and dependencies with other people, places and events. Geographers add a third axis to this difference-centered approach that recognizes a young person's multiple spatial relations. To the degree that Moosa-Mitha redefines children's rights relationally by examining if children are able to have a *presence* in the many interactions through which they participate, these relations must also recognize young people's *presence* through multiple spatial scales and within local heterotopias. By presence, Moosa-Mitha means the degree to which the "voice, contribution and agency of the child is acknowledged" (Moosa-Mitha 2005: 381). Not to recognize the presence of a political subject is itself a form of oppression. Presence, more than autonomy and individuation, acknowledges the self not only as relational and dialogical, but also as spatial. Young people always take up space.

An axis of multiple spatial relations suggests that it is problematic to consider children's rights outside of issues of global consumption, production and reproduction because, as noted in the previous section, in a connected world of flexible capital and instantaneous market adjustments local places are increasingly important for understanding the contexts of children's well-being. Of course, young people are not a simple *tabula rasa* upon which the will of capital is etched and rights are delimited as unviable. Children not only "become other" through the influences of these changing objects, they also bring something of themselves into cultural life as they actively participate in the day-to-day workings of places. In the same sense that the processes of globalization are neither unidirectional nor even, then it is impossible to characterize or position a uniform context for childhood because the local conditions of global children are so varied. In noting that local "*belonging* and *inclusion* are contested terms," Staeheli and Kofman (2004: 1) suggest that they are nonetheless a vital part of imbuing political subjects with rights. As a consequence, establishing the spatial rights of children may be about difference rather than inclusion, and positioning young people as relational citizen-selves rather than as non-adults may be about understanding cultural reproduction. By arguing for a focus on spatial rights within global heterotopias, this chapter pushes a little further the idea of children's rights as human rights elaborated in the Handbook's introduction. The introduction noted that just like human rights more generally, children's rights originate from the quest for human dignity and social justice, but the concrete meaning of the rights varies from person to person. Young people's needs also vary from place to place and their needs for space vary from person to person. So, too, rights should encompass this spatial variability and personal flexibility. The important point is that young people are afforded the right to make and remake spaces and themselves in an ongoing dialectical process.

Roger Hart (1997, 16) argues that the debate over children's rights is only important to the extent that it encompasses a discussion of fundamental changes in culture and how culture reproduces itself. Anne Trine Kjørholt (2002, 2008), for example, focuses on Norwegian projects that suggest a shift in focus from the "developing" child to the "competent" child; and from "pedagogy" to "culture". The problem, she notes, is that a culture made by children (children's own culture or play culture) is rapidly disappearing as they become what she calls "symbolic participants" in a larger neoliberal agenda. The larger neoliberal agenda, Harvey (2005) argues, was implemented by Thatcher and Reagan but began with Milton Friedman and the so-called Chicago Boys' school of economics. It is a coherently thought out economic plan for a particular form of global capitalism that takes decision-making away from individuals and families but nonetheless forces the responsibility for those decisions squarely on the shoulders of those individuals and families least able to support economic failures. Children are symbolic participants in this plan because they have no input into its formulation and implementation, and they are unwitting victims of the inevitable outcomes of greater spatial disparities and social inequalities. Gibson-Graham (2006) notes that although this system appears gargantuan, rigid, and unwaveringly tilted towards the already rich, there are nonetheless always contexts of subversion and transformation, and these most often occur at the local scale, in what they call *community economies*. A critical examination of what this means for young people is needed in a world where more and more children are growing up in complex multi-cultural and multi-scalar settings creating identities that have the potential to confound adultist neoliberal projects (Aitken 2001, 174). This is not about children being or becoming citizens but about *child formation, children's rights, sustainability* and *citizenship formation* (Marston and Mitchell 2004) that contests these terms as it critiques them.

4. Contesting universal children's rights and global discourses

Iris Marion Young (1990) suggests that identity politics are laid out along axes of difference, which are characterized through gender, age, race/ethnicity, disability, sexuality and so forth. Geographers add spatial as an axis of political identity (e.g. nation, border, that place, this town) and show how spaces are tied intimately to other axes of identity (e.g. adult, adolescent, student, child).[4] Kjørholt (2008) focuses on the impossibility of authenticity in children's voices and the nonetheless undaunted search for them by some national and global institutions. For example, the CRC's penchant for placing responsibility regarding particular kinds of rights on particular forms of childhood, argues Kjørholt, places it squarely in the realm of a neoliberal agenda that fixes individual categories of existence and identity. As a counter, she argues that children reproduce life on par with adults and, as such, they are co-creators of their childhoods. Questions remain about how much license children are given in their part of the creation. This problem is exacerbated by the specificity of CRC, which highlights a problematic subject/object dualism: the idea of children as objects of rights (the CRC's focus on protection and provision) and the idea of children as subjects of rights (the CRC's focus on participation and children making autonomous claims). Kjørholt (2008) suggests that the Western project of neoliberal globalization finds one of its most precise forms in the CRC and to the degree that this form also dominates national politics, the subject/object dualism fits nicely.

The CRC moved the rhetoric of child rights from moral to legal ground when it was ratified by most nations in the world and as attempts were made to implement its articles as national policy. There are several tensions that emanate from this top-down approach. First, and at a general level, there is tension regarding what specifically is meant by rights. As noted in the introductory chapter of this book, the CRC's categorization of protection, provision and participation does not align with the larger agenda of human rights advocacy, which focuses on civil and political rights on the one hand, and social economic and cultural rights on the other.

---

4 For example, Aitken *et al.* (2011) and Spyrou and Christou (2014) comprise studies that show how border regions affect the political identities of young people and how young people, in turn, shape the border places through which they pass.

Heller (2013) notes a geographic tension on what constitute appropriate rights' foci, with issues relating to civil and political rights predominating in Eastern Europe as opposed to social rights, which stand out in the demands of popular movements in the global South. He goes on to point out, crucially, that although there are "profound asymmetries in global civil society," there is also clear evidence that "while network linkages may be asymmetric, the outcomes are far less so ... and the playing field is in the process of being significantly leveled" (Heller 2013, 13). A well-worn critique points out that in the majority of transnational networks, including the CRC, agendas are set by actors from the global North who privilege certain concerns and norms. But, Heller goes on to point out, partners in the global South are far from passive, and international institutions and NGOs recognize the importance of access to domestic political spheres of influence. Although Kjørholt's (2008) denunciation of the CRC as neoliberal may be excessive, it is nonetheless true that the credibility and legitimacy of the Convention rests with its flexibility around the frames and objectives of national partners, and many of these frames are disturbingly neoliberal.

Kate Swanson (2010, 7–8), for example, notes this transformation for Ecuador in the context of economic restructuring. In 1990, Ecuador was the first country in the Americas, and the third in the world, to ratify the CRC. A year later, the *Foro por la Niñez y Adolescencia* was created to pressure the government to create laws that upheld children's rights. By 1998 several of these rights were written into the Ecuadorian constitution and within a year a new civil code was created that became, in 2003, the *Código de la Niñez y Adolescencia*. It is important to note that the code was created with input from children and teens, and it "recognizes the rights of all children and advocates for a more integrated, context-specific, child-centered approach" (Swanson 2010, 7–8) that embraces the legal need to protect children's rights. Focusing on the rights of marginalized populations, Swanson points out that these laws pay lip-service to a majority of young indigenous poor in Ecuador who find their way to the capital through an organized network, which pushes a variety of different forms of begging on the streets. She notes that a militarized policing of Quito's streets was imported from Rudy Giuliani's get tough stance on crime in a rapidly gentrifying NYC and, like Guiliani's policies, it looks a lot like revanchism against indigenous poor and homeless young people who are now banned from what they call the "gringo pampas", an area of the city that was created specifically to attract tourist dollars. The rights of indigenous poor children cannot compete with the right of neoliberal economic policy to create a global tourist city out of Quito.

Kallio and Häkli (2011) raise a different child rights context in Finland, a country like Ecuador with a strong precedent in socialism, which is also facing the reworking of local relations through neoliberal social doctrinarianism. After ratification of the CRC in 1991, Finnish child policies strove to become the most progressive in the world by mandating participation, protection and provision not only for children and youth, but also infants. In 1999 the *Finnish Constitution* was amended to acknowledge children's right to be heard in matters concerning them and, in 2006 the *Youth Act* declared that people under 29 had the right to participate in local and regional youth work and policy. This was followed by the *Youth Welfare Act* (2007), which detailed how the "will, views, opinions and wishes" of children between 0 and 17 years of age and young people between the ages of 18 and 20 "are to be canvassed and taken into account in all situations in which their well-being is considered" (Kallio and Häkli 2011, 101). A year later, the country enacted the governmental *Policy Program for the Well-Being of Children, Youth and Families* (2007), which focused not just on children's rights and democratic skills, but also on their "communal competencies". The program, however, was focused exclusively on what children offer community and democracy and not vice versa. To the extent that the young people who got involved in these programs were self-selecting, Kallio and Häkli (2011,

2013) found that they tended to create a particular class of child whose politics in the official Finnish settings were quite different from child politics in everyday settings.

In the cases of Ecuador and Finland, problems arose with neoliberal concepts of the universal autonomous child. Michael King's (2007: 206) critique of the CRC's dualism that constructs children as objects of rights (e.g. protection by adults) and subjects of rights (e.g. capable of autonomous claims) is to link it with the rhetoric of the new sociology of childhood, which, he argues, pushes the child from a rights holder to a citizen to be consulted and voice to be heard, to a "fully-fledged theoretical concept: that of the child as social agent." To the extent that the concept is fully-fledged, a universality is suggested that belies the complex relations and variability of children's lived worlds, and it denies their propensity to become different from something that adults imagine. The rhetoric of the child as "fully-fledged" shows up uncritically in academic and policy discourses (e.g. Verhellen 2004). A critical perspective on child rights notes that no child or adult is fully-fledged and that we are all, rather, in various processes of becoming that is dialogic and relational. Critical geographers point out that a focus on children's presence, voice and participation in these discourses requires an understanding of how the child "becomes other" in the sense that s/he can choose something different from adult norms and mores, and the absence of familial, community and state relations in those choices severely limits "… the wider fields of power within which children's lives unfold" (Vanderbeck 2008, 397; cf. Ansell 2009).

Tracey Skelton (2008) argues that we need to critically assess the CRC's focus on participation with particular concern for one of its sponsors, UNICEF, and its practice through the 2003 *State of the World's Children* report. In noting with King (2007) that the CRCs first set of emphases on protection and provision has of late been superseded by notions of child participation, Skelton sees a problem with forms of use that are never viewed uncritically or unfavorably; there is a presumption that child participation is always of value. Using critical discourse analysis, Skelton argues that the 2003 UNICEF report problematically focuses on children's naivety, and their forward-looking hopes and dreams. She shows how this rhetoric is problematically decontextualized and focused on an uncritical "deepening of democracy", which may be inclusive and responsive but is also linked to a progressive form of development. In a skilful historical analysis of progressive forms of development, Elizabeth Gagen (2008) points out a problematic link not just to Jean Piaget's work in child development in the mid-twentieth century but also to imperialism and the creation of a new world order beginning in the nineteenth century. Gagen contextualizes Piagetian development as an extension of the nineteenth century's elaborated hegemony of empire, at a time when colonialism and imperialism expanded the so-called metropolitan heartlands to colonial hinterlands. This expansion saw space as something to be controlled and history as a developmental given. Peripheral colonial spheres were "civilized" with the imposition of governmental, legal, economic and educational frames from the metropolitan heart. The links to child development are clear, and the specific spatial framing that Gagen elaborates focuses on the ways domestic US changes propelled psychology's suggestion of "normal" development. Gagen shows that the "infantilization" of so-called primitive colonial cultures is, in actuality, a discourse from the normative liberal developmentalism of nineteenth-century psychology. Joining with the critiques of King (2007), Kjørholt (2008) and Skelton (2008), Gagen makes an important argument about the ways liberal discourses of national and child development are insidiously intertwined, and are part of the same imperial project. Like nascent colonies in the nineteenth century and countries of the global South today, children move along a prescribed and normalized path from underdevelopment to development. Olga Nieuwenhuys (2008) brings Gagen's critique into the twentieth century by showing how institutions like the International Labor Organization

(ILO) and the CRC, dis-embedded from a wider context, help justify states' disengagement from sites of social and cultural reproduction in the direct interest of the global North and southern elites. This is the heart, she argues, of disciplining the "global womb". And it is a heart which is populated by a lifeworld we know little about because much of the international rhetoric and research is focused upon what is appropriate and what is inappropriate in terms of children's rights, while dismissing as inconsequential their work to support families and economies through day-to-day activities. Nieuwenhuys' argument is that a large part of the globalized discourses from the CRC and the ILO, when they land in local places, curtail children's choices in an attempt to tame them.

The issue of more choices for young people is intriguing and hotly debated within the context of universal children's rights. The argument that King, Kjørholt, Nieuwenhuys and others put forward is that fixed rights emanate from a progressive neoliberal individualism that assumes identities are always already constituted. What many geographers want to do is replace this rhetoric with a politics that takes as a central concern the constitution of young people's situated identities and the local and scaled relations through which they are constructed. What this means is to set aside ideas of universal fixes and neoliberal individualism presaged by assumptions of what we think we know about young people, and instead focus on the ways young people show up locally, and how they are shaped and in turn shape those local places. In terms of global politics, these local and scaled relations must be understood as embedded material spatial practices. Similarly, it is important to let go of our assumptions about space and instead see it too as a product of these local and scaled relations and as important as space is to young identities, it does not exist prior to children's material spatial practices.

One possible solution to getting passed the fixity of space and children is to create what Katz (2004, 2011) calls *counter-topographies* through the politics of play. For Walter Benjamin, emancipation through revolutionary imaginations arises from play. He understood play not as the capacity to imitate, or learn through imitation, but as the capacity to affect and be affected by the world. As such, young people's capacity to play is also a capacity to re-conceive history and geography, which in turn creates a "moment of revolutionary possibility" (Benjamin, cited in Buck-Morss 1991, 339). Benjamin (1978) suggests that from within children's playful activities comes not only the capacity to imagine things differently, but also the ability to experiment with cultural, social and political relations:

> [c]hildren's cognition had revolutionary power [to Benjamin] because it was tactile, and hence tied to action, and because rather than accepting the given meaning of things, children got to know objects by laying hold of them creatively, releasing from them new possibilities of meaning.
>
> *(Buck-Morss 1991, 264)*

Play as a space of "becoming other" may be reworked through the idea that it is mimetic not just in the sense of copying something but also as a radical flash of inspiration and creativity when something is performed or used differently. From this perspective, children's play is not just about identity making, it is about world making (Katz 2011).

5. Rights in place and rights to space: Where are we now?

According to David Harvey (2005, 39) neoliberalism was birthed in Chile when Pinochet's military coup, with US backing, ousted the democratically elected Allende government. An imposed neoliberal economic model from Milton Friedman and the Chicago Boys extended a pernicious form of social doctrinarianism where schools were privatized and free-market ethics were introduced. At the core of the ensuing Penguin Revolution were rights to a fair education system that encompassed all social and economic classes. Common wisdom deems as un-childlike young children protesting in the streets, and so the *Pingüinos* showing up in school uniforms was seen as out-of-place. To the degree that the protests were playful, something different was exposed with this revolution. In 2006, newly elected president Michelle Bachelet went on state television with a public announcement to the *Pingüinos* saying "We have realized that your demands are justified and reasonable." After three months of struggle and with many of their demands met, the *Pingüinos* disbanded in June 2006 and normal classes were resumed with the proviso that the government follow through with its promises. To the extent that the government did not follow through, deterioration of the Chilean education system continued and the *Pingüinos* re-engaged their protests. Many of the original protestors are now at university, and rather than donning school uniforms they take to the streets in costume and perform dance routines. Their performances are often met with tear-gas and water cannons. The *Pingüinos'* playful protests nonetheless are witnessed by a sympathetic national and international audience. In December 2013, Bachelet was re-elected on a platform that promised a reconstituted education system.

The *Pingüinos* performed new kinds of protest; playful and out-of-place. The *Izbrisani* lost their rights by fiat, in a vicious cycle where they could not leave their birth country to collect necessary documentation from elsewhere for fear of being unable to return; they were stateless and locked-in-place. Many *Izbrisani* were ethnic Bosnians, Serbs and Croats who were born in Slovenia and chose not to give up their transnational identities. It seems that in this case the quest for citizenship trumps the quest for rights and ties young people legally and geographically to a form of permanent residency that deprives certain freedoms. In extreme neoliberal terms, it creates a potential workforce for which the nation-state has no responsibility; a workforce upon whom is forced the costs not only for social welfare but also for basic human rights. It also broaches concerns about cosmopolitanism and universal rights as opposed to difference or, at the very least, a fixed ethic of difference that denies rights and counters the freedom and mobility that transnationalism confers. The issue of the *Izbrisani* creates a constitutional crisis for Slovenia, which struggles with how its peoples are contextualized and counted as nationals. The crisis raises the global issue of young people's mobilities and their rights to stay put. It highlights loss of control at national and international levels when neoliberal economic structures focused on autonomy, independence and free-market economies presage the rights of young people residing in disadvantaged places to move from one place to another or, if they choose, to stay put.

The *Izbrisani* and *Pingüinos* offer poignant examples of children locked-in-place and young people out-of-place that raise to high relief the importance of understanding spatial contexts as a basis of rights and young people's collective right to make and re-make space.

The clarion call from a relational and critical geography is for a realization and re-imagining of the full challenge of children's rights within spaces and scales that are not immutable, and their rights to create and re-create spaces and themselves. A central part of the questioning in this revolves around a critique of the seeming inevitability of global development (and, in particular, its neoliberal construction) and children's development (and, in particular, their normative cognitive development). In this formulation, both globalization and child development are problematically enframed by forces emanating always from "elsewhere". A critical geographic perspective on children's rights demands that the spatial frameworks of progress and development, for both young people and nations, is replaced with something more fluid and politically open.

Questions for debate and discussion

- How can we understand children's rights as the product of interrelations constituted through spatial and scalar interactions, from the immensity of the global to the intimacy of the local?
- How do we unravel the ways that these relations are necessarily embedded material practices?
- To the extent that we understand space as the sphere of possible multiple stories through which children are problematically fixed as objects and subjects of rights, how do we construct a post-developmental future where a multiplicity of children's stories-so-far are contextualized in a plurality of spaces and across all scales?
- Given that space and children's rights are always already under co-construction, and that there is never closure, how do we imagine and create a space for multiple possible futures that are not presaged by current neoliberal projects?
- To the degree that the significance of children's rights and how we understand them varies according to what aspects of children's lives and situations are focused upon, and given that children may be directly involved in neoliberal projects, with positive or negative outcomes, how do we recognize contexts of marginalization and exploitation?

References

Aitken, Stuart C. (1994). *Putting Children in Their Place.* Washington DC: Association of American Geographers Resource Publication Series. Boston: Edwards Bros.
Aitken, Stuart C. (2001). *Geographies of Young People: The Morally Contested Spaces of Identity.* London and New York: Routledge.
Aitken, Stuart C. (2010). Throwntogetherness: Encounters with Difference and Diversity. In Dydia DeLyser, Stuart Aitken, Steve Herbert, Mike Crang, and Linda McDowell (eds), *The Handbook for Qualitative Methods in Geography,* pp. 46–68. Thousand Oaks, CA: Sage.
Aitken, Stuart C. (2014). *The Ethnopoetics of Space and Transformation:Young People's Engagement, Activism and Aesthetics.* Farnham, UK: Ashgate.
Aitken, Stuart C., Silvia Lopez Estrada, Joel Jennings and Lina Aguirre (2006). Reproducing Life and Labor: Global Processes and Working Children in Tijuana. *Childhood* 13(3), 365–367.
Aitken, Stuart C., Kate Swanson, Fernando Bosco and Tom Herman (2011). *Young People, Border Spaces and Revolutionary Imaginations.* New York: Routledge.
Azmi, Fazeeha, Cathrin Brun and Ragnhild Lund (2013). Young People's Everyday Politics in Post-conflict Sri Lanka. *Space and Polity* 17(1), 106–122.
Ansell, Nicola (2009). Childhood and the Politics of Scale: Descaling Children's Geographies. *Progress in Human Geography* 25, 591–614.
Ansell, Nicola, Loraine van Blerk, Flora Hajdu, and Elsbeth Robson (2011). Spaces, Times and Critical Moments: A Relational Time-space Analysis of the Impacts of AIDS on Rural Youth in Malawi and Lesotho *Environment and Planning A* 43(3), 525–544.
Benjamin, Walter (1978). On the Mimetic Faculty. In P. Demetz and E. Jephcott (eds), *Reflections,* pp. 333–336. New York: Harcourt Brace.
Berglund, Ulla, and Nordin Kerstin (2007). Using GIS to Make Young People's Voices Heard in Urban Planning. *Children, Young People and Built Environments* 33(4), 469–481.
Bosco, Fernando, Stuart C. Aitken and Tom Herman (2011). Women and Children in a Neighborhood Advocacy Group: Engaging Community and Refashioning Citizenship in a Border Town. *Gender, Place and Culture* 18(2), 155–178.
Buck-Morss, Susan (1991). *The Dialectics of Seeing: Walter Benjamin and the Arcades Project.* Cambridge, MA: MIT Press.
Bunge William W. (1971). *Fitzgerald: Geography of a Revolution.* Cambridge, MA: Schenkman.
Bunge William W. (1973). The Geography. *The Professional Geographer* 25(4), 331–337.
Bunge, William W., and Robert Bordessa (1975). *The Canadian Alternative: Survival, Expeditions and Urban Change.* Geographical Monographs 2, Toronto: York University.

Connolly, Mark and Judith Ennew (1996). Introduction: Children Out of Place. *Childhood* 3(2), 131–145.
England, Kim (1993). Pink Collar Ghettoes: The Spatial Entrapment of Women? *Annals of the Association of American Geographers* 82(3), 225–242.
Gagen, Elizabeth (2008). Reflections of Primitivism; Development, Progress and Civilization in Imperial America, 1998–1914. In Stuart C. Aitken, Ragnhild Lund and Anna-Trine Kjørholt (eds), *Global Childhoods: Globalization, Development and Young People*, pp. 15–28. New York and London: Routledge.
Gibson-Graham, J.K. (1996). *The End of Capitalism (As We Knew It): A Feminist Critique of Political Economy.* London: Blackwell.
Gibson-Graham, J.K. (2006). *A Postcapitalist Politics.* Minneapolis: The University of Minnesota Press.
Haraway, Donna (1991). *Simians, Cyborgs and Women: The Re-invention of Nature.* London: Routledge.
Hart, Roger (1997). *Children's Participation: The Theory and Practice of Involving Young Citizens in Community Development and Environmental Care.* London: UNICEF/Earthscan.
Harvey, David (2005). *A Brief History of Neoliberalism.* Oxford: Oxford University Press.
Harvey, David (2008). The Right to the City. *New Left Review* 53(Sep/Oct), 23–40.
Harvey, Francis (2014). Mind the Gap: Reconsidering Geography's Twentieth Century Nihilist Technological Settlements. In Stuart C. Aitken and Gill Valentine (eds), *Approaches to Human Geography: Philosophies, Theories, People and Practices.* London: Sage.
Heller, Patrick (2013). *Challenges and Opportunities: Civil Society in a Globalizing World.* United Nations' Development Program. Human development Occasional Paper, 2013/6.
Holloway, Sarah and Gill Valentine (2000). *Children's Geographies: Playing, Living, Learning.* New York: Routledge.
James, Allison, Chris Jenks and Alan Prout (1998). *Theorizing Childhood.* Bristol, UK: Polity Press.
Kallio, Kirsi and Jouni Häkli (2011). Tracing Children's Politics. *Political Geography* 30, 99–109.
Kallio, Kirsi and Jouni Häkli (2013). Children and Young People's Politics in Everyday Life. *Space and Polity* 17(1), 1–15.
Katz, Cindi (1991) Sow What You Know: The Struggle for Social Reproduction in Rural Sudan. *Annals of the Association of American Geographers* 81, 488–514.
Katz, Cindi (2004) *Growing Up Global.* New York: Guilford Press.
Katz, Cindi (2011). Accumulation, Excess, Childhood: Towards a Countertopography of risk and waste. *Documents d'Anàlisi Geogràfica* 57(1), 47–60.
King, Michael (2007). The Sociology of Childhood as Scientific Communication. *Childhood* 14, 193–213.
Kogovšek, Neža (2010). The Erasure as a Violation of Legally Protected Human Rights. In Neža Kogovšek, Jelka Zorn, Sara Pistotnik, Uršula Lipovec Čebron, Veronika Bajt, Brankica Petkovi and Lana Zdravkovic (eds), *The Scars of the Erasure: A Contribution to the Critical Understanding of the Erasure of People from the Register of Permanent Residents of the Republic of Slovenia*, pp. 83–140. Peace Institute: Metelkova 60, 1000 Ljubljana, Slovenia.
Kjørholt, Anne-Trine (2002). Small is Powerful: Discourses on "Children and Participation" in Norway. *Childhood* 9(1), 63–82.
Kjørholt, Anne-Trine (2008). Childhood as a Symbolic Space: Searching for Authentic Voices in the Era of Globalization. In Stuart C. Aitken, Ragnhild Lund and Anne-Trine Kjørholt (eds), *Global Childhoods: Globalization, Development and Young People*, pp. 29–42. New York: Routledge.
LeFebvre, Henri (1991). *The Production of Space.* trans. Donald Nicholson-Smith. Oxford: Blackwell.
LeFebvre, Henri (1996). *Writings on Cities*, trans. Eleonore Kofman and Elizabeth Lebas. Oxford: Blackwell.
Martson, Sallie and Katharyne Mitchell (2004). Citizens and the State: Citizen Formations in Space and Time. In C. Barnett and M. Low (eds), *Space of Democracy: Geographical Perspectives on Citizenship, Participation and Representation*, pp. 93–112. London: Sage.
Marston, Sallie, J.P. Jones and Keith Woodward (2005). Human Geography without Scale *Transactions of the Institute of British Geographers* 30, 416–432.
Massey, Doreen (2005). *For Space.* London: Sage.
Matthews, Hugh (1992). *Making Sense of Place: Children's Understanding of Large-Scale Environments.* Lanham, MD: Rowman and Littlefield.
Mitchell, Don (2003) *The Right to the City: Social Justice and the Fight for Public Space.* New York: The Guilford Press.
Mitchell, Katharyne, Sallie Marston and Cindi Katz (2004). *Life's Work: Geographies of Social Reproduction.* New York: Blackwell-Wiley
Monk, Janice and Susan Hanson (1982). On Not Excluding Half of the Human in Human Geography. *The Professional Geographer* 34(1), 11–23.

Monk, Janice and Cindi Katz (1993). *Full Circles: Geographies of Women over the Life Course*. London and New York: Routledge.

Moosa-Mitha, Mehmoona (2005). A Difference-Centred Alternative to Theorization of Children's Citizenship Rights. *Citizenship Studies* 9(4), 369–388.

Nieuwenhuys, Olga (2008). Embedding the Global Womb: Global Child Labor and the New Policy Agenda. In Stuart C. Aitken, Ragnhild Lund and Anna-Trine Kjørholt (eds), *Global Childhoods: Globalization, Development and Young People*, pp. 149–164. New York and London: Routledge.

Qvortrup, Jens, Margatta Brady, Giavanni Sgritta and Helmut Winterbreger (eds) (1994). *Childhood Matters: Social Theory, Practice and Politics*. Vienna, Austria: European Centre for Social Policy and Research.

Robson, Elsbeth (2010) Children's Bodies Working and Caring in Sub-Saharan Africa', in R. Colls and K. Hörschelmann (eds), *Contested Bodies of Childhood and Youth*, pp. 148–162. Basingstoke, UK: Palgrave Macmillan.

Skelton, Tracey (2008). Children, Young People, UNICEF and Participation. In Stuart C. Aitken, Ragnhild Lund and Anna-Trine Kjørholt (eds), *Global Childhoods: Globalization, Development and Young People*, pp. 165–181. New York and London: Routledge.

Skelton, Tracey and Gill Valentine (1998). *Cool Places: Geographies of Youth Cultures*. New York: Routledge.

Spyrou, Spyros and Miranda Christou (2014). *Children and Borders*. Basingstoke, UK: Palgrave MacMillan.

Staeheli, Lynn and Elizabeth Kofman (2004). Mapping Gender, Making Politics: Toward Feminist Political Geographies. In Lynn A. Staeheli, Eleonore Kofman, and Linda Peake (eds), *Mapping Women, Making Politics: Feminist Perspectives on Political Geography*, pp. 1–14. London: Routledge.

Staeheli, Lynn and Don Mitchell (2008). *The People's Property: Power, Politics and the Public*. London: Sage.

Staeheli, Lynn, Kafui Attoh and Don Mitchell (2013). Contested Engagements: Youth and the Politics of Citizenship. *Space and Polity* 17(1), 88–105.

Swanson, Kate (2010). *Begging as a Path to Progress*. Athens, GA: University of Georgia Press.

Valentine, Gill and Sarah Holloway (2002). Cyberkids? Exploring Children's Identities and Social Networks in On-line and Off-line Worlds. *Annals of the Association of American Geographers* 92(2), 302–319.

Vanderbeck, Robert M. (2008). Reaching Critical Mass? Theory, Politics and the Nature of Debate in Children's Geographies. *Area* 40(3), 393–400.

Vanderbeck, Robert M. and Cheryl Dunkley (2004). Geographies of Inclusion, Exclusion and Belonging in Young Lives. *Children's Geographies* 2, 177–184.

Verhellen, Eugeen (2004). The Convention on the Rights of the Child. In A. Weyts (ed.), *Understanding Children's Rights. Collected Papers Presented at the Seventh International Interdisciplinary Course on Children's Rights*, pp. 17–34. Ghent: Children's Rights Centre.

Wridt, Pamela (2010). A Qualitative GIS Approach to Mapping Urban Neighborhoods with children to Promote Physical Activity and Child-friendly Community Planning. *Environment and Planning B* 37(1) 129–147.

Young, Iris Marion (1990). *Justice and the Politics of Difference*. Princeton, NJ: Princeton University Press.

Zorn, J. and Lipovec Čebron, U. (eds) (2008), *Once Upon an Erasure: From Citizens to Illegal Residents in the Republic of Slovenia*. Ljubljana, Slovenia: Študentska Založba.

9
Children's rights from a gender studies perspective
Gender, intersectionality and ethics of care

Katrien De Graeve

1. Introduction

Gender-biased inequality does not start from adulthood, but also shapes and limits the worlds of children.[1] From the moment a person is born (and even before), a particular gender is assigned to that person; and this classification of children as girls or boys goes hand in hand with different norms and expectations. Girls and boys learn how they are supposed to behave, act and react in expected ways, or resist or rebel against these norms, in this way constantly (re)producing gender and the gender order (Lorber, 1994, p. 60). Although both girls and boys can be constrained by gendered patterns of power and expectations, under current patriarchal conditions it is girls who are more likely to occupy subordinate positions. Girls for instance tend to be more often the victim of sex-selective abortion, infanticide and (sexual) violence than boys.[2] They often have less access to schooling or even to health care than their male peers and are more often expected to take up more care work and household duties. Girls often experience more (parental) control and supervision and often have less freedom of movement and expression.[3] They face more pressure of conforming to unattainable beauty standards and may undergo female genital cutting or other interventions (e.g. plastic surgery) aimed at managing and controlling the female body and sexuality.[4]

Yet, this reality may become obscured by a discourse that tends to collapse gender differences into the more generic rubrics of 'children' and 'youth'. Although, as stated in the

---

1   I use the term 'children' to refer to female and male children and adolescents; and the terms 'girls' or 'boys' when I aim to emphasise gendered dimensions. However, it must be kept in mind that these terms are not objective labels that refer to clearly delineated and homogeneous categories of people, but are socially constructed and highly differentiated.
2   According to Cai and Lavely (2003), for instance, in China approximately 8.5 million girls are missing in the cohorts born 1980 to 2000 due to sex-selective mechanisms.
3   Porter (2011), for instance, describes how the mobility of girls in African rural areas is constrained due to patriarchal discourses on girls' vulnerability and their perceived promiscuity.
4   For discussions on discursive constructions of choice and constraint around for instance female genital cutting and cosmetic surgery see e.g. Chambers (2008, pp. 21–44) (see also Leye and Middelburg, Chapter 17 in this Handbook).

introduction of this book, from the late 1970s, there is a shift in research and policy towards an increasing recognition of children as social actors, worthy of study in their own right (see also James and Prout, 1997a, p. 4), the intersection of children and gender is less commonly taken into account in policy design and implementation (Morrow, 2006). Discourses on children's rights and policy often start from the universality of childhood and frequently take a gender-neutral approach (Berman, 2003, p. 103; Taefi, 2009, p. 349), in spite of the fact that sex and gender profoundly shape and limit children's experiences. However, an emerging body of childhood research has begun to explore gender as an important factor when studying children, using a constructionist and performative approach. Furthermore, these studies have used insights from other fields, including gender studies, to further develop useful models for the study and conceptualisation of children and childhood.[5,6] Some of the new conceptualisations have been adopted by theorists of children's rights who embrace bottom-up approaches and contextual orientations.[7] Yet, tensions between universalist notions of children that tend to be used in traditional children's rights discourses and the recognition of the multiplicity and diversity of childhoods remain to be further addressed in future research and practice.

This chapter reviews a selection of relevant literature and discussions that have emerged at the interface of gender studies and childhood studies, and explores what a gender studies perspective may contribute to the theory and practice of children's rights. 'Intersectionality' and 'ethics of care', two concepts that stem from gender studies, are particularly relevant for further theorisation within childhood studies as well as for the development of children's rights research, policy and practice. Both concepts can contribute to a better understanding of children as social actors within a particular context shaped by a complex of intersecting social forces and interrelatedness. These understandings can provide important building blocks for the development of a bottom-up approach to children's rights, as well as to deepening the 'contextual orientation' that is pursued in this book as a means to moving beyond traditional paradigms in children's rights research.

In what follows, I first discuss the feminist concept of 'intersectionality' and how it has been applied for an understanding of childhood as plural, dependent on a child's positioning on various and interrelated axes of social stratification, such as gender, age, race, class, sexuality and religion. I also discuss some of the critiques of intersectionality, which warn against the danger of creating new monolithic categories, reinforcing (rather than undermining) race, class and gender inequalities or diminishing the power of the children's rights project. Then, I highlight the feminist 'ethics of care' that has been put forward as a tool for overcoming some of the problems that have been associated with the prevalent rights-based model. I discuss the main feminist critiques of a liberal rights-based approach and explore the applicability of ethics of care theory to childhood studies, as well as to the theorisation of children's rights. However, before considering these issues, it is necessary to say a few words on current definitions of gender. The

---

5   The term 'childhood' refers to a set of social, cultural and institutional structures, while the term 'children' refers to a variably defined group of individuals, distinguished on the basis of their age.
6   Throughout the article, I use the term 'gender studies' and 'feminist studies' interchangeably, to refer to the broad interdisciplinary academic field of feminist-inspired studies that focus on gender relations and women's subordinations.
7   I use the term 'childhood studies' to refer to anthropological and sociological studies of children, yet distinct from the study of children's rights. According to Freeman (1998, p. 433), childhood studies and children's right studies have divergent 'aims and perspectives, even world views' and 'little dialogue or collaboration between them'. However, recent contextual conceptualisations in children's rights seem to narrow this gap.

following section explores the various ways childhood studies as well as children's rights studies interact with gender theory. Not only does a growing number of childhood studies take gender into account as an important axis when analysing the lives of children, but the way gender is theorised and re-visioned by feminist studies also inspires the re-visioning of children in current childhood studies and in new conceptualisations of children's rights (and vice versa).

2. Gender studies and childhood images

Wekker and Lutz (2001, p. 36) define gender as 'the complex and ever-changing system of personal, social and symbolic relations through which men and women are created socially and through which they get access to roles, identities, status, power and material resources available in society'. Whereas there seems to be a consensus on the constructed nature of gender, its relation to sex is the subject of controversy. In much feminist theory, gender is conceptualised as the social interpretation of biological sex difference (e.g. Lorber, 1994), while more recent critiques further challenge the sex–gender distinction by arguing that there is no subject beyond what is socially produced. Judith Butler, for instance, argues that sex assignment is not 'a statement of fact but an interpellation that initiates the process of 'girling', a process based on perceived and *imposed* differences between men and women, differences that are far from "natural"' (Salih, 2007, p. 61, italics in original). She emphasises the performative nature of the gendered body. Although she does not deny that physical differences exist, she states that the body 'has no ontological status apart from the various acts which constitute its reality' (Butler, 2003, p. 185) and describes gender as 'a practice of improvisation within a scene of constraint' (Butler, 2004, p. 1).

Feminist understandings of gender, together with insights from racial-ethnic studies and studies of other marginalised groups, contributed to a shift in childhood images. They inspired a move from an image of childhood as a biological and universal stage in the life course to a 'performative theory of childhood' (Dickenson, 2011, p. 63), which sees 'child' as 'an identity constituted through institutions, discourses and everyday practices' (Dickenson, 2011, p. 37). The theoretical reciprocity between gender and childhood studies is related, as Thorne (1987, p. 86, italics in original) argues, not only to the '*parallels* between [children's] situations and those of women', but also to the *connections* between women and children. As 'the fates and definitions of children have been closely tied with those of women' (Thorne, 1987, p. 95), the 'ideological and actual *connections* between women and children' (Thorne, 1987, p. 86, italics in original) provide a fruitful domain for exploring theoretical connections.

The 'gender-constituting' nature of the relationships between the child and its significant other, or the way 'mother' or 'father' identities are co-constituted with that of the child (Baird, 2008, p. 298), has attracted considerable attention from feminist scholars, particularly in light of patriarchal 'women-and-children' discourses, which equate women's interests with those of children and relegate both women and children to the private sphere. Aiming to reveal the structured and pervasive nature of women's subordination in society, feminist studies deconstructed naturalised images of motherhood and childrearing (e.g. Hays, 1996; Rich, 1995), thereby also unpacking the historical and cultural contingency of childhood. They revealed that the current representations in middle-class milieus in so-called 'Western' countries that tend to conceptualise childrearing as an enterprise that should intensively be performed preferably by women within nuclear families (Forsberg, 2009; Hays, 1996), is not universally given, but socially constructed. They also showed that images of what is considered 'good' childrearing are historically and contextually co-constituted with images of children, childhood and children's rights. Representations of appropriate parenthood which strives for intense rearing practices as well as emotional and intimate relations between parents (typically mothers) and children (Forsberg, 2009, p. 29,44), are shaped and co-constituted in accordance with particular representations of child-centredness, the sacralisation of childhood, and a protectionist view of children's rights that emphasise for instance the right of children to grow up in a caring and (over)protective environment, preferably within the confines of the nuclear family (Glenn, 1994; Hays, 1996; Rich, 1995; Zelizer, 1985).

The main feature of the childhood paradigm that has dominated much policy and research since the end of the nineteenth century and that mainly understood children's rights as 'protection rights' (see the introduction of this Handbook) is 'the myth of the vulnerable child' (Furedi, 2008, p. 40), seeing the child as incompetent and totally dependent on the care of adults. Within such a view, children are predominantly seen in terms of their potentiality (Burman and Stacey, 2010, p. 231; Cockburn, 2005, p. 77), and the maximum development of that potentiality is considered mainly the parents' responsibility. A second and interrelated element in these representations of children is the separateness of the child, 'including the construction of the special site of "home" as the appropriate place for children, their exclusion from paid work and segregation into educational establishments, and the construction of particular dedicated public places such as playgrounds' (Ribbens McCarthy et al., 2000, p. 788). A third element is the construction of the child as innocent, outside moral agency and accountability (Ribbens McCarthy et al., 2000, p. 788). Yet, from the late 1970s on, the childhood image of the sacralised, vulnerable child has not only been uncovered as contingent, it also became a target of critique for its tendency to perpetuate unequal power relations between adults and children (Berman, 2003, p. 103).

Parallel to the conceptualisation of gender, in the so-called 'new childhood paradigm', being a child is no longer seen as a 'simple fact or static condition of a body, but a process whereby regulatory norms' (Butler, 1993: 2) '"materialize", give shape to, or define the boundaries of the "child"' (Dickenson, 2011, p. 63). A constructionist and performative understanding of childhood conceptualises childhood as 'an identity that is constituted through institutions, discourses and everyday practices' (Dickenson, 2011, p. 37). Prout and James (1997, p. 8) have outlined the key features of the new paradigm in childhood studies as follows:

- Childhood is understood as a social construction.
- Childhood is a variable of social analysis, along with other variables such as gender, class and ethnicity.
- Children's cultures and relationships are worthy of study in their own right.
- Children are active social agents.
- Studying children involves engaging in processes of reconstructing childhood in society.

It is important to note that a shift to a new paradigm does not mean that the old one has completely disappeared. On the contrary, both paradigms continue to be used and influence many policy and research perspectives. However, although further implications of the new childhood paradigm and how it should be translated into policy remain subject to debate, especially since the 1980s, this paradigm has become more firmly established in childhood studies (James and Prout, 1997b).

Although feminist studies have strongly contributed to the acknowledgement of childhood as a contingent and constructed category, feminist understandings have also been challenged by critical childhood studies (Baird, 2008, p. 297) for reinforcing the image of child vulnerability. Whereas feminist theory that 're-visioned women as active, speaking subjects' (Thorne, 1987, p. 88) has been inspiring for the re-conceptualisation of children's agency, feminist scholarship's emphasis on the agency of women in constructing their lives and identities often left children play the role of simply pre-social, dependent and passive recipients of care and education.

'Gender socialisation' studies of the 1970s and 1980s in particular, although successful in demonstrating that gender divisions are not natural and unchangeable (Thorne, 1987, p. 92), depicted childhood as a period in which children learn and internalise the rules of adult culture. These studies tended to put a strong emphasis on the role of parents and other caregivers in the gendering of children – leaving little room for children's agency – and understanding children primarily 'by their becoming, as adults-in-the-making' (Thorne, 1987, pp. 92–93).

Much of recent literature both on parenting and childhood, has challenged socialisation theory for its 'adult ideological viewpoint' (Speier, 1976) and 'its exaggerated view of children as unagentic, blank slates' (Martin, 2005, p. 457). It has started to adopt a performative and interactionist view of gender and childhood, leaving more room for considering children themselves as 'active meaning-maker[s] in a world constituted through intersubjective experience' (Mahoney and Yngvesson, 1992, p. 49), instead of seeing them as merely passive recipients of adult influence. This view of children as autonomous and agentic individuals also generated new views of children's rights, aiming to recognise children as entitled to the same rights to protection, provision and participation as adults.

Moreover, much writing has been critical of the central role of developmental psychology in the conceptualisation of children and childhood, rooted in a bio-essentialist view that sees the early years of life in terms of 'maturational stages' that need particular forms of care and attention (Ribbens McCarthy and Edwards, 2011, pp. 21 and 143). The traditional developmental view of the child has been criticised for being dominated by a male and 'Western' perspective (e.g. Burman and Stacey, 2010, p. 230; Prout and James, 1997, p. 10; Thorne, 2007, p. 150). Moreover, the view of individual development as a 'natural' succession of predictable phases towards adulthood has been challenged for producing pathologisation discourses (Rose, 1999, pp. 144–154; Walkerdine, 2000, p. 4). Describing the rise since the early 20th century of developmental psychology, Rose (1999, p. 146) argues:

> The gathering of data on children of particular ages over a certain period, and the organization of this data into age norms, enabled the norms to be arranged along an axis of time and seen as cross sections through a continuous dimension of development. Growth and temporality could become principles of organization of a psychology of childhood. And normalization and development enabled individual children to be characterized in terms of their position on this axis of time relative to that deemed 'normal' for their age.

Developmental understandings of normality were blamed for creating categories of 'abnormal' children and 'deviant' child behaviour in need of correction. Moreover, as normality is generated from what have been called 'Western', 'first world' and middle class contexts, these discourses have come to regulate and stigmatise children who live in other contexts, as well as the caring and parental practices of their parents (Burman and Stacey, 2010, p. 229). Lister (2006, p. 321) and Baird (2008, p. 300) criticise 'the iconization of the child in the "social investment state"' that tends to constrict childhood as a period of investment and thinks of children in terms of their future, leaving little room for children as 'beings' who have actual experiences (Baird, 2008, p. 300). Walkerdine (2000, p. 21) links the pathologisation discourses to 'long-established practices of regulation of the poor and the masses', as 'adult pathology is understood and expressed mostly by those who were poorly socialised as children' (Walkerdine, 2000, p. 21). Other studies locate these normative discourses on how children have to develop and have to be raised within (new) technologies of 'intimate colonialism' (Summers, 1991) that aimed to control the personal lives of colonial subjects and created new markets for capitalist exploitation (Lock and Nguyen, 2010).

The feminist critical work that has been done so far mainly 'focused on challenging women's positions in relation to children, rather than on feminist approaches to children and childhood per se' (Burman and Stacey, 2010, p. 229). However, engagements with the complexities of child–woman dependencies have also opened avenues for the further development of feminist theories that explicitly focus on children, as well as of childhood studies that are being conducted in close relation to current debates in feminist studies on sex/gender, citizenship, equality and difference, agency and care. Central to these studies is the further theorisation of children as '"differently equal" members of the public culture in which they are full participants' (Moosa-Mitha, 2005, p. 369). Among other feminist theoretical concepts, 'intersectionality' and 'care ethics' seem to be of utmost importance for the difference-centred and contextual approach that is pursued in recent children's rights studies. Intersectionality and care ethics can provide us with theoretical tools for enriching the analysis of children's experiences and rights with the contexts and relations in which children are embedded, the plurality of their identity, as well as the vectors of power and subordination that operate in the lives of children. In what follows, I discuss the two concepts, starting with intersectionality.

3. Intersectional theory and the study of children

In the early 1970s, in response to feminist theories that did not adequately address the divergent experiences of women, new ways of thinking about identity and agency emerged. Instead of treating women as a single category and ignoring the differences between women, intersectional theory was developed as a way of emphasising the ways various identity categories interact on multiple and often simultaneous levels. Intersectionality refers to the 'merging and mingling of multiple markers of difference' (Ludvig, 2006, p. 246) and holds that these markers do not act independently of one another, but, on the contrary, interrelate, make up 'intersections' of multiple forms of discrimination and privilege.

Kimberlé Crenshaw (1991) has coined the term 'intersectionality' to capture a critique that was voiced by black feminists in the 1970s, who felt they were not being represented by mainstream feminism, nor by antiracism. They argued that feminism was all about white, middle-class women and that it ignored the differences and different power positions women face. But black women did not feel represented by antiracism either, as the struggle against racism seemed to be solely about black men. The term intersectionality wanted to capture that intersectional identity of black women and critiqued the way feminist and antiracist discourses failed to consider the 'fact that women of color are situated within at least two subordinated groups that frequently pursue conflicting political agendas' (Crenshaw, 1991, pp. 1251–1252). Mari Matsuda (1990) developed an instrument to strengthen awareness of various normative structures that may be intertwined with gender. She encourages researchers to 'ask the other question' in every analysis in order to expose 'the ways in which patriarchy, racism, and heterosexism buttress each other' (Nash, 2008, p. 12):

> The way I try to understand the interconnection of all forms of subordination is through a method I call 'ask the other question'. When I see something that looks racist, I ask, 'Where is the patriarchy in this?' When I see something that is homophobic, I ask, 'Where are the class interests in this?'
>
> *(Matsuda, 1990, p. 1189)*

Although intersectionality originated in feminist theory as an attempt to theorise the multiple intersections of gender and race, in more recent years the concept has also been picked up by childhood scholars (e.g. Amoah, 2007; Morris, 2007; Taefi, 2009). Age has been identified as one of the many identity categories that shape our lives and influence the extent to which we are able to exercise agency. The idea of age as a variable of social analysis that must be considered in interrelation with other variables has even become one of the pillars of the new childhood paradigm in childhood studies. Yet, whereas in the last few decades children, childhood and children's rights have increasingly become the focus of research, and have increasingly been included in policy making, the intersection with other markers of difference has not always been clearly articulated. Children's rights discourse often reverts to gender-neutral language, while women's rights discourse focuses predominantly on adult women (Taefi, 2009, p. 349). As such, similar to the marginalisation of black women, girls' rights tend to be divided in separate entitlements for women and children (Taefi, 2009, p. 346), which risks obscuring their particular needs.

While some feminist scholars tend to centre on the particular position of 'multiply marginalised subjects' (such as black women or girl-children), others refer to intersectionality as a generalised theory of identity (Nash, 2008, pp. 9–10). They argue that we all have intersectional identities and plead in favour of 'a nuanced conception of identity that recognizes the way in which positions of dominance and subordination work in complex and intersecting ways to constitute subjects' experiences of personhood' (Nash, 2008, p. 10). Methodologically, Leslie McCall (2005) distinguishes three approaches in intersectionality, defined in terms of their stance towards the use of analytical categories. Whereas the 'anticategorical' approach entirely rejects the use of categories as it considers them as too simplistic to express the complexity of social life, the 'categorical' approach, which mainly relies on quantitative methods, believes that the strategic use of analytical categories is necessary to adequately study relationships of inequality. The third approach, the 'intracategorical complexity' falls in the middle between the other two models. Like the categorical approach, 'it acknowledges the stable and even durable relationships that social categories represent at any given point in time, though it also maintains a critical stance toward categories' (McCall, 2005, p. 1774).

Several critics (Jiwani and Berman, 2002; Nash, 2008) have warned against intersectional approaches that treat multiply marginalised groups, such as black women or girl-children, as unitary and monolithic entities. They argue that such approaches tend to replicate what they critique. Furthermore, the tendency of treating the different layers of the identity of marginalised groups as additive has been questioned because of the risk of construing 'the girl-child', like 'the black woman', as multiply burdened in all situations. Yet, such a conceptualisation passes over the complex ways in which different identity markers intersect and shape people's experiences of privilege and discrimination.

Postcolonial critics have rejected the monolithic construction of black women and girl-children on the ground that it tends to reinforce dichotomised constructions of the 'civilised' 'West' versus the 'primitive' 'Third World'. Chandra Mohanty (1991, p. 51), in her famous article 'Under Western Eyes', argues for a deconstruction of the category of 'the Third World woman'. She accuses 'Western' feminism of the mental and discursive colonisation of women in 'developing countries', reducing them to oppressed and voiceless victims while creating the mirror-image of emancipated, 'Western' women who have control over their own bodies and sexualities.

Jiwani and Berman (2002, p.2) formulate a similar postcolonial critique in relation to the 'Third World' girl-child:

> Typically, the girl child is portrayed as the desperate and reluctant victim of female genital mutilation in Africa; the poverty-stricken child labourer and child-bride in India; the child prostitute in Thailand; the undeserving victim of honour killing in the Middle East; the illiterate, uneducated, exploited, and uncared for child in Latin America; or the unwanted girl child in China. More recently, the girl child has entered the popular western imagination in the form of the fleeing, illegal, refugee who is in need of our protection on the one hand, and who signifies the barbarism of her country of origin on the other hand. All of these images are typically displayed prominently in the fundraising initiatives of international aid organizations and in the mass media. The unstated premise is that atrocities inflicted upon girls occur elsewhere – in backward nations outside the realm of the 'civilized' west.

Moreover, postcolonial feminist critique warns against the continued focus only on women and children in gender and development initiatives, as it tends to reinforce complex historicised masculinity constructions of 'lazy' or violent African men and 'non-Western' men as 'the problem' (Chant and Gutmann, 2002; Whitehead, 2000).

An example of a postmodern, deconstructionist stance towards intersectionality is the work of Jasbir Puar (2005). She criticises the analytical usage of different identity components in intersectional theory on the grounds that it tends to naturalise and essentialise categorisations. By using the concept of 'assemblage', she aims to stress the fuzziness and interwovenness of different markers of identity:

> As opposed to an intersectional model of identity, which presumes components – race, class, gender, sexuality, nation, age, religion – are separable analytics and can be thus disassembled, an assemblage is more attuned to interwoven forces that merge and dissipate time, space, and body against linearity, coherence, and permanency.
>
> *(Puar, 2005, pp. 127–128)*

While the multiplicity of identity in general and childhood in particular has gained ground in new childhood studies, it has also been the subject of critique. Adrian James (2010), for instance, cites Qvortrup (2005) who warns against too much emphasis on plurality, as it risks diverting attention away from childhood as a social category and diminishing the political power of the project of children's rights (James, 2010, pp. 487–488). Therefore, he pleads for an integration of both approaches:

> Thus, if we look at children's experiences of parenting, we can explore whether their experiences differ according to their gender or their position in the social hierarchy (be it caste, clan, socioeconomic status of parents, or whatever is the prevailing mode of social stratification); we can explore how and to what extent children (of different ages) are able to use their agency to mediate the effects of gender and social stratification, either in terms of their daily lives or their longer term life chances; we can consider how children of different genders and from different positions in the social hierarchy are regulated, both formally and informally; and we can ask questions about whether male and female children have the same or different rights and responsibilities and, if so, how this affects their experiences as children and extent to which their use of agency can be a factor in modifying their experiences. Such an approach not only avoids the pitfalls of dualistic thinking, it privileges neither the commonalities of childhood nor the diversities of childhoods and it allows our enquiries to range across the entire fabric of childhood studies,

from whatever our perspective, without asserting that any one element of the fabric is more important than any other.

(James, 2010, pp. 494–495)

It remains for further research to examine how such an integrated approach can be applied to a children's rights framework that enables us to study children's rights as part of the larger human rights agenda, while at the same time looking at its intersections with women's rights, minority rights, religious rights and other rights that intersect in the child's specific context. As Wall (2008) argues, this not only requires us to rethink children's rights, it also needs a re-grounding of human rights in general. Intersectionality's promise lies in its potential to contribute to a strengthening and deepening of the current rights framework, enabling people to respond to 'persons in their irreducible diversity or difference' (Wall, 2008, p. 537). A feminist ethics of care may contribute to pressing 'the ethics of otherness' in what Wall (Wall, 2008, p. 538) calls a 'circular' direction, towards including responsiveness and responsibilities.

4. A feminist ethics of care and the study of children

While our thinking about moral judgements and justice seems to be dominated by liberal conceptions of rights and the self-sufficient individual, since the 1980s feminist theory has begun to challenge the validity of this model. From the traditional experiences of women, feminist theorists have proposed a different approach to morality, one that takes into account care and responsibility in interpersonal relationships rather than abstract rules and principles. In this section I discuss the feminist 'ethics of care' that has been developed as a critique of traditional moral philosophy, and explore how the concept has been employed for the study of the concerns of children. As children are heavily dependent on the care of others, and caring is central to the well-being of children, it is not surprising that care ethics theory has been considered an interesting and relevant model for the study of children, and may be useful for a 'thicker' analysis of the contexts in which children's rights are situated.[8]

This section will be structured as follows. First, I discuss how the liberal 'rights model' has been thoroughly contested by feminist theorists. A moral founded on the universal and autonomous individual, as well as the conceptual split between the public and the private realm have been criticised for not providing the appropriate basis for ethical reflection and justice. Second, I describe the feminist ethics of care that, in contrast to a liberal rights-based approach, starts from the conceptualisation of the individual as concrete and relational and defines moral situations in terms of relations of care. I will then go on to discuss how academics from different fields working on care have conceptualised the relationship between care ethics and rights ethics, and how these discussions can be useful for the field of children's rights, and the critical approach towards dominant children's rights paradigms in particular. One of the most important issues raised by feminist scholarship in relation to liberal rights-based approaches concerns the universalism on which these approaches are premised. The 'rights model' tends to start from an abstract, or generalised other, and the idea that all individuals, irrespective their unique characteristics, possess universal political and other rights (Leys Stepan, 1986, p. 30). Feminist critics have challenged 'the myth of the unembodied subject' (Kittay et al., 2005, p. 445), that abstracts

---

8 The care of others seems to be of crucial importance for all children, and for children with higher levels of need in particular (e.g. young children, children with disabilities…). Yet, this is not to ignore children's agency, nor to diminish the importance of care in all people's lives.

'from the individuality and concrete identity of the other' (Benhabib, 1985, p.411), on the grounds that it applies a white, male, adult, 'Western', middle-class perspective to all circumstances and is insufficiently sensitive to the plurality of being human (Leys Stepan, 1986, p. 29). Dominant groups' viewpoints are deceptively disguised as 'everyone's', and 'consequently, differences distinctive of subordinated groups are labelled as inferiorities, liabilities, menaces, risks' (Silvers, 1995). Feminist scholars have argued that the complex, intersectional understanding of difference and identity demands equally complex understandings of morality and justice and understandings of the workings of domination (Hirschmann, 2008, p. 150). Moreover, the construction of the generic, universal individual, and the inability of some individuals to position themselves as this supposedly abstract individual, was criticised for implying the construction of particular races, genders, classes, sexualities or age groups as natural, biologically grounded entities, debarred from the right to full citizenship (Leys Stepan, 1986, p. 30).

A second feminist critique of the liberal rights model is that it sees individuals as autonomous, 'disembedded' (Benhabib, 1985, p. 405) subjects and that it takes the abstract and independent individual as the basic organising principle of polity and citizenship. The liberal rights model translates moral dilemmas into conflicts over rights, of one person against another, that must be solved by identifying the highest principle (Cockburn, 2005, p. 77). Feminist theory, conversely, developed the notion of '"relational autonomy" which incorporated a notion of autonomy not as opposed to relations with others, but dependent on them' (Hirschmann, 2008, p. 52). As such it incorporates a different understanding of what it means to be a person: 'not separate and inherently distinct from all others, but connected through networks of relationships, and through physical, material, psychological, and emotional interdependence' (Hirschmann, 2008, p. 52).

The underlying public–private dichotomy of the liberal rights model, and the ensuing denigration of the so-called private sphere, is another and equally important concern raised by feminist theory. Feminist critics (e.g. Fraser, 1990; Lister, 2007; Werbner and Yuval-Davis, 1999) argue that the distinction between public and private realms has served to sustain a patriarchal public order, and to justify gender hierarchy and inequality. They critique the construction of the public as 'the distinctively human realm in which man transcends his animal nature, while the private realm of the household is seen as the natural region in which women merely reproduce the species' (Held, 1990, pp. 334–335). The depiction of the public world as superior to the private, and the traditional relegation of women to the domestic sphere, feminists argue, have systematically supported and obscured the structural subordination of women. They claim that this has led to the undervaluation of care work (i.e. unpaid work within the family and caring jobs within the private sector) and to women and other subordinated groups being disproportionately represented in this kind of work, while (white) men take up more highly valued functions in the public domains of state, law and the marketplace. They also, for instance, point at the role of the public–private dichotomy in the protection of (male) domination and violence within the family from public scrutiny (e.g. Thomas and Beasley, 1993). This critique is highly relevant to discussions of children's rights as well, as the subordinate positions and almost complete relegation of children to the private sphere can hamper their ability to exercise their rights to bodily integrity and security.

In response to these concerns, a feminist theory of care has been developed since the 1980s. Gilligan's work, together with that of Nel Noddings (1986), is considered foundational for care ethics theory and has paved the way for a vast body of subsequent work. Carol Gilligan challenged Lawrence Kohlberg's cognitive theory of moral development, which considered women's moral reasoning as deficient. She revealed that the moral reasoning that is often associated with women is a different, but equally important way of thinking about moral problems, yet has been systematically undervalued by male-biased theories (Reiter, 1996, p. 34). Her critique is in line with other feminist work (e.g. Haraway, 1988; Harding, 1991; HyungYi Kang, 2009; Leys Stepan, 1986) that lays bare the androcentric nature of the traditional scientific method and epistemology. Yet, her conceptualisation of care ethics has been the source of subsequent debates on whether it is essentialising gender differences and reinforcing traditional stereotypes of a 'good woman' or not (Held, 2006; Tronto, 1993), and on how it needs to be reconceptualised.

While the 'ethics of care' is not a homogenous, unified theory, important common themes can be found across care ethics work. One of the most important commonalities is that an 'ethics of care' places care and relationships of care at the centre of ethical reflection. Therefore, it foregrounds the following principles: First, as opposed to the notion of a 'generalised' other, it adheres to the principle of the 'concrete' other (Benhabib, 1985). As Benhabib (1985, p. 411) argues, it 'requires us to view each and every rational being as an individual with a concrete history, identity, and affective-emotional constitution'. As such, it is a contextual theory. Second, it operates on the principle of the 'relational' self, being part of networks of 'care and dependence', in contrast to the independent and un-embedded individual of the liberal rights model. Third, it challenges traditional moral theory that solely defines moral situations in terms of rights and responsibilities. An ethics of care aims to look at moral situations as embedded in relationships of care.

Despite this consensus, there is some disagreement among care ethics theorists over how a theory of care must be conceptualised in order to be inclusive and empowering for subordinated individuals and groups. First, there is difference of opinion on how care ethics relates to justice ethics and liberal theory, and on the extent to which justice is relevant to care ethics. A first position thinks an ethics of care should replace the ethics of justice (Noddings, 1986) or argues for considering an ethics of care as an alternative moral theory, rather than a necessary corrective (Tronto, 1987, p. 655). Such an approach locates responsibility towards others 'not in the abstract universals of justice, but rather in the recognition of our intersubjective being' (Popke, 2006, p. 507).

A second position links a disposition of care to some notion of justice, and aims at integrating an ethics of care with an ethics of justice and rules (Held, 1990, p. 331). Held for instance believes that care relations (being the most basic moral value) 'should form the wider moral framework into which justice should be fitted' (Held, 2006, p. 71). This is also the position of many scholars who work on ethics of care in relation to children and argue for a balance between a children's rights model and a care model that takes into account the caring relationships in which children are embedded. A sole reliance upon justice ethics in policies and practices that relate to children, is believed to be 'at the expense of affirming and giving due regard to the complex emotional and practical caring (and sometimes uncaring) relationships within which the young person is situated' (Holland, 2010, p. 1665). Barnes provides the example of a sixteen-year-old girl in foster care, who filed a complaint about her foster carers and was consequently moved to a hostel. The girl was not happy with this settlement, in which rights considerations had taken precedence over care arrangements. Barnes uses this example to plead for the consideration of young people's relationships when dealing with children's rights. She adds:

> A basic ontological position of relationality implies seeing children and young people in necessary relation to others, that is their family, their environment, their 'carers' and their professional workers rather than in isolation.

(Barnes, 2007, p. 149)

Yet, these scholars seem to be reluctant to move away from a children's rights model, that is contended to be hard-won. They believe a rights framework should not be given up (Barnes, 2007, p. 149), but re-imagined as grounded in relationality, contextuality and experience. (Cockburn, 2005, p. 85).

A second point of disagreement among care theorists concerns care ethics' ability to move beyond gender dualisms and the public–private dichotomy. Early formulations of an ethics of care have been criticised for keeping care in its traditional place, i.e. the private, feminine sphere (Scuzzarello, 2009, p. 65; Tronto, 1993) with for instance a strong emphasis on mothers caring for children (see e.g. Held, 1990). Tronto is an important advocate for the development of an ethics of care into a moral theory that considers caring as a political practice that extends beyond the private level to the moral and political context (Myhrvold, 2006; Robinson, 2006; Scuzzarello, 2009, p. 62; Tronto, 1987). She also moves beyond the gender binary in care ethics by stating that moral difference is a function of social position rather than of gender (Tronto, 1987, p. 649). She argues that the daily caring experiences of white women and minority men and women provide these groups with better opportunities to develop moral sense than most white men (Tronto, 1987, p. 652). Yet, she rejects the celebration of care ethics as a factor of gender difference that points at women's superiority (Tronto, 1987, p. 662). Instead, she aims at redrawing care ethics as 'a full-fledged moral and political theory of care' (Tronto, 1987, p. 657). As she believes that the devaluation of care is connected with oppressive boundaries between the public and the private, she argues for a fundamental reconsideration of these boundaries so that women's moral and political participation can be improved.

This reconsideration of public/private boundaries can have important consequences for the study of children as well, since because of their supposed incapacity for public autonomy and reason, children – like women – are traditionally relegated to the private sphere. Children are typically identified as pre-political or non-political beings (Kallio and Häkli, 2011, p. 6). Furthermore, they are often depicted, even in works that draw on care ethics, as *passive recipients* of care, stripped of agency and voice (Cockburn, 2005; Holland, 2010, p. 1667; Lister, 2006, p. 323).

Childhood and children's rights studies shatter this stereotype by providing examples of children – especially girls – being carers for siblings, sick or disabled parents, family members or pets (Cockburn, 2005, p. 73; Holland, 2010, p. 1672) and explore how an ethics of care could be applied to the children's rights context. They show how children, although also dependent on their gendered, classed and raced position, are 'active co-participants in care' (Brannen and Heptinstall, 2003). They have denounced the conceptualisation in some care ethics work of children as solely in need of care, while the complexity and reciprocity of care relations are made invisible and little notion is left for a 'relationship' of caring (Cockburn, 2005, p. 80). This assessment is in line with a critique that warns against the dangers of a needs-based framework for prescribing care and education and upholding children's rights (Cunningham, 2005; Ribbens McCarthy et al., 2000; Woodhead, 1997; Zelizer, 1985). A needs-based approach, it is argued, tends to depart from contemporary 'Western' and middle class understandings of childhood, framing children as passive and vulnerable and childhood as a time of dependency, emptying the child of agency (Berman, 2003; Jenkins, 1998). Furthermore, and as Woodhead (1997) argues, it is concurred that it is primarily parents, experts, policy makers and service providers who define what the best interests of the child are, leaving little scope for children to define their own context (Cockburn, 2005, p. 82).

Some childhood scholars plead for the recognition of children as active agents within networks of relationships with parents, teachers, friends, etc. when making judgements of rights, needs or protection (Cockburn, 2005, p. 77). They argue that although an ethics of care offers a framework for recognising that everyone, including children, are 'relational' and 'interdependent', and as such actively contribute to 'caring *relational* practices' (Held, 2006, p. 54, italics added), the omnipresence of care relationships in our society and the importance of interrelatedness in everyone's life, not just in that of vulnerable or marginalised people (Holland, 2010, p. 1672) needs to be more fully considered. During the last decennia there has been increasing attention for children's participation rights in political processes in what is generally acknowledged as the public sphere, such as policy making in schools and civic activism. However, as Kallio and Häkli (2011) argue, so far childhood studies and the study of children's rights have refrained from explicitly studying children's everyday worlds as political arenas. Yet, studying children's worlds as 'spaces where the presence of human relations is organized by power' (Kallio and Häkli, 2011, p. 21) can contribute to a better understanding of children as active agents within a web of power relations.

5. Conclusion

This chapter has presented some of the critical debates in gender studies and has explored the way these debates have been picked up by childhood and children's rights studies. I have singled out two concepts that stem from feminist theory and that have already been cautiously adopted by some childhood scholars, yet their utility and relevance remain to be fully explored within the framework of children's rights scholarship and policy. While it is not the intention of this chapter to reject the children's rights framework, I point out the necessity of finding a way of re-balancing our priorities so that difference and interdependency are re-valued alongside and in relation with individual rights.

This chapter has argued that the concepts of intersectionality and ethics of care are particularly important for the further development and theorisation of children's rights, because of their ability to offer analytical tools for the development of a bottom-up approach to children's rights, as well as to strengthen the 'contextual orientation' that this Handbook pursues. A combined analysis of the way age interacts with gender, but also with other axes of social signification, can counteract adult-dominance and gender-bias (Taefi, 2009, p. 372), as well as other forms of discrimination. An intersectional approach that looks at children's specific positioning within intersections of different social markers and meaningful (care) relations, trying to incorporate the matrix of domination, interlocking inequalities and ideological assumptions that children might experience, can provide an important guideline for a critical analysis of children's rights. However, there remain many challenges for the integration of intersectional theory and ethics of care within the children's rights framework.

There is on-going discussion on how the complexity of a person's intersectional position can best be conceptualised (e.g. Puar's discussion of assemblage), 'conceiving of privilege and oppression as complex, multi-valent, and simultaneous' (Nash, 2008, p. 12). Rahman (2009, p. 353) points out the inherent analytical tension in aiming to understand the full diversity of experiences while at the same time seeking to derive common or theoretically generalisable analytical propositions from these intersectional standpoints. This touches upon the question of whether intersectionality can avoid reproducing the conceptual frameworks it tries to overcome. The infinite list of differences has been indicated as a weak point in intersectional theory, leading to difficulties operationalising research design. It also raises questions, as Ludvig (2006, p. 247, italics in original) argues, 'that are often avoided in published work: *Who* defines *when, where, which* and *why* particular differences are given recognition while others are not?' (see also: Warner, 2008). The researcher's own positionality can create power imbalances that can interfere with the ability to engage in meaningful interaction with research participants, especially when they are children. These critiques call for research procedures that take more deeply into account not only the inequalities in participants' lives, but also the power imbalances in the research framework and within the relationship between researcher and participants (Berman, 2003, p. 108).[9]

It must also be noted that the concept of care is not always a warm and empowering concept, but can become oppressive and abusive for both carers and cared-for. It seems crucial that any analysis takes into account the power differentials within relations of care. Therefore an analysis of care relations must be combined with intersectional analysis, which tries to grasp the intersecting power systems in children's lives. Yet it remains for further research to concretise how such an approach can be applied to and further developed in a children's rights framework, enabling us to study children's rights in interrelation with other rights, such as women's rights, cultural rights and religious rights, as well as with children's embeddedness in relations of care. However, although many challenges remain, and there seems to be no easy solution to balancing principles of rights and care, the integration in a children's rights framework of an analysis of the complexity of children's contexts, including their intersectional identities as well as their caring relations, seems to be a promising avenue to pursue.

Questions for debate and discussion

- In what concrete ways can intersectional theory and ethics of care be integrated in a children's rights framework?
- What does an intersectional approach of children's rights looks like? How can children's rights be studies in interrelation with other rights, such as women's rights, cultural rights and religious rights?
- In what ways can a children's rights approach be made more attentive to children's relations of care?
- How can we make our research more sensitive to the researcher's positionality and other issues of power inequality?
- How should we define which differences and relations of care are given recognition while others are not?

References

Amoah, Jewel. (2007). The world on her shoulders: The rights of the girl-child in the context of culture and identity. *Essex Human Rights Review*, 4(2), 1–23.
Baird, Barbara. (2008). Child politics, feminist analyses. *Australian Feminist Studies*, 23(57), 291–305.
Barnes, Vivienne. (2007). Young people's views of children's rights and advocacy services: A case for 'caring' advocacy? *Child Abuse Review*, 16(3), 140–152.
Benhabib, Seyla. (1985). The generalized and the concrete other: the Kohlberg-Gilligan controversy and feminist theory, *Praxis International*, 5(4), 402–424.
Berman, Helene. (2003). Getting critical with children: Empowering approaches with a disempowered group. *Advances in Nursing Science*, 26(2), 102–113.
Brannen, Julia, and Heptinstall, Ellen. (2003). Concepts of care and children's contribution to family life. In Julia Brannen and Peter Moss (eds), *Rethinking Children's Care* (pp. 183–197). Buckingham, UK: Open University Press.

---

9   For further discussion of issues of children's participation, rights and relationships in what could be called a 'children's rights-based' research process, see Lundy and McEvoy 2012.

Burman, Erica, and Stacey, Jackie. (2010). The child and childhood in feminist theory. *Feminist Theory*, 11(3), 227–240.
Butler, J. (1993). *Bodies that Matter: On the Discursive Limits of 'Sex'*. New York: Routledge.
Butler, Judith. (2003). Performative acts and gender constitution: an essay in phenomenology and feminist theory. In Carole R. McCann and Seung-Kyung Kim (eds), *Feminist Theory Reader: Local and Global Perspectives* (pp. 415–427). New York, NY: Routledge.
Butler, Judith. (2004). *Undoing Gender*. New York, NY: Routledge.
Cai, Yong and Lavely, William. (2003). China's missing girls: Numerical estimates and effects on population growth. *The China Review*, 3(2), 13–29.
Chambers, Clare. (2008). *Sex, Culture, and Justice: The Limits of Choice*. University Park, PA: Pennsylvania State University Press.
Chant, Sylvia, and Gutmann, Matthew C. (2002). 'Men-streaming' gender? Questions for gender and development policy in the twenty-first century. *Progress in Development Studies*, 2(4), 269–282.
Cockburn, Tom. (2005). Children and the feminist ethic of care. *Childhood*, 12(1), 71–89.
Crenshaw, Kimberle. (1991). Mapping the margins: Intersectionality, identity politics, and violence against women of color. *Stanford Law Review*, 43(6), 1241–1299.
Cunningham, Hugh. (2005). *Children and childhood in western society since 1500* (2nd ed.). Harlow, UK: Pearson Longman.
Dickenson, Dianne. (2011). *Performing Childhood: Media, Childhood and Identity*. Doctor PhD Thesis, Macquarie University, Australasian Digital Theses Program. Available at www.researchonline.mq.edu.au/vital/access/manager/Repository/mq:20136
Forsberg, Lucas. (2009). *Involved Parenthood: Everyday Lives of Swedish Middle-class Families*. PhD thesis, Linköping University, Linköping.
Fraser, Nancy. (1990). Rethinking the public sphere: A contribution to the critique of actually existing democracy. *Social Text*, 25–26, 56–80.
Freeman, Michael. (1998). The sociology of childhood and children's rights. *The International Journal of Children's Rights*, 6(4), 433–444.
Furedi, Frank. (2008). *Paranoid Parenting: Why Ignoring the Experts May Be Best for Your Child*. London: Continuum.
Glenn, Evelyn Nakano. (1994). Social constructions of mothering: A thematic overview. In Evelyn Nakano Glenn, Grace Chang and Linda Rennie Forcey (eds), *Mothering: Ideology, Experience, and Agency* (pp. 1–29). New York, NY: Routledge.
Haraway, Donna. (1988). Situated knowledges: The science question in feminism and the privilege of partial perspective. *Feminist Studies*, 14(3), 575–599.
Harding, Sandra. (1991). *Whose Science? Whose Knowledge? Thinking from Women's Lives*. Milton Keynes: Open University Press.
Hays, Sharon. (1996). *The Cultural Contradictions of Motherhood*. New Haven, CT: Yale University Press.
Held, Virginia. (1990). Feminist transformations of moral theory. *Philosophy and Phenomenological Research*, 50, 321–344.
Held, Virginia. (2006). *The Ethics of Care: Personal, Political, and Global*. New York, NY: Oxford University Press.
Hirschmann, Nancy J. (2008). Feminist political philosophy. In Linda M. Alcoff and Eva F. Kittay (eds), *The Blackwell Guide to Feminist Philosophy* (pp. 145–164): Malden, MA: Blackwell Publishing.
Holland, Sally. (2010). Looked after children and the ethic of care. *British Journal of Social Work*, 40(6), 1664–1680.
Hyung Yi Kang, Laura. (2009). Epistemologies. In Philomena Essed (ed.), *A Companion to Gender Studies* (pp. 73–86). Malden, MA: Wiley-Blackwell.
James, Adrian L. (2010). Competition or integration? The next step in childhood studies? *Childhood*, 17(4), 485–499.
James, Allison, and Prout, Alan. (1997a). Introduction. In Allison James and Alan Prout (eds), *Constructing and Reconstructing Childhood: Contemporary Issues in the Sociological Study of Childhood* (2nd ed., p. 1–6). London: Routledge.
James, Allison, and Prout, Alan. (1997b). Preface to second edition. In Allison James and Alan Prout (eds), *Constructing and Reconstructing Childhood: Contemporary Issues in the Sociological Study of Childhood* (pp. ix–xvii). London: Routledge.
Jenkins, Henry. (1998). Introduction. Childhood innocence and other modern myths. In Henry Jenkins (ed.), *The Children's Culture Reader* (pp. 1–37). New York, NY: New York University Press.

Jiwani, Yasmin, and Berman, Helene. (2002). Introduction. In Helene Berman and Yasmin Jiwani (eds), *In the Best Interests of the Girl Child. Phase II Report* (pp. 1–12). Vancouver: The Alliance of Five Research Centres on Violence, Status of Women.

Kallio, Kirsi Pauliina, and Häkli, Jouni. (2011). Are there politics in childhood? *Space and Polity*, 15(1), 21–34.

Kittay, Eva Feder, Jennings, Bruce, and Wasunna, Angela A. (2005). Dependency, difference and the global ethic of longterm care. *Journal of Political Philosophy*, 13(4), 443–469.

Leys Stepan, Nancy. (1986). Race, gender, science and citizenship. *Gender and History*, 10(1), 26–52.

Lister, Ruth. (2006). Children (but not women) first: New Labour, child welfare and gender. *Critical Social Policy*, 26(2), 315–335.

Lister, Ruth. (2007). Inclusive citizenship: Realizing the potential. *Citizenship Studies*, 11(1), 49–62.

Lock, Margaret, and Nguyen, Vinh-Kim. (2010). *An Anthropology of Biomedicine*. Malden, MA: Wiley-Blackwell.

Lorber, Judith. (1994). 'Night to his day': The social construction of gender. *Paradoxes of Gender*, 1, 1–8.

Ludvig, Alice. (2006). Differences between women? Intersecting voices in a female narrative. *European Journal of Women's Studies*, 13(3), 245–258.

Lundy, Laura, and McEvoy, Lesley. (2012). Childhood, the United Nations Convention on the Rights of the Child and research: What constitutes a 'rights-based' approach. In Freeman, Michael (ed.), *Law and Childhood Studies: Current Legal Issues*, 14, 75–91. Oxford: Oxford University Press.

Mahoney, Maureen A., and Yngvesson, Barbara. (1992). The construction of subjectivity and the paradox of resistance: reintegrating feminist anthropology and psychology. *Signs*, 18(1), 44–73.

Martin, Karin A. (2005). William wants a doll. Can he have one? Feminists, child care advisors, and gender-neutral child rearing. *Gender and Society*, 19(4), 456–479.

Matsuda, Mari. (1990). Beside my sister, facing the enemy: Legal theory out of coalition. *Stanford Law Review*, 43, 1183–1192.

McCall, Leslie. (2005). The complexity of intersectionality. *Signs*, 30(3), 1771–1800.

Mohanty, Chandra Talpade. (1991). Under Western eyes: Feminist scholarship and colonial discourses. In Chandra Talpade Mohanty, Ann Russo and Lourdes Torres (eds), *Third World Women and the Politics of Feminism* (pp. 52–80). Bloomington, IN: Indiana University Press.

Moosa-Mitha, Mehmoona. (2005). A difference-centred alternative to theorization of children's citizenship rights. *Citizenship Studies*, 9(4), 369–388.

Morris, Edward W. (2007). 'Ladies' or 'loudies'?: Perceptions and experiences of black girls in classrooms. *Youth and Society*, 38(4), 490–515.

Morrow, Virginia. (2006). Understanding gender differences in context: Implications for young children's everyday lives. *Children and Society*, 20(2), 92–104.

Myhrvold, Trine. (2006). The different other: Towards an including ethics of care. *Nursing Philosophy*, 7(3), 125–136.

Nash, Jennifer. (2008). Re-thinking intersectionality. *Feminist Review*, 89, 1–15.

Noddings, Nel. (1986). *Caring: A Feminine Approach to Ethics and Moral Education*. Berkeley, CA: University of California Press.

Popke, Jeff. (2006). Geography and ethics: Everyday mediations through care and consumption. *Progress in Human Geography*, 30(4), 504–512.

Porter, Gina. (2011). 'I think a woman who travels a lot is befriending other men and that's why she travels': Mobility constraints and their implications for rural women and girls in sub-Saharan Africa.', *Gender, Place and Culture*, 18(1), 65–81.

Prout, Alan, and James, Allison. (1997). A new paradigm for the sociology of childhood? Provenance, promise and problems. In Allison James and Alan Prout (eds), *Constructing and Reconstructing Childhood: Contemporary Issues in the Sociological Study of Childhood* (2nd ed., pp. 7–33). London: Routledge.

Puar, Jasbir K. (2005). Queer times, queer assemblages. *Social Text*, 23(3/4), 121–139.

Qvortrup, Jens. (2005). *The little 's' and the prospects for generational childhood studies*. Paper presented at the paper presented at the international conference, 'Childhood 2005', Oslo, 29 June–3 July.

Rahman, Momin. (2009). Theorising intersectionality: Identities, quality and ontology. In Emily Grabham, Davina Cooper, Jane Krishnadas and Didi Herman (eds), *Intersectionality and Beyond: Law, Power and the Politics of Location* (pp. 352–373). Abingdon, UK: Routledge-Cavendish.

Reiter, Sara Ann. (1996). The Kohlberg-Gilligan controversy: Lessons for accounting ethics education. *Critical Perspectives on Accounting*, 7(1), 33–54.

Ribbens McCarthy, Jane, and Edwards, Rosalind. (2011). *Key Concepts in Family Studies*. London: Sage.

Ribbens McCarthy, Jane, Edwards, Rosalind, and Gillies, Val. (2000). Moral tales of the child and the adult: Narratives of contemporary family lives under changing circumstances. *Sociology*, 34(4), 785–803.

Rich, Adrienne. (1995). *Of Woman Born: Motherhood as Experience and Institution*. New York, NY: Norton.

Robinson, Fiona. (2006). Care, gender and global social justice: Rethinking 'ethical globalization'. *Journal of Global Ethics*, 2(1), 5–25.

Rose, Nikolas. (1999). *Governing the Soul: The Shaping of the Private Self* (2nd ed.). London: Free Association Books.

Salih, Sara. (2007). On Judith Butler and performativity. In Karen Lovaas and Mercilee M. Jenkins (eds), *Sexualities and Communication in Everyday Life: A Reader* (pp. 55–68). Thousand Oaks, CA: Sage.

Scuzzarello, Sarah. (2009). Multiculturalims and caring ethics. In Sarah Scuzzarello, Catarina Kinnvall and Kristen R. Monroe (eds), *On Behalf of Others. The Psychology of Care in a Global World* (pp. 61–81). Oxford: Oxford University Press.

Silvers, Anita. (1995). Reconciling equality to difference: Caring (f)or justice for people with disabilities. *Hypatia*, 10(1), 30.

Speier, Matthew. (1976). The adult ideological viewpoint in studies of childhood. In A. Skolnick (ed.), *Rethinking Childhood* (pp. 168–186). Boston: Little, Brown.

Summers, Carol. (1991). Intimate colonialism: The imperial production of reproduction in Uganda, 1907–1925. *Signs*, 16(4), 787–807.

Taefi, Nura. (2009). The synthesis of age and gender: Intersectionality, international human rights law and the marginalisation of the girl-child. *The International Journal of Children's Rights*, 17(3), 345–376.

Thomas, Dorothy Q., and Beasley, Michele E. (1993). Domestic violence as a human rights issue. *Human Rights Quarterly*, 15(1), 36–62.

Thorne, Barrie. (1987). Re-visioning women and social change: Where are the Children? *Gender and Society*, 1(1), 85–109.

Thorne, Barrie. (2007). Editorial. Crafting the interdisciplinary field of childhood studies. *Childhood*, 14(2), 147–152.

Tronto, Joan C. (1987). Beyond gender difference to a theory of care. *Signs*, 12(4), 644–663.

Tronto, Joan C. (1993). *Moral Boundaries: A Political Argument for an Ethic of Care*. New York: Routledge.

Walkerdine, Valerie. (2000). Violent boys and precocious girls: Regulating childhood at the end of the millennium. *Contemporary Issues in Early Childhood*, 1(1), 3–22.

Wall, John. (2008). Human rights in light of childhood. *International Journal of Children's Rights*, 16, 523–543.

Warner, Leah R. (2008). A best practices guide to intersectional approaches in psychological research. *Sex Roles*, 59(5–6), 454–463.

Wekker, Gloria, and Lutz, Helma. (2001). A wind-swept plain. A history of gender and etnicity-thought in the Netherlands [translation of 'Een hoogvlakte met koude winden. De geschiedenis van het gender- en etniciteitsdenken in Nederland']. In Maayke Botman, Nancy Jouwe and Gloria Wekker (eds), *Caleidoscopische visies. De zwarte, migranten en vluchtelingenvrouwenbeweging in Nederland* (pp. 25–49). Amsterdam: Koninklijk Instituut voor de Tropen.

Werbner, Pnina, and Yuval-Davis, Nira. (1999). Introduction: Women and the new discourse of citizenship. In Pnina Werbner and Nira Yuval-Davis (eds), *Women, Citizenship and Difference* (pp. xii, 271). London: Zed Books.

Whitehead, Ann. (2000). Continuities and discontinuities in political constructions of the working man in rural sub-Saharan Africa: The 'lazy man' in African agriculture. *European Journal of Development Research*, 12(2), 23.

Woodhead, Martin. (1997). Psychology and the cultural construction of children's needs. In Allison James and Alan Prout (eds), *Constructing and Reconstructing Childhood: Contemporary Issues in the Sociological study of Childhood* (pp. 63–84). London: Routledge.

Zelizer, Viviana A. Rotman. (1985). *Pricing the Priceless Child: The Changing Social Value of Children*. New York: Basic Books.

10
Children's rights and citizenship studies
Re-theorising child citizenship through transdisciplinarity from the local to the global

Richard Mitchell

1. Introduction and cultural/historical context

The chapter presents theoretical and empirical analyses of children's[1] and young people's citizenship that starts in Canada but is representative of an evolution of citizenship visible throughout the world judging by the significant international literature focused on this contemporary discourse. The chapter had its genesis from recommendations found in a dismal research report from the Canadian Senate entitled *Children: The Silenced Citizens*[2] (Senate of Canada, 2005, 2007), an exhaustive investigation into implementation of the UN Convention on the Rights of the Child (CRC, 1989) in Canada, although underlying notions that young people's views are silenced from relevant discourses is a familiar one throughout the literature. As noted in the Introduction for this Handbook, conceptually children's rights have grown apart from human rights in general, and this pattern is reflected in discourses to do with the "worldwide resurgence of interest in questions about education and democratic citizenship" noted by Biesta and Lawy (2006, p. 63).

A secondary analysis drawn from a 2008–2010 ethnographic study in southern Ontario, Canada of both adult and child participants' experience of active citizenship[3] also informs the

---

1   The terms "children", "childhood", "young people" and "youth" are used interchangeably in this chapter and are meant to convey the definition found in UNCRC Article 1 – without prejudice – which states "a child means every human being below the age of eighteen years" (1989).
2   The Canadian Senate Standing Committee on Human Rights tabled a three-year study on UNCRC implementation entitled "Children: The Silenced Citizens" in 2007. See Senate recommendations and database: www.parl.gc.ca/Content/SEN/Committee/391/huma/rep/rep10apr07-e.pdf.
3   While a "Western" basis for citizenship is frequently understood and argued relative to a particular geopolitical space or nation-state, (see Cohen, 2005, and Kiwan, 2005, for examples), the UN Convention on the Rights of the Child (1989) has nonetheless become an international framework for child citizenship in an ongoing reconstruction of this discourse. Positive changes in domestic legislation to do with genital cutting, for example, in "non-Western" states such as Kenya, Senegal, Egypt and Ethiopia (*The Lancet*, 2010, p. 1800; see also Leye and Middelburg, Chapter 17 in this Handbook) offer evidence of this conceptual and political shift from a growing discourse re-defining the boundaries between childhood and citizenship.

chapter. That study anchored an edited volume on critical citizenship pedagogies (Mitchell and Moore, 2012) from which a small portion of the literature herein has been drawn, and is in keeping with at least two of our Handbook themes of a "bottom-up approach to children's rights" and our collective critique of "dominant paradigms in children's rights research". The study's central research question was: "What are some of the critical issues for young people as they attempt to exercise their rights to participatory citizenship in Canada and beyond?" The investigation focused on two years of events leading up to a youth rally hosted by international children's rights activist Craig Kielburger at my university (Brock Press, 2009; see also Kielburger and Kielburger, 2006; Wingrove, 2010). This same question serves as an opening to this chapter although from a globalised perspective and not solely from my own socio-historical context.

The rally drew 350 elementary, secondary and post-secondary students from Ontario's Niagara Region, which contrasted with the complete abandonment of child soldier Omar Khadr in the American prison camp at Guantánamo Bay in Cuba being reported that day in domestic and international media. I interviewed Mr. Kielburger and discussed Mr. Khadr's plight on that occasion since the federal government had also initiated the unprecedented step of appealing a Supreme Court of Canada ruling ordering Khadr's repatriation, the only Western citizen remaining in the prison until 2012 (University of Toronto Bora Laskin Law Library, 2014). While perhaps remote, the application of widely accepted "principles and provisions" of the CRC (Article 42) may have proven a more effective response to unravelling this young person's citizenship issues – a domestically born "child soldier" under complex international circumstances.

I also emphasize here that politically contentious and contested notions related to inclusive Canadian citizenship for First Nations, Aboriginal, Inuit and Métis first peoples and their children are mired inter-generationally in colonialist structures and struggles. These same structures and struggles are present in regions throughout the world as separate though integrally related discussions, beyond the scope of this chapter. Saul (2010, p. 136, citing Borgeault, 1988) recounts the historical development of South Africa's apartheid system using the Canadian approach:

> "South Africa turned to Canada in the first decade of the 20th century", since "Canada was probably the only advanced capitalist state that had an elaborate system of administration and territorial segregation of an internally colonized indigenous population, a possible exception being the United States". Indeed, Canada's Dominions Land Act of the 1870s (after which the South African Land Settlement Act of 1912 and 1913 was actually patterned, according to Bourgeault), and related acts including our very own *Indian Act*, restricted Indians, as they were then termed (now "First Nations" people), from acquiring property or trading their goods off the reserves. They also deprived Indians of the vote, and even established a kind of pass system for exit and re-entry to reserves. Small wonder that apartheid South Africa was interested (see Deer, 2009 and Cambre, 2007 for further historical analysis).

There are at least 370 million Indigenous people throughout the world – many of whom have large and growing populations of children and young people – whose ancestors have faced similar inter-generational colonialist predations over the past five centuries. The processes associated with subjugation and assimilation also gave impetus to the *UN Declaration on the Rights of Indigenous Peoples* (see also Arabena, 2008; Malott, 2008; Blanchet-Cohen, Chapter 21 in this Handbook; United Nations, 2007).

2. Globalisation of child citizenship

Craig and Marc Kielburger, co-founders of *Free the Children* are two leading figures in youth empowerment and child citizenship (Henderson, 2013). Their international non-governmental organisation (INGO) works with more than one million youth every year as the world's largest network of children helping children through education. The brothers are syndicated columnists and co-authors of the New York Times bestseller *Me to We* (2006), and *The World Needs Your Kid* (Kielburger et al., 2009). Their work has been widely featured on US-based *CNN*, *The Oprah Winfrey Show*, *60 Minutes* and *The Today Show*, and in news magazines such as *Time* and the *Economist*, as well as appearances on the *BBC*.

Sociologist Daiva Stasiulis (2002a, 2002b) was one of the first scholars to critically assess Kielburger's efforts to mobilise young people, and to comment on the truncated political efforts to reconfigure children's citizenship. She recounted layers of inertia and the "relative failure" of all governments combined with the manner in which state policy, Canadian courts, and children's politics have responded to "the imaginary of the active child citizen … . The reluctance of adult decision-makers to open up policy-making to the contributions of children has been further hindered by the current anti-democratic cast of neo-liberal governance" (Stasiulis, 2002b, p. 507).

In a doctoral investigation, the capacity of five- and six-year-old elementary students for "active citizenship" was analysed within a group of Australian students through both storytelling and social action (Phillips, 2010, particularly pp. 79–106). She also critically assesses Kielburger's work, and while young people from economically rich countries speaking for those in economically poor countries "raises potential risks of colonial-like practices … and neo-colonialist appropriations of third world issues", Phillips observes members of the organisation are "empowered, knowledgeable, compassionate and autonomous" (Phillips, 2010, pp. 37–38). Moreover, she cites Kielburger (1998, p. 75) who recalls "the struggle against child labour did not 'begin in the west, but rather began with organisations such as CWA (Child Workers of Asia)'" (Phillips, 2010, p. 38).

Scottish childhood scholars Malcolm Hill and Kay Tisdall (1997, p. 21) observe: "[r]ights, and the related concept of citizenship, constitute one of the most powerful discourses in today's world … definitions of children's rights, and debates around them, are reliant on two concepts – of 'childhood' and of 'rights' – and how these two are combined" (also Tisdall, 1994). Irish educator Dymphna Devine (2002, p. 303) argues that while locating rights within the context of adult–child relations, an education for citizenship based in schools must take into account dynamics of power and control between teachers and pupils, and the impacts on children's construction of themselves as citizens. As an attribute of such engaged citizenship, the question arises: what is critical thinking and how do children and young people develop those skills? Henry A. Giroux has frequently answered this by recalling Brazilian educator Paulo Freire's approach to pedagogy:

> What Freire made clear is that … education is a political and moral practice that provides the knowledge, skills and social relations that enable students to explore for themselves the possibilities of what it means to be engaged citizens, while expanding and deepening their participation in the promise of a substantive democracy.
>
> *(Giroux, 2010b, para. 5)*

In this chapter, my standpoint includes critically teaching and applying the CRC in a similar pedagogical approach – within and beyond schools – as both a researcher and a practitioner

(Moore and Mitchell, 2008, 2009; Mitchell and Moore, 2012), and from a "transdisciplinary" conceptual and methodological basis (Mitchell, 2013, p. 514). The pedagogical issue of teaching this nation's children about the CRC has eluded the majority of Canada's educators since signing and ratifying the CRC (Senate of Canada, 2005, 2007; also Howe and Covell, 2005, 2007; United Nations Committee on the Rights of the Child, 1995, 2003). Noted researchers Howe and Covell (2005, p. 63) observe that while "the enjoyment of rights is basic to citizenship", under the current regime Canadian children's citizenship is consistent with core human rights principles "only in part". They further observe (2007, p. ix) that domestic CRC implementation "has neither been as quick nor as comprehensive as we would have liked. In fact, in many ways we have been more successful on the international scene than at home".

Guantánamo prisoner Omar Khadr is an international exemplar who also represents the fluidity of citizenship and permeability of geopolitical borders. Captured in Afghanistan and held by the American military for war crimes, he is a child of the globe and not solely of a particular nation-state. While local experiences shaped Khadr's citizenship, these were also global and exemplified by the glare of international legal, political and media reaction to his mistreatment. Child soldiers such as Khadr are victims of war, and singular disciplinary or legal lenses are inadequate to address these complex issues. Both Khadr and Kielburger are Canadians by birth and began their activism as school children in Toronto-area classrooms. By virtue of differentiated power relations, both have now become archetypes for the "'child in danger' versus the 'dangerous child'" noted by our editors in the Introduction, as well as poster boys for the complexity of the current era (see also Bauman, 2000; Sassen, 2008; and Vrasti, 2009 for discussion).

Khadr's fate stretched to the Afghani war, a US prison camp, and a high court ruling before repatriation (Supreme Court of Canada, 2010 SCC 3) though his lawyers have recently filed a $60 million lawsuit against the government for contributing to his torture (Friscolanti, 2013). Kielburger's trajectory includes a Nobel nomination and rock star status among children and his peers well beyond his native land. In light of their subsequent emergence to global status, previous theoretical notions of how citizenship rights are constituted and applied appear inadequate. These constructs demonstrate why we can no longer analyse citizenship within the binaries of state or statelessness, citizenship or rights, or even "me to we" as the Kielburgers have written (Kielburger and Kielburger, 2006).

I'm reminded of Bauman's (2005, p. 1095) observation that we live now in a time of "liquid modernity ... among a multitude of competing values, norms, and lifestyles without a firm and reliable guarantee of being in the right [that] is hazardous and commands a high psychological price". Alan Prout's (2001, p. 19) analysis on the future of childhood is similar in that "[w]e live with the knowledge that modernity's project of rational control has limits... The mood is more cautious and reflexive about the status of our understanding, more aware of the complexity of nature and society, more alert to the unintended consequences of our social actions and less sure of our social institutions". This complexity is evidenced by the flood of images on traditional and social media that continue as grim reminders that millions of children are still being dispossessed of the most basic human rights simply to live and enjoy healthy development. As one of many examples, portions of Syria and its population burn as I write (British Broadcasting Corporation, 2013).

3. Re-theorising adult citizenship through child citizenship

Critical educators Hyslop-Margison and Thayer (2009, p. xv) note: "these are extremely tenuous times for modern democratic states and for democracy more generally", and students in advanced capitalist societies are bombarded daily "with ideological messages designed to convince them that self-worth and social status are dependent on appearance, purchasing power and conspicuous consumption". In Mitchell and Moore (2012, pp. 1–8) we highlight that similar to globalisation, "democracy" is still a highly contested and localized term. Nevertheless, with the apparent "impending neoliberal capitalist collapse" observed by Hyslop-Margison and Thayer (2009), the increasing interdependence of world society points to a "multitude of transformations and challenges across and despite borders" (Vrasti, 2009, p. 4; also Luhmann, 1997). An increasingly complex "global assemblage" (Sassen, 2008, p. 5)[4] of both childhood and adult citizenship is becoming visible though, one that is being crafted on human rights principles – a citizenship no longer solely encompassed by, or understood through, lenses of single disciplines or nation-states. In this local/global nexus, active citizenship continues to become uncoupled from traditional geopolitical borders and traditional frameworks (see Moosa-Mitha, 2005; and Castells, 1999, 2000a, 2000b for theoretical insights).

From a British perspective, Biesta and Lawy (2006) offer important distinctions they have encountered in the teaching of citizenship. "In new and emerging democracies the focus has, understandably, been on how education can contribute to the formation of democratic dispositions and the development of a democratic culture" (p. 63). They note that similar questions are being raised in more mature democratic nations, particularly on how to maintain and nurture both "democracy and democratic culture" (Biesta and Lawy, 2006, p. 63). In a companion paper, Lawy and Biesta (2006, p. 43) further emphasise:

> Citizenship-as-practice does not presume that young people move through a pre-specified trajectory *into* their citizenship statuses or that the role of the education system is to find appropriate strategies and approaches that prepare young people for their transitions into "good" and contributing citizens. Indeed it makes no distinction between what might otherwise be regarded as a status differential between citizens and *not-yet-citizens*. It is inclusive rather than exclusive because it assumes that *everyone* in society including young people are citizens who simply move *through* citizenship-as-practice, "from the cradle to the grave".

They contend that to conceptualise citizenship as an ongoing practice involves a fundamental change in the way we conceive such practices. "Citizenship is no longer a solely adult experience but is experienced and articulated as a wider shift in social relations common to all age groups" (Lawy and Biesta, 2006, p. 43). Notwithstanding, their analyses underscore an "adult-centric" construction of citizenship lingering in much of the discourse, which while alluding to "youth" nonetheless omits reference to global CRC implementation. Biesta (2008) corrects this omission, though their previous efforts to theorise the teaching of active citizenship are similar to that of Turner (2006), and to Isin and Turner's (2007, pp. 12–13) notions of "invigorating" this discourse through continued re-theorising of "global citizenship".

---

4 In the Introduction to her 2008 text (p. 5), Sassen acknowledges: "I use the concept assemblage in its most descriptive sense. However, several scholars have developed theoretical constructs around this term. Most significant for the purpose of this [her] book is the work of Deleuze and Guattari, for whom "assemblage" is a contingent ensemble of practices and things that can be differentiated (that is, they are not collections of similar practices and things) and that can be aligned along the axes of territoriality and deterritorialization…" I have also chosen Sassen's interpretation of "rights" as a global assemblage of "practices and things that can be differentiated", and as a descriptive construct to allow a re-theorising and reconstruction of relations associated with UNCRC implementation, including the new concept of young people as active citizens in an increasingly networked world society.

3.1. Human rights and child citizenship

A general inquiry using the ubiquitous *Google©* search engine as I write reveals 127 million results (in 0.29 seconds) for "child as citizen", and nearly 600,000 (in 0.09 seconds) with a more focused search using *Google Scholar©* beginning from the period the CRC was being introduced and implemented in the early 1990s. One such programme is exemplified in a 2006–2009 project initiated by the INGO *Childwatch International* in collaboration with well-known researchers in six nations (Taylor and Smith, 2009). The initiative was part of an international comparative research project focusing on children's perspectives on their rights, responsibilities and citizenship at home, in school and in the community. These researchers emphasise that with recent global trends towards democratization in all major regions of the world, economic, political, and social changes are also taking place in dramatic fashion. The widespread acceptance of the CRC offers an unprecedented global consensus on the nature and extent of participation rights of children and youth, they observe.

In the Foreward to Invernizzi and Williams' (2008) seminal text on child citizenship, former chair of the UN Committee on the Rights of the Child, Jaap Doek (2008, p. xii) recounts the struggle for nine million stateless humans, but also observes there are no provisions "in any international human rights treaty conferring on an individual the right to citizenship". However, in the context of children's rights, he highlights that CRC Article 7 (1) emphasises "every child has the right to acquire a nationality" (Doek, 2008, p. xii).

Similarly, the Annals of the American Academy of Political and Social Science contributed a collection of papers on the "child as citizen" from presentations at the host's institution marking the 20th anniversary of the CRC (Earls, 2011). In her analysis of Norwegian efforts, Anne Kjørholt (2002, p. 70) argues that the "socialization paradigm emphasizing children's development towards becoming mature human beings in the future … may… be seen as contradictory to the construction of the child as a right-holder in modernity, stressing children's rights as citizens here and now". British educators Audrey Osler and Hugh Starkey have amassed a significant scholarship linking the CRC with such a "here and now" style of teaching citizenship within schools (Osler and Starkey, 1998, 2005, 2010; also Carter and Osler, 2000; Trivers and Starkey, 2012; Mejias and Starkey, 2012).

Within the literature there is also disagreement with any notions of children as citizens in any context, and research by Dina Kiwan (2005, p. 37) offers one such analysis. While this paper excludes research directly with children, she argues convincingly that "conflating" the concept of citizenship with human rights is "not only conceptually incoherent, but may actually obstruct the empowerment and active participation of individual citizens in the context of a political community". She also challenges any notion that the CRC offers the "ideal basis for citizenship education", and citing Alderson (2000, p. 115) Kiwan claims she has failed to "engage with the conceptual distinction between human rights and citizenship rights" (p. 37). Kiwan's critique deserves serious consideration if only by virtue of the weight of research contradicting her analysis, a solid cross-section reviewed herein.

Kiwan (2005, p. 45) claims a "theoretical confusion" regarding whether CRC rights refer to human rights which are accorded to all individuals. She contends this arises because of the inclusion of "participation" and civic rights, which are theoretically a different kind of right to other CRC rights "such as the right to life (Article 6), the right to freedom of religion (Article 14) or the right to education (Article 28)". In this light, she analyses various constructs that provide the basis for adult citizenship (Kiwan, 2005, pp. 38–44) including moral, legal, identity-based, and participatory.

> While it may be important to acknowledge the important role of human rights within the practice of active citizenship and to recognize that the practice of human rights occurs within a political community, it is inaccurate to conflate the two concepts. This is because human rights discourses are located within a universalist discourse, in contrast to citizenship, which is located within a more particularist discourse. Underpinning human rights is the notion of common humanity, based on ethical conceptualisations of the individual. In contrast, citizenship rights are underpinned by their relation to a political community, based on political conceptualisations of the individual.
>
> *(Kiwan, 2005, p. 47)*

US-based political scientist Elizabeth Cohen (2005) takes a similar critical stance towards the construct of "child citizenship" in liberal democracies observing that with the introduction of CRC and globalisation, "new possibilities for membership in political communities that transcend the nation state" are clearly manifest. Nevertheless, she echoes Kiwan's concern that "without adequate national citizenship, children's citizenship will remain grounded in abstract guarantees created by well-meaning but powerless groups of adults ... that can enforce very little in regard to the political circumstances of children for whose physical safety they claim responsibility" (Cohen, 2005, p. 223). Similar to Biesta and Lawy (2006), these political relations are the crux of both Kiwan's (2005) and Cohen's (2005) arguments, and are clearly adult-centric.

There are two similar blind spots in these authors' analyses, and in the first instance I'll respond directly to Kiwan's critique of Alderson and truly "engage with the conceptual distinction between human rights and citizenship rights" (Kiwan, 2005, p. 37). Kiwan's most glaring omission is to do with the theoretical and methodological distinctions articulated by sociologists of childhood over the past two decades, many of whom are also contributing to the children's rights discourse (Christensen and James, 2000; Davis, 2011; Davis and Watson, 2000; James and Prout, 1997; James and James, 2004; James *et al.*, 2002; Mayall, 2000, 2002 [also Chapter 5 in this Handbook]; Matthews, 2007; Mitchell, 2003, 2005; Montgomery *et al.*, 2003; Moss and Petrie, 2002; Woodhead, 1999).

Various theoretical analyses into how "participation" works *in situ* continue to illuminate discourses related to childhood and active citizenship notwithstanding many early CRC critics. Such thinking provided the basis for textbooks by Heather Montgomery, Rachel Burr and Martin Woodhead entitled *Childhood: The Series*. In their volume "Changing Childhoods: Local and Global" a typical section on child citizenship (Montgomery *et al.*, 2003, pp. 262–270) emphasises once again that "participation is, at root, about extending the goals of democracy to ensure that all citizens – including the youngest – are prepared and able to contribute to shaping their own lives, their community and the wider society" (p. 262). These authors observe that while many initiatives have taken shape in "well-established democracies in the affluent countries of the North", they cite the Delhi labour campaigns by street children in India and Nepalese children's clubs for additional evidence that democratic children's groups organised through CRC teaching are visible throughout all regions of the globe. Sociologist Sara Matthews (2007, p. 329) offers an overview of this childhood literature, but observes most "scholars in the United States are on a somewhat different path than their colleagues in other Western countries".

A major problem encountered in applying the "new" sociology of childhood perspective in research is that children may have no independent right to participate in research. Although in the United States children must assent to participate, their parents have the right of first refusal and can withhold consent.... . In nations where issues related to children's rights are being addressed, researchers may have less difficulty with access. The proliferation of the "new" sociology of childhood can be read as one result of scholars in various countries taking up the challenge of the UN Convention by thinking carefully about how children experience institutions controlled by adults.

(Matthews, 2007, p. 329; see Corsaro, 2005, and Thorne, 1993 for contrasts)

In terms of Kiwan's second omission, James and Prout (1997, p. 8) note the type of reflexive social activity related to adults researching, teaching and engaging with children – in this context within rights-based pedagogies – as illustrative of Giddens' (1984) "double hermeneutic of the social sciences". I am positing here that by engaging in research and teaching of the CRC with young social actors, critical pedagogues are at the same time contributing to a "new" dimension of children's rights studies. Indeed, viewing the concept through the lenses of the double hermeneutic implies neither a uni-disciplinary nor a uni-directional knowledge exchange, but a co-constructed and reflexive experience of citizenship for both adults and young people alike.

Baroness Ruth Lister of Burtersett was appointed to England's upper house in 2010, and she has investigated and written widely on the construct of children's citizenship, indeed she remains one of the most widely referenced. She recounts the elements of a substantive citizenship include membership and participation, rights, responsibilities, and equality of status, respect and recognition. She considers the case for recognizing children as citizens is not so much arguing for wholesale extension of adult rights and obligations, "but recognition that children's citizenship practices constitute them as *de facto*, even if not complete *de jure*, citizens". More broadly, Lister urges, "this position points towards an understanding of citizenship which embraces but goes beyond that of a bundle of rights" (Lister, 2007, p. 693). Doek (2008, p. xii) charts the terrain from a similarly global perspective while articulating the dimensions of adult citizenship as nationality; the right to reside permanently on the territory of a State; the right to be protected by the State; the right to vote, to hold office and to participate in decision making; and the right to social action and to economic rights. He also considers the characteristics for young people in the context of the CRC by noting

> the citizenship of the child should not be dealt with only as a nationality issue. Nationality is undoubtedly an important element of citizenship. But I like to take a broader approach from the perspective of the child as a rights holder. Citizen Child may not vote or run for a public office, but is entitled to the enjoyment of all the rights enshrined in the CRC without discrimination of any kind.
>
> *(Doek, 2008, p. xii)*

This rights-based citizenship is exemplified in the ample literature on "participation" and "engagement" of young people (see Anget *et al.*, 2006, among many).

3.2. Human rights and global citizenship

While citizenship has evolved through historical, social, political and theoretical dimensions, until the current era it has been adapted and viewed mainly as an exclusionary device for gendered and racial binaries, in oppressive conditions exercised upon racialized minorities, women, children, the intellectually and physically challenged, and on those from South Africa's and Canada's original inhabitants, along with most other Indigenous populations. Writing from the Australian context again, Margaret Coady (2008) notes the range of political philosophers from "Aristotle through Aquinas, Augustine, Marsilius, Hobbes, Locke and Kant [who] have closely analysed the idea of citizenship", though again solely on behalf of adults, and most likely, on behalf of adult males.

Moreover, literally thousands of civil society organisations with consultative status at United Nations sessions in New York, Geneva and Paris have established their legitimacy longer than many contemporary democratic states and the transitory nature of their political and governance structures. As one example, English feminist Eglantyne Jebb's *Save the Children* established in 1919 is an international non-governmental organisation (INGO) currently at work in 120 nations (Montgomery *et al.*, 2003, pp. 196–199). This emergence of trans-national human rights and democratic governance are key features of global citizenship in late modernity theorised by German legal theorist Niklas Luhmann as "world society" (1997). Indeed, many university-based research initiatives and coursework include notions of global citizenship as learning objectives. Australia's University of New South Wales offers one example with their students becoming "global citizens":

- Capable of applying their discipline in local, national and international contexts.
- Culturally aware and capable of respecting diversity and acting in socially just/responsible ways.
- Capable of environmental responsibility.

University College London is another institution contributing to the discourse by touting itself as a "world-class, research-led, multi-faculty university, consciously and deliberately global and wide-ranging in its reach and ambition". University College London (2014) contends their global citizenship pedagogies will produce individuals characterised by the following attributes:

- Critical and Creative Thinkers
- Sensitive to Cultural Difference
- Ambitious, yet Idealistic
- Highly Employable and Ready to Embrace Professional Mobility
- Entrepreneurs with the Ability to Innovate
- Prepared to Assume Leadership Roles

Once again, the assumption that *criticality* in this context is easily understood by corporate educators and the educated needs to be challenged, as our editors have done in the Introduction to this Handbook. I turn here to Giroux's analysis of American culture (Giroux, 2010a) that could pass for most contemporary industrialised societies around the globe:

> Imposed amnesia is the *modus operandi* of the current moment. Not only is historical memory now sacrificed to the spectacles of consumerism, celebrity culture, hyped-up violence and a market-driven obsession with the self, but the very formative culture that makes compassion, justice and an engaged citizenry foundational to democracy has been erased from the language of mainstream politics and the diverse cultural apparatuses that support it. Unbridled individualism along with the gospel of profit and unchecked competition undermine both the importance of democratic public spheres and the necessity for a language that talks about shared responsibilities, the public good and the meaning of a just society (para. 2).

The type of "democratic public spheres" re-imagined here by Giroux offer a fitting description for those being co-constructed by adult mentors in rights-based relationships with young people. A doctoral investigation by Wangbei Ye (2012, pp. 9–34) offers another illustration of this "double hermeneutic" noted by James and Prout (1997, p. 8) in an analysis of school power and democratic citizenship education in Communist China. Drawing on interview, survey and observational data collected from three secondary schools in Shenzhen City, findings from this research indicate (rather counter-intuitively) that some Chinese school practices are congruent with critical pedagogy studies ongoing in other regions of the globe (see Shor and Freire, 1987; Freire, 1970, 1999; Kincheloe, 2010).

The investigator argues that local schools are capable of advancing democratic citizenship education by de-politicizing Communist Party-dominated citizenship education, decentralising curriculum decisions in order to take power from governments, and democratising school culture to better meet the growing needs of Chinese civil society. These practices do not, however, eliminate the CCP's politically-motivated values, centralised control and non-democratic education management style. Echoing Devine (2002), the study indicates that pedagogical relations even in a communist state may best be understood by viewing *power* as a semi-emancipatory relationship. It is also worth recalling here that China ratified the CRC in 1992, and submitted its third and fourth reports to the UN Committee on the Rights of the Child for review in 2010 (United Nations Office of the High Commissioner for Human Rights, 2013).

Writing in Bangkok in 2008 with children across East Asia and the Pacific, the *Interagency Working Group on Children's Participation* also tackled the question "Are children citizens?" By observing that all children are born with civil, political, social and economic rights, and these rights enable them to practice their citizenship "at least to some extent", they claim that children's entitlement to citizenship does not depend on their future contributions to society since their ability to exercise their rights evolves as they grow and learn (see Article 5 CRC). The researchers also observed that the CRC does not extend many political rights to children, though some countries such as Nicaragua and Iran go beyond to offer the right to vote to some teens. As children's rights continue to be adapted to the social, political and economic realities of fast-changing societies, they contend, increased demands to extend the right to vote to older youth in the coming decades may be features of regions around the world. "Irrespective of their lack of formal political rights, children are taking part in political actions, movements, campaigns, political and even armed struggles, and are members of political parties" (Interagency Working Group on Children's Participation, 2008, p. 5; see also Vanobbergen, Chapter 4 in this Handbook).

3.3. What are common dimensions of child citizenship?

Feminist scholar Erica Burman (2001, pp. 14–15) early on explored linkages between women's and children's rights by encouraging researchers to engage in a little "cultural and disciplinary tourism and experiment with ideas from outside western psychology". Lister (2007, p. 693) also claims "lessons may be learned from feminist critiques of mainstream constructions of citizenship, paying particular attention to the question of capacity for citizenship". Bacon and Frankel (2014) explore meanings of children's citizenship again from an English context by drawing attention to children's capacities to generate and negotiate their own and others' social meanings. They contend that to respect children as contributors, citizenship experiences must be re-configured from structures managed solely by adults in power to include products of personal agency, and involvement in the re-negotiation of norms and values (see also Bacon *et al.*, 2013; Jamieson *et al.*, 2010/2011; MacNaughton *et al.*, 2008; Taylor and Smith, 2009; Tomaševski, 2006; as well as the Interagency Working Group on Child Participation, 2008).

While I acknowledge that concepts such as rights, democracy and citizenship are far from neutral, this section builds on Biesta's (2008, p. 40) delineation with tendencies he views as problematic within the Scottish national curriculum for citizenship education. He identifies four characteristics – too strong a tendency towards *individualism*, an *all-encompassing concept* of citizenship that includes political, economic, social and cultural dimensions, *activity* with regard to the learning of citizenship through engagement, and finally, their strong emphasis on *community*. While his final dimension seems to contradict his first, his erudite analysis bears re-emphasising here.

> Thus, the Scottish approach is based on what we might call a social rather than an exclusively political conception of citizenship, one which understands citizenship in terms of membership of and concern for the many communities that make up people's lives. This includes the more narrowly political domain of citizenship, but extends to civil society and potentially includes any community. This is why "active and responsible citizenship" is said to have to do with "individuals having a sense of belonging to, and functioning in, communities".
>
> *(Biesta, 2008, p. 44)*

Biesta (2008) further notes the framing of the Scottish curriculum (Scottish Executive, 2004) by CRC texts but the attributes of adult citizenship in stable liberal democracies such as the right to vote, to sign contracts, to serve on juries and the armed forces, and in this case, the need to engage with political parties still seem to hold sway in his analysis. These adult-centric notions have been compared and contrasted in this selection of literature with the following dimensions of active child citizenship most commonly identified:

- Birth registration and the right to acquire a nationality both of which are obliged under CRC Article 7
- The prevention of children from becoming stateless which is a regular problem for children belonging to ethnic minorities, refugee or immigrant children, and for children born in times of conflict and war
- Engagement and application of CRC knowledge in community-based contexts
- Engagement in critical reflection within a local/global nexus through Internet technologies and social media
- Respect for individual and group agency in the exercise of adult power and active participation in decision-making (see also Hart, 2008)
- Access to ever-increasing levels of education
- Finally, the influential role of INGOs and NGOs in adult/child partnerships aimed at democratic, active local/global experiences of citizenship

In the following section, I argue for a relatively untapped framework for making clearer sense of interconnected phenomena within the child rights, human rights and citizenship literature in an effort to create common ground amongst those holding different paradigmatic, philosophical or disciplinary perspectives.

4. Re-theorising child and youth citizenship through transdisciplinarity

Along with Biesta and Lawy (2006), British sociologists O'Byrne (2003) and Turner (1993, 1997, 2006) have gone a considerable distance in re-theorising this discussion with their contribution of a "sociology of human rights" in the discourse, as has Belgian legal theorist Gert Verschraegen (2002). Nevertheless, viewing any system of interactions associated with "citizenship" or "globalisation" through solely legal, capitalist, environmental, scientific, philosophical, sociological or empirical lenses of any one paradigm obscures the interconnectedness and interdependencies within these discourses (see also Sen, 2004).

This much was clear from investigating contemporary child and youth citizenship in our own community: that the multi-layered phenomena associated with the Kielburger's *Free the Children* INGO offer hundreds of thousands of young people critical entry points into inclusive citizenship experiences throughout the world. To understand these phenomena from a perspective that appreciates inherent complexities, I have argued for a "transdisciplinary" standpoint (Mitchell, 2007, 2013; Moore and Mitchell, 2008; Mitchell and Moore, 2012). A similar argument was made by Ang *et al.* (2006, p. 39) for "transcending disciplines" to fully understand the nature and challenges to young people's "participation", among others. In this light, Harvard University's Steven Pinker (2011, pp. 378–481) has put forth a massive, counter-intuitive thesis contending that the various "rights revolutions" in the latter portion of the twentieth century are playing a pivotal role in the transformation of humanity – a role not yet fully understood.

Transdisciplinarity is defined by Nicolescu (2002) as moving beyond traditional scholarship through a critical way of knowing "that will be essential in the 21st and later centuries" (Koizumi, 2001, p. 219). The call for transdisciplinary research is coming from within and outside the academic machinery, and US-based sociologist Patricia Leavy (2011) has written an introductory text for academics, civil society stakeholders and the general public including chapters on design and evaluation of such projects. She starts by observing how universities and research institutes are hierarchically organized around a disciplinary model of knowledge-building such that different fields are separated from each other – fields such as internet technologies, law, sociology, education, neuro-endocrinology, physics, psychology, biology, business, literature, health studies, history, and so forth. She lists Indigenous, feminist, traditional scientific and social science researchers, along with critical race, queer, postmodern, post-structural, and postcolonial theorists, and interdisciplinary fields such as communications, gender, and cultural studies, each having a contemporary view of transdisciplinarity.

Most problems of the twenty-first century are complex systems issues that do not fit into the domain of singular disciplines, Leavy also observes, and trans-global issues such as sustainability, health care, violence against women and children, school-based bullying, and almost any contemporary issue of importance have multiple dimensions that require researchers from different disciplines to come together and share their expertise. It is a problem-centred approach instead of a discipline-centred approach, and thus, generally creates its own criteria and standards because of its unique, emergent qualities including greater legitimisation of knowledge creation by Indigenous stakeholders and other marginalised groups located in non-elite spaces outside the political confines of the increasingly corporate-industrial-academic complex.

Developmental psychologist Jean Piaget along with French sociologist Edgar Morin and Austrian astrophysicist Erich Jantsch are each credited with coining the term simultaneously in the 1970s, but the definition underpinning this section builds upon Romanian quantum physicist Basarab Nicolescu's elucidation. He observes that the term "retains a certain pristine charm, mostly because it has not yet been corrupted by time" (2002, p. 1), but that time may well be drawing nigh. Nicolescu (1999, p. 4) articulates his view succinctly: "The emergence of a new culture, capable of contributing to the elimination of tensions menacing life on our planet will be impossible without a new type of education which takes into account all the dimensions of the human being".

Australian health scientists Albrecht, Freeman and Higginbotham (1998) observe how complexity, change and permanent interrogation are focal points of transdisciplinarity, and while calamity may be nearby, through these lenses we may also observe how human populations are constantly being re-oriented towards interconnectedness. The most critical problems humanity faces today are complex problems, observe Apgar, Argumedo, and Allen (2009, p. 255), and they too observe these times are "characterized by high levels of uncertainty, multiple perspectives and multiple interlinked processes from local to global scales". These epistemological and methodological shifts can be aimed at resolving such dilemmas, and in an exhaustive review two Canadian health scientists note this definition:

> Transdisciplinarity integrates the natural, social and health sciences in a humanities context, and transcends their traditional boundaries. The objectives of multiple disciplinary approaches are to resolve real world or complex problems, to provide different perspectives on problems, to create comprehensive research questions, to develop consensus clinical definitions and guidelines, and to provide comprehensive health services. Multiple disciplinary teamwork has both benefits and drawbacks.
> *(Choi and Pak, 2006, p. 351)*

Giroux and Searls Giroux observe that "transdisciplinary work operates at the frontiers of knowledge" (2004, p. 102) prompting teachers and students alike to raise new questions while developing new models of analysis beyond the boundaries of established disciplines. While educators may be forced to work within academic silos, "they can develop transdisciplinary tools to challenge the limits of established fields and contest the broader economic, political, and cultural conditions that reproduce unequal relations of power" (Giroux and Searls Giroux, 2004, p. 102). I contend the CRC has exemplified this challenge since its 1989 ratification through a set of "transdisciplinary tools" for knowledge creation at the borderlands of both childhood and citizenship studies.

5. Some concluding thoughts

In closing, I return to Doek's (2008, p. xvi) erudite analysis.

> The recognition of the child as a citizen requires concrete measures such as an immediate registration at birth and the provision of a nationality. But from the CRC perspective a broader approach is needed. Every child, and not only those with a birth certificate and a nationality, should be treated as a citizen. This means inter alia the full respect for and implementation of the rights of every child in order to allow her/him to live an individual and decent life in society and to facilitate her/his active and constructive participation in the community...
>
> Quite often children are presented as the citizens of tomorrow. It is undoubtedly important that we invest to the maximum extent of our available resources in the implementation of the rights of the child in order – to quote Article 29 CRC – to prepare the child for a responsible life in a free society in the spirit of understanding, peace, tolerance, equality of sexes and friendship among all peoples ethnic, national and religious groups and persons of indigenous [sic] people.
>
> But that citizenship starts today and from birth. The Citizen Child is a citizen of today and the full recognition of this fact is one of the fundamental requirements of the CRC.

In light of Doek's global view of the notion, a critical question for educators throughout the world has been "how to understand and apply the CRC's interdependent components in the lived experiences of young people?" I have previously characterised these challenges as the *what?* and *so what?* phases of implementation, but the question still remains *now what?* (in Mitchell, 2013, pp. 510, 514). The key dimensions of transdisciplinarity as discussed in the literature – its attempt to manage *complexity* in local/global contexts; *non-academic* partnerships; a focus on *marginalised populations;* application of *Indigenous frameworks*; and *multiple disciplinary, methodological* and *paradigmatic perspectives* on a continuum from positivism to post-modernism – are offered here in response to the final question *now what?*

The unprecedented electronic evaporation of geopolitical and technological borders has opened up new areas for theorising in a number of related discourses such as childhood, human rights, and citizenship. While the chapter began with an overview of young people's citizenship with two young archetypes from a particular political and social context, the chapter included contributors to an emergent global assemblage from regions throughout the world. I have also made the case for considering transdisciplinarity in the citizenship debate for both children and adults, and posit at least the potential for the type of critical, democratic post-modernism envisioned by Giroux (2003, 2010a, 2010b), Giroux and Searls-Giroux (2004), Kincheloe (2010), and other critical educators.

The phenomena associated with two different teenaged Nobel nominees, Craig Kielburger and Pakistani student Malala Yousafzai, the latter shot for simply accessing her rights to education as a young woman (Yousafzai and Lamb, 2013), are additional indicators of the ongoing reconstruction of local/global child/adult citizenship and not outliers I would observe. Finally, I would reflect that thinking differently is the genesis of acting differently, and as both Pinker (2011) and Rosling (2006) have observed, it is just as possible that humans may be moving towards interconnectedness, health and well-being, and less violence in this liquid, late modern era of rights revolutions.

Questions for debate and discussion

- What are the opportunities and challenges for adults in any local community to mentor children and young people as active citizens' within complex, increasingly globalised social, political and economic contexts?
- How do various professional groups – those involved in political systems, physicians, nurses, counsellors, social workers, youth justice authorities, researchers, teachers, and INGO representatives, for example – reflexively engage children and young people in co-constructing experiences of active citizenship?
- What citizenship problems are most suited for CRC research and teaching utilising a transdisciplinary framework?
- What are appropriate indicators for evaluating transdisciplinary human rights projects with and for children?

References

Albrecht, G., Freeman, S., and Higginbotham, N. (1998). Complexity and human health: The case for a transdisciplinary paradigm. *Culture, Medicine and Psychiatry, 22,* 55–92.

Alderson, P. (2000). Citizenship in theory and practice: Being or becoming citizens with rights. In D. Lawton, J. Cairns, and R. Gardner (eds), *Education for citizenship* (pp. 114–135). London: Continuum.

Ang, F., Berghmans, E., Cattrijsse, L., Delens-Ravier, I., Delplace, M., Staelens, V., et al. (2006). *Participation rights of children.* Antwerp: Intersentia.

Apgar, J. M., Argumedo, A., and Allen, W. (2009). Building transdisciplinarity for managing complexity: Lessons from indigenous practice. *International Journal of Interdisciplinary Social Sciences,* 4(5), 225–270.

Arabena, K. (2008). *Indigenous epistemology and well-being: Universe referent citizenship* (Australian Institute of Aboriginal and Torres Strait Islander Studies Discussion Paper, Number 22). Canberra: Government of Australia. Available at www.aiatsis.gov.au/_files/research/dp/DP22.pdf (last accessed April 10, 2014).

Bacon, K., and Frankel, S. (2014). Rethinking children's citizenship: Negotiating structure, shaping meanings. *The International Journal of Children's Rights,* 22(1), 21–42.

Bacon, K., Frankel, S., and Faulks, K. (2013). Building the "big society": Exploring representations of young people and citizenship in the National Citizen Service. *The International Journal of Children's Rights,* 21(3), 488–509.

Bauman, Z. (2000). *Liquid modernity.* Oxford, UK: Blackwell.

Bauman, Z. (2005). Afterthought: On writing; on writing sociology. In N. K. Denzin and Y. S. Lincoln (eds), *The Sage handbook of qualitative research* (3rd ed., pp. 1089–1098). London, Thousand Oaks, CA, New Delhi: Sage.

Biesta, G. (2008). What kind of citizen? What kind of democracy? Citizenship education and the Scottish Curriculum for Excellence. *Scottish Educational Review,* 40(2), 38–52.

Biesta G., and Lawy R. (2006). From teaching citizenship to learning democracy: Overcoming individualism in research, policy and practice. *Cambridge Journal of Education,* 36(1), 63–79.

Bourgeault, R. (1988). Canada [and its] Indians: The South African connection. *Canadian Dimension,* 21(8), 6–10.

Brock Press. (2009). *Brock hosts "Be the change" conference.* St. Catharines, ON: Author. Available at http://emdjournalism.wordpress.com/2009/05/12/brock-hosts-be-the-change-conference/ (last accessed April 10, 2014)

British Broadcasting Corporation. (2013, December, 24). *Syria conflict: Who are the forces opposing Assad?* Available at www.bbc.co.uk/news/world-middle-east-17258397 (last accessed April 10, 2014).

Burman, E. (2001). Beyond the baby and the bathwater: Postdualistic developmental psychologies for diverse childhoods. *European Early Childhood Education Research Journal,* 9(1), 5–22.

Cambre, M.-C. (2007). Terminologies of control: Tracing the Canadian-South African connection in a word. *Politikon,* 34(1), 19–34.

Carter, C., and Osler, A. (2000). Human rights, identities and conflict management: A study of school culture as experienced through classroom relationships. *Cambridge Journal of Education* 30(3), 335–356.

Castells, M. (1999). Flows, networks and identities: A critical theory of the informational society. In M. Castells, R. Flecha, P. Freire, H. A. Giroux, D. Macedo, and P. Willis (eds), *Critical education in the new information age* (pp. 37–64). Boston, MA: Rowman and Littlefield.

Castells, M. (2000a). Materials for an exploratory theory of the network society. *British Journal of Sociology,* 52(1), 5–24.

Castells, M. (2000b). *The information age: Economy, society and culture* (Vols. 1–3). Oxford, UK: Blackwell.

Choi, B. and Pak, A. (2006). Multidisciplinary, interdisciplinary and transdisciplinarity in health research, services, education and policy: 1. Definitions, objectives, and evidence of effectiveness. *Clinical Investigation and Medicine* 29(6), 351–364.

Christensen, P., and James, A. (eds). (2000). *Research with children: Perspectives and practices.* London: Falmer Press.

Coady, M. (2008). Beings and becomings: Historical and philosophical considerations of the child as citizen. In G. MacNaughton, P. Hughes, and K. Smith (eds), *Young children as active citizens: Principles, policies and pedagogies* (pp. 2–14). Newcastle, UK: Cambridge Scholars.

Cohen, E. F. (2005). Neither seen nor heard: Children's citizenship in contemporary democracies. *Citizenship Studies,* 9(2), 221–240.

Corsaro, W. (2005). *The sociology of childhood.* Thousand Oaks, CA: Sage.

Davis, J. M., and Watson, N. (2000). Disabled children's rights in everyday life: Problematising notions of competency and promoting self-empowerment. *The International Journal of Children's Rights,* 8(2), 211–228.

Davis, J. M. (2011). *Integrated children's services.* Thousand Oaks, CA: Sage.

Deer, F. (2009). Aboriginal students and the delivery of citizenship education. *Canadian and International Education / Education canadienne et internationale,* 38(2), Article 3. Available at http://ir.lib.uwo.ca/cie-eci/vol38/iss2/3 (last accessed April 10, 2014).

Devine, D. (2002). Children's citizenship and the structuring of adult-child relations in the primary school. *Childhood,* 9(3), 303–320.

Doek, J. E. (2008). Foreward. In A. Invernizzi, and J. William (eds), *Children and citizenship* (pp. xii-xvii). Thousand Oaks, CA: Sage.

Earls, F. (2011, January). The child as citizen [Special Edition]. *The Annals of The American Academy of Political and Social Science, 633*, 6–264.

Freire, P. (1970). *Pedagogy of the oppressed.* New York: Herder and Herder.

Freire, P. (1999). Education and community involvement. In M. Castells, R. Flecha, P. Freire, H. A. Giroux, D. Macedo, and P. Willis (eds), *Critical education in the new information age* (pp. 83–92). Boston, MA: Rowman and Littlefield.

Friscolanti, M. (2013, November 27). Omar Khadr sues for $60 million. *Maclean's Newsmagazine.* Available at www2.macleans.ca/2013/11/27/omar-khadr-sues-government-for-60-million/ (last accessed April 10, 2014).

Giddens, A. (1984). *The constitution of society: Outline of the theory of structuration.* Berkeley, CA: University of California Press.

Giroux, H. A. (2003). *The abandoned generation.* New York: Palgrave Macmillan.

Giroux, H. A. (2010a, November 16). *Living in the age of imposed amnesia: The eclipse of democratic formative culture.* Available at www.truth-out.org/archive/item/92891:living-in-the-age-of-imposed-amnesia-the-eclipse-of-democratic-formative-culture (last accessed April 10, 2014).

Giroux, H. A. (2010b, November 23). Lessons to be learned from Paulo Freire as education is being taken over by the mega rich. *Truthout/OP-ED* [online]. Available at www.truth-out.org/archive/item/93016:lessons-to-be-learned-from-paulo-freire-as-education-is-being-taken-over-by-the-mega-rich (last accessed April 10, 2014).

Giroux, H. A., and Searls-Giroux, S. (2004). *Take back higher education: Race, youth and the crisis of democracy in the post-civil rights era.* New York: Palgrave Macmillan.

Hart, R. (2008). Stepping back from the ladder of participation: Reflections on a model of participatory work with children. In A. Reid, B. B. Jensen, J. Nikel, and V. Simovska (eds), *Participation and learning* (pp. 19–31). Amsterdam: Springer.

Henderson, S. (2013, October 30). Hashtag activism can help today's youth. *Winnipeg Free Press*, p. A6. Available at www.winnipegfreepress.com/local/coming-of-age-229822681.html (last accessed April 10, 2014).

Hill, M., and Tisdall, K. (1997). *Children and society.* Harlow, Essex, UK: Addison Wesley Longman.

Howe, R. B., and Covell, K. (2005). *Empowering children: Children's rights education as a pathway to citizenship.* Toronto: University of Toronto Press.

Howe, R. B., and Covell, K. (eds). (2007). *Children's rights in Canada: A question of commitment.* Waterloo, ON: Wilfrid Laurier University Press.

Hyslop-Margison, E. J., and Thayer, J. (2009). *Teaching democracy: Citizenship education as critical pedagogy.* Rotterdam: Sense.

Interagency Working Group on Children's Participation. (2008). *Children as active citizens: Commitments and obligations for children's civil rights and civic engagement in East Asia and the Pacific – A policy and programme guide.* Bangkok: IAWGCP, ECPAT International, Knowing Children, Plan International, Save the Children Sweden, Save the Children UK, UNICEF, and World Vision.

Invernizzi, A., and William, J. (eds). (2008). *Children and citizenship.* London: Sage.

Isin, E., and Turner, B. (2007). Investigating citizenship: An agenda for citizenship studies. *Citizenship Studies, 11*(1), 5–17.

James, A., and James A. L. (2004). *Constructing childhood: Theory, policy and practice.* Basingstoke, UK, New York: Palgrave Macmillan.

James, A., Jenks, C. and Prout, A. (1998). *Theorising childhood.* Cambridge: Cambridge University Press.

James, A. and Prout, A. (eds) (1997). *Constructing and reconstructing childhood: Contemporary issues in the sociological study of childhood* (2nd ed.). London: Falmer Press.

Jamieson, L., Pendlebury, P., Bray, R., and Smith, C. (2010/2011). *South African child gauge. Conclusion: Children as citizens.* Cape Town: Children's Institute, University of Cape Town. Available at www.ci.org.za/index.php?option=com_contentandview=articleandid=868andItemid=224#sthash.32Ob9Aiv.dpuf (last accessed April 10, 2014).

Kielburger, C. (1998). *Free the children: A young man fights against child labour and proves that children can change the world.* New York: Harper Collins.

Kielburger, C., and Kielburger, M. (2006). *Me to We: Finding meaning in a material world.* Mississauga, ON: John Wiley and Sons.

Kielburger, C., Kielburger, M., and Page, S. (2009). *The world needs your kid: How to raise children who care and contribute.* Vancouver, Toronto: Greystone Books.

Kincheloe, J. L. (2010). *Knowledge and critical pedagogy: An introduction.* New York: Springer.
Kiwan, D. (2005). Human rights and citizenship: An unjustifiable conflation? *Journal of Philosophy of Education, 39*(1), 37–50.
Kjørholt, A. T. (2002). Small is powerful: Discourses on "children and participation" in Norway. *Childhood, 9*(1), 63–82.
Koizumi, H. (2001). Transdisciplinarity. *Neuroendocrinology Letters, 22,* 219–221.
Lawy, R., and Biesta, G. (2006). Citizenship-as-practice: The educational implications of an inclusive and relational understanding of citizenship. *British Journal of Educational Studies, 54*(1), 34–50.
Leavy, P. (2011). *Essentials of transdisciplinary research: Using problem-centered methodologies.* Walnut Creek, CA: Left Coast Press.
Lister, R. (2007). Why citizenship: Where, when and how children? *Theoretical Inquiries in Law, 8*(2), 693–718. Available at www.degruyter.com/view/j/til.2007.8.issue-til.2007.8.2.1165/til.2007.8.2.1165.xml (last accessed April 10, 2014).
Luhmann, N. (1997). Globalization or world society: How to conceive modern society? *International Review of Sociology, 7*(1), 67–79.
MacNaughton, G., Hughes, P., and Smith, K. (eds). (2008). *Young children as active citizens: Principles, policies and pedagogies.* Newcastle, UK: Cambridge Scholars.
Malott, C. (ed.) (2008). *A call to action: An introduction to education, philosophy, and Native North America.* New York: Peter Lang.
Matthews, S. H. (2007). A window on the "new sociology" of childhood. *Sociology Compass, 1*(1), 322–334.
Mayall, B. (2000). The sociology of childhood in relation to children's rights. *The International Journal of Children's Rights, 8*(3), 243–259.
Mayall, B. (2002). *Towards a sociology of childhood: Thinking from children's lives.* Philadelphia, London: Open University Press.
Mejias, S., and Starkey H. (2012). Utopian visions and neoliberal uses of global education: A case study of an ngo-supported whole-school human rights education project in a secondary school in England. In R. C. Mitchell and S. A. Moore (eds), *Politics, participation and power relations: Transdisciplinary approaches to critical citizenship in the classroom and the community* (pp. 119–136). Rotterdam: Sense.
Mitchell, R. C. (2003). Ideological reflections on the DSM-IV-R (or Pay no attention to that man behind the curtain, Dorothy!). *Child and Youth Care Forum, 32*(5), 281–298.
Mitchell, R. C. (2005). Postmodern reflections on the CRC: Towards utilising Article 42 as an international compliance indicator. *The International Journal of Children's Rights, 13*(3), 315–331.
Mitchell, R. C. (2007). Towards a transdisciplinary model within child and youth rights education. In A. Alen, H. Bosley, M. De Bie, J. Vande Lanotte, F. Ang, I. Delens-Ravier, *et al.* (eds), *The UN children's rights convention: Theory meets practice. Proceedings of the International Interdisciplinary Conference on Children's Rights, 18–19 May 2006, Ghent, Belgium* (pp. 181–200). Antwerp, Oxford: Intersentia.
Mitchell, R. C. (2013). Reflections on the CRC's future from a transdisciplinary bricoleur. *The International Journal of Children's Rights, 21*(1), 510–522.
Mitchell, R. C., and Moore, S. A. (eds). (2012). *Politics, participation and power relations: Transdisciplinary approaches to critical citizenship in the classroom and community.* Rotterdam: Sense.
Montgomery, H., Burr, R., and Woodhead, M. (2003). *Changing childhoods: Local and global* [Book Four of Childhood Series]. Thousand Oaks, CA: Sage.
Moore, S. A. and Mitchell, R. C. (eds). (2008). *Power, pedagogy and praxis: Social justice in the globalized classroom.* Rotterdam: Sense.
Moore, S. A., and Mitchell, R. C. (2009). Rights-based restorative justice: Evaluating compliance with international standards. *Youth Justice, 9*(1), 27–43.
Moore, S. A., and Mitchell, R. C. (2012). Transdisciplinary approaches to young people's citizenship: From bystanders to action. In R. C. Mitchell and S. A. Moore (eds), *Politics, participation and power relations: Transdisciplinary approaches to critical citizenship in the classroom and the community* (pp. 183–205). Rotterdam: Sense.
Moosa-Mitha, M. (2005). A difference-centred alternative to theorization of children's citizenship rights. *Citizenship Studies, 9*(4), 369–388.
Moss, P., and Petrie, P. (2002). *From children's services to children's spaces: Public policy, children and childhood.* New York: RoutledgeFalmer.
Nicolescu, B. (1999, April). *The transdisciplinary evolution of learning.* Paper presented to the Symposium on Overcoming the Underdevelopment of Learning held at the annual meeting of the American Educational Research Association, Montreal, Canada.

Nicolescu, B. (2002). *Manifesto of transdisciplinarity*. New York: State University of New York Press.
O'Byrne, D. J. (2003). *Human rights: An introduction*. London: Pearson Education.
Osler, A., and Starkey, H. (1998). Children's rights and citizenship: Some implications for the management of schools. *The International Journal of Children's Rights, 6*(4), 313–333.
Osler, A., and Starkey, H. (2005). *Changing citizenship: Democracy and inclusion in education*. London: Open University Press.
Osler, A., and Starkey, H. (2010). *Teachers and human rights education*. London: Trentham Books.
Phillips, L.G. (2010). *Young children's active citizenship: Storytelling, stories and social actions*. Ph.D. study submitted in fulfilment of requirements for the degree of Doctor of Philosophy, Faculty of Education, Queensland University of Technology: Australia.
Pinker, S. (2011). *The better angels of our nature: Why violence has declined*. New York: Viking Press.
Prout, A. (2001). *The future of childhood*. First annual lecture of the Children's Research Centre. Dublin: Trinity College.
Rosling, H. (2006). Hans Rosling shows the best stats you've ever seen. *TED Talks*. Available at http://ed.ted.com/lessons/hans-rosling-shows-the-best-stats-you-ve-ever-seen (last accessed April 10, 2014).
Sassen, S. (2008). *Territory, authority, rights: From medieval to global assemblages*. Princeton, NJ: Princeton University Press.
Saul, J. S. (2010). Comment: Two fronts of anti-apartheid struggle – South Africa and Canada. *Transformation, 74*, 135–151. Available at www.socialistproject.ca/inthenews/ itn2429.pdf (last accessed April 10, 2014).
Scottish Executive. (2004). *A curriculum for excellence*. Edinburgh, UK: Scottish Executive.
Sen, A. (2004). Elements of a theory of human rights. *Philosophy and Public Affairs, 32*(4), 315–356.
Senate of Canada. (2005). Standing Committee on Human Rights hearings to examine and report upon Canada's international obligations in regards to the rights and freedoms of children. Available at www.parl.gc.ca/Content/SEN/Committee/381/huma/rep/rep19nov05-e.pdf (last accessed April 10, 2014).
Senate of Canada. (2007). *Children: The silenced citizens*. Ottawa: Standing Senate Committee on Human Rights, Government of Canada. Available at www.parl.gc.ca/Content/SEN/Committee/391/huma/rep/rep10apr07-e.pdf (last accessed April 10, 2014).
Shor, I., and Freire, P. (1987). What is the "dialogical method" of teaching? *Journal of Education, 169*(3), 11–31.
Stasiulis, D. (2002a). Introduction: Reconfiguring Canadian citizenship. *Citizenship Studies, 6*(4), 365–375.
Stasiulis, D. (2002b). The active child citizen: Lessons from Canadian policy and the children's movement. *Citizenship Studies, 6*(4), 507–538.
Supreme Court of Canada. (2010). Canada (Prime Minister) *v.* Khadr, 2010 SCC 3, [2010] 1 S. C. R. 44. Available at http://scc-csc.lexum.com/decisia-scc-csc/scc-csc/scc-csc/en/item/7842/index.do (last accessed April 10, 2014).
Taylor, N., and Smith A. (eds in partnership with *ChildWatch International*, 2009). *Children as citizens? International voices*. Dunedin, New Zealand: Otago University Press.
The Lancet. (2010, November 27). Female genital mutilation and social change. *376*(9755), 1800. [online]. Available at www.thelancet.com/journals/lancet/article/PIIS0140-6736%2810%2962149-6/fulltext (last accessed April 10, 2014).
Thorne, B. (1993). *Gender play: Girls and boys in school*. New Brunswick, NJ: Rutgers University Press.
Tisdall, E. K. M. (1994). Why not consider citizenship? A critique of post-school transitional models for young disabled people. *Disability and Society, 9*(1), 3–16.
Tomaševski, K. (2006). *The state of the right to education worldwide: Free or fee*. Available at www.katarinatomasevski.com/ (last accessed April 10, 2014).
Trivers, H., and Starkey H. (2012). The politics of critical citizenship education: Human rights for conformity or emancipation? In R. C. Mitchell and S. A. Moore (eds), *Politics, participation and power relations: Transdisciplinary approaches to critical citizenship in the classroom and the community* (pp. 137–152). Rotterdam: Sense.
Turner, B. S. (1993). Outline of a theory of human rights. *Sociology, 27*(3), 489–512.
Turner, B. S. (1997). Citizenship studies: A general theory. *Citizenship Studies, 1*(1), 5–18.
Turner, B. S. (2006). Classical sociology and cosmopolitanism: A critical defence of the social. *The British Journal of Sociology, 57*(1), 133–151.
United Nations. (1989). *Convention on the Rights of the Child*. New York, Geneva: Author.

United Nations Committee on the Rights of the Child. (1995). *Concluding observations/ comments: Canada*. Geneva: United Nations.

United Nations Committee on the Rights of the Child. (2003). *Concluding observations/ comments: Canada*. Geneva: United Nations.

United Nations Office of the High Commissioner for Human Rights. (2013). *Concluding observations on China by the UN Committee on the Rights of the Child*. Available at www.ohchr.org/EN/HRBodies/CRC/Pages/CRCIndex.aspx (last accessed April 10, 2014).

United Nations Office of the High Commissioner for Human Rights. (2007). *UN Declaration on the rights of Indigenous peoples*. New York: United Nations General Assembly. Available at www2.ohchr.org/english/issues/indigenous/declaration.htm (last accessed April 10, 2014).

University College, London. (2014). *Global citizenship programme*. Available at www.ucl.ac.uk/global-citizenship (last accessed April 10, 2014).

University of Toronto: Bora Laskin Law Library. (2014). *Khadr case resources page*. Available at http://library.law.utoronto.ca/khadr-case-resources-page (last accessed April 10, 2014).

Verschraegen, G. (2002). Human rights and modern society: A sociological analysis from the perspective of systems theory. *Journal of Law and Society, 29*(2), 258–281.

Vrasti, W. (2009). The politics of globalization studies: From the problem of sovereignty to a problematics of government. *Institute of Globalization and Human Condition: Working Papers Series, 9*(5), 1–21.

Wingrove, J. (2010, March 20). Marc and Craig Kielburger's do-gooding social enterprise. *The Globe and Mail*, pp. F1–F6. Available at www.theglobeandmail.com/news/national/marc-and-craig-kielburgers-do-gooding-social-enterprise/article4389008/?page=all (last accessed April 10, 2014).

Woodhead, M. (1999). Reconstructing developmental psychology: Some first steps. *Children and Society, 13*(1), 3–19.

Woodhead, M. (2000). Children's rights and children's development: Rethinking the paradigm. In E. Verhellen (ed.), *Understanding children's rights: Collected papers presented at the 5th International Interdisciplinary Course on Children's Rights* (pp. 113–127). Belgium: University of Ghent.

Ye, W. (2012). School power and democratic citizenship education in China: Experiences from three secondary schools. In R. C. Mitchell and S. A. Moore (eds), *Politics, participation and power relations: Transdisciplinary approaches to critical citizenship in the classroom and the community* (pp. 9–34). Taipei: Sense.

Yousafzai, M., with Lamb, C. (2013). *I am Malala – The girl who stood up for education and was shot by the Taliban*. New York: Little, Brown and Co.

Part II
Selected themes at the intersection of the global and the local

11
Children and young people's participation
A critical consideration of Article 12

E. Kay M. Tisdall

Children and young people's participation[1] did not begin with the United Nations Convention on the Right of the Child (UNCRC). Children and young people's involvement in decision-making, within their families and communities, can be traced historically: from children and young people's involvement within their household subsistence, to children's school strikes in the early twentieth century,[2] to a child's right to refuse or consent to being adopted in Scotland.[3] But the UNCRC galvanised adults to recognise children and young people's *rights* to participate, as part of a broader human rights agenda. This has encouraged changes in law, policy and practice to ensure children's rights to be heard; advocacy has developed across different contexts, from education to child labour to juvenile justice; numerous projects have been initiated, to encourage children and young people 'to have a say' in their services, their communities and in policy-making.

A range of UNCRC articles are grouped together as participation rights (one of the 3Ps, recognizing the criticisms raised in Chapter 1 in this Handbook, p. 6). These include Article 13 (freedom of expression), Article 14 (freedom of thought, conscience and religion), Article 15 (freedom of association and peaceful assembly) and Article 17 (access to information). Considered a key overarching principle of the UNCRC (UN Committee on the Rights of the Child, 2003), Article 12 states:

> 1. States Parties shall assure to the child who is capable of forming his or her own views the right to express those views freely in all matters affecting the child, the views of the child being given due weight in accordance with the age and maturity of the child.

---

1   This article generally uses the phrase 'children and young people', following young people's typical preference to be referred to as the latter in the UK. Broadly, 'children and young people' refers to children up to the age of 18, following the definition within the United Nations Convention on the Rights of the Child.
2   For example, in 1911, children went on strike demanding shorter school hours and the end of corporal punishment in schools. See http://libcom.org/history/childrens-strikes-1911 (accessed 27 May 2014).
3   From the age of 12, under the Adoption (Scotland) Act 1978.

> 2. For this purpose, the child shall in particular be provided the opportunity to be heard in any judicial and administrative proceedings affecting the child, either directly, or through a representative or an appropriate body, in a manner consistent with the procedural rules of national law.

This chapter particularly focuses on Article 12. Article 12, and children and young people's participation more generally, have been particularly hard to implement. Such participation frequently tests structures, policies and ways of relating that were not developed with children and young people. Even more fundamentally, participation challenges 'traditional' views of childhood and children based on dependency and vulnerability (see James *et al.*, 1998). Such views see children as 'in development', learning to become adults and full members of society. Thus their competencies, capacities, and citizenship are called into question – and as a result their rights to participate. Children and young people's participation presents different views of childhood and children, as social actors (Prout and James, 1990), which challenge hierarchical structures and ways of relating.

This chapter first explores definitions and typologies of children and young people's participation, in light of the UNCRC and the children's rights literature. The chapter then looks at two examples of children and young people's participation, based on research evidence from Scotland. First, it considers children's participation as *individuals*, in family law proceedings and, second, it considers children and young people's participation *collectively*, in school councils (see also Quennerstedt, Chapter 12, and Reynaert and Roose, Chapter 6, both in this Handbook). The chapter concludes by discussing the limitations as well as the potential of the concept and practices of participation.

1. What is participation?

Like many popularised concepts, participation has many and varied definitions (Leal, 2010). A dictionary definition of participation is very broad: for example, 'The act of taking part or sharing in something' (Free Dictionary, 2009, no page number). Hart's 1992 publication, *Children's Participation: From Tokenism to Citizenship*, is iconic in the children's rights field. Here, he defines participation as 'the process of sharing decisions which affect one's life and the life of the community in which one lives' (Hart, 1992, p. 5). This definition has both an individual component – decisions that affect one's life – and a collective one – the life of one's community. Participation is a 'process' rather than an event, suggesting development and change over time rather than a single point of decision-making. In this definition, process is emphasised rather than outcome: there is no requirement for the participation to have an impact on the decisions.

Impact on decision-making, however, is explicitly recognised by the UN Committee on the Rights of the Child. In its General Comment on Article 12, the Committee puts forward a description of participation:

> This term has evolved and is now widely used to describe ongoing processes, which include information-sharing and dialogue between children and adults based on mutual respect, and in which children can learn how their views and those of adults are taken into account and shape the outcome of such processes.
> *(UN Committee on the Rights of the Child, 2009, p. 3)*

Here, there is an emphasis on *mutual* respect, between children and adults (and not just respect for children). There is an element of development – children learn about how views are taken into account. While there is a leaning towards processes, which should be ongoing, there is also some recognition of having an impact – shaping the outcome.

The General Comment underlines that children have the right to be heard as an individual and as a collective (that is, the right to be heard as applied to a group of children). In its analysis of Article 12, the General Comment emphasises certain aspects of Article 12's wording and their implications. Of note particularly for this chapter are:

- Children's rights under Article 12 are not discretionary.
- A child should be presumed to have the capacity to form a view. It is not up to the child to prove this capacity. The right to express a view has no age threshold and a child need not have comprehensive knowledge to be considered capable.
- Non-verbal communication should be recognised as expressing a view and not just verbal communication.
- Children should be supported to participate – and they may well need information to clarify their views and assistance to express them. They should be able to express their views 'freely', without being unduly influenced or pressured.
- The reach of Article 12 is wide, relating to 'all matters affecting' the child. The child's views must be given 'due weight': that is, to be considered seriously when the child is capable of forming a view.
- Children should have feedback on how their views have been taken into consideration.

In providing this literal analysis of Article 12, the UN Committee on the Rights of the Child implicitly addresses many of the challenges faced in trying to implement children and young people's participation (see Lansdown, 2010; Tisdall, 2014). The Committee emphasises that *all* children have the right to participate (and not just older children or articulate children), that they should be supported to do so, that their views should be weighed seriously in decision-making and that they should know what has happened to their input.

2. Typologies of participation

In the promotion of children and young people's participation, particularly at a collective level, typologies have been often cited and very influential. Hart's ladder of participation (Hart, 1992, p. 8) is the most widely known; Hart's ladder was itself developed from Arnstein's (1969) ladder of citizen participation. Hart's ladder has eight rungs, with the bottom three (manipulation, decoration, and tokenism) categorised as non-participation. The subsequent rungs represent varying degrees of participation, going from the fourth rung of 'assigned and informed' up to the top rung of 'child-initiated, shared decisions with adults'. The ladder has proven itself in training and development, in catalysing groups and individuals to (re)consider how children and young people are involved in decision-making locally and nationally, across services, projects and communities. Perhaps because of its popularity, however, it has been subjected to considerable criticism. The image of a ladder suggests that the ideal participation form is at the top (Sinclair, 2004); while 'child-initiated, shared decisions with adults' may suit some decisions, it does not suit others. Treseder (1997) stripped out the bottom three categories and placed the remaining five in a circle, to emphasise the non-hierarchical nature between these degrees of participation. Both typologies, however, risk being static, without taking into account change over time (see Cornwall, 2008; Tisdall, 2014). Indeed,

Hart himself cautioned in 1992 not to use the ladder as a 'simple measuring stick of quality' (Hart, 1992, p. 11).

Returning to Arnstein's original 1969 article, she herself notes the usefulness of the citizen participation ladder to highlight the need for power re-distribution but also three limitations. First, the ladder divides people into two groups, the have-nots and the powerful. However, they are not homogenous groups, and power relationships exist within as well as between the groups. Second, the ladder does not incorporate the 'most significant roadblocks' to 'genuine' participation (Arnstein, 1969, p. 217), such as inadequate socio-economic infrastructure or racism and paternalism. Third, the ladder fails to recognise the potential mixing between rungs (e.g. a government programme hires certain 'have nots'). Such criticisms equally apply to Hart's ladder of participation, in relation to children and adults. Children and adults are divided into two groups, reifying the construction of childhood versus adulthood (see Shamgar-Handelman, 1994; Oswell, 2013) and dampening recognition of diversity, vested interests within the two groups or commonalities across them. A great deal of effort has been spent on developing fun, engaging ways of involving children and young people in projects and research, without recognising and addressing wider contextual issues – which may well be one reason for the criticisms of children and young people's participation as being culturally inappropriate in some contexts (Valentin and Meinert, 2009) and ineffectual in influencing decision-making in others (Tisdall, 2008; Lansdown, 2010). The third limitation illuminates the potential for tokenism, even when children and young people are in the 'limelight' (e.g. participation in the UN General Assembly Special Session on Children 2002 (Ennew, 2008)) or peer research (Tisdall, 2012a), being more a performance than influencing practice or decisions (see Tisdall and Davis, 2004).

Other models have developed, addressing certain of these issues. For example, Shier's (2001) model emphasises what organisations need to do in order to realise children and young people's participation. This begins to address the 'roadblocks' of organisational structures, practices and ethos that may prevent realising children and young people's participation. In 2009, he brings in experiences working with children involved in coffee-growing in Nicaragua, emphasising children's individual learning processes and development into community leaders. Johnson's (2011) Change-Scape model maintains a focus on institutional contexts but adds in considerations of culture, politics and policy, and the physical environment, which may impact on the effectiveness of children and young people's participation.

Thus, participation models are growing more complex, with wider recognition of institutional, social, political, cultural and economic influences, and the mechanisms to increase children and young people's involvement. Such models, however, still largely set up a dichotomy between children and adults and thus ignore the diversity of individuals and relationships. In part because of being written down on a page, they risk being perceived as static, without a sense of movement and evolution across time and space (see Tisdall, 2014). And they tend to posit children and young people's participation, as expressed in Article 12, as a normative good,[4] without deeply interrogating participation as a term or as a discourse nor fully addressing Cornwall's (2008) three questions: who is participating, in what are they participating and for whose benefit?

Below two contentious examples of involving children and young people are discussed: involvement in (1) disputed family law proceedings and (2) in school councils. They are used

---

4   Note that Hart (1992) is an exception, in recognising less benign self-organisation of children and young people, such as street gangs.

to illuminate the dilemmas of a children's rights approach to participation and to interrogate more deeply what is meant, or what could be meant, by the concept.

3. The right to be heard as an individual child: The example of family law proceedings

As family relationships have changed in the minority world,[5] with increasing rates of parental separation and divorce in many countries, so has attention to the impact of family breakdown on dependent children.[6] Legal processes, within family law, have developed to dissolve the marriage contract and address implications thereof, and to address parental rights; the idea of including children in such decisions developed later, and has been much debated. Such debates illuminate the fundamental challenge that children's participation poses to traditional attitudes towards children and childhood – at least in the minority world, where children are the private responsibilities (if not property) of their parents, perceived as dependent and vulnerable, and seen as lacking the capacity to contribute to decisions about where they will live, contact with family members, and property distribution.

Fuelled by Article 12 of the UNCRC, however, a number of legal jurisdictions have sought to ensure that children's rights to participation are realised in family law proceedings when parents separate or divorce. Developments have been numerous: from enthusiasm for judges to speak directly to children and young people; to greater advocacy and/or legal representation for children and young people; to 'softer' means of inclusion through mediation with parents (e.g. parents being advised to consider their children's views) (see Freeman, 2012; Birnbaum and Saini, 2012).

Scotland had leading legislation in this regard, with the Children (Scotland) Act 1995. First, the Act sets a wide (if largely unknown) duty on those with parental responsibilities to consider a child's view when making 'any major decision' in exercising parental responsibilities or rights (s.6). The duty is subject to a child's age and maturity, picking up the wording of Article 12 in the UNCRC. A child aged 12 or older is presumed to have sufficient age and maturity, although the duty does apply to all children. Thus, even if parents did not go to court, children's views should be considered in major decisions relating to parental divorce or separation.

Second, if a case did reach court, the court must consider a child's views when making an order:

> ... taking account of the child's age and maturity, shall so far as is practicable –
>
> (i) give him an opportunity to indicate whether he wishes to express his views;
> (ii) if he does so wish, give him an opportunity to express them; and
> (iii) have regard to such views as he may express. (s.11(7)(b))

---

5   The terms 'majority world' and 'minority world' refer to what has traditionally been known as 'the third world' and 'the first world' or more recently as 'the Global South' and 'the Global North'. This acknowledges that the 'majority' of population, poverty, land mass and lifestyles is located in the former, in Africa, Asia and Latin America, and thus seeks to shift the balance of our world views that frequently privilege 'western' and 'northern' populations and issues (Punch 2003).
6   In Scotland, a 'child' and 'young person' has a particular legal meaning in family and other legislation: a young person has legal capacity similar to an adult, albeit with some protections (Age of Legal Capacity (Scotland) Act 1991). Thus 'child' and 'children' are used in this section.

Again, a child aged 12 or over is presumed to have sufficient age and maturity to form a view. A child can sue or defend proceedings in relation to parental responsibilities and rights, and a child under the age of 16 has the legal capacity to instruct a lawyer in any civil matter when the child has a general understanding of what it means to do so (Age of Legal Capacity (Scotland) Act 1991, s. 2(4A)).

A child's views could be put forward to the court in numerous ways. For example, a child can send a form into the sheriff,[7] stating the child's views; the court can appoint someone to report on the child's views as well as the child's best interests (typically by someone with a legal and/or psychology background); the sheriff can ask to hear directly from the child; or a child may take independent legal advice, with the lawyer having a range of ways to present the child's views (from writing to the court, to seeking to have the child involved as a party to the action). If a child expresses a view, the sheriff or someone appointed by the sheriff must record this view. The sheriff may decide whether this record should be kept confidentially.

In Scottish legislation, then, children and young people's right to participate in decisions about parental responsibilities and rights is strong. There have been leading Scottish cases, which have developed the details. For example, the Court of Session observed in *Shields v Shields* (2002 SC 246) that the question is not *whether* a child's views should be gathered but *how:* 'But, if, by one method or another, it is "practicable" to give a child the opportunity of expressing his views, then, in our view the only safe course is to employ that method' (para 11). Practicability is the first, low threshold for a child's views to be considered by the court. After that step, the court weighs the child's views in the court's decision, subject to the child's age and maturity. Suitably taking into account children's views is now a recognised ground of appeal and, in some cases, has been the *sole* ground (see also *C v McM* 2005 Fam LR 36). Such pronouncements from senior courts have promoted children's rights to participate, with considerable alignment with General Comment No. 12 (UNCRC, 2009) and Article 12. A shift can be described in family law proceedings:

> The welfare paradigm, which sees children as lacking the capacity and maturity to understand and assert their own needs, has been challenged by new paradigms, including children's rights and children as social actors and citizens. Within these new paradigms, children are no longer seen as dependent, vulnerable, at-risk victims of divorce and passive objects of law, but are seen as subjects with agency.
>
> *(Hunter, 2007, p. 283 [writing about England])*

However, this positive, progressive description can be queried. The empirical research on children and young people's experiences of family law proceedings raises questions about the *quality* of their experiences (see Mackay, 2012; Tisdall and Morrison, 2012). Information for children remains problematic, from children knowing their rights, how such proceedings function and how they can become involved, to what the court's decision is and why (Potter, 2008). Procedures may be present, courts may ensure they take place and utilise children's views, but children may still not feel satisfied that their views are duly considered.

Professional reports are relied upon, to meet children's rights to be heard, and practice is not always exemplary (Tisdall and Morrison, 2012; Whitecross, 2011). Despite the 1995 Act, the courts have been ambivalent about children being directly involved in courts, particularly if the

---

[7] A sheriff is a professional judge, in the second tier of courts. A sheriff would hear most family law cases in the first instance.

children's views are seen as the same as one of their parents (e.g. *Henderson and Henderson* 1997 Fam LR 120) or if parents are believed to have manipulated the child (Barnes, 2008). Legal representation has become even more problematic for children due to changes in legal aid funding, where the financial resources of parents are now considered alongside children's, except if it were 'unjust or inequitable to do so' (see Morrison *et al.*, 2013). Family law proceedings thus still have difficulty recognising the legal status of children as separate from their parents – despite the rights to be heard enshrined in law and procedures.

Under the 1995 Act, the child's welfare is the paramount consideration of the court (s. 11(7)(a)), which is a stronger requirement even than Article 3 of the UNCRC (where a child's best interests is 'a primary consideration'). Within the reported case law, the courts tend to privilege views on what a child's best interests are in the long-term, over the children's current views. This draws on traditional views of childhood, which focus on children as 'human becomings' rather than as 'human beings' (Qvortrup, 1994). There is evidence, however, of courts also considering children's well-being, should they: move schools, friendships, need to travel between parents, and more (e.g. *M v M* 2000 Fam LR 84; *X v Y* 2007 Fam LR 153). Such considerations recognise children's present as well as their future.

The reported case law is not filled with court's pronouncements on children's capacity or competency, in weighing up their views. Instead, case law shows a divide between children's views deemed consistent, definite and clear – which would be more persuasive to the courts – and those described as ambivalent or anxious – which would be given substantially less weight (Tisdall and Morrison, 2012). Professional reports were frequently relied upon to support sheriffs' evaluations of the children's views and thus the weight given to children's views. Such practices raise questions. First, they suggest a presumption that there is a 'true' or 'authentic' statement of children's views (Hunter, 2007, p. 283), 'out there waiting to be collected' (Mantle *et al.*, 2006, p. 792). But, as Mantle and colleagues go on to argue, 'Interpretation is unavoidable and meanings are likely to be contested' (Mantle *et al.*, 2006, p. 792). Following the UNCRC, research and practice often purport to put forward 'children's voices', by direct verbal or written quotations from children and young people. But the selection of quotations, how they are framed and how they are analysed are very frequently carried out by adults. Adults are determining what constitutes 'voice' and interpret what the 'voice' might be saying.

To be persuasive to the courts, children's views should not be changeable, they should not be unduly influenced by others, and they should not be overly distressed or anxious in expressing their views (see *H v H* 2000 Fam LR 73). This privileges concepts of the autonomous individual and rationality, rather than recognising relationality and emotions. Yet the autonomous and rational individual has been questioned widely by feminism, communitarian philosophy and disability studies, as no one is fully autonomous and independent but instead all humans are social beings who are vulnerable and inter-dependent (see Arneil, 2002; Fineman, 2008). Emotions are artificially separated from rationality, as expressed by Williams and Bendelow:

> Even to the present day, emotions are seen to be the very antithesis of the detached scientific mind and its quest for 'objectivity', 'truth' and 'wisdom' ... Such a view neglects the fact that rational methods of scientific inquiry, even at their most positivistic, involve the incorporation of values and emotions.
>
> *(Williams and Bendelow, 1998, p. xvi)*

As Pinkney (2014) points out, the emotional and affective aspects of children's participation are often ignored. She encourages consideration of these aspects not only for children but also for professionals. She discusses the individual coping strategies of social workers, such as: avoiding seeing the child; avoiding touching the child; and focusing on managing violent or controlling parents. These strategies map surprisingly well to family law proceedings: sheriffs can be reluctant to meet with the child (*X v Y* 2007 Fam LR 153); the weight of children's views is undermined if they are considered manipulated by parents; and courts underplay the extent and impacts of domestic abuse in separation disputes (Morrison *et al.*, 2013).

Thus, the advancement of children's rights to be heard in family law proceedings demonstrate both the 'success story' of children's rights and its potential problems. It shows practical problems of the 'top-down' approach, as discussed in the introductory chapter (this Handbook, p. 2). Law and procedures lay down certain rules and practices, which are differentially enacted by those with power, experienced variably by children and young people, and have uneven impact on decisions. It shows the influence of different conceptualisations of childhood. These are still typically the more traditional views of children as human becomings, which side-line their current concerns. Or children may be seen as expressing agency but rationality and autonomy are privileged at the expense of acknowledging emotions and relationality. It shows the difficulties of respecting children as social actors, when they are participating in adult structures that were not originally developed with children and young people's participation in mind – with subsequent legislation seeking to insert them into what are fundamentally adult-oriented procedures and spaces (see Tisdall and Bell, 2006; Kesby, 2007).

4. School councils

Within schooling, school councils have been a popularised initiative to recognise pupils' collective right to be heard within their schools. While definitions may vary, the Welsh definition of school councils captures common understandings:

> ... a representative group of pupils elected by their peers to discuss matters about their education and raise concerns with the senior managers and governors of their school.
>
> *(Pupil Voice Wales, no date, para 1)*

School councils have become ever more popular in the United Kingdom, in many European countries and elsewhere (Dürr, 2005). While examples of influential and active school councils have been documented (Yamashita and Davies, 2010), research on school councils suggests more ambivalence about school councils in general and their enactment of Article 12. The subsequent section draws on research undertaken in Scotland, which covered all local government areas in Scotland, with surveys of all Scottish secondary schools and a representative sample of primary schools, and case studies of six schools.[8]

Fundamentally, those involved in school councils – such as headteachers, local government education advisers, adult advisers to school councils, school council members and pupils more generally – had different ideas of what school councils were for. Despite certain rights to be heard in education legislation (influenced by the UNCRC) and increasing promotion in national guidance and advice (Tisdall, 2012b), children's legal rights were not a dominant reason to have a school council. School councils were seen as having 'symbolic' value, showing adult interest in the views and 'voice' of pupils (Baginsky and Hannam, 1999). The symbolic

---

8 See www.havingasayatschool.org.uk/ for research methods.

value of school councils did not necessarily translate into school councils' impact on decision-making. A pupil councillor in the Scottish research raised his frustration:

> I don't know whether they thought we would be dealing with making sure there was more toilet roll or trying to work our prices for lunch ... I keep saying we are running out of small things to fix. It's the big things that are the problems.
>
> *(Secondary school, pupil councillor)*

School councils across the UK have been criticised for focusing on 'inconsequential issues' rather than more fundamental academic issues like staffing and learning (Wyse, 2001; Maithes and Deuchar, 2006; Yamashita and Davies, 2010).

By far the most common purpose of school councils, for school staff, was educational: they were 'laboratories of democracy', where children and young people could practice formal democratic practices. Pupil councillors themselves felt they gained skills and confidence. A significant minority of Scottish children do have a chance to be a pupil councillor: over one-third of respondents to a large-scale survey of secondary school pupils reported having been a pupil councillor at least once (Tisdall with Milne and Iliasov, 2007). As school councils become even more popular, this proportion is likely to increase further over time. Despite the survey having a representative sample by socio-economic and other background characteristics, there were no statistically significant differences by such characteristics, in whether or not a young person had experience of being a pupil councillor. Rather, children and young people in the case study schools cited other social factors like popularity and 'being cool' as influential on certain people becoming pupil councillors, while school staff reported some finessing of who stood and was elected to be a pupil councillor (e.g. many schools required both a boy and girl representative).

The research shows both the benefits and challenges of seeking to meet formal democratic requirements. In the surveys of school councils and adult advisers, there was a high correlation between perceiving the election/selection of pupil councillors as fair and perceiving the school council as effective. This was despite whether or not the school council was reported as accomplishing a great deal. The in-depth research in the six case-study schools showed the considerable time and effort it took to practice formal democracy, which crowded out time to discuss action and make decisions. The large-scale survey of secondary school pupils (Tisdall, Milne and Iliasov, 2007) found that some children and young people feel excluded by a competitive election process and were waiting to be invited to put themselves forward and/or were reluctant to do so.

The research findings suggest practical action can be taken to improve school councils in Scotland, which echo more general concerns with children and young people's participation. The model lacks continuity, as school councils tend to renew themselves every school year, with new pupil councillors elected and little institutional memory. Having some carry-over of membership, whether through peer mentors, training, and/or staggered membership changes, would help address this continuity. Like many participation projects, school councils are very reliant on the commitment of the 'participation workers' (for school councils, the adult adviser), who may not be rewarded nor supported in their task. Money does equate to power: even small budgets resulted in perceived effectiveness and demonstrable outcomes. Budgets could be allocated regularly to school councils.

More fundamentally, the research demonstrates that children and young people's participation can have different purposes. Each purpose can have its advantages and disadvantages, in terms of participation being meaningful to those involved and effective. The research underlines the benefits of discussing and debating what participation is *for*: given that pupil councillors were more focused on the outcomes of school councils and school staff more on the processes, a greater consensus could assist in avoiding staff and/or children and young people becoming frustrated by how their particular school council functions.

5. Learning from the practices of participation

In presenting her ladder of citizenship participation, Arnstein wrote:

> The idea of citizen participation is a little like eating spinach: no one is against it in principle because it is good for you. Participation of the governed in their government is, in theory, the cornerstone of democracy – a revered idea that is vigorously applauded by virtually everyone.
>
> *(Arnstein, 1969, p. 216)*

Children and young people's participation is similarly advocated as a normative good – as an inherently good thing. The avowal is more positive than spinach: it is not just a healthy but often unpopular nutrient, like spinach; children and young people's participation is celebrated for recognising their human rights, respecting and acknowledging their human dignity (see Chapter 1 in this Handbook, p. 5).

But like many other buzzwords, participation can stray from its aspirational roots and become conceptually and practically stretched beyond its original meanings and intentions. The development literature, for example, has strong critics of participation. Cooke and Kothari (2001) wrote of the 'tyranny of participation', when participatory approaches (i) override existing, legitimate decision-making processes, (ii) reinforce the interests of the already powerful, and (iii) drive out other methods with advantages, that participation cannot provide. Leal (2010) ties the ascendance of the participation buzzword with the promotion of neo-liberalism by the World Bank and the International Monetary Fund. Participation has become a way to control dissent, she argues, to co-opt people into the existing dominant order, rather than supporting transformative agendas of social movements. Participation, according to these critiques, is not necessarily a normative good.

The examples of family law proceedings and school councils show the continued influence of how childhood is constructed and perceived, which can constrain or enable children and young people's participation. In family law, the traditional view of children as human becomings is still evident, so that children's current concerns are side-lined when making a decision based on a child's welfare. Beyond law, the dominant expertise brought to weighing up children's views and welfare is psychological, so the focus on the individual child and child development predominates in the framing of expert reports, without critical reflection. The 'new' sociology of childhood has disparaged the normalisation and individualisation of child development and the undue reification of development stages (e.g. James et al., 1998). Work like Alderson's (2012), from a sociological and children's rights perspective, underlines the importance of context, information and experience for young children's capacities to participate in decision-making.

The examples in this chapter, of family law proceedings and school councils, show how current practices tend to separate out children from adults, reifying distinctions between childhood and adulthood. This lead to decisions about households and family life being fundamentally parent-oriented in family law proceedings, without recognising the 'care work' that children and young people frequently do to manage their family relationships during and afterwards (Morrison, 2014). Current practices reify the autonomous individual with agency, which can clash with a more collective ethos (Valentin and Meinert, 2009). Such practices identify adults specially mandated to involve children and young people, like the adult advisers for school councils or the court reporters in family law proceedings, without questioning the expertise, support and training they have for such a role. Others, like sheriffs or school management, need not feel they are responsible for involving children and young people as part of their regular skills set. This risks 'ghettoising' rather than mainstreaming children and young people's participation, failing to recognise that children and young people are already family, community and societal members. While protected spaces can give children and young people opportunities to interact in ways that suit them, and gain skills and confidence, too much isolation means they do not link to other stakeholders, learning from them, and coming together in greater collective strength (Kesby, 2007; Tisdall, 2014). This can result in children and young people's participation being accepted when it is palatable to the decision-makers but easily sidelined if other (more powerful) stakeholders have competing views (Tisdall and Davis, 2004).

If children and young people's participation is always treated as 'special', something to be done separately from adult participation, then barriers presented by adult-oriented structures, networks and ways of working are not challenged nor encouraged to change: courts are not required to be more user-friendly; schools need not be more participative for all involved, from staff to parents to children; policy-making remains the familiar terrain of the policy-savvy (Tisdall, 2014). Over recent decades, children, young people and adults have devised engaging and productive ways to involve children and young people in both individual and collective decision-making (see Percy-Smith and Thomas, 2010). The most substantial barrier is not having ways to engage positively and productively with children and young people, but whether their views are actually heard and duly considered in decision-making. Children and young people's participation risks fitting into a niche within bureaucratic structures, perhaps with good intentions but fundamentally kept within its place.

Other examples – and frequently examples that are *outwith* the institutional structures – have been documented with more transformative potential. For example, the radio project *Abaqophi BakwaZisize Abakhanyayo* in South Africa trained children and young people to become reporters on the popular local radio channel (see Meintjes, 2014). With the 'power of the microphone', children and young people were able to follow their interests and raise issues with other adults, that were normally not spoken about – such as parents moving away, deaths by HIV and AIDS, and discrimination. The radio project thus challenged and helped transform certain hierarchical and silencing relationships between children, young people and adults. A non-governmental organisation in India, the *Arunodhaya*-Centre for Street and Working Children, began to combat child labour (see Le Borgne, 2014). Over the years, taking a children's rights approach, the organisation has developed structures and ways of working to support children and young people's participation. Following up young adults, previously involved in the participation activities, shows how their experiences of participation have helped transform their lives – such as going onto to higher education, their career aspirations, etc. – and increasingly those of the next generation. An 'early years' service in Scotland sought to develop meaningful ways to engage with very young children, using tactile objects and group work over time, so that children are now regularly engaged in their individual and collective learning and environment (see Tisdall, 2013).

These three examples all were influenced by the children's rights paradigm and UNCRC agenda. They all involved creating spaces for children and adults to communicate together and not separately. They involved changing hierarchies between children, young people and adults. Children and young people were seen as part of their communities and capable of contributing to decisions and enacting change. When at their most successful, participation has been a challenging activity, one requiring changing ways of working and for adults to develop an ethos of respect for children. These are not 'tick box' exercises but rather ones of values and relationships.

6. Conclusion

Participation rights have been held up as the most radical and controversial contribution of the UNCRC (Reid, 1994; Smith, 2013); protection and provision rights are more readily accepted as duties towards dependent and vulnerable children (Freeman, 1983). Article 12 and associated rights have been challenging and are often cited within policy, practice and the literature for encouraging changes in power relationships between children, young people and adults, in creating opportunities for children and young people to have influence on decisions that affect them, and recognising their citizenship (Jans, 2004; Cairns, 2006; Cockburn, 2012).

However, Article 12 is not that radical. It does not recognise a child's right to vote in political elections (which can be seen as a central citizenship right in a democracy; Marshall, 1950). It facilitates children and young people to be involved in decision making and a wide range of decisions ('all matters that affect them') but it does not discuss self-determination. According to Article 12, the decision-maker must give 'due weight' to the child's views, qualified by a judgement about the 'age and maturity' of the child, but ultimately the decision can be incongruent or against the child's views. A familiar debate in the literature is the potential tension between Article 12 and Article 3, which requires a child's best interests to be a primary consideration in all actions concerning children (Marshall, 1997; Archard and Skivene, 2009). The discretionary nature of judging a child's best interests can easily lead to adults silencing a child, or side-lining a child's views, rather than fulfilling Article 12's obligations. This is evident in the two examples discussed in this chapter: family law proceedings, where children's welfare is the paramount consideration, so legally it must trump children's views; and school councils, where the focus can be on *training* children in democracy, for their well-being as well as society's, rather than children and young people's current participation rights.

The development studies literature reminds us of the (elusive?) transformative potential of participation, at both individual and collective levels. Some of the problems so frequently found by children and young people's participation arise from top-down, tokenistic and/or instrumentalist participation – which can narrow the agenda, suppress dissent, and at worse control children and young people. Participation is not necessarily comfortable and the results can be challenging.

Wyness (2014) suggests five emerging narratives, in the literature on children and young people's participation:

1   Participation can be seen as embedded in children's 'everyday lives', routine and on-going, rather than exceptional and event-based.
2   Participation is relational, enacted and created with others, rather than reifying the individual person with agency.
3   Participation is recognised as emotional and embodied, rather than solely rational and intellectual.
4   Participation is material as well as political, including the economic.
5   The distribution of participation should be considered, in how it follows or creates (in)equalities, identities and differences. (These points are expanded from Wyness, 2014.)

These narratives set up an agenda for children's participation rights, both practically and conceptually. They value the ground-up approach recommended by Shier (2009), recognising children and young people's participation in their 'everyday' spaces rather than seeking to extract them into adult, invited spaces (Percy-Smith, 2010). The narratives question the reification of 'voice' and discursive forms of participation, to value other forms of communication. They widen the 'participation' category, reminding us of the other participation rights in the UNCRC (like freedom of assembly), which are arguably more radical than Article 12, and even beyond that to consider interactions with the material and the economic. The divide between childhood and adulthood may have some merit in highlighting the discrimination so often experienced by children, based on their age; but the divide fails to recognise the diversity, differentiation and relationships between and within children and young people as well as adults. If there is growing recognition that children's rights should be seen as children's *human* rights and thus part of the broader human rights agenda, then we need to question why there are not more radical notions of children and young people's involvement in their social, economic, cultural and political contexts than to have due regard to their views.

Questions for debate and discussion

- Should children and young people's participation always have an impact on decision-making?
- Children and young people were not substantially involved in the creation of the UNCRC and thus the articulation of their participation rights. Does this matter?
- Is children and young people's participation appropriate for 'all matters affecting them' and in all contexts around the world?
- Do the 'participation rights', as expressed in the UNCRC, go far enough in recognising children and young people as social actors?

Acknowledgements

I would like to thank the generous contributions of children and young people, professionals and policy-makers throughout the studies referred to in this chapter. I want to emphasise the collaborative nature of these studies, with the above and with numerous academic colleagues. The chapter in particular makes reference to collaborative projects funded by the Big Lottery Fund, the British Academy, Economic and Social Research Council (R451265206, RES-189-25-0174, RES-451-26–0685), the European Research Council, the Leverhulme Trust, the Royal Society of Edinburgh and Scotland's Commissioner for Children and Young People.

References

Alderson, P. (2012). Young Children's Human Rights: A Sociological Analysis. *International Journal of Children's Rights*, 20(2), 177–198.
Archard, D. and Skivenes, M. (2009). Balancing a Child's Best Interests and a Child's Views. *International Journal of Children's Rights*, 17(1), 1–21.
Arneil, B. (2002). Becoming versus Being: A Critical Analysis of the Child in Liberal Theory. I n D. Archard and C.M. Macleod (eds), *The Moral and Political Status of Children* (pp. 70–96). Oxford: Oxford University Press.
Arnstein, S.R. (1969). A Ladder of Citizen Participation. *AIP Journal*, July, 216–224.
Baginsky, M. and Hannam, D. (1999). *School Councils: The Views of Students and Teachers*. London: NSPCC.
Barnes, L.A. (2008). 'A Child Is, After All, A Child': Ascertaining the Ability of Children to Express Views in Family Proceedings. *Scots Law Times*, 18, 121–127.
Barnes, M., Newman, J. and Sullivan, H. (2007). *Power, Participation and Political Renewal*. Bristol, UK: Policy Press.

Birnbaum, R. and Saini, M. (2012). A Scoping Review of Qualitative Studies on the Voice of the Child in Child Custody Disputes. *Childhood*, 20(2), 260–282.

Cairns, L. (2006). Participation with a Purpose. In E.K.M. Tisdall, J. M. Davis, M. Hill and A. Prout (eds), *Children, Young People and Social Inclusion* (pp. 217–234). Bristol, UK: Policy Press.

Cockburn, T. (2012). *Rethinking Children's Citizenship*. Basingstoke, UK: Palgrave.

Cooke, B. and Kothari, U. (2001). *Participation: The New Tyranny?* London: Zed Books.

Cornwall, A. (2008). Unpacking 'Participation. *Community Development Journal*, 43(3), 269–283.

Dörr, K. (2005). *The School: A Democratic Learning Community*. Strasbourg: Council of Europe. Available at www.edchreturkey-eu.coe.int/Source/Resources/Pack/School_democraticlearning_community_EN.pdf (last accessed 25 October 2013).

Ennew, J. (2008). Children as 'Citizens' of the United Nations (UN). In A. Invernizzi and J. Williams (eds), *Children and Citizenship* (pp. 66–79). London: Sage.

Fineman, M.A. (2008). The Vulnerable Subject: Anchoring Equality in the Human Condition. *Yale Journal of Law and Feminism*, 20(1), 1–18.

Free Dictionary Web site (2009). Available at www.thefreedictionary.com/participation (last accessed 6 May 2014).

Freeman, M.D.A. (1983). *The Rights and Wrongs of Children*. London: Francis Pinter.

Freeman, M.D.A. (ed.) (2012). *Law and Childhood Studies* [Current Legal Issues Vol. 14]. Oxford: Oxford University Press.

Hart, R. (1992). *Children's Participation: The Theory and Practice of Involving Young Citizens in Community Development and Environmental Care*. London: Earthscan.

Hunter, R. (2007). Close Encounters of a Judicial Kind: 'Hearing' Children's 'Voices' in Family Law Proceedings. *Child and Family Law Quarterly*, 19(3), 283–303.

James, A, Jenks, C, and Prout, A (1998). *Theorizing Childhood*. Cambridge: Polity Press.

Jans, M. (2004). Children as Citizens: Towards a Contemporary Notion of Child Participation. *Childhood*, 11(1), 27–44.

Johnson, V. (2011). Conditions for Change for Children and Young People's Participation in Evaluation: 'Change-Scape'. *Child Indicators Research*, 4, 577–596.

Kesby, M. (2007). Spatialising Participatory Approaches. *Environment and Planning A*, 39(12), 2813–2831.

Lansdown, G. (2010). The Realisation of Children's Participation Rights. In B. Percy-Smith and N. Thomas (eds), *A Handbook of Children and Young People's Participation* (pp.11–23). London: Routledge.

Le Borgne, C. (2014). Transformative Participation: Experiences of a Children's Sangam in Tamil Nadu (South India). In E.K.M. Tisdall, U. Butler and A. Gadda (eds), *Children and Young People's Participation and Its Transformative Potential*. Basingstoke: Palgrave.

Leal, P.A. (2010). Participation: The Ascendancy of a Buzzword in the Neo-liberal Era. In A. Cornwall and D. Eade (eds), *Deconstructing Development Discourse: Buzzwords and Fuzzwords* (pp. 89–100). London: Oxfam.

Mackay, K. (2012). *The child's Voice in Contact Disputes: Genuine Participation in Private Law Court Actions*. Saarbrücken, Germany: Lambert Academic Publishing.

Maithes, H. and Deuchar, R. (2006). We Don't Learn Democracy, We Live It! Consulting the Pupil Voice in Scottish Schools. *Education, Citizenship and Social Justice*, 1(3), 249–266.

Mantle, G., Moules, T., Johnson, K. with Leslie, J., Parsons, S. and Shaffer, R. (2006). Whose Wishes and Feelings? Children's Autonomy and Parental Influence in Family Court Enquiries. *British Journal of Social Work*, 37(5), 785–805.

Marshall, K. (1997). *Children's Rights in the Balance: The Participation Protection Debate*. London: The Stationery Office.

Marshall, T.H. (1950). Citizenship and Social Class. In *Sociology at the Crossroads and Other Essays* (pp. 1–85). Cambridge: Cambridge University Press.

Meintjes, H. (2014). Growing up in a Time of AIDS: The Shining Recorders of Zisize. In E.K.M. Tisdall, U. Butler and A. Gadda (eds), *Children and Young People's Participation and Its Transformative Potential*. Basingstoke, UK: Palgrave.

Morrison, F. (2014). *Children, Contact and Domestic Abuse*. PhD Thesis, University of Edinburgh, UK.

Morrison, F., Tisdall, E.K.M., Jones, F. and Reid, A. (2013). *Child Contact Proceedings for Children Affected by Domestic Abuse*. Available at www.sccyp.org.uk/downloads/Adult%20Reports/Child_contact_proceedings_March_2013.pdf (last accessed 27 May 2014).

Oswell, D. (2013). *The Agency of Children: From Family to Global Human Rights*. Cambridge: Cambridge University Press.

Percy-Smith, B. (2010). Councils, Consultations and Community. *Children's Geographies*, 8(2), 107–122.
Percy-Smith, B. and Thomas, N. (eds) (2010). *A Handbook of Children and Young People's Participation*. London: Routledge.
Pinkney, S. (2014). *Telling the Quiet Stories: Emotional Landscapes of Care-embodied Practices in Child Protection*. Presentation at Modena, Italy Symposium Theorising Childhood: Citizenship, Rights, Participation (23 May 2014). Available at http://esarn4modenasymposium.wordpress.com/program/ (last accessed 27 May 2014)
Potter, M. (2008). The Voice of the Child: Children's 'Rights' in Family Proceedings. *International Family Law*, 3, 140–151.
Prout, A. and James, A. (1990). A New Paradigm for the Sociology of Childhood? provenance, promise and problems. In A. James and A. Prout (eds), *Constructing and Reconstructing Childhood: Contemporary Issues in the Sociological Study of Childhood* (pp. 7–33). London: Falmer Press.
Pupil Voice Wales (no date). *The School Council*. Available at www.pupilvoicewales.org.uk/grown-ups/get-involved/the-school-council/ (last accessed 6 May 2014).
Punch, S. (2003). Childhoods in the Majority World: Miniature Adults or Tribal Children? *Sociology*, 37(2), 277–295.
Qvortrup J. (1994). Childhood Matters: An Introduction. In J. Qvortrup, M. Bardy, G. Sgritta, H. Wintersberger (eds), *Childhood Matters. Social Theory, Practice and Politics* (pp. 1–24). Avebury: Aldershot.
Reid, R. (1994). Children's Rights: Radical Remedies for Critical Needs. In S. Asquith and M. Hill (eds), *Justice for Children* (pp. 19–25). London: Martinus Nijhoff Publishers.
Shamgar-Handelman, L. (1994). To Whom Does Childhood Belong? In J. Qvortrup, M. Bardy, G. Sgritta, and H. Wintersberger (eds), *Childhood Matters. Social Theory, Practice and Politics* (pp. 249–256). Aldershot: Avebury.
Shier, H. (2001). Pathways to Participation: Openings, Opportunities and Obligations. *Children and Society*, 15(2), 107–117.
Shier, H. (2009). 'Pathways to Participation' Revisited. In B. Percy-Smith and N. Thomas (eds), *A Handbook of Children and Young People's Participation* (pp. 215–229). London: Routledge.
Sinclair, R. (2004). Participation in Practice: Making It Meaningful, Effective and Sustainable. *Children and Society*, 18(2), 106–118.
Smith, A.B. (2013). Links to Theory and Advocacy. *Australian Journal of Early Childhood*. Available at www.earlychildhoodaustralia.org.au/australian_journal_of_early_childhood/ajec_index_abstracts/childrens_rights_and_early_childhood_education.html)
Tisdall, K. and Davis, J. (2004). Making a Difference? Bringing Children's and Young People's Views into Policy-making. *Children and Society*, 18(2), 131–142.
Tisdall, E.K.M. and Bell, R. (2006). Included in Governance? Children's Participation in 'Public' Decision Making. In E.K.M. Tisdall, J.M. Davis, M. Hill and A. Prout (eds), *Children, Young People and Social Inclusion* (pp. 105–120). Bristol, UK: Policy Press.
Tisdall, E.K.M. (2008). Is the Honeymoon over? Children and Young People's Participation in Public Decision-making. *International Journal of Children's Rights*, 16(3), 343–354.
Tisdall, E.K.M. and Morrison, F. (2012). Children's Participation in Court Proceedings when Parents Divorce or Separate. In M. Freeman (ed.), *Law and Childhood Studies* (pp. 156–173). Oxford: Oxford University Press.
Tisdall, E.K.M. (2012a). The Challenge and Challenging of Childhood Studies? Lessons from Disability Studies and Research with Disabled Children. *Children and Society*, 26(3), 181–191.
Tisdall, E.K.M. (2012b). Taking Forward Children and Young People's Participation. In M. Hill, G. Head, A. Lockyer, B. Reid and R. Taylor (eds), *Children's Services: Working Together* (pp. 151–162). Harlow, UK: Pearson.
Tisdall, E.K.M. (2013). The Transformation of Participation? Exploring the Potential of 'Transformative Participation' for Theory and Practice around Children and Young People's Participation. *Global Studies of Childhood*, 3(2), 183–193.
Tisdall, E.K.M. (2014). Addressing the Challenges of Children and Young People's Participation: Considering Time and Space. In T. Gal and B.F. Duramy (eds), *Promoting the Participation of Children and Youth across the Globe: From Social Exclusion to Child-Inclusive Policies*, Oxford: Oxford University Press. (forthcoming)
Tisdall, E.K.M. with Milne, S and Iliasov, A. (2007). *School Councils and Pupil Participation in Scottish Secondary Schools*. Glasgow, U: Scottish Consumer Council.

Treseder, P. (1997). *Empowering Children and Young People Training Manual: Promoting Involvement in Decision-Making*. London: Save the Children, UK.
UN Committee on the Rights of the Child (2003). *General Comment No. 5 General measures of implementation of the Convention on the Rights of the Child*. Available at http://tbinternet.ohchr.org/_layouts/treatybodyexternal/Download.aspx?symbolno=CRC%2fGC%2f2003%2f5andLang=en (last accessed 27 May 2014).
UN Committee on the Rights of the Child (2009). *General Comment No. 12 The Right of the Child to be Heard*. Available at www2.ohchr.org/english/bodies/crc/docs/AdvanceVersions/CRC-C-GC-12.doc (last accessed 27 May 2014).
Valentin, K. and Meinert, L. (2009). The Adult North and the Young South. *Anthropology Today*, 25(3), 23–28.
Whitecross, R. (2011). *Scoping study to provide information on the commissioning, preparation and use of court reports in the Child Welfare Hearing System in the Sheriff Courts*. Available at www.scotland.gov.uk/Publications/2011/01/07142042/0 (last accessed 27 May 2014).
Williams, S.J. and Bendelow, G. (1998). Introduction: Emotions in Social Life. In G. Bendelow and S.J. Williams (eds), *Emotions in Social Life* (pp. xiii–xxvii). London: Routledge.
Wyness, M. (2014). *Mapping out the Field of Children's Participation: Meanings, Narratives and Disputes*. Presentation at Modena, Italy Symposium Theorising Childhood: Citizenship, Rights, Participation (21 May 2014). http://esarn4modenasymposium.wordpress.com/program/ (last accessed 27 May 2014).
Wyse, D. (2001). Felt Tip Pens and School Councils. *Children and Society*, 15(4), 209–218.
Yamashita, H. and Davies, L. (2010). Students as Professionals. In B. Percy-Smith and N. Thomas (eds), *A Handbook of Children and Young People's Participation* (pp. 230–239). London: Routledge.

12
Education and children's rights

Ann Quennerstedt

1. Introduction

Most people would agree that education is of great importance to humanity. The value of education for the individual is regarded high enough to declare it as a human right. Besides the role played in the development of knowledge and skills, education is also recognised as a conduit for other human rights (Johnson 2010; McCowan 2012). It is not only the individual that gains from education, but also society, since the education of people is a matter of society's continuity, development and prosperity (Lansdown 2001). Consequently, as a human right, education is not only essential for children and young people, but is also vital for adults and society at large.

However, for children and young people, the implications of the human right to education go beyond receiving necessary training for a good future life or for upholding and developing society. Many children and young people spend a large part of their time in educational settings, often more than with their families. The work they undertake in education is their main activity, and the educational setting is the basic platform for friendship and peer communication. It is also a place where children and young people may experience ostracism, humiliation and violence. For children and young people, education is life in all its facets. For this reason, from the perspective of children's human rights, education is not only a question of developing skills and knowledge for the benefit of individuals or societies, but is also about living and growing together with others.

The ambition in this chapter is to, from an educational perspective, grasp the relation between education and children's human rights and to clarify the complexity of this relation. The starting point is taken in an often used explanation of what is included in a rights perspective on education, namely a distinction between the right *to* education and rights *in* education (e.g. Lundy 2012). With the aim of further expanding what children's human rights may mean in relation to education, I suggest three specific aspects as tools for elaboration: *access* to education, *content* of education and *relations* in education. The right *to* education will be discussed in terms of access and content, whereas rights *in* education will be explored from the vantage point of content and relations. This structure is developed by the use of arguments and findings in recent educational children's rights research. This serves also to fulfil a second aim of the chapter, which is to give a broad account of the current knowledge about education and children's rights.

It should be noted that research into children's rights, generally as well as within the discipline of education, is largely undertaken by researchers in Western contexts. This influences the kinds of questions that are posed and which lines of enquiry are followed, for example: since Western societies mostly have comprehensive school systems, matters of access to education receive less attention than what happens in education. This chapter also departs from such a position, but available research from other regions has been carefully sought and represent scholarly work from other perspectives. Further, since the main interest in the chapter is to explore and understand the relation between education and children's human rights, detailed descriptions of the various studies or findings discussed are not given. Instead, references are provided for those who wish to pursue a topic further. In the last part of the chapter attention is directed more specifically towards the research field itself. The chapter therefore concludes with a critical reflection on the research undertaken so far into children's rights issues in education, and makes suggestions for the continued study of children's human rights and education.

Another important standpoint of this chapter that should be clarified is that children's rights are regarded as included in the human rights, a view that is also reflected in the introduction to this Handbook. Drawing on Bobbio's (1990) work, children's rights is seen as a proliferation, or specialisation, of the general human rights meaning that 'children's rights' is an interpretation of the human rights for a specific group of humans, namely children. The Convention on the Rights of the Child is consequently seen as the international community's interpretation of children's human rights. In this chapter, the various ways in which rights for children are conceptualised – children's rights, children's human rights, human rights for children – accordingly reflect the view that these refer to same thing.

1.1. Outlining a framework for understanding the relation between education and children's rights

The distinction between the right *to* education and rights *in* education is illuminating in that it specifies that education is both an abstract entitlement and an everyday setting where rights are lived. However, I would argue that the *right to–rights in* distinction is too simplistic a frame to facilitate a deeper understanding of what a rights perspective on education could mean. One way of catering for increased complexity would be to add to the framework three basic aspects of the relation between education and children's rights: access, content and relations. These aspects cut across the rights to–rights in distinction and elucidate the complexities.

First, one of the most basic rights issues in relation to education is *access*. However, even though education is declared a human right in a range of treaties, and this right is recognised as such by the states that are signatories to these treaties, many children around the world still do not have access to education and accordingly do not have any opportunity to enjoy their right to education. In regions where children have relatively easy access to education, problems with access may still arise, for example for disabled children. A comprehensive school system does not guarantee that there are no access-related rights issues to discuss.

Second, the right to education is not only a matter of access, but also of *content*. Here, the term content refers both to the teaching content (like facts and skills) and the pedagogical practices that are employed. In other words, what children and young people are given as possibilities to learn and how the teaching and learning is organised and carried out are as important for the fulfilment of the human right to education as access (United Nations 2001). It should be noted that content includes values. Indeed, one of the responsibilities of formal educational institutions is to encourage children and young people to embrace certain central values, such as democracy and the principles enshrined in the human rights. The learning of values relies both on teaching content and pedagogical practice. For example, learning to act in accordance with human rights requires knowledge about what human rights are (facts) and teaching that respects those rights (practice).

Third, children's *relations* to and with other people are essential to how they will experience their time in education and to how they will learn about social life. Some of the most important children's rights issues in education are connected to relations. Children's relations to and with their schoolmates are often a source of happiness and growing self-esteem, but for those children and young people who experience taunting, discrimination or violence in school, school is a fearful and dangerous place. Children's and young people's relations to and with their teachers also involve numerous children's rights issues. While most teachers are eager to create a child-friendly environment, the traditions in education that form teachers' views of children are not always in line with a children's rights perspective. In many instances, authoritarian patterns and insufficient respect for children's human dignity and rights characterise the relations between children and teachers.

Merging the distinction between the right to education and rights in education with the rights issues of access, content and relations could enable us to advance our understanding of the relation between education and children's rights. I accordingly suggest that discussions about the right to education need to include matters of access and of content. The right is not only an entitlement to participate in education per se, but also to take part in a certain kind of education (with a certain content). If the importance of the content of education to fulfil the child's right to education is not highlighted, it runs the risk of being overlooked and remaining unexamined. Talking about the child's rights in education accentuates the here-and-now character of education as an everyday location for children's and young people's human rights, which is a necessary stance for research in this field. However, I would argue that the *in* is somewhat vague, and would benefit from an employment of both content and relations as rights-related dimensions of the everyday life of educational institutions. This is the framework that will be used in the following to clarify what the relation between education and children's human rights might include and to make the complexity more visible.

2. The right to education: Access and content

2.1. The meaning of the right to education

At first glance the meaning of the right to education may not seem to be very complicated. This is illusory. McCowan (2010: 510) asks: 'to what exactly does the right to education actually relate? Does it correspond to access to educational institutions, to a particular form of educational experience, or to some educational effect?' McCowan is troubled by the almost non-existent discussion about the nature of the education that corresponds to the right, and urges us to pay more attention to the conceptualisation of the right.

It is important that both the quantitative and qualitative aspects are included in discussions about the right to education (e.g. Beeckman 2004; Johnson 2010; McCowan 2010). Some of the central quantitative aspects are that places offering education are sufficient and accessible to all children, that participation rates are high and that education is free of charge. Qualitative aspects may concern acceptable learning achievement, processes of education and a respectful educational environment. Most UN documents reflect this line of thinking. One such document is the Convention Against Discrimination in Education (UNESCO 1960, Art. 1), which states that the term education 'includes access to education, the standard and quality of education, and the conditions under which it is given.' In her search for indicators with which to evaluate the implementation of the child's right to education, Beeckman (2004) finds that those that are available consistently prioritise quantitative aspects rather than qualitative ones. When indicators do address qualitative elements they often end up turning into quantification exercises. Beeckman argues for the need to develop ways of measuring the extent to which the qualitative dimension of the right to education is implemented, for example whether teaching and learning processes are open, interactive and participatory.

In addition to the somewhat diverging messages concerning the access/content aspects of the right, as described above, there is a lack of clarity in international documents about *what* education is considered as a right. A shift in vocabulary over time can be noted (Johnson 2010): from the Universal Declaration of Human Rights' provision for free and compulsory education 'at least in the *elementary and fundamental* stages' (United Nations 1948, Art 26:1, emphasis added) to the International Convention on Economic, Social and Cultural Rights' (United Nations 1966, Art. 13, emphasis added) statement that '*primary* education' should be free and available to all. In more recent documents (UNESCO 1990, 2000) the term '*basic* education' has been introduced, and a distinction made between basic and primary education, with the former being the right and the latter the delivery system (McCowan 2010). Moreover, these later documents indicate that *pre*-primary education is also included in basic education (Mtahabwa 2010; Herczog 2012).

The ground for confusion is obvious. First, how are we to understand the parallel, and in meaning varying, use of *basic* and *primary* education – which is the right? Second, if 'basic' education most correctly defines the right, as some of the documents suggest, is pre-primary education also included in the right to education, or not? Third, can 'basic' education really be limited to a certain part of the education system labelled primary education (as a means of delivery of basic education)? Here, variations between different nations' educational systems must be taken into account. For example, the transition from pre-school to primary school occurs at varying ages – between the ages of 4–7, and as Johnson (2010) points out, the duration of primary education varies between 3 and 10 years. And what about secondary education? In many nations it would be very difficult to manage with only primary education, and in those places secondary education is seen as basic.

In short, the precise meaning of the right to education is not at all clear, and the interpretations in the various international treaties and other documents actually add to the continued confusion concerning how access to and content of education relates to the right and which education corresponds to the right – basic, primary, pre-primary, or secondary.

2.2. Some specific issues relating to the right to education

When considering the meaning of the right to education, a number of specific issues can be raised. One such issue is the tension between children's rights and parents' rights in relation to the right to education. Education is perhaps the societal arena in which the human rights held by parents and those held by children converge most, and where the interest that parents and children have in education does not always harmonise (Marples 2005; Grover 2006). When parents send their child to school, and in doing so hand over influence on their child's development to an educational institution, they may find that the education given to their children conflicts with their own convictions (Lundy 2005). This is especially evident in relation to religious beliefs, where parents' right to freedom of religion and their wish to bring up their child in that belief may clash with the child's right to an education that promotes religious autonomy

(Høstmælingen 2005; Jawoniyi 2012). Note here that it is not education per se that is suggested as the object of parental rights claims. The idea is not that parents should have a right to decide whether their children should participate in education or not. Instead, it is the *content* of education that for some is seen as a legitimate object of parental authority. The centrality of educational content in 'the right to education' is here brought to the fore.

When parents are given far-reaching authority over their children's education, for example through the design of school systems or specific legislation in these matters, and use such authority to limit the presence of life views or convictions other than their own in the child's educational surrounding, the child's right to education is violated, according to several authors (Høstmælingen 2005; Marples 2005; Almog and Perry-Hazan 2012). Englund (2010) and Grover (2006) both argue that the right to education is an entitlement to a pluralistic education that opens various perspectives for reflection and that provides a meeting point for ethnic, cultural and social groups. These authors argue that children's rights to be educated for tolerance and autonomy must trump parents' freedom rights. The standpoint of the global community on this matter is however not clarified. On the contrary, there is ambivalence both within and between various treaties, and between the treaties and how they are interpreted in human rights courts (Høstmælingen 2005; Quennerstedt 2009b; Wahlström 2009).

A second issue that is related to the right to education is educational segregation by the separation of children from mainstream education to special education institutions, for example children with disabilities or special educational needs, children belonging to an ethnic minority, or separation from school through exclusion. The Jomtien Declaration (UNESCO 1990) marked a shift in discourse, in that it accentuated and acknowledged that certain vulnerable and marginalised groups of children were not given equal opportunities to enjoy their human right to education. Some years later, the Salamanca Declaration (UNESCO 1994) discussed in more depth the implications of this for children with special educational needs. The main message of the Salamanca Declaration, which was later repeated in other human rights documents, is that all children have a right to attend a mainstream neighbourhood school – conceptualised in the term *inclusive education* (Miles 2009). Since then the inclusion of all children in mainstream schools has become a central feature of many nations' educational policy, despite there being a lot of uncertainty about what inclusion actually means (Allan 2010). Changing approaches over time to the education of children who need additional support has accordingly altered vocabulary and legislation, although the actual effects on educational practice seem to have been limited (Flatman Watson 2009; Runswick-Cole and Hodge 2009; Miles 2009; Allan 2010; Petriwskyj 2010). Almost without exception, this research shows that children with disabilities are still largely viewed from a deficit perspective and as deviant, and continue to suffer discrimination in the various education systems. Despite the ambition to include all children in mainstream schooling, a large number of children with disabilities, or who need additional support for other reasons, attend special schools, whether by choice or not.

Segregating and discriminative tendencies also affect the equality of access and outcomes for children from minority groups (Lundy 2012). In particular, the educational situation of Roma children has been brought to the fore. Roma children are described as those facing most inequality with regard to access to and benefits from education (O'Nions 2010). This group is disproportionally segregated from mainstream education, either within mainstream schools or by being placed in special schools (Roth and Moisa 2011; Murray 2012).

The exclusion or suspension of students from school as a response to challenging behaviour is a practice that can be questioned from the perspective of the child's right to education (access/content) and the principle of the best interest of the child. Suspension and exclusion have negative academic and social effects and increase the risks of academic failure and drop out, disengagement from school, alcohol and drug abuse, physical violence and other antisocial actions (Dávila and Naya 2007; Bryson 2010; Hemphill and Schneider 2013). Moreover, suspension and exclusion may augment existing disadvantages and societal inequality, since these measures are disproportionally used for students belonging to an ethnic minority group or of low socio-economic status (Osler and Starkey 2005; Quennerstedt 2009a; Bryson 2010; Hemphill and Schneider 2013). The use of suspension or exclusion as a disciplinary measure seems to have increased (Hemphill and Schneider 2013), and in some nations the state's responsibility to provide education has been 'solved' by the arrangement of alternative education for excluded students (Bryson 2010). On the one hand, alternative education provision may re-engage excluded children in education, although on the other hand, the students are often permanently separated from mainstream education. Bryson (2010) argues that alternative education in itself sustains exclusionary practices.

Refugee and migrant children's right to education is another burning issue which highlights how the enjoyment of human rights still depends on citizenship status: the rights we have as humans are not necessarily the same as those we have as citizens of a state (Benhabib 2004; Vandenhole et al. 2011; Quennerstedt 2012). Examinations of the educational situation of migrant children, and especially undocumented children, show that if they are given access to public education at all it is often of inferior quality, for example due to insufficient resources or unqualified teaching staff (Bacáková 2011; Wang and Holland 2011; Vandenhole et al. 2011).

To sum up this first section on *the right to education*, two main aspects can be highlighted. First, there is confusion about what the right to education actually means. It is reasonably clear that the right includes aspects of both access and content, although there is more focus on access issues. Moreover, the confusion surrounding *what* kind of education is a right is widespread, and here international documents offer little help. Second, a range of specific issues stem from the claim that education is a right for all children and include: how children's human rights relate to parents' human rights, how we are to view educational segregation, and how the situation of the non-citizen child is to be dealt with. None of these issues have been resolved. In the next section we will look at education and children's rights through a different lens – one that shifts the focus from a general international or national policy level to the everyday educational practices in early childhood education and schools.

3. Rights in education: Content and relations

The claim that children's and young people's human rights have to be considered as an aspect of the everyday life and activities *in* education highlights the responsibility of educational institutions to acknowledge and be responsive to the rights of children and young people here and now in practice. It is no longer only the human right to education that needs to be taken into account and interpreted, but rather the whole range of human rights. How, then, can we view the role and responsibility of educational institutions to respond to children's human rights *in* education?

I suggest that a first part of this responsibility is to *respect* children and young people as holders and practitioners of human rights. This means seeing and meeting children as legitimate holders of rights, and allowing them to exercise their human rights in the educational setting. This role includes safeguarding respectful relations between all participants in the educational environment, and a responsibility to protect children and young people from discrimination, violence and other negative actions that infringe their human rights and dignity. I further suggest that a second part of the responsibility of educational institutions to respond to the rights of children is closely related to the specific role assigned to education by society, namely to *educate* children. This would mean that children and young people are educated as holders and practitioners of human rights by being given opportunities to develop the knowledge, skills and capacities they need to more fully enjoy and exercise their human rights.

In everyday practice the acts of respecting children and educating children are intertwined. For example, the experience of being treated with respect for your human rights includes learning about what it feels like to be respected and the importance of respectful relations between humans, which in turn affects one's own actions. Acknowledgment and respect for children and young people as rights holders is in itself educating. In the following I will discuss rights *in* education as largely connecting to the respect for and education of children by means of *educational content* and to the nature of *relations* in educational settings.

3.1. Respecting and educating through the choice of educational content

As mentioned at the beginning of this chapter, *educational content* includes facts, values and skills, as well as the processes and interactions in teaching and learning. Ideas about respecting and educating children as holders and practitioners of human rights can be incorporated into the choice of educational content in various ways. A directly visible rights-related content of teaching and learning is when rights are made an object of teaching/learning – children are educated about and in rights. This is sometimes labelled 'children's rights education' (Covell 2010). Howe and Covell (2005) discuss how such children's rights education can help children to develop (i) knowledge about their own rights and the responsibilities that accompany those rights, (ii) knowledge about general human rights principles and the underlying values and attitudes, and (iii) skills and capacities that facilitate taking positive action as a holder of rights. The purpose of children's rights education is thus that children will develop their knowledge and gain action competence as rights holders. A recent shift in vocabulary can be noticed in this area to the extent that (in line with the standpoint declared in the beginning of this chapter) children's rights and human rights are increasingly merged. For example, Covell *et al.* (2011) have in their later works rephrased their former wording to 'children's human rights education', and Mitchell (2010) argues for a reconstruction of children's rights education within the framework of human rights, thereby aiming towards pedagogical integration between children's human rights and citizenship education. In my view, the shifting vocabulary reflects a more basic shift in thinking about children's rights – not separating them from the general human rights.

Also, pedagogical choices surrounding the framing and presentation of objects of study other than human rights can be more or less explicitly guided by a rights perspective. One example is religious education. In-depth knowledge about, and a critical understanding of, the role of religion in today's world is becoming increasingly necessary, and is why we need to carefully consider how religious education should be formed and presented (Jawoniyi 2012). Jawoniyi suggests that the human rights framework supports the standpoint that non-confessional and multifaith education is preferable. Another example is character and moral education. The role of education to foster a desired character and morals has always been held high, but how do we decide what 'good' character or morals are? In the search for a value base that guides the kind of character that we hope children will develop, Lake (2011) suggests that a human rights framework can provide a more universal way of understanding character education. Both these authors show how a children's human rights perspective can inform pedagogical choices of various kinds.

Important parts of the educational content reside in the processes of education. This means that procedures and interactions that are employed to deal with a particular object or topic will inevitably contribute to what is learnt. I would say that this is an overlooked aspect in the human rights documents, for example in the Universal Declaration of Human Rights (United Nations 1948) and the Convention on the Rights of the Child (United Nations 1989). These instruments elaborate on the aims of education, but do not address the kind of processes or experiences that need to occur in order to achieve those aims (McCowan 2012). There may be a risk that structures and processes in education are seen as less important for children's and young people's growth in knowledge and ability than the topics or objects of education. In my view, the discussion about what children's rights mean in education needs to engage more with the significance of educational processes and raise questions about which processes are important from a rights perspective.

From a rights perspective, one valuable educational process is experience-based learning. The importance of experience for children's learning and growing is highlighted by many educational scholars (Dewey 1938; Todd 2007; Covell et al. 2008; Quennerstedt and Quennerstedt 2013). In this, schools could make use of everyday situations to discuss 'lived rights' with the children. In their interactions with each other and with adults, children and young people will be faced with rights dilemmas, since human rights are not always at peace with each other. For example, how does the right to freedom of speech relate to the right to non-discrimination? In discussions based on self-experienced situations, children can be given opportunities to consider different ways of dealing with ambiguity in relation to human rights. Todd (2007) maintains that the real potential of educating children and young people as rights holders lies precisely in the capacity to extend their experience and knowledge by discussing the issues and having their ideas challenged.

Another kind of educational process that has been suggested by many authors as valuable from a rights perspective is that of participation (see also Tisdall, Chapter 11). However, the various ways in which the concept of participation has been used to discuss rights issues lead in somewhat different directions ('children's participation', 'student participation', 'participation rights' and 'right to participation'). Thomas (2007) describes how the term 'participation' can refer to taking part in an activity (physical presence) or, more specifically, to taking part in decision-making. Participation can also be used to characterise a process that engages children as autonomous and knowledgeable actors, or to describe the outcome of an activity. The expression 'children's participation in education' can accordingly refer to quantitative aspects of education, such as enrolment and drop out statistics, and qualitative ones, such as the extent and quality of children's engagement in educational activities (Smit 2013). Also, when participation is coupled with the term 'rights' the meaning varies. The use of 'participation rights' indicates that there are a number of such rights that need to be considered in education, while 'the right to participation' suggests that children have a particular right that is called participation. Although using the term participation to specify a certain kind of process can be problematical, it is nevertheless a widespread way of approaching and conceptualising how processes in education can be rights respecting and contribute to children's growth and learning as rights holders.

The value of participatory processes in education is mainly discussed in two ways: one that centres on the child's right to be heard and included in decision-making in education (Bae 2010; Theobald and Danby 2011; Dunphy 2012) and one that highlights the child as a participant in all aspects of school life – planning, learning and evaluating (I'Anson and Allan 2006; Smith 2007). Like all humans, children and young people have the political right to exercise influence over their own lives by having their opinions and views taken into account and by being invited into the arenas in which public opinion is formed and decisions are made (Quennerstedt 2010). Participatory processes in education, guided by respect for children's political rights and simultaneously aiming to provide opportunities for children and young people to develop their knowledge and abilities as holders and practitioners of political rights, may accordingly be of great importance from a rights perspective.

3.2. Respecting and educating through the relations in education

Reflecting on relations between the participants in an educational setting is central to a comprehensive understanding of children's rights in education. This includes the relations between children and between children and adults, in this case mainly teachers. These relations may be joyful and strengthen children's rights and human value, but may also be detrimental, diminishing children's and young people's human value and even violating human rights. In the following, some of the rights issues in education that are connected to relations will be discussed as relevant aspects of respecting and educating children as holders of rights.

Friendships and positive social relationships are vital for children and young people. For children, being among friends may be the main motivation for going to school. Difficulties in making and maintaining friendships not only affect children's well-being, but also their possibilities of academic achievement. Social relations that are affirmative contribute positively to children's and young people's development, learning and overall quality of life (MacArthur 2013). The Convention on the Rights of the Child states that for children, the right to life includes a right to develop (United Nations 1989, Art. 6). From such a rights perspective, we need to ask whether educational settings are places in which children experience positive social relations and human dignity, and consider the responsibility of educational institutions to support children who are struggling with friendships and are in danger of being excluded.

Regrettably, many children and young people are subjected to physical aggression, verbal aggression and/or exclusion in school. Some groups of children, such as those with disabilities, are particularly exposed to bullying and abuse (Mepham 2010). Bullying has been widely debated since the 1970s, but very few analyses of this phenomenon have been conducted from a rights perspective. Recently, it has been suggested that efforts to combat bullying would be greatly enhanced by making it synonymous with the defence of human rights (Greene 2006; Taylor 2008). Magendzo Kolstrein and Toledo Jofré (2013) make a strong case by relating the issue of bullying to the wording in central human rights instruments that *all humans are equal in dignity and rights*, and that *no one shall be subjected to cruel, inhuman or degrading treatment* (United Nations 1948, 1989). The authors maintain that in the act of bullying a person's dignity is stripped and the victim is humiliated and degraded. They conclude that all forms of bullying undermine human rights and that some are direct or even severe violations of human rights.

Some authors highlight that the discourse of bullying is largely separated from a discourse of rights (Greene 2006; Stein 2003). The anti-bullying laws and school programmes that many nations have adopted in order to combat bullying usually focus on establishing anti-bullying policies (national/local), on individuals' feelings and on the bully/victim. Connections are rarely made to the underlying norms that enable hostile environments in which such actions can occur and to the violation of human rights. In this sense, Stein (2003) argues that the discourse of bullying can minimise or obscure the severity of aggression and harassment. Through the discourse of rights, the violence, harassment, degrading treatment and exclusion that children and young people experience can be viewed against a different backdrop. Such change of discourse may provide new ways of addressing these problems.

Children's and young people's relations to and with adults in education are also of great importance from a rights perspective. In general teachers strive to create a warm and friendly atmosphere, where children are cared for and feel safe and happy and where learning conditions are beneficial. In spite of this, research indicates that within education there appears to be a reluctance to adopt children's rights thinking (Alderson 1999; Lansdown 2001; Quennerstedt 2011). The traditional view of the child as the property of its parents and as an object of the process of natural development has defined children as people with little autonomy and lacking in competence (Quennerstedt and Quennerstedt 2013). This view of the child has governed the structures and relations in education for a long time. However, the perception of the child as a dependent 'not yet' has been challenged by the rights discourse and by the theorising in the sociology of childhood (e.g. James *et al.* 1998), and the view of the child has gradually changed over the last few decades. Of course, teachers have also been affected by new thinking about children's social status. In Hudson's study (2012), when asked about how they view children and children's rights, teachers expressed agreement with these principles. However, turning principles into practice seems to be difficult – Hudson identified a significant gap between what teachers talked about in relation to children's rights and what actually happened in practice. How can we understand this reluctance to change in education?

A first aspect to consider is educational tradition. The core values that are reflected in traditional schooling are not always in line with contemporary children's rights thinking. Educational practices are commonly underpinned by hierarchical power structures, where time, space, bodies and activities are controlled by adults (Alderson 1999; John 2001). There is a strict separation between adults and children: adults have the right to make decisions and administer discipline, while children have to accept their subordinate position and lack of power. Furthermore, the imbalance of power is often combined with a view of learning in which children are seen as passive recipients of adult wisdom. Adults' ideas and perceptions are prioritised and form the basis for activities and interactions. Murris (2013) discusses that such 'epistemic injustice' often characterises the relation between teachers and children, in that children are regarded and treated as not yet full epistemic subjects (knowers) by their teachers. Research has demonstrated that children seem to be well aware of the unequal power structures and their inferior status in school and report on their experiences of this in a variety of situations (Allan and I'Anson 2004; Thelander 2009).

A second aspect to take into account when understanding the resistance in education to children's rights-oriented change is the theoretical foundation for teacher professionalism. Developmental psychology has traditionally formed the base in education for approaching the child as a learner and, despite decades of critique from other theoretical domains, it still dominates educational practice (Osler and Starkey 2005; MacNaughton *et al.* 2007; Murris 2013). Accordingly, the education provided in early childhood centres and schools has been informed by general beliefs about younger children's limited competencies, self-centredness and lack of capacity for abstract thinking. Developmental theories tend to essentialise and generalise about children and their capacities, thereby abstracting the child from his or her social context (Murris 2013). This universalist notion of child development has played an important role in teachers' professional expertise and has equipped teachers with a 'map' of childhood and the child's development of capacities and abilities at certain ages (MacNaughton *et al.* 2007). This view of the learning and developing child might actually weaken and undermine the notion of children's rights.

In short, the argument in this section has been that rights *in* education are closely connected to respecting and educating children – in all aspects of everyday school life – as fully-fledged holders of human rights. In this, one role of education is *choosing educational content*. A number of aspects related to choice of content have been highlighted: educating children about rights, framing other educational content with human rights and employing educational processes that promote children's human rights. Another role of education is cultivating *respectful relations* between all actors in education. A need to investigate the underlying norms that enable an environment in which bullying and discrimination occur has been pointed out, as has the potential of the human rights framework to work against hostility and discrimination. The seeming resistance within education to adopt a children's rights perspective, which maintains unequal power patterns between adults and children and a view of children as 'not-yets', has also been highlighted.

4. Some reflections on educational research into children's rights issues

So far in this chapter, research has been used to give substance to the exposé of what children's human rights mean in relation to education. In this final section, a more distanced position will be taken to the research hitherto conducted. Here critical reflections are outlined and possible new routes for the future of educational children's rights research are suggested.

In this chapter's portrayal of the relation between education and children's rights, little attention has been paid to the intensity of research interest into the various themes presented. However, two earlier review studies of children's rights research by Reynaert et al. (2009) and Quennerstedt (2011) have identified the following research focal points:

- the child's *right to participation* (alternatively 'participations rights') in education,
- the tension between *parental rights and children's rights* in the right to education,
- *implementation research* (in relation to the Convention on the Rights of the Child), for example in the case of disabled children, ethnic minorities or the right to participation,
- *teachers' views* on children's rights and structures in education that undermine children's human rights.

In all these matters our knowledge has been significantly extended and refined by the research that has been conducted. But other aspects of the relation between education and rights that have been pointed out in this chapter have received little attention in research, and, as a consequence, the knowledge about these matters is limited. These include:

- *what the right to education means*, what is included in the right and which concepts embody the right to and rights in education,
- the significance of *educational content* (topics and processes) in relation to the right to and rights in education.
- the significance of *relations* in education (to peers and adults) for what is learned.

An emerging interest in these later issues may be seen to represent new lines of inquiry in educational children's rights research that could open up new areas of research and contribute with important insights. This is particularly the case with regard to educational content; an area that is still largely unexplored from a rights perspective. These issues may also represent a more critical and specifically educational approach to the study of children's rights, and answer the calls from within the field for more critical investigations.

Reynaert et al. (2009) raise our awareness of a problematical general characteristic of children's rights research, namely that it is part of an international consensus building around children's rights. 'Children's rights' are presented in an unambiguous way, and a notion of social consensus is constructed. The authors' argument that the Convention on the Rights of the Child has been placed at the centre of children's rights as a definition and an instruction for policy and practice, without being questioned or analysed, is a warning that should be taken seriously. Continuing this line of argument, I have elsewhere suggested that the change sought for by Reynaert *et al.* needs to include a more critical stance towards the Convention as well as more theory driven research, where research questions are formulated in relation to theory rather than in relation to the Convention (Quennerstedt 2013). A critical perspective is also a starting point for this Handbook (see introduction). Both these approaches offer ways of breaking consensus, opening the field to contesting views and standpoints and facilitating constructive debate and new thinking.

Another change of direction that would make a significant difference is bringing the study of children's rights closer to particular academic domains. The top-down approach that is often employed in this field of research runs the risk of neglecting the expertise and specific knowledge interest that is at hand within a certain discipline. The context in which the rights are studied is then viewed as just an arena for implementation. Questions about children's rights are constituted as universally valid and equally relevant in all settings. I would instead suggest the opposite approach, namely that research into children's rights should depart from the particular knowledge interest of a certain academic field. The matter of human rights for children in relation to education accordingly needs to be incorporated into the core interests of educational research, and questions formulated from such a merged position. This would mean that questions about children's rights in e.g. law studies are substantially different from those raised in e.g. educational studies, because these disciplines have differing knowledge interests.

The work on participation issues, parents' rights–children's rights issues, implementation matters and teachers' views is not over. On the contrary, much remains to be done. However, this work would benefit from a more Convention-critical and theory driven approach. The exploration of deeper meanings of the right to education has only just begun, as has the significance of educational content to respond to children's and young people's human rights in educational settings. All this work could be given a new orientation if perspectives were changed, from a children's rights perspective on education, to an educational perspective on children's rights.

Questions for debate and discussion

- How can we understand the dominance of Western scholarship in the field of children's rights? And what can the consequences of this be?
- How can educational processes be discussed as significant to the role of educational institutions to respond to children's human rights?
- What is the difference between the role of education to respect children as rights subjects and to educate children as rights subjects?

References

Alderson, Priscilla (1999) Human rights and democracy in schools do they mean more than 'picking up litter and not killing whales'? *The International Journal of Children's Rights* 7, 185–205.
Allan, Julie (2010) Questions of inclusion in Scotland and Europe. *European Journal of Special Needs Education* 25(2), 199–208.
Allan, Julie and I'Anson, John (2004) Children's rights in school: Power, assemblies and assemblages. *The International Journal of Children's Rights* 12, 123–138.
Almog, Shulamit and Perry-Hazan, Lotem (2012) Conceptualising the right of children to adaptable education. *International Journal of Children's Rights* 20, 486–500.
Bacáková, Marketa (2011) Developing inclusive educational practices for refugee children in the Czech Republic. *Intercultural Education* 22(2), 163–175.

Bae, Berit (2010) Realizing children's rights to participation in early childhood settings: Some critical issues in a Norwegian context. *Early Years* 30(3), 205–218.

Beeckman, Katrien (2004) Measuring the implementation of the right to education: Educational versus human rights indicators. *The International Journal of Children's Rights* 12, 71–84.

Benhabib, Seyla (2004) *The Rights of Others*. Cambridge: Cambridge University Press.

Bobbio, Norberto (1990) *The Age of Rights*. Cambridge: Polity Press.

Bryson, Peter (2010) Alternative education, equity and compromise: dilemmas for practice development. *Child Care in Practice* 16(4), 347–358.

Covell, Katherine (2010) School engagement and rights-respecting schools. *Cambridge Journal of Education* 40(1), 39–51.

Covell, Katherine, Howe Brian and McNeil, Justin (2008) 'If there's a dead rat, don't leave it': Young children's understanding of their citizenship rights and responsibilities. *Cambridge Journal of Education* 38(3), 321–339.

Covell, Katherine, Howe, Brian and Polegato, Jillian (2011) Children's human rights education as a counter to social disadvantage: A case study from England. *Educational Research* 53(2), 193–206.

Dávila, Paulí and Naya, Luís María (2007) Education and the rights of the child in Europe. *Prospects* 37, 357–367.

Dewey, John (1938) *Experience and Education*. New York: Macmillan Publishing.

Dunphy, Elizabeth (2012) Children's participation rights in early childhood education and care: The case of early literacy learning and pedagogy. *International Journal of Early Years Education* 20(3), 290–299.

Englund, Tomas (2010) Questioning the parental right to educational authority: Arguments for a pluralist education system. *Education Inquiry* 1(3), 235–258.

Flatman Watson, Sheelah (2009) Barriers to inclusive education in Ireland: The case for pupils with diagnosis of intellectual and/or pervasive developmental disabilities. *British Journal of Learning Disabilities* 37, 277–284.

Greene, Michael (2006) Bullying in schools: A plea for measure of human rights. *Journal of Social Issues* 62(1), 63–79.

Grover, Sonja (2006) The right of the child to be heard in education litigation: An analysis of the 'intelligent design' Pennsylvania case on the separation of Church and State in the public schools. *Education and Law* 18(2–3), 149–160.

Hemphill, Sheryl and Schneider, Sharon (2013) Excluding students from school: A re-examination from a children's rights perspective. *International Journal of Children's rights* 21, 88–92.

Herczog, Maria (2012) Rights of the child and early childhood education and care in Europe. *European Journal of Education* 47(4), 542–555.

Høstmælingen, Njål (2005) Mandatory religious education that builds tolerance: Lessons to be learned from Norway? *The International Journal of Children's Rights* 13, 403–412.

Howe, Brian and Covell, Katherine (2005) *Empowering children. Children's Rights Education as a Pathway to Citizenship*. Toronto: University of Toronto Press.

Hudson, Kim (2012) Practitioners' views on involving young children in decision making: Challenges for the Children's rights agenda. *Australasian Journal of Early Childhood* 37(2), 4–9.

I'Anson, John and Allan, Julie (2006) Children's rights in practice: A study of change within a primary school. *International Journal of Children's Spirituality* 11(2), 265–279.

James, Allison: Jenks, Chris and Prout, Alan (1998) *Theorizing Childhood*. Cambridge, UK: Polity Press.

Jawoniyi, Oduntan (2012) Children's rights and religious education in state-funded schools: An international human rights perspective. *The International Journal of Human Rights* 16(2), 337–357.

John, Mary (2001) Achieving respect for children's views in education: Roles for adults and children. In S. Hart *et al.* (eds) *Children's Rights in Education*. London: Jessica Kingsley.

Johnson, Robert (2010) The child's right to an education: 'Consensus-minus-one?' *International Journal of Children's Rights* 18, 185–216.

Lake, Kristine (2011) Character education from a children's rights perspective: An examination of elementary students' perspectives and experiences. *International Journal of Children's Rights* 19, 679–690.

Lansdown, Gerison (2001) Progress in implementing the rights in the Convention: Factors helping and hindering the process. In S. Hart *et al.* (eds) *Children's Rights in Education*. London: Jessica Kingsley Publishers.

Lundy, Laura (2005) Family values in the classroom? Reconciling parental wishes and children's rights in state schools. *International Journal of Law, Policy and the Family* 19, 346–372.

Lundy, Laura (2012) Children's rights and educational policy in Europe: The implementation of the United Nations Convention on the Rights of the Child. *Oxford Review of Education* 38(4), 393–411.

MacArthur, Jude (2013) Sustaining friendships, relationships, and rights at school. *International Journal of Inclusive Education* 17(8), 793–811.

MacNaughton, Glenda, Hughes, Patrick and Smith, Kylie (2007) Early childhood professionals and children's right: Tensions and possibilities around the United Nations General Comment No.7 on Children's Rights. *International Journal of Early Years Education* 15(2), 161–170.

Magendzo Kolstrein, Abraham and Toledo Jofré, María Isabel (2013) Bullying: An analysis from the perspective of human rights, target groups and interventions. *International Journal of Children's Rights* 21(1), 46–58

Marples, Roger (2005) Against faith schools: A philosophical argument for children's rights. *International Journal of Children's Spirituality* 10(2), 133–147.

McCowan, Tristan (2010) Reframing the universal right to education. *Comparative Education* 46(4), 509–525.

McCowan, Tristan (2012) Human rights within education: Assessing the justifications. *Cambridge Journal of Education* 42(1), 67–81.

Mepham, Sarah (2010) Disabled children: The right to feel safe. *Child Care in Practice* 16(1), 19–34.

Miles, Susie (2009) Engaging with teachers' knowledge: Promoting inclusion in Zambian schools. *Disability and Society* 24(5), 611–624.

Mitchell, Richard (2010) Who's afraid now? Reconstructing Canadian citizenship education through transdisciplinarity. *The Review of Education, Pedagogy and Cultural Studies* 32, 37–65.

Mtahabwa, Lyabwene (2010) Provision of pre-primary education as a basic right in Tanzania: Reflections from policy documents. *Contemporary Issues in Early Childhood* 11(4), 353–364.

Murray, Colette (2012) A minority within a minority? Social justice for traveller and Roma children in ECEC. *European Journal of Education* 47(4), 569–583.

Murris, Karin (2013) The epistemic challenge of hearing child's voice. *Studies in Philosophy of Education* 32, 245–259.

O'Nions, Helen (2010) Divide and teach: Educational inequality and the Roma. *The International Journal of Human Rights* 14(3), 464–489.

Osler, Audrey and Starkey, Hugh (2005) Violence in schools and representations of young people: A critique of government policies in France and England, *Oxford Review of Education* 31(2), 195–215.

Petriwskyj, Anne (2010) Who has rights to what? Inclusion in Australian early childhood programs. *Contemporary Issues in Early Childhood* 11(4), 342–352.

Quennerstedt, Ann (2009a) Children's rights in education: Transforming universal claims into New Zealand policy. *New Zealand Journal of Educational Studies* 44(2), 63–78.

Quennerstedt, Ann (2009b) Balancing the rights of the child and the rights of parents in the Convention on the Rights of the Child. *Journal of Human Rights* 8(2), 162–176.

Quennerstedt, Ann (2010) Children, but not really humans? Critical reflections on the hampering effect of the "3 p's". *International Journal of Children's Rights* 18, 619–635.

Quennerstedt, Ann (2011) The construction of children's rights in education: A research synthesis. *International Journal of Children's Rights* 19, 661–678.

Quennerstedt, Ann (2012) Transforming children's human rights: From universal claims to national particularity. In M. Freeman (ed.) *Law and Childhood Studies*, 104–116.

Quennerstedt, Ann (2013) Children's rights research moving into the future: Challenges on the way forward. *International Journal of Children's Rights* 21, 233–247.

Quennerstedt, Ann and Quennerstedt, Mikael (2013) Researching children's rights in education: Sociology of childhood encountering educational theory. *British Journal of Sociology of Education* 35(1), 115–132.

Reynaert, Didier; Bouverne-de Bie, Maria and Vandevelde, Stijn (2009) A review of children's rights literature since the adoption of the United Nations convention on the rights of the child. *Childhood* 16(4), 518–534.

Roth, Maria and Moisa, Florin (2011) The right to education of Roma children in Romania: European policies and Romanian practices. *International Journal of Children's Rights* 19, 501–522.

Runswick-Cole, Katerine and Hodge, Nick (2009) Needs or rights? A challenge to the discourse of special education. *British Journal of Special Education* 36(4), 198–203.

Smit, Ben (2013) Young people as co-researchers: Enabling student participation in educational practice. *Professional Development in Education* 39(4), 550–573.

Smith, Anne (2007) Children and young people's participation rights in education. *International Journal of Children's Rights* 15, 147–164.

Stein, Nan (2003) Bullying or sexual harassment: The missing discourse of rights in an era of zero tolerance. *Arizona Law Review* 45, 783.

Taylor, Catherine (2008) A human rights approach to stopping homophobic bullying in schools. *Journal of Gay and Lesbian Social Services* 19(3–4), 157–172.

Thelander Nina (2009) *We are all the same, but... Kenyan and Swedish school children's views on children's rights.* Karlstads universitet: Karlstad University Studies 2009: 36. Dissertation.

Theobald, Maryanne and Danby, Susan (2011) Child participation in the early years: Challenges for education. *Australasian Journal of Early Childhood* 36(3), 19–26.

Thomas, Nigel (2007) Towards a theory of children's participation. *International Journal of Children's Rights* 15, 199–218.

Todd, Sharon (2007) Promoting a just education: Dilemmas of rights, freedom and justice. *Educational Philosophy and Theory* 39(6), 592–603.

UNESCO (1960) *Convention Against Discrimination in Education.*

UNESCO (1990) *World Declaration on Education for All. Meeting Basic Learning Needs.* (Jomtien Declaration)

UNESCO (1994) *The Salamanca Statement and Framework for Action on Special Needs Education.*

UNESCO (2000) *The Dakar Framework for Action. Education for All: Meeting our Collective Commitments.*

United Nations (1948) *Universal Declaration of Human Rights.* General Assembly resolution 217A(III), 10 Dec. 1948. U.N. Doc. A/RES/3/217/A.

United Nations (1966) *International Covenant on Economic, Social and Cultural Rights.* General Assembly resolution 2200A(XXI), 16 Dec. 1966.

United Nations (1989) *Convention on the Rights of the Child.* General Assembly resolution 44/25, 20 Nov. 1989. U.N. Doc. A/RES/44/25.

United Nations (2001) Convention on the Rights of the Child. Annex IX. *General Comment No. 1. Article 29 (1): The Aims of Education.* CRC/GC/2001/1.

Vandenhole, Wouter, Carton de Wiart, Estelle, Marie-Lou de Clerk, Helene, Mahieu, Paul, Ryngaert, Julie, Timmerman, Christiane and Verhoeven, Marie (2011) Undocumented children and the right to education: Illusory right or empowering lever? *International Journal of Children's Rights* 19, 613–639.

Wahlström, Ninni (2009) The struggle for the right to education in the European Convention on Human Rights. *Journal of Human Rights* 8(2), 150–161.

Wang, Lihua and Holland, Tracey (2011) In search of equity for the migrant children of Shanghai. *Comparative Education* 47(4), 471–487.

13
Health and children's rights

Ursula Kilkelly

1. Introduction

The importance of good health to all children is well recognised and under Article 24 of the UN Convention on the Rights of the Child (CRC), all children have the right to enjoy the highest attainable standard of health, to facilities for the treatment of disease and to access healthcare services. However, children face many, diverse challenges exercising their right to health and there is a huge gulf between the right to health and healthcare and its effective enjoyment by children around the world. The child's right to health is frustrated by healthcare systems that are inaccessible, expensive, inequitable or poor in quality (Harris *et al.*, 2011; Huber *et al.*, 2008). Child mortality, although improving, continues to be a serious problem, especially in sub-Saharan Africa where children under five are 16 times more likely to die than children in the developed world (WHO, 2013). The fact that more than half of the world's early child deaths (6.5 million in 2012) are due to conditions that could be prevented or treated with access to simple, affordable interventions, highlights the complexity of the problem (WHO, 2013). The challenge in implementing the right to health and healthcare thus varies from situations that frustrate the right to access health and healthcare, those that undermine the right to health and those that threaten the way in which the right is protected and realised.

In other ways too, children experience barriers to securing their right to health. For instance, healthcare is usually delivered to children in the presence of parents who frequently enable but sometimes frustrate the child's involvement in healthcare decision-making (Kilkelly and Savage, 2013). The situation is complicated by the intimate involvement of health professionals such as doctors, nurses or therapists. Children may struggle to have their voices heard or their perspective represented adequately in this adult dominated setting (Gabe *et al.*, 2004). Paternalism – where the focus is on the need to protect children from harm rather than enabling them to exercise their rights – is commonplace in children's healthcare. Children's lack of capacity – perceived or real – can sometimes undermine their involvement in healthcare decision-making and has implications for the development of the law relating to consent (Bainham, 1986; Eekelaar, 1986; Fortin, 2009).

The CRC has made a major contribution to the legal protection of children's rights by articulating children's needs and interests as legal claims and entitlements and giving children and those who work with and for them a basis for legal advocacy (Freeman, 2007). In addition to enshrining health and healthcare as a legal right of the child, the indivisibility of rights means that children's rights to education, play, contact with family, and to have a say must also be protected when children come into contact with the healthcare system. At the same time, the CRC says remarkably little about the scope of the child's right to health and how to ensure that children's healthcare is delivered in a rights compliant manner. Nor does the CRC direct states on the many sensitive and controversial issues in children's health, including consent to medical treatment, involvement in medical trials and the impact of poverty on child health. The Committee on the Rights of the Child has provided important guidance to states on these and other contemporary issues of child health but many questions remain. Some of these questions arise from the fact that children are not a homogenous group – they differ not only in age and levels of maturity but in other ways too related to socio-economic background for instance. This complexity is not reflected in the CRC, as the Introduction to this Handbook notes, yet it is crucial to the effective implementation of the child's right to healthcare as this chapter shows. Issues of capacity, perceptions of childhood and different professional attitudes and cultural traditions all add to the complex challenge of ensuring that every child enjoys their right to healthcare. Disparity in socio-economic circumstances also weighs heavily on the extent to which children enjoy their right to health. Poverty, famine and drought frustrate efforts to provide even basic healthcare to children in certain countries meaning that the children's rights issues vary dramatically from the developed to the developing world. On a more positive level, healthcare is a hugely important setting in which to promote and protect children's rights where children, families, health professionals and government agencies are necessary partners to effect children's healthcare rights. Inter-disciplinarity and inter-agency co-operation – at the core of the implementation of children's rights – is present here too. If made to work, however, the benefits are huge. Children's health is not only a right in itself, it enables children to enjoy their other rights to the full and if children's rights are effectively protected in the healthcare setting, the multiplier effects are significant.

Against the backdrop of this complexity, this chapter has two aims – first, it will sketch out the right of the child to health under the CRC. A summary of the key CRC provisions is provided and a brief analysis of the application of the CRC to some of the contemporary issues in child health is presented. Second, the chapter will then consider in more depth the challenges posed by children's rights in healthcare, and will examine with reference to research, the extent to which these rights are being protected in practice. Particular regard is had here to the right of the child to participate in healthcare decision-making, as this is a key barometer of child's rights compliant healthcare. The chapter concludes with an assessment of the challenges that prevent further implementation of children's rights in healthcare.

2. The child's right to health in international law

International law on the right to healthcare can be traced to the Constitution of the World Health Organisation of 1946 and shortly afterwards, the Universal Declaration of Human Rights in 1948. It was not until 1966, however, that the right to health was enshrined in binding international law in the form of the International Covenant on Economic, Social and Cultural Rights (ICESCR), Article 12 of which guarantees to 'everyone' the right to enjoy the highest attainable standard of physical and mental health. More specific to children, Article 12(2) of the ICESCR provides that states are specifically required to take steps to achieve the full realisation of this right including those necessary, *inter alia*, for 'the provision for the reduction of the stillbirth-rate and of infant mortality and for the healthy development of the child'.

In 2000, the UN Committee on Economic, Social and Cultural Rights adopted a General Comment on the right to health where it expanded upon the duty to protect, respect and fulfil the right without discrimination (UN Committee on Economic, Social and Cultural Rights, 2000). According to the General Comment, the right to health has four components – availability, accessibility, affordability and quality. The Committee's commentary on the child's right to health relies heavily on the CRC in highlighting the duty to ensure that, in all policies and programmes on the right to health, the child's best interests are a primary consideration. Specific mention is also made of the need to provide a safe and supportive environment for adolescents that enables them to participate in decisions affecting their health and acquiring information and counselling that helps them to negotiate health-behaviour choices (UN Committee on Economic, Social and Cultural Rights, 2000).

2.1. Convention on the Rights of the Child

In 1989, the adoption of the CRC by the General Assembly of the United Nations recognised explicitly the child's right to healthcare in international law. Article 24 of the CRC makes provision for the child's right to 'the highest attainable standard of health and to facilities for the treatment of illness and the rehabilitation of health' and provides that States shall 'strive to ensure that no child is deprived of his or her right of access to such healthcare services.' Thereafter, the provision focuses on what could be considered basic, minimum standards of child health in that states are required to take appropriate measures in respect of infant and child mortality; the development of primary healthcare; disease and malnutrition; pre- and post-natal care for mothers and health promotion. The emphasis on the needs of children in developing countries is accentuated by the final paragraph, which requires states to 'promote and encourage international co-operation with a view to achieving progressively the full realization of the right recognized in the present article', with particular account being taken of the 'needs of developing countries'. Interestingly, the African Charter on the Rights and Welfare of the Child, which was adopted in 1990 and came into force in 1999, contains very similar provision to the CRC. Article 14 of the Charter also focuses on the core minimum health standards for children including: primary care, prevention, healthcare for mothers and health promotion.

Article 24(3) of the CRC requires states to take 'all effective measures' to abolish traditional practices prejudicial to the health of children (see also Leye and Middelburg, Chapter 17 in this Handbook). The CRC recognises that traditional cultural practices have an impact on children's health and steps must be taken to eliminate them, but it stops short of naming various forms of mutilation or cutting carried out for religious, cultural or social reasons (Fortin, 2009). The Committee on the Rights of the Child has also been slow to define such practices and it is notable that the General Comment on the Right to Health does not deal with Article 24(3), while only a passing reference is made to the elimination of the practice of genital mutilation in the General Comment on Adolescent Health (UN Committee on the Rights of the Child, 2003b: 3). In the absence of explicit protection of the child's right to health in this context, legitimate concerns prevail about the dominance of competing rights claims – including parents' rights and religious/cultural rights – over those of the child in this area (DeLaet, 2012).

Article 24 of the CRC is not the only Convention provision relevant to child health. Also relevant is Article 6, which recognises the right of the child to life, and requires states to secure to children the right to survival and development to the maximum extent possible. This provision – one of the four general principles of the Convention (UN Committee on the Rights of the Child, 1991) – makes it clear that children are entitled to a standard of health that is commensurate with their healthy development. The UN Committee on the Rights of the

Child has carefully linked Articles 6 and 24 to the body of evidence on social determinants of health (Commission on the Social Determinants of Health, 2008). In particular, the Committee has highlighted that the 'many risks and protective factors that underlie the life, survival, growth and development of the child need to be systematically identified in order to design and implement evidence-informed interventions that address a wide range of determinants during the life course' (UN Committee on the Rights of the Child, 2013b: 6).

The CRC's three other general principles – under articles 2, 3 and 12 – resonate loudly in the healthcare setting too. Article 2, which requires states to ensure CRC rights to all children without discrimination on the grounds of 'origin' and 'property' makes it clear that poorer health or disadvantaged access to healthcare services derived from social origin, geographical location or poverty is contrary to the Convention. Conversely, it is argued that child rights and equity principles can help to deliver more effective child health in practice globally (Goldhagen and Waterston, 2007; Goldhagen and Mercer, 2011). But like socio-economic rights more generally, equal enjoyment of the right to health is a huge challenge that is far from met in reality (Marmot *et al.*, 2008; Berry *et al.*, 2010). Significantly though, as Tobin has noted, the drafters of the CRC recognised that the health of children is not compromised merely 'by gaps in medical knowledge, a lack of resources, or inadequacies in the social determinants of health such as housing and food' (Tobin, 2009: 374).

Article 3, which requires the best interests of the child to be a primary consideration in all actions concerning children, reinforces that healthcare policy and the organisation of healthcare must be informed by what is in children's interests, while also highlighting that healthcare must meet the needs of individual children (UN Committee on the Rights of the Child, 2013b: 12). The key question of course is how are the child's best interests or needs to be determined in the healthcare setting (Fortin, 2009). Some health professionals and health systems use a solely medical framework (the 'diagnose and treat dialectic') for determining what treatment or approach to apply to child health (Goldhagen and Mercer, 2011). However, under the CRC, individual children's best interests must be assessed in a holistic manner, based on their 'physical, emotional, social and educational needs, age, sex, relationship with parents and caregivers, and their family and social background, and after having heard their views according to article 12 of the Convention' (UN Committee on the Rights of the Child, 2013b: 13). The Committee on the Rights of the Child has made it clear that hearing the views of children and taking them into account in the decision-making process is the only way to ensure a rights-compliant approach to the implementation of Article 3 (UN Committee on the Rights of the Child, 2009: 15). To aid this process, the Committee has advised that states should develop 'procedures and criteria to provide guidance to health workers in this area' (UN Committee on the Rights of the Child, 2013b: 14).

Article 12 is pivotal to healthcare decision-making concerning children in two ways: the first concerns the involvement of the child in decisions about their individual healthcare treatment and the second requires that children's views are taken into account in healthcare policy and the planning, delivery and improvement of healthcare services (UN Committee on the Rights of the Child, 2009: 20). In relation to the former, views about the limits of children's capacity – specifically in the case of younger children who have no legal entitlement to consent – can inform professionals' attitudes towards them with the result that children may not be involved in any meaningful way in decisions about their healthcare. Yet, as the Committee on the Rights of the Child has pointed out, children should be included in decision-making processes in line with their evolving capacities (UN Committee on the Rights of the Child, 2009: 20). Moreover, children themselves want to be listened to, want more information about their healthcare and want to understand the information they are given (Kilkelly, 2011). To this end, children should be provided with information about 'proposed treatments and their effects and outcomes' (UN Committee on the Rights of the Child, 2009: 20).

There is recognition in Article 5 of the CRC that the role of the parent to support the child's exercise of his/her rights changes with the child's evolving capacity and maturity. At the same time, even very young children are capable of expressing their views if adults develop the skills to listen to them (Alderson, 2007; UN Committee on the Rights of the Child, 2009: 7). This is true for healthcare professionals too who should receive training in this area (UN Committee on the Rights of the Child, 2009: 12). Older children also have the right to be able to participate in healthcare decision-making and respect for their right to privacy under Article 16 requires professionals to create safe spaces to this end (UN Committee on the Rights of the Child, 2003b: 3). Children are not a homogenous group, however, and children who come into contact with the healthcare system have different needs and circumstances (Alderson, 2014). Depending on their age and understanding, their level of familiarity with their health and the healthcare system in which they are treated, children will have different levels of capacity to understand and participate in healthcare decision-making.

Taken together, the provisions of the CRC prescribe healthcare for children that is informed by equitable access, the best interests of the child and children's views and perspectives. This approach applies to individual healthcare decision-making as well as to the way in which healthcare policy and services are developed and implemented. Children of all ages have much to contribute to the development of healthcare policy and efforts to improve service delivery. Respect for children's right to participate requires their voices to be heard in this context also and for this reason, the Committee on the Rights of the Child has recommended that states introduce measures enabling children to 'contribute their views and experiences to the planning and programming of services for their health and development' (UN Committee on the Rights of the Child, 2009: 21). A broader approach requires children's involvement in policy making that has implications for children's health, like in the area of environmental health for example (Spady et al., 2008).

More generally, a children's rights approach to healthcare requires states to put in place a healthcare system that respects not only the child's right to health, but all the child's other rights too. Child-friendly healthcare, as defined by the Council of Europe Guidelines, is 'health care policy and practice that are centred on children's rights, needs, characteristics, assets and evolving capacities, taking into account their own opinion' (Council of Europe, 2011). A child rights approach to healthcare means that under the CRC, children who come into contact with the healthcare system have a right to access education (Article 28), to enjoy play, rest and leisure (Article 31), to enjoy their right to privacy (Article 16) and to have contact with and the support of their parents and carers (Articles 9, 18) throughout this process. Children continue to have the right to be protected from all forms of harm (Article 19) and exploitation (Article 36) and they are entitled to religious freedom (Article 14) and freedom of expression (Article 13). The child's right to information is particularly important in the healthcare context. Children have a general right to access information and material from a diversity of sources, especially information aimed at the promotion of the child's social, spiritual and moral well-being and physical and mental health (Article 17). In addition, the Committee on the Rights of the Child has encouraged states to adopt and implement 'a comprehensive strategy to educate children, their caregivers, policymakers, politicians and professionals working with children about children's right to health, and the contributions they can make to its realization' (UN Committee on the Rights of the Child, 2013b: 19). Healthcare decision-making requires that children are provided with 'adequate and appropriate information' to inform the choices being made are in the child's best interests and to

Health and children's rights

enable them to provide their consent in an informed manner, when possible (UN Committee on the Rights of the Child, 2013a: 17).

3. Contemporary challenges in child health

3.1. Consent

Although the CRC could not be expected to deal with every eventuality and issue affecting child health, it is remarkably silent on a large number of the contemporary dilemmas and controversies. For instance, it makes no explicit reference to what is arguably the key question in child health, i.e. the age at which children can consent to medical treatment without the consent of their parents or carers. Nor does it consider when children should be entitled to refuse such treatment or the limits that might be placed on such decisions (e.g. with regard to euthanasia, organ donation or non-therapeutic research). Although Article 5 recognises the role of parents in providing guidance to children in the exercise of their rights in line with the principle of evolving capacity, the CRC does not stipulate at what age children should be allowed to take responsibility for decision-making in healthcare or what say children should have where their legal consent is not required. Article 12 of the CRC requires that children's views are taken into account in matters that affect them and the Committee on the Rights of the Child has recommended that 'supportive policies are in place and that children, parents and health workers have adequate rights-based guidance on consent, assent and confidentiality' (UN Committee on the Rights of the Child, 2013b: 7). At the same time, health professionals, whose 'decisions and actions' 'impact on children's lives in profound, intimate, and powerful ways' (Lansdown, 2000) are not mentioned in the CRC, which is also silent on whether parents or health professionals should have the final say when consensus cannot be reached.

The CRC announced the recognition of the child's independent status as a rights-holder, making it clear that the traditional dynamic – whereby parents and health professionals alone took the decisions about children's health – had to change (Fortin, 2009). Recognition of children's rights has begun to increase awareness of children's capacity and competence in healthcare decision-making, with the criteria moving from age to understanding (Alderson, 2007). At the forefront of this shift was the 1986 judgment by the House of Lords in Gillick v West Norfolk and Wisbech Area Health Authority ([1986] AC 112), which decided that children under the legal age of consent can have capacity to consent if they are considered mature enough to understand the implications of the decision. A judgment still needs to be made as to whether the child is 'mature enough' and so such developments have not necessarily led to more widespread exercise of autonomy by children in the healthcare process. What autonomy does exist more frequently applies to children's right to consent to, rather than their right to refuse medical treatment (Gilmore and Herring, 2011) and adult-formed views of what is in a child's best interests continue to influence children's involvement in healthcare decision-making (Kilkelly and Donnelly, 2006). Admittedly, the CRC presents a somewhat cloudy picture here in requiring under Article 3 that the best interests of the child be a primary consideration in all actions (including healthcare). This, it is suggested, hands the power back to the adults to make this determination, notwithstanding the requirement under Article 12 that the child's views be taken into account. In this way, the issue of consent to or refusal of medical treatment must be distinguished from the right of the child to have a say in the healthcare decision-making process (Donnelly and Kilkelly, 2011) if greater compliance with children's rights is to be achieved.

Regardless, it is arguable that consideration of what is in a child's best interests outweighs the interference with bodily integrity that proceeding without consent would normally involve. The 'best interests' principle and sometimes even the public interest can outweigh the child's exercise of his/her autonomy in this area (Ribot, 2013). Aside from the many ethical issues here, the question of why it is legitimate to proceed without the consent of a child – indeed faced with the child's opposition to an intervention – when the same standard is not applied to an adult remains unanswered. Freeman has argued, based on Dworkin's theory of 'future orientated consent', that such restrictions on the child's autonomy can be justified because they enable children to mature to independent adulthood (Freeman, 1992). This approach clearly applies only where the autonomy is being limited to preserve life; it does not assist when the decision is to refuse life saving treatment or to hasten death. Should children's exercise of their right to health include a right to refuse medical treatment with the ultimate consequence? Situations like euthanasia (Vrakking *et al.*, 2005) are clearly much more difficult to resolve than where the child is choosing between two different types of life sustaining treatment (Gilmore and Herring, 2011). Similarly, where the medical treatment results in no benefit to the child – such as in areas like non-therapeutic research or organ or bone marrow donation – the search continues for a satisfactory framework to determine its legitimacy and its compliance with children's rights (Fortin, 2009; Lyons, 2011; Alderson, 2014).

3.2. Sexual health

Although Article 24 makes reference to pre- and post-natal care for mothers, it makes no explicit reference to when children themselves become mothers and what entitlements they have to autonomy over their bodies in this context. The Committee on the Rights of the Child has acknowledged the reality of 'high rates of pregnancy among adolescents globally' and recommended that health systems and services are able to 'meet the specific sexual and reproductive health needs of adolescents, including family planning and safe abortion services', ensuring that girls can make autonomous and informed decisions on their reproductive health (UN Committee on the Rights of the Child, 2013b: 13). Although the issue of confidential access to information and counselling on matters of sexual health might be considered too controversial for a binding international treaty, it is disappointing that the Committee's guidance is not more specific. For instance, although the Committee states a preference for privacy and confidentiality with respect to advice and counselling on medical matters, it reserves the right to privacy and confidential services, including treatment, to those 'adolescents deemed mature enough to receive counselling without the presence of a parent' (UN Committee on the Rights of the Child, 2003b: 4). The controversy that this has generated in the courts suggests, perhaps, that the Committee is correct not to establish minimum universal standards in this area (e.g. Bridgeman, 2006; Gilmore and Herring, 2011).

3.3. Health promotion

The importance of health promotion is specifically mentioned in Article 24(2)(e) of the CRC, which highlights the need to equip parents and children with basic knowledge on child health and nutrition. This links in with Article 17 also, which recognises the importance of children having access to information and material from a diversity of sources, especially those aimed at 'the promotion of his or her social, spiritual and moral well-being and physical and mental health'. The importance of providing health information to children in accessible, age appropriate forms and formats, is well recognised in the General Comments also (UN Committee on the Rights of the Child, 2003b, 2013b), where it is linked to preventive healthcare and promotion of healthy life choices. The relevance of 'nutrition' in contemporary times can be linked to obesity as the most significant health risk to children in both developed and increasingly developing countries (WHO, 2014).

The CRC is equally silent on other crucial aspects of child health promotion including children's involvement in medical trials and their access to life-saving medicines and vaccinations. Also unclear is how the CRC would apply when the risk to the child – say of HIV infection or foetal alcohol syndrome – comes from his/her mother (Dabis and Ekpini, 2002; Scott, 2000). Would the child's best interests and his/her right to health trump a mother's right to autonomy and bodily integrity in these circumstances? This issue has been addressed in the Committee's General Comment on HIV/AIDS and the Rights of the Child where states are encouraged to take steps to prevent mother to child transmission of HIV/AIDs including via the provision of essential drugs and medical intervention (UN Committee on the Rights of the Child, 2003a: 8). Given the scale of these threats to children's health and development, it is surprising that they have not been addressed much more directly in the Committee's guidance on the child's right to health.

4. Implementing children's rights in healthcare

In addition to these challenges to children's right to health, multiple barriers also prevent the realisation of children's rights in healthcare. Research provides a useful insight into the extent to which children's rights are implemented in the healthcare setting and multiple small studies on children's experiences and views on healthcare inform international compliance with children's rights norms in this setting. This next section considers this evidence in an effort to examine the progress made in the implementation of children's rights in health by focusing in detail on the specific aspect of children's right to participate in healthcare decision-making.

4.1. Children's right to participate in healthcare decision-making

As already noted, international law is clear about children's right to have a say in decisions that affect them. Healthcare clearly affects children and the centrality of Article 12 to healthcare is confirmed to be the most important right to children across all age groups (Bensted et al., 2014). However, the research presents a complex picture as to the extent to which children enjoy this right in practice (Moore and Kirk, 2010; Coyne, 2008; Martenson and Fagerskiold, 2007; Worrall-Davies and Marino-Francis, 2008).

Several studies show that children are often marginalised from the decision-making process across a range of settings including: hospital inpatient units (Lambert et al., 2008, 2010b; LeFrancois, 2007; Coyne et al., 2006; Alderson, 2014); outpatient departments (Savage and Callery, 2007) and community healthcare (Kilkelly and Donnelly, 2006; Tates et al., 2002). One study (Lambert et al., 2008, 2010b) noted that during healthcare consultations, children were either positioned as 'passive bystanders', as healthcare professionals communicated directly with parents or 'active participants', as healthcare professionals communicated directly with them. The impact of the 'passive' position was that children were left 'overshadowed', eavesdropping in the background, whereas children in the 'active' role were more prepared to ask questions. Observations made in the outpatient departments of two Irish hospitals found that the communication style of healthcare professionals – closed conversations and interrogative questioning – contributed to the largely marginalised position of children (Savage and Callery, 2007). These researchers found that parents' accounts of their children's health (cystic fibrosis) were often privileged over those of their children, and some children spoke of healthcare professionals not believing what they had to say. Staff were friendly towards the children and talked to them about social aspects of their lives, but conversations with them about their health were limited (Savage and Callery, 2007).

Although children have the right to participate in the healthcare process under Article 12 of the CRC, they have no obligation to do so. Striking the right balance between supporting children to be involved, but not requiring that participation can be difficult as children's needs and preferences vary. Apart from the differences between children, a child may move along the spectrum from active to passive involvement in the process requiring health professionals to be constantly attuned to their wishes and their development to ensure that the choice about what role they play lies with the child. Children's preferences about their level of involvement during consultations can vary with age, with younger children preferring their parents to communicate to health professionals, whereas older children mostly prefer to take the lead (Gibson et al., 2010; Garth et al., 2009; Savage and Callery, 2007; Kilkelly and Donnelly, 2006; Coyne et al., 2006). For the health professionals, age and cognitive ability can determine a child's level of involvement in consultations (Garth et al., 2009; Martenson and Fagerskiold, 2007). According to one Irish study, however, professionals were influenced more by a child's age, than his/her capacity to understand or be directly involved (Kilkelly and Donnelly, 2006), implying a belief that younger children are less capable of being involved during healthcare consultations compared to older children. Conversely, research has found that young children have a greater capacity to communicate about their health and well-being than adults are willing to believe (Garth et al., 2009; Savage and Callery, 2007; Alderson and Montgomery, 1996). The reality that one size does not fit all is reinforced by the fact that additional factors – illness experiences, social experiences of communicating with adults and a willingness to be involved – may influence the level of involvement that children want during consultations (Gibson et al., 2010; Alderson et al., 2006). Training and education to deal with the variety of situations that may arise is clearly vital in ensuring that all health professionals have the capacity to respond appropriately to the needs of the child in each individual case (UN Committee on the Rights of the Child, 2003c).

In some studies, children differentiate between making 'small' (those relating to everyday aspects of care, like diet and medication) and 'serious' decisions (relating to surgery for example) (Coyne et al., 2006; Coyne and Gallagher, 2011), presenting mixed views as to whether the latter are made by them alone or shared with carers. These findings suggest that children's participation in decision-making is a matter of degree and accordingly, there is a need for a flexible and individualised approach that meets the needs, choices and desires of the children concerned.

Access to information is important both to facilitate meaningful participation by children in healthcare decision-making and as a right in itself. Research shows that children appreciate the importance of information in the healthcare context. For example, in a survey of young people undertaken for the Council of Europe, 80.9% of the respondents considered it important that children should be given information about what is going to happen to them in the healthcare setting (Kilkelly, 2011; Bensted et al., 2014). In other studies (Kilkelly and Donnelly, 2011; Alderson, 2014), children readily identified that having things (e.g. proposed treatment) explained to them in advance made them less afraid. For children, therefore, there are important, practical reasons for ensuring that they have information that they can understand.

Participation in healthcare decision-making presupposes that children will be informed and will understand the issues being discussed, but providing information in a way that is understood by children and that is relevant to their needs is not straightforward. Using age appropriate language and props has been described by children as a component of their 'ideal model of participation' (Kilkelly and Donnelly, 2006); a finding supported in communication frameworks for working with children (Jaaniste *et al.*, 2007; Alderson and Montgomery, 1996). Yet, this component of an 'ideal model of participation' is not often experienced by children (Buckley and Savage, 2010; Lambert *et al.*, 2010b; Savage and Callery, 2007; Coyne *et al.*, 2006). Regarding language, children have identified the importance of professionals using child-friendly terminology when medical or healthcare information is being communicated to them. Studies have found that the use of 'simple' language in the child's own terms and the avoidance of medical 'jargon' better equips children to understand health information communicated to them (Mitchell-Lowe and Eggleston, 2009; Kilkelly and Donnelly, 2011; Coyne *et al.*, 2006). However, it is evident that as children get older, they want information in terminology that is more age appropriate (Gibson *et al.*, 2010).

There have been surprisingly few studies on information sharing practices with children in healthcare. Some studies – mainly relating to children's hospital experiences – have shown that children want information on what to expect especially in relation to procedures and medical treatments (Coyne and Gallagher, 2011; Migone *et al.*, 2008; Coyne *et al.*, 2006). One general study analysed unsolicited information requests made by children and young people to the Children's First for Health website in the UK, which is an online information resource for this population group (Franck *et al.*, 2008). Over an 18-month period, there were 2,865 hits for general information and 924 hits for specific inquiries. There were more hits from adolescents than younger children. The most common queries related to psychosocial issues, hospital and health services, and normal growth and development. These researchers, along with others (e.g. Gray *et al.*, 2005), illustrate that children are active agents in seeking out information about health and healthcare matters in their own time and space.

There is evidence that children are dissatisfied with the information received from healthcare professionals. One study found that children aged 5 to 11 years were generally dissatisfied with how they were informed about impending procedures such as injections and x-rays (Kilkelly and Donnelly, 2006). Although there was some evidence of procedures being explained, the practice of informing children was found to be sketchy overall and not a planned process. According to Jaaniste *et al.* (2007), healthcare professionals often experience uncertainty about informing children in relation to medical procedures. These researchers offer a framework on the scope of providing children with health-related information: *content* – what to tell them; *format* – how to convey information; *personnel* – who provides information; and *timing* – when to provide information. Using this framework, Buckley and Savage (2010) explored the pre-operative information needs of children (aged 6 to 9 years) undergoing tonsillectomy in one general teaching hospital in Ireland. Children, who were interviewed on the eve of surgery, spoke of having received little information in advance of admission for surgery. One consequence of children having limited information is that they may construct inaccurate mental representations of what might happen and these could be frightening.

Effective communication depends not only on the approach taken, it also depends on the nature of the relationship between those communicating. Children want healthcare professionals to be sympathetic towards them; children in one Irish study identified this quality as definitive of 'a good health professional' (Kilkelly and Donnelly, 2006, 2011). Children need healthcare professionals to empathise with them and their situation and to show some appreciation of what they are going through (Buckley and Savage, 2010; Coyne *et al.*, 2006; Smith and Callery, 2005). Communicating with children in the healthcare context differs from everyday social discourse because private, emotional, or intimate matters may need to be discussed such as talking about stigma around mental health or worrying about the seriousness of illness. In order to deal effectively with children's distressing situations, individual professionals need to exercise 'interpersonal sensitivity' i.e. affective behaviours that pay attention to, and interest in, the child's feelings and concerns (Levetown *et al.*, 2008). Based on a review of evidence of clinical communication in paediatric settings, Levetown *et al.* recommended general behaviours for effective communication practices with children among which are: begin conversation with a broad, non-threatening topic; pay attention to body language and tone of voice; listen actively; use creative communication tools such as drawings and games; talk with the child not at them; and use language that they can understand. The importance to children of their healthcare professional being child-friendly – in the sense of connecting with them through language and approach – is a hugely dominant one across all the literature.

5. Children's participation in policy making and service design

The CRC Committee advocates children's involvement in consultation on healthcare policy (UN Committee on the Rights of the Child, 2013b: 7). In contrast to the growing body of knowledge on children's participation in clinical consultations and decision-making regarding their health, there is less known about the role of children in health service planning, governance, and policy formulation. It is only in recent years that attention has focused on the 'service user' in the healthcare context and the idea of children being service users in healthcare is now slowly gaining momentum internationally. This is partly due to international law obligations under Article 12 of the CRC, and partly due to a wider political agenda concerning democratisation, citizenship and choice – all of which are applicable to all service users (Coad and Shaw, 2008). The evidence available to date on children as service users mostly relates to health service planning, especially children's views and expectations of services. A growth of interest in this area is particularly notable in the UK (Koller *et al.*, 2010; Hoole and Morgan, 2010; Robinson, 2010; Mainey *et al.*, 2009; Coad and Shaw, 2008; Day, 2008; National Children's Bureau, 2005; Dogra, 2005; Boylan, 2004). These reviews or studies collectively draw on children's views across a range of services – acute hospital care, long-term care, community, mental health, and intellectual disability (Spady *et al.*, 2008).

Taken together, the findings indicate a number of key areas that are important to children in service planning: service organisation and access; care delivery processes; staffing (qualifications and communication style); and environment. On service organisation and access, children want accessible, flexible and integrated services that allow for continuity of care. In addition, they want wider access to information about health matters and related services made available to them; the need for community drop-in centres was highlighted in one review (National Children's Bureau, 2005). A specific call for fairness and equality has been made by young people with intellectual disabilities (Hoole and Morgan, 2010). In this study, young people expressed the view that they were not being afforded the same rights to services as their counterparts without disabilities; this reference was specific to social care provision such as housing. Areas highlighted in relation to processes of care delivery have included provision of information and shared decision-making. In addition, children have highlighted that services need to be holistic in perspective to include emotional and social care and not just physical aspects of care; a point made specifically in relation to general and acute healthcare services (Koller *et al.*, 2010; National Children's Bureau, 2005; Goldhagen and Mercer, 2011).

5.1. Children's views on healthcare services

Studies have found that children connect their experience of a quality healthcare service strongly with their views on the qualities of healthcare professionals. In particular, they want staff to be knowledgeable, skilled, competent, and to have expertise specific to a child's health condition or problem (Robinson, 2010). Their relationships with their professionals are important – as noted above, the evidence clearly points to children wanting professionals that are friendly, good communicators, good listeners, empathetic and non-judgemental (Robinson, 2010; Mainey *et al.*, 2009; Coad and Shaw, 2008; Dogra, 2005; National Children's Bureau, 2005; Boylan, 2004). Significantly, these qualities have also been identified as important for others working in the healthcare system, like receptionists (National Children's Bureau, 2005).

Regarding the environment, the evidence points to a number of facilities and resources that children would like to see built into service planning. Play and recreation resources and activities have been highlighted as important to children across a range of healthcare settings (Lambert *et al.*, 2010a; Koller *et al.*, 2010; National Children's Bureau, 2005; Boylan 2004). This is an area reported by children to be inadequate (Migone *et al.*, 2008; Kilkelly, 2011). Play is not only important as a right of the child under Article 31 of the CRC, it is also a vital part of the child-friendly approach to healthcare in that it aims to secure healthcare services to children in a manner that respects their rights. Although there is little published research on the role of play specialists in promoting a culture of respect for children's rights in healthcare settings, there is evidence that organised and supervised play activities by such professionals help to alleviate children's distress and anxieties in relation to procedures such as day surgery (Fereday and Darbyshire, 2008). Their work clearly facilitates the fulfilment of the child's rights to health and to play in the healthcare setting.

Children and young people have also identified the need for developmentally appropriate facilities such as separate adolescent units, bright and colourful décor and age appropriate furniture (Lambert *et al.*, 2010a; National Children's Bureau, 2005; Boylan, 2004). For example, children's (5–8 years) views on the design of the new children's hospital in Ireland includes some important child-focused recommendations such as: quiet reading areas; stepping stone paths leading to play areas; open spaces to allow for physical activities e.g. jumping and dancing; bikes to move around on, and information and communication technology including game consols for playing games (Lambert *et al.*, 2010a). The many specially designed children's hospitals around the world are testament to how seriously this is now viewed. Children's needs regarding facilities and resources are not just recreational and aesthetic but also directly relate to the protection of their rights. For example, older children, in particular, have called for healthcare settings to be designed in ways that promote their privacy during consultations and treatment procedures (Tylee *et al.*, 2007; National Children's Bureau, 2005; Boylan 2004). The need for distinct child-friendly settings for different categories of children is also applicable to younger children (Lambert *et al.*, 2010a) and is an important illustration of the indivisibility of children's rights in the healthcare context.

Children's needs across all areas (e.g. organisation of and access to services; care delivery processes; staffing and the environment) have been highlighted (Boylan, 2004; National Children's Bureau, 2005). In order to promote respect for children and their rights, health services need to be planned and implemented in accordance with children's own identified needs. In reality, this aspiration is far from realised (Hoole and Morgan, 2010; Coad and Shaw, 2008; Dogra, 2005) and there is little substantive evidence on the long-term impact that children's views have on changing and improving services to meet their needs. If children are to be respected as service users, however, it is important to go beyond recording their views about services and their recommendations for how this should be changed. Although this is an important baseline, respect for children's rights in healthcare, and indeed the spirit of service user involvement, demands that children need to be supported to actively engage in service organisation, governance and policy formulation. Children's participation at this level is now beginning to emerge (e.g. Coad and Shaw, 2008; Godfrey, 2003; Owens, 2010; Burke *et al.*, 2010).

5.2. Challenges implementing children's rights to participate in healthcare decision-making

Progress is being made in the implementation of the child's right to participate in healthcare decision-making, but this is a complex and sensitive process. Barriers identified by the research include: poor communication skills among professionals who use medical jargon rather than child friendly language; lack of time and appropriate facilities; ignoring or disregarding children's preferences and professional and parental attitudes and beliefs about age and competence of children (Moore and Kirk, 2010; Kelsey et al., 2007; Runeson et al., 2007; Kilkelly and Donnelly, 2006). The absence or inadequacy of training for those who work with and for children in the healthcare setting is a dominant concern, identified by both health professionals and children themselves (Kilkelly and Donnelly, 2006). A range of measures are necessary to address these barriers and given their mutual dependency, the measures must be addressed simultaneously to: health professionals, parents and carers and children. While resources may be required to ensure that the healthcare environment and infrastructure (hospitals, waiting areas, equipment, materials, etc.) enables respect for children's rights, cultural and traditional barriers to children's rights are arguably more difficult to dismantle. For instance, parents opposed to having their child involved in healthcare decision-making – perhaps because they want to protect them from a negative prognosis (Coyne and Gallagher, 2011; Kilkelly and Donnelly, 2006; Runeson et al., 2002; Tates et al., 2002) – may not be aware of the benefits to children of being informed and supported to take on a greater role in decision-making. Education will help parents to understand the importance of listening to children in this context and what they can do to support their child to realise his/her rights. At the same time, parents who wish to promote their child's participation in decision-making may face obstacles in doing so, such as where the healthcare professional is the controlling influence (Hallstrom and Elander, 2004). Healthcare professionals need to find better ways to navigate through what can be a delicate process in order to ensure that children are spoken to directly, understand what is going to happen to them and agree to any interventions proposed (Moore and Kirk, 2010). They need to understand the significance of treating the child as a rights-holder in the healthcare process and to develop special skills to balance the right of parents to decide what is in their child's interests with their own professional understanding of the child's needs and rights. Child-friendly healthcare requires respect for children as the primary rights-holder; what children seek is accessible information and safe spaces in which they can express themselves freely and be supported to understand their health and healthcare better. Parents and professionals, on the other hand, should be made aware of the strength of children's ability to reflect on their experiences and to contribute in a meaningful way to decisions about their healthcare (Alderson and Montgomery, 1996; Alderson, 2014). Addressing the attitudes, roles and competencies of all three groups is thus necessary to maximise respect for the rights of the child in healthcare.

Implementing children's rights to healthcare depends to a large extent on the attitudes, skills and competence of those providing healthcare services at primary, secondary and tertiary levels. The scope and nature of professional training and ongoing development in child development, children's rights and communication with children will influence the extent to which children are treated as individuals with the capacity to understand information about their health and healthcare and to participate, directly or indirectly in healthcare decision-making (Kilkelly and Donnelly, 2006). For this reason, the Committee on the Rights of the Child has recommended that all healthcare professionals receive systematic training on children's rights and child development (UN Committee on the Rights of the Child, 2003c: 66–70, and 2010: 49). Raising awareness about children's rights among adults, notably parents and carers, and among children themselves is also vital to the implementation of children's rights (see Article 42). Research shows that the awareness of children's rights must also be generated among healthcare managers and policy makers in order to ensure that those who set the priorities for the development of the healthcare system and who decide how and where to deliver children's healthcare services are sensitive to the needs and rights of those most affected by their decisions (Kilkelly and Savage, 2013).

According to the Committee on the Rights of the Child, translating rights into good healthcare practice requires the adoption of legislative, administrative and other measures, expending the maximum extent of available resources (Article 4). The implementation of the Convention thus requires the adoption of relevant law and policy to promote the full enjoyment of children's rights in healthcare. It also requires the establishment of institutions, services and facilities responsible for the care or protection of children, and these must conform to the standards established by competent authorities, particularly in the areas of safety, health, in the number and suitability of their staff, as well as competent supervision (Article 3(3)). Data collection on the extent to which children are enjoying their rights in healthcare is vital to monitor progress and ensure on-going implementation of the Convention (Alderson, 2014). States are encouraged to develop indicators to this end and to ensure that children have the opportunity to feed their experiences into the evaluation process (UN Committee on the Rights of the Child, 2003c: 12). Similarly, the establishment of effective monitoring bodies will ensure that targets are being met and progress maintained in the delivery of child-friendly healthcare (UN Committee on the Rights of the Child, 2003c: 3).

Ensuring that children's rights are fulfilled in the healthcare system is thus a challenging process. It requires that:

- Healthcare law and policy and the organisation and delivery of health services recognises children as rights-holders, focuses on the child's best interests and on the full realisation of the child's right to health and healthcare while respecting the child's rights to family support, protection from harm, access to education, rest and play and privacy;
- Decision-making on matters that affect the child is informed by children's views and perspectives including individual clinical decisions and healthcare policy development and improvement to services;
- Services are organised and implemented in a manner that recognises children's special needs, circumstances and vulnerability, with reference to their evolving capacity and changing needs.

6. Conclusion

This chapter set out the international law on children's rights in healthcare, by providing an overview of the CRC provision on the right to health and the guidance of the Committee on the Rights of the Child and the Council of Europe Guidelines on Child-friendly Healthcare. Attention was drawn to several contemporary challenges of child health: consent, sexual health and health promotion and these complex issues were discussed from the perspective of children's rights.

The case study of the child's right to participate in healthcare illustrates the depth and range of research that identifies both the barriers to the implementation of children's rights in this setting and the lessons that show that healthcare is informed by children's interests, views and perspectives. Healthcare is a hugely important setting in which to promote and protect children's rights. Children's health is not only a right in itself, it enables children to enjoy their own rights to the full. Implementing children's rights in healthcare brings with it a range of challenges – from traditional attitudes to the availability of resources – that must be addressed if children are to be treated as rights holders in the healthcare system.

Questions for debate and discussion

- To what extent does the CRC provide a framework for responding adequately to contemporary challenges in child health?
- What does research tell us about children's right to have a say in healthcare decision-making?
- What are the barriers to the realisation of CRC rights in healthcare?
- What measures should be taken to promote greater compliance with children's rights in healthcare settings?
- What challenges does the specific context of healthcare bring to children's rights?

Acknowledgements

With thanks to all of the children who contributed to all of the studies cited here and to the Department of Children and Youth Affairs, the Ombudsman for Children and the Council of Europe who have supported my work in this area. This piece draws from research undertaken with my colleague Professor Eileen Savage, Head of the School of Nursing and Midwifery at University College Cork. All mistakes remain my own.

References

Alderson, P. (2014). Children as patients. In Melton, G., Ben-Arieh, A., Cashmore, J. Goodman, G. and Worley, N. (eds). *The Sage Handbook of Child Research*. London: Sage.

Alderson, P. (2007). Competent children? Minors' consent to health care treatment and research. *Social Science and Medicine*, 65(11): 2272–2283.

Alderson, P. and Montgomery, J. (1996). *Health Care Choices: Making Decisions with Children*. London: Institute for Public Policy Research.

Alderson, P., Sutcliffe, K., and Curtis, K. (2006). Children as partners with adults in their medical care. *Archives of Disease in Childhood*, 91, 300–303.

Bainham, A. (1986). The balance of power in family decisions, *Cambridge Law Journal*, 45, 262

Bensted, R., Hargreaves, D.S., Lombard, J., Kilkelly, U. and Viner, R.M. (2014). Comparison of healthcare priorities in childhood and early/late adolescence: Analysis of cross-sectional data from eight countries in the Council of Europe Child-friendly Healthcare Survey, 2011. *Child: Care, Health and Development*, 1–6.

Berry, J., Bloom, S., Foley, S. and Palfrey, J. (2010). Health inequity in children and youth with chronic health conditions. *Pediatrics*, 126(Suppl 3), s111–s119.

Boylan, P. (2004). Children's Voices Project. *Feedback from Children and Young People about their Experience and Expectations of Healthcare*. Commission for Health Improvement. National Health Service. Available at www.cqc.org.uk/_db/_documents/04012717.pdf

Bridgeman, J. (2006). Commentary: Young people and sexual health. Whose rights? Whose responsibilities? *Medical Law Review* 14(3), 318.

Buckley, A. and Savage, E. (2010). Preoperative information needs of children undergoing tonsillectomy. *Journal of Clinical Nursing*, 19, 2879–2887.

Burke, K., Owens, S. and Ghate, D. (2010). *Learning from Experience to Inform the Future: Findings Emerging from the Initial Phase of the Children's Services Committee in Ireland*. Dublin: Centre for Effective Services. Available at www.effectiveservices.org

Coad, J.E. and Shaw, K.L. (2008). Is children's choice in health care rhetoric or reality? A scoping review. *Journal of Advanced Nursing*, 64, 318–327.

Coyne, I., Hayes, E., Gallagher, P. and Regan, G. (2006). *Giving Children a Voice: Investigation of Children's Experiences of Participation in Consultation and Decision-Making in Irish Hospitals*. Dublin: Office of the Minister for Children.

Coyne, I. (2008). Children's participation in consultations and decision- making at health service level: A critical review of the literature. *International Journal of Nursing Studies*, 45, 1682–1689.

Coyne, I. and Gallagher, P. (2011). Participation in communication and decision-making: Children and young people's experiences in a hospital setting. *Journal of Clinical Nursing*, 20(15–16), 2334–2343.

Commission on the Social Determinants of Health (2008). *Closing the gap in a generation: Health equity through action on the social determinants of health*. Final Report of the Commission on Social Determinants of Health. Geneva, World Health Organization.

Council of Europe (2011). *Guidelines on Child-friendly Healthcare*. Adopted by the Committee of Ministers on 21 September 2011 at the 1121st meeting of the Ministers' Deputies. Available at www.coe/int/children

Dabis, F. and Ekpini, E.R. (2002). HIV-1/AIDS and maternal and child health in Africa. *The Lancet*, 359(9323), 2097–2104

Day, C. (2008). Children's and young people's involvement and participation in mental health care. *Child and Adolescent Mental Health*, 13, 2–8.

DeLaet, D. (2012). Genital autonomy, children's rights and competing rights claims in international human rights law. *The International Journal of Children's Rights*, 20(4), 554–583.

Dogra, N. (2005). What do children and young people want from mental health services? *Current Opinions in Psychiatry*, 18, 370–373.

Donnelly, M. and Kilkelly, U. (2011). Child friendly healthcare: Delivering on the right to be heard. *Medical Law Review*, 19(1), 27–54.

Eekelaar, J. (1986). The emergence of children's rights. *Oxford Journal of Legal Studies*, 6, 161–182.

Fereday, J. and Darbyshire, P. (2008). Making the wait easier: Evaluating the role of supervised play in a surgical admission area. *Neonatal., Paediatric and Child Health Nursing*, 11(1), 4–9.

Fortin, J. (2009). *Children's Rights and the Developing Law* (3rd ed.). Cambridge: Cambridge University Press.

Franck, L., Noble, G. and McEvoy, M. (2008). Enquiring minds want to know: Topics requested by users of a children's health information website. *Patient Education and Counselling*, 72, 168–171.

Freeman, M. (1992). Taking children's rights more seriously, in Freeman, M. (ed.), *The International Library of Essays on Rights: Children's Rights*. England: Dartmouth.

Freeman, N. (2007). Why it remains important to take children's rights more seriously. *International Journal of Children's Rights*, 15, 5–23.

Gabe, J., Olumide, G. and Bury, M. (2004). 'It takes three to tango': A framework for understanding patient partnership in paediatric clinics. *Social Science and Medicine*, 59, 1071–1079.

Garth, B., Murphy, G.C. and Reddihough, D.S. (2009). Perceptions of participation: Child patients with a disability in the doctor-parent-child partnership. *Patient Education and Counselling*, 74, 45–52.

Gray, N.J., Klein, J.D., Noyce, P.R., Sesselberg, T.S. and Cantrill, J.A. (2005). Health information-seeking behaviour in adolescence: The place of the internet. *Social Science and Medicine*, 60, 1467–1478.

Gibson, F., Aldiss, S., Horstman, M., Kumpunen, S. and Richardson, A. (2010). Children and young people's experiences of cancer care: A qualitative research study using participatory methods. *International Journal of Nursing Studies*, 47, 1397–1407.

Gilmore, S. and Herring, J. (2011). No is the hardest word: Consent and children's autonomy. *Child and Family Law Quarterly* 3.

Godfrey, A. (2003). Children's service planning: The process and implications for wider partnership working. *Child Care in Practice*, 9, 181–198.

Goldhagen, J. and Waterston, J. (2007). Why children's rights are central to international child health. *Archives of Disease in Childhood*, 92: 176–180.

Goldhagen, J. and Mercer, R. (2011). Child health equity: From theory to reality, in A. Invernizzi and J. Williams (eds), *The Human Rights of Children: From Visions to Implementation*. Aldershot, UK: Ashgate.

Hallstrom, I. and Elander, G. (2004). Decision-making during hospitalization: parents' and children's involvement. *Journal of Clinical Nursing*, 13, 367–375.

Harris, B., Goudge, J. Ataguba, J.E., McIntyre, D. Nxumalo, N., Jikwana, S. and Chersich, M. (2011). Inequities in access to health care in South Africa. *Journal of Public Health Policy*, 32, 102–123.

Hoole, L. and Morgan, S. (2010). 'It's only right that we get involved': Service-user perspectives on involvement in learning disability services. *British Journal of Learning Disabilities*, 39, 5–10.

Huber, M., Stanciole, A., Wahlbeck, K., Tamsma, N., Torres, F., Jelfs, E. and Bremner, J. (2008). *Equality in and Equality of Access to Healthcare Services*. Brussels: European Commission.

Jaaniste, T., Hayes, B. and Von Baeyer, C.L. (2007). Providing children with information about forthcoming medical procedures: A review and synthesis. *Clinical Psychology Science and Practice*, 14, 124–143.

Kelsey, J., Abelson-Mitchell, N. and Skirton, H. (2007). Perceptions of young people about making in the acute healthcare environment. *Paediatric Nursing*, 19, 14–18.

Kilkelly, U. and Donnelly, M. (2006). *The Child's Right to be Heard in the Healthcare Setting: Perspectives of Children, Parents and Health Professionals*. Dublin: Office of the Minister for Children.

Kilkelly, U. (2011). *Child Friendly Healthcare: The Views and Experiences of Children and Young People in the Council of Europe*. Strasbourg: Council of Europe.

Kilkelly, U. and Donnelly, M. (2011). Participation in healthcare: The views and experiences of children and young people. *International Journal of Children's Rights*, 19, 107–125.

Kilkelly, U. and Savage, E. (2013). *Child-friendly Healthcare: A Report Commissioned by the Ombudsman for Children*. Dublin: Ombudsman for Children.

Koller, D., Nicholas, D., Gearing, R. and Kalfa, O. (2010). Paediatric pandemic planning: Children's perspectives and recommendations. *Health and Social Care in the Community*, 18, 396–377.

Lambert, V., Glacken, M., and McCarron, M. (2008). 'Visible-ness': The nature communication for children admitted to a specialist children's hospital in the Republic of Ireland. *Journal of Clinical Nursing*, 17, 3092–3102.

Lambert, V., Coad, J., Hicks, P. and Glacken, M. (2010a). *Physical Places and Social Spaces for Young Children in Hospital*. Dublin: National Paediatric Hospital Project.

Lambert, V., Glacken, M. and McCarron, M. (2010b). Communication between children and health professionals in a child hospital setting: A child transitional communication model. *Journal of Advanced Nursing*, 67, 569–582.

Lansdown, G. (2000). Implementing children's rights and health. *Archives of Disease in Childhood*, 83, 286–288.

LeFrancois, B.A. (2007). Children's participation rights: Voicing opinions in inpatient care. *Child and Adolescent Mental Health*, 12, 94–97.

Levetown, M. and the Committee on Bioethics (2008). Communicating with children and families: From everyday interactions to skill in conveying distressing information. *Pediatrics*, 121(5), e1441–e1460.

Lyons, B. (2011). Obliging children. *Medical Law Review*, 19(1), 55–85.

Mainey, A., Ellis, A. and Lewis, J. (2009). *Children's Views of Services: A Rapid Review*. London: National Children's Bureau.

Marmot, M., Friel, S., Bell, R., Houweling, T. and Taylor, S. (2008). Closing the gap in a generation: Health equity through action on the social determinants of health. *The Lancet*, 372(9650), 1661–1669.

Martenson, E.K., and Fagerskiold, A.M. (2007). A review of children's decision-making competence in health care. *Journal of Clinical Nursing*, 17, 3131–3141.

McPherson, A.C., Glazebrook, C., Forster, D., James, C. and Smyth, A. (2006). A randomized, controlled trial of an interactive educational computer package for children with asthma. *Pediatrics*, 117, 1046–1054.

Migone, M., McNicholas, F. and Lennon, R. (2008). Are we following the European charter? Children, parents and staff perceptions. *Child: Care, Health and Development*, 34, 409–417.

Mitchell-Lowe, M. and Eggleston, M. (2009). Children as consumer participants of child and adolescent mental health services. *Australasian Psychiatry*, 17, 287–290.

Moore, L. and Kirk, S. (2010). Literature Review of children's and young people's participation in decisions relating to healthcare. *Journal of Clinical Nursing*, 19, 2215–2225.

National Children's Bureau (2005). *Children and Young People's Views on Health and Health Services: A Review of the Evidence*. London: National Children's Bureau.

Owens, S. (2010). *An Introductory Guide to the Key Terms and Interagency Initiatives in Use in the Children's Services Committees in Ireland*. Centre for Effective Services. Available at www.effectiveservices.org.

Ribot, J. (2013). Underage abortion and beyond: Developments of Spanish law in competent minor's autonomy. *Medical Law Review*, 20(1), 48–66.

Robinson, S. (2010). Children and young people's views of health professionals in England. *Journal of Child Health Care*, 14, 310–326.

Runeson, I., Hallstrom, I., Elander, G. and Hermeren, G. (2002). Children's participation in the decision-making process during hospitalization: an observational study. *Nursing Ethics*, 9, 583–598.

Runeson, I., Mårtensson, E. and Enskär, K. (2007). Children's knowledge and degree of participation in decision making when undergoing a clinical diagnostic procedure. *Pediatric Nursing*, 33, 505–511.

Savage, E. and Callery, P. (2007). Clinic consultations with children and parents on the dietary management of cystic fibrosis. *Social Science and Medicine*, 64, 363–374.

Scott, R. (2000). Maternal duties toward the unborn? Soundings from the law of tort *Medical Law Review*, 8(1), 1

Smith, L. and Callery, P. (2005). Children's account of their pre-operative information needs. *Journal of Clinical Nursing*, 14, 230–238.

Spady, D., Ries, N., Ladd, B.D., Buka, I., Osornio-Vargas, A.R. and Soskolne, C.L. (2008). Governance instruments that protect children's environmental health: Is enough being done? *Environmental Law Review*, 10(3), 200–217.

Tates, K., Meeuwesen, L., Elbers, E. and Bensing, J. (2002). 'I've come for his throat': Roles and identities in doctor-parent-child communication. *Child Care Health and Development*, 28, 109–116.

Tobin, J. (2009). The international obligation to abolish traditional practices harmful to children's health: What does it mean and require of states? *Human Rights Law Review*, 9(3), 373–396.

Tylee, A., Haller, D., Graham, T., *et al.* (2007). Youth-friendly primary care services: How are we doing and what more needs to be done? *Lancet*, 369(9572), 1565–1573.

UN Committee on Economic, Social and Cultural Rights (2000). *General Comment No 14: the Right to the Highest Attainable Standard of Health*. E/C.12/2000/4.

UN Committee on the Rights of the Child (1991). *General Guidelines Regarding the Form and Content of Initial Reports to be Submitted by States Parties under Article 44, Paragraph 1(a) of the Convention.* CRC/C/5/1991.

UN Committee on the Rights of the Child (2003a). *General Comment No 3. HIV/AIDS and the Right of the Child.* CRC/GC/2003/3.

UN Committee on the Rights of the Child (2003b). *General Comment No 4. Adolescent Health and Development in the Context of the Convention on the Rights of the Child.* CRC/C/GC/4/2003.

UN Committee on the Rights of the Child (2003c). *General Comment No 5. General Measures of Implementation of the Convention on the Rights of the Child.* CRC/C/GC/5/2003.

UN Committee on the Rights of the Child (2009). *General Comment No 12 on the Rights of the Child to be Heard.* CRC/C/GC/12/2009.

UN Committee on the Rights of the Child (2013a). *General Comment No 14 on the right of the child to have his or her best interests taken as a primary consideration.* CRC/C/GC/14/2013.

UN Committee on the Rights of the Child (2013b). *General comment No 15 on the right of the child to the enjoyment of the highest attainable standard of health.* CRC/C/GC/15/2013.

Vrakking, A., van der Heide, V. Frans, W. Arts, W., Pieters, R., van der Voort, E., Rietjens, J., Onwuteaka-Philipsen, D., van der Maas, P. and van der Wal., G. (2005). Medical end-of-life decisions for children in the Netherlands. *Archives of Pediatrics and Adolescent Medicine*, 159(9), 802–809.

World Health Organisation (2013). *Children: Reducing Mortality.* Factsheet No 178. Available at www.who.int/mediacentre/factsheets/fs178/en/

World Health Organisation (2014). *Obesity and Overweight.* Factsheet No 311. Available at www.who.int/mediacentre/factsheets/fs311/en/

Worrall-Davies, A. and Marino-Francis, F. (2008). Eliciting children's and young people's views of child and adolescent mental health services: A systematic review of best practice. *Child and Adolescent Mental Health*, 13, 9–15.

14
Juvenile justice from an international children's rights perspective

Ton Liefaard

1. Introduction

1.1. Juvenile justice: A children's rights issue

Since the adoption of the UN Convention on the Rights of the Child (CRC) in 1989 and its entry into force in 1990, juvenile justice[1] can be considered an international children's rights issue. The 195 countries that have endorsed the CRC are under the obligation to safeguard the rights of 'every child alleged as, accused of, or recognized as having infringed the penal law' (art. 40 (1) CRC), which boils down to 1) fair treatment, with respect for children's inherent dignity and the right to a fair trial, and 2) treatment in a manner that takes into account children's age (child-specific treatment).

The CRC has served as a catalyst for additional standard setting at the international (UN) and regional level (note that there is no other human rights area that has resulted in so many standards at the international level; see below), for law reform in many domestic jurisdictions and for a growing body of jurisprudence, internationally and domestically. Yet, despite the increased attention for juvenile justice and almost universal endorsement of the CRC, the rights and freedoms of children in conflict with the law are often not adhered to, with devastating impact on their lives, development and future perspectives. There is, in other words, a significant gap between international and national human rights standards applicable to

---

[1] This chapter refers to juvenile justice as the system established to respond to children who (allegedly) committed criminal offences (i.e. everyone under the age of 18 when committing the (alleged) criminal offence; art. 1 CRC). A rough and simplified distinction can be made between systems that primarily have a *welfare* orientation, that is: focusing more on care and protection of children and less on the competence, accountability and rights of children, and systems with a *justice* orientation, in which the competence and accountability of children have a prominent position.

children (allegedly[2]) in conflict with the law and the administration of juvenile justice in practice.

1.2. Complexity of juvenile justice and children's rights implementation

The challenges concerning the implementation of children's rights in the context of juvenile justice are related to the complexity of this particular area and its inherent tensions, ambiguities and controversies. A first important challenge relates to the objectives of juvenile justice, which are plural and serve different and potentially conflicting interests. In general, interventions towards juvenile delinquency are primarily designed to serve the interests of society, that is: to protect society against violent and dangerous offenders through incapacitation, deterrence and prevention, to restore legal order and/or to realize some level of retribution (accountability), restoration or reparation for victims[3] and communities. At the same time, many juvenile justice systems are based on the assumption that juvenile offenders are different from adults and require special, pedagogically oriented interventions, which focus on the (short and long term) interests of the child offender and aim to prevent recidivism through education and reintegration. Balancing the different interests and related objectives is far from easy. Although one could defend that the interests of child offender and society are strongly connected, particularly in the long run, they are often perceived as conflicting opposites, which relates to a second challenge underscoring the particular complexity of juvenile justice.

Juvenile justice is an area that finds itself in the very heart of public interest and debate. It is significantly influenced by perceptions (true or false), (public) opinions and stigmas. As a consequence it is an easy prey for 'tough on crime' or 'zero tolerance' approaches (see e.g. Smith 2014; Cavadino and Dignan 2006), often at the cost of a nuanced, evidence- and rights-based imagery of juvenile offenders and offending. In general, children in and around the juvenile justice system belong to the most stigmatized children of society, together with children belonging to minorities, immigrant children, street children and children in need of (mental health or alternative) care. In addition, there are persistent misconceptions regarding the incidence and prevalence of juvenile delinquency, its impact on public safety and effective strategies to prevent or respond to juvenile offending.

The challenges concerning children's rights implementation in the area of juvenile justice are furthermore related to the wide variety of juvenile justice practices throughout the world and within countries. Comparative and systematic analyses of juvenile justice systems reveal the absence of a universal notion of what a juvenile justice system should look like and what this means for critical juvenile justice issues, including, among others: accountability, proportionality, participation, prevention and sentencing (see e.g. Cavadino and Dignan 2006; Cipriani 2009; Dünkel et al. 2010; Rap 2013). One comes across stark differences in the way children in conflict with the law are dealt with; differences that can be explained by the historical background of systems, perceptions with regard to childhood, children's capacity, punishment, protection, etc., the context of juvenile delinquency, including social factors such as poverty,

---

2 Children in the juvenile justice system are often referred to as 'children in conflict with the law'. While using this terminology, one should not disregard that until a judicial body convicts the child of committing a criminal offence he or she is under the allegation of being in conflict with the law.
3 The position of victims has gained significant attention in many domestic jurisdictions as well as at the international level. This includes the position of child victims; see e.g. art. 39 CRC and the Guidelines on Justice in Matters Involving Child Victims and Witnesses of Crime, ECOSOC Res. 2005/20.

social exclusion and stigmatization, existing institutional structures and the availability of financial and human resources.

Finally, it is important to highlight that juvenile justice systems as such are rather complex systems, with different stages and related interests (from the initial arrest, police interrogations and pre-trial investigations to the trial in court and the enforcement of sentences), with different actors with different roles, and with different implications for the way children are and should be treated. When assessing the implementation of children's rights, one cannot disregard the complexity of the juvenile justice system and its variety of stages and institutions.

1.3. Focus of the chapter

This non-exhaustive list of challenges underscoring the complexity of the area of juvenile justice and the implementation of children's rights in this particular area raises the question to what extent international children's rights provide authoritative guidance on how to approach the (legal) position of children in conflict with the law at the domestic level. International children's rights standards relevant for juvenile justice and the way they have evolved since the 1980s are strongly interrelated with the (development of) domestic juvenile justice systems (see e.g. Trépanier 2007). Developments at the domestic level have also shaped the development of international standards. At the same time, international children's rights are designed to set an international benchmark concerning the treatment of children in conflict with the law and the protection of their rights and freedoms (see also Goldson and Muncie 2012).

This chapter aims to clarify what this benchmark looks like, how clear and unambiguous it is (i.e. one of the requirements for providing authoritative guidance) and to what extent it can contribute to a common (or universal) understanding of a child rights oriented juvenile justice system. It focuses on the key issues of juvenile justice from an international children's rights perspective, which can be divided into three categories. The first category revolves around the requirement to set up a specific justice system for children in conflict with the law and relates to the need for specificity and specialization, the objectives of the juvenile justice system and age limits (see section 3). The second category of key issues is about fair proceedings and the safeguarding of the right to a fair trial for children, including the right to effective participation and the broader and more recent notion of child-friendly justice (see section 4). The third category concerns dispositions in juvenile justice cases and includes diversion, non-custodial sentences (often referred to as alternative sentences), extreme sentences and deprivation of liberty (see section 5). This chapter starts with an overview of the development of the frame of international juvenile justice standards and related non-legal and domestic developments that have shaped the global juvenile justice agenda (see section 2).

2. Legal framework of international and regional juvenile justice standards[4]

2.1. Child-specific standards at the international (UN) level

As highlighted in the introduction, the number of international and regional standards with regard to the administration of justice is relatively high.[5] The first relevant set of international

---

4   For a more elaborated analysis of the relevant international and regional juvenile justice standards see Liefaard 2008, Chapter 2.
5   See e.g. the list of standards regarding human rights in the administration of justice exceeds all other lists on www.ohchr.org/EN/ProfessionalInterest/Pages/UniversalHumanRightsInstruments.aspx (last visited 29 May 2014).

juvenile justice standards was the UN Standard Minimum Rules for the Administration of Juvenile Justice, also known as the Beijing Rules.[6] Dating from 1985, this set of rules preceded the CRC and provides detailed guidance on the administration of a special justice system for children. Article 40 of the CRC has codified the Beijing Rules, obviously in a less detailed manner, and it generated two additional UN resolutions: the UN Rules for the Protection of Juveniles Deprived of their Liberty (unofficially known as the Havana Rules)[7] and the UN Guidelines for the Prevention of Juvenile Delinquency (the Riyadh Guidelines).[8] All three UN resolutions are as such not legally binding, but they are to be used for the interpretation and implementation of article 40 CRC and related CRC provisions, including article 37 CRC that enshrines the prohibition of torture and other forms of cruel, inhuman or degrading treatment or punishment, the prohibition of capital punishment and requirements with regard to deprivation of liberty, including life imprisonment (see e.g. UN Committee on the Rights of the Child 2007, para. 4 and 88). The CRC and the UN resolutions provide a comprehensive legal framework concerning the rights of children subject to criminal justice proceedings and dispositions, including rules regarding the objectives of juvenile justice and strategies for prevention and diversion (see section 5). Another significant document that has been developed at the international level is the 10th General Comment of the UN Committee on the Rights of the Child (hereafter: CRC Committee) on 'Children's rights in juvenile justice', adopted in 2007 (CRC Committee 2007). This document provides States parties detailed guidance on how to administer a juvenile justice system that is in conformity with international children's rights. The CRC Committee underscores that a national juvenile justice that is compliant with the CRC and related international standards, both legally binding treaties and related soft law instruments 'will provide States parties with possibilities to respond to children in conflict with the law in an effective manner serving not only the best interests of children, but also of the short- and long-term interests of the society at large' (CRC Committee 2007, para. 3). The CRC Committee has not supported this claim with empirical evidence, but it represents the Committee's belief that a children's rights-based approach contributes to a more effective juvenile justice system.

The UN's *general* human rights instruments that preceded the CRC remain of relevance for juvenile justice. The International Covenant on Civil and Political Rights (ICCPR), for example, provides rules with regard to fair trial (art. 14 and 15), punishment (art. 6 and 7) and deprivation of liberty (art. 9 and 10). In addition, the Convention against Torture (CAT), as well as resolutions, such as the 1955 Standard Minimum Rules for the Treatment of Prisoners[9] and the United Nations Standard Minimum Rules for Non-custodial Measures (The Tokyo Rules) are relevant for children.[10]

2.2. Child-specific standards at the regional level

There are many relevant instruments at the regional levels, although they more or less set similar standards. At the European level, for example, the Council of Europe has issued a number of recommendations and guidelines that are relevant for the juvenile justice systems of its 47

---

6   GA Res. 40/33 of 29 November 1985.
7   GA Res. 45/113 of 14 December 1990.
8   GA Res. 45/112 of 14 December 1990. Prevention is of great significance, but will not be addressed in this chapter.
9   See ECOSOC resolutions 663 C (XXIV) of 31 July 1957 and 2076 (LXII) of 13 May 1977.
10 GA Res. 45/110 of 14 December 1990.

member states. The most important ones are the 2003 Recommendation concerning new ways of dealing with juvenile delinquency and the role of juvenile justice[11] and the 2008 European Rules for juvenile offenders subject to sanctions or measures[12] (hereafter: European Rules for juvenile offenders). The latter provides detailed guidance on how to enforce custodial and non-custodial sanctions and measures. A more recent development concerns the development of 'Guidelines on child-friendly justice' by the Council of Europe. These guidelines 'aim to ensure that, in any [justice] proceedings all rights of children, among which the right to information, to representation, to participation and to protection, are fully respected with due consideration to the child's level of maturity and understanding and to the circumstances of the case' and without jeopardizing the rights of other parties involved (Guidelines, para. I.3). Justice for children in a broad sense, including juvenile justice, should be 'accessible, age appropriate, speedy, diligent, adapted to and focuses on the needs and rights of the child, respecting the rights of the child including the rights to due process, to participate in and to understand the proceedings, to respect for private and family life and to integrity and dignity' (Guidelines, para. II.c). The Guidelines on child-friendly justice have served as an example for the Guidelines on Action in the Justice System for Children in Africa, adopted in Kampala in 2011 together with The Munyonyo Declaration on Justice for Children in Africa.[13] It is to be expected that the concept of child-friendly justice will be endorsed in other parts of the world as well.[14]

Another important development at the regional levels concerns the case law of the treaty bodies in the European and Inter-American human rights systems. The European Court of Human Rights has issued significant case law, among others, on the participation of children in trial (see section 4.2), the right to legal counsel during police interrogations (see section 4.1) and the use of (pre-trial) detention.[15] The European Court has included UN children's rights standards, including soft international and regional standards, such as resolutions, recommendations and general comments, in its jurisprudence under the European Convention on Human Rights. In addition, it has drawn upon the standards and reports of the European Committee on the Prevention of Torture (CPT), which have been of significance for the position of children in detention and their protection under art. 3 ECHR.

The Inter-American Court of Human Rights and Inter-American Commission on Human Rights have also developed a growing body of judgements and decisions, respectively, with relevance for the administration of juvenile justice, including deprivation of liberty and arrest, detention and ill-treatment of children by the police (see Feria-Tinta 2014 and Rapporteurship on the Rights of the Child 2008).

2.3. Non-legal developments shaping the international juvenile justice agenda

The plethora of international and regional instruments regulating the administration of juvenile justice is complemented by numerous reports of bodies or representatives from

---

11 Rec(2003)20, 24 September 2003.
12 Rec(2008)11, 5 November 2008.
13 The declaration was adopted by representatives of governments, CSOs, INGOs, the African Committee of Experts on the Rights and Welfare of the Child, the UN Committee on the Rights of the Child, the African Union, UN agencies, UN experts and other experts, from all over Africa and other parts of the world. See www.kampalaconference.info (accessed 29 May 2014).
14 See furthermore UN High Commissioner for Human Rights, *Access to justice for children*, 16 December 2013, UN Doc. A/HRC/25/35.
15 See e.g. ECtHR 20 January 2009, *Appl. No. 70337/01* (Güveç v. Turkey) and ECtHR 19 January 2012, *Appl. No. 39884/05* (Korneykova v. Ukraine).

international organizations such as the UN (Human Rights Council, Office of the High Commissioner for Human Rights (OHCHR), UN Office on Drugs and Crime (UNODC), Special Representative on Violence against Children, UNICEF; see e.g. Joint Report 2012[16]), the Inter-American Commission on Human Rights (see in particular the Rapporteurship on the Rights of the Child) or the Council of Europe (e.g. the Commissioner for Human Rights) and reports of (I)NGO-coalitions or individual NGOs, such as the Inter-Agency Panel on Juvenile Justice, International Juvenile Justice Observatory (IJJO), Defence for Children International or Penal Reform International (PRI) that provide guidance on how to safeguard the generally vulnerable position of children in conflict with the law. These reports or statements are also part of the international frame of reference affecting the interpretation of international standards and their implementation, and have shaped the global juvenile justice agenda.

3. Specific justice system for children

The first category of key issues of juvenile justice from an international children's rights perspective revolves around the requirement to set up a specific justice system for children in conflict with the law. It enshrines the call upon States parties to safeguard specificity and specialization, the objectives of the juvenile justice system and the issue of age limits.

3.1. Separation, specificity and specialization

Article 40 (3) of the CRC stipulates that States parties promote the establishment of a juvenile justice system through laws, procedures, authorities and institutions specifically applicable to children. The CRC provides little guidance about what this should entail, unlike, for example, the American Convention on Human Rights, which explicitly calls for separate criminal proceedings for minors before specialized tribunals (art. 5 (5)). Under the CRC, it remains unclear what is precisely meant by the call for specificity. With regard to national law, it is questionable whether States should draw up separate legislation regulating the justice system for children, as for example done by a number of countries at the African continent, after ratification of the CRC (UNICEF Innocenti Research Centre 2007, p. 81ff). States will meet the requirements of art. 40 (3) CRC if they include special juvenile justice provisions in existing substantive and procedural legislation regulating the criminal procedure and penal law. The discretion for States is understandable in light of the global variety of criminal justice systems affecting children. At the same time, the absence of more guidance explains the prevalence of a wide variety of methods of incorporating children's rights in domestic law. In Europe, for example, all countries have special arrangements for children in conflict with the law. There are countries that have special penal or procedural laws for children (e.g. Austria, France, Germany, Serbia and Switzerland), countries that have special regulations in the general criminal justice acts (e.g. the Netherlands, Romania and Lithuania) and countries that have special legal provisions for children concerning specific aspects of the criminal justice system, in addition to general criminal justice legislation (e.g. Estonia) (Pruin 2010, pp. 1523–1525). States' efforts to adopt special acts on juvenile justice seem very much dependent on the (quality of the) already

---

16 See also UN Economic and Social Council, *United Nations Model Strategies and Practical Measures on the Elimination of Violence against Children in the Field of Crime Prevention and Criminal Justice*, 15 May 2014, UN Doc. E/CN.15/2014/L.12/Rev.1.

existing legal frameworks and the need to incorporate international law into domestic law in order to have legally binding effect (e.g. in dualistic systems).

Specificity seems to be more a matter of specialization rather than of separation, although article 37 (c) CRC does explicitly stipulate that children should be separated from adults if they are deprived of their liberty and article 40 (1) CRC proclaims that children should be treated in a fundamentally different way than adults (see below). The CRC Committee underscores that States Parties are required 'to develop and implement a comprehensive juvenile justice policy' (CRC Committee 2007, para. 4), which should not be limited to the implementation of the specific CRC provisions – articles 40 and 37 CRC – but also concern the proclaimed general principles of the CRC (art. 2, 3, 6 and 12) as well as other relevant provisions such as art. 39 CRC on the recovery and reintegration of victims and art. 4 CRC on general implementation measures. Based on art. 4 CRC, States Parties ought to consider the need to 'undertake all appropriate legislative, administrative and other measures for the implementation of the rights recognized in the [CRC]', as part of their comprehensive juvenile justice policy. Specialization of authorities and institutions, such as law enforcement authorities, judicial authorities, lawyers, probation services and institutions, clearly should be part of this policy as well (CRC Committee 2007, para. 92ff; see also e.g. rule 12.1 Beijing Rules).

States have much discretion when it comes to the establishment of a specific juvenile justice system. With some important exceptions, the CRC does not proclaim a system that is completely separated from the adult system. Separation has the advantage of sending out the clear message that the classical approach towards delinquent behaviour as generally applied to adults (i.e. a punitive response aiming at retribution and deterrence) is unfit for children. However, one could also argue that too much focus on *separation* runs the risk of disregarding that children are like adults entitled to be treated fairly (see section 4). If a State, for example, develops separate national legislation on juvenile justice (e.g. a separate juvenile justice Act), it has to consider the applicability of fair trial rights as well, either by incorporating these rights in the new legislation or by referring to general legislation or a constitutional framework. Even if a State does not have a specific justice system for children, but instead a child protection or welfare system meant to respond to juvenile offending, it should be concerned about the recognition of the right to be treated fairly. It might not be realistic to expect more guidance from the CRC on this: at the same time children's rights implementation would undoubtedly have benefitted from it.

3.2. Objectives of juvenile justice

Article 40 (1) CRC stipulates that children subjected to criminal justice proceedings should be treated in a manner that takes into account the age of the child and that aims at the child's reintegration in society, in which he or she can play a constructive role. This implies in the first place that the juvenile justice system recognizes that 'children differ from adults in their physical and psychological development, and their emotional and educational needs', which 'constitute the basis for the lesser culpability of children in conflict with the law' (CRC Committee 2007, para 10) and which requires that children should be treated differently from adults. In its landmark case on the abolition of the death penalty for minors (Roper v. Simmons[17]) the US Supreme Court noted that children are not only 'categorically less culpable', but also more likely to be open for reform than adults, which underscores the potential

---

17   *Roper v. Simmons*, 543 U.S. 551 (2005).

of reformative approaches towards delinquent behaviour. According to the Supreme Court's majority opinion 'it would be misguided to equate the failings of a minor with those of an adult, for a greater possibility exists that a minor's character deficiencies will be reformed'.

The call for age-specific treatment of children also means that one should take into account differences between children in terms of age and maturity (i.e. developmental stage; note that art. 40 (1) CRC does not refer to maturity; cf. art. 5 CRC) and differentiate accordingly. This is relevant for children's assumed accountability, for their capacity to participate in proceedings and for the determination of an appropriate response to the child's behaviour. In addition, it has implications for the way children are treated in the different stages of the juvenile justice system, which also affects the way parents are involved (art. 5 CRC), the age at which children should (or should not) be deprived of their liberty (see e.g. rule 11a Havana Rules, which calls for a minimum age of deprivation of liberty[18]) and the way children are informed about the proceedings (incl. information on charges and the possible outcomes of the case, incl. sentences).

Second, article 40 (1) CRC stipulates that juvenile justice must aim at the child's reintegration in society, in which he or she can play a constructive role. This represents the pedagogical objective of juvenile justice, placing the child offender's individual interests and his future role in society at its core, and which makes the juvenile justice system fundamentally different from the adult criminal justice system. It rules out a purely repressive approach, aiming at retribution or deterrence, as this is considered not to be in the child's best interests (and his reintegration), nor serving his or her right to development (art. 6 CRC). According to the CRC Committee, 'the protection of the best interests of the child means, for instance, that the traditional objectives of criminal justice, such as repression/retribution, must give way to rehabilitation and restorative justice objectives in dealing with child offenders', which 'can be done in concert with attention to effective public safety' (CRC Committee 2007, para. 10).[19] Article 40 (1) CRC's reintegration objective furthermore implies that one should acknowledge the potential negative impact of the justice system on the child's development and short- and long-term interests and use it only as a last resort. This means that one should develop and enforce diversion mechanisms (see section 5), scrutinize discrimination in the context of juvenile justice (art. 2 CRC)[20] and prevent prosecution of status offences (CRC Committee 2007, para. 8; see also article 56 of the Riyadh Guidelines). Moreover, States should develop a comprehensive policy to prevent juvenile delinquency (CRC Committee 2007, para. 16ff).

The pedagogical objective of juvenile justice is furthermore substantiated by article 40 (1) CRC stipulating that juvenile justice aims at the reinforcement of the child's respect for the human rights and fundamental freedoms of others, for example through education aiming at the development of respect for human rights and freedoms in general (cf. art. 29 (1) (b) CRC and General Comment No.1 on the aims of education). The CRC Committee notes that '[i]t

---

18 See e.g. Switzerland; Commentary to the European Rules for juvenile offenders subject to sanctions or measures, CM(2008)128 addendum 1, p. 47.
19 The reintegration objective of art. 40 (1) has also been incorporated in the case law of the European Court of Human Rights under art. 8 ECHR's protection of family life in case of expulsion. In the case Maslov v. Austria (23 June 2008, *Appl. No. 1638/03*) the Court found a violation because the reintegration objective as stipulated by art. 40 CRC was neglected by the Austrian authorities; para. 83.
20 For example of stigmatized groups of children, such as street children, girls, children with disabilities and children belonging to racial, ethnic, religious or linguistic minorities (CRC Committee 2007, para. 6ff).

is obvious that this principle of juvenile justice requires a full respect for and implementation of the guarantees for a fair trial recognized in article 40 (2) [CRC]' (CRC Committee 2007, para. 13). It also observes that the juvenile justice system should respect the child's inherent dignity and it raises the following question: 'If the key actors in juvenile justice, such as police officers, prosecutors, judges and probation officers, do not fully respect and protect these guarantees, how can they expect that with such poor examples the child will respect the human rights and fundamental freedom of others?' (CRC Committee 2007, para. 13.) Moreover, it can be argued that the pedagogical objective means that the child should be equipped with means and assistance to reintegrate constructively, which implies that the State should offer education and vocational training and forms of (medical) treatment, for example to address substance abuse or psychological or psychiatric problems.

It can be argued that article 40 CRC does not provide much substantive guidance on how to realize the objectives of juvenile justice. At the same time, article 40 CRC assumes a high reliance on state services in responding to juvenile offending. This certainly is problematic in many countries due to lack of financial and human resources. It can also be problematic because of the existence of a certain distrust in governmental services for citizens in general or children in particular. In addition, article 40 CRC does not clarify how far the State can go in offering or imposing interventions that aim at the child's re-education and reintegration, which may open the door to an overly paternalistic approach towards juvenile delinquency. What if the State authorities, for example, consider it necessary for the prevention of recidivism and in the best interests of the particular child to impose a placement in a reform school, which can be prolonged until the child is regarded fit to reintegrate into society? What if the child can be subjected to (compulsory) medical treatment, if considered necessary for his reintegration? And what if a pedagogical intervention implies a whole range of non-custodial interventions, including intensive probation, counselling, restraining orders, etc., which may very well be perceived by the child as a disproportionate and even repressive sentence?

Article 40 CRC is clear, however, in excluding a purely repressive approach towards children in conflict with the law, even if they have committed heinous criminal offences. It is also clear in proclaiming that reintegration through education, and if needed through special care and assistance, should be at the core of any response to juvenile delinquent behaviour, without discrimination of any kind. It is furthermore clear in arguing that fair treatment should be at the core of the juvenile justice system, not only because this concerns a right of the child, but also because it is perceived to be conducive to the realization of the objectives of juvenile justice. This principle of fair treatment is also meant to prevent tipping of the scale towards an overly paternalistic approach by the State towards children in conflict with the law.

3.3. Age limits

The administration of a specific juvenile justice system implies a distinction between the juvenile justice system on the one hand and the adult criminal justice system on the other. This touches upon the upper age limit of juvenile justice, which is currently subject to debate and which will be addressed below. Another important, but highly controversial age limit, is the minimum age of criminal responsibility, also known as the MACR. The applicability of the juvenile justice system is determined by these two age limits.

Before looking into the details of both age limits, it is important to underscore that the setting of age limits to define the scope of the juvenile justice system is inherently artificial and to a certain extent arbitrary. However, legal constructions like this do serve relevant legal interests such as equality and legal certainty. At the same time, they require specific justification and clarification in order to avoid unlawful treatment and to be able to respond adequately to the inevitable borderline cases.

3.3.1. Minimum Age of Criminal Responsibility (MACR)

According to Article 40 (3)(a) CRC 'State Parties shall seek to promote ... establishment of a minimum age below which children shall be presumed not to have the capacity to infringe the penal law'. States parties should set a MACR, which is not so much about the capacity of a child to infringe the penal law (as the wording of article 40 (3) CRC suggests), but about the age at which a child who commits an offence can be held criminally accountable and at which he or she can be prosecuted for alleged criminal behaviour (Doek 2008, p. 236). Regarding children under the MACR there is an irrefutable assumption that they cannot be held criminally responsible for their behaviour and that they cannot be formally charged. Despite the weak wording of the provision ('shall seek to promote'), the CRC Committee 'understands this provision as an obligation for State parties to set a minimum age of criminal responsibility' (CRC Committee 2007, para. 31).

The CRC does not indicate what an acceptable minimum age is, neither do other international instruments. According to rule 4.1 of the Beijing Rules, the MACR 'shall not be fixed at too low an age level, bearing in mind the facts of emotional, mental and intellectual maturity'. The reason for this lack of clarity lies in the highly controversial nature of the issue and the wide variety of MACRs throughout the world. At the international political level there was no consensus at the time of drafting of both the Beijing Rules and the CRC. According to the commentary to rule 4.1 of the Beijing Rules 'the minimum age of criminal responsibility differs widely owing to history and culture' and that '[t]he modern approach would be to consider whether a child can live up to the moral and psychological components of criminal responsibility; that is whether a child, by virtue of her or his individual discernment and understanding, can be held responsible for essentially antisocial behaviour'.

Despite its controversy and global variety (Cipriani 2009), the CRC Committee has argued that a MACR below the age of 12 years is considered not to be internationally acceptable, and it has encouraged States parties 'to increase their lower MACR to the age of 12 years as the absolute minimum and to continue to increase it to a higher level' (CRC Committee 2007, para. 32). In addition, the CRC Committee has urged States parties not to lower their MACR to the age of 12 (i.e. the world's median MACR; Cipriani 2009), but to opt for a MACR of 14 or 16 instead.[21] This final remark has proven to be important, because some States considered lowering it and some States have actually done so (CRIN 2013). It is furthermore important to highlight that the CRC Committee has strongly recommended against a flexible MACR, that is: lower than 12 in case of certain serious offences or if the child is considered mature enough to be held criminally responsible *(doli (in)capax* rule; CRC Committee 2007, para. 34). Finally, the CRC Committee noted that '[i]f there is no proof of age and it cannot be established that the child is at or above the MACR, the child shall not be held criminally responsible' (CRC Committee 2007, para. 35).

Much can be said about the MACR (see Cipriani 2009, for a comprehensive analysis of the issue; see also Vandenhole, Chapter 2 in this Handbook), but it is clear that the position of the

---

21 In Europe, most of the countries have a MACR of 13 or 14; Commentary to the European Rules for juvenile offenders subject to sanctions or measures, CM(2008)128 addendum 1, p. 47.

CRC Committee has not made the issue less controversial.²² On the contrary, the MACR remains at the heart of political debate and 'tough on crime' approaches (see e.g. Downes and Morgan 2012). This is particularly true in times of elections, law reform (see the debate and compromise in the 2008 South African Child Justice Act; Gallinetti 2009, pp. 20–21) or when young children committed serious crimes (see e.g. the Bulger case in England in the 1990s). Some argue that the international minimum as proclaimed by the CRC Committee is too low and should be raised to at least 14, particularly because children under the age of 14 cannot be assumed competent to understand criminal proceedings or fit to stand trial (see Rap 2013; see also under section 4); others argue that one should not prosecute children at all (CRIN 2013; see also Inter-American Commission 2011, para. 59), a position that is often connected to the assumption that the criminal justice system is not an appropriate setting for addressing children's responsibility. Such an approach implies that one does not set a MACR and that there actually is no specific justice system for children. This runs the risk of denying children's agency and responsibility, which does not correspond with the imagery of childhood that can be derived from the CRC and that is built upon the concept of the child's evolving capacities, and can have a negative impact on the recognition of children as rights holders in a broader sense (Cipriani 2009). Moreover, the absence of a MACR may very well imply that the State responds to juvenile delinquency in a purely welfare-oriented manner, without paying due regard to a fair and rights-based treatment. It has also been argued that one needs to move beyond the setting of the MACR and focus more on the way one addresses children's responsibility, including the way children younger than the MACR are treated (Cipriani 2009; Hammarberg 2009, quoted in CRIN 2013). This way should be based on unconditional respect for the rights of the children involved with the aim of furthering their chances to reintegrate and play a constructive role in society, while installing their respect for the rights and freedoms of others.

The setting of a MACR serves important interests, including the recognition of the child's evolving capacities and his evolving autonomy and accountability. At the same time, defining the appropriate age at the international level in legal standards turned out to be a bridge too far due to the lack of consensus and the wide variety of practices; it will probably always remain like that. It is therefore remarkable that the CRC Committee chose to define a *minimum* MACR in 2007, based on what it considered to be the internationally acceptable minimum. One could argue that by doing so the CRC Committee defined a universal MACR, which opens the door to prosecution. However, one could also argue that the CRC Committee has actually defined the age at which children can be considered (criminally) accountable to a certain but lesser extent, which on the one hand protects children underneath that age against prosecution and on the other hand sets the scene for a child-specific and fair system designed to respond appropriately to children in conflict with the law. By doing so, the CRC Committee has clarified one of the core minimum standards for juvenile justice.

3.3.2. Upper age limit

The upper age limit of the juvenile justice system is 18 years of age, which is connected to the definition of the child as provided in article 1 of the CRC. Even though the CRC does not

---

22 See e.g. the Special Issue of *Youth Justice* (Church et al., 2013). The Council of Europe's Guidelines on Child-Friendly Justice, dating from 2010, do not provide a MACR, but provide that '[t]he minimum age of criminal responsibility should not be too low and should be determined by law' (para. 23). In other words, the Council of Europe has not endorsed the recommendation of the CRC Committee.

explicitly provide so, it is safe to assume that article 40 CRC and related international children's rights standards are applicable to individuals under the age of 18 at the time they committed the alleged offence ('crime date criterion'; Liefaard 2008). Consequently, the upper age limit of juvenile justice is not so much defined by the transition from minority to majority (i.e. a child could attain majority before he or she reaches the age of 18 and if national law provided this, he or she is no longer considered a child under the CRC; see art. 1). The crime date criterion is related to the justification of a juvenile justice intervention based on the culpability of children and can also be found in article 37 (a) CRC which *inter alia* provides that 'neither capital punishment nor life imprisonment without the possibility of release shall be imposed for offences committed by persons below 18 years of age'. This implies that the juvenile justice system is applicable to all children of the MACR or older, but younger than 18 at the time of the offence. It also means that these children remain entitled to a constructive response to their delinquent behaviour and to treatment, as stipulated by article 40 CRC as children, even if they turned 18 during prosecution or during the enforcement of sentences. Consequently, the requirements concerning deprivation of liberty remain applicable as well, that is: arrest, detention or imprisonment may only be used as a measure of last resort and for the shortest appropriate period of time (art. 37 (b) CRC) and that 'a child placed in a facility for children [does not need] to be moved to a facility for adults immediately after he/she turns 18' (CRC Committee 2007, para. 86). According to the CRC Committee '[c]ontinuation of his/her stay in the facility for children should be possible if that is in her/his best interest and not contrary to the best interests of the younger children in the facility' (CRC Committee 2007, para. 86).

The question remains to what extent the actual age of the individual should be taken into account. The CRC is not clear on this point, but the actual age is, for example, relevant for the question to what extent the child's parents or legal guardian remain involved, since from a legal perspective a young adult no longer falls under parental custody or guardianship. Furthermore, the actual age can be relevant in order to determine the appropriate response to the delinquent behaviour of the child, who may have become a young adult in the meantime. It is also relevant to differentiate between young people, for example within a custodial institution and to tailor the regime and, more importantly, the individual programme in order to achieve the objectives of the (juvenile) criminal justice intervention, which, with regard to former children, may not be merely repressive.

The upper age limit of 18 also implies that young adults (e.g. between 18 and 25) who commit criminal offences do not fall under the protection of the CRC. This can be problematic on a practical level, for example when an 18-year-old commits a criminal offence together with a 17-year-old. However, it is also a matter of justifying why you treat young adults just above the age of majority differently from children. This issue has become more apparent under the influence of recent scientific insights indicating that the cognitive development of adolescents continues roughly until the age of 25 years, which has implications for their involvement in criminal behaviour and their level of culpability. The assumption that young adults can be held fully accountable is no longer self-evident (Liefaard 2012). In many countries, the position of young adults has gained significant attention. Yet, the recognition of their position under international human rights laws remains marginal.

In the context of criminal justice, some references to young adults can be found in international standards. In 2003, the Council of Europe recommended that 'reflecting the extended transition to adulthood, it should be possible for young adults under the age of 21 to be treated in a way comparable to juveniles and to be subject to the same interventions, when the judge is of the opinion that they are not as mature and responsible for their actions as full adults'.[23] In 2008, the Council of Europe took the concern for young adults further by recommending in the European Rules for juvenile offenders that 'young adult offenders may, where appropriate, be regarded as juveniles and dealt with accordingly' (rule 19). In addition, the Council recommends that 'juveniles shall not be held in institutions for adults, but in institutions specially designed for them', although it leaves room for exceptional circumstances in which a child has to be held in an institution for adults. In such an event, 'they shall be accommodated separately unless in individual cases where it is in their best interest not to do so' (rule 59.1). Furthermore, it recommends that 'juveniles who reach the age of majority and young adults dealt with as if they were juveniles shall normally be held in institutions for juvenile offenders or in specialized institutions for young adults unless their social reintegration can be better effected in an institution for adults' (rule 59.3). It is interesting that the Council of Europe calls upon its member states to pay particular attention to the special position of older children and young adults in order to avoid transitions taking place in a rigid manner.[24] In light of this, the CRC Committee noted with appreciation 'that some States parties allow for the application of the rules and regulation of juvenile justice to persons aged 18 and older, usually till the age of 21, either as a general rule or by way of exception' (CRC Committee 2007, para. 38).

Finally, there is one significant issue that concerns the practice of transfer or waiver of children (generally ages 16 or 17) to adult criminal courts (e.g. largely practised in the US), and the practice of sentencing children as adults, with subsequent confinement in adult facilities (e.g. in the Netherlands). Application of such a mandatory or discretionary waiver or transfer (hereinafter: transfer) goes against the point of departure that all persons below the age of 18 fall under the protection of the juvenile justice system as well as the CRC. In addition, transfers often result in (mandatory) long custodial sentences, which jeopardizes the requirement to use imprisonment regarding children only as a last resort and for the shortest appropriate period of time (art. 37 (b) CRC). The CRC Committee, therefore, recommends States parties 'which limit applicability of their juvenile justice rules to children under the age of 16 (or lower) years, or which allow by way of exception that 16- or 17-year-old children are treated as adult criminals, [to] change their rule to a full application of the rules and regulations of juvenile justice to persons aged 18 and younger' (CRC Committee 2007, para. 38). Despite the strong (legal) arguments against the practice of transfers, it is important to recognize that this practice is often perceived as an inevitable tool to respond to older children who commit serious offences, sometimes with young adults, not only by politicians but also by legal professionals, including for example judges. At the same time, the application of transfer or waiver does not always result in much severer sentences (see e.g. Weijers 2006; in many countries transfer does result in severer sentences). In addition, it should be noted that legal systems that do not allow transfer or waiver might very well have higher maximum sentences for children (among others related to the absence of an 'escape' to the adult system; Killias et al. 2012, p. 315ff).

4. Fair trial with special focus on the right to effective participation

The second category of key issues concerns the fairness of juvenile justice proceedings and the safeguarding of the right of the child to a fair trial, including the right to effective participation.

---

23   Rec(2003)20 concerning new ways of dealing with juvenile delinquency and the role of juvenile justice, 24 September 2003, para. 11.
24   In addition, in the European Prison Rules meant for adult facilities, the Council recommends that young adults be kept separately from older prisoners (rules 18.8 and 18.9).

4.1. Fair trial in general

Article 40 (2) CRC stipulates that children are entitled to a fair trial and it provides a range of fair trial principles, which can also be found in other general human rights treaties; the children's rights provision was founded on art. 14 and 15 ICCPR (Detrick 1999). The relevance of human rights for criminal justice has always revolved around the concept of fair trial and the treatment of the accused, prosecuted and sentenced individual with humanity and with respect for their inherent human dignity. In this regard, international human rights law does not distinguish between adults and children. Both 'shall be equal before the courts and tribunals' (art. 14 (1) ICCPR) and are entitled to the same rights and freedoms (see also art. 6 and 8 ECHR). General fair trial rights that are equally applicable to children concern: the principle of legality (art. 40 (2)(a) CRC; see also art. 15 (1) ICCPR with regard to the prohibition of retroactive sentencing); the presumption of innocence (art. 40 (2)(b)(i) CRC); the right not to incriminate oneself (art. 40 (2)(b)(iv) CRC); the right to prompt information on the charges in a language one understands (art. 40 (2)(b)(ii) CRC); the right to be tried before a competent, independent and impartial authority or judicial authority (art. 40 (2)(b)(iii) CRC; the right to (cross-)examine witnesses (art. 40 (2)(b)(iv) CRC) and the right to free assistance of an interpreter (art. 40 (2)(b)(iv) CRC).

Article 40 (2) CRC adds a number of fair trial principles specifically for children. A child is entitled to have the criminal trial determined 'without delay by a competent, independent and impartial authority' (art. 40 (2)(b)(iii) CRC). By using the wording *without delay* rather than 'without undue delay' (cf. art. 14 ICCPR), it assumes that children are entitled to a speedier trial (CRC Committee 2007 para. 51; see also para. 83 in which the committee recommends a maximum term of six months for a juvenile case in first instance, if the child is detained). This assumption is based on the '[international] consensus that for children in conflict with the law the time between the commission of the offence and the final response to this act should be as short as possible' in order to prevent that the response loses its desired positive, pedagogical impact, and that the child will be stigmatized (CRC Committee 2007, para. 51).

Furthermore, a child must be 'informed promptly and directly of the charges against him or her' (i.e. 'as soon as possible'; CRC Committee 2007, para. 47). If appropriate this must happen 'through his or her parents or legal guardians'. The parents can also be present during the proceedings to provide general psychological and emotional assistance to the child. Article 40 CRC, thus, recognizes the special position of the child's parents, which conforms to the general recognition of the child's family and parents as primary caretakers under the CRC (arts. 18 and 5 CRC).

A child is also entitled to legal or other appropriate assistance (art. 40 (2)(b)(iii) CRC), which has received quite some attention at the European level, in relation to the position of the child during police interrogations. The European Court of Human Rights has developed case law implying that an arrested child has the right to legal counsel during the initial police interrogations, as part of his right to a fair trial under art. 6 of the European Court of Human Rights.[25] In addition, the European Commission is currently developing specific EU law on procedural safeguards for children suspected or accused in criminal proceedings (Liefaard and Van den Brink 2014).

In general, international standards strongly focus on the legal protection of children, particularly in the earliest stages of the criminal justice process. Despite its significance, there may

---

25 ECtHR, 27 November 2008, *Appl. No. 36391/02* (Salduz v. Turkey); ECtHR 11 December 2008, *Appl. No. 4268/04* (Panovits v. Cyprus).

very well be a tension between providing safeguards (e.g. legal assistance) and responding diligently and in pedagogically sound way. The latter might suffer from too much focus on legal safeguards, which for example slows down the process (and might even result in detention, because the lawyer cannot be present in time) or can be counterproductive in the sense that the child is assisted by a non-specialized lawyer, who is not aware of the possibilities of diversion (see e.g. Liefaard and Van den Brink 2014). At the same time, the initial stages of criminal justice proceedings are too critical to argue that the child should have no right to legal assistance or can waive his right to consult a lawyer (see also Liefaard and Van den Brink 2014). In light of this, it would have been better if art. 40 CRC stipulated that a child has the right to legal *and* other appropriate assistance (*cf.* art. 37 (d) CRC).

Another child-specific feature of article 40 (2) CRC is that the child's privacy must be 'fully respected at all stages of the proceedings' (art. 40 (2) (b) (vii) CRC; art. 16 CRC). According to the CRC Committee this stretches out over the disposition phase as well and implies, among others, that criminal records should not be used in adult proceedings regarding the same offender. Preferably, criminal records should be erased (e.g. once the child reaches age 18; CRC Committee 2007, para. 67). Above all, the full respect of privacy implies, according to the CRC Committee, that a juvenile justice trial should 'as a rule' be held behind closed doors (*in camera*; cf. art. 6 (1) ECHR), which is also supported by the right of the child to participate effectively in justice proceedings. This requires some further elaboration.

4.2. Right to effective participation

According to the CRC Committee '[a] fair trial requires that the child (…) be able to effectively participate in the trial' (CRC Committee 2007, para. 46), which makes effective participation, stemming from article 12 CRC and implied in article 40 CRC, a prerequisite for a fair trial. Obviously, this has implications for every stage of the juvenile justice process (CRC Committee 2007, para. 12). This position of the CRC Committee has been inspired by the European Court of Human Rights, which has developed significant case law connecting the right to a fair trial and the right to participate effectively during trial (Kilkelly 2014). The court ruled that 'it is essential that a child charged with an offence is dealt with in a manner which takes full account of his age, level of maturity and intellectual and emotional capacities, and that steps are taken to promote his ability to understand and participate in the proceedings' (T v. UK, para 84).[26] In this particular case (i.e. the Bulger case in which two 11-year-olds (T. and V.) were tried for the murder of toddler) the court held the young boy(s) was (were) unable to participate effectively because it is was 'highly unlikely' that they would have felt 'sufficiently uninhibited, in the tense courtroom and under public scrutiny, to have consulted with [their lawyers] during the trial or, indeed, that, given [their] immaturity and [their] disturbed emotional state, [they] would have been capable outside the courtroom of cooperation with [their] lawyers and giving them information for the purposes of [their] defence' (T. v UK, para. 88). In another case, S.C. v. the UK,[27] the European Court held that article 6's right to a fair trial does not require that a child on trial should 'understand or be capable of understanding every point of law or evidential detail' (para. 29). In this regard, the court underscores the significance of legal representation (see also art. 6 (3)(c) ECHR). According to the court '"effective

---

26 ECtHR, 16 December 1999, *Appl. No. 24724/94* (T. v. the United Kingdom); see also ECtHR, 16 December 1999, *Appl. No. 24888/94* (V. v. the United Kingdom).
27 ECtHR, 15 June 2004, *Appl. No. 60958/00* (S.C. v. the United Kingdom).

participation" in this context presupposes that the accused has a broad understanding of the nature of the trial process and of what is at stake for him or her, including the significance of any penalty which may be imposed' (para. 29). The European Court has, thus, defined critical steps that ought to be considered when assessing the possibilities of children to participate effectively in trial proceedings as part of their right to a fair trial. By doing so, it has incorporated article 40 CRC and related children's rights standards in its case law under article 6 ECHR.

Inspired by this case law and with reference to rule 14 of the Beijing Rules providing that proceedings 'shall be conducted in an atmosphere of understanding, which shall allow the juvenile to participate therein and to express herself or himself freely', the CRC Committee has recognized the right to participate effectively in trial and that the child 'needs to comprehend the charges, and possible consequences and penalties, in order to direct the legal representative, to challenge witnesses, to provide an account of events, and to make appropriate decisions about evidence, testimony and the measure(s) to be imposed' (CRC Committee 2007, para. 46). The committee adds that '[t]aking into account the child's age and maturity may also require modified courtroom procedures and practices' (CRC Committee 2007, para. 46). The CRC Committee has also provided further guidance on the significance of article 12 CRC for criminal justice proceedings in its General Comment No. 12 on the child's right to be heard. It observed that 'a child cannot be heard effectively where the environment is intimidating, hostile, insensitive or inappropriate for her or his age' and that '[p]roceedings must both be accessible and child-appropriate', which means that '[p]articular attention needs to be paid to the provision and delivery of child-friendly information, adequate support for self-advocacy, appropriately trained staff, design of court rooms, clothing of judges and lawyers (…)' (CRC Committee 2009, para. 34). It furthermore held with regard to the juvenile justice context that '[i]n order to effectively participate in the proceedings, every child must be informed promptly and directly about the charges against her or him in a language she or he understands, and also about the juvenile justice process and possible measures taken by the court' (CRC Committee 2009, para. 60). In addition, 'the proceedings should be conducted in an atmosphere enabling the child to participate and to express her/himself freely' and, as mentioned earlier, '[t]he court and other hearings of a child in conflict with the law should be conducted behind closed doors' (CRC Committee 2009, para. 60–61).

The above-mentioned developments have to a large extent set the scene for the development of the guidelines for child-friendly justice (see section 2), which provide detailed guidance on how to enforce child-friendly (or child-sensitive) proceedings. Recent interdisciplinary and comparative research conducted by Rap (2013) also provides concrete steps to safeguard the right to effective participation in youth court proceedings. In addition to what has been mentioned already, she underscores the need for specialized and active judges who are trained in conversational techniques suitable for communicating with adolescents and in avoiding jargon, active parental involvement that contributes to young people's feelings being taken seriously, explanations and clarification of the order proceedings, the purpose of the hearings and the persons present in the court room, as well as of the decisions made (e.g. the imposition of a sentence) in a concrete manner and in way that the child can determine how his views have been taken into account (Rap 2013, pp. 321–322). Rap recommends investing in the specialization and training of other professionals in the juvenile justice system as well (prosecutors, lawyers, probation officers etc.) (Rap 2013, p. 355). She also questions the MACR standard set at 12 by the CRC Committee in relation to the assumption that from this age children cannot only be considered accountable but also capable of participating effectively in trial (CRC Committee 2007, para. 45). Rap strongly recommends against prosecuting children younger than 14 years of age. Only children of 14 and older can in general be considered fit to stand trial. Children younger than 14 should not be subjected to formal proceedings since her study reveals that in general children cannot rely on adequate assistance, which becomes more problematic when younger children are concerned (Rap 2013, pp. 356–357).

As mentioned earlier there might be a tension between safeguarding the right to a fair trial and the pedagogical objectives of juvenile justice or, more broadly, the call for child specificity, and much more can be said about it (see e.g. section 5); neither the CRC nor the CRC Committee touch upon it. At the same time, there are areas, such as the area of effective participation, in which the striking of the balance between fair trial and child-specific arrangements has developed quite well, among others stimulated by the use of interdisciplinary insights on children's needs and capacities, which helped to interpret the implications of international standards. This shows that the tension is not so much a fundamental problem. It seems more a matter of implementation, enforcement and time, which underscores the need for the development of interdisciplinary strategies to acquire knowledge of and insight in how to merge a fair trial into the specific features of the juvenile justice system.

5. Disposition in juvenile justice

The third and final category of key issues that will be addressed in this chapter concerns the disposition of juvenile justice cases. This category can roughly be distinguished into diversion (and restorative justice), non-custodial sentences (often referred to as alternative sentences, although one could argue that deprivation of liberty as a sentence should be regarded as an alternative[28]), extreme sentences and deprivation of liberty.

5.1. Diversion and restorative justice

Both article 40 and 37 CRC have implications for the disposition of juvenile justice cases, which should be understood in light of the objectives of juvenile justice (see para. 3). Article 40 (3)(b) CRC advocates that States parties should promote measures for dealing with children in conflict with the law without resorting to judicial proceedings, also known as diversion, '[w]henever appropriate and desirable'. Diversion aims to avoid exposing children to the negative impact of formal judicial proceedings, such as stigmatization, that could jeopardize their reintegration, and to enable a quick response to criminal behaviour, which is considered important for the effectiveness of justice interventions (CRC Committee 2007, para. 25; diversion is generally also considered to be more cost-effective; see Dünkel *et al.* 2010, pp. 1626–1628). States parties have much discretion in how to establish diversion mechanisms. Diversion can take place at the different levels and in different phases of the criminal justice proceedings. It can be used by the public prosecutor, but also by the police and even by (pre-trial) judges. In practice, there is a wide variety of diversion mechanisms, including warnings, conditional dismissal of cases, supervision orders, including forms of community service, forms of restorative justice, including restoration of damage, victim compensation, victim-offender mediation or family group conferences. There are many differences between countries in how they operationalize diversion, and different studies indicate that diversion can have a positive impact on

---

28 Statement of Mr. Benoit van Keirsbilck, President Defence for Children International, at the conference 'Growing with children's rights', Dubrovnik, Croatia, 27–28 March 2014.

children's behaviour as well as the prevention of recidivism (Dünkel 2009, pp. 155–160; see also Doek 2008, p. 238).

Restorative justice is often mentioned as a form of diversion as well (CRC Committee 2007, para. 10). The Special Representative on Violence Against Children considers restorative justice relevant for the prevention of violence against children in the justice system and underscores the growing importance of it for the realization of the objectives of juvenile justice, including taking responsibility and changing behaviour, respecting the right of the child to be heard, the avoidance of the harmful effects of deprivation of liberty and the prevention of stigmatization, including the tackling of the negative imagery of child offenders (Special Representative on VAC 2013, pp. 3ff and 27ff).

The CRC Committee draws attention to the protection of human rights, including procedural safeguards, when using diversion (CRC Committee 2007, para. 22; see also some critical remarks in section 4). It underscores that diversion should only be used if there is 'compelling evidence that the child has committed the alleged offence' and that the child admits responsibility freely and voluntarily without pressure. In addition, the child should give informed consent to the diversion and he or she should be entitled to consult legal or other appropriate assistance (it is suggested that parents of younger children should consent as well; see Council of Europe, Recommendation 2003(20), para. 8 and rule 11.3 Beijing Rules). Another important point made by the CRC Committee concerns the need to formally close the case if the child has successfully completed the programme and the need to avoid unnecessary stigmatization through registration of the diversion programme in criminal records (CRC Committee 2007, para. 27). The CRC Committee highlights that diversion should not be reserved for first offenders only; recidivist and even serious offenders should also benefit from appropriate diversion programmes (CRC Committee 2007, paras. 23 and 25).

5.2. Sentences: Non-custodial sentences and extreme sentences

States parties must ensure, if formal charges have been lodged and the child is tried in court, that the court has a variety of dispositions at its disposal, including 'care, guidance and supervision orders; counselling; probation; foster care; education and vocational training programmes and other alternatives to institutional care' (art. 40 (4) CRC; see also rule 18 Beijing Rules and Part II of the European Rules for juvenile offenders). This non-exhaustive list underscores the pedagogical objective of the juvenile justice system and is meant to stimulate the use of non-custodial sentences over forms of deprivation of liberty, such as imprisonment (see below). It can be argued that article 40 (4) confirms that a strictly punitive approach is not in conformity with the CRC, in particular with article 40 (1) (Doek 2008, p. 241). It furthermore is important to note that the principle of proportionality is explicitly referred to in article 40 (4) CRC, which means the intervention should always be proportionate to the seriousness of the criminal offence and the circumstances of the case, including the age of the child, his or her assumed lesser culpability, his or her special needs and circumstances and the interests of society, particularly on the long run (CRC Committee 2007, para. 71). In light of this, it is important to reiterate that children could experience non-custodial sentences, due to their intensity, as disproportionate and even repressive. This should also be taken into account when defining a proportionate sentence.

Article 37 CRC provides further guidance on sentencing, particularly on the imposition of extreme or the most severe sentences. Art. 37 (a) CRC clearly prohibits capital punishment for persons below 18 years when committing the offence (cf. art. 6 (5) ICCPR). Despite this prohibition, there are a number of States parties to the CRC that still execute children.[29] As mentioned earlier, in 2005, the US Supreme Court ruled the death penalty for minors unconstitutional with reference, among others, to international standards, including this one.[30]

Article 37 (a) also prohibits life imprisonment without the possibility of release. This rather weakly formulated provision (i.e. the result of a political compromise included in the final stages of the drafting; Detrick 1992) leaves room for the imposition of life with the possibility of parole. In essence, the article 37 (a) CRC provision with regard to life imprisonment has led to an inconsistency within article 37 CRC, since paragraph (b) stipulates that imprisonment may only be used as a measure of last resort and for the shortest appropriate period of time (see below) and also with the overall objectives of juvenile justice as enshrined in article 40 (1) CRC. The CRC Committee underscores that despite this room for discretion in favour of the use of life imprisonment, States Parties are under the obligation to safeguard the realization of the objectives of article 40 (1) CRC, in particular the child's reintegration. According to the CRC Committee this means that a child sentenced to imprisonment 'should receive education, treatment, and care aiming at his/her release, reintegration and ability to assume a constructive role in society' and it 'strongly recommends the States parties to abolish all forms of life imprisonment for offences committed by person under the age of 18', because it is very likely that 'a life imprisonment of a child will make it very difficult, if not impossible, to achieve the aims of juvenile justice despite the possibility of release' (CRC Committee 2007, para. 77).

Finally, article 37 (a) CRC prohibits torture or other forms of cruel, inhuman or degrading treatment or punishment. This prohibition concerns all children, including those within the juvenile justice system. In terms of sentencing, the CRC Committee has stipulated that States parties should prohibit all forms of corporal punishment as a sentence (CRC Committee 2007, para. 71; see also CRC Committee 2006), a position which has gained global support.

5.3. Special focus: Deprivation of liberty of children

A highly topical and global issue is the use of deprivation of liberty with regard to children under the juvenile justice system, including arrest, pre-trial detention and imprisonment after disposition (i.e. custodial sentences). It is estimated that at least one million children are deprived of their liberty (United Nations Violence Study 2006, p. 191), although this estimation arguably is too modest. Research shows that children deprived of their liberty are at serious risk and confronted with gross violations of their rights and freedoms, including denial of family contact, lack of access to basic services including medical care and lack of protection against various forms of violence by other inmates or staff (see e.g. United Nations Violence Study 2006; Joint Report 2012; Council of Europe 2014). In light of this 'manifest tension between international human rights standards and the practical realities of child imprisonment' (Goldson and Kilkelly 2013), it is fair to conclude that children deprived of their liberty belong to the most disadvantaged groups of children and that gap between human rights standards and the reality of child imprisonment arguably is too big to be closed. As Goldson and Kilkelly observe that '[i]rrespective of reform efforts and no matter how the practices of penal detention are 'dressed up' in human rights and/or penal reform 'talk', ... to punish a child by way of

---

29 According to Amnesty International. Available at www.amnesty.org/en/death-penalty/executions-juvenile-offenders (last accessed 29 May 2014).
30 *Roper v. Simmons*, 543 U.S. 551 (2005).

imprisonment ultimately amounts to the deliberate imposition of 'organised hurt' (Goldson and Kilkelly 2013, p. 370[31]). Despite all this, it is worthwhile to look into the features of international children's rights standards on this issue, since it provides a significant benchmark that has found its way to regional as well as domestic standard-setting.

Article 37 CRC's primary focus concerns deprivation of liberty of children, not limited to the context of juvenile justice (Liefaard 2008). It recognizes the impact of deprivation of liberty on children, as well as the need for a child-specific human rights approach for children deprived of their liberty. Article 37 CRC contains legal requirements regarding deprivation of liberty on the one hand and provisions concerning the treatment of children deprived of liberty and their (procedural and substantive) legal status, on the other. Article 37 (b) CRC prohibits unlawful or arbitrary deprivation of liberty and introduces two additional requirements for children by stipulating that 'the arrest, detention or imprisonment ... shall be used only as a measure of last resort and for the shortest appropriate period of time'. Both requirements have no precedent in international treaty law (cf. rules 13, 17 and 19 Beijing Rules) and their introduction can be considered as 'among the most notable improvements and innovations which the [CRC] sets out' (Cantwell 1992, pp. 28–29). States parties, thus, are under the obligation to use deprivation of liberty regarding children with the utmost restraint and only after careful consideration, that is: based upon an individual assessment regarding the appropriateness and duration of the deprivation of liberty while giving due weight to the best interests of the child, including *inter alia* his age and maturity (Liefaard 2008; Schabas and Sax 2006). The implications of article 37 (b) CRC differ for the different forms of deprivation of liberty in the context of juvenile justice (such as arrest, police custody pre-trial detention and custodial sentences). As far as sentencing is concerned, it rules out, among others, minimum or mandatory sentences (see furthermore Liefaard 2008), which has been confirmed by the South African Constitutional Court that has ruled the minimum sentencing legislation for 16- or 17-year-olds unconstitutional since it would make imprisonment a first resort rather than a last resort.[32]

Particularly with regard to the requirements of last resort and shortest appropriate period of time, the CRC does not give much guidance (nor does the CRC Committee) and many question remain unanswered. It is up to the States to develop their legislation, create alternatives and to foster the incorporation of the requirements in the actual decision-making (see Liefaard 2008 for detailed recommendations). Moreover, article 37 (b) CRC's requirement of the shortest appropriate period of time is not unambiguous, since appropriateness is not necessarily short and therefore leaves room for longer forms of detention if regarded appropriate (see Liefaard 2008, p. 195ff).

In light of the legality of the deprivation of liberty, article 37 (d) CRC provides a number of procedural safeguards for children who are (at the risk of) being deprived of their liberty, such as the right to challenge the legality of the deprivation of liberty (*habeas corpus*) and the right to prompt access to legal *and* other appropriate assistance. The latter right is not so much related to the criminal justice proceedings (cf. art. 40 (2)(b)(ii) and (iii) CRC as mentioned earlier), but to the status of the child (i.e. deprived of his liberty).

If a child is deprived of his liberty, he must be treated with 'humanity and respect for the inherent dignity of the human person, and in a manner which takes into account the needs of persons of his or her age'. This 'right to be treated with humanity' as stipulated by article 37

---

31 With reference to H. von Henting (1937). *Punishment: Its Origins, Purpose and Psychology,* London: Hodge.
32 *Centre for Child Law v Minister of Justice,* 2009 (6) SA 632 (CC). See art. 28(1)(g) of the South African Constitution.

(c) CRC, can be considered the core article regarding the treatment of children deprived of liberty. It embodies a positive obligation for States parties to ensure minimum guarantees for the humane treatment of detained children and stipulates that children cannot be detained with adults and have the right to maintain contact with their family, which implies that the family will be informed about the detention of the child (art. 37 (c) CRC; see also art. 9 (3) CRC). In general, it implies that each child deprived of his liberty must be recognized as entitled to all rights under the CRC and that limitations of the enjoyment of the rights may only take place if necessary in light of the objectives of the deprivation of liberty, while taking into account the best interests of the child as well as the views of the child (arts. 3 (1) and 12 CRC). In addition, a child should have effective remedies available (such as the right to lodge complaints) to address (alleged) unlawful or arbitrary treatment (for a more detailed analysis of the legal status of the child deprived of his liberty, see Liefaard 2008). While bearing in mind the objectives of juvenile justice, article 40 (3) CRC furthers the creation of special institutions for children, which include 'distinct, child-centred staff, personnel, policies and practices' (cf. rule 10.3 Beijing Rules; CRC Committee 2007, para. 85). The minimum conditions of detention have been worked out in detail in the 1990 Havana Rules, which should be implemented and incorporated into domestic law (CRC Committee 2007, para. 88–89).

Again there is quite some room for interpretation and diversity in implementation. However, it is important to note that there is an increasing level of sophistication in filling in the requirements for the treatment of children deprived of their liberty. For example, the European Committee for the Prevention of Torture has developed its CPT standards, which provide detailed guidance on the treatment of detainees and prisoners, including children and which have been endorsed by the European Court of Human Rights in its case law. Moreover, the Council of Europe has adopted the European Rules for juvenile offenders subject to sanctions or measures (i.e. the European Havana Rules), which provide a similar set of rules that enables states to safeguard the rights of children deprived of their liberty.

6. Conclusion

The CRC has generated a substantial number of standard-setting initiatives at the international and regional level, resulting in a growing recognition of juvenile justice as a children's rights issue that revolves around fairness and child specificity. The CRC and related standards at the international and regional level undoubtedly provide an international benchmark for the treatment of children in conflict with the law. Despite the many open norms and its weaknesses, ambiguity or lack of clarity at certain points, the CRC does, supported by the CRC Committee, provide guidance on critical issues concerning the objectives of juvenile justice, the requirements of a fair trial, including the right to effective participation, and children deprived of their liberty. Many of the CRC provisions have been further developed in resolutions, recommendations, guidelines and case law, supported by interdisciplinary research. There clearly is an on-going effort to address the position of children in conflict with the law in a child-specific and fair manner within the particular complexity and diversity of the juvenile justice system throughout the world.

At the same time, there remains great discomfort concerning the (so far during the past 25–30 years) limited impact of these standards on the justice systems at the domestic level. Even if domestic law reform were initiated, often, significant challenges such as the absence of financial and human resources and lack of political will to implement domestic law and international legal standards, stand in the way of realizing a system that unconditionally respects the fundamental rights and fundamental freedoms of children, even if they have broken the law. Children in conflict with the law do not receive the attention and respect they are entitled to under international law and this seriously jeopardizes the short- and long-term interests of both the children and society.

Questions for debate and discussion

- Does the CRC provide sufficient guidance on the implications of a specific justice system for children? What are the most important gaps, controversies and uncertainties?
- Is there a tension between the right of the child to be treated fairly and the right to be treated in a manner that takes into account the child's age? And to what extent can both be accommodated in one justice system for children?
- What is the significance of (not) setting a MACR and is there common ground for a universal MACR? Should the CRC Committee reconsider its position? Why or why not?
- Should young adults (age 18–25) be protected under the CRC as well?
- Art. 37 (b) CRC requires that arrest, detention and imprisonment must only be used as a last resort and for the shortest appropriate period of time. What does shortest appropriate period of time mean and how does that relate to different objectives of juvenile justice?

Acknowledgement

The author would like to thank Maryse Hazelzet, LL.M for her research assistance.

References

Cantwell, N. (1992). 'The origins, development and significance of the United Nations Convention on the Rights of the Child', in S. Detrick (ed.), *The United Nations Convention on the Rights of the Child: A Guide to the 'Travaux Préparatoires'*, Dordrecht: Martinus Nijhoff, pp. 19–30.
Cavadino, M. and Dignan, J. (2006). *Penal Systems: A Comparative Approach*, London: Sage.
Church, R., Goldson, B. and Hindley, N. (eds) (2013). The minimum age of criminal responsibility: Clinical, criminological/sociological, developmental and legal perspectives [Special Issue]. *Youth Justice*, 13(2).
Cipriani, D. (2009). *Children's Rights and the Minimum Age of Criminal Responsibility. A Global Perspective*, Aldershot, UK: Ashgate.
Council of Europe/PC-CP (2014). Violence in Institutions for Juvenile Offenders, Strasbourg, 7 November 2014 (PC-CP (2014) 13 rev2). Available at www.coe.int/t/DGHL/STANDARDSETTING/CDPC/CDPC%20documents/PC-CP%20(2014)%2013E_REV%20Draft%20report%20on%20Violence %20in%20Institutions%20for%20Juvenile%20OffendersFinal.pdf
(CRC) UN Committee on the Rights of the Child (2006). *General Comment No. 8: The right of the child to protection from corporal punishment and other cruel or degrading forms of punishment* (Arts. 19; 28, para. 2; and 37, inter alia), UN Doc. CRC/C/GC/8, 2 March 2006.
(CRC) UN Committee on the Rights of the Child (2007). *General Comment No. 10: Children's rights in juvenile justice*, UN Doc. CRC/C/GC/10, 25 April 2007.
(CRC) UN Committee on the Rights of the Child (2009). *General Comment No. 12: The right of the child to be heard*, UN Doc. CRC/C/GC/12, 20 July 2009.
CRIN (2013). 'Making children criminals…'. Available at https://www.crin.org/en/library/publications/stop-making-children-criminals (last accessed January 2013).
Detrick, S. (ed.) (1992). *The United Nations Convention on the Rights of the Child: A Guide to the 'Travaux Préparatoires'*, Dordrecht: Martinus Nijhoff.
Detrick, S. (1999). *A Commentary on the United Nations Convention on the Rights of the Child*, Dordrecht: Martinus Nijhoff.
Doek, J.E. (2008). 'Juvenile justice: International rights and standards', in R. Loeber *et al. Tomorrow's Criminals. The Development of Child Delinquency and Effective Interventions*, Aldershot, UK: Ashgate, pp. 229–246.

Downes, D. and Morgan, R. (2012). 'Waiting for Ingleby: The minimum age of criminal responsibility – a red line issue', in T. Newburn and J. Peay (eds), *Policing: Politics, Culture and Control*, Oxford: Hart, pp. 245–264.

Dünkel, F. (2009). 'Diversion: A meaningful and successful alternative to punishment in European juvenile justice systems', in J. Junger-Tas and F. Dünkel (eds), *Reforming Juvenile Justice*, Dordrecht: Springer, pp. 147–164.

Dünkel, F., Pruin, I. and Grzywa, J. (2010). Sanctions systems and trends in the development of sentencing practices, in F. Dünkel, I. Pruin, J. Grzywa, J. and P. Horsfield (eds), *Juvenile Justice Systems in Europe: Current situation, reform developments and good practices*, Mönchengladbach, Germany: Forum Verlag Godesberg, pp. 1623–1690.

Feria-Tinta, M. (2014). 'The CRC as a litigation tool before the Inter-American System of Protection of Human Rights', in T. Liefaard and J.E. Doek (eds), *Litigating the Rights of the Child*, Dordrecht: Springer.

Gallinetti, J. (2009). *Getting to Know the Child Justice Act*, Bellville, South Africa: The Child Justice Alliance.

Goldson, B. and Kilkelly, U. (2013). 'International human rights standards and child imprisonment: Potentialities and limitations', *International Journal of Children's Rights*, 2, 345–371.

Goldson, B. and Muncie, J. (2012). 'Towards a global "child friendly" juvenile justice?', *International of Law, Crime and Justice*, 40(1), 47–64.

Inter-American Commission on Human Rights/Rapporteurship on the Rights of the Child (2011). *Juvenile Justice and Human Rights in the Americas*, 13 July 2011, OEA Ser.L/V/II Doc.78 Eng.

Joint Report (2012). Joint Report of the Office of the High Commission for Human Rights on prevention of and responses to violence against children within the juvenile justice system, 27 June 2012, UN Doc. A/HRC/21/25.

Killias, M., Redondo, S. and Sarnecki, J. (2012). 'European perspectives', in R. Loeber et al. (eds), *Persisters and Desisters in Crime from Adolescence Into Adulthood: Explanation, Prevention, and Punishment*, Aldershot, UK: Ashgate, pp. 291–334.

Kilkelly, U. (2014). 'CRC in litigation under the ECHR', in T. Liefaard and J.E. Doek (eds), *Litigating the Rights of the Child*, Dordrecht: Springer.

Liefaard, T. (2008). *Deprivation of Liberty of Children in Light of International Human Rights Law and standards*, Antwerp: Intersentia.

Liefaard, T. (2012). 'Juvenile in transition from juvenile justice to adult criminal justice', in R. Loeber et al. (eds), *Persisters and Desisters in Crime from Adolescence Into Adulthood: Explanation, Prevention, and Punishment*, Aldershot, UK: Ashgate, pp. 159–200.

Liefaard, T. and van den Brink, Y. (2014). 'Children's right to legal counsel during police interrogations', *Erasmus Law Review*, 7(4) (forthcoming).

Pruin, I. (2010). 'The scope of juvenile justice systems in Europe', in F. Dünkel et al. (eds), *Juvenile Justice Systems in Europe*, Mönchengladbach: Forum Verlag Godesberg, pp. 1514–1555.

Rap, S.E. (2013). *The Participation of Juvenile Defendants in the Youth Court: A Comparative Study of Juvenile Justice Procedures in Europe*, Amsterdam: Pallas.

Rapporteurship on the Rights of the Child of the Inter-American Commission on Human Rights (2008). *Children and their Rights in the Inter-American System of Human Rights* (2nd ed.), 29 October 2008, OEA/Ser.L/V/II.133, Doc. 34. Available at www.cidh.oas.org/countryrep/Infancia2eng/Infancia2Toc.eng.htm (last accessed 29 May 2014).

Schabas, W. and Sax, H. (2006). *Article 37: Prohibition of Torture, Death Penalty, Life Imprisonment and Deprivation of Liberty*, Leiden: Martinus Nijhoff.

Smith, R. (2014). *Youth Justice. Ideas, Policy, Practice*, Abingdon, UK: Routledge.

Special Representative on Violence Against Children (2013). *Promoting Restorative Justice For Children*, New York.

Trépanier, J. (2007). 'Children's right in juvenile justice: A historical glance', in A. Alen et al. (eds), *The UN Children's Rights Convention: Theory Meets Practice*, Antwerp: Intersentia, pp. 509–530.

United Nations Secretary-General's Study on Violence against Children/Paulo Sérgio Pinheiro (2006). *World Report on Violence Against Children*, Geneva 2006.

UNICEF Innocenti Research Centre, *Law Reform and Implementation of the Convention on the Rights of the Child*, Florence.

Weijers, I. (2006). *Jeugdige dader, volwassen straf?*, Deventer: Kluwer.

15

The human rights of children in the context of formal alternative care

Nigel Cantwell

The alternative care of children comprises all measures taken, once a child cannot be looked after by his or her parents, for whatever reason. These measures may have to respond to anything from sudden emergencies and short- or medium-term incapacities of various kinds to more durable situations such as the death of the parents, the abandonment of the child or the definitive withdrawal of parental rights and responsibilities. This variety of circumstances and, consequently, of the aims and nature of a given placement indicates the complexities of providing suitable alternative care and, even more, doing so in compliance with the overall human rights of the child. The term "alternative care for children" should never mask the fact that what is at stake is the most appropriate care solution for each individual child.

In most countries, the great majority of alternative care for children in situations such as these is arranged on an informal basis. Members of the extended family or others in the community who are known to them take over day-to-day parental tasks for the time and to the degree required, with no outside decision-making involved and invariably no special supervision or support on the part of official services.

A smaller, but often significant, proportion of children deemed to need alternative care are subject to formal arrangements. Broadly, these are of two main kinds: family-based settings, such as foster care, and placements in residential facilities, ranging from small group homes to larger establishments. In these formal cases, the State – usually through its official services and sometimes in conjunction with the courts – has ultimate responsibility both for assessing the need for the placement and for ensuring the suitability and quality of the care provided.

It is important to note that legalised adoption is generally not viewed as a *form* of alternative care but rather as a potential *outcome* for children in formal or informal alternative care who will never be able to return to the care of their parents but could benefit from living in another "permanent" family. Thus, an adopted child is considered to be once again in (new) parental care, not in "alternative" care. At the same time, of course, there is such an intimate linkage between adoption and alternative care that reference to the former cannot be entirely dismissed from the discourse on alternative care measures themselves.

The alternative care (and adoption) of children is a sphere that crystallises, and creates much debate on, crucial issues regarding the realisation of a wide range of the human rights of children, as well as attitudes towards children themselves.

A key background feature to this debate is undoubtedly the particularly high significance of "localisation" factors, alluded to in the Introduction, for interpreting rights' implications and how the best interests of the child are perceived (Bessell and Gal, 2008). Every society has developed its own informal ways of responding to children without parental care, with social and religious tenets often influencing how that care can or cannot be envisaged in practice. Those same tenets, together with historical, political and economic factors, have also determined the way that formal alternative care has come to be organised in each society, resulting in what are now vastly divergent systems throughout the world. Similarly, both informal and formal care provision reflect diverse "child images" (Bessell and Gal, 2008) – though too often the image of total dependency and of needs limited to little more than basic survival – not to mention discriminatory images of specific groups, such as children with disabilities and those of ethnic minorities. Consequently, and notwithstanding what might generally be promoted as "good" or qualified as "bad" practices, context-specific considerations are particularly vital in the field of alternative care, meaning that a constructively critical review of global conventional wisdom on children's rights is necessary if those rights are to be seen as relevant and applicable in each situation.

This chapter therefore first looks at how the rights of the child "in relation to formal alternative care" (i.e. not only regarding the provision of alternative care but also through explicit recognition of the need to prevent recourse to it) have evolved. It then considers in more detail what efforts are to be made before formal alternative care can be seen as justified from a children's rights standpoint and, from that same perspective, what factors might determine the degree to which such care provision is acceptable once it is shown to be necessary. In so doing, it seeks to give examples of how practice and approaches vary widely, and often reflect different images of the child, but should be seen in a broader context before they are assessed and reacted to in the light of children's rights criteria. It concludes by pointing to a number of issues that need to be tackled – or at least to be tackled differently – in order to enhance respect in practice for the human rights of children in this sphere.

1. Changing approaches, developing standards

It is instructive to review briefly how alternative care has been broached in international human rights instruments over the course of time. As in other spheres, these instruments trace a gradual move away from considering the child purely as a vulnerable being in need of protection to someone who is a member of a family and community and who, in particular, must be consulted and involved in decisions about, in this instance, by whom and where he or she wants to be cared for, and with what aim.

Initially, the focus was indeed a purely charitable one, limited to responding to the situation of parentless and destitute children. Thus, the first allusion to the question in an internationally approved text was a reference to "the orphan and the waif" who "must be sheltered and succoured" (League of Nations, 1924, Principle 2).

The subsequent 1959 UN Declaration of the Rights of the Child gave some needed perspective to the provision of alternative care by stipulating notably that "[the child] shall, wherever possible, grow up in the care and under the responsibility of his parents and, in any case, in an atmosphere of affection and of moral and material security; a child of tender years shall not, save in exceptional circumstances, be separated from his mother." This Declaration noted that "society and the public authorities shall have the duty to extend particular care to children without a family and to those without adequate means of support…" (United Nations, 1959, Principle 6). That provision expanded somewhat the range of situations in which children might be seen as needing some form of alternative care provided by others – "without a family" is wider than "orphan" – and it introduced the concept of "duty", stressing accountability as opposed to moral obligation. What was notably missing, from a rights standpoint, was any indication of the way in which provision of such "particular care" should be envisaged.

Subsequent general human rights instruments reinforced the "duty" aspect but also shed no light on what kinds of alternative care would be deemed acceptable. The only child-specific article of the 1966 International Covenant on Civil and Political Rights (ICCPR) notes the child's right "to such measures of protection as are required of his status of minor, on the part of his family, society and the State" (Art. 24). For its part, Article 10(3) of the 1966 International Covenant on Economic, Social and Cultural Rights (ICESCR) simply calls for "special measures of protection and assistance".

These lacunae were tentatively addressed in broad terms by a far more focused UN text that followed in 1986: the Declaration on Social and Legal Principles Relating to the Protection and Welfare of Children, with special reference to Foster Placement and Adoption Nationally and Internationally (United Nations, 1986). The principles set out in this text, approved during the period when the 1989 Convention on the Rights of the Child (CRC) was being drafted, had a substantial influence on the way the relevant rights in that treaty were shaped. First, it states unequivocally that "[t]he first priority for a child is to be cared for by his or her own parents" (United Nations, 1986, Art. 3). Second, in comparison to previous instruments, it broadens considerably the scope of situations covered to comprise any child for whom parental care is "unavailable or inappropriate" (United Nations, 1986, Art. 4). Third, it refers for the first time to how alternative care is to be provided, strongly promoting recourse to family-based alternative care "by relatives of the child's parents [or] by another substitute – foster or adoptive – family", with placement in an "appropriate institution" only to be considered "if necessary" (United Nations, 1986, Art. 4), thereby establishing a first appreciation of the overall relative desirability of the different options. In addition, its Preamble recognises the role of *kafala* of Islamic law as an alternative care option, the very first mention of this measure in an international instrument. All of these elements find reflection in the CRC, as does, albeit on a more general level, the principle that, "as appropriate", the child should be "involved" in all matters relating to a foster placement (United Nations, 1986, Art. 12), which clearly signalled a first step towards acceptance of a child's agency rather than the child image founded essentially on protection needs.

At the same time, this Declaration inadvertently introduced a degree of confusion into the debate, not least by dealing with a single form of alternative care – foster care – alongside a potential outcome of such care, adoption. This confusion was unfortunately maintained in the CRC (Art. 20.3). In contrast, the 1986 Declaration diverges from the CRC by making a clear distinction between parental care and care within the child's wider family, since it groups "relatives of the child's parents" with "another substitute – foster or adoptive – family" (United Nations, 1986, Art. 4) rather than espousing the overall notion of "family environment" that, as noted below, characterises the approach in Article 20.1 of the CRC. The latter's implicit – though only implicit – recognition of the importance of the informal role of the extended family in providing alternative care in most societies is more in line with context-specific interpretations. It also shores up the child's right to live in his or her "family environment" as the first option wherever possible, and can thus be viewed as constituting grounds for efforts to minimise recourse to formal extra-familial placements.

Otherwise, the CRC essentially reinforces the various recommended thrusts of the 1986 Declaration in binding form. It sets great store in upholding the child's right "as far as possible to know and be cared for by his or her parents" (Art. 7.1) and obligates States Parties to take a variety of measures designed to enable this. It stipulates in essence that alternative care must be foreseen for any child who is "temporarily or permanently deprived of his or her family environment" or "cannot be allowed to remain" there, and gives non-exclusive examples of such care as being "foster placement, *kafala* of Islamic law, adoption or if necessary placement in suitable institutions…" (CRC, Art. 20). Through Article 12.2, it establishes the child's right to be consulted in "any judicial and administrative proceedings affecting the child", which obviously includes placement in formal alternative care. In addition, Article 20.3 requires that the "continuity of the child's upbringing" and his or her cultural background be given due consideration in decision-making, which again might be seen, *inter alia*, as the implicit promotion of kinship care. The CRC also institutes a previously non-existent obligation to review the necessity and appropriateness of any placement on a regular basis (CRC, Art. 25), for which any changes in the family situation would be relevant. Interestingly, however, while the CRC indeed talks of the need for alternative care of children who cannot be in their "family environment" – a term clearly wider than "parental care" – it in fact makes no explicit reference to the role of the extended family as a provider of informal kinship care (their role as per Art. 5 of the CRC in providing "appropriate direction and guidance" for the child to exercise his/her rights cannot be interpreted *prima facie* – or on the basis of the *Travaux préparatoires* – as extending to this; Cantwell and Holzscheiter, 2008, pp. 32–36). This and certain other questions raised by the tenor of Article 20 of the CRC regarding the proper approach to alternative care are discussed later.

Notwithstanding the CRC, the lack of detailed and concrete internationally-agreed standards in this sphere led to a UNICEF-inspired initiative calling for the development of such an instrument. The result was the 2009 Guidelines for the Alternative Care of Children, which the UN General Assembly approved by consensus, that seek to build on the rights set out in the CRC and to give detailed policy indications on three main issues: how can recourse to alternative care be avoided, when should alternative care be deemed necessary and, in that case, how is an appropriate care setting to be ensured (United Nations, 2009).

The initial draft of the 2009 Guidelines was prepared by international NGOs and UNICEF, with numerous direct inputs from individual experts and young people with experience of alternative care, and finally negotiated with and among governmental representatives. As noted in the Guidelines themselves, they are designed to "[take] account of the developing knowledge and experience in this sphere" (United Nations, 2009, §2) and they indeed arguably constitute the best available compilation, and accessible synopsis, of state-of-the-art thinking and approaches to the promotion and protection of the human rights of "children who are deprived of parental care or who are at risk of being so" (United Nations, 2009, §1). Along with the CRC, these Guidelines naturally form the main backdrop to the issues reviewed in this chapter.

2. Necessity and suitability

The 2009 Guidelines contain a raft of recommended policy orientations directed towards family strengthening and support, underscoring the upstream linkage of the alternative care system with overall social and economic policy. It is not sufficient to foresee "quality care" as such; tackling the factors behind family breakdown is now an integral part of strategies on alternative care.

This implies efforts at both the macro level of primary prevention – ranging from providing access to basic services and social security through to combating societal problems such as stigmatisation, discrimination and marginalisation – as well as targeted, secondary prevention measures to support families that are vulnerable or in crisis. It also involves setting limits on when "child protection" concerns should lead to decisions to withdraw a child from parental care: material poverty alone, for example, is no longer considered good cause to do so (United Nations, 2009, §15). This has given rise to the idea that placements in formal alternative care settings must conform to the *"necessity principle"*, i.e. they should not be ordered or allowed unless it is shown that, despite support, the child genuinely cannot be maintained in his or her family environment.[1]

If recourse to formal alternative care is deemed necessary for a child, it must take place in an appropriate setting, in other words the concomitant *"suitability principle"* has to be respected. This principle is grounded in a variety of criteria involving both the setting's compliance with the human rights of the child as a whole and its fitness to meet the specific needs of the individual child in question (Cantwell *et al.*, 2012). It underpins a major aspect of current policy: the move towards deinstitutionalising the alternative care system, with a clear emphasis on promoting family-based or family-type settings where the child can forge a bond with surrogate parental figures. At the same time, the fundamental importance to be given to the child's own family means that alternative care is seen primarily and ideally as a temporary measure, designed above all to look after a child until he or she can return to the family environment or, failing that, move to a "permanent" family setting such as through adoption (Human Rights Council, 2009, §II(13)).

This has challenging implications for the child protection system. It is often difficult, for example, to identify families that are both willing and able to look after children for undetermined but relatively short periods, providing care and affection without becoming overly-attached, as well as in many cases taking on the delicate task of ensuring constructive relations with the child's parent(s). In addition, as discussed later, deinstitutionalisation is an objective that is by no means always shared, particularly (though by no means only) by private care providers running large residential facilities. But *grosso modo*, the quality of an alternative care system is currently assessed largely on the basis of its ability to plan for, and then put into practice under appropriate conditions, the child's departure from it as soon as possible. The main exceptions to this will be the relatively small proportion of children who need long-term specialist treatment, those for whom neither return to the family nor adoption is feasible or desired, and those who freely express their preference to remain in their alternative care setting.

Two mechanisms are key to ensuring that both the necessity and suitability principles are adhered to and to safeguarding children's rights when formal alternative care is envisaged or undertaken. The first is a "gatekeeping" body that is in a position to examine systematically whether all options have been pursued to avoid a formal care placement – which itself requires the existence of community-based support services – and determines which kind of care setting is likely to respond best to the individual child's needs, characteristics and circumstances, in turn presupposing the availability of a range of settings from which to choose. The second is a placement review process that regularly evaluates both the continuing need for the placement in the light of any significant changes or in the family circumstances, and its on-going appropriateness for meeting the child's specific (and potentially evolving) needs. Both mechanisms are notably to foresee full consultation with the child concerned before reaching decisions. According to the country situation, however, effective mechanisms of this kind are

---

1   For a discussion of the principles of "necessity" and "suitability", see Cantwell *et al.*, 2012, pp. 22–23).

avowedly difficult to set in place, not only in terms of resource allocation as such but also in view of what may be only nominal implication of the State in alternative care provision.

All of these basic policy orientations seem clear and well-founded in rights considerations but, as in other spheres affecting children, there are dangers that they be taken as unassailable principles for blanket implementation and unquestioned watchwords for "best practice". In line with the critical approach proposed in this Handbook, many deserve to be analysed in greater depth if responses to the alternative care needs of children are to correspond both to the fullest enjoyment of their human rights and to the realities in which that is to be effected. The range of issues that are pertinent to alternative care provision, as reflected in the wide scope of the 2009 Guidelines, clearly defies comprehensive examination here. The following pages focus on three key areas where it seems particularly important to emphasise context, dig deeper and potentially adopt a more nuanced approach:

1   The role of informal kinship care in preventing the need for formal placements
2   The limits of family-based formal alternative care
3   Strategies for deinstitutionalisation

3. Reducing recourse to placements in formal alternative care

As noted above, the State's obligation to "ensure alternative care" (CRC, Art. 20.2) first implies primary and secondary prevention measures to enable the child to remain with his or her family wherever possible. These should include support for informal solutions as a means of avoiding the need for placements in formal alternative care. Indeed, in most countries, industrialised and developing alike, the great majority of children who are unable to live with their parents are cared for on an informal basis by relatives (kin) or, in some cases, close members of their community (United Nations, 2009, §18). At the same time, from a children's rights standpoint, there remains both confusion and debate as to the role that the State might validly play regarding such informal arrangements, in terms of support, protection and making certain that the child agrees with the kind of arrangement offered.

3.1. The role and recognition of informal kinship care

The vital role played by kinship care is widely acknowledged. This is reflected, for example, in concerns expressed about the ramifications of the growing inability of such traditional coping mechanisms to cater to the needs of children who have lost one or both parents as a result of the AIDS pandemic, or in contexts where extended families are geographically separated due to younger members migrating to urban areas (Nyambedha et al., 2003). In a different vein, it is also demonstrated by the fact that statutory services in a number of countries, such as Australia and New Zealand, have been increasingly formalising kinship foster care arrangements instead of placing children in designated unrelated foster families (Boetto, 2010).

As intimated previously, States' precise obligations under the CRC regarding recognition of, and support for, kinship care are quite difficult to discern. While the requirement to provide "special assistance and protection" kicks in when it is not viable that the child remains in his or her "family environment" (CRC, Art. 20.1), other assistance and protection demands of the State set out in the treaty refer not only to parents and family but also to others having legal or *de facto* responsibility for the child. Thus, among many examples, a child has the right, as far as possible, to know and be cared for by his or her *parents* (CRC, Art. 7.1) and States are to assist *parents and legal guardians* in their child-rearing responsibilities (CRC, Art. 18.2), whereas the child's right to benefit from social security may depend on the resources and circumstances of *the persons having responsibility for the maintenance of the child* (CRC, Art. 26) and the *parents or others responsible for the child* have primary responsibility to provide appropriate conditions of living, with the State obligated to assist them, where necessary, to implement that right (CRC, Arts. 27.2 and 27.3).

Against that background, the 2009 Guidelines make a special effort both to recognise the role played by kinship care and other informal traditional arrangements, and to set out the kinds of support that States should grant to those caring for a child in this way (United Nations, 2009).[2] There is, however, a palpable – and somewhat understandable – tension in the document regarding the level and form of State intervention that would be both warranted and acceptable in what is essentially viewed as a "private" sphere. While informal coping mechanisms should be "respected and promoted to the extent that they can be shown to be consistent with the children's rights and best interests" (United Nations, 2009, §75), at the same time "special and appropriate measures designed to protect children in informal care" (United Nations, 2009, §79) are to be devised.

Among the identified advantages of kinship care are: preservation of the child's family, community and cultural ties; avoidance of trauma resulting from moving in with strangers; and less likelihood of multiple placements. However, kinship or friendship is no guarantee of welfare, protection and ability to cope.[3] Although "available research suggests that most children are at least as safe in kinship care as they are in non-relative foster-care" (National Resource Center for Foster Care and Permanency Planning, 1995, p. 83), this means that a minority are not, and "some relatives may be abusive or neglectful toward the children because they come from the same 'troubled' family" (National Resource Center for Foster Care and Permanency Planning, p. 5). Other identified risk factors and problems associated with this form of care include: children being less likely to receive services than in non-kin foster care; relatives unable to access services and support available to formal foster carers; and risk of intra-familial conflict over the division of responsibilities and decision-making powers. Further, if kinship care is formalised or carers receive special allowances, there may be financial disincentives to returning the child to parental care.[4]

Taking account of these issues and making certain that kinship care takes place in positive conditions of course poses numerous practical problems. In most countries, State resources are vastly inadequate for ensuring protective support and supervision in informal kinship care, especially where such arrangements carry known risks yet are fully accepted by the communities concerned. In addition, resources made available through foreign donors are invariably devoted to the development of formalised care provision, which only tends to weaken the kinship care option.

Overall, the protection of children's rights through and in kinship care starkly highlights – even in industrialised countries – the difficult relationship between customary coping mechanisms and duties of the State, all the more so in that State obligations in this case are not fully clarified in the CRC.

---

2   Notably § 75, 76–79 and § 18.
3   Analogously, while it was agreed in discussions during the drafting of the 1993 Hague Convention on Intercountry Adoption that preference should normally be given to potential adopters who are family members, the treaty contains no dispensation from the normal vetting process in their respect.
4   These and other issues are discussed in National Resource Center for Foster Care and Permanency Planning (1995).

3.2. Child-headed households

If it had been finalised a few years later, the CRC might well have included explicit reference to child-headed households, as it does to child refugees and asylum seekers. Households composed of minor siblings and, in some cases, other children from the extended family or community, in the absence of available adult caregivers, are a long-standing phenomenon, particularly in Africa and Asia. However, child-headed households only captured international attention once the ramifications of the AIDS pandemic became clear in the late 1980s, subsequently reinforced by the consequences of events such as the genocide in Rwanda in the mid-1990s. This attention came too late for reflection in the CRC (Sloth-Nielsen, 2004, p. 6). As it stands, therefore, the CRC has had to be "interpreted" as regards State obligations to these households and the most appropriate response to the children concerned. The debate on these issues provided a particularly evocative example of the dispute between those espousing the "protective" approach to children's rights, with the children concerned being seen solely through a vulnerability lens, and those more inclined towards a participatory perspective where children have agency and are recognised as being actors in the exercise of their rights (CRC, Art. 5) and involved in decision-making (CRC, Art. 12).

Not surprisingly, the immediate reaction – in the industrialised countries at least – tended to be "protective" and "paternalistic": such households were "automatically [...] judged as unacceptable" (Dube, 2011, p. 1). These children were without parental care and vulnerable to exploitation, with the household head taking on tasks and responsibilities incompatible with the status of "child".

Gradually, however, "participation" issues began to prevail, as more attention was paid to the child's "right to be heard" (CRC, Art. 12.2) and understanding increased of both the motives behind children's choice of remaining together and the ways in which the support they required might be foreseen. Various studies[5] documented their fears about being separated if taken into a formal care setting, being exploited if placed with extended family members, and losing the family house, land, and other possessions if they were moved elsewhere. At the same time, they complained of lacking resources, protection and guidance. Attention thus turned towards enhancing coping strategies and finding appropriate ways of satisfying those needs: taking these concerns into account, it could be posited that, from a children's rights standpoint, these children were in a family environment and therefore eligible, as a family, for assistance and protection *in situ* from the State (Sloth-Nielsen, 2004, p. 5 ff).

South Africa played a key role in moving this second approach forward. Its Law Reform Commission decided to assimilate child-headed households with informal kinship care rather than looking at them as an "extraordinary" phenomenon by virtue of a child being responsible for the group (South African Law Reform Commission, 2002). It found that there was general agreement that child-headed households "have the advantage of enabling siblings to remain together and provide mutual support, while also providing for continuity of relationships with and support from their community" (South African Law Reform Commission, p. 561) as well as for their continued residence in their family home and control of family assets (Tolfree, 2004). The Commission proposed their legal recognition "as a placement option for orphaned children in need of care" (South African Law Reform Commission, 2002, p. 561) and consequently for provision to be made to ensure adequate supervision and support by persons or entities selected or approved by, and accountable to, an official body. This stand

---

5   See, among many: University of South Africa (2008) and Masondo (2006).

informed the relevant provisions of the Children's Act of 2005 and has had considerable impact on the way child-headed households are viewed globally today.

4. How should formal alternative care be provided?

Once the necessity of a formal alternative care placement has been demonstrated, a decision has to be made as to the care setting that should correspond best to the needs, situation and wishes of the child.

This last factor – the child's wishes – is a nascent element in decision-making, growing in importance according to where and when the language of rights becomes more accepted by the alternative care system, but as yet is totally ignored by most. Given the wide variety of reasons for children coming into formal alternative care (from orphanhood and relinquishment through to maltreatment and poverty), the temporary or longer-term nature of the envisaged placement, and the fact that the latter may have been instigated by the family, offered by a facility or ordered by the competent authorities, it is unsurprising that children will express diverse expectations regarding their care environment – if they are invited to do so. Peterson-Badali *et al.* (2008), for example, have found that, as a group, "[c]hildren with histories of maltreatment who are living in care may find abuse and safety issues less salient than non-maltreated youth because they have already experienced violations of their rights to physical and emotional integrity…" (p. 114). Individual children within each group will also have differing concerns and priorities that should help determine the most appropriate care setting for them.

At a recent meeting, a workshop of young people with experience of out-of-home care characterised what children and young people are looking for in a placement as: "safety, stability and support", in order to give them "a sense of confidence and security" (Quality in Alternative Care Conference, 2011). They thus implicitly recognised that settings have to differ and also may unavoidably change – not least as a result of the placement review process – but those realities should not in themselves constitute an obstacle to the child being able to benefit from "safety, stability and support" in each placement.

There is undoubtedly a need to look more closely at how well that vision corresponds to the ultimate goal of "permanency" that placements should be seeking to achieve according to the mission statement, or its policy equivalent, of most organised alternative care systems. As just one example:

> Permanency is a priority area to provide stability for children and young people in care. Governments should provide all children with the right to a comprehensive range of permanency options, including adoption. Decisions about permanency should be made as soon as possible to provide the child/young person with a sense of belonging and security. Early decision-making is important to avoid deleterious delays in establishing permanency.
>
> *(Association of Children's Welfare Agencies, n.d.)*

"Planning for permanency", through family reintegration or a durable (usually family-based) alternative, thus figures large in the 2009 Guidelines (United Nations, 2009, § 60–63). Of course permanency can be foreseen but never guaranteed. Up to 8% of children adopted from foster care in the USA "were placed out of the home after 4 years" (Child Welfare Information Gateway, 2012, p. 6). In the UK, it is estimated that breakdown rates for children adopted at age 6 or over are around 25%, and for those aged 1 to 5 years at adoption, the figure is 10% (UK Parliament, 2012). Concern is increasingly being voiced that the overriding quest for "permanency" as such is leading to rushed decisions and undue pressures on all involved (families, social workers, courts and the child protection system as a whole), coupled with inadequate assistance in subsequently ensuring the viability of the "permanent" arrangement. Importantly, the call for permanency as the ultimate goal may detract attention from the more immediate goal of "safety, stability and support" through alternative care provision itself and its outcome.

In addition is the "wicked" problem that, as Bessell and Gal (2008, p. 283) point out, "[c]hildren in the care and protection system do not fare well on a range of indicators, when compared to the overall population". Poor outcomes might be expected for young people leaving institutional care: in Russia according to a study cited by Holm-Hansen et al. (2003), for example, 20% resorted to crime, 14% ended up in prostitution and fully 10% committed suicide (p. 83). But in Scotland, children leaving the largely family-based formal alternative care system are at least ten times less likely to go on to higher education than their peers and in England and Wales, 11.5% of young offenders are, or have been, looked-after children (Scottish Government, 2014; Patel, 2004).

It follows that decisions on formal alternative care placements as a protection measure may respond to valid children's rights concerns but can equally create children's rights problems themselves, and these are not resolved simply by preferring family-based settings to residential care.

4.1. The promotion of formal family-based alternative care

While the development of foster care and similar family-based settings is a key thrust of initiatives to improve alternative care for children, in many societies taking an unrelated child into one's home, whether on an informal or formal basis, is by no means an anodyne act. It may be, variously, culturally unacceptable, or subject to certain conditions, or generally undertaken for reasons likely to be incompatible with the aims of foster care or similar practices.

An assessment carried out in Syria, just prior to the outbreak of conflict there in 2011, showed that the way that certain religious tenets were interpreted and applied in that country meant that, in principle, fostering unrelated children is seen as counter to Islamic traditions and values (Cantwell and Jacomy-Vité, 2011). Only "foundlings" (babies or young children abandoned with complete anonymity) are entitled to family-based care, under the practice called *el haq*. Children who are orphaned, relinquished or deprived of parental care for other reasons have little prospect of living in a family-based setting unless they are taken in by the extended family (Cantwell and Jacomy-Vité, 2011). In other countries of Islamic Law, there can be more flexibility in this regard. In Sudan, for example, it has proved possible to set up programmes to identify, prepare and support families willing and able to provide alternative care on either an emergency or a more permanent basis, as well as for "specialist" care for children with special needs (UNICEF Sudan, 2007). Algeria has long recognised *kafala*[6] for both orphans and children "abandoned" (not necessarily anonymously) and the *kafil* undertakes to care for the child as he would his own.

An (unpublished) assessment of the situation in Ghana by this author in 2013 provided only slightly more nuanced findings. Thus, in general, "stranger children" could and would be taken

---

6   The term "*kafala*" is a generic concept roughly equivalent to "sponsorship". As applied to child protection in countries of Islamic law, the implications of this "sponsorship" vary significantly from one to another. Reference to *kafala* in the CRC and 2009 Guidelines is clearly intended to denote the child's physical presence in the home of the (*kafila*) family concerned, and the latter's responsibility for all aspects of his/her care and welfare on a day-to-day basis.

into a household, but invariably with the intention of creating a long-term relationship in the form of customary adoption. Not only does this mean that the notion of providing temporary foster care to "stranger children" has been virtually unknown, but also that, if the child proves "unsuitable" for any reason, care in the family will end. Alongside this practice, in significant parts of the country, women who inherit the title of, or are designated as, Queen Mothers shoulder responsibility for the care of unaccompanied children who arrive in a community from elsewhere, sometimes in their own home but more usually by placing them with other families – whose motives, it is sometimes alleged, lie more with a desire for domestic or other help than to fulfilling the child's need for alternative care, but as yet there is no documented evidence in this respect.

Clearly, as internal migration to cities has increased in countries such as Ghana, the physical proximity of extended family members – and hence even affective links within families – has been eroded. Societies, communities and families that are otherwise used to relying on kinship responses to children's needs in these situations are suddenly – within less than a generation – confronted with predicaments concerning their children that were previously almost unknown.

It is against such backdrops, where the significance of "localisation" in efforts to promote children's rights seems crystal clear, that the almost unquestioned global effort to promote formal foster care has to be assessed.

Formal foster care is defined by the 2009 Guidelines as the placement of children by social services with families that are "selected, qualified, approved and supervised" to look after them for the period required (United Nations, 2009, § 29.c.ii). It is widely considered to be the preferred form of alternative care if informal kinship care is unavailable or inappropriate.

Without putting it into doubt as such, this standpoint has to be examined more closely. Over and above obstacles to caring for "stranger children", the elements of the above-quoted definition ("selected, qualified, approved and supervised") are particularly important: setting up and maintaining a functional foster care system requires considerable investment and expertise for ensuring that carers are selected on the basis of recognised criteria and then validly "supervised" – a term that can be taken to include support – during placements. Matching for each placement must be ensured, so that the capacities of the carers can be determined as meeting the needs of the child. Serial and destructive foster placements are indicative both of a policy imperative that family-based alternative care be prioritised in all cases, regardless of a child's needs and characteristics, as well as of inadequacies in the matching and support processes.

Foster care demands an unusual level of commitment, flexibility and professionalism, usually including the willingness and ability to engage positively with a child's parent(s) with a view to family reintegration. This means that the potential pool of foster carers may be small as compared with the perceived need: a government-backed recruiting drive in Britain in 2000, for example, reportedly resulted in just 1,000 applications compared with a target of 7,000 (McVeigh, 2001). Reliance on a formal foster-care system can become exaggerated, especially in the context of moves towards deinstitutionalisation. One result can be the recruitment of insufficiently prepared and supported foster carers, another the over-burdening of existing foster carers.

Countries considering the establishment or development of formal foster care clearly need to be made aware of the dangers of pinning their hopes significantly on this system. The resource and other implications of ensuring its operation in accordance with international standards and the protection of children's rights are very considerable, as are the risks for children of not doing so. These considerations must never be marginalised in the "rights-based" promotion of family-based alternative care.

4.2. Deinstitutionalisation

The only explicit example of non-family-based care given in both the 1986 Declaration and the CRC is an appropriate or suitable "institution". This has to some extent fuelled an unhelpful and unwarranted amalgam between residential care and institutional placements, where anything other than a family-based care setting tends to be unjustifiably decried, not to say demonised.

The 2009 Guidelines have managed to clarify this issue to some degree, by limiting the meaning of "institutions" to "large residential care facilities" (United Nations, 2009, § 23).[7] Only these facilities are to be targeted by deinstitutionalisation, whereas residential care in general is recognised as a necessary component of the range of options to be foreseen to cater to the varied needs and circumstances of individual children, provided it is used only for positive reasons, i.e. when it is seen to correspond better to those needs and circumstances than would a family-based setting (United Nations, 2009, § 54 and 21).

It would be difficult to identify any current evidence-based study that takes issue with the finding that, not only do placements in institutional care generally have less favourable outcomes than those in family-based settings, but also that those placements often have a negative impact on children's overall development that may be serious and irreversible.

As noted previously, the subsidiarity of institutional placements was established by Article 4 of the 1986 Declaration and echoed in the CRC which notes, as the final item in a list of alternative care options, that these could include "if necessary placement in suitable institutions for the care of children" (CRC, Art. 20.3). The CRC Committee has interpreted both the substance and the positioning of this wording to indicate that this solution is a last resort, and consistently advocates in its Concluding Observations on States Parties' reports that active measures be taken to phase out recourse to institutional care.

The 2009 Guidelines go further. They suggest that, "in accordance with the predominant opinion of experts" (United Nations, 2009, § 22) and with limited exceptions, alternative care for young children, especially those under 3, should be provided only in family-based settings. They also propose that each State puts in place "an overall deinstitutionalisation strategy" aimed at the "progressive elimination" of such facilities (United Nations, 2009, § 23).

A report adopted by the Inter-American Commission on Human Rights in 2013 sees this approach as not only responding to research findings but also as being grounded in "the child's right to grow up, develop and be cared for in a favourable family environment [...]" (Comisión Interamericana de Derechos Humanos, 2013, p. 302). References such as this to a "right to [live in] a family" are, however, not necessarily helpful to rights-based advocacy regarding alternative care. First, as Van Bueren (1998, p. 93) has stated very clearly, "[a]lthough children have a right under a variety of treaties to respect for family life, [...] children, as with adults, understandably, do not have a right to a family *per se* under international law". Second, such a "right" would imply that any child not being cared for in a family setting – for example in a "suitable" residential facility as foreseen under the CRC – would automatically be considered as a victim of a rights violation, thereby invalidating the approach based on a "range of options", including residential settings, espoused by the 2009 Guidelines. It is thus wise to disregard any

---

7   However, a facility's size is only one factor that might define it as an "institution". No less important as a characteristic is the impersonal, regimented routine that is applied, with staff having a technical rather than affective relationship with the children in their care. "Institutions" also tend to be isolated – often geographically, but sometimes simply in terms of lack of contact with the outside world. Such conditions clearly do not meet the standards set by the 2009 Guidelines for appropriate residential care.

so-called "right to a family" argument in promoting deinstitutionalisation; embracing the recognised policy objective of securing a family-based placement wherever possible and appropriate is a far sounder basis on which to proceed.

4.2.1. Varied contexts of the development of institutions

Action to pursue the goal of phasing out institutions has to take account of the history of their implantation and development in each country, the role they currently play, socio-cultural factors and resources that governments are potentially able to devote to child protection and alternative care provision. This means, *inter alia*, that only a limited number of direct lessons can be learned from the experience of economically privileged countries that have moved away from placements in institutions. In addition, it follows from the earlier discussion that promoting deinstitutionalisation cannot be reduced to pointing out the potentially negative effects of institutional placements but has to be accompanied by feasible substitute proposals. The reasons why institutional care has developed and persists therefore vary, with several (significant) points in between, from the strict application of an ideologically based policy to the effective absence of any policy whatsoever. Recognising this, acknowledging the varied aims and outcomes of institutional placements, and identifying the consequently very different issues to be addressed, is an essential first step in any strategy towards their being phased out.

There are many different scenarios, but most instances where institutional care persists can be reasonably categorised under three broad headings.

4.2.1.1. The alternative care system in private hands with foreign support

The most challenging realities are undoubtedly the many countries where alternative care is essentially in private hands, often financed wholly or in good part from abroad and invariably in the form of so-called "orphanages". Here, the involvement of the State is minimal not only in terms of direct provision, but very frequently also as regards the regulation and monitoring of the sector and development of policy. In some cases, such as Ethiopia, Guatemala, Haiti and Nepal, significant numbers of these institutions have been linked directly or indirectly to the procurement and/or channelling of children for intercountry adoption. When the government is unable to ensure or promote effective preventive services and options to institutional placements, private providers are in a strong position to maintain their activities. They resist initiatives to reduce recourse to placements in the facilities they own or manage since their income from foreign financial backing is dependent on the number of children in their care.

4.2.1.2. Institutional care financed in-country

In many Islamic countries, for example, as a logical consequence of various degrees of societal resistance to the idea of families taking in a "stranger" child, alternative care provision is also mainly "institution"-based. While some facilities may be State-run, most tend to be run by religious entities, with the active agreement of the State though with more or less direct oversight. In contrast to the previous category, however, their financing invariably comes from charitable sources within the country. Although these facilities are often large, they may in practice be less isolated (in all senses) than elsewhere and seek to avoid the worst excesses of impersonal regimes, with more emphasis on preparing a child for future life in the community than simply meeting minimum basic day-to-day needs. The benefits of such facilities are rarely questioned in-country, and alternatives to residential care are often difficult to envisage in the specific context concerned.

4.2.1.3. The alternative care system in State hands

The situation is completely different in countries such as those of Central and Eastern Europe and the former USSR, where institutions were set up, run and financed solely by the State, and were considered to be a logical reflection of its responsibility for children who could not be looked after by their parents. With, in essence, no other formal options being available for almost two generations, society has still viewed the placement of children in such institutions – including temporarily – as normal practice well after the onset of "transition" in the early 1990s. The fact that the State remains the direct provider of most alternative care, on the basis of policies that it sets, means that moves towards deinstitutionalisation can in principle be more immediately effective, once political will is engaged. This is being demonstrated to some degree by uptake on a region-wide initiative launched by UNICEF and OHCHR designed to ensure that no child in the 0–3 years age-range be the subject of a placement in an institution (the campaign is largely grounded in the findings of UNICEF, 2012).

4.2.2. The common logic underlying institutional placements

While there are many variations of the above scenarios, one factor is common to all, albeit for often different reasons: a child who is deemed, by whomsoever and on whatever basis, to require formal alternative care is more than likely to be automatically placed in a "large residential facility" regardless of his or her specific needs and situation, and similarly regardless of his or her wishes and opinions.

Thus, over and above issues relating to whether or not such care could in fact be avoided (the necessity principle) and whether it responds effectively to the child's individual circumstances (the suitability principle), systems such as these reflect the "image" of a child as being simply one of a vulnerable group for whom a single form of "protection" can validly be applied.

Undoubtedly this generalised and depersonalised perception of the child has to be kept very much in mind when envisaging the already complex task of drawing up "localised" strategies for deinstitutionalisation that take account of the diverse contexts in which institutional care has developed.

4.3. Strategies for deinstitutionalisation

This diversity of how and why institutional care is provided underpins the call in the 2009 Guidelines for each State to develop its own strategy for reducing both the actual and perceived need for placements in these facilities, in response to the specificities of its context and system. If we accept this call on children's rights grounds, account must be taken of three issues in particular.

First, what is required above all is a strategy for deinstitutionalising the alternative care system, not one for deinstitutionalising children who are currently in those facilities: it is primarily designed to install a system that replaces the one whereby children are more or less automatically pushed or sucked into institutional care when parental or kinship care is not available.

Second, and a direct consequence of the above, the strategy has to begin well up-stream and be wide-ranging in scope. Beginning up-stream implies focusing efforts on enabling the child to remain within his or her family and, if that fails, disrupting the complex "institutionalising circuits" that can pervade social systems and implicate poor families, social services, the judicial system and municipalities, among others. Policy and legislative measures must be supplemented by creating a propitious climate for that change. This will involve, *inter alia*: influencing community attitudes regarding families in difficulty and responses that will be in the child's best interests; securing the understanding and cooperation of professionals; alleviating the employment fears of current institutional staff; setting in place a gatekeeping mechanism; as well as ensuring the prior development of substitute community-based care settings and making certain that budgeting and financing are such as to promote and enable their use.[8]

Third, in terms of financial resources, the key issue to be addressed may often be less one of reallocating funding and more one of facing up to the ramifications of how that funding is currently sourced. A system essentially comprising "orphanages" funded by foreign charities will not willingly reallocate funds for family strengthening programmes or the development of foster care. Other strategies have to be sought, such as long-term effective awareness-raising in the donor countries and requesting bilateral assistance to develop family-based care that can demonstrate a diminishing need for residential facilities and justifies hastening their closure. At the other end of the spectrum, where all or most of the system is publicly funded, the problem may lie in division of responsibilities between, for example, central funding for institutional care and local funding for family-based and family-type care settings. This was the case in Ukraine, where it was not only administratively far easier to place a child in an institution than to seek a suitable foster home, but also that solution created no additional burden for cash-strapped municipalities. The perverse effects of how, as opposed to how much, financing of alternative care takes place are regularly overlooked.

Examining all these issues within the specific context in which institutions have been maintained to date is clearly a major exercise. Despite the CRC Committee being "concerned that the institutionalisation of children is used systematically" (United Nations, 2006, §27) and its general push in favour of family-based alternative care, it recognises that "dogmatic implementation of the principle that placement in an institution must be the last resort" could "leave the institution in which the child is ultimately placed with an impossible mission" (United Nations, 2006, §22). The Committee also "acknowledges that it is challenging to change the deep rooted ideology behind the institution model" (United Nations, 2006, §23). Comments of this nature from the Committee are too rarely taken into account in analyses of how to move forward to improve respect for children's rights in relation to alternative care.

5. By way of conclusion: The essential challenge

This chapter has sought above all to demonstrate that, while there has been substantial progress in establishing a solid internationally recognised children's rights base in relation to the provision of formal alternative care, the context-specific interpretation and application of those rights is of special significance in this particular sphere.

The range of reasons for which formal alternative care may be envisaged or undertaken for children is vast, and the relative importance of each such reason, in practice, differs considerably among countries and regions, with clear implications for how care provision is, can or should be envisaged. Approaches, attitudes and systems currently in place also vary widely,

---

8   The issues reviewed in this paragraph are documented in detail in the case studies of deinstitutionalisation efforts in Argentina, Chile, Uruguay, Italy and Spain, see UNICEF (2002).

largely in response to socio-cultural, economic, political and historical realities. The chapter has hopefully shown that advancing the rights of children against backdrops of such a diverse nature cannot be achieved simply through global advocacy grounded in the rigid conventional wisdom of children's rights and the watchwords adopted to date, which have often led, for example, to the out-and-out promotion of formal family-based care together with, in many cases, its counterpart of demonising residential care provision.

This need for circumspection is all the greater in that, even in countries with long-standing programmes of formal fostering and similar measures, for example, the documented difficulties in ensuring effective systems and positive outcomes for children should put into question the legitimacy of consistently promoting this path where the practice is to all intents and purposes unknown. A better guide to our assessment of solutions proposed and provided could surely be whether or not they represent a society's best efforts to ensure the perceived "safety, stability and support" that children concerned say they are looking for from their alternative care setting. Here, as suggested in the chapter, it will be necessary to take a closer look, *inter alia*, at how "stability" in alternative care links coherently with the concept of "permanency" as an outcome of that care, and at the ramifications of any such linkage.

Building as they do on the rights set out in the CRC, the 2009 Guidelines for the Alternative Care of Children have arguably set the stage for a more nuanced view of how efforts might be oriented towards the context-specific viewpoint put forward in the Introduction. Thus, they emphasise the need for a "range of options" that includes residential care, not only noting the conditions to be met if the latter is to be suitable but also setting out stringent requirements for a well-functioning foster care system. They also encourage States to draw up strategies for deinstitutionalising their respective alternative care systems, but in a bespoke fashion that takes account of the very different contexts of – and reasons for – the existence of institutional care in each country.

The 2009 Guidelines do a lot more for advancing the children's rights agenda. By emphasising initiatives to prevent recourse to formal alternative care, they highlight the broader rights issues that must be tackled if formal out-of-home placements are, as they should be, destined for use only as a truly exceptional measure. Such prevention includes support for the child to remain in his or her family environment through informal kinship care, a rights-based practice not always sufficiently recognised given the frequent Western obsession with formalised arrangements as the best means for "ensuring" protection and assistance, even though such formal solutions in many cases could not be envisaged anyway because of human and material resource restrictions. That said, and as noted in the chapter, there are tensions between recognising informal customary practices and enabling the State to meet its protective and other obligations towards children: these need to be resolved on a context-specific basis.

The requirement that children be meaningfully consulted before any decisions related to alternative care are made also figures large in the 2009 Guidelines. Effective children's agency, however, cannot be promoted and developed in a vacuum, in relation to alternative care alone, although it might serve as one acceptable entry point or a trigger for wider consideration of the child's right to be heard. Yet again, context-specific sensitivity must clearly underlie any approach to bolstering the rights of the child in this regard.

The chapter has also shown that the 2009 Guidelines deal with issues that, while significant for moving forward the children's rights agenda, have tended to escape sufficient attention to date. One example of these concerns the financial motives that can influence – far more than pure children's rights questions – how alternative care is provided, such as the fact that in many economically underprivileged countries, there has been a major reliance on residential facilities wholly or substantially financed from foreign private sources, with generally inadequate State regulation and oversight. Despite the paradox involved in "orphanages" being funded from countries where institutional care has been roundly criticised and often almost eliminated, there is unlikely to be spontaneous reallocation of those "charitable" contributions to family strengthening, support for informal care arrangements or even – to the extent that these might be feasible in the context – for family-based alternative care programmes. In such cases, any argument based on children's rights needs to be put forcefully to the donors rather than to the "beneficiaries". Simultaneously, governments concerned should negotiate bilateral and multilateral development aid for programmes that will reduce the need for recourse to institutional placements, as a means of improving their compliance with international standards.

But "children's rights" arguments anyway need to be subject to more scrutiny. To begin with, there is a regrettable and dangerous tendency towards "human rights inflation" where children are concerned. This chapter has pinpointed one such instance in particular concerning alternative care – a so-called "right to a family" unwarrantedly extrapolated from what is no more than an agreed policy objective. In addition, a "purist" view of genuine rights can lead to simplistic representations that, however unassailable they are from a juridical standpoint, may be directed (often for reasons of sheer facility) towards the wrong actors – as in the abovementioned case of residential care financed from abroad – or make futile assumptions as to the automatic justification for their acceptance (in the face of, for example, entrenched societal resistance to family-based care for "stranger children").

In sum, the essential challenge may be less a question of marshalling general arguments for the human rights of children to be respected as regards formal alternative care, but more one of identifying, proposing and enabling viable means for making that possible in each situation.

Questions for debate and discussion

- What realistic measures can be envisaged to ensure that children are not placed in formal alternative care settings simply because of their family's material poverty?
- How can customary care arrangements be simultaneously encouraged and supported by the State yet also adequately monitored without unduly compromising their informal nature?
- What effective gatekeeping mechanisms can be envisaged in countries where formal alternative care is essentially in the hands of private providers?
- What feasible measures can be taken to prohibit or dissuade foreign donors from funding large residential facilities in developing countries?
- How do the practical implications of a "permanency planning" imperative correspond to the need for "safety, stability and support" expressed by children in alternative care settings?

References

Association of Children's Welfare Agencies. (n.d.). *Children and Young People in Care Growing up Strong, Safe and Connected*. Discussion Paper. Available at www.communityservices.act.gov.au/ocyfs/out-of-home-care-strategy-2015-2020/submissions/acwa-discussion-paper-submission

Bessell, S. and Gal, T. (2008). Forming Partnerships: The Human Rights of Children in Need of Care and Protection. *International Journal of Children's Rights, 17*, 283–298.

Boetto, H. (2010). Kinship Care: A Review of Issues. *Family Matters (85)*. Australian Institute of Family Studies. Available at www.aifs.gov.au/institute/pubs/fm2010/fm85/fm85g.html

Cantwell, N. and Holzscheiter, A. (2008). Article 20: Children Deprived of Their Family Environment. In *A Commentary on the United Nations Convention on the Rights of the Child*. Leiden: Martinus Nijhoff.

Cantwell, N. and Jacomy-Vité, S. (2011). *Assessment of the Alternative Care System in the Syrian Arab Republic*. Report prepared on behalf of International Social Service for UNICEF Syria. UNICEF/Ministry of Social Affairs and Labour, Damascus.

Cantwell, N., Davidson J., Elsley S., Milligan, I. and Quinn, N. (2012). *Moving Forward: Implementing the 'Guidelines for the Alternative Care of Children'*. Centre for Excellence for Looked-After Children in Scotland, UK.

Child Welfare Information Gateway. (2012). *Adoption Disruption and Dissolution*. Available at https://www.childwelfare.gov/pubs/s_disrup.pdf

Comisión Interamericana de Derechos Humanos. (2013). *El Derecho del niño y la niña a la familia. Cuidado alternativo: Poniendo fin a la institucionalización en las Américas* [The Right of Boys and Girls to a Family. Alternative Care: Ending Institutionalization in the Americas]. Available [in Spanish] at www.oas.org/es/cidh/infancia/docs/pdf/Informe-derecho-nino-a-familia.pdf [Press release in English, 19 February 2014. Available at www.oas.org/en/iachr/media_center/PReleases/2014/014.asp].

Dube, C. (2011). *The Child Head of Household as a Meaning Maker: The Opinions (Ideas, Desires, Wishes and Thoughts) of Children Heading Households on Service Accessibility, Specific Risks and Protective Processes as they Affect Their Basic Development and Realization of Their Rights – The Case of Swaziland*. (Unpublished masters thesis). Institut Universitaire Kurt Bösch, Switzerland.

Hague Conference on Private International Law. (1993). *Convention on Protection of Children and Co-operation in respect of Intercountry Adoption*. Available at www.hcch.net/upload/conventions/txt33en.pdf

Holm-Hansen, J., Kristofersen, L. B. and Myrvold, T. M. (eds) (2003). *Orphans in Russia: Policies for Family-like Alternatives*. Norwegian Institute for Urban and Regional Research. Available at www.nibr.no/filer/2003-1.pdf

Human Rights Council. (2009). *Promotion and Protection of all Human Rights, Civil, Political, Economic, Social and Cultural Rights, including the Right to Development*. UN Doc. A/HRC/11/L.13. Available at www.unicef.org/aids/files/UN_Guidelines_for_alternative_care_of_children.pdf

League of Nations. (1924). *Geneva Declaration of the Rights of the Child*. Available at www.un-documents.net/gdrc1924.htm

Masondo, G. (2006). *The Lived-experiences of Orphans in Child-headed Households in the Bronkhorstspruit Area: A Psycho-educational Approach*. Unpublished masters dissertation, University of Johannesburg, South Africa. Available at https://ujdigispace.uj.ac.za/bitstream/handle/10210/1155/masondo.pdf?sequence=1

McVeigh, T. (2001). Fostering in Crisis as Children Are Left at Risk in Unsafe Homes. *The Guardian*. Available at www.theguardian.com/uk/2001/jun/03/theobserver.uknews2

National Resource Center for Foster Care and Permanency Planning (1995). *Tool for Permanency: Kinship Care*. Hunter College School of Social Work. Available at www.hunter.cuny.edu/socwork/nrcfcpp/downloads/tools/kinship-tool.pdf .

Nyambedha, E. O., Wandibba, S. and Aagaard-Hansen, J. (2003). Changing Patterns of Orphan Care due to the HIV Epidemic in Western Kenya. *Social Science and Medicine*, 57, 301–311.

Patel, N. (2004). *Accommodation Needs of Young Offenders*. Youth Justice Board for England and Wales.

Peterson-Badali, M., Ruck M. D. and Bone, J. (2008). Rights Conceptions of Maltreated Children Living in State Care. *International Journal of Children's Rights*, 16, 99–119.

Quality in Alternative Care Conference (2011). Prague. Available at www.quality-care-conference.org/general-information/about-the-conference/pages/default.aspx

Scottish Government (2014). *Post-school Destinations of Looked-after Children*. Available at www.scotland.gov.uk/Publications/2014/06/6518/3

Sloth-Nielsen, J. (2004). *Realising the Rights of Children Growing up in Child-headed Households: A Guide to Law Policies and Social Advocacy*. Community Law Centre, University of Western Cape, Cape Town. Available at www.communitylawcentre.org.za/projects/socio-economic-rights/Research%20and%20Publications/SER%20Publications/Child-headed%20households.pdf

South African Law Reform Commission. (2002). *Discussion Paper (103)*, 561. Available at www.justice.gov.za/salrc/dpapers/dp103.pdf

Tolfree, D. (2004). *Whose Children? Separated Children's Protection and Participation in Emergencies*. Stockholm: Save the Children Sweden.

UK Parliament (2012). *Memorandum from the Department for Education*. Available at www.publications.parliament.uk/pa/ld201213/ldselect/ldadopt/127/12719.htm

UNICEF. (2002). *Children in Institutions: The Beginning of the End?* Florence: Innocenti Research Centre.

UNICEF Sudan. (2007). *Technical Briefing Paper No. 1*. Sudan: UNICEF Sudan. Available at www.unicef.org/sudan/UNICEF_Sudan_Technical_Briefing_Paper_1_-_Alternative_family_care.pdf

UNICEF. (2012). *Children under the age of three in formal care in Eastern Europe and Central Asia: a rights-based regional situational analysis*. Available at www.unicef.org/ceecis/UNICEF_Report_Children_Under_3_FINAL.pdf

United Nations. (1959). *Declaration of the Rights of the Child*. UN Doc. A/RES/1386 (XIV). Available at www.un.org/cyberschoolbus/humanrights/resources/child.asp

United Nations. (1986). *Declaration on Social and Legal Principles relating to the Protection and Welfare of Children, with special reference to Foster Placement and Adoption Nationally and Internationally*. UN Doc. A/RES/41/85. Available at www.un.org/en/ga/search/view_doc.asp?symbol=A/RES/41/85andLang=EandA rea=RESOLUTION

United Nations. (2006). *Report of the Committee on the Rights of the Child*. UN Doc. A/61/41. Available at http://daccess-dds-ny.un.org/doc/UNDOC/GEN/G06/431/68/PDF/G0643168.pdf?OpenElement

United Nations. (2009). *Guidelines for the Alternative Care of Children*. UN Doc. A/RES/64/142. Available at www.un.org/en/ga/search/view_doc.asp?symbol=A/RES/64/142

University of South Africa. (2008). *A Situational Analysis of Child-Headed-Households in South Africa*. Available at www.dsd.gov.za/Nacca1/index.php?option=com_docmanandtask=cat_viewandItemid=39andmosmsg=You+must+login+and+be+authorized+to+access+this+document.

Van Bueren, G. (1998). *The International Law on the Rights of the Child*. Leiden: Martinus Nijhoff.

16
Violence against children

Gertrud Lenzer

1. Introduction: The children's rights turn – an interdisciplinary challenge

In 1991 the new interdisciplinary field of Children's Studies (Lenzer, 2001)[1,2] was founded at The City University of New York. The field rested on the connected philosophical, methodological and empirical premises that children must be understood, represented and heard in their wholeness as human beings. It was not sufficient to have a conglomeration of disciplines focusing on different and often disparate aspects of children, ranging from child psychology, children's literature, pedagogy and education, the sociology of children, the history of children to child protection or juvenile justice, medical science and the law. An aggregation of the findings from these disciplines, while perhaps multidisciplinary, does not offer the fullness of understanding we owe to children and young people. In light of the fragmentation of knowledge, a novel and interdisciplinary approach was seen as a new challenge and mandate for the world of scholars, reformers and policy makers.

From its inception, the field of children's studies adopted the human rights of children, as articulated in the holistic UN Convention on the Rights of the Child (CRC), as its overarching framework. The adoption of the CRC in 1989, based on the conception of the civil, political, economic, social and cultural rights of children, represented a turning point in the study of, for and with children. Even though advocacy for the rights of children has a long history, the Convention ushered in what, for want of a better term, must be called a holistic "children's rights turn" – historically as well as locally, regionally and globally. For when viewed in its articulation of the civil, political, economic, social and cultural rights of children as their human rights, the Convention represents the best interests of the child in the totality of her/his abilities, propensities and needs for provision, protection and participation. This human rights

---

1   In the same year, the author founded the Sociology of Children as a Section in the American Sociological Association.
2   In the subsequent development of Childhood Studies with its primary focus on social science, especially sociology and anthropology and often to the exclusion of developmental psychology, childhood is "understood as a permanent form of any generational structure." (Qvortrup et al., 2009: 23). Much of the childhood studies literature assumes as a given that childhood as well as the child are social constructions, which raises Ian Hacking's (1999) question: *The Social Construction of What?*

instrument was thus itself a call to interdisciplinary attention and action on the part of scholars, advocates and policy makers (Lenzer, 1996, 1998, 1999, 2009). The universality and interdependence of human rights represent a challenge to all involved in comprehensively promoting the human rights of children and of human justice.[3] This chapter offers a history of this turn, and its impact and implications for both the theory and practice of the field of children's rights.

2. Violence against children: An expansion of the CRC

Close to a decade ago, in October 2006, Paulo Sérgio Pinheiro's[4] *World Report on Violence against Children* (hereafter, *World Report*) was published under the imprimatur of United Nations Secretary-General Kofi Annan. "In 2001, on the recommendation of the Committee on the Rights of the Child, the General Assembly in its resolution 56/138 requested the Secretary General to conduct an in-depth study on the question of violence against children and put forward recommendations for consideration by Member States for appropriate action." Launched on November 20, 2003, the *World Report*[5] represents the comprehensive outcome of international, regional, sub-regional and national consultations, as well as surveys of expert thematic meetings on this topic. From the outset, the investigation involved children and young people and youth facilitators at all levels, making their active involvement a priority. The Study's major foci, according to Pinheiro, "combined the perspectives of human rights, public health and child protection" and called for the establishment of the office of the Special Representative of the Secretary General (SRSG) on Violence against Children. The *World Report* and its recommendations provided the foundational framework for the mandate of the Special Representative. The office was established in September 2009 with the appointment of the first UN Special Representative, Marta Santos Pais. Most importantly, the campaign to end Violence against Children foregrounds one pillar of the CRC – the *protection* of children worldwide from maltreatment in any form by way of policy, legal efforts and public educational measures. This emphasis on protection represents an historic shift in the approach to children's rights.

---

3   Although there are numerous debates in the literature about the definition of a child, for the purpose of this essay, the author is using Article 1 of the CRC according to which "a child means every human being below the age of 18 years unless, under the law applicable to the child, majority is attained earlier." If legal and policy measures are required to eliminate violence against children or their maltreatment, the binding legal definitions of what constitutes a child in a society are of importance. For example, in the United States all laws, regulations and national statistics define a child as being under the age of 18. There are of course exceptions such as in the case of adult criminal responsibility which in the states of North Carolina and New York starts at age 16.
4   A 34-page summary of the Report of the Independent Expert for the United Nations Study on Violence against Children, A/61/299, was submitted by the UN Secretary General to the General Assembly in October 2006. United Nations, General Assembly (2006). *Rights of the Child*. Note by the Secretary General, p. 5.
5   "The participatory processes that led to this report brought together the experience of governments, international organizations, civil society organizations, research institutions and children." (*World Report*, 2006: xiii). Independent Expert for the United Nations Secretary General's Study on Violence against Children.

2.1. The history of the emergence of the new paradigm within the children rights arena

It should be noted at the outset that the introduction of the term "violence" is not simply a terminological change. In fact, the term was used for the first time in the entire CRC in Article 19; before that the preferred terminology in most legal, social science and policy discussions was "child abuse and neglect." In other words, the introduction of the domain of "violence against children," was a significant expansion in the perception of a real world problem, and thematic, and one that must not be overlooked or seen as a simple shift in usage. In fact, it was this broadened conceptualization of a global phenomenon that is responsible for the expanded treatment of "violence against children" both in the global study and the *World Report*. In other words, the children's rights movement and its literature underwent a paradigm shift: the recognition that the phenomenon of violence in its numerous manifestations represents a global and comprehensive assault on the human dignity of children and young people – a violation of their human rights.

Just as child poverty represents a global phenomenon, so violence against children represents a present and mostly invisible global reality sustained by a variety of cultural, social and religious practices, beliefs and norm systems that may support and even legitimate it. Moreover, violence against children opens up the inequitable structures of Western and non-Western societies to full view, making them visible as infrastructures of the world of children and young people who suffer the deleterious effects of the violence they are exposed to – either as direct victims or as witnesses.

Although the Committee on the Rights of the Child initiated its in-depth study on violence against children in 2003, the background of the CRC's recommendations begins with the Committee's general discussion days in September 2000 and September 2001. In its deliberations in 2000, the CRC focused on "State Violence against Children."[6] In 2001, the focus was on "Violence against Children, within the Family and in Schools."[7] And since that time, the conceptualization of violence against children as an assault on the rights and human integrity of the child has led to a continuing expansion of the CRC and the work of the Committee in order to make visible an "underworld," as it were, in which children worldwide live with little recourse and few remedies. Thus the addition of violence against children and the call for their protection from it must be seen as a radical shift and step forward in the interpretation and implementation of the CRC in the best interests of the child.

2.2. World Report on Violence Against Children

In the three-year study that resulted in the *World Report on Violence against Children*, Article 19[8] of the CRC is of signal importance.[9] Article 19(1), reads:

---

6   www.ohchr.org/Documents/HRBodies/CRC/Discussions/Recommendations/Recommendations 2001.pdf. As Pinheiro put it in the "Summary": "The definition of violence is that of Article 19 of the CRC: 'all forms of physical or mental violence, injury and abuse, neglect or negligent treatment, maltreatment or exploitation, including sexual abuse.'" (*World Report*, 2006: 4). www.ohchr.org/Documents/HRBodies/CRC/Discussions/Recommendations/ Recommendations2000.pdf

7   www.ohchr.org/Documents/HRBodies/CRC/Discussions/Recommendations/Recommendations 2001.pdf

8   Other relevant Articles are 37, 40, and the general principles of Articles 2, 3, 9 and 12.

9   As Pinheiro put it in the "Summary": "The definition of violence is that of Article 19 of the CRC: 'all forms of physical or mental violence, injury and abuse, neglect or negligent treatment, maltreatment or exploitation, including sexual abuse.'" (*World Report*, 2006: 4).

States Parties shall take all appropriate legislative, administrative, social and educational measures to protect the child from *all forms of physical or mental violence*,[10] injury or abuse, neglect or negligent treatment, maltreatment or exploitation, including sexual abuse, while in the care of parent(s), legal guardian(s) or any other person who has the care of the child.[11]

According to Pinheiro, moreover, "Each child has the right to his or her physical and personal integrity and protection from all forms of violence. Children, as human beings, are entitled to enjoy all the rights guaranteed by the various international human rights treaties that have developed from the Universal Declaration of Human Rights." (*World Report*, 2006: 31). The *World Report* discusses violence against children in the context of international human rights law and standards. In addition to the protections contained in the CRC, children are also entitled to the protections contained in international legal instruments relating to international criminal, humanitarian, refugee and labor law; regional human rights systems; and in any non-binding instruments. Moreover, children are "entitled to the rights and procedures set out in the International Bill of Rights, consisting of the International Covenants on Economic, Social and Cultural Rights, and that on Civil and Political Rights" (*World Report*, 2006: 31).

As we shall see, the *World Report* and the three-year global study on which it is based mark a milestone in the children's rights movement. Its historical significance cannot be underestimated, for it "discovered" and made visible an invisible reality that from then on could no longer be ignored. It helped to expand and radically transform the interpretation of the CRC and with it the responsibilities of all state parties to the Convention to take all measures to protect children from all forms of physical and emotional violence and maltreatment.

2.3. Principles and recommendations of the World Report

The Report emphasizes as the guiding principle of the Study the ideas that "no violence against children is justifiable"; that violence can be prevented and that states have the "primary responsibility to uphold children's rights to protection and access to services." (Kofi Annan, 2006: xi). It is important to note as well Kofi Annan's emphasis on prevention, "protection" and "access to services" – as the major mission of the campaign to end Violence against Children. In addition, the Study includes the affirmation that "Children have the right to express their views, and to have these views taken into account in the implementation of policies and programs." (*World Report*, 2006: 17).

The twelve overarching recommendations of the Study (*World Report*, 2006: 18–24) are:

1 Strengthen national commitment and action.
2 Prohibit all violence against children.
3 Prioritize prevention.
4 Promote non-violent values and awareness-raising.
5 Enhance the capacity of all who work with children.

---

10 Italics added.
11 Article 19, however, represents only one human rights instrument effective in the Report, since according to Pinheiro "the notion of child protection in the CRC goes well beyond non-exploitation. Within its holistic framework for the upbringing, well-being and development of the child. ... numerous other articles are of importance to the Study."

6   Provide recovery and social reintegration services.
7   Ensure participation of children.
8   Create accessible and child-friendly reporting systems and services.
9   Ensure accountability and end impunity.
10 Address the gender dimension of violence against children.
11 Develop and implement systematic national data collection and research.
12 Strengthen international commitment.

2.4. Scope of the World Report

As far as the central socio-cultural and economic violence domains in the *World Report* are concerned, Pinheiro summarizes:

> Violence against children cuts across boundaries of geography, race, class, religion and culture. It occurs in homes, schools and streets; in places of work and entertainment, and in care and detention centers.
>
> Perpetrators include parents, family members, teachers, caretakers, law enforcement authorities and other children. Some children are particularly vulnerable because of gender, race, ethnic origin, disability or social status.
>
> The consequences of violence can be devastating. Above all, it can result in early death. But even children who survive must cope with terrible physical and emotional scars. Indeed, violence places at risk not only their health, but also their ability to learn and grow into adults who can create sound families and communities.
>
> Violence against children is thus a major threat to global development and our work to reach the Millennium Development Goals.
>
> *(World Report, 2006: xi)*

The *World Report* examines in detail violence against children in their five major settings: "home and family, schools, care and justice systems, workplaces and the community" (*World Report*, 2006: 7). The *Report* provides estimates of violence against children for all five settings, ranging from homicides to non-fatal physical violence, with special emphasis on corporal punishment, neglect, sexual exploitation, psychological violence, and harmful traditional practices among others, differentiating them according to age groups. The account also discusses short-term and long-term disorders resulting from violence. One of the most significant findings relates to the risk factors of age and sex. As far as violence against children in the home and family is concerned, Pinheiro reports: "In general, children under 10 are at significant greater risk than children aged 10 to 19 of severe violence perpetrated by family members and people closely associated with the family." (*World Report*, 2006: 50). While approximately 50% to 75% of murders of children aged under 10 are by family members, this proportion drops to about 20% of murders of children aged 10 to 14, and 5% of murders of children aged 15 to 19." (*World Report*, 2006: 50). And when it comes to the sex of a child, a "US study found that female victims were twice as likely as male victims to have been killed by a family member." (*World Report*, 2006: 50).

Despite the often invisible nature of violence against children, its international range and extent was a major concern for the Report, largely because such violence had, in the judgment of experts, reached epidemic proportions. It is telling that the Report's first table presented the (very limited) extent to which children are legally protected from corporal punishment, revealing that only 2 percent of children are protected from corporal punishment in the home, 4 percent in alternative care, 42 percent in schools and between 42 and 81 percent in penal institutions either as form of a sentence or as disciplinary measures.[12] In other words, the phenomenon of corporal punishment was from the outset a major concern in the *World Report,* and it will be further discussed below in more detail as a central component of violence against children. It is worth noting here that historically physical and emotional punishment by parents or family members has been widely considered a matter of "disciplining" children for their improvement – and has been seen as a private parental prerogative, particularly when it occurs in in the home.

In order to demonstrate the "range and scale of violence against children," Pinheiro also referred to data provided by the WHO and the ILO for 2002: according to their estimates 53,000 child fatalities were homicides (*World Report,* 2006: 11). Of particular importance here are risk factors according to age:

> In countries where homicide statistics are analyzed according to age of the victim, 15–17-year-olds are the age group that is most at risk. The second high-risk group are infants. Data from OECD countries suggests that the risk of death is about three times greater for children under one year old than for those aged 1 to 4, who in turn face double the risk of those aged 5 to 14. The younger the child, the more likely their death will be caused by a close family member.
>
> (World Report, 2006: 51)

In addition, 218 million children were involved in child labor in 2004, 126 million of whom were engaged in hazardous work. Estimates from 2000 suggest that 5.7 million were in forced and bonded labor, 1.8 million in prostitution and pornography, and 1.2 million were victims of trafficking (*World Report,* 2006: 12). When it comes to the number of children who witness violence in the home, the estimates for all MDG (Millennium Development Goals) Regions range from 133 to 275 million children (*World Report,* 2006: 71).

In his transmittal of the *World Report* to the UN General Assembly (United Nations, General Assembly, 2006: 9), then Secretary General Kofi Annan highlighted the following statistics: "up to 80 to 98 per cent of children suffer physical punishment in their homes, with a third or more experiencing severe physical punishment resulting from the use of implements."[13] "WHO estimates that 150 million girls and 73 million boys under 18 experienced forced sexual intercourse or other forms of sexual violence during 2002." (United Nations, General Assembly, 2006: 10).

2.5. The institution of the Special Representative of the Secretary General on Violence Against Children

The issuance of the *World Report* led in May of 2009 to the appointment of Marta Santos Pais, Esq. as the "Special Representative of the Secretary General on Violence Against Children" (SRSG). Ms. Santos Pais's mandate was renewed for three years in 2013. Over the last five years, Santos Pais has pursued numerous missions across the globe and organized many meetings with

---

12 Source, *Global Initiative to End All Corporal Punishment of Children (2006),* and *Global Summary of the Legal Status of Punishment of Children, 28 July 2006,* cited in *World Report,* 2006: Figure 1.1, p.11.
13 The circumstance of physical punishment in the home assumed a major role in the *World Report,* and we shall come back to this below, in the section on Corporal Punishment. For reasons of space, discussion of such other forms of violence against children as sexual exploitation, child soldiers, and children in legal systems had to be omitted.

governments, legislators, policy makers, children and youth organizations, NGOs and other civil society bodies.

Since 2006, the *World Report* has been a guiding document for all subsequent developments in the field of children's human rights, developments that have been chronicled in annual reports by the SRSG to the General Assembly since 2010. There are also numerous documentations of the missions of the SRSG and her accomplishments. In addition, the Office of the SRSG has published numerous documents and thematic reports including *Prevention of and Responses to Violence against Children within the Juvenile Justice System* (Office of the SRSG, 2012a); *Safe and Child-sensitive Counseling, Complaint and Reporting Mechanisms to Address Violence Against Children* (Office of the SRSG, 2012b); *Political Commitments by Regional Organizations and Institutions to Prevent and Address Violence against Children* (Office of the SRSG, 2012c); *Protecting Children from Harmful Practices in Plural Legal Systems* (Office of the SRSG, 2012d); *Tackling Violence in Schools: A Global Perspective Bridging the Gap Between Standards and Practice* (Office of the SRSG, 2012e), *Promoting Restorative Justice for Children* (Office of the SRSG, 2013a) and most recently *Toward a World Free from Violence: Global Survey on Violence Against Children* (Office of the SRSG, 2013b). These reports represent major and detailed commentary and offer recommendations on topics from violence against children in such different settings as schools and juvenile justice institutions to the promotion of restorative justice mechanisms.

In one instructive report, *Political Commitments by Regional Organizations and Institutions to Prevent and Address Violence against Children* (SRSG, 2012c), the SRSG chronicled the results of her work with governments, policy makers, NGOs and children. This report provided a detailed account of Marta Santos Pais's international missions and policy accomplishments from 2009 through 2012. They ranged from the "Council of Europe Policy Guidelines on integrated national strategies for the protection of children from violence (2009)," reports from Africa, Asia, South Asia, Latin America, the Caribbean and declarations of Kingston, Santo Domingo, Cairo, Marrakesh, Doha, Beijing, to the declaration of young persons of the Caribbean and the Council of Europe Strategy for the Rights of the Child (2012–2015).

Wherever and whenever possible, the SRSG involves children and young people in her global mission and makes sure that even younger children have their voices heard, understand what maltreatment of children is all about and know how to engage in its abolition.

3. Corporal punishment as a central component of violence against children

Although corporal punishment was not explicitly mentioned in the CRC, it emerged as a major theme in the Committee from its fourth Session in 1993 forward. According to CRC documents, the committee members noticed the widespread existence of corporal punishment in the reports from individual state parties. The Committee documented their observations carefully. Writing its own history, as it were, the Committee pointed out that

> Already by 1993, the Committee noted in the report of its fourth session that it "recognized the importance of the question of corporal punishment in improving the system of promotion and protection of the rights of the child and decided to continue to devote attention to it in the process of examining States parties' reports."[14]

(Bitensky, 1996)

---

14 Committee on the Rights of the Child, Report on the fourth session, 25 October 1993, CRC/C/20, para. 176.

Later, the Committee explained the relationship between its concerns about corporal punishment and its later inclusion under the enlarged conception of violence against children in its General Comment 8 as follows:

> 1. Following its two days of general discussion on violence against children, held in 2000 and 2001, the Committee on the Rights of the Child resolved to issue a series of general comments concerning eliminating violence against children, of which this [General Comment No.8] is the first. The Committee aims to guide States parties in understanding the provisions of the Convention concerning the protection of children against all forms of violence. This comment focuses on corporal punishment and other cruel or degrading forms of punishment, which are currently very widely accepted and practiced forms of violence against children. (CRC/C/GC/8, page 3).

> 2. The Convention on the Rights of the Child and other international human rights instruments recognize the right of the child to respect for the child's human dignity and physical integrity and equal protection under the law. The Committee is issuing this general comment to highlight the obligation of all States parties to move quickly to prohibit and eliminate all corporal punishment and all other cruel or degrading forms of punishment of children and to outline the legislative and other awareness-raising and educational measures that States must take. (CRC/C/GC/8, page 3).

The wording of General Comment 8 is as follows:

> **General Comment No. 8 (2006)** "The right of the child to protection from corporal punishment and other cruel or degrading forms of punishment (arts.19; 28, para. 2; and 37, inter alia)" was the first planned general comment to focus on the elimination of violence against children.[15]

The wide-reaching definitions provided by the Committee on physical and degrading punishment are worth noting. The Committee defines

> "corporal" or "physical" punishment as any punishment in which physical force is used and intended to cause some degree of pain or discomfort, however light. Most involves hitting ("smacking", "slapping", "spanking") children, with the hand or with an implement – a whip, stick, belt, shoe, wooden spoon, etc. But it can also involve, for example, kicking, shaking or throwing children, scratching, pinching, biting, pulling hair or boxing ears, forcing children to stay in uncomfortable positions, burning, scalding or forced ingestion (for example, washing children's mouths out with soap or forcing them to swallow hot spices). In the view of the Committee, corporal punishment is *invariably degrading*. In addition, there are other non-physical forms of punishment that are also cruel and degrading and thus incompatible with the Convention. *These include, for example, punishment that belittles, humiliates, denigrates, scapegoats, threatens, scares or ridicules the child.*[16]

---

15 http://srsg.violenceagainstchildren.org/sites/default/files/documents/docs/GRC-C-GC-8_EN.pdf. It was released during the Forty-second session, 15 May – 2 June 2006.
16 Emphases added.

The CRC's decision to enumerate, in detail, acts that it considered physical and emotional maltreatment clearly demonstrates both its commitment to increasing awareness of the numerous ways in which the human rights and the dignity of a child are violated and its resolve to convince the global community that these were societal issues rather than private ones. Moreover, the Committee's General Comment 8 is clearly descended from the groundbreaking *World Report*, the document that, it can be said, "discovered" the extent and range of violence against children and asserted that there was a state responsibility to protect children from violence. For these reasons, Comment 8 must be seen as a significant new chapter in the history of this work.

Both before and subsequent to General Comment 8, a literature on the elimination of corporal punishment has emerged (Bitensky, 1998, 2009, 2010, 2013; Gershoff, 2002; Kemme *et al.*, 2014; Straus and Donnelly, 2005) and organizations have been created internationally to advocate its abolition. One of the most important, the "Global Initiative to End all Corporal Punishment of Children (hereafter, Global Report)," was launched as early as 2001 in Geneva and has been active ever since under the leadership of Peter Newell. Similar organizations have sprung up elsewhere such as the Every Child Matters Education Fund and The National Coalition to End Child Abuse Deaths in the United States, along with conferences and symposia addressing the topic of corporal punishment.[17]

As of the Global Report 2013 and the latest documents received, "44 states have prohibited corporal punishment in all settings, including the home."[18] In addition, global child populations are protected by law from corporal punishment in the following settings: in 41 countries in alternative care, in 41 in day care, 122 in schools, 124 in penal institutions and in 159 as sentences for a crime. These statistics, however, may be deceptive since the Report indicates that, for example, 94.6 percent of children globally can still be lawfully hit and hurt in their own homes (*Global Report*, 2013: 6).

4. The United States of America: A case study in the violence against children

While the data and estimates across the world may be problematic, the statistics from the United States alone are sobering. We include these data here both to highlight violence against children in a Westernized, industrial country, and to offer more recent information than is included in the *World Report*. The case study also serves as a model for the kind of data that is needed – and that is typically missing in the discussion of violence against children – for other countries.

Perhaps the most compelling data come from research and national surveys undertaken by David Finkelhor, Professor of Sociology, Director of the Crimes Against Children Research Center, and Co-Director of the Family Research Laboratory of the University of New Hampshire (Finkelhor, 2008). Known for his work on child victimization and maltreatment, Finkelhor coined the term "poly-victimization" to address the fact that most children and

---

17 For example: Symposium on "Creating a Non-Violent Future: Children's Rights and Advances in Protection from Corporal Punishment," Loyola University Chicago and co-sponsored by Southern Methodist University and Children's Studies Center for Research, Policy and Public Service, May 23–24, 2014.
18 June 5, 2014: Brazil will become the 38th country to ban corporal punishment of children awaiting signature from the President. Brazil (child population 59,000,000) will be the first very large state to achieve prohibition.

juveniles "experience multiple victimizations." (Finkelhor, Ormrod, *et al*., 2009a). Correctly, he has highlighted the problem of fragmenting types of victimization, given the "considerable overlap" (Finkelhor, 2008) between individual forms of victimization.

Finkelhor was commissioned by the US Office of Juvenile Justice and Delinquency Prevention (OJJDP) and supported by the Centers of Disease Control and Prevention (CDC) to conduct a national survey of "Children's Exposure to Violence," between January and May 2008.

> [The survey] measured the past-year and life-time exposure to violence for children age 17 and younger across several major categories: conventional crime, child maltreatment, victimization by peers and siblings, sexual victimization, witnessing and indirect victimization (including exposure to community violence and family violence), school violence and threats, and Internet victimization. ... This survey is the first comprehensive attempt to measure children's exposure to violence in the home, schools, community across all age groups from birth to age 17, and the first attempt to measure the cumulative exposure to violence over the child's lifetime.
>
> *(Finkelhor, Turner, et al., 2009b: 1)*

The extraordinary results of this survey reveal the extent of violence against children in the United States.

> The survey confirms that most of our society's children are exposed to violence in their daily lives. More than 60 percent …were exposed to violence within the past year, either directly or indirectly. … Nearly one-half of the children and adolescents surveyed (46.3 percent) were assaulted at least once in the past year, and more than 1 in 10 were injured in an assault; 1 in 4 (24.7 percent) were victims of robbery, vandalism, or theft; 1 in 10 suffered from child maltreatment (including physical and emotional abuse, neglect, or a family abduction); and 1 in 16 (6.1 percent) were victimized sexually. More than 1 in 4 (25.3 percent) witnessed a violent act and nearly 1 in 10 (9.8 percent) saw one family member assault another. Multiple victimizations were common: more than one-third (38.7 percent) experienced 2 or more direct victimizations in the previous year, more than 1 in 10 (10.9 percent) experiences 5 or more direct victimizations in the previous year, and more than 1 in 75 (1.4 percent) experiences 10 or more direct victimizations in the previous year.
>
> *(Finkelhor, Turner, et al., 2009b: 1f)*

The figures and number of incidents must be reported in detail to convey the overall picture of violence against children in America. One of Finkelhor's latest surveys (Lincoff, 2013: 1) informs us that "two out of five children surveyed, or more than 40 percent, were physically assaulted in 2011. One in 10 children sustained an injury, and experienced sexual assault or sexual abuse, though the rate was nearly 11 percent for girls ages 14 to 17. The results also show that more than 13 percent of children and teens repeatedly experienced abuse by a caregiver, including 3.7 percent who suffered physical harm." It was data like these that led US Attorney General Eric Holder to characterize the situation as one of "epidemic" proportions, when in September 2010 he initiated his "Defending Childhood Initiative" and established a National Task Force on "Children Exposed to Violence." (US Department of Justice, 2012).

4.1. Child fatalities

When it comes to the number of child fatalities due to abuse and neglect, the US has the onerous distinction of being the leading country in the industrialized world. In fact, "federal data show that 10,440 children in the US died from abuse and neglect between 2001 and 2007, but experts say the real number may be as many as 5,000 higher." (National Coalition to End Child Abuse Deaths). It was these realities that led to the *Protect our Kids Act*, passed by Congress in January 2013. This Act established a bi-partisan Federal Advisory Commission to Eliminate Child Abuse and Neglect Fatalities, CECANF) whose 12 members were appointed jointly by the President and congressional leaders. Its mandate is to develop a "comprehensive national strategy to reduce and prevent child abuse and neglect fatalities." (National Coalition to End Child Abuse Deaths). The first public meeting of the Commission took place on February 24, 2014.

4.2. Other national data on child abuse and neglect, schools, foster care, and child poverty in the United States

Some of the most reliable data on *child abuse and neglect* are collected by the Child Welfare Information Gateway of the US Department of Health and Human Services, (USHHS) Administration of Children, Youth and Families (www.childwelfare.gov) via the National Child Abuse and Neglect Data System (NCANDS). The NCANDS reports that, in all, 6.3 million children were reported to Child Protective Services (CPS) during the period of October 2011–September 2012, 62% were screened in, and 3.2 million children received a CPS response in the form of an investigation or alternative response. Of these 686,000 unique victims, 1,640 were *fatalities*.

Moreover, *Maltreatment* (US Department of Health and Human Services, 2012, xi) reports "nearly three-quarters (70.3%) of all child fatalities were younger than 3 years old." These data confirm that one of the largest age cohorts suffering from and experiencing abuse and adversity consists of very young children. According to Pinheiro's *World Report* they were the second largest age group after 14–17-year-old children. The statistics and research on child victimization with non-fatal consequences document that in 2011 two in five children suffered maltreatment at the hands of adults. Relatedly, the incidence of children experiencing and witnessing violence in the home, in institutions and in the community is also at "epidemic" proportions.

As far as *beating in schools* is concerned, according to US Congresswoman Carolyn McCarthy (D-NY4), "19 states still allow school personnel to beat students." She joined other Representatives to introduce H.R.3027 "Ending Corporal Punishment in Schools Act, of 2011" (www.opencongress.org/bill/hr3027-112/text). The bill cited US Department of Education statistics to the effect that "each year in the United States, hundreds of thousands of school children are subjected to corporal punishment in public schools. School corporal punishment is usually executed in the form of "paddling", or striking students with a wooden paddle on their buttocks or legs, which can result in abrasions, bruising, severe muscle injury, hematomas, whiplash damage, life-threatening hemorrhages, and other medical complications that may require hospitalization." With significant racial and ethnic disparities among the affected students, corporal punishment is "used in many instances for minor disciplinary infractions, such as being tardy or violating the dress code." Also "children with disabilities are subjected to corporal punishment at disproportionally high rates, approximately twice the rate of the general student population in some States." (Text of H.R. 3027). The bill was never enacted and died in Committee.

The number of children in child protective institutions such as *foster care and group homes* is very large. According to the children's Bureau of the US Administration of Children, Youth and Families as of September 30, 2012, "there were an estimated 399,546 children in foster care."[19] *Child poverty* in the United States in addition represents another form of maltreatment. To provide only a brief overview, we turn to the Children's Defense Fund (2014: 22) *The State of America's Children 2014*.

> Children are the poorest group in the nation. ... Over 16 million children were poor in – 2012 – more than 1 in 5 children. More than 40 percent of them lived in extreme poverty, at less than half the poverty level of $11,746 a year for a family of four.[20] The youngest children are the poorest: over 1 in 4 children under age 5 were poor – nearly 5 million. Almost half of them –2.4 million – were extremely poor.

This brief case study of a leading industrialized and rich society is intended to demonstrate the extent and depth of violence against children in American society. Although we have focused on the United States, similar case studies for other societies would reveal the extent and number of children experiencing violence in them. As we know from the World Report, violence against children and the related infringement of their human rights is ubiquitous, and in the absence of reliable data it is difficult to gain a more comprehensive picture. This collection of data from a country that has made some efforts to collect it is thus important as a snapshot of the larger problem across the globe.

5. Schools of children's rights: Critical reflections

Since among the aims of this *Handbook* is to present a "bottom-up" approach in line with recent developments in the conceptualization of children's rights and general human rights scholarship, this essay must speak to that approach. Broadly speaking, this approach promotes the idea that children, as subjective right holders, should themselves organize and be assisted with this organization. This more recently advanced notion about children's rights – so the argument goes – is considered to be in contradistinction to the CRC and related regional and national children's rights instruments. Manfred Liebel and his co-authors' recent work, *Human Rights from Below* (2012),[21] can be seen as foundational and representative for this approach, which has "aimed at identifying the weaknesses and growing fragility of a children's rights project primarily focused on the state and the existing mechanisms of the international children's rights system." As Liebel states in his introduction[22]: "*One key question we want to discuss in this book ... is ... ways children's rights can be understood as subjective or agency rights of children and*

---

19 Child Welfare Information Gateway, November 2013, p.1.
20 Child poverty is defined at an annual income for a family of four of $23,492. Extreme poverty at half the dollar amount.
21 Manfred Liebel. *Children's Rights from Below: Cross-Cultural Perspectives*. Other authors of chapters,
22 In this connection, an important and relevant article by Didier Reynaert, Maria Bouverne-de-Bie and Stijn Vandevelde provides "A review of children's rights literature since the adoption of the United Nations Convention on the Rights of the Child," (*Childhood*, 2009). In this critical exploration of scholarly work on the UN CRC, the authors identify three themes that "predominate" in it: "(1) autonomy and participation rights as the new norm in children's rights practice and policy, (2) children's rights vs. parental rights and (3) the global children's rights industry." Karl Hanson, Ivan Saadi, and Wouter Vandenhole.

whether they can be enforced by children themselves." (Liebel, 2012: 2, italics added). And as he puts it elsewhere:"One key question is how rights could be understood as subjective rights, and *how they could possibly be enforced by children themselves, particularly those in experiencing specifically severe situations of social disadvantage and exclusion."* (Liebel, 2012: 4, italics added).

In line with the author and his collaborators' focus on participatory rights of children rather than the state or other entities' duty to protect them, "protection" and "provision" are viewed as "welfare rights" of children rather than what the authors refer to as "agency rights."

In this literature – the triad of protection, provision and participation has clearly shifted to liberation, with a major emphasis on competence, autonomy, participation and equal rights of children, and away from what Karl Hanson (2012) in his four ideal types of schools of thought classifies as an earlier emphasis on paternalism, welfare, and emancipation. This new emphasis stands in contrast to the CRC in which, according to Liebel,

> [B]esides rights to secure the basic needs of children, rights that serve to ensure the development of children are emphasized. Therefore children's rights can be understood as "welfare rights" which are enforced by adults on behalf of, and in the interest of, children *or* as "agency rights" which are used and enforced by children themselves.
>
> *(Liebel, 2012: 29: italics added)*

What then is the role of adults and advocates in a "bottom up" approach? Here is a formulation from the book's conclusion:

> Adults who want to act as advocates for children in this way, will not only insist on their independence ... but must also understand themselves – as in the case of the children's movement in Latin America – as *"co-protagonists"* of the children.
>
> *(Liebel, 2012: 239, italics added)*

As appealing as that formulation can sound, the scope of violence against children worldwide, whether in homes, schools, institutional settings, or elsewhere, as shown in this essay, indicates how many children and young people need protection by the state, and by laws and regulations as a central first remedy. While the arguments advanced in the "bottom-up" approach put this author and chapter squarely in Hanson's paternalistic and welfare school of thought, the data documented earlier make it impossible for children – especially since, as we have shown, infants and very young children are among the largest cohorts of victims – to organize on their own behalf to achieve any diminution in or remedies for the violence they encounter or are forced to endure.

The cases provided, for example, by Liebel and Hanson, including street children in Nicaragua, the African Movement of Working Children and Youth (141 ff) and movements in other regions, are situations in which indeed young people manage to organize to pursue the realization of their own rights. But these examples are in no way applicable to children who are physically and emotionally disciplined to the point of murder. For the hundreds of thousands of children, especially those who also suffer from disabilities, for those disciplined in school systems, for the children and young people encountering brutality in jails and prisons, for those locked up in solitary confinement, or the children, who by actions of the state are separated from their parents or family caregivers and put in foster care systems – to name only a few examples – such "self-organization" is impossible.

In other words, in light of the child maltreatment and human violence perpetrated against so many children, Liebel's desideratum and description of how they should be able to organize to realize their rights of participation read like a search for a children's rights El Dorado. Indeed the merest possibility of participation, autonomy, emancipation and social justice are denied to these children and young people. No matter how desirable it would be for children to participate in their own liberation, the hard social, economic and legal realities are an iron cage that makes such participation impossible.

In the context of the discussion about human rights from below (Liebel, Hanson, and others), the question arises as to how indeed children could make human rights claims against the violence they experience worldwide. Even though children and young people's voices were prominently represented in the study that led to the *World Report*, the major responsibility for ensuring their safety must rest in convincing societies and their national governments, policy and legislative bodies to prohibit violence against all children in the first place. Additionally a further focus must be on the caregivers in the home, the schools, in foster care, jails and prisons, at work, and in the community.

If indeed, as Liebel and others postulate, a new era in which children are expected to organize as human rights subjective right holders on their own is coming or can be built – this era would be one in which they are thus called upon to protect themselves with adults as "co-protagonists" on their side. What such an era would entail, is a down- or out-sourcing of adult responsibilities to the children themselves. Such a devolution, however well-intended, would make children an independent and isolated social class, and thus de facto an unprotected one.

6. Findings from neuroscience, epigenetic research and behavioral sciences

Recent findings from the neurosciences, epigenetic research and the behavioral sciences deliver some of the most powerful arguments in support of the global violence against children campaign. What this literature demonstrates are the generational and trans-generational effects of early childhood adversity, distress, maltreatment, abuse, neglect and violence (Finkelhor, 2008; Finkelhor *et al.*, 2009a, 2009b; Karr-Morse and Wiley, 2013; McEwen, 2011; Meaney, 2010; Shonkoff and Phillips, 2000; Shonkoff *et al.*, 2009).[23]

There is an entire recent literature that emphasizes the seriousness of the problem of the behavioral and medical effects of early child maltreatment. According to Bruce S. McEwen,[24] since "the brain is a very plastic and changeable organ," "stressors or stressful experiences, especially during early life, can change brain architecture. It can cause some brain structures to become underdeveloped and underactive, which causes an imbalance in how the brain functions and how the person behaves." (Lenzer and Grochowalski, 2012: 97).[25] Or as the epigenetic researcher Frances A. Champagne of Columbia University puts it:

> I think that some of the key findings that have come out in recent years really describe *the biological impact of early childhood adversity*, both the meaning and the timing of that impact. … We know a lot more now about how the experience of abuse and neglect may become

---

23 A major panel discussion on this topic took place at the National Consultation. *Social Justice for Children: To End Child Abuse and Violence against Children* (Lenzer and Grochowalski, 2012).
24 The Alfred E. Mirsky Professor and Head, Harold and Margaret Millikin Hatch Laboratory of Neuroendocrinology, The Rockefeller University, New York.
25 This and the following quotations are from interviews with and presentation by these scholars for the Children's Studies Center National Consultation. *Social Justice for Children: To End Child Abuse and Violence against Children* (Lenzer and Grochowalski, 2012).

> embedded at a biological level in the neurons within the brain, in the cells and in the genes within those cells, and how that can have a lasting effect on function.
>
> *(Lenzer and Grochowalski, 2012: 103, italics added)*

And she stresses the trans-generational effects of child maltreatment:

> I think the lifelong and trans-generational consequences of early adversity are something that we do know a lot more about. The question is what to do about them and certainly the basic clinical work and basic animal research now suggests that these effects of early *life adversity do become incorporated into our biology, that they can have implications for the next generation of offspring*, and for their functioning as parents as it relates to the care of their offspring.
>
> *(Lenzer and Grochowalski, 2012: 103, italics added)*

Given these findings, it makes sense to consider violence against children as a kind of socio-cultural affliction of extraordinary magnitude – with a multitude of different symptoms and causes. Although theoretically curable, this disorder can be found in epidemic proportions. This is how James A. Mercy, from the Division of Violence Prevention in the US Centers for Disease Control and Prevention, put it at the opening of his presentation at the National Consultation on Social Justice for Children: To End Child Abuse and Violence against Children, catching the audience by surprise (Lenzer and Grochowalski, 2012: 44):

> I want you to imagine something with me for a second. Imagine that you woke up this morning and in the headlines of the *New York Times* ... the headline was that scientists discovered a new Disease. This was a disease that affected children and about 60 per cent of children every year were exposed to this disease. Scientists also reported that those exposed were at greater risk for mental health problems. ... for physical health problems ... such as diabetes, heart disease and cancer. In addition, they were at greater risk for social problems, like crime and drug abuse, during their lives. Scientists also noted that they even could pass this on in the future to their own children in some way. If we had a disease that was in the headlines, framed like that, what you think we would do about it.... The truth is ... we do have such a disease: it's called violence against children.

Given these recent findings, the question that arises is how infants, younger and even older children can organize a movement to establish their agency and human rights from below, when in fact their "participation" is that they are the victims of violence? And given the new biological information about the ways that violence injures children above and beyond the actual physical injuries they may sustain, it seems particularly problematic to insist that victimized children can or should be their own protectors and clinicians.

7. Coda

All this is not to deny the desideratum that children and young people as social subjects should be afforded whenever possible participation rights in all affairs that are of direct concern to them, that infringe upon their human rights as well as constitute forms of violence against them in any setting. In fact, despite the critiques advanced against both the CRC and the Committee, a careful analysis of the CRC since its inception demonstrates the Committee's commitment to enlarging children's participatory sphere of autonomy. Rather than characterize the Committee as a part of the "global children's rights industry" (Reynaert et al., 2009, based on a review of the literature since 1989), what should be emphasized is a dual evolution, not only that of international jurisprudence with regard to children's rights, but also the linked and proactive evolution of the Committee's work and its interpretation of the CRC. In addition, both UNICEF and numerous NGOs have made active "participation" not just in the form of "tokenism" into a central part of their programs and initiatives for some years. The same is true of the missions by the Special Representative of the Secretary General on Violence against Children.

Moreover since its inception, the 18–member Committee has issued 17 General Comments that are binding on state parties to the CRC. These topics include such as General Comment 8, "The Right of the Child to Protection from Corporal Punishment and Other Cruel and Degrading Forms of Punishment," General Comment 9, "The Rights of Children with Disabilities," General Comment 10, "Children's Rights in Juvenile Justice," General Comment 12, "The Right of the Child to be Heard," General Comment 17, "Right to Play" – to name only a few. In addition, the Committee is responsible for three Optional Protocols to the UNCR all of which address Violence Against Children. They are the Optional Protocol to the CRC on Sale of Children, Child Prostitution and Child Pornography (OPSC) and on Children in Armed Conflict (OPAC) as well as the third Optional Protocol (OP3 CRC on a Communications Procedure, which entered into force on April 14, 2014. All three Protocols represent signal contributions by the Committee on the Rights of the Child in the domain of Violence against Children.[26]

By way of conclusion, and unfortunately so, both provision and protection remain central imperatives that *enable* children and young people to realize their human rights and development. And that means that adults will – and should – continue to be held accountable for providing provision, protection *and* participation to help children realize their autonomy, respect and agency. Given the epidemic of violence against children, the multiplicity of its forms, its cross-border nature, and the fact that children are not safe even in their own homes, the campaign to abolish it is still in its early stages. Although achievements have been made, as SRSG Santos Pais stated as recently as May 2014, it is important to "recognize that progress has been too slow, too uneven, and too fragmented to make a genuine breakthrough."[27] The elimination of all violence against children and freedom from violence in all its forms will, therefore, remain the human rights imperative of the next decades to come, if not of the twenty-first century.

8. Post scriptum

In September 2014, UNICEF released a new report, *Hidden in Plain Sight: A Statistical Analysis of Violence Against Children*. This report represents the first major worldwide documentation of violence against children with data mostly from middle- and low-income countries. UNICEF describes it as

---

26 It goes without saying that the enforcement capacities of the Committee of the CRC and of both their general comments and optional protocols are indeed limited. Its Concluding Observations to State party reports take the form of recommendations of changes to be instituted.
27 "Children's Rights, Freedom of Violence and Criminal Justice," contribution on the occasion of the International Conference on Child-Friendly Justice, University of Stockholm, 16–18 May 2014, mss. p. 3.

the largest compilation to date of statistics on violence against children, drawing on data from 190 countries. By examining global patterns of violence against children as well attitudes and social norms, it sheds light on an issue that has remained largely undocumented. Its objective is to use data to make violence against children more visible, bringing about a fuller understanding of its magnitude and nature and offering clues to its prevention.

(UNICEF, 2014a: 165)

Especially based on Article 19 of the CRC, the report states that "[E]nsuring that all forms of violence are recognized as a fundamental violation of children's human rights is a first step in moving towards their elimination." (UNICEF, 2014a: 165). The major categories of interpersonal violence in the report are physical, sexual and emotional, and the key findings include data about homicide, violent discipline, violence among peers and by intimate partners and sexual violence. For example, the "data show that far more children experience violence in the form of discipline – usually in their own homes and from a very young age. On average, about 6 in 10 children worldwide (almost 1 billion) between the ages of 2 and 14 are subjected to physical (corporal) punishment by their caregivers on a regular basis. For the most part, children are exposed to a combination of physical punishment and psychological aggression." (UNICEF, 2014a: 165f). In addition to the 200-page report, UNICEF also published in September 2014, *Ending Violence Against Children: Six Strategies for Action #ENDviolence* – a 63-page report (UNICEF, 2014b).

Questions for debate and discussion

- How important is a multi- or interdisciplinary approach to violence against children?
- Does context (poverty; cultural attitudes) matter when discussing violence against children?
- Is there any possibility to apply a "bottom-up" human rights approach to solve the apparently intractable human realities of children and young people and the power relations between adults and children, especially very young children?
- Is the emphasis on children's agency detrimental to the protection of children against violence?
- How can children and young people themselves contribute to the abolition of violence in the home, schools, state institutions and in the community? Or is this primarily the responsibility of adults to protect children and young people from maltreatment and violence?

Acknowledgement

This research was supported by a grant from the New York Community Trust and the Reuben Mark Family Fund.

References

Annan, K. (2006). Preface. In P.S. Pinheiro (ed.), *World Report on Violence Against Children* (p. xi). Geneva: United Nations. Secretary-General's Study on Violence against Children. Available at www.unicef.org/lac/full_tex(3).pdf

Bitensky, S.H. (1998). The child's right to humane discipline under the U.N. convention on the rights of the child: The mandate against all corporal punishment of children. *Loyola Poverty Law Journal, 4*, pp. 47–53.

Bitensky, S.H. (2009). The poverty of precedent for school corporal punishment's constitutionality under the eighth amendment. *University of Cincinnati Law Review, 77*(4, summer).

Bitensky, S.H. (2010). The Mother of all human rights: The child's right to be free of corporal punishment as hard international law. *Ohio Northern University Law Review XXXVI*, 6.

Bitensky, S.H. (2013). An analytical ode to personhood: The unconstitutionality of corporal punishment of children under the thirteenth amendment. *Santa Clara Law Review, 53*(1).

Children's Defense Fund. (2014). *The State of America's Children 2014*. Washington, D.C.

Finkelhor, D. (2008). *Childhood Victimization: Violence, Crime, and Abuse in the Lives of Young People*. New York, NY: Oxford University Press.

Finkelhor, D., Ormrod, R.K. and Turner, H.A. (2009). Lifetime assessment of poly-victimization in a national sample of children and youth. *Child Abuse and Neglect 33*, 403–411.

Finkelhor, D., Turner, H., Ormrod, R., Hamby, S. and Kracke, K. (2009). Children's exposure to violence: A comprehensive national survey of children's exposure to violence. Washington, DC: *Juvenile Justice Bulletin* (October).

Gershoff, E.T. (2002). Corporal punishment by parents and associated child behaviors and experiences: A meta-analytic and theoretical review. *Psychological Bulletin, 128*, 539–579.

Global Initiative to End All Corporal Punishment of Children (2013). *Ending legalized violence against Children. Global Report*.

Hacking, I. (1999). *The Social Construction of What?* Cambridge, MA: Harvard University Press.

Hanson, K. (2012). Schools of thought in children's rights. In M. Liebel (ed.), *Children's Rights from Below: Cross-cultural Perspectives* (pp. 63–79). New York, NY: Palgrave MacMillan.

Hanson, K. and Nieuwenhuys, O. (eds) (2013). *Reconceptualizing Children's Rights in International Development: Living Rights, Social Justice, Translation*. New York, NY: Cambridge University Press.

Karr-Morse, R. and Wiley, M.S. (2013). *Ghosts from the Nursery: Tracing the Roots of Violence* (Rev. and updated ed.). New York, NY: The Atlantic Monthly Press.

Kemme, S., Hanslmaier, M. and Pfeiffer, M. (2014). *Experience of Parental Corporal Punishment in Childhood and Adolescence and its Effect on Punitiveness*. New York, NY: Springer Science and Business Media, online, January 14th.

Lenzer, G. (1996). Children's studies and the arts and sciences: Recent trends. In E. Verhellen (ed.), *Understanding Children's Rights: Collected Papers Presented at the First International Interdisciplinary Course on Children's Rights* (pp. 169–173). Ghent, Belgium: Children's Rights Center, University of Ghent.

Lenzer, G. (1998). The importance of children's rights programs in academic institutions. *Loyola Poverty Law Journal, 4*, 251–261.

Lenzer, G. (1999). The human rights agenda and the rights of children: Towards a unified approach. *Whittier Law Review, 21*, 107–117.

Lenzer, G. (2001). Children's studies: Beginnings and purposes. *The Lion and the Unicorn, 25*, 181–186.

Lenzer, G. (2009), (ed.). Implementation and monitoring of the optional protocol to the united nations convention on the rights of the child on the sale of children, child prostitution, and child pornography. *Proceedings of the Third Child Policy Forum of New York*. Brooklyn, NY: Children's Studies Center for Research, Policy and Public Service.

Lenzer, G. and Grochowalski, J. (eds) (2012). *Social Justice for Children: To End Child Abuse and Violence Against Children*. A national consultation, 20th anniversary of the founding of the field of children's studies, November 2011. Proceedings. Brooklyn, NY: Children's Studies Center for Research, Policy and Public Service.

Liebel, M. (2012). *Children's Rights from Below: Cross-cultural Perspectives*. New York, NY: Palgrave MacMillan.

Lincoff, N. (2013). Survey finds two in five US children suffer abuse. *HealthlineNews*, May 13.

McEwen, B.S. (2011). *Effects of Stress on the Developing Brain*. Adapted from a Dana Foundation Report on Progress, September.

Meaney, M.J. (2010). Epigenetics and the biological definition of gene x environment interactions. *Child Development, 81*, 41–79.

Office of the SRGS [Office of the Special Representative of the Secretary General on Violence against Children] (2012a). *Prevention and Responses to Violence against Children within the Juvenile Justice System*. New York. NY: Author.

Office of the SRSG (2012b) *Safe and Child-sensitive Counseling, Complaint and Reporting Mechanisms to Address Violence against Children*. Joint report of the SRSG and the Special Rapporteur on the sale of children, child prostitution and child pornography. New York, NY: Author.

Office of the SRGS, (2012c). *Political Commitments by Regional Organizations and Institutions to Prevent and Address Violence against Children.* New York, NY: Author.

Office of the SRGS, (2012d). *Protecting Children from Harmful Practices in Plural Legal Systems.* New York, NY: Author.

Office of the SRGS, (2012e). *Tackling Violence in Schools: A Global Perspective Bridging the Gap Between Standards and Practice.* New York, NY: Author.

Office of the SRGS. (2013a). *Promoting Restorative Justice for Children.* New York, NY: Author.

Office of the SRGS. (2013b). *Toward a World Free from Violence: Global Survey on Violence against Children.* New York, NY: Author.

Qvortrup, J., Corsaro, W.A. and Honig, M.-S. (2009). (eds) *The Palgrave Handbook of Children's Studies.* New York, NY: Palgrave Macmillan.

Reynaert, D., Bouverne-de Bie, M. and Vandevelde, S. (2009). A review of children's rights literature since the adoption of the United Nations Convention on the Rights of the Child. *Childhood, 16,* 518–534.

Shonkoff, J.P. and Phillips, D.A., (eds). (2000). *From Neighborhoods to Neurons: The Science of Early Childhood Development.* National Research Council, Institute of Medicine. Washington, DC: National Academy Press.

Shonkoff, J.P., Boyce, W.T. and McEwen, B.S. (2009). Neuroscience, molecular biology, and the childhood roots of health disparities. *Journal of the American Medical Association, 301,* 2252–2259.

Straus, M.A. with Donnelly, D.A. (2005). *Beating the Devil out of Them: Corporal Punishment in American Families and its Effects on Children.* London: Transaction.

UNICEF (2014a). *Hidden in Plain Sight: A Statistical Analysis of Violence Against Children.* Available at http://files.unicef.org/publications/files/Hidden_in_plain_sight_statistical_analysis_EN_3_Sept_2014.pdf

UNICEF (2014b). *Ending Violence Against Children: Six Strategies for Action.* Available at www.unicef.org/publications/files/Ending_Violence_Against_Children_Six_strategies_for_action_EN_2_Sept_2014.pdf

United Nations, General Assembly (2006). *Rights of the Child.* Note by the Secretary-General, August 29. (On the occasion of transmission of Paulo Sérgio Pinheiro's *World Report.*)

US Department of Health and Human Services, Administration for Children and Families, Administration on Children, Youth and Families, Children's Bureau (2012). *Child Maltreatment 2012.* Washington, DC, 2013, p. XII.

US Department of Justice (2012). *Report of the Attorney-General's National Task Force on Children Exposed to Violence.* [Office of the Justice Program]. Washington, DC: Office of Juvenile Justice and Delinquency Prevention.

World Report on Violence Against Children. (2006). (Edited by P.S. Pinheiro). Geneva: United Nations. Secretary-General's Study on Violence against Children. Available at www.unicef.org/lac/full_tex(3).pdf

17

Female genital mutilation in Europe from a child right's perspective

Els Leye and Annemarie Middelburg

1. Introduction

Female Genital Mutilation (FGM)[1] is a harmful practice that remains widespread. The most recent statistical overview of 27 countries in Africa[2] and the Middle East[3] shows that more than 125 million girls and women live with FGM and 30 million girls are at risk of being cut in the next decade. Due to migration, FGM has also been spread to other continents including Europe, the Americas, Australia and Asia (UNICEF, 2013b; Eneng Darol Afiah, 2013). In Europe, no comparable data for each Member State are available, making a total estimate for the European Union impossible (Leye *et al.*, 2013). The European Parliament estimates that at least 500,000 women and girls in Europe have been subjected to FGM and that 180,000 girls and women are at risk of undergoing FGM every year (European Parliament, 2009). However, the methods used for this estimate are not clear (European Institute for Gender Equality [EIGE], 2013).

For a couple of decades, FGM has been framed within a human rights framework, viewing the practice as a form of Violence Against Women (VAW) and violating the rights of both the girl child and the adult woman. However, despite the wide range of human rights documents that make reference to FGM, there is a slow pace in the decline of the prevalence of FGM. Indeed, the Report "Violating Children's Rights: Harmful Practices Based on Tradition, Culture, Religion or Superstition", observes a "devastating failure of international and regional human rights mechanisms to provoke the necessary challenge to these practices and their

---

[1] The practice was initially referred to as "female circumcision", which drew a direct parallel with male circumcision. The term "female genital mutilation" was used to highlight the fact that there are important differences between male circumcision and the procedure that is practiced on women. The word "mutilation" emphasizes the gravity of the act and underscores the fact that the practice is a violation of the rights of girls and women. As FGM has been a successful advocacy tool to underline the gravity of the action, we prefer to use the term FGM.

[2] Benin, Burkina Faso, Cameroon, Central African Republic, Chad, Côte d'Ivoire, Djibouti, Egypt, Eritrea, Ethiopia, Gambia, Ghana, Guinea, Guinea-Bissau, Kenya, Liberia, Mali, Mauritania, Niger, Nigeria, Senegal, Sierra Leone, Somalia, Sudan, Togo, Uganda, United Republic of Tanzania.

[3] Yemen and Iraq.

effective prohibition and elimination in all regions" (International Council on Violence against Children, 2012).

This chapter first provides an overview of the basic facts about FGM, before sharing some insights about the human rights at stake. The case study described in this chapter focuses on how FGM is dealt with in the EU from a child rights' perspective with a particular focus on protection, provision of services and participation. It provides a critical reflection on how the rights of the girls are (not) fulfilled. In line with the introductory chapter of this Handbook – where it is argued that the reality of children's rights is much richer than the legal instruments and its implementation – this chapter argues that the limited impact might be due to an inadequate transformation of the children's rights framework at national level and into the daily practice of those confronted with FGM. We will argue that there is a lack of a comprehensive approach that can join all stakeholders, tools and instruments as well as policies put in place for the prevention of FGM, protection against it, and the provision of services, in a coordinated strategy to put the human rights framework into practice. We will equally provide suggestions to tackle FGM more adequately.

2. Key facts about FGM

FGM is defined as a procedure that involves the "partial or total removal of the external female genitalia or other injury to the female genital organs for non-medical reasons" and includes four categories (WHO, 2008):

- Type I or clitoridectomy involves the partial or total removal of the clitoris and/or the prepuce.
- Type II or excision involves the partial or total removal of the clitoris and the labia minora, with or without excision of the labia majora.
- Type III or infibulation is the narrowing of the vaginal orifice with the creation of a covering seal by cutting and appositioning the labia minora and/or the labia majora, with or without excision of the clitoris.
- Type IV includes all other forms of harmful procedures to the female genital genitalia for non-medical purposes, for example pricking, piercing, incising, scraping and cauterization.

FGM can be considered as a social norm in a particular context, when individuals are aware of the rule of behaviour regarding the cutting of girls and know that it applies to them, and if individuals prefer to conform to this (UNICEF, 2013b). The reasons why FGM persists vary among communities. It may be considered to be necessary to raise a girl properly and to prepare her for adulthood and marriage. In communities where the practice is viewed as a prerequisite for marriage, economic necessity can be a determinant. FGM is often believed to be necessary to control women's sexuality, to preserve a girls' virginity, to ensure marital fidelity, to make girls clean and beautiful or as a necessity to eliminate "masculine" parts (such as the clitoris) of the genitalia. In many communities, religious arguments are put forward, although none of the monotheistic religions prescribes FGM (WHO, 2008).

The age at which FGM is performed varies between communities or regions, depending on local traditions and circumstances (WHO, 2008). The largest proportion of girls and women are cut between infancy and the age of fifteen (UNICEF, 2013a). A trend of decreasing the age of cutting was noted in some countries, while in other countries the age remained fairly stable (UNICEF, 2013a). This tendency to reduce the age is believed to be associated with parents wanting to reduce the trauma for their girls and to avoid older children reporting an excision or denouncing their parents or excisors to the authorities, and to avoid interference from judicial authorities (UNICEF, 2005). Traditional practitioners perform most of the cases of FGM, although the so-called medicalization of FGM – the performance of FGM by medically skilled personnel – is on the rise in a number of countries (UNICEF, 2013b).

The health consequences vary according to the type of FGM (the extent of the cutting), the circumstances in which it was performed (in a health setting by medical skilled personnel versus a traditional excisor with non-sterile material at particular traditional FGM-sites), and the general condition of the girl. Immediate consequences include severe pain (the procedure is often performed without anaesthesia), bleeding (haemorrhage), shock (caused by pain and haemorrhage), tetanus or sepsis (bacterial infection), urine retention (due to the pain, swelling or oedema and to avoid urine having to pass the edges of the fresh wound), open sores in the genital region and injury to nearby genital tissue. The act can even lead to death due to haemorrhage, infections or shock (WHO, 2008). Long-term consequences include formation of scar tissue, cysts and abscesses, difficulties with menstruation and sexual intercourse, fertility problems, chronic infections of urinary tract, infections of the reproductive tract, and obstetric consequences (WHO, 2008; Banks et al., 2006).

Although evidence on the psychological and social consequences of FGM is weak (Berg, Denison and Fretheim, 2010), some of the documented psychological consequences include fear of sexual intercourse; post-traumatic stress disorder, anxiety, depression and memory loss (WHO, 2008; Vloeberghs et al., 2012). The impact on sexuality includes pain during intercourse, reduced sexual desire and reduced sexual satisfaction (Berg et al., 2010). The true extent of morbidity and mortality related to FGM remains blurred, due to a lack of population-based surveys to document the adverse outcomes of FGM, ethical issues, the unavailability or inaccessibility of health care, ignorance (problems considered normal in communities where FGM is common practice) or fear of legal retribution (Leye, 2008; Jackson et al., 2003; Obermeyer, 1999, 2003).

3. FGM as a human rights violation

Initially, FGM was placed beyond the scope of international human rights law, because VAW in general and FGM more specifically was seen by the international community as a private matter carried out by individuals – rather than state officials. This changed in the 1990s with the global movement against VAW. Landmark events were the adoption of General Recommendation No. 14 on Female Circumcision[4] (1990) where the Committee on the Convention on the Elimination of All Forms of Discrimination against Women (CEDAW Committee) strongly condemned FGM and recommended States parties to take appropriate and effective measures with a view to eradicating the practice of FGM. The adoption of General Recommendation No. 19 on Violence Against Women (1992)[5] was equally important, because the CEDAW Committee explicitly included VAW more generally within the scope of CEDAW and thus international human rights law. The Vienna Declaration and Programme of Action (1993) expanded the international human rights agenda to include gender-based violence. It advocated the importance of "working towards the elimination of violence against

---

4   UN Committee on the Elimination of Discrimination Against Women (CEDAW), *CEDAW General Recommendation No. 14*, 1990, A/45/38 and Corrigendum.
5   UN Committee on the Elimination of Discrimination Against Women (CEDAW), *CEDAW General Recommendations No. 19*, 1992, A/47/38 (contained in Document A/47/38).

women in public and private life, [...] and the eradication of any conflicts which may arise between the rights of women and the harmful effects of certain traditional or customary practices [...]." (Vienna Declaration on Human Rights 1993, point 38). With the adoption of the Declaration on the Elimination of Violence against Women,[6] for the first time FGM was recognized as a form of VAW. Article 2 of the Declaration explains that "[v]iolence against women shall be understood to encompass, but not be limited to, the following: [...] female genital mutilation and other traditional practices harmful to women."[7] Although not legally binding, this declaration strengthened the growing international consensus that FGM of any type is a human rights violation. In 1994, the human rights implications of FGM were again addressed at the International Conference on Population and Development in Cairo: "In a number of countries, harmful practices meant to control women's sexuality have led to great suffering. Among them is the practice of female genital mutilation, which is a violation of basic rights and a major lifelong risk to women's health."[8] UN agencies reinforced the classification of FGM as a human rights violation as well (WHO, 1997, 2008).

As explained in the introductory chapter of this Handbook, children's rights are understood as fundamental claims for the realization of social justice and human dignity for children – just like human rights more generally. As FGM is commonly performed upon girls between 0 and 15 years, any violation of women's rights may in principle be said to amount to a children's rights violation too. However, the legal qualification of FGM as a children's rights violation under the CRC is less straightforward than it may seem at first sight.

In the CRC, FGM is addressed most explicitly in the right to health. Article 24(3) CRC includes the obligation for States Parties "to take all effective and appropriate measures with a view to abolishing traditional practices prejudicial to the health of children." The CRC Committee adopted a general comment on the right to health in 2013,[9] but deliberately excluded any discussion of harmful practices. The latter will be the subject of a separate general comment that is under preparation. It is therefore too early to say how the CRC Committee will interpret "traditional practices prejudicial to the health of children". The article-wise scholarly commentary on the CRC does not offer much interpretative guidance either on this point (pp. 46–48). The UN Special Rapporteur on the right of everyone to the enjoyment of the highest attainable standard of physical and mental health has argued that "Rape and other forms of sexual violence, including [...] female genital mutilation, and forced marriage all represent serious breaches of sexual and reproductive freedoms, and are fundamentally and inherently inconsistent with the right to health."[10] FGM may bring the right to life (Art. 6 CRC) into bearing when a girl dies when undergoing FGM due to excessive bleeding, or when a woman dies during childbirth as a consequence of a tight infibulation or other related FGM problem. FGM may also contribute to neonatal death. Article 21 of the African Charter

---

6 UN General Assembly, Declaration on the Elimination of Violence against Women of 20 December 1993 (A/RES/48/104).
7 UN General Assembly, Declaration on the Elimination of Violence against Women of 20 December 1993 (A/RES/48/104), Article 2.
8 Programme of Action of the International Conference on Population and Development, Cairo, Egypt, Sept. 5–13, 1994, U.N. Doc. A/CONF.171/13/Rev.1 (1995), para. 7.35.
9 CRC Committee (2013), General comment No. 15, The right of the child to the enjoyment of the highest attainable standard of health (Article 24), UN Doc. CRC/C/GC/15.
10 Commission on Human Rights, Economic, Social and Cultural Rights, The right of everyone to the enjoyment of the highest attainable standard of physical and mental health, Report of the Special Rapporteur, Paul Hunt, E/CN.4/2004/49, 16 February 2004, p. 9, para. 25.

on the Rights and Welfare of the Child (ACRWC) explicitly links harmful social and cultural practices with not only the health but also the life of the child, as well as with the child's welfare, dignity, normal growth and development.

Another way of qualifying FGM under children's rights law is to consider it as a form of violence against children, or as torture, cruel, inhuman and degrading treatment. Article 19 CRC obliges States Parties to take all appropriate measures to protect the child from all forms of physical or mental violence (for an elaborate discussion on Art. 19 CRC, see Lenzer, Chapter 16 in this Handbook). Article 37 CRC prohibits torture or any other cruel, inhuman or degrading treatment. In its general comment on violence, the CRC Committee mentions female genital mutilation as a harmful practice that comes under the notion of violence.[11] FGM may be construed as a form of torture, cruel, inhuman and degrading treatment (Art. 37 CRC). The Committee Against Torture stated in its General Comment No. 2 that FGM falls within the mandate of the Committee.[12] Likewise, the UN Special Rapporteur on VAW[13] and the UN Special Rapporteur on torture[14] have both recognized that FGM can amount to torture under the Convention Against Torture and Other Cruel, Inhuman or Degrading Treatment or Punishment (CAT) if states fail to act with due diligence to protect, prevent, investigate and, in accordance with national legislation, punish FGM.[15] However, the classification of FGM as torture is complex (Wood, 2001; Chinkin, 1998). Moreover, the CRC Committee has only occasionally and rather vaguely mentioned sexual violence against children under Article 37 CRC, but it has not made the equation (Schabas and Sax, 2006, 20).

Support for a children's rights argument against FGM could also be sought in the CRC general principles. Article 3 CRC stipulates that "the best interests of the child" must be a primary consideration. However, different cultures have different understandings of what is in a child's best interest (Freeman, 2007, p. 2). Parents may perceive of FGM as an act in their child's best interest. Whereas support can be found in order not to interpret best interests in an overly culturally relativist way and deny (other) rights guaranteed to children by the CRC,[16] a convincing cross-cultural best interests argument remains to be made.

---

11 CRC Committee (2011), General comment No. 13, Article 19: The right of the child to freedom from all forms of violence, UN Doc. CRC/C/GC/13, para. 27.
12 UN Committee against Torture, General Comment No 2, UN Doc CATFGM/GC/2 (2008), para. 18.
13 The previous UN Special Rapporteur on Violence against Women has clearly stated that FGM amounts to torture. See "15 Years of the Special Rapporteur on Violence Against Women, Its Causes and Consequences" (2009): the Special Rapporteur "views cultural practices that involve pain and suffering and violation of physical integrity as amounting to torture under customary international law, attaching to such practices strict penal sanctions and maximum international scrutiny regardless of ratification of CEDAW or reservations made thereto". See also the Report of the Special Rapporteur on violence against women, its causes and consequences, Ms. Radhika Coomaraswamy, Commission on Human Rights, Fifty-eighth session, 31 January 2002, EFGMN.4/2002/83, para. 6.
14 Report by the Special Rapporteur on torture and other cruel, inhuman or degrading treatment or punishment, Mr. P. Kooijmans, EFGMN.4/1986/15, para. 38; Report of the Special Rapporteur on torture and other cruel, inhuman or degrading treatment or punishment, Manfred Nowak, 15 January 2008 (UN Doc. A/HRC/7/3), paras 50–54.
15 UN General Assembly, *Convention Against Torture and Other Cruel, Inhuman or Degrading Treatment or Punishment*, 10 December 1984, United Nations, Treaty Series, vol. 1465, p. 85.
16 Starting points may be found in the CRC Committee's (2013) General Comment No. 14 on the right of the child to have his or her best interests taken as a primary consideration (Art. 3, para. 1).

Another entry point could be found in Article 12 CRC, which ensures the right of the child to express his or her views freely in all matters affecting him or her, and to have these views being given due weight. Whereas a right to express one's views cannot be understood as a right to consent, the CRC Committee has in its general comment on Article 12 CRC explicitly welcomed the right to consent at a fixed age in health care.[17] The social pressure to undergo FGM is usually very high, and in the rare case of a girl refusing to be excised, she will most likely be ostracized from her family and community, with very little possibilities to seek refuge. The question could therefore be raised whether it is possible to reasonably talk about real consent or autonomy when the social pressure in the community to undergo FGM is so high. Interestingly, the international children's rights framework acknowledges the role of the parents and the family in making decisions for children (see inter alia Art. 5 CRC), although it places ultimate responsibility for protecting the rights of the child with the State.

FGM may also be construed as a violation of the right to be free from discrimination (Art. 2 CRC). A child has the right to be protected from all forms of discrimination irrespective of his or her sex or other status. Article 21 ACRWC explicitly mentions customs and practices "discriminatory to the child on the grounds of sex or other status". From a women's rights perspective, FGM fits within the definition of "discrimination against women" that follows from Article 1 of the CEDAW. The practice itself reflects deep-rooted inequality and power imbalances between the sexes. FGM is a practice applied to women and girls that has the effect of nullifying their enjoyment of fundamental rights. FGM aims, amongst others, at controlling women's sexuality, which carries a fundamental discriminatory belief of the subordinate role of women and girls in society. Less attention has been paid to the particular ways in which children experience discrimination, notwithstanding the fact that the discrimination of girls has gradually become a separate issue from that of women and hence has been addressed through different standards (Besson, 2005).[18] Notwithstanding the differences between FGM and male circumcision, there are important similarities in that both involve the removal of healthy parts of one's most intimate sexual organs, without a medical necessity and without informed consent.[19] The emphasis on consent with regard to male circumcision may provide support to the argument that in case of more intrusive acts, even more emphasis should be put on consent.

4. State duties in relation to FGM

The campaign against FGM has gained considerable momentum at policy-level. But what exactly are the duties for states that follow from the human rights framework with regard to FGM?

At the international level, traditional practices are specifically mentioned in CEDAW and the CRC. Article 5 of CEDAW requires States parties to "…take all appropriate measures: (a) To modify the social and cultural patterns of conduct of men and women, with a view to achieving the elimination of prejudices and customary and all other practices which are based on the idea of the inferiority or the superiority of either of the sexes or on stereotyped roles

---

17 CRC Committee's (2009) General Comment No. 12, The right of the child to be heard, para. 102.
18 Besson points out the ambiguity of these girl-specific discrimination approaches: "Although this may have benefited girls, it also means that gender-oriented measures lack coherence overall …"
19 First of all, the reasons given for the practice are different. FGM violates the right to be free from discrimination, because FGM is linked to a reduction in women's sexual desire and an irreversible loss of capability of sexual functioning (WHO and UNAIDS, 2008). This is not the case for male circumcision. There is also a major difference in the amount of harm done. It has often been argued that the equivalent of FGM types I, II and III equals gradual amputation of the penis.

for men and women." Article 24(3) of the CRC provides that "States Parties shall take all effective and appropriate measures with a view to abolishing traditional practices prejudicial to the health of children." Neither the CEDAW nor CRC elaborated what exactly would be "effective and appropriate measures."

At the regional level, the Maputo Protocol addresses the elimination of harmful practices, including FGM. Article 5 says that "States Parties shall prohibit and condemn all forms of harmful practices which negatively affect the human rights of women and which are contrary to recognized international standards. States Parties shall take all necessary legislative and other measures to eliminate such practices". These measures are: (a) awareness-raising through information campaigns, formal and informal education, and outreach; (b) prohibition, through legislative measures backed by sanctions, of all forms of FGM, including the medicalized procedure; (c) support for victims of FGM in the form of health care, legal counsel, psychological care and support, and education and training; and (d) protection of women who are potential victims of FGM or other forms of violence, abuse or intolerance.

The so-called "soft law" instruments elaborate further on what action is expected from States' parties against FGM. Article 4 of the Declaration on the Elimination of Violence against Women submits that states should refrain from invoking any custom, tradition or religious consideration to avoid their obligations with respect to FGM.[20] States are urged to prohibit all forms of FGM (including the medicalized procedure), through the enactment and effective enforcement of national laws.[21] Legal obstacles to prosecution of FGM cases need to be removed and therefore laws need to be reviewed and revised, adjusted or amended as appropriate. This has been stated in several documents, including General Assembly resolutions,[22]

---

20 UN General Assembly, *Declaration on the Elimination of Violence against Women*, 20 December 1993, A/RES/48/104; Similar wordings can be found in other General Assembly resolutions (GA Resolution 61/143 on Intensification of efforts to eliminate all forms of violence against women, para. 5; GA Resolution 63/155 on Intensification of efforts to eliminate all forms of violence against women, para. 9.), the Beijing Declaration (Beijing Declaration and Platform for Action, para. 124(a)), the reports of the Special Rapporteur on violence against women (Report of the Special Rapporteur on violence against women, its causes and consequences(A/HRC/4/34), para. 30; Report of the Special Rapporteur on violence against women, its causes and consequences(A/HRC/7/6), para. 5.) and the agreed conclusions of the Commission on the Status of Women (Agreed conclusions on the elimination and prevention of all forms of violence against women and girls, 57th session (4–15 March 2013), E/2013/27, E/CN.6/2013/11, para. 14.).

21 Programme of Action of the International Conference on Population and Development, Cairo, Egypt, Sept. 5–13, 1994, U.N. Doc. A/CONF.171/13/Rev.1 (1995), para. 4.22; Beijing Declaration and Platform for Action, para. 124(i) and 283(d); ESCR General Comment No. 16 on the equal right of men and women to the enjoyment of all economic, social and cultural rights, para. 29; GA Resolution 53/117 on Traditional or customary practices affecting the health of women and girls, A/RES/53/117, 1 February 1999, para. 3(c); GA Resolution 52/99 on Traditional or customary practices affecting the health of women and girls, para. 3(e); GA Resolution 54/133 on Traditional or customary practices affecting the health of women and girls, para. 3(d); GA Resolution 56/128 on Traditional or Customary Practices Affecting the Health of Women and Girls, para. 3(d); GA Resolution 58/156 on The Girl Child, para. 9; GA Resolution 60/141 on The Girl Child, para. 9; GA Resolution 61/143 on Intensification of efforts to eliminate all forms of violence against women, para 8(c); GA Resolution 62/140 on The Girl Child, para. 13; GA Resolution 63/155 on Intensification of efforts to eliminate all forms of violence against women, para. 16(b); GA Resolution 67/146 on Intensifying global efforts for the elimination of female genital mutilations, para. 4.

22 GA Resolution 52/99 on Traditional or customary practices affecting the health of women and girls, para. 3(e); GA Resolution 54/133 on Traditional or customary practices affecting the health of women and girls, para. 3(d); GA Resolution 56/128 on Traditional or Customary Practices Affecting the Health of Women and Girls, para. 3(d); GA Resolution 58/156 on The Girl Child, para. 9; GA

general comments of treaty bodies,[23] reports of special rapporteurs,[24] UN Secretary-General reports[25] and World Health Assembly resolutions.[26] In addition, several human rights documents[27] and reports of treaty monitoring bodies[28] recommend that states put in place adequate and concrete national accountability mechanisms for implementation and monitoring of legislation law enforcement and national policies. There is also a need to adopt effective and appropriate measures aimed at preventing and abolishing FGM.[29] Various bodies have called upon states to develop national action plans and strategies to eradicate FGM.[30] States have also

> Resolution 60/141 on The Girl Child, para. 9; GA Resolution 61/143 on Intensification of efforts to eliminate all forms of violence against women, para 8(c); GA Resolution 62/140 on The Girl Child, para. 13; GA Resolution 63/155 on Intensification of efforts to eliminate all forms of violence against women, para. 16(b); GA Resolution 67/146 on Intensifying global efforts for the elimination of female genital mutilations, para. 4.
> 23 ESCR General Comment No. 16 on the equal right of men and women to the enjoyment of all economic, social and cultural rights, para. 29; CEDAW General Recommendation no. 24 on Women and health, para. 15(d);
> 24 Report of the Special Rapporteur on violence against women, its causes and consequences (E/CN.4/2002/83), para. 125; Report of the Special Rapporteur on violence against women, its causes and consequences (E/CN.4/1996/53), paras 102 and 142; Report of the Special Rapporteur on violence against women, its causes and consequences (A/HRC/7/6), para. 81; Report of the Special Rapporteur on violence against women, its causes and consequences (A/HRC/7/6/Add.5), paras 258 and 338; Report on Torture and Other Cruel, Inhuman or degrading treatment or punishment (E-CN/4-1986-15), para. 49. Report of the Special Rapporteur on torture and other cruel, Inhuman or degrading treatment or punishment (A/HRC/7/3), para. 76.
> 25 Report of the Secretary-General on Traditional or customary practices affecting the health of women and girls (A/53/354, of 10 September 1998), para. 10; Report of the Secretary-General on Traditional or customary practices affecting the health of women and girls (A/58/169, of 18 July 2003), para. 12; Report on Ending Female Genital Mutilation (E/CN.6/2010/6), para. 1; Report on Ending Female Genital Mutilation (E/CN.6/2012/8), para. 47.
> 26 Resolution on Female Genital Mutilation (WHA61.16), para. 1(2).
> 27 GA Resolution 53/117 on Traditional or customary practices affecting the health of women and girls, para. 3(c); GA Resolution 67/146 on Intensifying global efforts for the elimination of female genital mutilations, para. 12; Commission on the Status of Women: Ending female genital mutilation E/CN.6/2010/L.8, para. 15; Report on Ending Female Genital Mutilation (E/CN.6/2012/8), para. 48.
> 28 CRC, 49th Sess. *Concluding observations: Djibouti* (CRC/C/DJI/CO/2). 7 Oct 2008; CEDAW, 45th Sess., Summary record of the 918th meeting. *Combined sixth and seventh periodic reports of Egypt* (CEDAW/C/SR.918). 1 Apr 2010; CRC, 43rd Sess. *Concluding observations: Ethiopia* (CRC/C/ETH/CO/3). 1 Nov 2006; CEDAW, 39th Sess., Summary record of the 795th meeting. *Consideration of reports submitted by States parties under article 18 of the Convention, Guinea,* (CEDAW/C/SR.795 (A)). 25 Jul 2007; CRC, 44th Sess. *Concluding observations: Kenya* (CRC/C/KEN/CO/2). 19 Jun 2007; *(CAT)*CAT, 44th Sess., *List of issues prior to the submission of the third report of Senegal.*
> 29 CCPR General Comment No. 28 on Equality of rights between men and women (Article 3), para. 3; ESCR General Comment No. 14 on The right to the highest attainable standard of health, para. 22; CRC General comment No. 13 on The Right of the Child to Freedom from all Forms of Violence (CRC/C/GC/13), para. 72(g); GA Resolution 56/128 on Traditional or Customary Practices Affecting the Health of Women and Girls, para. 3(h); GA Resolution 61/143 on Intensification of efforts to eliminate all forms of violence against women, para. 8(f); Report and Programme of Action of the International Conference on Population and Development, Cairo, 5–13 September 1994 A/CONF.171/13/Rev.1, para. 5.5; Report of the World Summit for Social Development, Copenhagen, 6–12 March 1995, para. 79(b); Commission on the Status of Women: Resolution 51/1 on Women, the girl child and HIV and AIDS, para. 13.
> 30 Report of the Special Rapporteur on violence against women, its causes and consequences (E/CN.4/2002/83), para. 126; GA Resolution 67/146 on Intensifying global efforts for the elimination of female genital mutilations, para. 12.

been urged to allocate sufficient financial resources for implementation of policies and legislative frameworks aimed at abandoning FGM.[31] States should also introduce appropriate educational and training programmes and seminars, as well as awareness-raising campaigns,[32] based on research findings about the problems arising from FGM to systematically reach the general public, relevant professionals, families and communities, including through the media and featuring television and radio discussion.[33] The importance of education and the dissemination of information in raising awareness of FGM is emphasized in the Maputo Protocol[34] and many UN human rights documents.[35] States should facilitate the establishment of multidisciplinary information and advice centres regarding the harmful aspects of FGM, as noted by the Committee on the Rights of the Child.[36] States should recognize the important role that

31 GA Resolution 67/146 on Intensifying global efforts for the elimination of female genital mutilations, para. 14; Commission on the Status of Women: Ending female genital mutilation E/CN.6/2010/L.8, paras 3, 27 and 22; UN SG Report on Ending Female Genital Mutilation (E/CN.6/2010/6), para. 40.
32 ICCPR. 83rd Sess. Concluding observations of the Human Rights Committee: Kenya (CCPR/CO/83/KEN). 29 Apr 2005; CEDAW, 39th Sess. Concluding comments on the Committee on the Elimination of Discrimination against Women: Kenya (CEDAW/C/KEN/CO/6). 10 Aug 2007; CRC, 44th Sess. Concluding observations: Kenya (CRC/C/KEN/CO/2). 19 Jun 2007; ICCPR, 61st Sess. Concluding observations of the Human Rights Committee: Senegal (CCPR/C/79/Add.82). 19 Nov 1997; CAT, 41st Sess. Consideration of reports submitted by States Parties under Article 19 of the CCAT, 41st Sess. Consideration of reports submitted by States Parties under Article 19 of the Convention, Concluding observations of the Committee against Torture: Kenya, (CAT/C/KEN/CO/1), 19 January 2009; CRC, 43rd Sess. Concluding observations: Senegal (CRC/C/SEN/CO/2). 20 Oct 2006; Universal Periodic Review Senegal – Review in the Working Group: 6 February 2009 Adoption in the Plenary: 11 June 2009.
33 CEDAW General Recommendation no. 14 on Female Circumcision; GA Resolution 67/146 on Intensifying global efforts for the elimination of female genital mutilations, para. 9.
34 See Article 5(a) of the Maputo Protocol: "States Parties shall take all necessary legislative and other measures to eliminate such practices, including: a) creation of public awareness in all sectors of society regarding harmful practices through information, formal and informal education and outreach programmes."
35 GA Resolution 52/99 on Traditional or customary practices affecting the health of women and girls, para. 2(d); GA Resolution 53/117 on Traditional or customary practices affecting the health of women and girls, para. 3(d); GA Resolution 54/133 on Traditional or customary practices affecting the health of women and girls, para. 3(g); Report and Programme of Action of the International Conference on Population and Development, Cairo, 5–13 September 1994 A/CONF.171/13/Rev.1, para.13.14(b); Beijing Declaration, Platform for Action and the Report of the Fourth World Conference on Women, paras. 107(a), 124(k) and 276(b); Commission on the Status of Women: Ending female genital mutilation E/CN.6/2010/L.8, paras. 3, 7, 10 and 23; Report of the Special Rapporteur on violence against women, its causes and consequences (E/CN.4/2002/83), para. 114; Report of the Special Rapporteur on violence against women, its causes and consequences (E/CN.4/1996/53), para. 112 and 114; Report of the Special Rapporteur on the right of everyone to the enjoyment of the highest attainable standard of physical and mental health (A/66/254), para. 57; Report of the Secretary-General on Traditional or customary practices affecting the health of women and girls (A/53/354, of 10 September 1998), para. 2, 7, 17, 40 and 54; Report of the Secretary-General on Traditional or customary practices affecting the health of women and girls (A/56/316, of 22 August 2001), paras. 9 and 40; Report of the Secretary-General on Traditional or customary practices affecting the health of women and girls (A/58/169, of 18 July 2003), para. 24 and 49; Report of the Secretary-General on Ending Female Genital Mutilation (E/CN.6/2010/6), para. 21; Report of the Secretary-General on Ending Female Genital Mutilation (E/CN.6/2012/8), para. 50; Resolution on Female Genital Mutilation (WHA61.16), para. 1(1).
36 CRC General Comment No. 4 on Adolescent Health and Development in the Context of the Convention on the Rights of the Child (CRC/GC/2003/4), para. 20.

NGOs play in the eradication of FGM and give them all necessary support and encouragement.[37] States are also recommended to establish or strengthen comprehensive and accessible sexual and reproductive health support services to respond to the needs of girls and women and to provide adequate training for health-care workers (nurses, midwives, doctors and other relevant personnel) at all levels on issues raised in the context of FGM.[38] Finally, states are recommended to collect and disseminate basic data about the prevalence, trends, attitudes and behaviour regarding FGM, as well as on reported cases and enforcement of legislation.[39] Universities, medical or nursing associations, national women's organizations or other bodies, can do the data collection.[40]

Although the United Nations, the African Union, the Council of Europe and the European Union have played a significant role in recognizing FGM as a human rights violation, the challenge of ending FGM ultimately rests at the national level. The case study of Europe demonstrates some of the challenges faced when translating the human rights framework regarding FGM into daily practice, and is described in the following sections.

5. Translating human rights into practice: The case of FGM in Europe[41]

Below, we provide some reflections on how human rights are put into practice in the EU, based on research performed in 2012 in all 28 EU Member States. This research aimed at mapping the situation and trends of FGM in the EU and to provide the European Commission with recommendations on how to tackle FGM in several areas (prevention, prosecution, protection,

---

37 CEDAW General Recommendation no. 14 on Female Circumcision; GA Resolution 52/99 on Traditional or customary practices affecting the health of women and girls, para. 3(f); Report of the Secretary-General on Traditional or customary practices affecting the health of women and girls (A/53/354, of 10 September 1998), para. 25; Report of the Secretary-General on Traditional or customary practices affecting the health of women and girls (A/56/316, of 22 August 2001), para. 12; Report of the Secretary-General on Ending Female Genital Mutilation (E/CN.6/2012/8), para. 49; World Health Assembly Resolution on Female Genital Mutilation (WHA61.16), para. 1(4); Report of the Special Rapporteur on violence against women, its causes and consequences (E/CN.4/2002/83), para. 132.
38 GA Resolution 67/146 on Intensifying global efforts for the elimination of female genital mutilations, para. 5; Commission on the Status of Women: Ending female genital mutilation E/CN.6/2010/L.8, para. 14; GA Resolution 58/156 on The Girl Child, para. 9; GA Resolution 60/141 on The Girl Child, para. 9; GA Resolution 62/140 on The Girl Child, para. 13; Beijing Declaration, Platform for Action and the Report of the Fourth World Conference on Women, para. 93; Report of the Secretary-General on Ending Female Genital Mutilation (E/CN.6/2012/8), para. 52; Resolution on Female Genital Mutilation (WHA61.16), para. 1(5).
39 GA Resolution 54/133 on Traditional or customary practices affecting the health of women and girls, para. 3(c); GA Resolution 56/128 on Traditional or customary practices affecting the health of women and girls, para. 3(c); Commission on the Status of Women: Resolution 51/3 Forced marriage of the girl child, para. 3(e); Report of the Special Rapporteur on violence against women, its causes and consequences (E/CN.4/2002/83), para. 130; Report of the Special Rapporteur on torture and other cruel, inhuman or degrading treatment or punishment(A/HRC/7/3), para 76; Report of the Secretary-General on Traditional or customary practices affecting the health of women and girls (A/53/354, of 10 September 1998), paras 15 and 34; Report of the Secretary-General on Traditional or customary practices affecting the health of women and girls (A/58/169, of 18 July 2003), para. 49.
40 CEDAW General Recommendation no. 14 on Female Circumcision.
41 The authors wish to acknowledge the following researchers that assisted in the EIGE study, on which this section is based: Lut Mergaert, Catarina Arnaut, Jessika Deblonde, Anke Van Vossole and Sioban O'Brien Green.

provision of services and prevalence of FGM in the EU).[42] The paragraphs below focus on child protection, the provision of services and participation, following the CRC Committee's general principles framework, as explained in the introductory chapter of this Handbook.[43]

5.1. Protecting the rights adequately

FGM is performed on non-consenting girls – in most cases before the age of fifteen – and has severe consequences on their health and wellbeing. These facts have urged many countries to classify FGM as a form of child abuse. In all EU Member States, general child protection laws exist and can be used in case of FGM (EIGE, 2013). When there is a suspicion of FGM, either voluntary (e.g. a hearing with the family) or compulsory measures (i.e. withholding the passports of parents to avoid them travelling; upheaval of parental authority) can be taken; the latter are subject to court order (Leye and Sabbe, 2009). The fact that interventions to protect girls from FGM have been taken in nine countries[44] (EIGE, 2013), underscores that girls in the EU are at risk of the practice. However, few countries developed specific policies to protect girls from FGM (EIGE, 2013).[45] These policies support the implementation of child protection laws for professionals, and include risk assessment protocols and referral procedures. Proper risk assessment is key to adequately protect girls, as it can assist those professionals confronted with risk situations (police officers, teachers, health professionals, etc.) to adequately assess the level of risk and provide guidance on adequately responding to risk situations. In the majority of the EU countries, policies for teachers as well as risk assessment instruments were notably lacking (EIGE, 2013). Registration of child protection cases of FGM is weak in all EU Member States, due to lack of adequate registering of FGM in child protection records.[46] Registrations could however be very helpful in monitoring and evaluating child protection services, and provide conclusive data on the number of cases reported, subsequent investigations or outcomes of investigations and as such, better target and steer the development of child protection policies and services.

Criminal laws have been put in place that make FGM illegal.[47] In Europe, thirteen countries developed specific criminal law provisions dealing with FGM.[48] In all other EU Member States, legal provisions dealing with bodily injury, mutilation and removal of organs or body tissue may be used for criminal prosecution of FGM (EIGE, 2013). However, the

---

42 For a full overview of this research, please consult the Report "Female Genital Mutilation in the European Union and Croatia", at the website of the European Institute for Gender Equality: www.eige.eu (EIGE, 2013).
43 "Guided by what has gradually come to be seen as the four underlying principles, i.e. of non-discrimination, best interests of the child, survival and development, and participation (Committee on the Rights of the Child, 2003, §12), the CRC grants children rights relating to protection, provision and participation."
44 These included interventions in Denmark, France, Finland, Germany, Italy, the Netherlands, Spain, Sweden and the UK. In Denmark, Germany, Italy and Spain, the interventions were court cases regarding child protection measures for FGM.
45 The countries with such policies are Denmark, France, The Netherlands and the UK.
46 Only France, the Netherlands, Spain and the UK seem to have some recording procedures put in place within the child protection sector (EIGE, 2013).
47 UN Division for the Advancement of Women. Supplement to the Handbook for Legislation on Violence Against Women. "Harmful Practices against Women", 2011, United Nations, New York.
48 These countries are: Austria, Belgium, Croatia, Cyprus, Denmark, Germany, Ireland, Italy, Malta, The Netherlands, Spain, Sweden and the UK.

implementation of the law – or the fulfilment of the protection rights by a State – remains problematic in European Member States as only six countries had criminal court cases (EIGE, 2013).[49]

Even if a country succeeds in prosecuting cases of FGM, this points to the fact that overall the system is not adequate enough in detecting and preventing FGM and that professionals and civil society organizations (CSOs), in charge of child protection and prevention of FGM, were not successful in avoiding FGM from happening. Court cases are only one indicator of the law enforcement process; the implementation of laws constitutes a totality of actions that are undertaken de facto, to give effect to the legal provisions at distinct levels of interactions by a number of stakeholders, who make use of multiple strategies: health and child protection officials who report cases, police officers and prosecutors who investigate cases, and judges and lawyers in the court room. The reality of the implementation of a law is characterized by the involvement of all these stakeholders and strategies (Leye et al., 2007; Ford, 2005). Major challenges with regard to the implementation of the criminal laws in the EU involve difficulties in the reporting/denouncing of cases of girls at risk or performed FGM, and finding sufficient evidence to bring a case to court (EIGE, 2013).

5.1.1. Reporting of cases

Several barriers have been documented in reporting and denouncing cases of FGM earlier (Leye et al., 2007), that were confirmed by the European case study (EIGE, 2013). One of these barriers includes the lack of willingness of family and community members to report cases of girls at risk, due to loyalty issues towards the community and family. Girls might be reluctant to report parents, as they are dependent on their family and community. Communities also need to be aware of the law and its repercussions when breaching it. When performing FGM, they have committed a crime, which is contrary to their intention of acting in the best interest of the girl. If parents are aware of the law, the benefits of having a daughter excised, i.e. conforming to the social norm might outweigh the negative effects of acting against the law. Furthermore, FGM is also performed in communities that are sometimes hard to reach by health and social services, making the detection of cases difficult (Leye et al., 2007).

Indeed, several professionals (such as doctors, nurses, teachers or social workers) play a critical role in identifying girls at risk, in reporting to the relevant authorities and in initiating protective measures (EIGE, 2013). In order to be able to play this role, these professionals have to be knowledgeable about FGM, and about the subsequent actions to take, in the case of a girl at risk or the case of performed FGM. Research showed that such knowledge is lacking (EIGE, 2013; Leye et al., 2007), resulting in an underreporting of cases and girls not offered adequate protection. Attitudes of health and child protection professionals, police officers and prosecutors, as well as judges and lawyers, equally influence the adequate implementation of laws. In particular, the fear of being labelled a racist and the respect for other cultures have resulted in the inaction of these professionals (Leye et al., 2007). Such attitudes have been noticed elsewhere as well (see for example Moynihan and Webb, 2009; Raman and Hodes, 2012). France has countered the "respect for other cultures"-argument in its court cases. French law considers that every person living in France is subject to the law, making no difference between origin and nationality; hence, all children enjoy the same rights, including the right to protection from

---

49 These countries were: Denmark, France, Italy, the Netherlands, Spain and Sweden; the majority of the court cases took place in France.

abuse (Leye *et al.*, 2007). According to Weil-Curiel, FGM should not be considered differently than any other form of child abuse, and that, should the court take into consideration this cultural argument, some children within French jurisdiction would be discriminated against as only children of African origin are subjected to FGM (Weil-Curiel, 2003, 2004b).

In cases where FGM has been performed, professionals need to consider protection of other female siblings from undergoing the same procedure. However, professionals who deal with girls at risk of FGM, struggle with finding the right balance between prosecution and prevention. The prevention of FGM entails seeking collaboration with the family to prevent FGM from taking place on a girl and her sisters, and this is sometimes conflicting with prosecution, where penalties such as imprisonment of parents, might jeopardize a family that is functioning well and is usually acting in the best interest of its children. Child protection officers act from a different angle than judicial authorities when assessing possible protective actions. The police might act according to the rule of law to protect a girl, for example, by taking compulsory measures such as withholding the passports of the parents or imprisoning them, while a child protection officer is reluctant to report a girl at risk as he or she might prefer to continue working with the family in a relation of trust, in order to protect other female siblings from FGM and not to destabilize. A report published in the UK underlines the importance of recognizing FGM as a form of child abuse and to integrate it into all UK child safeguarding procedures in a systematic way (Royal College of Midwives, Royal College of Nursing, Royal College of Obstetricians and Gynaecologists, Equality Now, and UNITE, 2013).

Professional's secrecy provisions and related disclosure regulations, that deal with the right or duty to report cases of child abuse among others, need to be taken into consideration as well. These are important mechanisms to ensure the implementation of the law and the protection of girls at risk. Professionals should be aware of it, as well as of the sanctions for non-reporting, the risk indicators of FGM, the procedures to be followed in the case of a risk situation, relevant referrals to be made and their time frame (EIGE, 2013).

5.1.2. Finding evidence

Some of the difficulties in finding evidence are equal to those concerning the reporting of cases, in particular the lack of knowledge about FGM, the attitudes of professionals and the secrecy surrounding FGM (Leye *et al.*, 2007). Finding sufficient proof of FGM is difficult, as generally speaking, there is no written proof of it. Medical examinations of the genital area are possible, and have been done or proposed in some EU countries to establish whether or not the genitals are intact and as a means to enforce the law. For example, in France, the "Protection Maternelle et Infantile"[50] received instructions to perform inspections of the external genitalia of all girls during medical follow-up and monitoring of the child until she is six years old, and to note and date the state of the (normal) genitalia in the "Carnet de Santé".[51] In cases where

---

50 The PMI is a governmental organization, set up by the Ministry of Health. It provides a national system to protect mother and child, and takes preventive measures (at medical, educational, psychological and social level), monitors and controls services for children from 0 to 6 years and provides family assistance (http://wikipedia.org/wiki/Protection_maternelle_et_infantile).
51 Protection Maternelle et Infantile, Direction de l'Action Sociale et de l'Enfance et de la Santé, Sous-Direction de la Petite Enfance, Département de Paris. Note à l'Attention des médecins d'arrondissement de PMI, des sages-femmes, des puéricultrices-coordinatrices de crèches, des puéricultrices de secteur, des médecins vacataires, des directrices de consultations. 'Conduite à tenir face à l'excision des petites filles.

the girl comes from a community that practices FGM, it is also advised to write down and date when the parents have been informed about the potential dangers related to FGM and the illegality of the practice (Leye et al., 2007). This medical follow up of newborns and children up to six years is not compulsory, and not all health professionals follow these instructions (Weil-Curiel, 2004b). In the Netherlands, in 2005, a special commission "Fight Against Female Genital Mutilation" investigated the possibility of compulsory gynaecological screening of girls of African origin. After this inquiry, the Dutch Minister of Public Health, Welfare and Sports, concluded that the Dutch government does not have the legal power to oblige citizens to cooperate with gynaecological examinations of underaged girls of a specific population group. The main arguments are that it is against the individual's right to freedom and only perpetrators, not victims, can be obliged to undergo such examinations. Moreover, this can only be done when the public health is in danger, which is clearly not the case in this instance. The Commission also states that imposing such a measure on a specific population group is against the principle of non-discrimination (Commissie Bestrijding Vrouwelijke Genitale Verminking, 2005). Leye et al. have already pointed out that such compulsory examinations of the genitals have not been suggested to detect systematically cases of child sexual abuse among the entire population (Leye et al., 2007). Hence, why such a measure for African girls is considered discriminatory and intrusive. Moreover, questions can be raised regarding the feasibility of it, as such screening would require skilled health professionals that can detect even the slightest alteration in the genitals and might need consent of the parents.

Finally, finding evidence when FGM is performed in Africa, will need cross-border investigations, which are highly complex. As the extended family is often involved in decision-making, finding the perpetrators and/or facilitators of the act is problematic, as well as gathering criminal evidence to prosecute when non-family members have performed FGM. The fact that the onus is put on girls who have undergone FGM to testify against their parents and/or families in court, attributes to this complexity.

The issues identified above regarding the implementation of legislation indicate that the provision of a legislative framework, i.e. a specific criminal law and a child protection policy on FGM, do not suffice to curb the practice of FGM. Criminalizing FGM might also have non-intended effects. It has been argued that the practice might go underground and hence deprive girls from adequate protection (Vandenhole, 2012). Another effect that was noted was the lowering of the age of cutting. Among the cited reasons for this earlier age, is being able to do the cutting more discreetly, particularly when people have been sensitized to end FGM or where the practice has been criminalized (Hernlund, 2000; Shell Duncan et al., 2011; UNICEF, 2013b).

In conclusion, the national legal framework, based on international human rights, is necessary to set the standard and provide an enabling environment for CSOs to act. It also provides professionals an additional tool to prevent FGM from happening. However, given FGM is considered a social norm, enacted by groups, that interacts with legal norms (enacted by States) and moral norms (internalized values of right and wrong), "any analysis undertaken to inform policies and programmes aimed at abandoning FGM needs to explore the 3 types of norms and how they interact with one another" (UNICEF, 2013b). In order to adequately change attitudes and behaviour on FGM, i.e. changing the social norm, laws are considered to be one of a set of interventions by governments that should be accompanied by other measures that target behaviour change in communities, as well as measures that target stakeholders. Such behaviour-change measures should address FGM within its broader social context, and take into account the degree of social support for the practice (Raman and Toubia, 2000; UNICEF, 2010;

Shell-Duncan *et al.*, 2013). Measures for professionals should aim at increasing knowledge on FGM and its legal framework, build intercultural competencies and skills and develop instruments and/or protocols to support their actions.

5.2. Providing appropriate services for girls at risk of FGM and those with FGM

When looking at services provided for girls at risk or for those who have already undergone FGM, it is important not only to consider the capacity building for professionals, to optimize service delivery, but equally, the available services. Most commonly, it is the health sector that will be confronted with women and girls who have undergone FGM, and the child protection sector with cases of girls at risk. Most of the services in Europe that cover protection, prevention, provision of training and support are delivered by CSOs and health professionals. Specialized health services, such as the African Well Women Clinics in the UK that provide a multidisciplinary approach, have been put in place.[52,53] CSOs provide training to a wide range of professionals, offer protection to girls and women, provide prevention activities among communities and professionals, raise awareness on the issue, etc. This service provision is supported by a variety of manuals, guidelines and protocols that have been developed for professionals and organizations that provide services (EIGE, 2013).

However, the main focus of service provision in the EU lies on gynaecological services, and there is a lack of services providing psychological care and psychosexual counselling. Health services that are available are provided through the existing health system, and specialized services such as the African Well Women Clinics are rather exceptional. Other issues include the concentration of services in larger urban areas, the ad hoc nature of service provision (mainstreaming FGM in existing services and institutionalization of services for victims of FGM are lacking) and training, the non-inclusion of FGM in curricula of health professionals and a lack of assessment of quality and effectiveness of existing tools that support service provision. Moreover, CSOs, as the major actor for service provision, struggle with a lack of financial and human resources, which is a major impediment to effective service delivery (EIGE, 2013).

As FGM is considered a form of child abuse in European Member States, such states should provide adequate child protection services. Existing services should be able to assess the risk that a girl will be excised, but they should equally be able to respond adequately in case FGM has been done. Professionals involved should be knowledgeable about how to deal effectively with cases of FGM, who to contact, how to determine risk factors and the legislative and protective mechanisms that are in place at a country or regional level. Some guidelines that support professionals in protecting girls have been developed. One example is the "Multi-Agency guidelines: female genital mutilation", developed by the Home Office in the UK. These include information on identifying when a girl (including an unborn girl) or young woman may be at risk of being subjected to FGM and responding appropriately to protect them; identifying when a girl or young woman has been subjected to FGM and responding appropriately to support them; and measures that can be implemented to prevent and ultimately eradicate the practice of FGM. However, training for child protection officials is rare in the EU and if such training exists, it does not seem to be conducted on a continual, structured and national basis, and very often CSOs are relied on to provide training on FGM (EIGE, 2013).

52 African Well Women Clinics are services in the UK that provide specialist services, including clinical management, counseling and prevention. For more information see http://eige.europa.eu FGMontent/african-well-woman-clinics
53 Such services are equally provided in Belgium, Italy, Sweden and France.

As argued above, in order to prevent all forms of FGM, sustainable changes in social and cultural norms and behaviour among women and men, and children, are required. This cannot be achieved by adopting laws and a repressive enforcement. Sustainable behaviour change strategies and interventions regarding FGM have been discussed elsewhere (Leye et al., 2005; Brown et al., 2013). The creation of an enabling environment for behaviour change should equally include training of professionals in close contact with women who have had FGM or girls at risk, as well as regular awareness-raising campaigns, and providing teaching materials that include gender equality.

In the EU, most of the instruments that are developed have focused on prevention, in particular on awareness raising and providing training to professionals and advocacy efforts. The main issues in the EU Member States with prevention are that engaging with women, girls and communities that are most at risk, appears less pronounced, and there are insufficient efforts done towards lasting behaviour change. Especially working with young girls at risk of FGM (and with men and religious leaders) seems to be lagging behind to working with women. As said before, most of the prevention work is done by CSOs, and their chronic lack of sufficient funds and resources hamper an adequate long-term strategy to change social and cultural norms related to FGM. Finally, most prevention activities are done in the absence of accurate FGM prevalence data and firm evaluations, which makes assessment of success factors and areas in need for more work, problematic (EIGE, 2013).

One of the proposals for a service that has raised considerable controversy was the proposition of the American Association of Paediatrics, to perform a ritual nicking of the clitoris, to meet cultural requirements but at the same time limit health consequences (Song, 2010). Ever since the early nineties, debate has been ongoing on providing such "light" forms of FGM to avoid health complications of more severe forms of FGM. Providing this service by medically skilled personnel is considered, by those advocating for it, to be a necessary step towards total eradication of all forms of FGM. In the Netherlands, in 1992, two researchers argued that there were mutilating and non-mutilating forms of FGM, and that the government should allow for the non-mutilating forms (incisions in clitoris). The same was proposed in 1999 in Germany, by a medical doctor, who saw incisions in the clitoral hood as the only solution as the ritual itself would never change, and in Italy, in 2003, a medical doctor argued such incisions would prevent illegal infibulations conducted during school holidays, when girls are taken to Africa (Leye et al., 2006). Those opposed to such "harm-reduction strategy" have repeatedly pointed to the fact that performing "light" versions of FGM by medical health professionals is against medical deontology, that such incisions are equally violating the right to bodily integrity and that in some communities, girls are "redone", if they notice that only an incision has been done (Baumgarten and Gahn, 2002). The assumption that a ritual will never change has been countered by recent statistics, which show that in some countries, younger generations do not undergo infibulations (UNICEF, 2013a), or that the meaning of the ritual changed: in some communities where it was part of the coming of age ritual, the cutting has been taken out of this initiation ritual – which is maintained – while FGM is performed on younger girls (Johansen et al., 2013). In Europe, some communities have switched from infibulations to Type II or Type I. However, in most countries, the type of FGM has not changed much across generations, which suggests that promoting less severe forms of FGM "does not hold much promise" and that the "benefits of a marginal decrease in harm resulting from less severe forms of FGM need to be weighed against the opportunity cost of promoting the end of FGM as one of many harmful practices that jeopardise the well-being of girls and infringe upon their rights" (UNICEF, 2013a).

The recurrent suggestion of pricking or incising the genitals, as a harm reduction strategy, seems to stem predominantly from health professionals. It is a short-term solution, viewed from a health perspective only, and ignores the human rights dimension. Addressing FGM as a health issue only is believed to be one of the reasons of the increasing medicalization of the practice.[54] Health professionals are generally considered as respectful individuals that have authority when it comes to health issues. When professional health organizations such as the AAP are publicly advocating for performing FGM by health professionals (in this case paediatricians), the effect of such a statement and its impact on the global campaign for the abandonment of all forms of FGM should not be underestimated. Maintaining FGM by performing ritual nicking does not contribute to the debate and questioning of the practice by the communities, which is a result of decades of campaigning against FGM. On the contrary, it legitimizes and contributes to upholding the practice.

5.3. The poor participation of girls and women in the FGM dialogue

It is of vital importance that policies and interventions are developed in full partnership with the communities that practice FGM. Partnerships with community-based organizations and professionals likely to be confronted with FGM, are also a prerequisite to develop and implement sustainable policies to tackle FGM. In the EU, a few countries have made efforts to include the communities in policy development or in the design of interventions, most commonly by collaborating with community based organizations that work towards the abandonment of FGM. The EIGE study identified several practices with potential, notably where such partnerships were formed to develop national action plans on FGM, to exchange experiences, to lobby national or international organizations, to provide services or to raise funds. However, in most cases, FGM-affected communities are not actively involved in policy dialogues on FGM, in the design of support services or in the drafting of specific criminal laws. The EIGE study found no evidence of involvement of minor girls in such partnerships in any of the EU countries. Finally, and as mentioned before, it is particularly striking to note that efforts in preventing FGM are rarely targeted at the communities themselves, but rather at professionals (EIGE, 2013). This might be a direct consequence of the fact that communities do not participate fully in dialogues with regard to the most effective strategies to deal with FGM.

In the field of FGM, a top-down approach is not effective, as outreach to communities that practice FGM is crucial in prevention work (Leye and Mergaert, 2012). Hence, why a community-based, participatory approach is paramount when developing interventions, policies or research studies. A notable practice with potential in the EU in this area is the END FGM-European Campaign, led by Amnesty International Ireland. This campaign (2009–2014) aims to put FGM on the EU agenda and "to echo voices of women and girls living with FGM and those at risk of being subjected to it" (End FGM European Campaign, 2009). The campaign is based on and advocates for the recognition of the principles of the human rights-based approach. This approach frames FGM as a human rights violation, aims at empowering rights holders, who are defined as women and girls living with or at risk of FGM, and seeks active and meaningful participation of those directly affected by the practice of FGM. According to the Campaign, active participation of rights holders in the development of policies affecting them and their communities is crucial to the success of any measures proposed at EU level. To

---

54 Medicalization of FGM refers to situations in which FGM is practised by any category of health care provider, whether in public or private clinic, at home or elsewhere (WHO, 2010. Global strategy to stop health care providers from performing female genital mutilation).

achieve its objectives, the Campaign has worked in partnership with 14 (community-based) organizations in 13 EU countries.

6. The need for a comprehensive approach to tackle FGM

FGM constitutes a violation of the rights of young girls and women. The human rights framework provides guidance for setting standards at national level and in creating an enabling environment for governments and CSOs to develop actions to tackle FGM. However, the implementation of international human rights law at national level and community level is facing multiple challenges. The case study of Europe showed that even in a context where policies and laws regarding FGM have been put in place, with available resources and an enabling political environment, implementation is not an automatic and easy process. It demonstrated that despite robust child protection policies being in place in the EU, the existing systems for protecting girls from child abuse show shortcomings when it comes to protecting girls from being subjected to FGM. Service provision lacks resources, and is often not provided in a structural way, but rather on an ad hoc basis, focused on awareness raising and sensitization, and is not provided at all levels. Although important first steps when tackling FGM are taken, more needs to be done to achieve sustainable behaviour change. Furthermore, girls and women affected by FGM participate poorly in the FGM dialogue: they are seldom actively involved in policy dialogues, in designing interventions of services or in drafting legislation. However, states alone are not able to deal with FGM, the particularities of FGM require full partnership with community-based organizations in the planning and implementation of all actions. They can liaise with and speak for the affected communities, and are crucial to make the work for abandoning FGM more effective (Leye and Mergaert, 2012). It should also be noted that in the EU there is an absence of baseline data and insufficient monitoring and evaluating mechanisms that can assist in following up on progress made by governments and states with regard to FGM. Robust data help in better targeting resources, in monitoring and steering the implementation of policies and activities, and consequently in making any action that deals with FGM more efficient and effective. The difficulties demonstrated when looking at prosecuting FGM, showed that many actors and strategies are involved when enforcing a criminal law. The call for more prosecutions regarding FGM, as is noted for example in the UK, should be regarded with caution. Having no court cases on FGM does not necessarily mean that the law is not being implemented. It might also point out that prevention and protection strategies are actually working. Having parents stand in court means that – ultimately – governments, CSOs and other stakeholders have failed in protecting a girl from being subjected to FGM. The ultimate goal of any intervention is to reach sustainable behaviour change, i.e. the abandonment of all forms of FGM. In order to take the above-mentioned elements into consideration, a comprehensive, multidisciplinary approach is necessary to deal with FGM. Such an approach should be adapted to each local context – this means that prior to an intervention a baseline assessment should be done to gain in-depth knowledge of the meaning of FGM in that particular context – and should focus not only on protection, provision and partnership, but equally have reliable prevalence estimates, while also trying to find the right balance between prosecution and prevention.

A coherent and comprehensive policy framework should not be limited to awareness raising or to successfully prosecuting FGM. Such an approach requires attention for the protection of girls and women at risk, the investigation of cases and subsequent prosecution of persons found guilty of practising FGM, the provision of services (health care, psycho-sexual care, psychological, social and medical counseling, legal advice) to those affected by FGM, as well as the building of and support for partnerships between actors involved in dealing with FGM (including statutory and non-statutory actors, public bodies and private actors, including CSOs and community based organizations) (Leye and Mergaert, 2012).

Questions for debate and discussion

- A view opposing the belief that FGM constitutes a human rights violation is that of cultural relativism. What are arguments in favour and against such a cultural relativist approach – compared to the universalist approach?
- To what extent may the consideration of "the best interests of the child" be subject to cultural interpretation?
- To what extent is it possible to reasonably talk about real consent or autonomy when the social pressure in the community is so high to conform to the social norm of practising FGM?
- Would you consider the "light" or "non-mutilating" forms of FGM (incisions in clitoris) a human rights violation? If so, why? Would it be a good strategy to introduce "non-harmful" FGM?
- Would male circumcision amount to a violation of the rights of the child?
- How should a comprehensive framework dealing with FGM look like?
- Why is adaptation to the local context important, when designing an intervention that deals with FGM?

References

Banks, E., Meirik, O., Farley, T., Akande, O., Bathija, H. and Ali, M. (2006). Female genital mutilation and obstetric outcome: WHO collaborative prospective study in six African countries. *Lancet*, 367, 1835–1841.

Baumgarten, I. and Gahn, G. (2002). *Stellingnahme zum "Leitfaden der neuen Strategie gegen die weibliche Genitalverstümmelung: Incisio Praeputii (IP), Verfassen Dr Arnold Groh"* [Position statement regarding the "Guideline for the new strategy on female genital mutilation: Incisio Praeputii (IP)]. Eschborn, Deutsche Gesellschaft für Technische Zusammenarbeit (GTZ).

Berg, R.C., Denison, E. and Fretheim, A. (2010). *Psychological, social and sexual consequences of female genital mutilation/cutting (FGM/C): A systematic review of studies. Report from Kunnskapssenteret nr 13–2010.* Oslo: Nasjonalt kunnskapssenter for helsetjenesten.

Besson, S. (2005). The Principle of non-Discrimination in the Convention on the Rights of the Child. *International Journal of Children's Rights*, 13, 445.

Brown, K., Beecham, D. and Barrett, H. (2013) The applicability of behaviour change in intervention programmes targetged at ending female genital mutilation in the EU: integrating social cognitive and community level approaches. *Obstetrics and Gynecology International*, Volume 2013, Article ID 324362. Available at http://dx.doi.org/10.1155/2013/324362

Chinkin, C. (1998). Torture of the girl child In G. van Bueren (ed.) *Childhood Abused: Protecting Children Against Torture, Cruel, Inhuman and Degrading Treatment and Punishment*. Aldershot, UK: Ashgate: 99.

Committee on the Rights of the Child (2003). *General Comment No. 4. Adolescent health and development in the context of the Convention on the Rights of the Child*. CRC/GC/2003/4. Geneva: United Nations.

EIGE (European Institute for Gender Equality) (2013). *Female genital mutilation in the European Union and Croatia. Report* Vilnius: European Institute for Gender Equality.

END FGM European campaign, led by Amnesty International Ireland (2009). *Ending Female Genital Mutilation: A Strategy for the European Union Institutions*. Available at www.endfgm.eu/content/assets/END_FGM_Final_Strategy.pdf

Eneng Darol Afiah (2013). Female circumcision: Practice, policies by religious organisations in the state of Indonesia. In *High-level Meeting on the Worldwide Ban on FGM*, Rome 3–5 February 2013.

European Parliament (2009). Resolution of 24 March 2009 on combating female genital mutilation in the

EU (2008/2071(INI)). Available at www.europarl.europa.eu/sides/getDoc.do?pubRef=-//EP//TEXT+TA+P6-TA-2009-0161+0+DOC+XML//V0//EN

Ford, N. (2005). Communication for abandonment of female genital cutting: An approach based on human rights principles. *International Journal of Children's Rights*, 13, 183–199.

Freeman, M. (2007). *A Commentary on the United Nations Convention on the Rights of the Child, Article 3: The Best Interests of the Child*, Leiden: Martinus Nijhoff: 2.

Hernlund, Y. (2000). Cutting without ritual and ritual without cutting: Female "circumcision" and the re-ritualisation of initiation in the Gambia. In B. Shell-Duncan and Y. Hernlund (eds), *Female "Circumcision" in Africa: Culture, Controversy, and Change*. Boulder, CO: Lynne Rienner Publishers.

International Council on Violence against Children (2012). *Violating Children's Rights: harmful practices based on tradition, culture, religion or superstition. A report from the International Council on Violence against Children*. United States of America: International NGO Council on Violence against Children.

Jackson, E. F., Akweongo, P., Sakeah, E., Hodgson, A., Asuru, R. and Phillips, J. F. (2003). Inconsistent reporting of female genital cutting status in northern Ghana: Explanatory factors and analytical consequences. *Studies in Family Planning*, 34, 200–210.

Johansen, R. E. B., Diop, N. J., Laverack, G. and Leye, E. (2013). What works and what does not: A discussion of popular approaches for the abandonment of female genital mutilation. *Obstetrics and Gynaecology International*.

Leye, E., Bauwens, S. and Bjälkander, O. (2005). *Behaviour Change towards Female Genital Mutilation: Lessons Learned from Africa and Europe*. ICRH.

Leye, E. and Sabbe, A. (2009). *Responding to Female Genital Mutilation in Europe: Striking the Right Balance between Prosecution and Prevention*. Gent: International Centre for Reproductive Health.

Leye, E. (2008). *Female genital mutilation in some countries of the European Union*. PhD in Comparative Sciences of Culture International Centre for Reproductive Health, Gent.

Leye, E, Deblonde, J., Garcia-Anon, J., Johnsdotter, S., Kwateng-Kluvitse, A., Weil-Curiel, L., et al. (2007). An analysis of the implementation of laws with regard to female genital mutilation in Europe. *Law, Culture and Social Change*, 47, 1–31.

Leye, E. and Mergaert, L. (2012). *Study to map the current situation and trends of female genital mutilation*. Final Report. Unpublished Work.

Leye, E., O'Brien Green, S., Arnaut, C. and Mergaert, L. (2013). Towards a better estimation of prevalence of female genital mutilation in the European Union: An overview of existing evidence in all EU Member States. *Genus*. Published in GENUS, LXX (No 1), 99–121.

Leye, E., Powell, R. A., Nienhuis, G., Claeys, P. and Temmerman, M. (2006). Health care in Europe for women with genital mutilation. *Health Care for Women International*, 27, 362–378.

Moynihan, S. and Webb, E. (2009). An ethical approach to resolving value conflicts in child protection. *Archives of Disease in Childhood*, 95, 55–58.

Obermeyer, C. M. (1999). Female genital surgeries: The known, the unknown, and the unknowable. *Medical Anthropology Quarterly*, 13, 79–106.

Obermeyer, C. M. (2003). The health consequences of female circumcision: Science, advocacy, and standards of evidence. *Medical Anthropology Quarterly*, 17, 394–412.

Raman, S. and Hodes, D. (2012). Cultural issues in child maltreatment. *Journal of Paediatrics and Child Health*, 48(1), 30–37.

Rahman, A., and Toubia, N. (2000). *Female Genital Mutilation: A Practical Guide to Laws and Policies Worldwide*. London: Zed Books.

Royal College of Midwives, Royal College of Nursing, Royal College of Obstetricians and Gynaecologists, Equality Now, and UNITE (2013). *Tackling FGM in the UK: Intercollegiate Recommendations for Identifying, Recording, and Reporting*. Available at www.rcph.ac.uk/news/tackling-female-genital-mutilation-uk

Schabas, W. and Sax, H. (2006). Article 37, Prohibition of Torture, Death Penalty, Life Imprisonment and Deprivation of Liberty. In A. Alen, J. Vande Lanotte, E. Verhellen, F. Ang, E. Beghmans and M. Verheyde (eds), *A Commentary on the United Nations Convention on the Rights of the Child*. Leiden: Martinus Nijhoff.

Shell-Duncan, B., Wander, K., Hernlund, Y. and Moreaub, A. (2011). Dynamics of change in the practice of female genital cutting in Senegambia: Testing predictions of social convention theory. *Social Science and Medicine*, 73(8), 1275–1283.

Shell-Duncan, B., Hernlund, Y., Wander, K. and Moreau, A. (2013). Legislating change? Responses to criminalising female genital cutting in Senegal. *Law and Society Review*, 47(4), 803–835.

Song, S. (2010). Pediatricians group withdraws statement on female circumcision. *TIME, Health and Family*. Available at http://healthland.time.com/2010/05/27/pediatricians-group-withdraws-statement-on-female-circumcision/

UNICEF (2005). *Changing a Harmful Social Convention: Female Genital Mutilation/Cutting*. Florence, UNICEF.

UNICEF (2010). *Legislative Reform to Support the Abandonment of Female Genital Mutilation/Cutting*. New York: UNICEF.

UNICEF (2013a). *Female genital mutilation/cutting. A statistical overview and exploration of the dynamics of change. Executive summary*. New York: UNICEF.

UNICEF (2013b). *Female genital mutilation/cutting: a statistical overview and exploration of the dynamics of change*. New York: UNICEF.

Vandenhole, W. (2012). Localising the human rights of children. In M. Liebel (ed.), *Children's Rights from Below*. London: Palgrave, 88–89.

Vienna Declaration on Human Rights (1993). Vienna, 14–25 June 1993, UN Doc. A/CONF.157/24 (Part I) at 20 (1993), point 38.

Vloeberghs, E., van der Kwaak, A., Knipscheer, J. and van den Muijsenbergh, M. (2012). Coping and chronic psychosocial consequences of female genital mutilation in The Netherlands. *Ethnicity and Health*, 17, 677–695.

Weil-Curiel, L. (2003). Weibliche Genitalverstümmelung aus Sicht einer französicher Rechtsanwältung und Aktivistin [Female genital mutilation from the perspective of a French lawyer and activist]. In Terre des Femmes (ed.), *Schnitt in die Seele. Weibliche Genital verstümmelung – eine fundamentele Menschenrechtenverletzung* [Cut in the soul: Female genital mutilation – a fundamental human rights violation]. Frankfurt am Main: Mabuse-Verlag.

Weil-Curiel, L. (2004a). In Leye, E., De Bruyn, M. and Meuwese, S. (eds). *Proceedings of the expert meeting on female genital mutilation*. Ghent-Belgium November 5–7, 1998. International Centre for Reproductive Health, Ghent, ICRH Publications N°2. Lokeren: The Consultory.

Weil-Curiel, L. (2004b). *French Legislation Regarding FGM and the Implementation of the Law in France*. Paris: CAMS.

Wood, A. N. (2001). A cultural rite of passage or a form of torture: Female genital mutilation from an international law perspective. *Hastings Women's Law Journal*, 12, 347–386.

WHO (1997). *Female Genital Mutilation: A Joint WHO/UNICEF/UNFPA Statement*. Geneva: World Health Organisation.

WHO (2008). *Eliminating Female Genital Mutilation. An Interagency Statement. OHCRH, UNAIDS, UNDP, UNECA, UNESCO, UNFPA, UNHCR, UNICEF, UNIFEM, WHO*. Geneva: World Health Organisation.

WHO and UNAIDS (2008). *Male Circumcision: Global Trends and Determinants of Prevalence, Safety and Acceptability*. Geneva: World Health Organisation.

18
Child labour, working children and children's rights

Karl Hanson, Diana Volonakis and Mohammed Al-Rozzi

1. Introduction

Over the last two decades, and increasingly since the adoption of ILO Convention No. 182 on the Worst Forms of Child Labour in 1999, the question of how the children's rights framework relates to child labour has been the subject of intense debates, not only between child rights advocates and policy makers, but also amongst academics (for an excellent overview of the debate, see Bourdillon, 2006). The dominant and most widespread view is that child labour denies children the right to enjoy their childhood and chances for a better future, and in particular deprives them of their schooling and therefore needs to be abolished. This position is aptly illustrated by the slogan 'School is the best place to work', with which a large international coalition of development organizations, trade unions, education unions and local NGOs campaign to eliminate all forms of child labour and to ensure quality full-time formal education for all children, at least until the age of 15.[1] Such a straightforward position that all child labour needs to be abolished and all children sent to school has been questioned, in particular by working children's organizations that argue that age-appropriate work in dignified conditions can play a positive role in childhood. For instance, the Concerned for Working Children, an Indian NGO which is a member of the international movement of working children's organizations, claims that it is their rights as workers that need to be recognized and that efforts should be undertaken to improve children's working conditions, rather than abolishing their work.[2]

These contrasting viewpoints illustrate that the relation between children's rights and child labour is more complicated than the commonplace understanding that all forms of child labour or work are, in all circumstances and in all contexts, an obvious violation of children's rights, and

---

[1] The campaign to stop child labour is coordinated by Hivos, a Dutch NGO for development cooperation. Available at the campaign's website www.stopchildlabour.org/ (accessed 1 April 2014).
[2] Available at the organization's website www.concernedforworkingchildren.org/; for their stance on child labour, go to: www.concernedforworkingchildren.org/empowering-children/child-work-and-child-labour/our-stance-on-child-labour/ (accessed 1 April 2014).

that it can only be addressed by abolishing child labour and sending children to school. In order to better understand the issues at stake, the present chapter aims to review some of the central themes in the current discussions on child labour. We will thereby critically engage with dominant perspectives on child labour upheld by the majority of actors in the broad international children's rights field. In the present discussion, we use the terms 'child labour' and 'child work' interchangeably. The debate surrounding the perceived distinction between the two terms will be discussed in detail in a subsequent paragraph. In line with the basic tenets of this Handbook, we approach the relation between child labour, working children and children's rights from a critical, emancipatory perspective which is grounded within current interdisciplinary approaches to children's rights and human rights studies. (On children's rights studies, see for instance: Hanson and Nieuwenhuys, 2013; Liebel, 2012; Reynaert et al., 2009. On human rights studies, see for example: Goodale, 2009; Merry, 2006; Stammers, 2009.) The chapter hence adopts an interdisciplinary perspective for which it will rely on combined insights from history, anthropology, childhood sociology, international labour law, human rights law and children's rights studies.

We will begin by pointing out some of the themes that were addressed during the drafting of Article 32 of the CRC and that give a first general idea of the topics to be considered in relation to the right of the child to be protected against economic exploitation. The next section looks at the way in which child labour has been addressed in history, thereby emphasizing how the Industrial Revolution was a critical period during which child work dramatically increased. Our perspective will then shift to an anthropological one, whereby we will also reconsider the debates raging upon the definition of child work as being often opposed to child labour. In the same section we will attend to efforts to provide relevant statistics of the phenomenon. Given the wealth of policy issues and viewpoints on the subject of child labour, the section thereafter aims to reflect on the differences in attitudes towards child work, ranging from the usual calls to boycotts and abolition of child work, to reactions to the phenomenon of recognizing working children's right to work in dignity. We will also present and discuss international legislation on child labour, placing special emphasis on the right of children to work in dignity, a claim brought forward by organizations of working children that originated about 20 years ago in Africa, Asia and Latin-America. In our conclusion, we will summarize the main themes that come out of our analysis and point at the importance of the child labour debate for children's rights studies more generally.

2. Drafting Article 32 of the UN Convention on the Rights of the Child

Some of the complexities involved when addressing child labour from a children's rights perspective came up during the drafting of Article 32 of the Convention on the Rights of the Child (hereafter: CRC), which is the Convention's provision specially dedicated to the right of the child to be protected from economic exploitation, including child labour. The article calls upon member States to take legislative, administrative, social and educational measures to protect children from economic exploitation and, in particular, to set a minimum age or minimum ages for admission to employment, provide regulations on the hours and conditions of employment and foresee appropriate sanctions. The drafting process of the CRC spanned over a decade and also involved discussion as to the precise wording of Article 32.

Despite general agreement of the need to ban children's economic exploitation, the drafters did not intend to totally prohibit all forms of child work. For example, in a comment on the first Polish draft of 1978, the delegation from New Zealand voiced the opinion that 'the introduction of legislation prohibiting young persons (under 15) from engaging in occasional or part-time employment … would have neither parental nor public support in New Zealand'

(Office of the United Nations High Commissioner for Human Rights, 2007: 694). The delegation was referring to forms of child work socially accepted in New Zealand, such as vending confectionery and newspapers. In a similar vein, it was argued during the Working Group discussions in 1986 that the establishment of a minimum age to employment should not prevent the participation of children in activities undertaken under the direction of their parents and that do not interfere with their education, such as hunting, fishing or occasional agricultural activities by non-family members, nor prohibit family subsistence activities (Office of the United Nations High Commissioner for Human Rights, 2007: 704). On proposal by the US delegation, the drafters agreed that the establishment of minimum ages only applies to admission to (formal) employment, but not to work in or for the family. Instead of requiring to provide for minimum ages for admission to employment or work, it was therefore agreed to delete the words 'or work' at the end of the phrase (Office of the United Nations High Commissioner for Human Rights, 2007: 704). The Food and Agriculture Organization of the United Nations (FAO), in a comment on the draft text issued in 1988, equally stressed its own implicit recognition of children's productive activity on small family farm enterprises, which are important production units in the world's food supply (Office of the United Nations High Commissioner for Human Rights, 2007: 706).

In its proposals submitted to the Working Group in 1981 and in 1984, even the International Labour Organization (ILO) raised concern about the unduly rigid character of a proposed provision to prohibit all child employment before the age of 15 years (Office of the United Nations High Commissioner for Human Rights, 2007: 698; 700). The ILO found that the CRC provision on protection against economic exploitation should be consistent with the existing international standards, in particular with the Minimum Age Convention, 1973 (No. 138). Furthermore, the ILO argued that a standard setting the minimum age at 15 years for admission to employment would insufficiently distinguish between different types of work, and that elements of flexibility needed to be introduced when regulating admission to employment, for instance by establishing different age levels for admission to hazardous work and to light work. Also, an overly strict provision would exclude work in connection with education or training, disconnect minimum age to school-leaving age and would preclude a progressive raising of the minimum age, nor take into account the particular situation of less developed countries who are allowed, under Article 2, paragraphs 4 and 5 of the Minimum Age Convention, 1973 (No. 138) to initially specify a minimum age of 14 years.

During the drafting process, an NGO also suggested including provisions that deal with legally permitted work that concern the freedom of choice of employment, the right to fair remuneration and decent working conditions (Office of the United Nations High Commissioner for Human Rights, 2007: 701). This suggestion was written into the final adopted text during the 1986 Working Group's discussion via a proposal drafted by the delegations of Finland, Canada and the United States. States now demanded not only to provide (a) minimum age(s) for admission to employment and sanctions to ensure the article's effective enforcement, but also to provide for appropriate regulations concerning the hours and conditions of employment of children (Office of the United Nations High Commissioner for Human Rights, 2007: 704). The obtained consensus significantly left out any explicit reference to working children's right to freedom of choice of employment, a claim that was later to be taken up by working children's movements such as the Concerned for Working Children.

Many of the issues raised during the drafting of Article 32 CRC are not new and have been informed by insights from the study of the history of child labour (Cunningham and Viazzo, 1996a), to which we turn now as a valuable source for a contemporary understanding of the phenomenon and the general policy and practice around it.

3. Child labour in history

Throughout history, child labour has been a much politicized phenomenon with numerous contentious debates often leading to more disagreement and less consensus on the different aspects of child work. In addition, the history of child labour has been researched only sparsely and therefore remains relatively poorly understood. Humphries explains this by referring to the lack of good sources of information on the era preceding, and the earlier stages of, the Industrial Revolution (Humphries, 2010: 6). Despite the increasing attention being given to the *study of children in work*, which has exploded in recent years (Myers, 1999), little account has been given to the exclusive *historical study of child labour*.[3] As child work has developed in a diverse manner across continents, we cannot talk about a single history of child labour, but about parallel histories that have certain shared themes. Our objective is hence not to cover the precise emergence and development of child labour across spatial and temporal settings, but to highlight some of the common historical trends.

There is evidence to start the contemporary history of child labour even before the explosion of industrialization and/or industrial capitalism where it is usually located (De Herdt, 1996; White, 1994). Despite disagreement on the prevalence and conditions of workers, most historians agree that children were contributing significantly to the family workforce in the era preceding the Industrial Revolution (Cunningham and Viazzo, 1996a, 14). This period is also called the 'proto-industrialization' phase (Mendels, 1972), which took place across Europe from the late seventeenth to the early nineteenth century and saw the spread of rural domestic manufacturing, leading an increasing number of families, including children, to work for emerging national and international markets (Hudson, 1990). In this period before and even immediately after the nineteenth-century Industrial Revolution, child work was welcomed and even promoted at the social/public and official levels for many reasons. Child work was seen as vital to prevent *idleness*, with its negative connotation and future implications (Abbott, 1908; Cunningham, 1996: 41) as well as an essential apprenticeship needed for the subsequent stages of life. In addition, the economic return of child work was contributing to the economy of the household and thus relieving widespread poverty. Historical evidence suggests that across America as well as in the British colonies the work of children was even encouraged and sometimes reinforced by the power of law (Abbott, 1908).

Notwithstanding changes in the push of children as labour force in family-based manufactures as early as the seventeenth century, it is in particular in the years of the industrialization, an epoch which led to unprecedented changes in economic activity, social life, and family structures across Europe, that child labour saw an apparent high rise (Humphries, 2010). This is evidenced by a wealth of literature on the history of child labour during that period, to the extent that it is even common to trace back the emergence of child labour, as a phenomenon, by tracing the development of industrial capitalism (Cunningham and Viazzo, 1996b, White, 1994). Humphries argues that children were considered important to the industrial revolution in England (Humphries, 2010: 366). Also for Abbott (1908), who investigated child labour in America more than a century ago, child labour was perceived as a necessary and important way to develop the colonies. The author also refers to the changes, as part of industrialization, which contributed to the increase of working children. He outlines that:

---

3   Few exceptions include Cunningham and Viazzo, 1996b; Humphries, 2010. But note that several studies have highlighted the history of child labour in their specific context, for example: Nieuwenhuys, 1994 (India); White, 1994 (The Netherlands); Abebe and Kjørholt, 2009 (Ethiopia); Grier, 1994 (Zimbabwe); Kirby, 2003 and Bolin-Hort, 1989 (Great-Britain).

With the introduction of machinery and the opening up of new and great possibilities of manufacturing industries, the employment of children became more and more profitable and we find that their labor is always counted on as a valuable resource with which to meet the deficiency and high cost of male labor in this country.

(Abbott, 1908: 23)

Children became more profitable as they received lower wages and were able to run the machines that do not need 'able-bodied men' (Abbott, 1908: 24). At the same time, the transition from household industry to factory, and from human to steam power contributed to reduce the hazards children were exposed to in the work setting (White, 1994: 855). These could be seen as the factors that made 'child labour ... endemic in the early industrial economy, entrenched in both traditional and modern sectors and widespread geographically' (Humphries, 2010: 366). However, the widespread practice of child labour would not have been possible without social approval and acceptance. Nardinelli argues that workers and their families had the choice to work or not to work, and yet chose employment, thus 'it must have been that child labour was preferred' (Nardinelli, 1990, cited in Humphries, 2010: 1). In fact, industrial life was not seen as 'an assault' on childhood, but as an opportunity for their present and future (Cunningham, 1996: 42). Not to forget, children also continued to work due to increased demand for labour in the emerging industrial nations. Also, children's relatively high wages contributed to the family economy (De Herdt, 1996) at times when poverty was a reality for the majority of the population for whom child work was a mechanism to overcome the widespread poverty. As White puts it: 'Children's employment was considered natural (for the poor) and even beneficial; local authorities and charities were themselves active in setting the children of the poor to full-time work in semi-philanthropic institutions' (White, 1994: 855). In contrast with contemporary dominant international policies on child labour, governments and organizations devoted their efforts to ensure that children had work, which continued until the late nineteenth century (Cunningham, 1996: 41).

Since the end of the nineteenth century and throughout the twentieth century, child labour in the industrialized Western countries has drastically declined, but there is disparity in views on the main reasons behind this decline. In general, the decline in child labour, especially in the North, can be attributed to the interaction between a variety of factors. These include change in the perception and image of childhood in Europe and North America (Cunningham, 1991, cited in Cunningham and Viazzo, 1996a: 14), change in the composition of the family (White, 1994; Cunningham and Viazzo, 1996b; Humphries, 2010) and the introduction of stringent labour standards and particular child labour legislation. Many historians argue that the introduction of schooling and compulsory education was, in fact, the most effective way to *end* child labour (Cunningham, 1996: 43; Mizen et al., 1999; Leonard, 2003) as it enabled raising the age of entry into employment as a norm (Cunningham, 1996). The number of children in work declined significantly when schooling was enforced, for instance in the case of Great Britain, where following the introduction of compulsory schooling in 1880 the number of working children (10–14 years) declined by about half between 1851 and 1911 (Cunningham, 1996: 43). However, the most compelling reasons advanced for understanding the drastic decline of child labour in the North at the turn of the nineteenth and twentieth centuries relate to changes in the organization of the economy and the economic production. As Qvortrup (2001) explains, child work is system-immanent: children's role as economic agents is embedded in the prevalent economy and modes of production. In the course of Western industrialization, children's useful activities have changed from manual work in the household economy into symbolic work at school where children learn the required skills to be effective in more sophisticated national economies. According to this account, children's work therefore did not decline, but was *transformed* from economically useful and needed work in the factories in the early period of industrialization into equally economically useful and needed work at school. Children's school work is indeed intrinsically tied to the prevalent economic system; in a convoluted economic system, highly skilled workers who master complex skills are indispensable to maintain and further develop the economy. Fundamental changes in the economic mode of production, rather than the adoption of legislation on compulsory education and/or the imposition of minimum ages for admission to employment have impacted the number of children needed as actual or future members of the workforce.

Some general insights, rather than historical lessons can be gained from our brief review of the history of child labour. First, as aptly summarized by Morrow (2010: 436), 'we know that child labour was used widely in a range of industries in the heyday of industrialization in virtually all developed countries, though it was used in differing ways, at differing intensities, and drew a range of responses from governments, educationists, industrialists, Trades Unions, and philanthropists'. A number of political measures that were inspired by the social reform movement of the late nineteenth century and beginning of the twentieth century (Abbott, 1908: 37; Dimock, 1993), have been common in policies aimed at the eradication of child labour. These include setting a minimum age for child employment, the introduction of legislation upholding part-time work and the enforcement of compulsory education. In addition to these measures, a number of social changes also contributed to the decline of child labour in the Global North, such as the decrease in family size and the spread of the nuclear family, the rise of adult wages and the decline of general poverty levels (White, 1994; Cunningham, 1996; Humphries, 2010). Second, the forms of child labour have evolved throughout history, from the exclusive dominance of specific sectors that were believed to be important to the industrial revolution, to other forms that emerged and dominated the economy in later stages. The transformation of child work in Europe went through a series of country-specific but also similar stages. One of the commonalities is that child work increased and became more visible due to the spread of the Industrial Revolution across Europe, especially during the proto-industrialization period characterized by labour intensive work in family-based manufactories. Child labour played an active role in 'developing divisions of labour and organizational readjustments that sustained traditional units of production and maintained their competitiveness' (Humphries, 2010: 366), comparable to the significant role played by child labour in the present-day economies of the countries of the Global South. Later on, as industrialization in Europe and North-America intensified, manual child labour became less of an imperative for the economy that needed skilled workers instead, leading to a drastic decline of child labourers along with the massive schooling of children at the beginning of the twentieth century. Third, after the 'end' of child labour in the industrialized North during the first decades of the twentieth century, the issue of child labour seemingly went into a deep hibernating state until the 1980s, after the end of colonialization.

The revival of the child labour theme on the international agenda at the end of the 1980s was greatly stimulated by the International Year of the Child in 1979 (Fyfe, 2007: 21; Cantwell, 2004: 397), an event which also triggered the drafting of the CRC. It was, however, only since the beginning of the 1990s, which witnessed the launch of the ILO Programme for the Elimination of Child Labour (IPEC), that a 'worldwide movement against child labour' effectively took off (Fyfe, 2007: 21) and continues its existence to this day. The global character of this campaign does not however mean that there is one single global perspective on child labour, in fact quite the contrary, as we will see in the next section.

4. The multifaceted realities of child labour

During the drafting process of Article 32 of the CRC, as discussed above, the FAO had stressed the importance of children's work on small family farm enterprises for food production. A recent historical study by Mayall and Morrow (2011) on child work in England during the Second World War makes an interesting parallel concerning the importance of children's work for guaranteeing food supply. In their study, the authors document how a vast number of British school children were involved in agricultural production throughout the war period, and that it was even officially acknowledged that without their help, specific crops such as potatoes would not have been planted or harvested. Both situations not only illustrate the importance of children's work for subsistence, but also that, depending on the circumstances, children's work has even been officially recognized and valued. Detailed ethnographic research on the circumstances and conditions of child work in the context of development by Nieuwenhuys (1994) and Reynolds (1991) stand out as examples of how anthropologists and childhood studies researchers have opened up new ways for engaging with the subject of 'child labour'. We can broadly situate this strand of research within the interdisciplinary field of childhood studies (see Qvortrup *et al.*, 2009), which has opened up perspectives for thinking of different childhoods that are distinguished across time and place. Leaving aside the policy concerns of international organizations, these studies have paved the way for an approach to the study of children's work from a perspective that is respectful of children and their families' own viewpoints on the meanings of their work, on children's social and economic contributions, on the value of work for survival and livelihood, and on children's personal achievements as a result of work. Child work came under scrutiny, especially in the Global South, including in Asia (see for instance Nieuwenhuys, 1994, 2007), in Africa (see for instance Omokhodion *et al.*, 2006; Abebe and Kjørholt, 2009), and in Latin America (see for instance Grugel and Ferreira, 2012). The results of these studies demonstrate that child work is a reflection of social norms, kinship support, intergenerational debt, and/or life training and vocational apprenticeship (Liebel, 2004; Nieuwenhuys, 2005; Alber, 2011). Furthermore, it is not only culturally and socially embedded, but also has a significant value for children's education and health, family survival, and household maintenance (Levine, 2011). Child work can even be perceived as a means of asserting the self, negotiating structural subordination in society, and practising high levels of autonomy and agency (McKechnie *et al.*, 2000; Leonard, 2003).

Notwithstanding the expansion of contextualized and nuanced understandings of historical and contemporary forms of children's work, the term 'child labour' primarily continues to be politically and socially linked to the images of tiny children in factories. Be it during the Global North's past industrialization period or in the present-day Global South's survival economies, working children are predominantly considered as being subject to brutal treatment and exploitation, whose childhood is stolen by heartless employers. These contrasting viewpoints on child labour lead us to consider debates over definitions. The definition of child labour is indeed highly important, as it is a determinant issue for many aspects in policy and practice. This is particularly because the definition is of a political nature, 'posing an emotionally charged choice of social values and objectives' (Myers, 1999: 22). It is not easy to reach a universal agreement on the definition of child labour (White, 1999; Giri, 2007; Edmonds, 2009) not only because both of the terms composing child labour (i.e. child and labour) are quite controversial and debated themselves, but also because of the diverse forms the phenomenon takes on. Child labour varies widely in the conditions of work, in forms of returns, in settings, in different spatial and temporal settings, etc. (James *et al.*, 1998; Lavalette, 1999b; Edmonds 2009). Or as stated by Myers, '[t]he debate over what is meant by "child labour" represents fundamental disagreement over what the social problem is that should be eliminated, and the stakes are high for key interest groups divided between the positions' (Myers, 1999: 22).

Nieuwenhuys points out that the term child labour 'came to be closely related to the notion of exploitation and fuelled a growing public sensitivity to the wrongs it implied in respect to the children' (2009: 289). This negative notion of child labour as a welfare-reducing activity is clearly indicated in diverse international conventions (Edmonds, 2009). This is well illustrated by the ILO's definition of child labour as:

> work that deprives children of their childhood, their potential and their dignity, and that is harmful to physical and mental development. It refers to work that is mentally, physically, socially or morally dangerous and harmful to children; and interferes with their schooling.
>
> *(ILO, 2004: 16)*

In policy documents and for programming efforts, the term 'child labour', which is usually used to indicate more exploitative, abusive and hazardous kinds of work, is often contrasted with the term 'child work', used to indicate the tolerated categories of work performed in the social domestic context (Nieuwenhuys, 1994; Giri, 2007; Edmonds, 2009). However, Woodhead (1999) points out two problems inherent to this clear-cut distinction: first, the parameters of child welfare are provisional, and second, hazard – which is the basis of this distinction – cannot be determined by only one indicator, as the level of hazard is determined by context, cultural meaning and other complex sets of indicators. In the same vein, Lavalette sees the distinction as unhelpful and 'theoretically unsustainable' (Lavalette, 1999a: 17). He argues that the work/labour distinction reflects 'political value judgments about how we treat our children' but is not based on solid research (Lavalette, 1999a: 38). Bourdillon goes even further and suggests, drawing on Mary Douglas' study on taboo and O'Connell Davidson's writing on the sexual exploitation of children, that:

> We structure the world into binary categories, such as children and adults, with binary sets of characteristics and appropriate behaviour. These categories are supported by mythologies and defended vigorously against any behaviour or discourse that may threaten them by crossing cognitive boundaries.
>
> *(Bourdillon, 2006: 1203)*

Based on this, a term like 'child labour' becomes a moral category of activities, which should be abolished regardless of the impact on children's lives (Bourdillon, 2006: 1203). Researchers, who are aware of the contention, suggested avoiding the use of the terms 'labour' and 'work' (Giri, 2009: 33) as it is difficult to sustain the distinction between them in the face of changing representations of childhood and research evidence that utilizes the views of children who work (James and James, 2008). The term 'working children' is increasingly being used, instead, as it encompasses both (bad) labour and (good) work activities. Thus, using this last term, researchers can avoid the moral judgment that is clearly drawn from this distinction (Boyden *et al.*, 1998; Giri, 2009; Nieuwenhuys, 2009). For similar reasons, the term 'child employment' appears in recent publications on work of children in the UK, to contrast 'the perceived pejorative sense of the expression 'child labour' (Lavalette, 1999b; Heesterman, 2005: 79). This alternative may help to understand the work of children, away from its historical usage, which tends to be negative (Bourdillon, 2006), even though the ILO uses the term to indicate only the *legal* work undertaken by children based on its Conventions (ILO, 2004). Finally, Myers argues that to use the term 'child labour' is inevitable. In his claim, 'the term is a permanent fixture in official usage, and we have to deal with it even if we do not want to' (Myers, 1999: 22).

Another contentious issue along with debates over definitions has to do with the precise number of children in work. A main reason for this is that the vast majority of children work in informal sectors, which are hard to access and where figures are therefore difficult to obtain. The argument developed by Qvortrup (2001) that we explained above on the need to consider children's activities as useful in connection to the dominant organization of the economy equally illustrates the intimate relation between problems over definitions and problems over statistics. If all children work, but not under the same conditions that depend on the dominant mode of economic production, we would only have to count the number of children to also know the number of 'working children'.

Notwithstanding these conceptual problems related to counting working children, the ILO has since the 1980s been producing detailed estimates and trends of child labourers around the world (see for the most recent statistical data: ILO, 2013). For the ILO, whether or not particular forms of 'work' can be called 'child labour' depends on the child's age, the type and hours of work performed, and the conditions under which it is performed (ILO, 2004). The ILO defines child labour as: all activities undertaken for profit under the age of 12 years (sometimes 13 years), all non-hazardous activities undertaken before the age of 15 years (sometimes 14 or 16 years depending on national legislation and the age of compulsory school education) except light work, and all hazardous activities undertaken before the age of 18 years old. Based on these operational definitions, the ILO estimates that around 168 million children worldwide are engaged in child labour, composing 11 percent of the total child population worldwide (ILO, 2013: vii). The largest number of child labourers is found in Asia and the Pacific region. However, the proportion of child labourers is the highest in Sub-Saharan Africa (21 percent). It is estimated that the 168 million labouring children are distributed regionally as follows; 77.7 million in Asia and the Pacific, 59.0 million in Sub-Saharan Africa, 12.5 million in Latin America and the Caribbean, and 9.2 million in the Middle East and North Africa (ILO, 2013: 17). The majority of children in employment are in the 5–11 age cohort and compose around 44 percent of the overall estimation of child labourers, while child labourers aged 12–14 years compose 28 percent of the overall estimated child labourers, with another 28 percent of labourers in the 15–17 age cohort (ILO, 2013: 18). There is almost no difference based on sex in the involvement of 5–11-year-old children in child labour. Boys and girls each make up roughly half of the overall child labour population for this age group. A gender gap begins to appear in the 12–14 age range, and continues to rise dramatically in the 15–17 age range, where boys account for 81 percent of all child labourers and outnumber girls by 29.8 million (ILO, 2013: 18). Regarding the distribution of child labour in economic sectors, almost 60 percent of children are officially recorded as involved in work in the agriculture sector (ILO, 2013: 7–8). The share of the other sectors is 7 percent in the industrial sector (including construction, mining and manufacturing) and 32 percent in the service sector (including hotels and restaurant, wholesale and retail trade (commerce); maintenance and repair of motor vehicles; transport; other community, social and personal service activities; and domestic work). These estimates per sector show that only a minority of child labour is to be found in the export-oriented manufacturing industry, a sector that has paradoxically received the bulk of the attention by international campaigns against child labour, and which has also been the main sector targeted by consumer boycotts. Absent from the ILO's official child labour statistics are the industrial countries in the Global North, where it is wrongly assumed, because these countries have achieved universality in levels of school enrolment, that child labour is a 'thing of the past'.

Growing research evidence suggests that work is, on the contrary, the experience of the majority (Lavalette, 1999b; Mizen *et al.*, 1999; Leonard, 2003; Heesterman, 2005; McKechnie *et al.*, 2009). Many studies indeed reaffirm that it is common for children to work below the minimum age determined by ILO Conventions and national laws.

Discussions within academia and among the general public over what kind of activities count as child labour, over numbers of working children or over the appropriate age limitations for admission to employment demonstrate that there is no general agreement upon the nature and extent of the phenomenon. Given the diversity of the assessment of the phenomenon, it is equally of little surprise that the attitudes and strategies on the means to address child labour, a topic to which we now turn, are highly controversial.

5. Attitudes towards child labour

The general attitude adopted in reaction to child labour is more often than not one of rejection and compassion, as was the case for the majority of interventions by the delegates during the drafting of Article 32 CRC. At best, child labour is a successfully defeated phenomenon of the past, at worst an indignant story of children trapped in sweatshops waiting to be rescued by compassionate welldoers. Given these views, it is of little surprise that most policies and programmes aim at abolishing child labour as a matter of urgency. However, other attitudes towards child labour do in fact exist, which are different from the staunch anti-child labour attitude. From a neo-liberal perspective, a high incidence of child labour is directly related to the poor level of economic development. Child labour can only be addressed indirectly, most obviously by investing in the development of the economy. Yet another perspective calls to regulate the conditions under which children have to work – a view that has been most outspokenly defended by organizations of working children. These movements, which include the aforementioned organization The Concerned for Working Children in India, have emerged during the 1990s in Latin-America, Africa and Asia, and have voiced concern about the protectionist, paternalistic character of the anti-child-labour positions, claiming in contrast that their right to work in dignity should be recognized (Liebel, 2013). Based on a discussion by White (1994) of the shifting ways of thinking about the problem of youth and child labour, we suggest that a distinction between four different stances in reaction to child labour can help clarify understanding of the debates. We will further discuss these four positions: 'laissez-faire', 'abolitionism', 'regulation' and 'empowerment'.[4]

The *laissez-faire* attitude stems from the idea that child labour is an evolving and auto-regulating phenomenon, which increases and subsides depending on the economic climate of a given region. In favourable economic conditions, adults' work allows to provide for the entire family, whereas in times of hardship, children work in order to supplement adult wages. The laissez-faire approach would therefore appear to entirely attribute the rise and fall of child labour to adjustments in family strategy, which seems to reflect the thought of Bolin-Hort, who asserted that 'children worked in factories because their families were poor; as family income increased, child labour decreased' (Bolin-Hort, 1989). This approach thus advocates for a 'policy of waiting, on the assumption that economic changes will enable individual families to adopt strategies that place more emphasis on investment in children than on the use of their labour' (Cunningham and Viazzo, 1996a: 12).

---

4   White makes a distinction between three positions on child labour, which he labels 'abolitionism', 'protectionism', and the 'liberationist' or 'empowerment' perspective (White, 1994: 853).

The most common approach is the *abolitionist* perspective as defended by ILO's tripartite constituents (governments, employers' and workers' organizations), large development organizations and NGOs including UNICEF and Save the Children (White, 1999). This position is also upheld by the majority of the greater public, which is supportive of public policy and legislation tht drastically limits the working opportunities of children and young people, and sometimes resorts to the boycott of goods manufactured by children. From an abolitionist perspective, to allow working children to pursue their activities is equated with abandoning them to a life of lowly exploitation. Work is entirely incompatible with childhood, and it is undeniably the role of adults to extricate children from their toils, offering them brighter future prospects, such as those attained through education or vocational training.

The *regulation* approach advocates for the regulation of child labour, as for instance expressed in paragraph 2, (b) of Article 32 CRC that requires States to 'provide for appropriate regulation and hours and conditions of employment'. The position to regulate child labour first concerns children who are above the minimum age for admission to employment, for instance young persons between 15 and 18 years that are engaged in full-time labour activities that do not amount to hazardous labour. Second, the adoption of measures aimed at protecting working children and improving their working conditions has also been defended as a transitional measure, pending the total abolition of all child work. Such a view was for instance adopted during the early years of the ILO's International Programme on the Elimination of Child Labour (IPEC), leaving space for the recognition of the labour rights of working children of an even younger age than the age limits imposed by the international labour standards (Hanson and Vandaele, 2013). Calling to regulate children's work by granting children the right to work 'in dignity' can also be seen as an aim in itself, which would seek to reduce the exploitative character of child labour, thus making the prohibition of child labour superfluous (Hanson and Vandaele, 2013).

The *empowerment* perspective views children as active subjects or agents of change and focuses on promoting working children's participation via their organizations. In this way working children claim the right to participate in discussions on child labour policies and programmes. These organizations, which can be conceptualized as grass-root social movements (Liebel, 2013; Bourdillon *et al.*, 2010), have made the child's right to work in dignity a central claim. Notwithstanding the relative absence of working children's perspectives from the international agenda, their organizations did take part in the debate, at times even very intensively, as illustrated by their participation in high-level meetings leading up to the ILO Convention on the Worst Forms of Child Labour. Their interpretation of rights talk has found its way into academic and advocacy circles (Bourdillon, 2006; Hanson and Vandaele, 2013). From an empowerment perspective, the real problem is not the fact that children work, but rather that working children are powerless against their employers, parents or other individuals who may seek to exploit them for their own selfish benefit. Proponents of this position disagree with efforts to ban child labour, and instead wish to regulate children's work. In order to do this, they explicitly rely on working children's own views and opinions. Child participation is therefore at the centre of empowerment concerns.

Understanding these diverse approaches to child work allows the critical evaluation of legislation and policy, or the absence thereof, which aims to regulate, reduce or abolish child labour. Also, the regulation and empowerment perspectives on child work demonstrate that abolitionism cannot be said to be the sole path towards social justice in relation to child work. The contrast between prohibition, which is the dominant view in child labour law, and the way in which labour law functions in the case of exploitative work performed by adults, is striking. In the case of adult labour, legislation has been elaborated not to prohibit but to regulate their labour. As stated by Hanson:

International labour standards aim at strengthening the position of workers by providing them particular rights, such as the right to decent conditions at work, fair wages, non-discrimination or to freedom of association. These work-related rights all contribute to guaranteeing respect for a person's fundamental right to work. Conversely, child labour legislation is deployed, not to regulate children's work or to foster respect for children's fundamental rights, but to prevent children from working against a wage. Save for some intermittent activities such as child acting or modelling, the prevalent international child labour regime makes children's paid work illegal.

(Hanson, 2014: 10)

However, it is not because the law prohibits child labour that children no longer work. From a legal perspective, children under the established age limits have to work clandestinely, outside a protective regulative framework. In this respect, Bonnet (1998) even argues that the legal ban on child labour has obstructed the adoption of legislation which provides working children with a number of safeguards to guarantee a fair wage and decent working conditions, restricting the possibility for working children to rely on fundamental workers' rights to eliminate the exploitative character of their work. We must therefore critically assess all too simple interventions aimed at 'rescuing' children from work, which may considerably worsen children's position and even risk forcing them into hidden and far more hazardous forms of work.

6. Conclusion

By way of summarizing the many issues raised in discussions on the relation between the children's rights framework and child labour and working children, we wish to draw attention to at least five themes that are central to understanding the debate. First, 'child labour', 'child employment' and 'child work' are general terms used to designate a great number of different situations, whereby distinctions are made according to the types of work, whether the work is undertaken within or outside the family unit, if it is linked with food production and/or tied up with subsistence and to what degree the work is considered culturally specific. Given persistent discussions over definitions of what is to be counted as child work, child labour or child employment, debates over which forms of children's economic activities should be banned or not also remain on the political agenda to this day. Second, as is the case for other child rights related themes such as criminal responsibility, marriage, child soldiering, children's political rights, etc., there is discussion over setting and enforcing minimum ages and what those minimum ages should be in the case of admission to employment or work. The CRC urges States to set minimum ages in accordance with the relevant provisions of other international instruments, in particular the international labour standards developed by the ILO. The reference in the CRC to extant international labour standards illustrates the pre-eminence of the ILO and its International Programme for the Elimination of Child Labour (IPEC) for international legal, policy and programme efforts in the field of child labour. This is our third observation: no discussion over said definitions, statistics or policy reactions to child labour has yet set aside the ILO's dominant position on the theme, and will, depending on the stance taken in the debate, lead to the endorsement or disagreement with the views upheld by the ILO. A fourth theme is the seemingly inseparable link between child labour and education, which are mostly thought of as mutually exclusive fields. Work that is impeding children's schooling should be prohibited, so the reasoning goes, precisely because it would prevent children's education; conversely, the motive why children need a proper education is because this will allow them to smoothly integrate into the labour market and have access to proper jobs. A fifth theme, which, in contemporary debates is particularly emphasized by grassroots working children's organizations, is that notwithstanding the principled ban on child labour, there is also a need to address issues related to wages and working conditions. If some forms of child work and the employment of young people above a certain age limit are internationally admissible, then regulation of remuneration and working conditions is needed. The same applies for working children who are legally under age to be officially employed, but who will, in reality, continue working as long as the economic, social and cultural conditions remain unaltered. In other words, how should we conceptualize and address the rights of the vast number of working children?

The emergence of organized working children's movements, who claim the right to work in dignity, has drawn attention to the value of child work from the children's own perspectives on their realities and their lives. With large numbers of children across the world who are actively and sometimes even enthusiastically engaged in work activities, the question remains: Does the current international policy framework and standards, including Article 32 CRC, truly and adequately protect the rights and interests of the working children they are supposed to defend? The child labour debate, then, also provides an emblematic case for discussions on the central features of the international children's rights framework. These deal with ways to balance a protective framework with the emancipatory promises to take children's perspectives seriously.

Questions for debate and discussion

- How do discussions over definitions of what counts as 'child labour' influence the positions taken in reaction to child labour?
- How can the complexities and differences inherent to working children's everyday lives be taken into account in the international legal and policy frameworks on child labour?
- How should international organizations respond to working children's claims for participation in the child labour debate, and to their claim of the right to work in dignity?
- Are child labour and schooling mutually exclusive, or should schooling be considered as a contemporary form of child work?
- How can research on child work contribute to discussions in childhood and children's rights studies (agency, participation, protection, etc.)?

References

Abbott, E. (1908). A study of the early history of child labor in America. *The American Journal of Sociology*, *14*, 15–37.

Abebe, T. and Kjørholt, A. T. (2009). Social actors and victims of exploitation: Working children in the cash economy of Ethiopia's South. *Childhood*, 16(2), 175–194.

Alber, E. (2011). Child trafficking in West Africa? In A. M., Gonzalez, F. Oloo and L. Derose (eds) *Frontiers of Globalization: Kinship and Family Structures in Africa*. Trenton: Africa World Press.

André, G. and Godin, M. (2014). Child labour, agency and family dynamics: The case of mining in Katanga (DRC). *Childhood*, 21(2), 161–174.

Bolin-Hort, P. (1989). *Work, Family, and the State: Child Labor and the Organization of Production in the British Cotton Industry, 1780–1920*. Lund: Lund University Press.

Bonnet, M. (1998). *Regards sur les Enfants Travailleurs. La Mise au Travail dans le Monde Contemporain: Analyse et Etudes de Cas* [Perspectives on Child Workers. Child Employment in the Contemporary World; Analyses and Case Studies]. Lausanne: Page deux.

Bourdillon, M. (2006). Children and work: A review of current literature and debates. *Development and Change*, 37(6), 1201–1226.

Bourdillon, M., Levison, D., Myers, W. and White, B. (2010). *Rights and Wrongs of Children's Work.* New Brunswick: Rutgers University Press.
Boyden, J., Ling, B. and Myers, W. (1998). *What Works for Working Children.* Stockholm: Rädda Barnen and UNICEF.
Cantwell, N. (2004). The Convention on the Rights of the Child, Vini, vici… et vinci ? In E. Verhellen (ed.), *Understanding Children's Rights* (pp. 395–407). Ghent University: Children's Rights Centre.
Cunningham, H. (1991). *The Children of the Poor: Representations of the Childhood since Seventeenth Century.* Oxford: Blackwell.
Cunningham, H. (1996). Combating child labour: The British experience. In H. Cunningham and P. P. Viazzo (eds) *Child Labour in Historical perspective 1800–1985: Case Studies from Europe, Japan and Colombia.* Florence: UNICEF.
Cunningham, H. and Viazzo, P. P. (1996a). Some issues in the historical study of child labour. In H. Cunningham and P. P. Viazzo (eds) *Child Labour in Historical Perspective 1800–1985: Case Studies from Europe, Japan and Colombia.* Florence: UNICEF.
Cunningham, H. and Viazzo, P. P. (eds) (1996b). *Child Labour in Historical Perspective 1800–1985: Case Studies from Europe, Japan and Colombia.* Florence: UNICEF.
De Herdt, R. (1996). Child labour in Belgium (1800–1914). In H. Cunningham and P. P. Viazzo (eds) *Child Labour in Historical Perspective 1800–1985: Case Studies from Europe, Japan and Colombia* (pp. 23–39). Florence: UNICEF.
Dimock, G. (1993). Children of the mills: Re-reading Lewis Hine's child-labour photographs. *The Oxford Art Journal, 16*(2), 37–54.
Edmonds, E. V. (2009). *Defining Child Labour: A Review of the Definitions of Child Labour in Policy Research.* IPEC Working Paper. Geneva: International Labour Office.
Fyfe, A. (2007). *The Worldwide Movement Against Child Labour: Progress and Future Directions.* Geneva: International Labour Office.
Giri, B. R. (2007). A reflexive autobiography of child work. *Childhood Today, 1*(2), 1–21.
Giri, B. R. (2009). *Bonded Labour in Nepal: Life and Work of Children in Communities.* PhD dissertation, Milton Keynes, UK: The Open University.
Goodale, M. (2009). *Surrendering to Utopia. An Anthropology of Human Rights.* Stanford, CA: Stanford University Press.
Grier, B. (1994). Invisible hands: The political economy of child labour in colonial Zimbabwe, 1890–1930. *Journal of Southern African Studies, 20*(1), 27–52.
Grugel, J. and Ferreira, F. P. M. (2012). Street working children, children's agency and the challenge of children's rights: evidence from Minas Gerais, Brazil. *Journal of International Development, 24*(7), 828–840.
Hanson, K. (2014). Separate childhood laws and the future of society. *Law, Culture and the Humanities, 10*(2) (Published online 13 April 2014, DOI: 10.1177/1743872114529502).
Hanson, K. and Nieuwenhuys, O. (eds) (2013). *Reconceptualizing Children's Rights in International Development: Living Rights, Social Justice, Translations.* Cambridge: University Press.
Hanson, K. and Vandaele, A. (2013). Translating working children's rights into international labour law. In K. Hanson and O. Nieuwenhuys (eds) *Reconceptualizing Children's Rights in International Development: Living Rights, Social Justice, Translations* (pp. 250–272). Cambridge: University Press.
Heesterman, W. (2005). Child labour and children's rights: Policy issues in three affluent societies. In J. Goddard, S. Mcnamee, A. James and A. James (eds) *The Politics of Childhood.* Basingstoke, UK: Palgrave Macmillan.
Hudson, P. (1990). Proto-industrialisation. *Recent Findings of Research in Economic and Social History, 10*, 1–4. Available on the Economic History Society website at www.ehs.org.uk/dotAsset/1d40418e-b981-4076-8974-b81686a9d042.pdf (last accessed 1 March 2014).
Humphries, J. (2010). *Childhood and Child Labour in the British Industrial Revolution.* New York: Cambridge University Press.
ILO (2004). *Child Labour: A Textbook for University Students.* Geneva: International Labour Office.
ILO (2013). *Marking Progress Against Child labour. Global Estimates and Trends 2000–2012.* Geneva: International Labour Office.
James, A. and James, A. (2008). *Key Concepts in Childhood Studies.* London: Sage.
James, A., Jenks, C. and Prout, A. (1998). *Theorizing Childhood.* Cambridge: Polity Press.
Kirby, P. (2003). *Child Labour in Britain, 1750–1870.* London: Palgrave Macmillan.
Lavalette, M. (1999a). The 'new sociology of childhood' and child labour: Childhood, children's rights and

'children's voice'. In M. Lavalette (ed.) *A Thing of the Past? Child Labour in Britain in the Nineteenth and Twentieth Centuries*. Liverpool: Liverpool University Press.

Lavalette, M. (ed.) (1999b). *A Thing of the Past? Child Labour in Britain in the Nineteenth and Twentieth Centuries*. Liverpool: Liverpool University Press.

Leonard, M. (2003). Children's attitudes to parents', teachers' and employees' perceptions of term-time employment. *Children and Society*, 17(5), 349–360.

Levine, S. (2011). The race of nimble fingers: Changing patterns of children's work in post-apartheid South Africa. *Childhood*, 18(2), 261–273.

Liebel, M. (2004). *A Will of Their Own: Cross-cultural Perspectives on Working Children*. London: Zed Books.

Liebel, M. (2012). *Children's Rights from Below: Cross-cultural Perspectives*. Basingstoke, UK: Palgrave Macmillan.

Liebel, M. (2013). Do children have a right to work? Working children's movements in the struggle for social justice. In K. Hanson and O. Nieuwenhuys (eds), *Reconceptualizing Children's Rights in International Development: Living Rights, Social Justice, Translations* (pp. 225–249). Cambridge: University Press.

Mayall, B. and Morrow, V. (2011) *You Can Help Your Country: English Children's Work during the Second World War*. London: Institute of Education, University of London.

McKechnie, J., Hobbs, S. and Anderson, S. (2009). Can child employment legislation work? *Youth and Policy*, 101, 43–53.

McKechnie, J., Lavalette, M. and Hobbs, S. (2000). Notes and issues: Child employment research in Britain. *Work, Employment and Society*, 14(3), 573–580.

Mendels, F.F. (1972). Proto-industrialization: The first phase of the industrialization process. *The Journal of Economic History*, 32(1), 241–261.

Merry, S.E: (2006). *Human Rights and Gender Violence: Translating International Law into Local Justice*. Chicago: University of Chicago Press.

Mizen, P., Bolton, A. and Pole, C. (1999). School age workers: The paid employment of children in Britain. *Work, Employment and Society*, 13(3), 423–438.

Morrow, V. (2010). Should the world really be free of 'child labour'? Some reflections. *Childhood*, 17(4), 435–440.

Myers, W. (1999). Considering child labour: Changing terms, issues and actors at the international level. *Childhood*, 6(1), 13–26.

Nardinelli, C. (1990). *Child Labor and the Industrial Revolution*. Bloomington: Indiana University Press.

Nieuwenhuys, O. (1994). *Children's Lifeworlds: Gender, Welfare, and Labour in the Developing World*. London: Routledge.

Nieuwenhuys, O. (2005). The wealth of children: Reconsidering the child labour debate. In J. Qvortrup (ed.) *Studies in Modern Childhood*. New York: Palgrave Macmillan.

Nieuwenhuys, O. (2007). Embedding the global womb: Global child labour and the new policy agenda. *Children's Geographies*, 5(1–2), 149–163.

Nieuwenhuys, O. (2009). From child labour to working children's movement. In J. Qvortrup, W. A. Corsaro and M.-S. Honig (eds) *The Palgrave Handbook of Childhood Studies*. London: Palgrave Macmillan.

Office of the United Nations High Commissioner for Human Rights (2007). Article 32 (Economic exploitation, including child labour). In *Legislative History of the Convention on the Rights of the Child. Vol. II*. (pp. 693–708). New York/Geneva: United Nations.

Omokhodion, F. O., Omokhodion, S. I. and Odusote, T. O. (2006). Perceptions of child labour among working children in Ibadan, Nigeria. *Child Care Health and Development*, 32(3), 281–286.

Qvortrup, J. (2001). Children's schoolwork: Useful and necessary. *Brood and Rozen*, 6(4), 145–162.

Qvortrup, J., Corsaro, W. A. and Honig, M.-S. (eds) (2009). *The Palgrave Handbook of Childhood Studies*. London: Palgrave Macmillan.

Reynaert, D., Bouverne-De Bie, M. and Vandevelde, S. (2009). A review of children's rights literature since the adoption of the United Nations Convention on the Rights of the Child. *Childhood*, 16(4), 518–534.

Reynolds, P. (1991). *Dance, Civet Cat: Child Labour in the Zambesi Valley*. London: Zed Books.

Stammers, N. (2009). *Human Rights and Social Movements*. London: Pluto Press.

White, B. (1994). Children, work and 'child labour': Changing responses to the employment of children. *Development and Change*, 25(4), 849–878.

White, B. (1999). Defining the intolerable: Child work, global standards and cultural relativism. *Childhood*, 6(1), 133–144.

Woodhead, M. (1999). Combatting child labour: Listen to what the children say. *Childhood* 6(1), 27–49.

19

The human rights of children in the context of international migration

Pablo Ceriani Cernadas

1. Introduction

Children and adolescents are increasingly migrating in search of family reunification, survival, security, improved standards of living, education, or protection from abuse and violence. Millions of children and young people are on the move, both within and between regions, accompanied by their families or on their own.[1] Also when not migrating themselves, they are affected, because migrating parents often leave them behind or because they are born to migrant parents in destination countries.

However, until very recently children in the context of international migration remained largely invisible in several aspects (policy making, legislation, research,[2] among others). For this reason, no proper attention has been given to the particularities of child migrants, whether with parents or unaccompanied, or to other categories of children whose lives are impacted by their parents' migration. This invisibility has been particularly prevalent in the field of public policy (Bhabha, 2008; UNLa/UNICEF, 2009), and has in many cases led to ineffective, inadequate, or illegal responses from a human rights perspective.

The Convention on the Rights of the Child (CRC) is the most comprehensive international legal instrument for the protection of the human rights of all children under a State's jurisdiction. As it establishes in Article 2, states must respect and ensure these rights without discrimination of any kind, irrespective of the child's, child's parents' or legal guardian's race, colour, sex, language, religion, political or other opinion, national, ethnic or social origin, property, disability, birth or other status.

---

1 Although comprehensive and comparable data is lacking, it has largely been shown that youth and child migration are important phenomena. While available data indicates that developing countries host a higher proportion of young migrants overall, the percentage of children and young migrants is considerably higher in less developed regions, where 26 percent of international migrants are under the age of 20. This is double the percentage found in the more developed regions (Cortina and Hovy, 2009).
2 A key publication on human rights and migration is Chetail and Bauloz (2014). It does not explicitly focus on children.

In addition, in General Comment No. 6, on unaccompanied and separated children, the Committee on the Rights of the Child (CRC Committee) asserted that "the enjoyment of rights stipulated in the Convention is not limited to children who are nationals of a State Party and must therefore, if not explicitly stated otherwise in the Convention, also be available to all children – including asylum-seeking, refugee and migrant children – irrespective of their nationality, immigration status or statelessness." (CRC Committee, 2005: §12).

Following the rapid approval and ratification of the CRC by most states – currently there are 195 member states – most countries have developed a set of policies, legislation, programmes, and practices aimed at ensuring the rights of children under their jurisdiction. Of course, the extent to which each state actually fulfils these obligations differs, and in all countries, many challenges remain regarding the effective realization of all the rights enshrined in the Convention.

When it comes to the rights of children in the context of migration, the tasks ahead are far-reaching. As will be argued in this chapter, the many issues currently pending reveal to what extent changes are still needed to apply children's rights principles and standards to migration policies and other related policies that impact the rights of child migrants and children affected by migration.

A child rights-based perspective is generally absent from migration laws and policies in countries of origin, transit and destination. The Special Rapporteur on the Human Rights of Migrants (2009), as well as other literature (Bhabha, 2008; UNICEF-UNLa, 2010), has argued that there is a general absence of an "age" approach in migration policies. Migration has been mainly discussed in terms of adult male movement, and children have been considered dependents: passive, vulnerable and exploited (Touzenis, 2008). A lack of distinction between adults and children in migration policies may lead to the denial or arbitrary restriction of migrant children's rights.

Additionally, the youth policies of many countries (as well as related public policies in key areas such as education, health care and employment) do not take the implications for and connections to migration into account. In host countries, this absence leads to failed integration policies, or to practices so restrictive that they might contribute to the social exclusion of child migrants and children born to migrant parents. In countries of origin, failure and deficiency of such policies may impact on the decision to migrate of children and/or their parents.

This chapter aims to depict some of the key international principles and standards on the human rights of children in the context of migration, with the objective of developing from a critical perspective alternative ideas and proposals on children's rights. It will also describe some of the main challenges and gaps between the CRC and migration policies and practices, especially in the field of migration control mechanisms such as detention and deportation. In addition, it will point out how other public policies, e.g. education or health care, may negatively impact child migrants' rights, particularly, but not exclusively, when they are undocumented.

First, this chapter will identify the categories of children affected by migration in order to reveal the variety of situations in which children's rights are linked to international migration (policies). Next, a brief section will be devoted to reflecting on some of the root causes of child migration in the current context of globalization. Thereinafter, the analysis focuses on the main aspects of international human rights standards both with regard to the root causes of migration and the deficiencies of and challenges to children's rights in the context of migration. In particular, it is based on the four guiding principles of the Convention on the Rights of the Child: best interests of the child, right to participation, right to survival and development, and non-discrimination.

2. Categories of children in the context of migration

Children are impacted by migration in at least two ways: 1) by migration itself: migration of children or migration of their parents or other relatives is a fact that may substantially impact children's lives, and 2) by migration policies: state responses to migration, and particularly the level of recognition and granting of migrants' rights, might be essential to either reducing or increasing the vulnerability of these children.

Various categories of children and adolescents affected by migration can be distinguished. It is important to note that in all these categories, the impact of both migration and policies will vary considerably according to the immigration status of children and/or their parents. While this condition will differ depending on the region and country, it has been widely evidenced that the degree of vulnerability of children in the context of migration – their capability to effectively exercise their human rights – is conditioned by their immigration status and whether states consider this status as a relevant condition for restricting or denying their rights (Rafferty 2007: 408).

Migrants become irregular in a number of ways: by irregularly entering the country of destination, by staying in the country after a rejected asylum application or after the expiration of a temporary status, by having residence documents arbitrarily confiscated by employers, or by losing their job. Some people decide to migrate irregularly because of a lack of lawful options, but others find themselves in an irregular situation due to administrative barriers or a lack of information (IOM, 2010). Actually, legal entry followed by overstaying the terms of entry is one of the main paths into irregularity. Irregular entry, on the other hand, occurs least frequently and is the exception rather than the norm (Düvell, 2011).

2.1. Unaccompanied and separated children

Unaccompanied children are children who have been separated from both parents and other relatives and are not being cared for by an adult who, by law or custom, is responsible for their welfare. Separated children have been separated from both parents or from their previous legal or customary primary caregiver, but not necessarily from other relatives. Both separated and unaccompanied children are in a particularly vulnerable situation and face a number of protection deficits. Their migrations occur for a number of reasons including family reunification, domestic violence, and a number of forms of persecution of the child. They may also leave their country due to international conflict and civil war; discrimination based on ethnic origin, sexual orientation and other prohibited grounds; trafficking in various contexts and forms; and the search for economic opportunities unavailable in countries of origin – namely, access to key social rights.

In 2005, the Committee on the Rights of the Child adopted General Comment No. 6, which describes a set of principles and standards that states must respect in order to ensure and protect the rights of unaccompanied and separated children outside their countries of origin (CRC Committee 2005). At regional level, for instance, the Parliamentary Assembly of the Council of Europe adopted a resolution setting out a number of guidelines on this issue (Council of Europe, 2011). In addition, MERCOSUR[3] member states have recently requested

---

3   MERCOSUR, created in 1991, is an economic and political integration mechanism among Argentina, Bolivia, Brazil, Paraguay, Uruguay and – since 2012 – Venezuela to promote the free movement of goods, services and people among member states. The MERCOSUR associated states are Bolivia, Chile, Colombia and Ecuador.

an Inter-American Court of Human Rights Advisory Opinion on children and migration. This opinion was adopted in August 2014 and will contribute to underpinning a number of regional human rights standards on the treatment of child migrants, including some guiding principles on unaccompanied and separated children (Inter-American Court of Human Rights, 2014).[4]

2.2. Children who migrate with their families

During the last decades, there has been an increase in the number of adults who migrate with all or some of their children, both regularly and irregularly. Children's migration status usually depends on that of their parents. While in some cases these children are likely to be deported if the entire family is in an irregular status, in other situations, they may be able to regularize the family's status or their own one, based on grounds such as studies or length of residence in the country.[5]

2.3. Children left behind by migrant parents

Many migrant parents leave their children in the country of origin. In several situations, legal restrictions in destination countries impede migration with the entire family. Often, countries of origin do not properly take into account the particular vulnerabilities and needs of children left behind. If their parents do not have a regular migration status, the children left behind may lack financial and emotional support, impacting their development and often placing them at risk of losing substantial access to social protection. Under such residence status, children are not entitled to family reunification in their parents' host country. Moreover, parents are not likely to regularly visit their children in the country of origin, due to the fear of being unable to return to the host country. These circumstances may increase the vulnerable situation of the children, prolong family disruption and, in many cases, push children and adolescents seeking to reunite with their parents into irregular migration.

2.4. Children born to migrant parents in host countries

This category concerns children born to parents who have migrated to the host country. Parents may have migrated through either regular or irregular channels. They may have a residence permit, have entered irregularly, or may have overstayed a residence authorization in the destination country. Even if they possess regular status, in some countries the parents may not have a work permit, or they may face restrictions regarding the freedom of seeking and choosing a job. In this case, as in the case of children that migrate with their parents, the migration and labour status of parents, as well as migrants' own opportunities in the labour market tend to considerably impact children's development and living conditions. The irregular status of parents may result in family separation due to deportation measures enacted against them.

---

4   The original request made by MERCOSUR Member States, as well as the information and *Amici Curiae* sent by several American states, international UN agencies, universities and non governmental organizations are available on the official website of the Inter-American Court of Human Rights, www.corteidh.or.cr/soloc.cfm.
5   One example of this is the US Government's decision aimed at regularizing the migration status of hundreds of thousands of young migrants who had arrived in the country years before and had studied in the US (see Gonzales and Bautista-Chavez, 2014).

Moreover, according to nationality regulations in each host country, children born to migrant parents could be recognized as nationals (*ius soli*[6]) or not (*ius sanguinis*[7]). Restrictive, arbitrary practices at registration offices may lead to a stateless condition for children.

2.5. Returned and deported children

Children who are returned, repatriated or deported to their country of origin (the terminology may vary according to the regulation of each country or the legal nature of the decision) could be in a particularly vulnerable condition, especially those who had migrated unaccompanied.

Several factors could have a critical impact on the living conditions of the children after their return to their countries of origin. Among others, the following can be mentioned: their experiences in transit and their stay in host countries, the existence of a Best Interest Determination Procedure in the country that decided the repatriation or a lack thereof, the extent of rights-based policies in the countries of origin and destination aimed at ensuring these children's reintegration in both the short and long term.

These categories are not mutually exclusive, and children may fit into different ones at various times. For instance, unaccompanied children may start out as children left behind and, if successful in their migration project for family reunification, they may end up with their parents in the host country. They can also move between regular and irregular situations.

If estimating the overall number of irregular migrants around the world is a challenge, it is even more difficult to estimate the percentage of children living without lawful residence or migrating through irregular channels in both transit and destination countries. It is equally problematic to identify the number of children left behind by irregular migrant parents and those born to parents with no regular status in host countries, even if some of those children are nationals of the countries where they are born.

Some national and regional studies try to estimate the percentage of children within the overall number of migrants in an irregular situation based on data obtained through border detentions.[8] However, data on border detention or data on deportation procedures in general, underestimate the number of migrant children in an irregular situation, given that they may not take into account those who successfully cross the border. In addition, it does not take into account those children whose administrative situation becomes irregular once they are in receiving countries, although they had originally entered in a regular way. Finally, there are no statistics for children born to migrant parents and nationals of host countries who are themselves in an irregular migration status. In these cases, again, data only become available to the extent that they relate to deportation measures taken against the parents (Applied Research Center, 2011; Beckles Flores, 2011).

Both individual and objective circumstances of each case, along with some characteristics of migration policies and regulations in receiving countries, are critical for shaping the experience and outcome of migration. In particular, these determine whether a migrant enters or stays in a host country regularly or irregularly.

---

6   *Ius soli* (Latin: right of the soil) is the right of anyone born in the territory of a state to nationality.
7   *Ius sanguinis* (Latin: right of blood) is a principle of nationality law by which nationality is not determined by place of birth but by having one or both parents who are nationals of the state.
8   See ICMPD (2001–2011). See also Mexico National Migration Institute statistics, on www.inm.gob.mx, and INM-CEM (2011).

In the case of children, there are a number of factors that drive children to migrate through irregular channels, such as: increasingly restrictive migration policies in host countries, absence of family reunification programmes, or bureaucratic, illegitimate conditions for family reunification, the growth of informal and unregulated labour markets, which demand an adolescent and young labour force, unprotected jobs for adolescent and young girls based on gender inequity, the growth of smuggling networks that take advantage of this context, and, last but not least, trafficking of persons. Trafficking is an issue that especially impacts children and women; it is exacerbated by, amongst other factors, restrictive migration policies, social exclusion and misinformation to victims in origin countries, and sexual and labour exploitation practices in host countries.

Irregular migration of unaccompanied and separated children, many of whom have been left behind by their parents, has increased in part due to the obstacles for access to a legal residence in countries of destination and the restrictions to family reunification. In many countries unaccompanied children are not authorized to enter if they do not have a formal permit given by their parents; this practice attests to the absence of policies driven by a child protection approach. Also, the phenomenon of circular migration programmes is another closely related problem. Many low-skilled temporary labour programmes do not permit migrants to bring relatives with them, leading to irregular migration, mainly by children, for the purpose of family reunification.

In addition, the absence of regularization policies – either extraordinary programmes or permanent channels – has led millions of migrants to stay in the destination country permanently, even though their plan had originally been temporary migration. As they might stay irregularly for a long period of time, the impossibility of even occasionally visiting the children left behind, may contribute to aggravating family separation and pushing families into the irregular unaccompanied migration of children (Kuhner, 2010).

Irregularity impacts children in many other ways. While several countries provide a residence permit to adults whose children are born in their territory, on the grounds of family unity, others do not embrace programmes that grant regular status to irregular migrant parents of child nationals, despite the fact that the right to family protection is widely enshrined in several core international human rights treaties.

3. Children's rights and root causes of migration: Ensuring the right to development in a globalized world

A comprehensive rights-based approach to the phenomenon of children in the context of migration should address the entire process of migration, starting with the root causes in the country of origin. The latter constitute one of the cornerstone issues that must be addressed in order to achieve effective, long-term, and legitimate responses to the existing challenges. In this regard, the Human Rights Council (2009) has stated that policies and initiatives on migration "should promote holistic approaches that take into account the causes and consequences and challenges and opportunities of the phenomenon and full respect for the human rights and fundamental freedoms of migrants, with due regard for the specific needs of children in vulnerable situations, such as unaccompanied children, girls, children with disabilities and those who may be in need of international refugee protection."

Individuals decide to migrate for many different reasons, whether through regular or irregular channels. Root causes of adult migration are not necessarily different from those that drive child migration. Moreover, root causes of irregular migration generally do not differ greatly from the determinants of regular migration. These include poverty, a lack of opportunities,

Table 19.1 Determining factors that influence children's irregular migration status

Crossing borders (through irregular channels)	In destination countries (becoming irregular)
• Limited and overly-selective possible categories for regular migration (visas, departure/entry regulations worldwide)	• Absence of regularization policies, both extraordinary plans and permanent avenues
• Demand for irregular migration by informal areas of the labour market	• Absence of regularization avenues for workers in informal and precarious jobs
• Deprivation of social rights in origin, social exclusion, and vulnerable conditions	• Loss of employment or termination of a labour contract
• Lack of long-term opportunities and family migration within circular/temporal migration programs	• Omission of the right to family unit as sufficient grounds for granting regular status to irregular migrant parents of child nationals
• Absence of information and awareness campaigns in countries of origin	• Increased severity of detention, deportation and criminalization policies leading to invisibility, and non-regularization
• Obstacles or lack of policies for family reunification, irregular migration of unaccompanied children	• Unaccompanied children facing a lack of special procedures for access to regular status, based on child protection approach
• Rise of smuggling networks in the above mentioned context.	• Unaccompanied children with regular status becoming irregular upon reaching 18 years of age.
• Gender stereotypes and discrimination against women in the labour market.	
• Increase of trafficking networks in the aforementioned context.	

Source: UNICEF-UNLa, 2011.

socio-economic inequality, regional disparities, political instability, gender inequity, discrimination, effects of climate change, armed conflict, labour market demands (including informal economy and unprotected jobs, amongst others). Addressing the root causes of migration requires engagement with the social, economic, and political patterns that drive migration, in both origin and host countries. This necessarily leads to facing structural causes such as poverty and inequality between and within countries and regions. It implies examining and addressing the factors that currently impede millions of people from enjoying the right to human development.

Human development, root causes of migration, and migration are inseparably linked, as has been acknowledged for almost two decades. Indeed, this issue was raised during the Programme of Action of the 1994 International Conference on Population and Development: "International economic imbalances, poverty and environmental degradation, combined with the absence of peace and security, human rights violations and the varying degrees of development of judicial and democratic institutions are all factors affecting international migration … The long-term manageability of international migration hinges on making the option to remain in one's country a viable one for all people. Sustainable economic growth with equity and development strategies consistent with this aim are a necessary means to that end" (ICPD, 1994: §10.1). More recently, the Global Commission for International Migration affirmed that the world's most prosperous states need to acknowledge the impact of their policies on the dynamics of international migration, for instance through trade reform that would give developing countries better and fair access to global markets (GCIM, 2005).

From a human rights perspective, Skogly has pointed out that if states are to take seriously their responsibility to the right to development, they will need to pay attention to the human rights effects of their development cooperation, the consequences of international trade rules and the results in the international community of their behaviour in intergovernmental institutions (Skogly, 2002). Similarly, reflecting on states' obligations on the right to development,[9] Salomon asserts that the gross inequality that characterizes world poverty today, the power differential that accompanies it, and the reality of global economic interdependence, should lead to a principle of shared responsibility. This means that developed states should contribute to fulfilling basic rights – for example, to food, water, and health – of people elsewhere, beyond international cooperation (Salomon, 2008).

Despite the fact that these root causes may apply to all kinds of current migration flows, it is important to note that there are root causes that specifically drive the regular and irregular migration of children, such as family reunification,[10] improved education and labour opportunities, escaping from family, social, or institutional violence and abuse, or in some contexts, social violence impacting adolescents (UNHCR, 2014). Addressing both the rights of children in origin and destination countries and the causes that generate migration – not only regular, but mainly irregular – is critical for comprehensively coping with the challenges linked to migration in the short and long term. The duty to ensure the right to development for everyone, which entails the full realization of all human rights, and the commitment to ensuring sustainable development, with its three pillars of economic development, social development and environmental protection, are principles that should be fully incorporated into a comprehensive approach aimed at effectively addressing the needs and vulnerabilities of children within the migration-development nexus (Abramovich et al., 2011).

One of the four general principles of the CRC is children's right to life, survival and development (as textually reflected in Art. 6 CRC). This right relates to a continuum of well-being that begins at maximum survival and progresses to an endpoint represented by children's optimum development, ensuring the conditions that enable them to develop to their full potential. In addition, this right informs the interpretation of the Convention, as it is intrinsically linked with the effective exercise of all the rights laid down in the CRC (Dutschke and Abrahams, 2006). The denial of this core right is one of the major root causes of migration for children, adolescents or their parents. Therefore, every aspect that undermines child survival and development in countries of origin must be taken into account in any analysis, discussion and initiative aimed at addressing the causes of migration, its characteristics (regular/irregular), and its consequences and impact on children, families, receiving and sending societies, as well as public policies meant to respond to this phenomenon.

Similarly, the violation of the other CRC general principles – best interests of the child, non-discrimination, and the right to participation – is always associated with factors that impact child migration. For instance, discriminatory practices that affect children on grounds such as

---

9   It is important to bear in mind the definition of the right to development given by the 1986 United Nations Declaration on the Right to Development: "States have the right and the duty to formulate appropriate national development policies that aim at the constant improvement of the well-being of the entire population and of all individuals".
10 Many children are left behind by parents that migrate alone due to increasing restrictions to family migration. After few or many years, those children seek to reunite with their parents in destination countries.

ethnic origin or sexual orientation, amongst others, may force them to migrate. The same result might be produced by the absence or failure of childhood policies and mechanisms aimed at ensuring children's right to participate in policies and programmes that affect them. And, in many countries, the omission of the best interests principle as a guiding rule for every policy, practice, and decision impacting the rights of children, is behind most children's decisions to migrate.[11]

4. The rights of children in the context of migration: International standards and key challenges

4.1. The primacy of children's rights: Implementing CRC principles in migration policies

The implementation of CRC obligations and principles in the context of migration is supported by an underlying principle: that the standards set out by the CRC should have primacy over any other aspect or policy involved. As was asserted by the CRC Committee and other stakeholders, childhood policies and legislation take precedence in a normative and policy migration framework (CRC Committee, 2012; Mercosur Member States, 2011; UNICEF, 2012: §27). This statement has many implications.

For one, children's rights should never be subjected to migration goals defined by a state. In other words, children must be treated first and foremost as children, rather than migrants. Despite the discretionary margin that states have traditionally held in regulating and managing migration and although the ends sought through migration policies by a particular state may be considered legitimate, the rights of children potentially affected by such policies and practices must be a primary consideration. In other words, children's rights (including principles and standards that guide the effective realization of these rights) should be explicitly included in any migration policy, piece of legislation, and decision that might impact them. The Office of the High Commissioner for Human Rights has argued that all authorities and institutions in contact with children in the context of migration should be required to assess whether their actions unequivocally protect the interests of each individual child. This principle should override all others, and be decisive in cases when conflicting provisions of migration policy arise (OHCHR, 2010: §24).

In reality, there are major gaps between migration policies and legislation, on the one hand, and the principles and obligations enshrined in the CRC, on the other. Therefore, one of the key challenges today is widely and correctly introducing all the CRC provisions into every migration policy and programme as well as related areas that may impact the rights of child migrants and other categories of children affected by migration. Clearly, this objective must also take into account the core principles of the Convention mentioned above.

First, all policies, programmes, decisions, practices on migration and related matters, both at the general level and on a case-by-case basis, must apply "the best interests of the child" principle. For instance, policies on detention, deportation of migrants (children and/or their parents), decisions aimed at addressing parents' irregular status, practices on access to health care and education in host countries, social, intercultural integration policies, and family reunification programmes, among other issues, should be guided by the best interest principle. As was stated by the CRC Committee, non rights-based arguments, such as those relating to general

---

11 For an in-depth analysis of the Best Interest Principle, see UN CRC Committee (2013).

migration control, cannot override a child's best interests consideration (CRC Committee, 2005: §86).

Below we explain how this principle should be applied to particular issues, including through the so-called Best Interests Determination Procedure (BID) in the case of unaccompanied children. Of course, as the UN Office of the High Commissioner for Human Rights (OHCHR) noted, the meaning of what constitutes "best interest" will necessarily change in different contexts, depending on the situation of the individual child. This makes it necessary to ensure that the individual circumstances (including his or her nationality, upbringing, cultural and linguistic background, vulnerability and particular protection needs) of the child be taken into account when determining what is in his or her best interests (OHCHR, 2010: §25).

Second, the principle of non-discrimination (a *jus cogens* principle, according to the Inter-American Court of Human Rights, 2003) forbids arbitrary distinctions based on grounds such as nationality or migration status of children or their parents when it comes to the entitlement and effective realization of any right enshrined in the Convention.[12] In issues such as undocumented migrants' access to social rights – either by children or their parents – access to justice, child birth registration, ensuring due process of law, or getting a residence permit, amongst others, the non-discrimination principle can play a key role in ensuring the rights of children in the context of migration. The European Court of Human Rights (ECtHR) has accepted, however, that differential treatment on the basis of immigration status may be justified under certain conditions, in particular with regard to public services (ECtHR 27 September 2011, Bah v. the United Kingdom, §§ 38–52).

Third, regarding the right to participation, it is important to note that there are a number of programmes and procedures directly or indirectly related to migration that should provide effective mechanisms for children's participation. In the specific area of migration, it is evident that children should be entitled to participate in procedures that may have consequences to them, such as: entering a country, applying for a residence permit, repatriation, and detention and deportation of their parents. The extent and mode of this participation might vary in each case due to various factors, including the principle of progressive autonomy of the child (IIN, 2010).

Additionally, the right to participation of these child migrants and children born to migrant parents in host countries could also include: participation in designing and implementing integration policies as well as in inter-cultural programmes at the educational system, initiatives on labour opportunities for adolescents, plans aimed at preventing xenophobia, and, of course, discussions on migration policy and legislative reform. In countries of origin, some examples would be: child participation in defining child-sensitive consular assistance policies, in evaluating processes on the impact of reintegration mechanisms for repatriated children, in designing and implementing child development policies meant to ensure adequate standards of living aimed at the prevention of migration due to necessity, and in drawing bilateral and regional strategies directed at upholding more regular avenues for migration, including fairly accessible family reunification programmes.

The previous section addressed children's rights to survival and development and their intrinsic relationship with key current discussions on migration. It is also important to note that these rights are also at stake when host countries regulate migrants' access to other basic rights.

---

12 For a thorough analysis of non-discrimination and children's rights, see inter alia Abramson (2008). For an analysis of discrimination in migration, see Vandenhole (2013).

Restrictions on the rights to health care, education, or social security based on grounds such as nationality or migration status often have direct consequences for child migrants and children born to migrant parents, or even for those children left behind. For instance, parents' access to labour rights and opportunities under conditions equal to those available to nationals is a key factor for social integration, and hence for child development in the broader sense, as emphasized above. The right to development for children in migrant families might also be positively or negatively affected according to whether or not regularization programmes exist, and if so, whether as extraordinary measures or permanent mechanisms.

Finally, it is worth remembering that other core principles of international human rights law should be explicitly taken into account for any policy or decision that may impact children in the context of migration. The principle of *Pro Persona* (*pro homine*), entailing an obligation to apply the regulation most favourable for the child's rights or best interest, as reflected for example in Art. 41 CRC,[13] is essential for policy and legislative interpretation on a case-by-case basis. Similarly, the principle of progressiveness[14] should lead to in-depth discussions on the approach of current migration policies and their impact on children's rights and welfare. In a climate of increased vulnerability of migrants, particularly children, are policies being designed from a rights-based perspective? Are they aimed at ensuring child protection? Or are these policies rather dominated by preventive and punitive considerations that regressively affect basic rights?

The principle of dynamism requires that, since human rights treaties are "living instruments", they should be implemented according to present-day challenges. Therefore, to what extent are states currently adequately responding to migration? And how is human rights law being enforced in this context? Is it being applied – by different stakeholders – in a way that ensures all migrants' rights, or by contrast, is it interpreted in a restrictive sense in order to justify migrants' rights constraints?[15] Finally, yet of great importance, although international standards require that vulnerable social groups be protected by special measures, migrants – especially undocumented children, the weakest of this group – are being subjected to several restrictions of their most basic rights, such as education, health care and the right to family.

The following sections will explore how the interpretation and implementation of the abovementioned principles and provisions are leading towards the establishment of a number of international human rights standards about the rights of children in the context of migration. These standards, as will be explained, are related to some of the most pressing problems and challenges that these children are currently facing.

4.2. Children's rights within migration control policies

One area that conspicuously lacks a children's rights perspective within migration policies is that of immigration control policies and practices. As a traditional manifestation of state

---

13   Article 41 CRC provides that

>   Nothing in the present Convention shall affect any provisions which are more conducive to the realization of the rights of the child and which may be contained in:
>   (a) The law of a State party; or
>   (b) International law in force for that State.

14   The principle of progressiveness means that States must adopt measures aimed at continuously improving the level of realization of all human rights to every individual under to their jurisdiction.

15   For instance, the European Court of Human Rights has adopted a narrow interpretation of Article 8 of the European Convention on Human Rights, on the right to family life, when it comes to issues related to migrants' rights (see Ceriani Cernadas, 2009).

sovereignty, immigration control has long been detached from the strides made in human rights protection. Only very recently, some key human rights obligations have been progressively incorporated in immigration control in many countries to prevent rights restrictions due to the enforcement of border control mechanisms, deportation measures, etc. As will be explained next, this progress, though, remains inadequate because a number of serious challenges remains, and when it comes to the protection of children's rights, the deficiencies are considerably greater. Some of the most acute violations of rights occur in the detention and deportation of children and/or their parents.

In particular with regard to unaccompanied or separated undocumented children, the CRC Committee has stated that "at any of these stages, a best interests determination must be documented in preparation of any decision fundamentally impacting on the unaccompanied or separated child's life" (CRC Committee, 2005: §19). The Best Interest Determination (BID) Procedure, originally envisaged for addressing asylum seeker cases (see UNHCR, 2008), is the most important tool for ensuring the respect, protection and fulfilment of the rights of unaccompanied migrant children, by means of a uniform process at the national and international level to determine what constitutes the best interests of the child on a case-by-case basis.

The BID Procedure entails the adoption of a public policy that includes a focus on the holistic protection of children in the responses of states towards the migration of unaccompanied children. Therefore, its effective implementation requires a series of factors to be contemplated, such as human and budgetary resources, training in children's rights, and inter-institutional coordination (UNICEF, 2012: §48).

In practice, details about conformity and implementation (including which governmental agencies can or should take part in the BID Procedure) should be specifically tailored to each country. Aspects such as structure and institutional organization, the impact of the phenomenon of unaccompanied child migration and institutional capabilities, among others, determine the concrete measures in each place. Nevertheless, the principles and objectives that guide the BID Procedure and its specific application in each case must not vary from country to country.

Moreover, in order to be able to duly satisfy the fundamental principles that characterize the BID Procedure, other core requirements must also be fulfilled. Among these are the guarantees of due process, including the children's right to be heard and right to participate, which should be gradually implemented according to the age and maturity of the child. Another section of this chapter is dedicated to the indispensable rights to legal assistance and a guardian. Additionally, the right to be permanently informed, the right to an interpreter, if necessary, as well as a right to an effective remedy and access to the justice system must also all be guaranteed.

The guarantee of consular assistance may also be greatly relevant in many cases. This guarantee and other elements of BID Procedures should include specific duties for the country of origin, as will be analysed further on. The consular action should, in turn, be part of effective cooperation between the country of origin and the destination (or transit) country in which the unaccompanied child is found. The information that the authorities in the country of origin can provide may be essential for effectively determining the best interests of the child, by revealing whether the family, social, or community conditions are adequate for the return and reintegration of the child.

4.2.1. The principle of non-deportation of children

Adapting migration policies so that they conform to the CRC involves revising all the mechanisms that can affect the rights of children. One of the issues that require a significant reformulation is that of the treatment of irregular migration, namely, the question of deporting a child, or not, under circumstances of migratory non-compliance, i.e. illegal entry, remaining after the period of stay or residence in the country expires, etc.

Deportation is a measure that emphasizes the infraction, implicitly assigns blame, and on this basis imposes a penalty. It has a legal nature and has motivations very different from the rights-related goals described above. Worse yet, in the majority of cases, deportation re-victimizes the child or even replicates the possible threat to his/her life, freedom, or physical health. Different semantics – "deportation", "expulsion", "return", "repatriation" – do not alter the effect; rather, what is pertinent is the type of procedure applied, the ends that such a decision seeks, and the means that are used to achieve this goal.

Many agree that children should not face deportation as a punitive measure (Human Rights Council, 2009; Special Rapporteur, 2009; OHCHR, 2010; Abramovich et al., 2011). The principle of non-deportation states that the proper response to irregular migration is not found among traditional measures provided by immigration policies, such as expulsion or deportation. On the contrary, the response to irregular migration must be consonant with the spirit, principles, and guidelines that derive from the CRC. A focus on holistic protection and key principles, such as the best interests of the child, the right to participation along with the principle of progressive autonomy and the principle of non-discrimination are core components for reaching a decision in every case.

The principle of non-deportation applies to all categories of migrant children, i.e. unaccompanied children, those separated from their parents, and children that migrated together with their families and happen to be in circumstances of irregular migration. This last situation is one which, in various countries, may lead to expulsion (as a disciplinary measure) for the entire family. Nevertheless, this decision does not conform to the precepts of the CRC. If the state determines that the adult parents should be expelled due to an immigration infraction that they have committed, the expulsion of their children should not automatically follow; rather, their fate must derive from principles that underlie the rights of children.

For example, a child will leave the country with her parents not because she or he is being expelled, but rather because the interests of the child (among other rights, like the right to life and family unity) is best served by maintaining the family unit intact. This also implies that any penalty that usually accompanies expulsion, such as prohibition of re-entry for a specified time, should not be applied to the child. Such a change of perspective is not only based on the fact that the response should be directed towards the rights of child – rather than the criteria of immigration control – but also on the fact that children should never be held responsible for the irregular migration.

When families migrate irregularly or when they fall into an irregular status in the host country, the irregularity might be the result of a mix of factors, such as: the increasing number of obstacles and permits for regular family migration, for access to a residence, or for renewing a regular residence; the loss of the job by their parents (when residence permit is tied to a particular job); the denial of an asylum application; among many others. It is a combination of objective factors (in origin and destination) and subjective decisions taken by the parents. In these cases, in general, children are in a vulnerable, passive position, and they face a number of challenges in many aspects of the daily life in origin, transit and the host countries.

Therefore, when the status of the family is addressed, the particular treatment of the child should be done through a child-protection lens. As it was noted, even if the ultimate decision is the deportation of the parents due to their migration status, the individual resolution in the case of the children shouldn't have a punitive approach. Then, a repatriation decision would be based in family unit and best interest principles. On the contrary, issuing them a deportation measure – which also usually includes a prohibition of entry for a period of time – seems a disproportionate, unreasonable response that prioritizes migration control over child protection.

Respecting the rights of children may also lead to the conclusion that no family member should be expelled. As UNICEF has observed, a holistic interpretation of the CRC may result in abstaining from ordering the expulsion of a migrant family based on the irregular migration status of the parents or children. On many occasions, children have migrated with their parents in early childhood or been born in destination countries that do not recognize the principle of *ius soli*. In these circumstances or similar ones (like that of adolescents completely integrated into the destination country), the expulsion can severely affect the rights and development of a child (UNICEF, 2012: §156). The ECtHR has been willing to more or less equate a long-term immigrant who has lawfully spent all or the major part of his or her childhood and youth in the host country with a national (ECtHR 23 June 2008, *Maslov v. Austria*, §75).

It might be more appropriate that in order to ensure the holistic protection of children, alternative responses to expulsion be sought for administrative infractions such as irregular migration, for example, the regularization of the children's status in the destination country, and by extension, through the principle of family unity, regularization of the parents' status as well (UNICEF, 2012: §157).

The principle of non-deportation should also prevail in the case of unaccompanied and separated children. Beyond the general obligation to protect all children, unaccompanied children should be given greater protection in light of their particularly vulnerable circumstances (compare the ECtHR who has argued that the vulnerability of an irregular child may take precedence over her migration status, ECtHR 12 October 2006, *Mubilanzila Mayeka and Kaniki Mitunga v. Belgium*, §55).

First, this is necessary because frequently these children have migrated in an irregular way or without adequate documentation for migration. Second, because both the causes that drove their migration, as well as the conditions of the route, reveal a context of extreme vulnerability due to a number of rights deprivations and abuses. Third, the mere fact that they turn up alone at a border or outside of their country of origin reveals that the situation requires special measures: protection, reparation of rights that have been violated, and of course, mechanisms that will permit these children the dignified and adequate exercise of all of their rights in the short and long term.

The Best Interest Determination (BID) Procedure, originally envisaged for addressing asylum seekers' cases (see UNHCR, 2008), is the most important tool for ensuring the respect, protection and fulfilment of the rights of unaccompanied migrant children. The information to be gathered in each case within the framework of the BID Procedure from different sources – including the testimony of the child – can shed light on the existence of risks and opportunities that would decide the case, for example, if there are sufficient rights-based reasons for returning the child. This information could, among other things, indicate whether the child has escaped from abuse or family violence, or from institutional or social violence, or abandonment, or whether the child seeks reunification of the family in the country in which he/she has been found or in some other country; it could also uncover a wide range of other circumstances that must be duly considered in order to arrive at the decision that will be most consonant with the best interests of the child.

A BID Procedure must fully respect the core international principle of *non-refoulement*. This means that under no circumstance should the return of a child be contemplated in the case where he or she would be sent to a country where there are substantial grounds for fearing real risk of irreparable harm. Moreover, the CRC Committee has pointed out that the assessment of the risk of such serious violations should be conducted in an age and gender-sensitive manner and should, for example, take into account the particularly grave consequences of inadequate food or health services (CRC Committee, 2005: §26–28, 58, 82, 84). Where children are at these kinds of risks, both short- and long-term alternatives suited to their best interests should be sought within the BID Procedure.

In this sense, if the causes that led to the unaccompanied migration are not sufficiently considered, it is very probable that the child will shortly migrate again, as has recently been documented.[16] This is the case, for example, when repatriation is determined on the simple basis of family unity, but without a larger analysis of the individual, family and social circumstances.

Lasting solutions should be determined based on an individual assessment within the BID Procedure. Thus, according to the specific circumstances of each case, what constitutes a durable solution can vary substantially. Some of the options are: family reunification in the country of origin (immediate or delayed), family reunification and integration in the country of transit or destination,[17] integration in the country of transit or destination (either independently, with foster family or child-care institutions[18]), and resettlement in a third country.

4.2.2. The principle of non-detention of child migrants

The non-detention of migrant children found in a country without authorization for residence, is another of the essential principles that derive from an adequate adjustment of migration policies to a standard based on the rights of the child. As noted by UNICEF (2012: §92), in such cases, even Article 37.b of the CRC, which allows for depriving children of their liberty "in conformity with the law and only as a measure of last resort…" could not be applied appropriately. For Article 37.b was conceived to be applied to cases in which children have committed criminal offences, not infractions of an administrative nature, such as irregular migration. The CRC Committee has been very clear on this point:

> International law provides that the detention of children, including children in the context of migration, should be avoided (Article 37 CRC). Article 37(b) of the CRC allows the detention of children in the context of juvenile justice, exclusively as a last resort and for the shortest appropriate period of time. However, the detention of children on the sole basis of migration status is not in accordance with the CRC.
>
> *(CRC Committee, 2012: 22)*

UNICEF (2012: §93) echoes that the principle of non-detention of child migrants is an essential standard for all cases which require, conversely, the adoption of special protective measures according to the sensitive position in which these children are found.

This principle is valid for both unaccompanied children and child migrants who are with (one of) their parents. In the latter case, it has been erroneously argued that for reasons of

---

16 A couple of examples are the cases of Moroccan children repatriated from Spain and Central American children from Honduras, Guatemala and El Salvador repatriated from the United States and Mexico. On the case of Mexico, see Ceriani Cernadas (2013).
17 Both the CRC Committee (2005: §83) and the UN Special Rapporteur (2009: §58) stated that the possibility of reunification in the country of destination should also be considered, and if in child's best interest, should be implemented, as per Articles 9 and 10 CRC.
18 On this, see the UN General Assembly (2010) *Guidelines for the Alternative Care of Children*.

family unity, children could be detained along with their parents. Nonetheless, a correct reading of the CRC and its principles – best interests, family unity, and non-detention (except as last resort in the case of juvenile justice) among others – must lead to releasing the entire family unit, and, if necessary, housing it in social protection centres, whose purpose is to ensure the protection of the child and its family; these centres, plainly, are not locked facilities (UNICEF 2012, OHCHR, 2010, Special Rapporteur, 2009, 2012).

Having observed the impact of detention on children, the European Committee for the Prevention of Torture and Inhuman or Degrading Treatment or Punishment (CPT) considers that the deprivation of liberty of an irregular migrant child is rarely justified and can certainly not be motivated merely by a lack of resident status (CPT, 2009). The CRC Committee has stated that "detention cannot be justified solely on the basis of the child being unaccompanied or separated, or on their migratory or residence status, or lack thereof," and that "all efforts, including acceleration of relevant processes, should be made to allow for the immediate release of unaccompanied or separated children from detention and their placement in other forms of appropriate accommodation" (CRC Committee, 2005: §61). Somewhat more cautiously, the ECtHR has argued that detention of children for reasons of migration control can only be justified if deprivation of liberty can be shown to be *necessary*. So far, it has not accepted that the necessity standard was ever met (see, e.g., ECtHR 19 January 2010, *Muskhadzhiyeva e.a. v. Belgium*, §74).

In the exceptional case that children are located in a facility for families or unaccompanied children, it should be designed (and additional safeguards put in place) in order to cater to the specific needs of children (CPT, 2009: §97; ECtHR 13 December 2011, *Kanagaratnam et alii v. Belgium*, §§61–69). The placement of migrant children in detention should be addressed from the approach of child protection, rather than a punitive or disciplinary approach. Authorities in charge of facilities should not be security guards or immigration authorities, but inter-institutional agencies, trained in children's rights and with a specific mandate for child protection, rather than migration control.

Moreover, it has been shown that when children are detained with their families, trauma is caused to the child by the violent circumstances intrinsic to the process of detention (American Psychological Association, 2013). It is traumatizing for a child to observe authority transferred from a parent to a security official, thus rendering the role of the father and/or mother weakened. In this way, detention also undermines the primacy of the family, in that family dynamics change due to the state interference.

Nevertheless, currently, many countries, such as the United States, detain both unaccompanied children and migrant families. Sometimes, family unity is mistakenly invoked. In others, like Mexico, it has been argued that detention is a protective measure for the children in vulnerable circumstances (Ceriani Cernadas, 2013). Arguments of this kind apply traditional pre-CRC policies in which the child is an object of assistance rather than being a subject of rights. Such policies were, and in many countries continue to be, an amalgam of welfare programmes and mechanisms of social control – in this case, of border control. In a number of countries, the situation is even more serious, since detention can be resorted to without any justification and can thus be directly utilized to meet the objectives of immigration control and the supposed interests of national and international security.

The principle of non-detention leads to the design of alternative measures, guided by the principles and obligations of the CRC, rather than the objectives of migration control. This entails the inclusion of alternative measures in legislation, and requirement from the competent authorities to implement these alternative measures effectively and to ensure mechanisms for permanent and independent monitoring for compliance. Ultimately, in the case of unaccompanied children, if policies are to be oriented towards determining the best interests of the child, then it is essential that the child be sheltered in a place that has adequate conditions for carrying out this purpose.

4.2.3. Due process of law guarantees in detention and deportation procedures

As long as a migration procedure may lead to a repatriation or deportation measure against a child and/or his or her parents, it is essential to ensure as the very minimum an entire series of guarantees of due process. Correspondingly, if a detention measure is ordered for an unaccompanied child or a family (based upon the migration circumstances or even by way of an alternative measure applied in lieu of detention, the decision should be adopted within the framework of legal due process.

Therefore, due process of law should be guaranteed to migrant children both *de jure* and *de facto* in all decisions – border admission, deportation or repatriation, detention or alternative measures, etc. The set of guarantees includes, firstly, *the right to be heard and participate*, critical in every procedure, particularly those involving unaccompanied children. In this regard, the OHCHR (2010) has stated that with respect to border control, orders for return, or access to social services, decisions should not be reached without consulting the affected children. Migrant children should also be able to be heard in a variety of judicial or administrative settings including in all aspects of immigration and asylum proceedings. The irregular status of children should not limit their right to participation. On the contrary, in order to fully guarantee and implement a Best Interest Determination process, children's opinions and voices must be considered.

Other key guarantees that all child migrants should effectively be able to exercise are: the right to be informed of all matters concerning their rights, migration procedures and safeguards; the right to an interpreter, critical for ensuring children's right to be heard; the right to access justice and effective remedies, in both administrative and judicial procedures; and the right to consular assistance.

In the case of unaccompanied children – whether there is a BID Procedure or not – two additional essential guarantees are the right to a legal representative and a guardian. In order to effectively secure the rights provided, migrant children must be granted adequate, prompt, and free legal assistance, including the assignment of a guardian or legal representative to defend their rights, interests and secure their welfare (CRC Committee, 2005: §21, 33–37). Children should have access to legal aid services that specifically deal with migration issues and the rights of migrants. Even so, these guarantees should also be taken into account in the framework of other procedures, especially those determining the most adequate option for the case. It is equally important that legal advisers be properly trained in children's rights and that they work with professionals from other disciplines, including child psychologists.

In addition, in order to give substance to the right to be heard and to participate, it is vital that all relevant personnel are adequately trained in applying a child-sensitive, rights-based approach to their tasks. This includes the figure of the guardian, who should be an independent advocate for the child's best interest both when the process takes place and in any decision to be adopted.

4.2.4. Children's rights and parents' detention and deportation

Detention and deportation of migrant parents greatly impacts children's lives and their human rights. Parents caught up in immigration enforcement processes are separated from their young children and often disappear into the detention system. If no relative is identified who can take the children, at the time of an immigrant parent's apprehension, these children may be placed in state custody or foster homes, abruptly unable to communicate with their parents or even to know where their parents are living. If parents choose to accept deportation (often at the encouragement of immigration officials), they run the risk of being forever separated from their children, given that in all likelihood these children will be unable to accompany them as long as they remain in state custody.

Recent reports have shown how the enforcement of immigration control policies – detention and deportation of parents – without consideration of the child's best interest, has led to thousands of shattered families and a correspondingly dramatic impact on children's rights and welfare. These reports also describe the lack of policies facilitating family reunification between child nationals born in destination countries and their deported parents, not only in the countries where parents have been removed, but also in their countries of origin (Applied Research Center, 2011; University of Arizona, 2011), and reveal the strong impact on child development and family bonds (Beckles Flores, 2011).

In these situations, a children's rights perspective implies that alternative measures for parents must be developed in order to protect children. In this regard, when analysing parents' status, authorities must fully consider the right to family life and the situation of the child, especially if ties to the host country have been developed or if the child was born in the country contemplating a deportation measure. A more comprehensive response considering the overall interests of the child and the future of the whole family is preferred. A child's best interests requires the adoption of alternative policies addressing the migration status of the parents, including alternatives to detention and mechanisms protecting the family unit and child development, mental health etc., through regularization rather than deportation.

Ultimately, as has already been mentioned, the best interests of the child in conjunction with other rights at play, can lead to a situation in which the state grants residence to a migrant family in an irregular situation rather than imposing a punishment of expulsion. The development of the child in the destination country, her personality, identity, social and community relationships, among others factors, will be seriously affected by an expulsion, impacting her mental and emotional health as well. In these circumstances, it does not appear that the mere state goal of punishing (administrative) infractions is serious enough to justify meddling in the lives of these children. Neither, of course, does it justify separating the family through the expulsion of the parents.

4.3. Children's right to family life

In the previous section we have seen how the right to family life should be taken into account by immigration control mechanisms. This right is recognized in numerous international and regional human rights treaties.[19] Nevertheless, in the domain of immigration policies and practices, or even in the decisions of international tribunals regarding migration (such as the European Court of Human Rights; Ceriani Cernadas, 2009),[20] it seems that this right carries less weight.

---

19 Articles 8, 9, 10, 16, 20 and 22 of the Convention on the Rights of the Child; Article 10, International Covenant on Economic, Social and Cultural Rights; and Articles 17 and 23, International Covenant on Civil and Political Rights; Article 8, European Convention on Human Rights and Fundamental Freedoms; Article 17, American Convention on Human Rights.
20 More recently, the European Court of Human Rights has acknowledged that the right to respect for family life may be violated by detaining children accompanying their parents (ECtHR 19 January 2012, *Popov v. France*, §§116–117).

An important aspect of the right to family life in the context of migration is family reunification. The procedures on family reunification can be decisive for achieving a regular migration process under dignified and appropriate conditions for the child. By contrast, the inexistence of such mechanisms or the imposition of unreasonable restrictions may lead to the weakening of rights and other risks.

For instance, the principle of family unity has an important protective function for children in the context of migration, particularly in the case of irregular migrant children. However, increasing restrictions on the right to family reunification in destination countries have led to the irregular migration of children and adolescents seeking to reunite with their parents.

Moreover, children's right to family life has been increasingly impacted by policies that prioritize migration control goals over the protection of children's rights. In the United States, more than 70,000 migrants that were removed from the country in 2013, alleged they had one or more US-born children.[21] An estimated 4.5 million US citizen children have at least one parent who is undocumented (Human Impact Partners, 2013).

Parents' irregular migration status at destination, along with restrictive regularization mechanisms (and absence of regularization programmes) may present long-term obstacles for family reunification. This situation can prolong or augment the social exclusion of migrant families, may impact on child development, and lead to family disruption. In this regard, it is important to stress that other migrants' rights issues, such as access to a regular residence, access to social rights regardless of residence status, the extension of migration control mechanisms at work, at social services and other public spaces, may considerably impact the right to family life and other related children's rights enshrined in the CRC of child migrants and children born to migrant parents. Addressing such issues could be critical for ensuring that parents are able to fulfil their responsibilities for child development (UNICEF, 2012).

4.4. Social rights of migrants: A key for child development and social integration

The CRC recognizes social rights[22] for all persons less than 18 years of age on the basis of the principles of universality, non-discrimination, and best interests (among others, in Articles 23–32). The exercise of these rights is indispensable, in turn, for the right to survival and development, and the right to an adequate standard of living. The International Covenant on Economic, Social and Cultural Rights also recognizes these rights, which may not be subjected to any kind of discrimination, including nationality or immigration status (ESCR Committee, 2009).

However, migrants, particularly those with irregular migration status, often work in precarious and dangerous jobs; they are excluded from health, education, and other social welfare institutions, or else their access to these systems is subject to additional conditions compared to nationals and they are often victims of exploitation in the housing market (Special Rapporteur, 2010; Cuadra, 2011). In countries of transit and destination, children who hold irregular immigration status are often discriminated against; they face restrictions in accessing basic rights and services such as education, housing, health care, and social security.

Unaccompanied children who migrate irregularly often live in precarious situations and are especially vulnerable to discrimination and difficulties when accessing basic social services.

---

21 www.huffingtonpost.com/2014/06/25/parents-deportation_n_5531552.html.
22 Social rights include a range of human rights such as the right to health, education, social security, and the right to an adequate standard of living.

Without documented status, in many countries they face difficulties acquiring education and health care, and risk facing hunger, homelessness, and sexual or labour exploitation. Moreover, they may end up living with poor or undocumented migrant caregivers, living and working on the streets, or becoming domestic or seasonal farm or mine workers.

Even when countries have laws providing rights and protection to undocumented migrant children and adolescents, there are often huge discrepancies between policy and practice that prevent these groups from enjoying their rights. These barriers, include, *inter alia*, administrative obstacles, linguistic hurdles, the complexity of the administrative, judicial, and other systems, discrimination, lack of information, fear of being reported, etc. For instance, the law may guarantee universal access to primary education, but schools may request documents prior to enrolling students (see also Vandenhole *et al.*, 2011 on education).

The rights and development of children in the context of migration are often tied to the condition of their migrant parents. The situation and safeguards provided to their parents may critically impact children' lives. Children born to irregular migrant parents in host countries are at risk of being denied legal status. There are countries – such as the Dominican Republic – in which children of undocumented workers and refugees are automatically classified as undocumented by virtue of the irregular status of their parents, a situation that may lead to the statelessness of children.

Removing these policies in host countries will assist in the effort to fulfil the economic and social rights of undocumented migrant adults, including the right to work; this right not only has a critical impact on other human rights, but is also paramount for ensuring the right to development and the right to an adequate standard of living for the migrants' children, who may have migrated regularly or irregularly, may have been left behind, or may be nationals of host countries. In addition, the lack of regularization programmes to benefit parents could negatively impact their children's rights and undermine their opportunities for improving their socio-economic conditions.

Moreover, it is important to note that the social rights of migrants can also be directly or indirectly affected by the mechanisms of immigration control. Some States have laws and policies that impose a duty on public officials and also on private actors – e.g., health care and education workers, and landlords, among others – to report undocumented migrants to immigration authorities (HUMA Network, 2009; UNICEF-UNLa, 2010). Such policies deter irregular migrants, including children, from accessing fundamental social rights. These constraints negatively impact children's right to development and right to an adequate standard of living, and contribute to the social exclusion and marginalization of migrant families.

These practices are difficult to reconcile with international standards. First, it is completely unjustifiable and discriminatory, explicitly or implicitly, to consider an irregular migration status (an administrative infraction) as a ground for denying access to social services. Second, this distinction based on migration status – much like the restrictions on the social rights of migrants in general – is yet more evidence not only of discriminatory treatment, but also of the absence of a child's rights-based perspective. The impact on the life and rights of children, whose basic rights are already severely limited, can be decisive to their physical and mental health, and appropriate and worthwhile development in the short and long terms. These restrictions on social rights are usually populist devices to send messages to the host society, suggesting on the one hand, that these measures will improve the living conditions of the national population, and on the other, that they will lower the cost of social services. In this regard, it should be noted that affecting the social rights of children may impede the process of social integration and increase the rates of social conflict and segregation – effectively mortgaging the future of the whole society and increasing the overall (monetary and non-monetary) toll on the society.

Ensuring access to basic social rights of migrants is a *sine qua non* condition for social integration and cohesion in host societies, thus facilitating the contribution of migrants to the human development of destination countries and countries of origin, and preventing social exclusion, poverty, and economic disparities (Mahal and Marks, 2007: 36). As to the costs-based argument, trustworthy data do not only prove this reduction of layout, but they also point to the contrary: the abridgement of social rights – for example, the right to health – tends to have a negative impact in the middle and long term, including in terms of "economic profitability". For instance, granting undocumented migrants access to only emergency health services, could lead to higher costs of these services due to the treatment of illness that could have been easily prevented if all migrants could have access to preventive health services.

To sum up, in light of the impact of denying social rights and of migration control mechanisms on social services, it is appropriate to highlight the key functions that migration regularization can fulfil. This refers not only to extraordinary regularization plans, but rather, especially, the permanent mechanisms for accessing a regular status, including those that prevent the transition to irregular status by those persons who already have residence. The recognition of labour connections, roots in society, family ties, or concretely, the state of vulnerability of child migrants and children of migrants, should lead to the granting of residence, as does indeed occur in some South–South destination countries (such as Argentina), rather than expulsion from the country or the denial of social rights.

For these reasons, it is appropriate to focus on several positive effects that these regularization mechanisms can have for migrants, states, and the societies of both origin and destination countries.

(a) Benefits *for migrants*: the family unit is ensured and family reunification is permitted, migrant workers are entitled to work and improve their families' socio-economic conditions; children may not face risks and limitations at schools, and adolescents can apply for education, training, and employment opportunities under equal conditions; migrants are in a better position to challenge abuses; it becomes easier to integrate migrants into society; migrants can access public services, including services to protect children at risk; migrants also can obtain fair wages.

(b) Benefits *for host societies*: governments are able to better record the number and circumstances of migrants in their territory; they can better promote formal, protected employment and prevent exploitation and human trafficking; they can meet public security goals; they can improve tax revenues and fiscal gains; they can benefit through the increased contribution of migrants to human and economic development; they can strengthen family protection and migrants' integration, reducing attrition rates within the education system; they can benefit from qualified adolescents and their contribution to future generations; they can improve salaries and labour conditions through migrants' empowerment and the exercise of labour and union rights.

(c) Benefits *to countries of origin* include: regularized migrants can increase their remittances positively affecting their families' living conditions and hence their consumption levels and contributions to society; similarly, migrants' willingness and capability to contribute to the development of their country of origin will improve; family reunification will be facilitated and family ties and communication maintained; conditions will be promoted for migrants to return to their country with new, improved skills (UNICEF-UNLa, 2011).

4.5. Children's rights and the duties of countries of origin

The countries of origin should be responsible for different types of necessary action in ensuring children's human rights in the context of migration. This section will briefly point out some measures that these states should develop or strengthen.

First, of course, countries of origin have an essential role to play in guaranteeing the rights of the child in order to prevent migration arising from necessity, the deprivation of basic rights, or the absence of public policies for children. The social programmes that protect the rights of children (either directly, or by ensuring parents' rights through facilitating and monitoring compliance of parental obligations) require a series of public policies; for instance, the state must be the primary guarantor of the rights of the persons within its jurisdiction, regardless of the obligations of other more developed states or the international community in general, as was seen in the analysis of the root causes of migration.

Regarding the children left behind, the countries of origin should, on the one hand, design public policies that take into account their needs and vulnerabilities that are direct consequences of the migration of their parents. On the other hand, these states should adopt measures to facilitate – if that is the wish of the family and/or in the best interests of the child – the regularization of the entire family or eventually familial reunification in the destination country. Unquestionably, the latter requires bilateral, regional, and global foreign policy initiatives.

In transit and destination countries, countries of origin must comply with the pivotal duty of consular assistance, which, like all public policy must have a human rights-based focus, including a children's rights perspective; this requires having a legal framework, budget, and personnel trained in children's rights. Consular assistance is also a strategic tool for enabling origin countries to compile and systematize the information necessary for constructing public policies that address children's rights in the context of migration. Key information about the causes of migration emerges from consular protections and their link to child migrants (accompanied or not), especially with regard to abuses in the origin, transit, or destination country, human trafficking networks, policy shortcomings in the destination country, etc.

It is important to note that consular protection may be necessary for avoiding the arbitrary detention and deportation of unaccompanied children or migrant families, or familial separation as a consequence of the deportation of the parents. As such, it performs a central function in the BID Procedure. In effect, in order to ensure the rights of unaccompanied children within these procedures, origin countries should not only guarantee consular assistance, but also design policies and practices that allow the compiling of necessary information in every case, so that agencies in the destination countries are able to determine best interests in light of all possible factors, thereby avoiding risks and securing the adoption of appropriate short- and long-term decisions.

Finally, though this is by no means an exhaustive list, the obligation of designing policies ensuring the return of unaccompanied children must be mentioned. This should be the beginning of a process of social reintegration within a context of effective exercise of rights, one that allows children to enjoy the right to development and an adequate standard of living.[23]

5. Final thoughts and issues for discussion

The situation of children in the context of migration has been increasingly included in the agenda of a number of key stakeholders: states, international organizations, civil society, academic institutions and media, among others. This chapter has sought to analyse some of the

---

23 Regarding the deficiencies of reintegration processes, such as the shortcomings of current policies of consular protection in some Central American countries, see Ceriani Cernadas (2013) and Casa Alianza Honduras (2012).

basic characteristics of the children and migration nexus, paying special attention to how children's rights should be taken into account in migration, childhood and other related policies that affect the life and rights of migrants and their families. Some of the main challenges and threats to the effective exercise of these rights have been pointed out.

There is a paramount challenge on how to address the different aspects of the current situation of children affected by migration. A comprehensive and rights-based approach is critical for properly coping with such challenges in the short and long term. Introducing the human rights of children to the field of migration policy entails a paradigm shift, which, among other factors, replaces the traditional machinery of the immigration agencies with children's protection bodies and services, complemented by other social policies aimed at ensuring human rights to all individuals.

There are many social, economic, cultural and political challenges to achieving this paradigm change; it requires the creation of opportunities for dialogue and debate among the different sectors: states, civil organisms, academic factions, international agencies, and, of course, the participation of children. It also needs the adoption of policies and measures at local, national, regional and global level by the countries of origin, transit and destination. Addressing the root causes of migration is essential not only regarding poverty, unemployment and other causes in origin countries, but also in host countries, such as demographic necessities and the increasing demand of informal, unprotected sectors of the labour market. Inequalities within and between countries must also be addressed in depth.

In destination countries, public policies should fulfil human rights to every person regardless of their nationality and residence status. These duties would imply a shift of the paradigm that reigns in the field of migration policies. In this regard, a comprehensive approach should lead to reducing the migration control focus and replace it by a rights-based lens, including a children's rights perspective.

Questions for debate and discussion

- What could or would be the implications of an age approach or child rights-based approach to migration? In your view, would it lead to a paradigm shift in migration policies, as this chapter has argued?
- Does the children's rights framework contain all the necessary elements (principles, standards, mechanisms) to provoke a paradigm change in migration policies? Are there gaps, if any, in the children's rights framework, or in the CRC in particular?
- Which principles or standards of the children's rights framework hold most potential to lead to a paradigm shift in migration policies? How could a plea for regularization policies be underpinned by a children's rights argument?
- Which image of childhood prevails in a children's rights approach to migration policies? Do you see a need for changing that? Why or why not?
- Should children and adults be treated differently in migration? Should different human rights principles and norms apply to both groups?

References

Abramovich,V. and Ceriani P. Morlachetti (2011), *The Rights of Children, Youth and Women in the Context of Migration. Conceptual Basis and Principles for Effective Policies with a Human Rights and Gender Based Approach*, UNICEF, Social and Economic Policy, Working Paper, New York.
Abramson, Bruce (2008), "Article 2: The Right of Non-Discrimination" in Alen, A., Vande Lanotte, J.,

Verhellen, E., Ang, F., Berghmans, E. and Verheyde, M. (eds), *A Commentary on the United Nations Convention on the Rights of the Child*, Martinus Nijhoff, Leiden.
American Physiological Association (2013), *The Psychosocial Impact of Detention and Deportation on U.S. Migrant Children and Families*, A Report for the Inter-American Human Rights Court, August, 2013.
Applied Research Center (2011), *Shattered Families: The Perilous Intersection of Immigration Enforcement and the Child Welfare System*, Publisher of Colorlines.com, November 2011.
Beckles Flores, Erika (2011), *Waiting for your return: A phenomenological study on parental deportation and the impact on the family and the parent child attachment bond*, Marriage and Family Therapy, Dissertations and Theses, Paper 42. Available at http://surface.syr.edu/mft_etd/42.
Bhabha, Jaqueline (2008), *Independent Children, Inconsistent Adults: Child migration and the legal framework*, UNICEF Innocenti Research Centre Discussion Paper, IDP No. 2008-02.
Casa Alianza Honduras (2012), *Análisis de la situación de Derechos de la Infancia Migrante No Acompañada en el marco de los procedimientos de deportación y retorno a Honduras*, Tegucigalpa, junio de 2012.
Ceriani Cernadas, Pablo (ed.) (2013), *Niñez Detenida. Los derechos de niños, niñas y adolescentes migrantes en la frontera México-Guatemala* [Detained Childhood. The Human Rights of Migrant Children and Adolescents in the Mexican-Guatemalan Border], Fontamara, Distrito Federal, México.
Ceriani Cernadas, Pablo (2009), *Los derechos de migrantes sin residencia legal en la jurisprudencia del Tribunal Europeo de Derechos Humanos: un balance complejo ante la realidad y los retos de la inmigración en la región*, in Ceriani and Fava (Coords.), *Políticas Migratorias y Derechos Humanos*, Ed. UNLa, Buenos Aires.
Chetail, Vincent and Bauloz, Céline (eds) (2014), *Research Handbook on International Law and Migration*, Cheltenham, Edward Elgar.
Cortina, Jeronimo, and Hovy, Bela (2009), *Boosting Cooperation: UNICEF, UNDESA and SU/SSC Joint Studies on Migration*, in South-South in Action, Summer 2009, Media Global, Voice of the Global South, United Nations Secretariat, New York.
Council of Europe, Parliamentary Assembly (2011), *Unaccompanied children in Europe: issues of arrival, stay and return*, Report Committee on Migration, Refugees and Population, Doc. 12539, 21 March 2011.
CPT (European Committee for the Prevention of Torture and Inhuman or Degrading Treatment or Punishment) (2009), *20 years of combating torture, 19th General Report*, 1 August 2008–31 July 2009.
CRC Committee (UN Committee on the Rights of the Child) (2013), General comment No. 14, *On the right of the child to have his or her best interests taken as a primary consideration* (Art. 3, para. 1), CRC/C/GC/14, 29 May.
CRC Committee (UN Committee on the Rights of the Child) (2012), *The Rights of All Children in the Context of International Migration*, 2012 Day of General Discussion Background Paper, Geneva, August 2012.
CRC Committee (UN Committee on the Rights of the Child) (2005), General Comment No. 6, *Treatment of Unaccompanied or Separated Children outside their Country of Origin*, CRC/GC/2005/6, 1 September.
Cuadra, Carin Björngren (2011), *Right of access to health care for undocumented migrants in EU: a comparative study of national policies*, The European Journal of Public Health Advance Access, Oxford University Press, June 9.
Dutschke, Mira, and Abrahams, Kashifa (2006), *Children's Right to Maximum Survival and Development*, Children's Institute, University of Cape Town, August 2006, Cape Town.
Düvell, Franck (2011), Paths into Irregularity: The Legal and Political Construction of Irregular Migration, *European Journal of Migration and Law*, 13, 275–295.
Duvell, Franck (2008), Clandestine migration in Europe. *Social Science Information*, 47(4), 479–497.
ESCR Committee (UN Committee on Economic, Social, and Cultural Rights) (2009), *Non-discrimination in economic, social and cultural rights (Art. 2, para. 2, of the International Covenant on Economic, Social and Cultural Rights)*, General Comment No. 20, E/C.12/GC/20, 2 July 2009.
GCIM (Global Commission on International Migration) (2005), *Migration in an Interconnected World: New Directions for Action*, Report of the Global Commission on International Migration, Geneva. Available at www.gcim.org/en/finalreport.html
Gonzales Roberto G. and Angie M. Bautista-Chavez (2014), *Two Years and Counting: Assessing the growing Power of DACA*, American Immigration Council, June 2014.
HUMA Network (2009), *Access to Health Care for Undocumented Migrants and Asylum Seekers in 11 EU countries*, September 2009.
Human Impact Partners (2013), *Family Unity, Family Health. How Family-Focused Immigration Reform Will Mean Better Health for Children and Families*, Oakland, June 2013.

Human Rights Council (2009), *Human rights of migrants: migration and the human rights of the child*, Session 12, A/HRC/12/L.16.

ICMPD, International Centre for Migration Policy Development (2001–2011), *Annual Yearbook on Illegal Migration, Human Smuggling and Trafficking in Central and Eastern Europe*, Vienna.

ICPD, International Conference on Population and Development (1994), *Program of Action*, Cairo.

IIN, Inter-American Children's Institute (2010), *Menu of Indicators and Monitoring System for Children's Right to Participation*, Organization of American States, Montevideo, October 2010.

INM-CEM, Instituto Nacional de Migración – Centro de Estudios Migratorios (2011), *Migración centroamericana de tránsito irregular por México. Estimaciones y características generales*, in *Apuntes sobre migración* [Survey on migration at the southern border of Mexico. 2008. Historic Series 2004–2008], No. 1, July 2011.

Inter-American Court of Human Rights (2003), *Advisory Opinion OC-18/03, Juridical Condition and Rights of Undocumented Migrants*, San José, 17 September 2003.

Inter-American Court of Human Rights (2014), *Advisory Opinion OC-21/14, Rights and Guarantees of Children in the Context of Migration and/or in Need of International Protection*, 19 August 2014.

IOM, International Organization for Migration (2010), *The Future of Migration. Building Capacities for Change*, World Migration Report, Geneva.

Kuhner, Gretchen (2010), *El impacto de la migración irregular en la familia. Mujeres y Niñas, Niños y Adolescentes (NNA) en tránsito por México: Un reto regional* [Irregular migration and its impact on families. Women, children and adolescents in transit through Mexico: a regional challenge], presentación realizada en la XV Conferencia Regional sobre Migración (CRM), Seminario Regional sobre Migración y Familia, Colegio de la Frontera Norte, Tijuana, 21–23 abril de 2010.

Mahal, Ajay, and Stephen Marks (2007), *Goals and Instruments of Poverty Reduction: Economic and human rights perspectives on children's rights and development strategies*. Cambridge, MA: University of Harvard.

Mercosur Member States (2011), *Request for Advisory Opinion on Migrant Children before the Inter-American Court of Human Rights*, Buenos Aires, April 2011

OHCHR, UN Office of the High Commissioner for Human Rights (2010), *Study of the Office of the United Nations High Commissioner for Human Rights on challenges and best practices in the implementation of the international framework for the protection of the rights of the child in the context of migration*. submitted to the Human Rights Council, A/HRC/15/29, 5 July 2010, Geneva.

Rafferty, Yvonne (2007), Children for Sale: Child Trafficking in Southeast Asia. *Child Abuse Review*, 16, 401–422.

Salomon, Margot (2008), "Legal Cosmopolitanism and the Normative Contribution of the Right to Development", in Marks, Stephen E. (editor), *Implementing the Right to Development: the role of International Law*, FriedrichEbert-Stiftung, Geneva.

Skogly, Sigrun (2002), *The Human Rights Obligations of the World Bank and the International Monetary Fund*, Cavendish Publishing Limited, London.

Special Rapporteur on the Human Rights of Migrants (2012), *Report of the Special Rapporteur on the situation on the Human Rights of Migrants*, A/HRC/20/24, 2 April 2012.

Special Rapporteur on the Human Rights of Migrants (2009), *Report of the Special Rapporteur on the Human Rights of Migrants*, submitted to the Human Rights Council, A/HRC/11/7, Geneva, 14 May 2009.

Touzenis, Katerina (2008), *Human Rights of Migrant Children*, edited by the International Organization for Migration, Geneva.

UN General Assembly (2010), *Guidelines for the Alternative Care of Children: resolution / adopted by the General Assembly*, 24 February 2010, A/RES/64/142. Available at www.refworld.org/docid/4c3acd162.html

UNHCR, UN High Commissioner for Refugees (2014), *Children on the Run. Unaccompanied children leaving Central America and Mexico and the Need for International Protection*, Washington, DC: Author.

UNHCR, UN High Commissioner for Refugees (2008), *UNHCR Guidelines on Determining the Best Interests of the Child*, Geneva: Author.

UNICEF (2012), *Amicus Curiae submitted by UNICEF Latin American Regional Office before the Inter-American Court of Human Rights*, San José, Costa Rica, 17 February 2012. Available at www.corteidh.or.cr/ soloc.cfm (in Spanish).

UNICEF-UNLa (2011), *Children and Adolescents in the Context of Irregular Migration*, Working Paper (In Progress), Draft, November 2011, New York-Lanús.

UNICEF-UNLa (2010), *Estudio sobre los estándares jurídicos básicos aplicables a niños y niñas migrantes en situación migratoria irregular en América Latina y el Caribe. Estándares jurídicos básicos y líneas de acción para su protección*, Panamá.

UNLa/UNICEF (2009), Estudio sobre los estándares jurídicos básicos aplicables a niños y niñas migrantes en situación migratoria irregular en América Latina y el Caribe. Available at www.unla.edu.ar/rectorado/centros/cdh/index.php

University of Arizona (2011), *Disappearing Parents: A Report on Immigration Enforcement and the Child Welfare System*, Southwest Institute for Research on Women and the James E. Rogers College of Law University of Arizona, May 2011.

Vandenhole, Wouter, Carton de Wiart, Estelle, Marie-Lou de Clerck, Helene, Mahieu, Paul, Ryngaert, Julie, Timmerman, Christiane, and Verhoeven, Marie (2011), The right to education of undocumented children: illusory right or empowering lever? *International Journal of Children's Rights*, 19(4), 613–639.

Vandenhole, Wouter (2014), "Migration and Discrimination: Non-Discrimination as Guardian against Arbitrariness or Driver of Integration?" In V. Chetail and C. Bauloz (ed.), *Research Handbook on International Law and Migration*, Cheltenham, UK: Edward Elgar, 216–238.

20
Child poverty in the context of global social development

Francine Mestrum

Specific actions against child poverty are most welcome. However, they should be framed within a broader context that looks beyond poverty and beyond age-determined groups. From a sociological point of view, poverty is a social relationship that cannot be de-linked from the societal context in which it originates and exists. The new focus of international organisations on universal social protection instead of on 'poverty reduction' may help to achieve this. Working exclusively at the level of child poverty entails a serious risk of ignoring or neglecting its broader causes and consequences. Reducing child poverty cannot be a solution when poverty in general and impoverishment processes continue to exist.

According to UNICEF, the United Nations (UN) Children's Fund, 1.4 million young people between 10 and 19 years old die every year because of accidents, suicides, criminality and aids. Around 50,000 young women under 19 die during pregnancy or while giving birth. One fourth of girls between 15 and 19 in developing countries are married. For young children under 10, the main causes of death in developing countries are diarrhea and measles. A quarter of young children are not getting enough nutrients to grow properly. Three hundred of them die every hour because of malnutrition. In many families children have to skip school to help their parents at work. Over the past five years, the price of food has soared across the globe, due to extreme weather conditions, diverting farmland to grow bio-fuels, speculative trading of food commodities and the global financial crisis (UNICEF, 2012; FAO, 2013).

This list is endless. We can complete it with the number of children at work – more than 200 million – children in forced labour – more than one million – and high percentages of youth unemployment – up to or more than 55 percent in rich countries like Greece and Spain, or even more than 50 percent in some municipalities of the rich region of Brussels (ILO, 2012a; European Commission, 2013; Irisnet, 2013).

At the June 2012 UN Conference Rio+20 on sustainable development, the focus was on solidarity with future generations, and rightly so. But it is clear there should be no hope for this as long as we do not succeed in organising intra-generational solidarity and care for the generations that are with us already, the world's children.

While the Bretton Woods institutions – World Bank and International Monetary Fund (IMF) – continue to stress the importance of poverty reduction and the progress that has been reached in reducing extreme poverty, UN organisations have realised this cannot be the only answer. It is impossible to fight poverty while leaving the poverty-creating economic policies unchanged and without tackling inequality. Several UN services and organisations are now promoting a transformative universal social protection. The International Labour Organisation (ILO) has adopted at its 2012 International Labour Conference a recommendation on 'Social Protection Floors' (UNRISD, 2010; United Nations, 2010a, 2010b; CEPAL, 2011; ILO, 2012b).

In an immensely rich world with all the possibilities and resources to solve social problems, the current social situation cannot be justified. It shows the urgency of adopting new policies and questioning some of the most 'obvious' ideas about poverty in general and child poverty in particular. In this contribution, I want to adopt a critical approach, challenging some of the most 'obvious' ideas and questioning some of the practices that characterise work on child poverty. In this way, space can be created for alternative ideas and for a more holistic approach to poverty and wealth.

While children's rights are extremely important in trying to solve some of the most urgent problems children are faced with, the solutions will not sustainably help if they are not linked to the broader context of human rights. Moreover, this legal approach will have to be completed with a sociological perspective in order to take into account the societal context in which children are living.

1. Poverty and globalisation

I want to argue that globalisation is the best remedy to fight poverty. But in order to avoid all misunderstandings, let me add immediately that it is a totally different kind of globalisation I want to promote and that child poverty will not be tackled as a separate problem from poverty in general and more particularly from inequality. I am not an anti-globalist, but an alter-globalist and a Kantian internationalist. This means I do consider the world to be a 'global village' in which nation-states only have a limited relevance, and that international cooperation based on respect and the awareness of our interdependence are crucial.

The globalisation we have known in the past decades was focused on the economy, global trade and deregulated finances. While global trade can indeed be useful to develop economies, it can never do so without taking into account the power relations. 'Kicking away the ladder' when you arrived at the top and shouting to those waiting on the ground that they only have to come up and join you, is not the best and most honest way to promote global economic development (Chang, 2002). Deregulating finance in such a way that profit maximising with citizen's bank deposits becomes the only objective, while banks can blackmail governments, is the most direct way to crisis and collective impoverishment of populations. This neoliberal globalisation has reached its limits and should urgently be put to an end (Crouch, 2011).

The same goes for political globalisation. The global institutions that were set up after the Second World War have reached their limits. In spite of changing economic relations, 'emerging' countries like India, Brazil, South Africa or Nigeria have no real say in world affairs as they are decided on in the UN Security Council. China and Russia are members of the UN highest body, but have insufficient votes to weigh on decisions in the World Bank or the IMF. Dominant countries from Europe and America are declining, but do keep the power to decide on war and peace, on development or social regression. The time has come to re-balance power relations and to respect the right to self-determination as well as to re-examine the sovereignty of nations and peoples.[1] Current multilateralism is in crisis and the newly created G20 does not make any real difference (Wahl, 2012).

It has become clear by now what neoliberalism means. It is a political programme more than an economic programme. It aims at promoting markets and corporations and basically wants to shape a new kind of state in favour of protecting global markets, competitiveness, property rights and consumer welfare. It is not concerned anymore with domestic markets, social integration or equality and that is why it promotes poverty reduction and breaks away from social protection – economic and social rights. An analysis of the poverty discourse of the World Bank of the 1990s shows that its focus on poverty was not meant to improve or complete existing social security, but on the contrary to replace it with poverty reduction policies. These policies then are not the 'human face of globalisation' but its masterpiece for dismantling welfare states (Mestrum, 2002). Current developments in the European Union confirm these findings (Mestrum, 2014).

Putting an end to neoliberal globalisation and to Washington Consensus policies[2] does not mean falling back on autarchy and closed borders. On the contrary, it means an honest negotiation on how we can keep humankind alive in a world with the threats of climate change, on how we can share responsibilities and resources, on how we can organise global solidarity.

I want to argue that globalisation and development should be synonymous, by which I mean that development, in the North and South, should be re-thought in order to take into account climate change, the needs of poor populations, and (also in the North and South), the levelling out of industrial and agricultural productive capacities. In the same way, taking into account the worldwide protest movements of these past years, solidarity should be looked at again, in order to give people the protection they need and deserve, wherever they live and in whatever political regime they live. An alternative globalisation should mean the eradication of poverty and of impoverishment processes, as well as the drastic reduction of inequalities. Together with a shift in power relations, this should lead to comparable development levels in all countries while maintaining people's sovereignty. In other words, it means global and shared responsibilities for managing the Earth and its peoples, articulated to regional, national and local responsibilities for practically organising states, economies and societies.

This is a Kantian, idealistic vision because the realistic vision based on interests will, in a world with scarcer basic resources like water and food, necessarily lead to more and harsher conflicts between states and people competing for them. It is not a matter of 'common interests' – the interests of rich and poor countries, of rich and poor classes are different – but of 'balanced interests' – the result of negotiations on whose interests can be promoted and to what extent. What we need, then, is an enlightened vision on what is possible and necessary to respect everyone's human rights, supposing these rights are universally accepted. Such a vision will not be achieved overnight and may always remain a faraway dream. But in order to start and work at the necessary reforms and changes, we need a utopia; we need to know what we work for and what the objective can be. Promoting children's rights requires this fundamental

---

1 UNCTAD LDC-reports have been pleading for a long time for more policy autonomy for poor countries.
2 'Washington Consensus' is the name used for the neoliberal policies and reforms introduced after the external debt crisis of the 1980s (see Williamson, 1990). The main thrust of these policies has been maintained throughout the following decades and are now applied in Europe.

change, since these rights cannot be de-linked from human rights in general and human rights cannot be de-linked from the political and societal context in which they exist.

This is the background against which I propose to look at children's poverty today. In the following section, I want to take a brief look at global poverty reduction policies and their results. In section three I look at the semantic confusion around 'poverty' and the difficulties this entails for the measurement of child poverty and for specific policies for children. Section four looks at the ideology of poverty, which means that more often than not poverty reduction policies are not meant to help poor people in the first place. We have to search for other reasons to explain the current focus on child poverty. In the conclusion I repeat that child poverty cannot be de-linked from poverty in general and from its societal context. While academic research may need to single out specific issues, their policy implications should include the broader context in which they are present.

2. Poverty reduction policies

The international community has now two parallel strategies to fight poverty. The first one is the 'Poverty Reduction Strategy Paper' (PRSP) process, introduced by the IMF and World Bank in 1999. It requires poor countries to present to the institutions a poverty strategy, defined through participation with major stakeholders. The 'ownership' principle on which it is based is limited, however, by the fact that the strategy has to be accepted by the Joint Staff of the institutions. Analysis of the process shows that most proposals concern in the first place institutional and macro-economic reforms. The poverty dimension itself is seriously limited by a lack of resources, imposed caps on expenditures, and reliable and comparable data in most countries.[3]

The second one is the 'Millennium Development Goals' (MDG) process adopted by the UN Millennium Summit in 2000. Its main objective is to reduce extreme poverty by half by 2015, compared to 1990. It is clear that this objective will be met at the global level, thanks to serious poverty reduction in India and China. Nevertheless, other countries in which MDG policies were proclaimed, such as those of Sub-Saharan Africa, seriously lag behind. While the lack of sufficient development aid by rich countries certainly has to be blamed, it also has to be stressed that the goals, however important they are, are not linked to any coherent economic or social development strategy or to a strategy for respecting human rights (UNDP, 2010; UNCTAD, 2010).

It also has to be stressed that the two poverty reduction processes are implemented in parallel. It took almost ten years before the first references to the MDG process were to be found in some PRSPs.

Both processes are subject to severe criticism (Pogge; Mestrum and Özden). Knowing that extreme poverty is poverty that kills people, the main point I want to stress here is the unbelievable 'lightness' with which rich countries are buying themselves a 'good conscience' with a promise of halving extreme poverty over a period of 25 years. Faced with the failure of seriously reducing extreme poverty in Sub-Saharan Africa, the World Bank President, now repeats an old promise. Whereas President McNamara promised in 1973 to eradicate extreme poverty by the year 2000, President Kim now suggests it might be eradicated by 2030 (Mestrum, 2013), with exactly the same arguments as forty years ago.

---

3   Apart from the numerous NGOs that have published critical reports on the PRSP process, three 'official' reports from UN institutions can be mentioned: UNCTAD (2002); IMF (2007); UNRISD (2010).

Table 20.1 Extremely poor people (< $1.25/day) per region (in %)

Region	1981	1984	1987	1990	1993	1996	1999	2002	2005	2008
East Asia and Pacific	78.8	67.0	54.4	56.0	51.2	37.1	35.5	29.6	17.9	14.34
East Europe and Central Asia	1.6	1.2	1.0	1.5	3.8	4.5	5.4	5.6	5.0	0.47
Latin America and Caribbean	12.3	13.9	12.4	10.7	10.8	11.5	11.6	10.1	8.2	6.47
Middle East and North Africa	8.6	6.8	6.9	5.4	5.2	5.3	5.8	4.7	4.6	2.7
South Asia	59.4	55.6	54.1	51.1	46.1	46.9	44.1	43.8	40.3	35.9
Sub-Saharan Africa	50.8	54.7	53.4	54.9	54.8	57.5	56.4	52.7	50.4	47.5
Mean average	52.0	47.1	41.8	41.6	38.9	34.8	33.7	31.0	25.7	22.43

Source: Chen, S. and Ravallion, M. (2008). *The Developing World Is Poorer Than We Thought, But No Less Succesful in the Fight against Poverty*. WB Policy Research Working Paper 4703, August 2008.

Table 20.2 Extremely poor people (< $125/day) per region (in millions)

Region	1981	1984	1987	1990	1993	1996	1999	2002	2005	2008
East Asia and Pacific	1,088	969	826	893	852	642	636	544	337	284
East Europe and Central Asia	6.6	5.0	4.3	7.0	17.8	21.1	25.7	26.7	23.9	2.23
Latin America and Caribbean	44.9	54.3	51.4	46.7	49.7	56.0	58.8	53.7	45.1	36.85
Middle East and North Africa	14.9	12.9	14.3	12.2	12.7	13.7	16.0	13.5	14.0	8.64
South Asia	548.3	547.7	569	572	550	593	589	616	596	571
Sub-Saharan Africa	202	237	253	239	306	348	370	373	384	386
Total	1,904	1,826	1,718	1,816	1,787	1,674	1,695	1,627	1,400	1,289

Source: http://web.worldbank.org/WBSITE/EXTERNAL/TOPICS/EXTPOVERTY/0,,menuPK:336998~pagePK:149018~piPK:149093~theSitePK:336992,00.html (accessed March 2012).

3. Tackling child poverty and semantic confusion

How can one look at child poverty in this context? How can we tackle it? The first major document we have to look at is the Convention for the Rights of the Child (CRC), based on a concept of children as social subjects with their own rights. If we consider these rights as fundamental claims for the realisation of social justice and human dignity, they certainly are the most direct way to solving children's poverty. The second approach is the one now proposed by all major international development organisations, that is, a system of universal social protection, with a particular focus on children. Children do need special attention, since they are more vulnerable than adults.

However, one of the problems with a specific focus on child poverty is the definition of poverty. While statistics are necessarily made up in terms of income and consumption poverty, a global consensus exists on the 'multidimensional' nature of poverty. It means that the income deficit is not the only or main characteristic of poor people, but that other problems, such as a lack of education and training, of health care, of decent housing, of 'empowerment', of 'voice' and in general a greater vulnerability are to be taken into account.

Especially for children this seems to be very important, since it is obvious that no one will expect children to earn a living or to achieve a decent standard of living for themselves. The question then arises what specific dimensions should be taken into account for children? Education? Housing? Health care? And the question that arises spontaneously when examining these points is to what extent these dimensions are different from adult's poverty. Or in what way are these dimensions different from the needs of non-poor children?

These questions are all directly related to the semantic confusion around 'poverty'. Speaking of 'multidimensional poverty' is less obvious than it seems at first sight. The different 'dimensions' linked to poverty can be causes as well as consequences of income poverty, and according to the dimensions that are emphasised, the research and/or policy practice will be directed towards specific groups in society: female heads of household, the elderly, the disabled, children, migrants and asylum seekers, etc. The existence of different NGOs each concerned with one specific group of people also testifies to this fragmentation in social protection and poverty reduction.

The problem with poverty research as well as with policy practice is the difficulty in de-linking them from the normative approach to poverty. All definitions point to some 'deficit' and are influenced by what one thinks is economically sustainable, socially desirable or psychologically feasible. There is a lack of 'objective' poverty definitions, since the perceived 'deficit' can only be defined in relation to an arbitrary 'enough' (Novak, 1996; Mestrum, 2002; Chapter 1 in this Handbook, p. 2).

I want to argue then that while poverty reduction or eradication policies will necessarily have to be multidimensional, poverty *is*, in every market economy, an income deficit. Working on aspects like education, health, housing, etc. will need to aim at giving people an adequate income, be it in terms of allowances – in cash or in kind – or in terms of wages. Integrating the causes and consequences of poverty into its definition directly leads to an enormous semantic confusion that also exempts people from analysing the root causes of poverty and from looking at its direct consequences for different groups of people. Training people if there are no jobs or if people have to remain 'working poor' is rather useless. Empowering people in a disempowering political context can only lead to frustration.

Defining poverty in terms of income is also the only way to stay in line with the human rights of poor people. International human rights instruments clearly recognise the right to 'an adequate standard of living' (article 11 of the International Covenant on Economic, Social and Cultural Rights; art. 27 CRC). In any market economy, this is impossible without an income. This is why the ILO in its recommendation for Social Protection Floors mentions 'basic income security for children', as well as for older persons and people not active on the labour market (ILO, 2012c: point 5B).

What does this all mean for children? I want to make a distinction between specific *measurements* of child poverty and specific *policies* for them. Statistical instruments are always the first need when one plans to develop policies for a specific group of people. Even if it is far from sure that statistics on poverty can help to solve the poverty problem, for all those who want to take specific measures in favour of children, a better idea on how many children are poor and where to find these poor children is an important first step.

Income poverty clearly is not relevant to measure child poverty. But what about the measurement of multidimensional poverty? It is certainly possible to measure different types of deprivation, in terms of education, health care, housing, etc. Here, two problems arise. The first one is, to what extent do these dimensions differ from adult's poverty? Unless we assume that parents consciously discriminate against their children or unless we want to help children without helping their parents – which would be morally difficult to defend – the objective advantages of knowing how many children suffer from specific deprivations that also affect their families remain unclear. Certainly, making visible the problems of poor children may raise the awareness and point to the urgency of eradicating poverty. It also may help to break the 'vicious circle' of poverty, since children who live in poverty will carry this psychological and material burden for the rest of their lives.

The second problem is the always very difficult issue of defining the cut-off point for multidimensional measurements. How much health care and how many years of schooling are necessary for being considered non-poor? What number will trigger the 'help' that poor children are entitled to? This question is impossible to solve in an objective way and always implies arbitrary decisions.

Allow me to give an example: the UNICEF Innocenti Research Paper, *Measuring Child Poverty* (UNICEF, 2012) measures child deprivation based on 14 indicators, and children are identified as 'poor' if they lack 2 or more of these items. This gives for The Netherlands a child poverty percentage of 2.7, for Germany 8.8, for France 10.1, for the UK 5.5 and for Romania 72.6. However, if we look at relative income poverty – that is families with less than 50% of median income in their countries – The Netherlands scores 6.1 percent, Germany a comparable 8.5 percent, France 8.8 percent, the UK 12.1 percent and Romania 25.5 percent. These numbers are difficult to interpret and do not allow for general conclusions. Furthermore, the results may be very different if you start to count as 'poor' from 3 instead of 2 indicators, an arbitrary choice. And the third comment is that all these indicators, meals per day, fresh fruit, internet access, books and leisure are as applicable to adults as they are to children.

More generally, I wonder to what extent statistics help us to better organise poverty reduction. Certainly, in countries where poverty is a 'residual' problem because of generalised wealth and good systems of social protection, it can be useful to go and look for specific remaining problems in order to solve them. But when more than half of the population of a country is 'poor', does it help to know exactly what the number of poor or of poor children is? Is it not some economic and social development for the whole population these countries need in the first place?

As for specific policies for poor children, do we need a separate approach for children at all? Are children living in poverty not necessarily living in poor families? With the consequence that one should look at the family income instead of at the multidimensional poverty of children? Can one imagine non-income-poor families with poor children? Or income-poor families with non-poor children? In order to answer these questions, I propose to look at some of the arguments in favour of a separate poverty approach for children.

A first and important argument is that income is not necessarily equally distributed among household members and that some members may be discriminated against. This is certainly true and has been pointed out by feminist researchers who would like to know more objectively whether there is a so-called feminisation of poverty. Women and girls certainly are discriminated against in many areas and we have statistics about their disadvantages in terms of health, education and wages.[4] But that is no reason to say they are more

---

4 This is why UNDP proposed in its Human Development Report of 1995 a 'Gender-related Development Index' (GDI) and a 'Gender Empowerment Measure' (GEM). In its Human Development Report of 2013 it proposes a 'Gender Inequality Index' (p. 156).

'poor' in terms of income. We simply don't know; there are almost no disaggregated income poverty statistics.

It will be clear however, that gender discrimination is not directly linked to 'poverty' but is a matter of cultural traditions and attitudes that will not change with anti-poverty policies. Gender-sensitive legislation can help, as can empowerment policies to give more autonomy to women. This being said, girls – more than children in general – are discriminated against in many countries,[5] but again, this is not an exclusive matter for poverty policies. Poverty is, however, a gendered problem, different for men and women. If one truly wants to reduce poverty, one will have to work differently at the level of mothers and daughters than at the level of men and boys, because yes, there are poor mothers and poor girls in non-income-poor households (Chant, 2007).

A second argument in favour of a child poverty approach concerns the specific poverty dimensions of children, such as immunisation and child labour. For immunisation it will be clear that all children should receive it, this is not a specific need of poor children, so it can be useful in a general immunisation policy to pay particular attention to poor children, but this is not limited to poverty problems. On the contrary, it clearly shows the need for universal policies instead of a targeted approach with the always existing risk of stigmatisation and informational distortion.

Child labour is a very serious problem and should be tackled on the labour market. Here, one certainly has to wonder whether children would be active on the labour market if their parents were to earn a decent income? Child labour is less a problem of poor children than a problem of children in poor families. If parents get an allowance or a job with a decent income, chances are high they will send their children to school, possibly leave them at home to take care of younger children.[6] Child labour very often is a coping mechanism in case of extreme poverty, and it diminishes when parents have other opportunities (Del Carpio and Loayza, 2012).

Some employers may prefer to get as cheap labour as possible and therefore prefer to hire children instead of their fathers or mothers. Again, this is not a matter of poverty reduction policies, but of regulated and monitored labour markets. Because families may escape poverty thanks to the additional income of their children's labour, whether it is income or multidimensional poverty. If looked at exclusively from a poverty perspective, not being registered as being poor, these families and these children will not be taken care of.

At any rate, child labour is a very difficult topic and research has shown that its abolition is not necessarily the best solution (see Hanson, Volonakis and Al-Rozzi, Chapter 18 of this Handbook). Working conditions clearly have to improve and child exploitation in factories or in families with domestic work obviously has to be condemned (ILO, 2013). But the so-called 'wealth paradox', which shows that child labour is higher when parents have productive assets, such as land, also shows that children can develop their skills by helping their parents. The main problem is then to have sufficient time and resources left for school and leisure (Del Carpio and Loayza, 2012; Lieten, 2005).

---

5   Sen, A. (1990). More than 100 million Women are missing. *The New York Review of Books*. Available at www.nybooks.com/articles/archives/1990/dec/20/more-than-100-million-women-are-missing/?pagination=false.

6   A decline in child labour and more household expenditures on education have been noticed in families receiving a Conditional Cash Transfer, such as Brazil: World Bank (2009); Hanlon *et al.* (2010).

All other dimensions of a multidimensional poverty approach for children are not different from those for adults: food, shelter, clothes, health, water and sanitation. They can all be tackled in a poverty reduction policy at the level of households since it is difficult to see a difference between adults and children in terms of access to them. Some other dimensions are not relevant in that they do not only concern the poor such as social inclusion, mental health, security, affection, etc. These 'intangible' dimensions of poverty are in fact not poverty related but concern all adults and children. 'Affection poverty' certainly is not absent from wealthy families since these have no monopoly on love and care.

Finally, there is the argument of the special vulnerability of children to environmental degradation, such as lack of drinking water, bad air from in-house cooking, etc. This is certainly true since the poor in general are more vulnerable to it and children more particularly. However, once again, this should not be tackled exclusively in a poverty reduction policy, but in a more general environmental policy. It would be rather meaningless to just solve the child-specific problems, and not the other ones.

Does this help to answer the questions we put? Is it possible to have poor children in non-poor households? I think not, except for girls that may be discriminated against, but if that is the case, their mothers will be suffering gender discrimination as well. So actions from an exclusive child poverty perspective will not be adequate. Is it possible to have non-poor children in poor households? Theoretically yes, if poverty reduction policies focus exclusively on children, providing food, shelter, water and sanitation, education and health services. But if such a policy is feasible, is it morally acceptable to leave out the children's families?

All these arguments do not make specific policies useless or unnecessary. Specific actions against child labour, in favour of immunisation and in favour of good education may be most welcome. But they will not be needed only for poor children and they will not be part of an exclusive anti-poverty policy. Rather, they are an additional argument for universal policies, avoiding the pitfalls of targeting (Grosh, 1994; Sen, 1995). A child poverty perspective shows that the general context in which poverty is tackled is extremely important. Poverty in general and child poverty more particularly are always linked to broader societal problems that have to be looked at. Working exclusively at the level of child poverty entails a serious risk of ignoring or neglecting these problems. Possibly, one may reduce child poverty, but not poverty in general, let alone labour market competition and inequality, to name just a few.

4. The ideology of poverty

If my reasoning is correct, then one might wonder why so much attention today is given to child poverty. It is true that children are often not taken into account in general poverty reduction policies. This points to the weakest spot of all poverty reduction policies: they are mostly not meant to reduce poverty in the first place, but arrived on the national and international political agenda because of other reasons than the actual existing poverty. These reasons are still predominant today.

According to Georg Simmel, the father of the sociology of poverty, 'poverty' is a teleological problem that never is in line with the needs of the poor but always with the needs of society or of the dominant classes. The 'exclusion' of the poor is due to the refusal to consider them the ultimate goal of poverty policies. 'Caring for the poor' is very often a moral obligation that the wealthy accept and put on the forefront, forgetting about the rights of poor people. If assistance to the poor was given in the first place, as a right, there would be no limit to the transfer of wealth, and it would rapidly lead to the total eradication of poverty. But that, clearly, does not happen, nor is it the objective, though everyone will agree there is more than enough wealth on this planet (Simmel, 1988). This also refers back to the neoliberal philosophy as mentioned before. States do not have to protect economic and social rights anymore, but only civil and political rights, such as the right to life. They do have to see to it that people do not die from hunger, but not that they have jobs and decent wages. This becomes a responsibility of the poor themselves.

This point also opens the difficult discussion on whether poverty is a human rights violation or not. From a strictly legal point of view, article 6 of the International Covenant on Civil and Political Rights – the right to life – only applies to the death penalty, torture or ill-treatment by States. In a more extended political perspective, one might also consider State policies preventing people from producing or acquiring food, shelter and health care as life-threatening practices. In that light, fighting extreme poverty can be seen as defending the civil right to life. In preparing the Guiding Principles on human rights and extreme poverty at the UN Human Rights Council, the rapporteurs have been struggling with the different concepts. Whereas the Vienna Conference on Human Rights of 1993 defined extreme poverty as a 'violation of human dignity', the Special Rapporteur on extreme poverty and human rights speaks in her final draft on poverty as 'a cause and a consequence of human rights violations', economic and social rights as well as civil and political rights.[7]

It is this general context and the confusion around the meaning of 'poverty' that can explain the search for ever poorer and more vulnerable people. The UN and the UN Development Programme (UNDP) first put the focus on women, the 'poorest of the poor', the 'human face of poverty'… (for a long series of statements of this kind, see Mestrum, 2002: 159). It explains the focus on extreme poverty instead of on poverty… It explains the focus on 'chronic poverty' instead of current poverty. And it explains, I am afraid, the current focus on children. As Gilbert Rist would explain: women and children are the ones that have to be saved first when the ship is sinking … (Rist, 1996)

Another reason that is now used in the context of child poverty is also used for promoting some types of social protection in general, namely 'social investment'. It is a costly mistake for societies to allow child poverty, says UNICEF (2012). It leads to reduced skills and productivity, lower levels of health and educational achievement, increased likelihood of unemployment and welfare dependence, higher cost of juridical and social protection and a loss of social cohesion. This is a purely economic argument, as can also be found in many documents around the newly promoted 'social protection floor'. There is no reason of course to refute these arguments if they can help to defend social protection and mobilise resources for it, but one should wonder what happens if the 'return on investment' is not to happen or is not the expected one? Why should one invest in pensions, if old people are not productive anymore? And why should one invest in child care if the labour market is already more than saturated? Should children be entitled to an education for which there is no demand on the labour market?

The focus on child poverty also corresponds to another characteristic of neoliberalism, which is its exclusive attention on individuals. Children are not seen as members of a family or of a community, the level at which poverty should be tackled, but as individuals. This may be in line with the CRC, though individual human rights do not cancel the collective rights of

---

7 United Nations, General Assembly, Human Rights Council (2007). Written statement by CETIM, *Is Poverty a Human Rights Violation?* A/HRC/6/NGO/48, 6 December 2007; United nations (2012). *Final Draft of the Guiding Principles on Extreme Poverty and Human Rights.* Human Rights Council, Doc A/HRC/21/39, 18 July 2012.

communities and societies, on the contrary, these are complementary (Flahault, 2011). Individual human rights are extremely important, but poverty can only be eradicated if seen as a social relationship, and this needs collective social and economic rights as well as a certain measure of redistribution in order to tackle inequality. Without the huge inequality that there is in our immensely rich world, there would be no poverty. Also, at the level of families, if men are jobless and poor, very probably their wives will be poor and their children will be poor. There is no possibility of separating them. The best way to save children from poverty may be to give a pension to aged people (Hanlon et al., 2010). As it may be useful to save children from poverty by better regulating global food prices or stop the global land-grabbing practices that rob farmers of their livelihood. In short, poverty in general and child poverty more particularly will only be eradicated with other development policies that do not rob poor countries and peoples of their livelihoods (Chang, 2002).

All this is also evidence of the lowered level of ambition of donor countries and of governments in developing countries. While 'development cooperation' started in the 1960s with 'economic development' and was later coupled to 'social development', now both have been abandoned and poverty eradication became poverty reduction and in fact the reduction – halving – of extreme poverty. But without economic and social development, without rules to govern world trade and to stop the exploitation of poor countries and people, impoverishment processes continue and worsen (Chang, 2002).

This leads to two other reflections. Focusing on women and child poverty has a major advantage. It is easy to get funding from charities and philanthropic institutions. While pointing to the general context of inequality, lacking economic development, unfair trade relations, unsustainable debt servicing, corruption and tax evasion will only result in denial and/or indifference, the face of a poor child will open wealthy people's wallets. Poverty reduction, especially when it is focused on women and children, allows for unfair economic and social structures to be maintained and even strengthened. It even gives these structures a moral legitimacy while leaving room for compensatory action by the wealthy.

Focusing on women and children also has the advantage of looking for 'innocent' victims. Children more particularly cannot help being born poor; they bear no responsibility at all, so they should be helped. The same does not apply to poor jobless men, who *certainly* have rejected good opportunities to work or did not develop the right attitudes to work.[8] Implicitly, this points to a deep-rooted cultural view on poverty: innocent poor children should not remain in the culturally deprived surroundings of poor families, who are too poor to avoid the poverty trap and to seize the opportunities that are offered to them. This is what explains the calls for pre-school enrolments and the many attempts to separate poor children from their families.

5. Conclusion

Alternatives will have to be looked for that will allow children, and all other people, all over the world, to live a life in dignity. While specific attention for poor children certainly is necessary, the usefulness of specific measurements of child poverty can be questioned. Children's rights as well as the rights of their families, should always be put in the forefront without losing sight of society's background.

---

8 This conservative point of view is defended by authors like Dalrymple (2010) and also links up with the ancient distinction between 'deserving' and 'non deserving' poor.

A first condition seems to me not to de-link child poverty from other people's poverty and from society as a whole. Even if, theoretically, child poverty can be dissociated from the poverty of their families and their communities, it goes without saying that for poverty reduction policies to be perceived as being fair, all poor people should benefit from them and be allowed social progress, which is not possible without involving society's non-poor.

Second, this means that labour market policies and social protection will come at the forefront. A very positive development in recent years can been seen in the work of the ILO and the UN who now plead for 'decent work', a 'social protection floor' and 'universal social protection'. More research should be done into the transformative potential of social protection policies in the fields of the economy, social relationships, democracy and the environment. If parallel processes in these different fields can be put into place, a positive interaction between them might enhance the needed systemic changes.

Third, all research points to the fact that poverty reduction strongly needs women and gender-sensitive policies. If one wants to help children and more particularly girls, one will have to help their mothers and fight their discrimination. A gender agenda goes far beyond poverty, but it is the major element that can help to promote social change, empowering women, giving them economic autonomy, education and health services.

Fourth, it should be clear that poverty cannot be de-linked from economic and social development. Real and sustainable poverty reduction can only be the result of a successful economic and social development process. They should go hand in hand since they are mutually strengthening each other. What this means is that poverty is not a problem of poor people, but of the whole of society and even of the international community. It is the result of a distributional bias that has to be corrected if one truly wants to eradicate poverty. Poverty can never be solved if one does not stop the impoverishment processes that are inherent to the current neoliberal policies of deregulating labour markets, privatising public services, dismantling social protection, etc.

While poverty has always existed and probably will never be totally eradicated, today's societies certainly have better ways and resources to fight it than what is currently being proposed by international organisations. Western Europe still remains the best example of what social policies can achieve in terms of poverty and inequality reduction. The structural and organic solidarity mechanisms that Western European countries introduced almost a century ago – and which are now being dismantled – have helped to prevent poverty and to eradicate extreme poverty. These values remain utterly important and should guide international development cooperation policies. Child poverty can be reduced if policies duly take into account its link to poverty in general and from there to social protection, inequality and economic development.

Finally, the important problem of child poverty also shows how crucial it is to stop fragmenting the different problems we are faced with. While academic research may need to single out specific issues, their policy implications should include the broader context in which they are present. Research into 'the poorest of the poor' is one thing, designing policies to help them is impossible without taking into account the other poor and the non-poor. To give some recent examples: is it acceptable to condemn child slavery practices at cocoa plantations in Ivory Coast, without condemning at the same time the child labour and the working conditions in general at these plantations? Or to give the example of austerity policies in Greece: is it acceptable to help poor Greek children, without looking at the living conditions of their parents and the equity of the government austerity measures imposed on them?

Poverty eradication policies in general and child poverty policies in particular can never succeed if families have no economic or social security, if societies are not protected against markets, if countries cannot compete on an equal footing with others. However well-intended the political focus on child poverty is, we also have some arguments to suspect that it is meant to make us just ignore and forget this broader dimension. This is why I want to put the focus on 'globalisation', which should be synonymous with 'development'. In fact, the problem of climate change, which threatens us all, should be an opportunity to re-think the development models of Northern and Southern countries. While the failures of the current economic system, causing poverty, hunger and conflict, might be an opportunity to re-think the ways we might do better. But then, of course, this involves power relations, and these are less easy to remodel.

Questions for debate and discussion

- What do children's rights have to say about poverty?
- Does it make sense to exclusively focus on child poverty? In policy? In research?
- Is specific attention for child poverty part of the problem or part of the solution?
- Why is it better to focus on social protection than on poverty reduction?
- What image of childhood prevails in the global poverty debate?

References

CEPAL (2011). *Protección social inclusiva en América latina* [Inclusive social protection in Latin America]. Santiago de Chile: United Nations.
Chang Ha-Joon (2002). *Kicking Away the Ladder*. London: Anthem Press.
Chant, S. (2007). *Gender, Generation and Poverty. Exploring the 'Feminisation of Poverty' in Africa, Asia and Latin America*. Cheltenham, UK: Edward Elgar.
Crouch, C. (2011). *The Strange Non-death of Neoliberalism*. Cambridge, UK: Polity Press.
Dalrymple, T. (2010). *Life at the Bottom*. London: Monday Books.
Del Carpio, X.V. and Loayza, N.V. (2012). *The Impact of Wealth on the Amount and Quality of Child Labor*. Policy Research Working Paper 5959, January 2012. Washington, DC: World Bank.
European Commission, (2013). *EU Employment and Social Situation Quarterly Review*, March 2013, Brussels.
FAO (2013). *Statistical Yearbook 2013*. Rome: Food and Agriculture Organization of the United Nations.
Flahault, F. (2011). *Où est passé le bien commun?* [What happened to the common good?] Paris: Mille et une Nuits.
Grosh, M.E. (1994). *Administering targeted social programs in Latin America. From Platitudes to Practice*. Washington, DC: The World Bank.
Hanlon, J., Barrientos, A. and Hulme, D. (2010). *Just Give Money to the Poor: The Development Revolution from the Global South*. Sterling, VA: Kumarian Press
ILO (2012a). *World Day Against Child Labour 2012*. Available at www.ilo.org/ipec/ Campaignandadvocacy/wdacl/ 2012/lang—en/index.htm
ILO (2012b). *Social Protection Floors for Social Justice and a fair globalisation*. ILC 101st session, 2012.
ILO (2012c). *Recommendation Concerning National Floors of Social Protection*. International Labour Conference, Provisional Record, 14A, June.
ILO (2013). *Ending Child Labour in domestic work and protecting young workers from abusive working conditions*. Geneva: ILO.
IMF (2007). *The IMF and Aid to Sub-Saharan Africa*. Independent Evaluation Office, Washington, DC.
Irisnet (2013). *Cijfers per wijk* [Numbers per quartier.] Available at www.bisa.irisnet.be/cijfers/cijfers-per-wijk
Lieten, K. (2005). *Estudiando el Trabajo Infantil*. The Hague: IREWOC.
Mestrum, F. (2002). *Mondialisation et Pauvreté. De l'utilité de la pauvreté dans le nouvel ordre mondial* [Globalisation and Poverty. On the usefulness of poverty in the new world order]. Paris: L'Harmattan.
Mestrum, F. (2013) *The World Bank and its New Poverty Approach*. Available at www.globalsocialjustice.eu/ index.php?option=com_content&view=article&id=431:the-world-bank-and-its-new-poverty-approach&catid=10:research&Itemid=13 (last accessed 7 May 2013).

Mestrum, F. (2014, 25 October). *An Emerging New Social Paradigm for Europe*. Available at www.globalsocialjustice.eu/index.php?option=com_content&view=article&id=397:an-emerging-new-social-paradigm-for-europe&catid=10:research&Itemid=13

Novak, M. (1996). Concepts of Poverty. In E. Øyen *et al.* (eds), *Poverty. A Global Review. Handbook on International Poverty Research*. Oslo: Scandinavian University Press.

Pogge, T., *The First UN Millennium Development Goal: A Cause for Celebration?* Available at www.etikk.no/globaljustice; Mestrum, F. and Özden, M., *The Fight against Poverty and Human Rights*, CETIM, Geneva. Available at www.cetim.ch/en/documents/report_11.pdf

Rist, G. (1996). *Le développement. Histoire d'une croyance occidentale* [Development: History of a Western Belief]. Paris: Presses de la Fondation nationale des sciences politiques.

Sen, A.K. (1995). The Political Economy of Targeting. In D. Van De Walle *et al.* (eds), *Public Spending and the Poor: Theory and Evidence*. Baltimore, MD: Johns Hopkins University Press.

Simmel, G. (1988). *Les pauvres* [The Poor]. Paris: PUF (Originally published in 1908).

UNCTAD (2002). *Escaping the Poverty Trap*. LDC Report 2002, Geneva.

UNCTAD (2010). *Towards a New International Development Architecture for LDCs*, LDC Report 2010. Geneva, UNCTAD.

UNICEF (2012). *Progress for Children. A Report Card on Adolescents*, n° 10, April 2012. Geneva: UNICEF.

UNICEF (2012). *Measuring Child Poverty*. Innocenti Research Centre, Report Card 10, 2012.

United Nations (2010a). *Re-Thinking Poverty*. Report on the World Social Situation 2010, New York: United Nations.

United Nations (2010b). *World Economic and Social Survey 2010*. New York: United Nations.

UNDP (2010). *What Will it Take to Achieve the MDGs?* New York: UNDP.

UNRISD (2010). *Combating Poverty and Inequality. Structural Change, Social Policy and Politics*. Geneva: UNRISD.

Wahl, P. (2012). *The G20. Overestimated and Underperforming*. Berlin: WEED.

Williamson, J. (1990). *The Progress of Policy Reform in Latin America*. Washington, DC: Institute of International Economics.

World Bank (2009). *Condition Cash Transfers*. Washington, DC: World Bank.

21

Indigenous children's rights

Opportunities in appropriation and transformation

Natasha Blanchet-Cohen[1]

1. Introduction

The United Nations Convention on the Rights of the Child (CRC) is the first international human rights treaty that specifically protects the rights of the Indigenous child. After unsuccessfully struggling at the international level for the recognition of their unique rights, Indigenous peoples and their allies welcomed this inclusion hoping it would address the historical breach of their rights (Price Cohen, 1995). What can be said about the significance of the CRC for Indigenous children, a quarter of a century after its adoption?

On the one hand, progress actualizing Indigenous children's rights remains stalled. The rampant violation of Indigenous peoples' rights constitutes a distressing reality. A United Nations (UN) document on the state of progress 25 years after ratification of the CRC continues to report that, "Indigenous children suffer extreme forms of exclusion and discrimination" (United Nations, 2012, par. 9). A scan through the titles of a myriad of research publications confirms this view: *Our greatest challenge: Aboriginal children and human rights* (McGlade, 2012) and *The rights of Indigenous children around the world: Still far from a reality* (Woolley, 2009). Clearly, state-based assimilation policies and histories of colonization will not be undone overnight; international recognition of Indigenous peoples and their rights has not yet resulted in an overall improvement of Indigenous children's lived realities.

Taking a critical perspective, this chapter posits that despite a grim situation, the CRC presents an opportunity to advocate for an alternative worldview *for*, *with* and *by* Indigenous children. Although the CRC has been critiqued for promoting Eurocentric conceptions of childhood that have resulted in paternalistic policies and programmes which are often disrespectful and detrimental to Indigenous ways of life (Boyden and Mann, 2005), given the proper conditions, the CRC can support Indigenous children's best interests in ways that respect

---

[1] The author is Associate Professor at Concordia University. *Acknowledgments:* This paper draws on the research, field experiences and participation in international processes related to the promotion of Indigenous children's rights over the past two decades. I wish to thank the many Indigenous mentors and relationships that have helped inform this paper, and the advice and feedback from Mutang Urud, Vanessa Currie, Peggy Herring and literature review by Kristy Franks.

dignity rather than negating identity. This is evidenced today in the way Indigenous peoples are putting into practice certain aspects of the CRC and other international human rights laws, redefining the legal terms and ideas behind them, posing deeper questions, and finding new meaning. In other words, when Indigenous children and communities are able to interpret the Convention and be actively involved in implementation, universal and paternalistic applications can be avoided. Through the process of appropriation and transformation by stakeholders, the CRC is being brought to life, realizing its "emancipatory objective" and becoming a "lever to change societal conditions" (see Chapter 1 in this Handbook, p. 11).

To illustrate this process of appropriation and transformation, I examine three overarching areas of the CRC that Indigenous peoples are actively involved in defining and interpreting to actualize their rights. These are (a) defining the concept of Indigenous, (b) understanding the significance and implications of the phrase "to enjoy his or her own culture," and (c) identifying duty-bearers and right-holders. This section is followed by a review of education and child protection, two sectors in which Indigenous peoples are putting into practice CRC principles.

Setting the tone for this chapter is Noeli Pocaterra explaining how she presents the CRC to children and mothers in the community. As a Wayuu leader from Venezuela and former vice-president of the World Council of Indigenous Peoples and member of the Venezuela Senate, I also credit her for introducing me to the potential of Indigenous children's rights twenty years ago.

> I often begin a presentation on children's rights by drawing a pregnant mother, and asking what an unborn child needs to be healthy when it is born. … We write the points down, and invite the children to mention those that have been omitted. It is then explained how all that has previously been said is essentially what constitutes the CRC. The CRC articles as such may never be mentioned; emphasis is placed on content and meaning rather than exact terminology.
>
> The introduction is followed by a discussion on the Indigenous world and non-Indigenous world, and the tensions between them. A drawing is made of two circles, and the group identifies what constitutes Indigenous ways (i.e., oral tradition, traditional clothing, honour system) in one circle and in the other non-Indigenous ways (i.e., written, legalistic, individual). Then, the CRC is presented as a tool that comes from the non-Indigenous world, but that offers the possibility to support children's well-being and some of the Indigenous ways and views.
>
> I then raise the question: who is responsible for implementing these rights? Children often mistakenly begin by mentioning the government or teachers. What about us? I sometimes need to point out. The idea of organizing children's rights committees is then introduced.
>
> (Noeli Pocaterra, personal communication, June 8, 2007)

While children correctly identified governments as the primary duty-bearers, Pocaterra's intentional emphasis on communities' role reflected her view that actualizing the CRC would depend largely on the participation of Indigenous children and communities. As an educator and community developer, I shared her interest in the role and possibilities of empowering communities to give meaning to their rights.

Indeed the CRC provides an opportunity for non-Indigenous and Indigenous worlds to come together, but this meeting of two worlds poses challenges because of a non-alignment of worldviews, and nation-states' lack of commitment toward respecting Indigenous peoples' rights. As discussed herein, working through the tensions is part of "broadening cross-cultural understanding and gaining a broader capacity to take competing views into account when thinking about or establishing international human rights treaties" (Libesman, 2007, pp. 285–286). Acknowledging a diversity of meanings and embracing questioning is a way of finding "out in which way further development of children's rights can promote culturally specific ways of living and the equality and acceptance of children" (Liebel, 2012, p. 21). This is part of moving away from the "technalization" and "decontextualization" that has characterized the CRC (Reynaert, Bouverne-de Bie, and Vandevelde, 2009, p. 358), and better serving Indigenous children. In discussing the activism (in or with Indigenous communities) surrounding seeking and giving meaning to the CRC, this chapter hopes to demonstrate the potential of this international document to advocate for the positive advancement of Indigenous children's rights, and to reverse generations of oppressive and discriminatory state policies and practices.

2. Indigenous children's rights

2.1. The United Nations Convention on the Rights of the Child

The 42 substantive rights of the CRC apply equally to all children; however, specific reference to Indigenous children appears in three articles. Article 30 protects the cultural, religious, and language rights of Indigenous children:

> In those States in which ethnic, religious or linguistic minorities or persons of indigenous origin exist, a child belonging to such a minority or who is indigenous shall not be denied the right, in community with other members of his or her group, to enjoy his or her own culture, to profess and practise his or her own religion, or to use his or her own language.
>
> *(United Nations, CRC, 1989)*

This article was introduced into the draft of the Convention by an Indigenous organization, the Four Directions Council, which pointed to the unique situation of Indigenous children and the importance of their cultural rights (Hodgkin and Newell, 2007). Inclusion of Article 30 also reflected the human rights community embracing a diversity of cultures.

Article 17(d) on access to mass media also makes specific reference to Indigenous children: "Encourage the mass media to have particular regard to the linguistic needs of the child who belongs to a minority group or who is Indigenous." Finally, Article 29.1(d) identifies that education shall be directed to "the preparation of the child for responsible life in a free society, in the spirit of understanding, peace, tolerance, equality of sexes, and friendship among all peoples, ethnic, national and religious groups and persons of indigenous origin."

Since the ratification of the CRC in 1989, several events have served to bring further attention to Indigenous children's rights. A General Discussion on the Rights of Indigenous Children was held by the CRC Committee in 2003. The preamble to its recommendations stated that "indigenous children were disproportionately affected by specific challenges ... yet are not sufficiently taken into consideration in the development and implementation of policies and programmes for children." Its 24 recommendations covered a range of topics including a call on State parties to strengthen data collection on Indigenous children, the right to identity, access, and appropriate education and health, as well as a call for international cooperation and follow-up. The following year, UNICEF's Innocenti Research Centre dedicated an issue of

Digest[2] to Indigenous children stating in its editorial that "indigenous children have not always received the distinct consideration they deserve," and closing with a recognition that "indigenous children carry with them a reserve of knowledge that is their special inheritance, and from which we can all benefit" (UNICEF, 2004, p.1).

Six years later, the Committee on the Rights of the Child (2009) published *General Comment No. 11: Indigenous Children and Their Rights under the Convention*. The General Comment identified that states needed direction on interpreting and implementing this Convention, given the "insufficient attention" (para. 20) paid to the rights of Indigenous children in state parties' reports. The General Comment considers that the right established in Article 30 "is an important recognition of the collective traditions and values in indigenous culture. … [and that] the right to exercise cultural rights among indigenous peoples may be closely associated with the use of traditional territory and its resources" (para. 16). Relevant issues for Indigenous children are also identified as they relate to (a) the general principles, (b) civil rights and freedom, (c) family environment and alternative care, (d) basic health care, (e) education, and (f) special protection measures. Considering the importance of working with Indigenous peoples, the General Comment also states: "In order to develop policy and programming efforts in a culturally sensitive manner, state parties should consult with indigenous communities and directly with indigenous children" (para. 80).

In a reflection of more skilled leadership and recognition of Indigenous peoples internationally, Indigenous organizations were actively involved in the development of the General Comment (Rae, 2006). For instance, the expert writer who was appointed to undertake the drafting was an Indigenous person who was recommended by the sub-group on Indigenous Children and Young People that reports to the UN Committee. As well, consultations were carried out with Indigenous groups and youth on four continents. This involvement provided opportunities to influence the framing and content of the General Comment, while creating awareness and ownership of the CRC among Indigenous peoples.

2.2. Supportive developments in international law

In the introductory chapter, the editors point out that human rights and children's rights regrettably have grown apart; conversely, positive developments in international law with respect to Indigenous peoples have contributed to furthering Indigenous children's rights. Indeed after receiving scant attention from the international community for most of the twentieth century, Indigenous peoples in the last two decades have gained an international personality with legal recognition and presence (Meijknecht, 2001). Numerous mechanisms at the UN have supported this, including the establishment of the UN Permanent Forum on Indigenous Issues with a thematic focus on Indigenous children and youth, the presence of the Special Rapporteur on the rights of Indigenous peoples, and the proclamation of two International Decades of Indigenous Peoples (1995–2004 and 2005–2014). Other important international treaties are the International Labour Organization (ILO) Convention No. 169 Indigenous and Tribal Peoples Convention (1989), and earlier ILO No. 107 The Indigenous and Tribal Populations Convention (1957), as well as the Convention on Biological Diversity (1992), which includes specific references to Indigenous peoples.

---

2 The Innocenti Digests provide summaries of current knowledge and debate on specific child rights issues, written in an accessible style for use by a wide range of audiences.

A major breakthrough in international law for Indigenous peoples took place after more than twenty years of negotiation and lobbying with the adoption of the United Nations Declaration on the Rights of Indigenous Peoples (UNDRIP) in 2007 by the General Assembly (Charters and Stavenhagen, 2009). Victoria Tauli-Corpuz, of the Igorot people of the Philippines and former Chairperson of the United Nations Permanent Forum on Indigenous Issues, stated in her opening remarks:

> This Declaration has the distinction of being the only Declaration in the UN which was drafted with right holders, themselves, the Indigenous Peoples. We see this as a strong Declaration which embodies the most important rights we and our ancestors have long fought for.

While Indigenous children would of course be covered by the entire Declaration, there are also several specific provisions for them in the document. The preamble recognizes in particular "the right of Indigenous families and communities to retain shared responsibility for the upbringing, training, education and well-being of their children, consistent with the rights of the child." Among the other five articles that mention Indigenous children is Article 7(2), which indicates that "Indigenous peoples have the collective right to live in freedom, peace and security as distinct peoples and shall not be subjected to any act of genocide or any other act of violence, including forcibly removing children of the group to another group." Furthermore, Article 14 acknowledges Indigenous peoples' right to "establish and control their education systems and institutions" and states that all Indigenous individuals "particularly children" should "have access, when possible, to an education in their own culture and provided in their own language".[3]

Given that declarations are not legally binding on states, implementation remains uncertain. Indigenous activists and their allies see the Declaration as a "framework of reference, a point of departure" (Charters and Stavenhagen, 2009, p. 357) that will lead to a new recognition of Indigenous peoples' rights. Implementing the Declaration includes promotion; to this effect an adolescent-friendly version of the Declaration was co-produced by UNICEF and the Indigenous Youth Caucus (2013). This document is being distributed among Indigenous organizations worldwide to raise awareness among youth.

The rise of the Indigenous movement internationally has been a source of power, increasing the ability to resist the abuses of states as well as providing a "source of moral appeal shared with that large part of humanity" (Niezen, 2003, p. 216). In his address to the UN Human Rights Council on the 60th anniversary of the Universal Declaration on Human Rights, Chief Wilton Littlechild of the Cree Nation in Canada stated, "[w]hen Indigenous Peoples WIN, the whole world WINS" (Charters and Stavenhagen, 2009, p. 375). Indigenous movements have reached out to broader society considering common values and shared interests. In the *Idle No More* campaign in Canada for instance, which was led largely by Indigenous youth, Canadian citizens were invited to join the vision for "just, equitable and sustainable communities".[4] Indeed, increased presence of Indigenous peoples on the international stage and support from allies have created a favourable context for bringing attention to the provisions relating to Indigenous children in the CRC.

---

3   The other three articles: Article 17 (2) on protecting indigenous children from economic exploitation, Article 21 on the right to economic and social conditions and Article 22 on the rights and needs of vulnerable groups including children.
4   For more information, see: www.idlenomore.ca/manifesto.

3. Appropriation and transformation through the challenges of implementation

While international law may at its foundation agree on the principles of Indigenous children's rights to survival, to respect, and to communicate (Price Cohen, 1995), the significance of many such notions is undetermined and undesignated. Below, developments in three areas are discussed: the concept of *Indigenous*; the meaning of *culture*; and *assuming responsibility for implementing* the CRC. In each area, I discuss how dealing with the challenges of implementation have involved some appropriation and transformation of the CRC. Though understanding the significance and implications of concepts remains complex and uneven across societies, the fact that they are being addressed in diverse contexts is to be welcomed, as it is indicative of an active dialectic process with the involvement of multiple stakeholders.

3.1. Defining indigenous

The term *Indigenous* – while commonly used in both international fora and the CRC – raises challenges because it lacks universal and easily applicable criteria.

The most cited definition of Indigenous peoples comes from the *Study on the Problem of Discrimination against Indigenous Populations* (UN Commission on Human Rights, 1986) by José R. Martinez Cobo:

> Indigenous communities, peoples and nations are those which, having a historical continuity with pre-invasion and pre-colonial societies that developed on their territories, consider themselves distinct from other sectors of the societies now prevailing on those territories, or parts of them. They form at present non-dominant sectors of society and are determined to preserve, develop and transmit to future generations their ancestral territories, and their ethnic identity, as the basis of their continued existence as peoples, in accordance with their own cultural patterns, social institutions and legal system.

While capturing core aspects of defining Indigenous peoples, its universal application has been considered problematic because of the absence of a universal and exclusive characteristic of Indigenous peoples (United Nations, 2009), such as a history of European colonialism and marginalization.

A conceptual note by the Secretariat of the Permanent Forum on Indigenous Issues (United Nations, 2004) states that, "the prevailing view today is that no formal universal definition of the term is necessary" (para. 8). The Working Group on Indigenous Populations in 1997, after meeting regularly since 1982 concluded that a common definition was neither possible, nor necessary. A definition would "inevitably be either over- or under-inclusive, making sense in some societies but not in others" (United Nations, 2009, pp. 6–7). Instead of a definition, the UNDRIP asserts in Article 33(1) that self-identification is the only consideration: "Indigenous peoples have the right to determine their own identity or membership in accordance with their customs and traditions. This does not impair the right of indigenous individuals to obtain citizenship of the states in which they live" (United Nations, 2007b). The ILO Convention No. 169 also considers self-identification in Article 1.1 as a fundamental criterion along with other criteria such as "social, cultural and economic conditions distinguish them from other sections of the national community" (ILO, 1989, Article 1(a)).

The absence of a standard definition is however problematic because states often do not recognize self-identification. Many countries under-account for Indigenous peoples, lacking mechanisms to self-identify; national surveys regularly do not include the category of Indigenous origin. In several cases, Indigenous children do not hold birth certificates, violating their right to identity and to a name as identified in Article 7 and in Article 8 of the CRC. In Bolivia for instance, as much as one-quarter of the Indigenous population in rural areas has no birth registration and therefore cannot fully enjoy their individual and collective rights (UNICEF, 2010). Challenges to birth registration include lack of awareness about its importance among communities, difficulty of access including language barriers and costs, as well as the coexistence of cultural norms that may discourage birth registration for newborn babies. In Chiapas, Mexico, for instance, many Indigenous children are not registered because children are born at home, and obtaining birth certificates requires journeying long distances (Gupta, 2012). In the absence of formal recognition of citizenship by the government, many Indigenous children in Mexico are prevented from accessing basic services in education, health, and social services.

Histories of discrimination and exclusion have meant Indigenous peoples have also chosen to deny their identity. Confronted with the predominance of a "Western" capitalist way of living, young people have chosen to deny their indigenous origin. This negation of identity can become a source of tension within communities, particularly with the older generation who value remaining connected to their roots.

As a result of globalization and mixed-marriages, Indigenous identities have become more complex. In Canada, for instance, women and their children would lose their Indian status upon marrying a non-status person. After aboriginal women's organizations pointed out the discriminatory nature of these provisions in the Indian Act, the women's and their children's status were reinstated with Bill C-31 in 1985 (Henry et al., 2000). Conversely, resource shortages have resulted in Indigenous communities requesting evidence of Indigenous origin. In a Mohawk community in Quebec, Canada, DNA testing was required to claim rights to community resources. These examples show that the ambiguity and variety around definitions of the term *Indigenous* will continue to be a question that Indigenous peoples and societies will grapple with; its resolutions and impact on children will also vary greatly depending on Indigenous people's political and economic positioning within a given context. It is expected that appropriation will unfold differently in contexts where recognition of Indigenous identity signifies increases in resource allocation from state parties compared to where indigenous identity remains a source of shame and discrimination.

3.2. Scope and implications of "to enjoy his or her own culture"

Another challenge raised in the CRC is the meaning of the right to *enjoy his or her own culture* in Article 30. What is included (or excluded) will determine the scope of Article 30. For many Indigenous peoples, children's right to culture is all-encompassing. The Wayuu in Venezuela, for example, translate children's rights as *sujutu tepichi* which means "the integral value of humanity." It incorporates the spiritual and physical, as well as the wisdom of the individual and collective knowledge (Blanchet-Cohen and Fernandez, 2003). This holistic view broadens the meaning of culture.

One critical question is whether the right to land, territories, and natural resources is implied in children's rights (see also Desmet and Aylwin, Chapter 22 in this Handbook). This could be assumed given that connection with the land, territory, and natural resources is considered to be the foundation of Indigenous culture. Upholding children's rights is often considered interconnected with defending the right to land. As Mutang Urud of the Kelabit people from Malaysia shared in his speech to the opening of the UN International Decade on Indigenous Peoples when speaking about the implications of logging and deforestation:

> A woman I know who has seven children once came to me and said, "This logging is like a big tree that has fallen on my chest. I often awake in the middle of the night, and I and my husband talk endlessly about the future of our children. I always ask myself, when will it end?"
>
> *(Wade et al., 1995, p. 140)*

As pointed out by Hodgkin and Newell (2007), while Article 30 may not be intended to cover economic and political rights, these cannot be separated easily. For example, in its concluding observations for Nicaragua, the Committee on the Rights of the Child "notes with concern that, despite constitutional recognition of indigenous customary rights, indigenous communities still suffer from institutional neglect, historic abandonment and indiscriminate pillaging of natural resources, especially in the Caribbean region" (United Nations, 2005a, para. 75). This is equally the case for Colombia's report: "The Committee welcomes the legal steps taken to recognize ethnic diversity, autonomy and collective land rights of minorities, in particular the Afro-Colombian and indigenous peoples" (United Nations, 2006, para. 94). In response to the Malaysia report, "the Committee recommends that the State party carefully and regularly evaluate existing disparities in the enjoyment by children of their rights and undertake on the basis of that evaluation the necessary steps to prevent and combat discriminatory disparities against children belonging to vulnerable groups, such as the Orang Asli, indigenous and minority children" (United Nations, 2007a, para. 32). Such interpretations by the Committee can become advocacy tools for Indigenous peoples when negotiating with governments in countries where there is a colonial history of appropriation of land, territories and natural resources, although effectiveness will depend on local mobilization and lobbying (Save the Children, 2008).

On the other hand, some cultural practices could be detrimental to children. The General Comment (United Nations, 2009) makes clear the distinction, stating: "Should harmful practices be present, *inter alia* early marriages and female genital mutilation (Leye and Middelburg, Chapter 17 in this Handbook), the State party should work together with indigenous communities to ensure their eradication" (para. 22).

While some cultural practices may not be in children's best interests, others may need to be redefined to better reflect contemporary realities. For instance, children's participation is a core principle of the CRC, with Article 12 stating the right to "express those views freely in all matters affecting the child", and its meaning is evolving. Traditionally in Indigenous communities, each stage of life was associated with distinct roles and responsibilities, with children participating by observing and being involved in the affairs of the family and the community (Blanchet-Cohen and Fernandez, 2003). Among Indigenous communities in Canada, care was generally provided according to a holistic worldview that deemed children important and respected members of an interdependent community and ecosystem (Blackstock, 2009). However, this form of children's participation is often more indirect than what is implied in the UNCRC. Still, modernity, colonization, and discrimination have shattered traditional structures, and have displaced children as they traverse life stages. As a result, new forms of expression are emerging. Indigenous young people seek new forms of engagement, and adopt a variety of means of expression that provide for empowerment and well-being that reflect their contemporary realities (Blanchet-Cohen et al., 2011). Young people are not just perpetuating culture but becoming creators of culture: "Youth recognize that meaningful engagement is not simply about returning to the past, but rather building on the past to accommodate to their changed and contemporary realities" (Blanchet-Cohen et al., 2011, p. 106).

In sum, the right to enjoy culture in Article 30 is an evolving concept, and as Indigenous young people and their communities take leadership, they are broadening its scope and creating new meanings. As warns Libesman (2007, p. 298), "the relationship between article 30 rights and Indigenous children's rights to their identity requires a subtle and nuanced interpretation of the Convention if inadvertent domination is not to occur". The process of young people claiming other forms of expressing themselves is a response to external conditions that should be welcomed as part of healthy development, even if it may give rise to difficult questions. A similar point was made by Alston (1994) in his analysis of the possible incompatibility between culture and best interests, and recognition that although the CRC provides broad signposts, in practice the Convention needs to be interpreted by local communities.

3.3. Identifying responsibility

A third challenge relates to the question of who assumes the responsibility for implementing the CRC, given that the Convention addresses state parties with whom Indigenous peoples are often in conflict. This context makes it problematic for an Indigenous community to rely on the state to act as duty-bearer, obligated to implement, monitor and report on progress.

Recognizing that non-state actors should also be duty-bearers with responsibility to implement the principles of the CRC, there is growing emphasis on non-state duty-bearers recognizing shared responsibility for implementation (Lundy and McEvoy, 2009). In the case of Indigenous peoples, this would involve Indigenous organizations, non-Indigenous organizations that are allied and Indigenous children (Rae, 2006). These actors are increasingly taking an active role in advocating for Indigenous children's rights, and pressuring governments to take the CRC and other relevant international human rights law seriously.

One example of Indigenous organizations taking on this role is in Canada, where First Nation organizations filed a human rights complaint against the government claiming discrimination in child welfare funding on reserves, given the over-representation of First Nation children in state care (Blackstock, 2011; Federal Court, 2012). Despite explicit references in the case documents to children's right to participate in matters affecting them, the government has refused to include the public in the hearings. "Consistent with the UNDRIP and CRC, First Nations are eager to have the case decided on the evidence of the discrimination allegation but Canada has repeatedly tried to derail a full hearing" (Blackstock, 2012, p. 2505). Indigenous organizations have been calling on the international community to pressure the government to open up the hearings to the public. The case has shed light on the difficulties of challenging government; five years in the federal court granted an application for judicial review following the earlier decision by the Canadian Human Rights Tribunal to dismiss the case on the grounds of lack of evidence.

To denounce abuse by governments, Indigenous organizations have also submitted reports to the UN Committee on the Rights of the Child. Complementary reports by organizations in Canada and Australia (Harris and Gartland, 2011) have brought attention to the situation of Aboriginal children and resulted in the Committee making several references in its concluding observations to the state about the need to address discrimination against Aboriginal children (United Nations, 2012). Throughout, Indigenous organizations have been reaching out, seeking alliances with non-state actors in order to increase the pressure on governments to comply with their international obligations.

Alongside Indigenous organizations and other non-state actors, Indigenous children and young people have become active, showing that children can also be right-holders claiming their rights (Liebel, 2012). Interestingly however, youth empowerment and requests for partnering with adults have not always been welcomed in their own communities (Blanchet-Cohen, 2010). For example, a Cree youth explained how youth issues were viewed by leaders in his community: "The youth agenda has fallen to the bottom of the list. Our leaders are, ironically, fighting against each other. We youth work together ... We need to control the agenda, to set the pace, to learn how to work together" (personal communication, April 18, 2012). In recognition of this reality, an adult who works with youth in Canada reflects: "We shut down as leaders ourselves ... [though] when kids are yelling and screaming they are telling us something. ... We don't give [them] the opportunity to fight and give back. We are not good at that. We don't hear the anger" (Blanchet-Cohen et al., 2011, p. 105).

At a conference on Indigenous social determinants of health held in Canada (National Collaborating Centre for Aboriginal Health, 2009), a youth participant spoke before an adult audience of the need for better support: "Youth feel weak; position us to learn to become strong." Another youth participant added, "We want to learn from you, so please extend your hand to us so we hold it." Indeed, youth call for capacity-building at all levels. Indigenous youth think that their communities should see resources spent on youth as an investment, not an expense, and that young people should be more involved in all community issues, not just those that are youth-specific. Youth feel able to transcend beyond the political divisions that curtail leaders. In confronting their own communities, Indigenous children and young people may transform culture.

Thus, with responsibility for implementation comes a need for partnering with Indigenous organizations and young people themselves. Young people's participation, consistent with a core principle of the CRC, may give rise to conflicting views between generations, but if children's rights is not to be prescriptive it must invite dialogue and reflection and consider embracing tensions rather than ignore them. The significance and priorities of each actor or the specific nature of actualization will therefore need to be figured out, claimed, and then often negotiated, paying particular attention to context which, as pointed out in the introductory chapter, is central to a critical approach to children's rights.

4. Examples of appropriation and transformation

To illustrate the unfolding of the process of appropriation and transformation, this section presents examples of how Indigenous children's rights are being actualized in the fields of education and child protection. This overview points to the complexities and possibilities in implementing alternative programming, given the situation of Indigenous peoples within specific contexts, but it also highlights the multiple systemic issues that impede Indigenous peoples' well-being.

4.1. Education

According to the CRC Article 28, states are obligated to provide primary education (Swadener et al., 2013) and Article 29 outlines the aims of education including a specific reference to respecting Indigenous culture (Quennerstedt, Chapter 12 in this Handbook). Education has however often been used as a means of assimilation to promote singular dominant models of knowing, at the cost of ethnic minority and Indigenous languages, and ways of knowing (Battiste, 2010). The UN Special Rapporteur on the situation of the human rights and fundamental freedoms of indigenous peoples observes that formal education has been a "two-edged sword," aimed at knowledge and skill acquisition, while at the same time removing Indigenous children from their culture (United Nations, 2005b). In many countries boarding schools were established for assimilation. As a result, Indigenous identities have been shattered: children have been "caught in a no man's land whereby they lose an important aspect of their identity while not fully becoming a part of the dominant society" (para. 15). An analysis of Indigenous children's school experience in Peru shows, for instance, that disregard of Indigenous language and culture is detrimental to education performance: "School experience not only contributes to the disempowering of Indigenous students and communities, but also prompts their academic failure by denying them the tools and motivation for cognitive engagement and identity investment" (Ames, 2012, p. 460).

Generally, subtractive education where Indigenous children are taught at the cost of their mother tongue has been shown to be harmful to the child linguistically and psychologically (Skutnabb-Kangas and Dunbar, 2010). The absence of Indigenous perspectives in formal curricula results in feelings of exclusion and low self-esteem, contributing to discrimination and racism. Indigenous students experience lower enrolment rates, higher drop-out rates, and poorer educational outcomes than non-Indigenous persons (United Nations, 2009).

Despite these facts, there have been in recent decades a growing number of positive developments in supporting Indigenous education as a result of state policies and leadership of Indigenous organizations (United Nations, 2005b). These examples illustrate implementations of Article 29.1(d) CRC and UNDRIP Article 14 to provide indigenous children with an "education in their own languages in a manner appropriate to their cultural methods of teaching and learning". Bilingual education, developing Indigenous curricula, and recognizing non-formal education as well as having Indigenous peoples managing their own schools (self-determination) illustrate Indigenous communities – with the approval and cooperation of the government in question (or, if not exactly approval, then at least they are not standing in the way) – "appropriating" Article 30 of the CRC (and UNDRIP Article 14), and after processing it through their own contexts "transforming" their rights.

However, experiences in creating a culturally relevant programme have not been devoid of challenges. In New Zealand, formal progress has been made in adopting Indigenous children's education rights, but narratives with Māori educators suggest that more training, resources, as well as parental support are necessary (see Swadener et al., 2013). Similarly, in South Africa, despite a policy that supports instruction in their primary language, and evidence that learning in the mother tongue in the early years will improve the future schooling experience, many parents chose to send their children to formerly White-only schools where instruction was given in English instead of their own African mother tongue (see Swadener et al., 2013). In Canada, the absence of accompanying infrastructure has often resulted in poor quality of First Nations controlled education, where parents complain about the catch-up required to transition to the general public system, and acquire the language skills necessary for obtaining employment (Senate of Canada, 2011). Success in appropriation in education is difficult without also attending to other systems, including training and resources for education and employment sectors.

Placing emphasis on mainstream education institutions that respect and accommodate Indigenous languages and cultures, and prioritizing Indigenous control of education with programmes specifically tailored to Indigenous children remains difficult. While there is perceived value in integrating traditional Indigenous teaching methods into mainstream education because it will "not only become more likely to serve the developmental needs of Aboriginal children and youth; it will also improve society in fostering a culture of human rights" (Cook and White, 2001, p. 345), others fear integration presents risk to Indigenous identity and culture.

Implementing the CRC requires focusing on more than just access to education. Attention also needs to be paid to the quality and place of education, and provision of other basic human rights including prospects for future employment. An analysis of experiences in Botswana and

Namibia suggests that context as well as involvement of Indigenous communities is critical in designing education that respects Indigenous rights (Hays, 2011). This will require a "focus on increasing the options available to Indigenous communities – as well as their ability to negotiate on their own behalf and thus to decide for themselves what is the best approach to take – through a variety of complementary approaches" (p. 149). Giving meaning to the provisions of Article 29.1(d) requires empowering Indigenous communities in seeking how to find a balance between supporting Indigenous children's cultural identities on the one hand, and their economic and social needs on the other.

4.2. Child protection

Another key sector of concern for Indigenous children is child protection, which deals with preventing and responding to violence, exploitation, and abuse against children (UNICEF, 2006, p. 1). Multiple articles in the CRC provide for children's right to protection, including dealing with hazardous work (Article 32), illicit production and drug trafficking (Article 33), sexual exploitation (Article 34), sale, trafficking and abduction (Article 35), as well as armed conflict (Article 38). Child protection includes the right not to be separated from parents unless it is in the child's best interests (Article 9), as well as the right to state assistance and protection in the absence of a family environment (Article 20).

The question of protection is most relevant to Indigenous children given that their families and communities experience high levels of violence, exploitation and abuse. Historically, Indigenous children have suffered from slavery and forced labour, and been at risk for the worst forms of child labour, commercial sex trafficking, and exploitation (United Nations, 2012). They are also particularly vulnerable to migration caused by conflict-induced displacement, loss of traditional livelihoods, armed conflicts, and environmental degradation (United Nations, 2012).

While there is a need to be concerned with protection of Indigenous children, a closer examination shows that underpinning child protection programmes and services are perspectives on childhood that may not be consistent with Article 30 CRC. As argued by Myers and Bourdillon (2012), the application of international law has often resulted in a standardization of policies and programmes that are "assumed to be technical and moral standards for all. They show no concern to place protection of children in the contexts of the communities in which they live. ... Although they affirm children's rights to a say in decisions that affect them, these decisions are clearly determined by adults from outside" (Myers and Bourdillon, 2012, p. 440). The prevailing child protection models – child rescue, social services, and medical models – commonly neglect local community assets, including the role of children themselves. An alternative approach considers that these assets play a critical role, particularly when family and community are the primary line of defence to protect children from violence. Research shows that child protection approaches can be ineffective, and even counterproductive, when local context is not given sufficient attention (Bissell *et al.*, 2007; Hand, 2006).

One key area of tension has been the removal of children from their culture as a result of biases in child welfare programmes. The impact in Australia (Douglas and Walsh, 2013), Canada (Blackstock, 2009), and the United States (Hand, 2006) has led to Indigenous children being taken into the care of the state at alarming rates. Appropriation is happening with Indigenous peoples denouncing this practice, declaring that it violates Article 30 CRC. There is transformation as greater recognition is being made of different cultural practices, including the crucial role of extended family and community members in child development, which has often been misconstrued as neglect in the current nuclear family-based system.

Just as it is in the education field, there have been a growing number of positive experiences in child protection where Indigenous communities have assumed greater control in child protection programmes and policies (Long and Sephton, 2011). Several Indigenous communities have been reviving traditional practices. The Dane-zaa people in northeastern British Columbia, for instance, are bringing traditional decision-making practices into the child welfare system (Ney *et al.*, 2014). Engaging community members in reviving local knowledge and rebuilding child protection capacity and protocols are ways of helping create institutions that resonate with what people view as appropriate for them. In Australia, Aboriginal and non-aboriginal understandings of *best interests* differ, requiring a better integration of indigenous perspectives into child welfare programming (Hays, 2011). In Māori communities, more restorative approaches to care, protection, and youth justice that move away from individual-based responses are being explored. At issue is not returning to the past but defining approaches that build on cultural practices. As Libesman (2014) argues, decolonizing Indigenous child welfare requires a sensitive approach that engages and builds on Indigenous ways while ensuring that children's rights are met and these rights reflect the principles of the CRC.

5. Reflecting on moving forward

The CRC provides opportunities for enhancing Indigenous children's lived realities. Along with other international human rights law, this instrument holds power because states have an obligation to report on implementation, and in a globalized world, they care about their international image. But as voiced by Noeli Pocaterra, one cannot depend solely on the government for implementation. The difference the CRC will make in the lives of Indigenous children will depend on non-state actors, namely Indigenous communities and children, as well as their allies, upholding these rights. For the Convention to become a catalyst for raising the status of Indigenous communities, non-state actors internationally and locally need to be active duty-bearers, and Indigenous children and young people must become active right-holders. This is essential to reverse the bleak realities of the more than 370 million Indigenous peoples worldwide (United Nations, 2009) who continue to be discriminated against by assimilation-based state policies and programmes that violate their basic rights.

This chapter has shown that breathing life into the CRC has involved Indigenous peoples finding and giving meaning to various components of the Convention. In becoming involved, Indigenous communities have broadened and deepened understandings of key concepts such as the definition of Indigenous, and the meaning of culture, while considering the actors required for implementation and their roles. In the important sectors of education and child protection, Indigenous peoples have designed and implemented programmes and services that reflect Article 30 and contemporary realities. Indeed, contrary to what is often claimed, the CRC is not uni-dimensional, nor does it provide a single recipe to resolve the tensions that arise in implementing different rights (Alston, 1994; Liebel, 2012).

In moving forward, seeking and nurturing partnerships appear critical because in today's globalized world, Indigenous peoples cannot realize their rights in isolation. As illustrated above, providing for a cultural lens in education and child protection requires the support and resources of the state system, including the infrastructure, as well as capacity-building, and recognition. In claiming rights, any changes or accommodations need to be negotiated, and within this, youth themselves need to be involved. The road to take is a complex one that will encompass strengthening communication within and between Indigenous organizations, communities, and young people, creating collaborations with allies in the multiple sectors that affect Indigenous children and young people's livelihood, and building capacity.

As discussed in this chapter, the emancipatory objective in a critical perspective to children's rights (see Chapter 1 in this Handbook) entails both appropriation and transformation. For children's rights as protected under the CRC to become a lever of social change, Indigenous peoples have to take possession of the Convention. In taking on this active role, alternative methods of providing for Indigenous children's dignity and well-being given diverse histories and cultural contexts are emerging; a contextual orientation is indeed central as pointed out in the introductory chapter.

The road ahead may appear blurry, but the point made in this chapter is that the CRC provides positive signposts that can significantly contribute to making this hope a reality, if taken on by Indigenous peoples and provided with the necessary supports. Finally as Chief Dan George (1974), Coast Salish from Canada, wrote, the youth "will be our new warriors; their training will be much longer and more demanding than it was in the olden days…but they will emerge with their hand held forward not to receive welfare, but to grasp a place in society that is rightly ours."

Questions for debate and discussion

- How can international and local non-state actors support local Indigenous communities who are discriminated against by state parties despite being signatories to the CRC and other international human rights instruments?
- What is the best process for cultural rights to be implemented in ways that reflect Indigenous children and young people's best interests? In what ways do Indigenous cultural rights need to be balanced with other human rights?
- What enabling environment is required to enhance Indigenous children's right to culturally appropriate education and child protection? Are there some unintended consequences of such a focus that would need consideration?
- How can Indigenous children and young people be supported to sustain their role in shaping an alternative perspective on children's rights? What would be (or not) relevant to non-indigenous children?
- What role can children's rights play in helping Indigenous children navigate across intergenerational conflicts, to strike a balance between conserving and redefining their identities given modern and urban realities?

References

Alston, P. (1994). The best interests principle: Towards a reconciliation of culture and human rights, *International Journal of Law, Policy and the Family, 8*(1), 1–25. doi: 10.1093/lawfam/8.1.1

Ames, P. (2012). Language, culture and identity in the transition to primary school: Challenges to Indigenous children's rights to education in Peru. *International Journal of Educational Development, 32*(3), 454–462. doi:10.1016/j.ijedudev.2011.11.006

Battiste, M. (2010). Indigenous knowledge and Indigenous peoples' education. In S.M. Subramanian and B. Pisupati (eds), *Traditional knowledge in policy and practice: Approaches to development and human well-being* (pp. 31–51). Tokyo, New York, Paris: United Nations University Press.

Bissell, S., Boyden, J., Cook, P., and Myers, W. (2007). *Rethinking child protection from a rights perspective: Some observations for discussion*. Unpublished White Paper, prepared for the International Child Protection and Rights Consortium.

Blackstock, C. (2009). After the apology why are so many First Nation children still in foster care? A summary of the research on ethnic overrepresentation and structural bias. *Children Australia, 34,* 22–3.

Blackstock, C. (2011). The Canadian Human Rights Tribunal on First Nations Child Welfare: Why if Canada wins, equality and justice lose. *Children and Youth Services Review, 33*(1), 187–194.

Blackstock, C. (2012). Aboriginal child welfare self-government and the rights of Indigenous children: A book review. *Children and Youth Services Review, 34*(12), 2504–2506. doi:10.1016/j.childyouth.2012.08.005

Blanchet-Cohen, N. (2010). Changing the landscape: Bottom up/top down approaches. In M. Pare, and S. Bennett (eds), *20th Anniversary of the Convention on the Rights of the Child – University of Ottawa, November 18–20th, 2009* (pp. 77–83). Ottawa: STM Learning, Saint Louis.

Blanchet-Cohen, N., and Fernandez, A. (2003). Women as generators of children's rights. The story of promoting Indigenous children's rights in Venezuela. *International Children's Rights Journal, 11*(1), 33–49. doi: 10.1163/092755603322384010

Blanchet-Cohen, N., McMillan, Z., and Greenwood, M. (2011). Indigenous youth engagement in Canada's health care. *Pimatisiwin: A Journal of Aboriginal and Indigenous Community Health, 9*(1), 89–113.

Boyden, J., and Mann, G. (2005), Children's risk, resilience and coping in extreme situations. In M. Ungar (ed.), *Handbook for working with children and youth: Pathways to resilience across cultures and contexts* (pp.3–25). Thousand Oaks, CA: Sage.

Charters, C., and Stavenhagen, R. (2009). *Making the Declaration work: The United Nations Declaration on Indigenous Peoples*. IWGIA.

Chief Dan George. (1974). *My heart soars*. Toronto: Clarke, Irwin.

Committee on the Rights of the Child. (2009). *General Comment No. 11. Indigenous children and their rights under the Convention*. Geneva, Switzerland: Office of the United Nations High Commissioner for Human Rights.

Cook, P., and White, W. (2001). Thunderbirds, thunder-beings, thunder-voices: The application of traditional knowledge and children's rights in support of Aboriginal children's education. *American Review of Canadian Studies, 31*(1), 331–347.

Douglas, H., and Walsh, T. (2013). Continuing the stolen generations: Child protection interventions and Indigenous people. *International Journal of Children's Rights, 21*(1), 59–87. doi:10.1163/157181812X639288

Federal Court. (2012). *Canadian Human Rights Commission V. the Assembly of First Nations, The Attorney General of Canada, the First Nations Child and Family Caring Society of Canada, Chiefs of Ontario and Amnesty International Canada (Docket T-578-11)*. Ottawa: Federal Court.

Gupta, A. (2012). Hazme visible Indigenous children's rights in Chiapas. *DePaul Journal for Social Justice, 5*(2), 379–391.

Hand, C.A. (2006). An Ojibwe perspective on the welfare of children: Lessons of the past and visions for the future. *Children and Youth Services Review, 28*(1), 20–46.

Harris, M., and Gartland, G. (2011). *Children of the Intervention: Aboriginal Children Living in the Northern Territory of Australia*. A Submission to the UNCRC. Concerned Australians.

Hays, J. (2011). Educational rights for Indigenous communities in Botswana and Namibia. *International Journal of Human Rights, 15*(1), 127–153. doi:10.1080/13642987.2011.529695

Henry, F., Tator, C., Mattis, W. and Rees, T. (2000). Perspectives on racism. *The colour of democracy: Racism in Canadian society* (2nd ed., pp. 119–142). Toronto: Harcourt Brace.

Hodgkin, R., and Newell, P. (2007). *Implementation handbook for the Convention on the Rights of the Child*. UNICEF.

International Labour Organization. (1989). *C169 – Indigenous and Tribal Peoples Convention*. Geneva.

Libesman, T. (2007). Can international law imagine the world of Indigenous children? *International Journal of Children's Rights, 15*(2), 283–309. doi:10.1163/092755607X206524

Libesman, T. (2014). *Decolonizing indigenous welfare: Comparative perspectives*. Routledge.

Liebel, M. (ed.). (2012). *Children's rights from below: Cross-cultural perspectives*. New York: Palgrave Macmillan.

Long, M., and Sephton, R. (2011). Rethinking the "best interests "of the child: Voices from Aboriginal child and family welfare practitioners. *Australian Social Work, 64*(1), 96–112. doi:10.1080/0312407X.2010.535544

Lundy, L., and McEvoy, L. (2009). Developing outcomes for educational services: A children's rights-based approach. *Effective Education, 1*(1), 43–60. doi: 10.1080/19415530903044050

McGlade, H. (2012). *Our greatest challenge: Aboriginal children and human rights*. Canberra, Australia: Aboriginal Studies Press.

Meijknecht, A. (2001). *Towards international personality: The position of minorities and Indigenous people in international law*. Oxford: Intersentia.

Myers, M., and Bourdillon, M. (2012). Introduction: Development, children and protection. *Development in Practice, 22*(4), 437–447.

Ney T., Currie, V., Maloney, M., Reeves, C., Ridington, J., Ridington, R., and Zwickel, J. (2014) Traditional decision-making in contemporary child welfare: Relying on Dane-zaa laws to care for and protect children and families. In A. Adebayo, J. Benjamin, and B. Lundy (eds) *Indigenous conflict management strategies: Global perspectives*. New York: Lexington Books, Rowman & Littlefield.

Niezen, R. (2003). *The origins of Indigenism: Human rights and the politics of identity*. Berkeley: University of California Press.

Price Cohen, C. (1995). International protection of the rights of the Indigenous child. *St. Thomas Law Review, 7*, 557–566.

Rae, J. (2006) *Indigenous children: Rights and reality: A report on indigenous children and the UN Convention on the Rights of the Child*. Ottawa: First Nations Child and Family Caring Society of Canada.

Reynaert, D., Bouverne-de Bie, M., and Vandevelde, S. (2009). A review of the children's rights literature since the adoption of the United Nations Convention on the rights the child. *Childhood, 16*(4), 518–34.

Save the Children. (2008). *Review of the concluding observation made by the Committee on the Rights of the Child. Non-discrimination, disability and ethnic rights*. Sweden.

Senate of Canada. (2011). *Reforming First Nations education: From crisis to hope*. Report of the Standing Senate Committee on Aboriginal Peoples.

Skutnabb-Kangas, T., and Dunbar, R. (2010). *Indigenous children's education as linguistic genocide and a crime against humanity? A global view. GálduČála: Journal of Indigenous Peoples' Rights, 1*. Available at www.e-pages.dk/grusweb/55/ (last accessed May 1, 2013).

Swadener, B., Lundy, L., Habashi, J., and Blanchet-Cohen, N. (eds). (2013). *Children's Rights in Education: International Perspectives*. New York, NY: Peter Lang.

UNICEF and Indigenous Youth Caucus. (2013, January). *Know your rights! United Nations Declaration on the Rights of Indigenous Peoples for Indigenous adolescents*. New York, NY: UNICEF.

UNICEF. (2006). *What is Child Protection?* [Child Protection Information Sheet]. Available at www.unicef.org/protection/files/What_is_Child_Protection.pdf

UNICEF. (2010). *Systematization of experiences on the right to identity and birth registration of Indigenous children in Bolivia, Ecuador, Guatemala and Panama*. Plan and UNICEF.

UNICEF. (2004). *Ensuring the Rights of Indigenous Children*. Innocenti Digest No. 11.

UN Commission on Human Rights. (1986). *Study of the problem of discrimination against indigenous populations*. E/CN.4/RES/1986/35.

United Nations. (2004). *The concept of Indigenous peoples. Background paper presented by the Secretariat of the Permanent Forum on Indigenous Issues*. PFII/2004/WS.1/3.

United Nations. (2005a). *Committee on the rights of the child. Concluding observations Nicaragua*. CRC/C/15/Add.265.

United Nations. (2005b). *Indigenous issues: Human rights and Indigenous issues. Report of the Special Rapporteur on the situation of human rights and fundamental freedoms of Indigenous people, Rodolfo Stavenhagen*. Geneva: Economic and Social Council. E/CN.4/2005/88.

United Nations. (2006). *Committee on the rights of the child. Concluding observations Colombia*. CRC/C/COL/CO/3

United Nations. (2007a). *Committee on the rights of the child. Concluding observations Malaysia*. CRC/C/MYS/CO/1.

United Nations. (2007b). *Declaration on the rights of Indigenous Peoples*. New York, NY: United Nations.

United Nations. (2009). *State of the World's Indigenous Peoples*. Department of Economic and Social Affairs: New York, NY.

United Nations. (2012). *Status of the Convention on the Rights of the Child. Report of the Secretary-General*. New York, NY: United Nations.

Wade, D., Mackenzie, I., and Kennedy, S. (1995). *Nomads of the dawn: The Penan of the Borneo rain forest*. San Francisco, CA: Pomegranate Artbooks.

Woolley, S.L. (2009). The rights of Indigenous children around the world: Still far from a reality. *Archives of Disease in Childhood, 94*(5), 397–400.

22
Natural resource exploitation and children's rights

Ellen Desmet and José Aylwin

1. Introduction

One of the greatest challenges for many countries today, mainly but not exclusively in the Global South, concerns the exploitation of their natural resources. The last decades have witnessed an increased pressure on, particularly non-renewable, resources worldwide, invigorated by the continued rise of raw material prices in a globalized world.[1] In the rush for short-term profits, human rights and environmental considerations are often swept under the carpet or only paid lip service to. This chapter explores the relevance of children's rights (law) in the context of natural resource exploitation, with focus on Latin America.

In contrast to "classical" children's rights themes such as juvenile justice or alternative care, an established research tradition on "children's rights and natural resource exploitation" does not – yet – seem to exist. This may be explained by the relative novelty of (attention to) the issue, triggered by the resource rush as well as growing environmental awareness and concerns. At both the normative and scholarly level, the relationship between children's rights and natural resource exploitation has been commonly approached from a particular point of view instead of from a holistic perspective. However, as will become evident throughout this contribution, natural resource exploitation is a transversal phenomenon, cutting across many traditional foci of children's rights analysis, among which child labour, health and education.

The chapter will also show that resource exploitation is an area that highlights the ambivalence of a separate "domain" of children's rights, and in which the current legal conceptualization of children's and human rights runs up against its limits. It is moreover argued that children's rights need to be understood in a holistic, intercultural and context-specific way, in order to adequately address extraction-related challenges.

The relationship between children and young people and natural resource exploitation is multidimensional and variable because of at least three factors: the wide range of resource

---

1 Global use of natural resource materials increased by over 40 percent between 1992 and 2005. By 2008 world trade in natural resources was equivalent to 24 percent of the total value of world trade (UNEP, 2012).

exploitation activities; the different roles of children and young people therein; and the diversity among children and young people.

For a start, there is a large variety of resource exploitation activities, differentiated in function of, among other things: the natural resource exploited (e.g., coffee, sugarcane, timber, oil, gas, mineral resources); the objectives of the exploitation (subsistence or profit-making); the executive agent (a business enterprise, a collectivity or an individual); the scale (small- or large-scale); and the impact on the population and the natural environment. Although "natural resource exploitation" in principle covers all these dimensions, the term is often used to refer to resource extraction with a profit-making objective by business actors. Within business enterprises, a distinction is commonly made between transnational companies (TNCs) and small and medium enterprises (SMEs). Research has mostly focused on the human and children's rights treatment by TNCs, paying – inappropriately – less attention to the role of SMEs and the informal economy (ICJ and OHCHR, 2011, p. 9; Mena et al., 2010, p. 183).

Second, children and young people may be involved in or impacted by natural resource exploitation in several ways. These different "roles" can be grossly divided into three categories: children may be participants, beneficiaries or victims of resource exploitation. As participants, children may be extracting fruits from the forests or working on coffee plantations. As beneficiaries, they may profit from hunting and agricultural activities undertaken by adult relatives, or from the revenues earned by their parents through timber extraction. As victims, children may suffer from pollution caused by oil company activities or from conflicts that the latter trigger with their communities. These various roles will often converge in one child, and boundaries between these are thus not clear-cut. Identifying the role of children in resource exploitation may also be ambiguous, as is illustrated with the issue of child labour (see in general Hanson, Volonakis and Al-Rozzi, Chapter 18 in this Handbook): depending on the context and working conditions, but also on their employer's, parents' and society's attitude and perceptions, children may feel "victims" (of exploitative labour) or "participants" (as "working children") in resource exploitation. Others (parents, employers) will also perceive children as taking up one of these roles – whereby their views will not necessarily coincide with those of children. The identification of the different roles that children can play in the context of resource exploitation may thus interplay with the construction of child images and the protection–agency dichotomy (see introduction). More concretely, interaction seems particularly plausible between the role of "victim" and the child image of a vulnerable child, and between the role of "participant" and the child image of an autonomous child.

Third, the relationship between resource exploitation and children and young people also varies because of the latter's internal diversity. Children and young people are not a homogeneous group, but differ with respect to, among other things, age, gender, class, ethnicity, socio-economic status and geographical location. Indigenous children, for instance, face particular challenges. Indigenous peoples generally live in resource-rich regions and have a profound, albeit dynamic (Desmet, 2011), relationship with their lands, territories and natural resources. They are among the groups most severely affected by the activities of the extractive and agro-industrial sectors (UN General Assembly 2013, §1).

These three factors characterizing the relationship between children and young people and natural resource exploitation will interplay in determining the impact of resource exploitation on the rights and well-being of children and young people. This impact greatly varies. Resource exploitation may contribute to the improvement of children's living standards and to the realization of their rights, for instance, when it concerns small-scale sustainable exploitation, or when states invest revenues in education and health care systems in a transparent and effective way. On the other hand, resource exploitation activities may also negatively impact on children's well-being and infringe their rights in multiple ways. It has been demonstrated that countries that rely on oil and mineral exports suffer from higher rates of mortality for children under the age of five than other states at the same income level. In addition, oil dependence is linked to higher rates of child malnutrition and lower results in the fields of education and health care, whereas mineral dependence is associated with higher levels of income inequality (Ross, 2001; Save the Children, 2003). This disconnect between natural resource wealth, on the one hand, and economic growth and development outcomes, on the other, has become commonly known as the "resource curse" (Auty, 1993).

The way (the impact of) resource exploitation is perceived and dealt with, will moreover vary with how children and young people are conceptualized. As elaborated in this Handbook's introduction, various child images can be distinguished, underpinning different policies and practices. If children are constructed as fragile and incompetent, protective and paternalistic policies will get the upper hand. If, on the other hand, children are conceptualized as active social agents, capable of expressing their views and contributing to their own development, policies and practices will take more account of this input of children and young people (Tranter and Sharpe, 2007). It will be demonstrated that in resource exploitation, the image of a vulnerable child seems predominant, leading to a "protective reflex" of (human rights) actors involved. Indications of recognition of children's and young people's agency are nonetheless increasingly emerging.

To contextualize and concretize the challenges faced by children and young people in relation to natural resource exploitation, the chapter zooms in on the Latin American continent. After an introduction on resource exploitation policies, the experiences of children and young people with regard to natural resource industries in Latin America are discussed on the basis of various case studies. Thereinafter, relevant legal standards are reviewed, with particular attention for business-related standards, the Inter-American human rights jurisprudence and the approach of the UN Committee on the Rights of the Child (hereinafter also CRC Committee). The chapter then discusses two fields of tension, on child-specificity and on incorporating insights from other disciplines, to round up with some future-oriented reflections.

2. Natural resource exploitation in Latin America: Policies and trends

The case of Latin America is interesting to analyse here due to the high dependency of its economy on natural resource exploitation, and the adverse implications this has had on human rights, including children's rights, in particular of indigenous peoples and local rural communities (RRI, 2012; Bass, 2008; Ensing, 2008). Although since colonial times mining and agriculture have been central activities in the region's economy, the dependency on natural resource exploitation has steadily grown in recent decades as a consequence of neoliberal policies adopted by most of its states (UNEP, 2012; CEPAL, 2012a). In accordance with these policies, which have been promoted by multilateral financial institutions such as the World Bank and the Inter-American Development Bank, many states in Latin America have abandoned previous policies of industrialization and import substitution, and opened their economies to foreign investment, mainly in natural resource exploitation (Leiva, 2011).

Such investment has been facilitated by free trade and bilateral investment agreements. These agreements generally contain provisions that protect investors against political risks and promote the enjoyment of financial benefits (RRI, 2012; Aylwin, 2010). Moreover, several of them contain "stabilization" clauses that can either insulate investors from new environmental and social laws or entitle them to seek compensation for compliance, restricting the ability of states to implement their international human rights obligations (Ruggie, 2010; Pahis, 2011).

As a result of these policies and agreements, Latin America is currently the main international destination of foreign direct investment in mining and oil. As exploration and exploitation increase, so do conflicts triggered by these activities. This is due to their significant environmental and social impact, in particular on local and indigenous communities (CEPAL, 2012a; RRI, 2012). Agriculture has equally experienced a significant growth in the region in recent years, leading to a considerable expansion of irrigated lands and areas destined for cultivation. Land grabbing processes associated with these activities have seriously threatened collective land rights of indigenous peoples and rural communities. Such activities have also undermined their food security based on local agricultural production. Environmental impacts include deforestation, land degradation and erosion, biodiversity loss and contribution to greenhouse gases. In the last two decades, Latin America has contributed one third of the world's deforestation (CEPAL, 2012a). In addition, South America in particular has emerged as a main destination of investments in forest plantations, largely monocultures, mostly oriented to the production of paper pulp (CEPAL, 2012a). The implications of these plantations for land rights and food security are similar to or even worse than those of agricultural activities, as illustrated below. Opportunities, such as employment, services and taxation, which are generally promoted as benefits of resource exploitation, in particular of mining, are unevenly distributed in Latin America. This unequal distribution helps to explain social conflicts that emerge in many areas where resource exploitation is undertaken (Bebbington, 2011).

3. Children('s rights) and natural resource exploitation: Cases from Latin America

Adverse impacts of resource exploitation on children and their rights are common to most countries in Latin America. One of the elements contributing to the internal diversity of children and young people is their geographical location, i.e. whether they are living in rural or urban areas. In rural areas, where access to social services and state presence are limited, child poverty is higher than in urban environments. It is also in rural areas that resource exploitation often takes place, and consequently, that children are more exposed to its direct impacts. Indigenous children, due to their intersected identity of being indigenous and a child, are generally even more exposed to negative consequences of resource exploitation. A total of 63 percent of Latin American children are poor; a percentage that increases to 88 percent in the case of indigenous children (Del Popolo, 2012).

For instance, indigenous (Aymara and Quechua) children in the Andes are actively engaged in small-scale and artisanal mining. In Peru, the International Labour Organization (ILO) estimates that 50,000 children are involved in mining. A study undertaken in two mining villages in Ayacucho and the Puno region shows that children working in this activity lack running water and a sewage system, as well as adequate health care and access to education. In the Puno region, they live in extreme climate conditions at high elevations (5,400 meters) and are at risk due to violence and alcoholism, practices widespread in the area. In both cases, mines lack advanced technology, subjecting children to health and security risks because of exposure to mercury, dust and toxic gases (Ensing, 2008).

Although large-scale mining generally does not employ children, it has severely impacted on children too. Serious environmental problems, which endanger children's health, are prevalent across the region, and have led to some cases before the Inter-American human rights system, as discussed below.

Agribusiness and forest plantations have also had serious impacts on indigenous children's rights. Such is the case of soybean and sugarcane plantations in Mato Grosso do Sul (MS), Brazil, in the ancestral territory of the Guarani Kaiowa people. Land acquisition by large corporations triggered by the 2007 biofuel agreement between Brazil and the US, has resulted in deforestation, the eviction of the Guarani Kaiowa from their natural habitats, and their inability to plant food, fish and hunt for a living (Aylwin, 2009; Miranda, 2012). By 2008, almost 8,000 indigenous persons, mainly Guarani, including children, were working in deplorable conditions on sugarcane plantations and alcohol distilleries in MS (Aylwin, 2009; Cultural Survival, n.d.). Soybean farms have also expanded into lands claimed by the Guarani. Homicides among them have increased from 19 in 2004 to 53 in 2007, being a result of internal and external tensions directly or indirectly related to the land struggle (Anaya, 2009). Infant mortality rate among Guarani children in 2007 was 49.23 per 1,000 live births compared to 21.2 per 1,000 live births in Brazil in general. Malnutrition among Guarani children caused 65 deaths in 2006 and 2007 (Aylwin, 2009).

In South Chile, forest monocultures for the production of timber and cellulose for the US and Chinese market, have severely impacted on Mapuche children and young people. Land dispossession as well as environmental and social impacts, among which biodiversity loss, diminished water supply, poverty and migration, have triggered Mapuche social protest (CEPAL-Alianza Territorial Mapuche, 2012b). Such protest – largely peaceful – has been contested by the state with police repression, resulting in many cases of torture and cruel, inhuman and degrading treatment affecting community members, including hundreds of children and young people between 9 months and 17 years old as well as elderly people. In 2002, police agents were responsible for the homicide of a child involved in acts of protest against forest companies. Even in Mapuche homes and schools, the police frequently uses rubber bullets and tear gas bombs, injuring many children. Numerous cases of arbitrary detention and illegal interrogation of Mapuche children have also been reported (ANIDE, 2012). Such practices continue to take place, notwithstanding the fact that the Supreme Court of Chile has ordered the police on several occasions to establish a special protocol for their action on Mapuche communities, taking particular care of Mapuche children and women (INDH, 2013).[2] Moreover, the Anti-terrorist law (No. 18,314) has been used to prosecute indigenous children. Notwithstanding a 2010 legal reform prohibiting prosecution of minors, Mapuche children continue to be prosecuted under charges of having committed terrorist crimes. Several children have spent long periods in preventive prison while anti-terrorist trials were taking place (ANIDE, 2012).

Not only in Chile have children and young people been expressing their concern about the impact of natural resource exploitation on the environment and on their rights. In a declaration to the 2005 Ibero-American Summit Meeting, for instance, boys and girls from 34 indigenous peoples called on their governments to "eradicate the illegal use of our traditional crops and support the development of other productive crops". In May 2014, hundreds of Kukama children of the Marañón river in Peru sent letters and drawings to President Humala, demanding his support to tackle the serious contamination of their environment, caused by more than four decades of oil exploitation (PUINAMUDT, 2014). Although the initiative was taken by local indigenous organizations, the parish and local schools, and can be considered a somewhat "superficial" form of participation, it at least provided children an opportunity to express their concerns directly to the highest person in charge in their country, giving them a voice in Peru and – via the world wide web – across the globe. To move beyond tokenistic

2   Supreme Court of Chile, decisions of 5 January 2012, 26 September 2012, 9 December 2012.

participation, inspiration can be drawn from experiences with child coffee-plantation workers in Nicaragua, where the approach implied supporting "children's gradual 'bottom-up' processes of learning, sharing, organising and mobilizing, so that when children demand a voice in the big decisions that affect their lives, they arrive at the table as a force to be reckoned with" (Shier, 2009, p. 226).

In urban environments, the consequences of increased resource exploitation may manifest themselves quite differently than among rural and indigenous communities. For instance, the availability of cheap oil has induced parents to drive their children to school and to rush them from one extracurricular activity to the next, in order to counter perceived risks of traffic and stranger danger – a protective impulse. This transport mode has had adverse effects, depriving children and young people from physical exercise and independent mobility, as well as from play opportunities and their street culture (Tranter and Sharpe, 2007). Consequently, a decline in oil availability and a rise of its price may give children more time and free play, albeit within more limited spaces of the local neighbourhood. This may then increase children's sense of connection to their local communities (Tranter and Sharpe, 2007, p. 192).

4. Legal standards

The cases mentioned above illustrate that virtually every human right of children and young people may be threatened or violated in the context of natural resource exploitation – confirming the interdependence and indivisibility of human rights. Whereas social, economic and cultural rights (e.g., right to health, right to protection from economic exploitation, right to an adequate standard of living, right to education, right to play) may be more immediately linked to or impacted by resource extraction, the Mapuche case especially demonstrates that also civil and political rights (e.g., right to life, prohibition of torture or other cruel, inhuman or degrading treatment, right to a fair trial) may be at stake. For indigenous children, the right to their lands, territories and natural resources and the right to enjoy their culture are particularly relevant. Moreover, states have an obligation to consult indigenous peoples in order to obtain their free, prior and informed consent before the adoption of legislation or administrative measures that may affect them (art. 19 UN Declaration on the Rights of Indigenous Peoples (UNDRIP); art. 6 ILO Convention 169), as well as when undertaking projects that affect their land, territory and resources, including mining and utilization or exploitation of other resources (art. 32 UNDRIP; art. 15(2) ILO Convention 169). In some circumstances, such as relocation, there is an obligation to obtain the consent of the indigenous peoples concerned, beyond the general obligation of consultation (arts. 10 and 29 UNDRIP; art. 16(2) ILO Convention 169). In the case *Saramaka People v. Suriname*, the Inter-American Court of Human Rights (IACtHR) also identified two criteria to establish the duty of the State to obtain free, prior and informed consent, namely when it concerns "large-scale" development or investment projects that would have a "major impact" within the people's territory (IACtHR, 2007, §134). Natural resource exploitation activities will often comply with these two conditions.

The Convention on the Rights of the Child (CRC) does not mention natural resource exploitation as such. The impact of environmental degradation is explicitly referred to in the context of the right to health. Article 24(2)(c) provides that States Parties, when pursuing the full implementation of the child's right to the enjoyment of the highest attainable standard of health, shall take measures "[t]o combat disease and malnutrition, ... taking into consideration the dangers and risks of environmental pollution". As illustrated above, almost any provision of the CRC may however come into play in a resource exploitation context. Since this complicates a comprehensive review of all possibly relevant standards, a threefold, necessarily limited, approach is adopted.³ Given the importance of business actors in resource extraction and the recent normative developments in this domain, the first subsection focuses on business-related standards in human rights and children's rights law. Thereinafter, it is analysed how natural resource exploitation in Latin America has been dealt with by presumably the most relevant human rights organs in this respect, namely the Inter-American Court of Human Rights, the Inter-American Commission on Human Rights (IACHR) and the UN Committee on the Rights of the Child – bearing in mind their different goals, the first ones charged with monitoring compliance with human rights in general, the Committee focusing on children's rights.

4.1. Business-related standards

Whereas business-related standards will often play a central role in the context of natural resource exploitation, both issues should not be identified with each other. Business actors may engage in resource extraction, but also in a wide array of other activities. On the other hand, although resource exploitation admittedly in many (and often the most impactful) cases belongs to the realm of corporate actors, exploitation may also be carried out by individuals, informal groups, non-profit associations or government actors themselves.

Current international (human rights) law considers states as the primary duty bearers. The growing impact of business actors in a globalized world, accompanied by a decreasing power of national states, have induced a vigorous debate on the relationship between human rights and business. Within the confines of this chapter, it is impossible to do justice to the breadth and depth of this debate (but see, e.g., Clapham, 2006; De Schutter, 2006; Deva and Bilchitz 2013; Mares, 2012). Hereinafter, both human and children's rights standards are analysed, to avoid their further growing apart, pointed to in this Handbook's introduction.

4.1.1. Human rights and business

Since the 1970s, the relationship between human rights and business has been increasingly addressed via voluntary and multi-stakeholder initiatives. As of today, no international legally binding instrument on human rights and business exists. The Guidelines for Multinational Enterprises of the Organisation for Economic Co-operation and Development (OECD) were adopted in 1976 and updated for the fifth time in 2011 (OECD, 2011). The Guidelines contain recommendations that the adhering governments promote among their enterprises, wherever they operate. A system of National Contact Points (NCPs) supports the implementation of the Guidelines, among others through assisting corporate actors in taking appropriate measures and by providing a mediation and reconciliation platform. The potential contribution of the Guidelines and the NCP system to the realization of children's rights is hampered by various shortcomings. The only children's rights issue explicitly included in the Guidelines is child labour, as a consequence of which the complaints received by the NCPs have mostly concerned this topic (Sheahan, 2011, p. 29). In addition, the Guidelines have far from

---

3   Issues falling outside the scope of this section include, among others, the norms on child labour and the debate concerning the rights of working children (see Hanson, Volonakis and Al-Rozzi, Chapter 18 in this Handbook), the complexities arising from resource exploitation in (post-)conflict areas (see, e.g., Buhmann and Ryngaert, 2012) and the specific rights of indigenous children (see Blanchet-Cohen, Chapter 21 in this Handbook).

worldwide coverage, the capacity of NCPs to investigate and mediate is weak, and the compliance level of companies with recommendations issued by the NCPs low (Sheahan, 2011, p. 30).

In 2000, the UN Global Compact was established, consisting of Ten Principles regarding human rights, labour standards, the environment and anti-corruption. Pursuant to Principle Five, businesses should "uphold the effective abolition of child labour". Companies are invited, on a voluntary basis, to sign up to these principles and align their strategies and activities with them. The lack of an effective monitoring mechanism impedes, however, a substantial impact.

The Norms on the Responsibilities of Transnational Corporations and Other Business Enterprises (TNC Norms), proposed by the UN Sub-Commission on the Promotion and Protection of Human Rights (2003), caused a lot of controversy. Whereas states bore the primary responsibility concerning human rights, it was proposed to apply the same typology of obligations – "to promote, secure the fulfilment of, respect, ensure respect of and protect human rights" – to transnational corporations, albeit limited to "their respective spheres of activity and influence". Given the resistance this proposal evoked especially within the business sector, the Human Rights Commission desisted from adopting the TNC Norms.

In 2005, John Ruggie was appointed as Special Representative of the Secretary-General on the Issue of Human Rights and Transnational Corporations and other Business Enterprises (SRSG). He engaged in broad consultations with a wide range of stakeholders, on the basis of a "principled pragmatism" approach. His work resulted in the "Protect, Respect and Remedy" Framework, which consists of three pillars: (i) the duty of the state to *protect* against human rights violations by third parties, including business enterprises; (ii) the responsibility of business enterprises to *respect* human rights, which implies acting with due diligence to avoid infringing on the rights of others as well as addressing adverse human rights impacts with which they are involved; and (iii) more effective access by victims to *remedies*, both judicial and non-judicial (UN Human Rights Council, 2008). In 2011, the Guiding Principles on Business and Human Rights (Guiding Principles) were issued to facilitate the implementation of the Framework (UN Human Rights Council, 2011a). In its 2011 resolution endorsing the Guiding Principles, the Human Rights Council (2011b) established an expert Working Group (WG) on the issue of human rights and transnational corporations and business enterprises, with a 3-year mandate to implement and disseminate the Guiding Principles. In a 2013 report, the WG addressed the implementation of the Guiding Principles in relation to indigenous peoples, providing recommendations to enhance the Principles' effective operationalization (UN General Assembly, 2013). The report reaffirms the duty of states to protect human rights, which implies that states must take measures to prevent or end infringement upon the enjoyment of a given human right caused by third parties, recognizing that in the context of the rights of indigenous peoples, such third parties are often business enterprises. Among others, the WG highlights the relevance of customary laws and practices as a form of non-judicial grievance mechanisms (UN General Assembly, 2013, §§ 45–47).

The Framework and Guiding Principles have generally been well received by states and corporate actors. Many civil society actors and scholars on the other hand, have criticized the texts for being too minimalist, missing "the opportunity to push states and business actors out of their comfort zone" (Simons, 2012, p. 41, see also Vandenhole, 2012a). After the failure of the TNC Norms, the SRSG aimed to achieve consensus and maintain all stakeholders on board (Bilchitz, 2010). Therefore, from the outset, the SRSG emphasized the state as the only legal duty-bearer, refraining from formulating direct legal obligations for enterprises. This is clear from the wording in the 2008 Framework, where states have an *obligation* to protect human rights, against the corporate *responsibility* to respect (Jägers, 2011, pp. 161–162).

An additional limit of current business-related standards concerns the lack of domestic and international mechanisms to address human rights violations committed by multinational enterprises outside the states in which they are registered (IFHR, 2012). Many resource exploitation companies operate abroad, however. The UN Committee on the Elimination of Racial Discrimination (UN CERD) has noted this reality and issued recommendations on this matter to several industrialized countries, including Australia (UN CERD, 2010), Norway (UN CERD, 2011a), the United Kingdom (UN CERD, 2011b) and Canada (UN CERD, 2012), with particular reference to indigenous peoples. Norway for instance was recommended to "take appropriate legislative or administrative measures to ensure that the activities of transnational corporations domiciled in the territory and/or under the jurisdiction of Norway do not have a negative impact on the enjoyment of rights of indigenous peoples and other ethnic groups, in territories outside Norway" (UN CERD, 2011a, §17). The WG has also recognized the need for states to regulate the extraterritorial activities of businesses domiciled in their territory and/or jurisdiction, and affirms that "States should take into account the specificities of indigenous peoples and ensure that any barriers to their access to [grievance] mechanisms are addressed and removed" (UN General Assembly, 2013, §37).

Another attempt to address this limitation are the "Maastricht Principles on Extraterritorial Obligations of States in the area of Economic, Social and Cultural Rights", which were adopted at a meeting convened in late 2011 at the University of Maastricht (the Netherlands). This document, while lacking endorsement by the UN Human Rights Council, has been supported by a large number of present and past UN mandate holders, members and former members of UN treaty bodies as well as members of academia and many civil society organizations. As regards the scope of jurisdiction, the Maastricht Principles hold that "a State has obligations to respect, protect and fulfil economic, social and cultural rights in any of the following: a) situations over which it exercises authority or effective control, whether or not such control is exercised in accordance with international law" (e.g. when a state-controlled enterprise is engaged in resource exploitation abroad); "b) situations over which State acts or omissions bring about foreseeable effects on the enjoyment of economic, social and cultural rights, whether within or outside its territory" (e.g. when lack of state control on environmental behaviour of resource extraction companies leads to adverse health impacts on the population); "c) situations in which the State ... is in a position to exercise decisive influence or to take measures to realize economic, social and cultural rights extraterritorially, in accordance with international law" (e.g. state omission to take measures to respect cultural rights in relation to resource exploitation) (§9). Applying these (non-binding) principles would considerably increase the accountability of states for violations of (children's) human rights in relation to resource exploitation.

In June 2014, the UN Human Rights Council (2014) adopted a resolution with the support of 20 member states, to "elaborate a binding instrument to regulate the activities of transnational corporations and other business enterprises". This decision may be an important step in the process of protecting against corporate-related human rights violations, and in clarifying extraterritorial obligations to regulate TNCs overseas.

In all these general human rights documents, children are only occasionally and briefly referred to, mostly in relation to child labour (cf. OECD Guidelines and UN Global Compact). Moreover, children seem to be predominantly conceptualized as "vulnerable", which limits an appropriate recognition of their agency. For instance, pursuant to the Commentary on Principle 3 of the Guiding Principles, state guidance to enterprises on respecting human rights should include advice on how to consider "vulnerability and/or marginalization, recognizing the specific challenges that may be faced by ... children".[4] The WG is requested to "give special attention to persons living in vulnerable situations, in particular children" (UN Human Rights Council 2011b, §6(f)), and has identified indigenous children as a group at risk of multiple discrimination in relation to business activities (UN General Assembly, 2013, §2).

4.1.2. Children's rights and business

The UN Committee on the Rights of the Child has been paying increased attention to the relationship between the rights of children and business. In 2002, the Committee discussed the role of the private sector as service provider during a General Day of Discussion. More recently, a new paragraph on "child rights and business" has been included in the section "General measures of implementation" of many concluding observations (see also below). In April 2013, the Committee (UN Committee CRC, 2013a) adopted General Comment No. 16 "On State obligations regarding the impact of the business sector on children's rights" (GC 16), after a broad consultation process with many stakeholders, including children (see Save the Children, 2012). GC 16 can be considered innovative in various ways. First, in contrast to the traditional approach of General Comments of discussing the interpretation of a particular article of the CRC, a broader – and more challenging – approach is adopted, involving the Convention as a whole. Moreover, the CRC Committee is the first UN treaty body to address the relationship between human rights and business in a General Comment (Martin-Ortega and Wallace, 2013, p. 121). Finally, submissions received during the consultation process that accompanied the drafting of GC 16 were published online, which contributed to the transparency of the process (Gerber et al., 2013, p. 13). Somewhat remarkably, Gerber et al. (2013) pay no particular attention in their discussion of the drafting process to (the degree and impact of) the participation of children and young people.

GC 16 aims to clarify the obligations of states regarding the impact of the business sector on children's rights, which arise from the CRC and its Optional Protocols. Like the Guiding Principles, GC 16 adopts a state-centred focus. Only very briefly, it mentions that private actors and business enterprises have "duties and responsibilities" to respect children's rights (UN Committee CRC, 2013a, §8). This can be considered a missed opportunity to address business actors directly.

The General Comment consists of four main parts. A first part analyses the four general principles of the CRC in relation to business activities. Regarding the impact of business activities on children's rights to life, survival and development, the Committee states:

> The activities and operations of business enterprises can impact on the realization of article 6 in different ways. For example, environmental degradation and contamination arising from business activities can compromise children's rights to health, food security and access to safe drinking water and sanitation. Selling or leasing land to investors can deprive local populations of access to natural resources linked to their subsistence and cultural heritage; the rights of indigenous children may be particularly at risk in this context.
> *(UN Committee CRC, 2013a, §19)*

These considerations are especially relevant in the case of businesses engaged in natural resource exploitation. Second, the Committee spells out the nature and scope of state obligations in

---

4   See also Commentary on Principle 12.

relation to the business sector based on the general framework of international human rights law, according to which states have three types of obligations: to respect, to protect and to fulfil. States also have "an obligation to provide effective remedies and reparations for violations of the rights of the child, including by third parties such as business enterprises" (UN Committee CRC, 2013a, §30). Third, the General Comment identifies specific contexts that require additional attention. Regarding the issue of businesses operating globally, GC 16 interestingly goes further than the Guiding Principles. Whereas the Guiding Principles did not include mandatory language in this respect, GC 16 clearly states that "[h]ome States also have *obligations* ... to respect, protect and fulfil children's rights in the context of businesses' extraterritorial activities and operations" (UN Committee CRC, 2013a, §43). This approach is more reflective of the current status of international law (Gerber *et al.*, 2013, p. 34). Finally, GC 16 provides a framework for implementation, distinguishing between five types of measures: legislative, regulatory and enforcement measures; remedial measures; policy measures; coordination and monitoring measures, including child rights impact assessments; and collaborative and awareness-raising measures.

Another standard-setting initiative addresses the business sector itself: in March 2012, UNICEF, Save the Children and the UN Global Compact (2012) presented the "Children's Rights and Business Principles" (CRB Principles), which aim to elaborate the role of the business sector in respecting and supporting children's rights in the community, marketplace and workplace. On the basis of a Child Participation Strategy, more than 400 children and young people in nine countries were consulted. The conceptualization of children's rights seems somewhat ambiguous, and in this way illustrates the tensions noted in this Handbook's introduction regarding children's rights and/as human rights. Whereas it is first more restrictively mentioned that "[c]hildren's rights are outlined by the Convention on the Rights of the Child, and [ILO Conventions 138 and 182]" (UNICEF, Save the Children and the UN Global Compact, 2012, p. 5), it is subsequently more broadly stated that "[i]n this document, the phrase 'children's rights' is synonymous with the 'human rights of children'" (UNICEF, Save the Children and the UN Global Compact, 2012).

The ten Principles do not create new international legal obligations, but are derived from the internationally recognized human rights of children (UNICEF, Save the Children and the UN Global Compact, 2012, p. 12). They are structured along two main types of actions: next to the "corporate responsibility to respect" (constructed in a similar way as in the UN "Protect, Respect and Remedy" Framework), stands the "corporate commitment to support", which refers to voluntary actions seeking to advance human and children's rights. By introducing another type of engagement ("commitment"), the CRB Principles contribute to a further conceptual distinction between the expectations from corporate actors ("responsibilities" and "commitments") and states ("obligations") (Martin-Ortega and Wallace, 2013, p. 117).

Principle 7, according to which all business should "respect and support children's rights in relation to the environment and to land acquisition and use", appears very pertinent for our analysis, and has been characterized as "particularly innovative" (Martin-Ortega and Wallace, 2013, p. 119). The corporate responsibility to *respect* the environment implies ensuring "that business operations do not adversely affect children's rights, including through damage to the environment or reducing access to natural resources" and that "the rights of children, their families and communities are addressed in contingency plans and remediation for environmental and health damage from business operations, including accidents". The responsibility to respect children's rights in relation to land acquisition and use requires avoiding or minimizing displacement of communities, seeking the free, prior and informed consent of indigenous peoples for any project that affects their communities, as well as respecting children's rights in cases of resettlement. The corporate commitment to *support* children's rights in relation to the environment includes taking measures to reduce gas emissions, promoting sustainable resource use, and supporting communities to adapt to the consequences of climate change. It is however remarkable that Principle 7 does not include a reference to child-sensitive consultation processes, in contrast to elsewhere in the document (Martin-Ortega and Wallace, 2013, p. 120).

Summing up, both GC 16 and the CRB Principles recognize children as bearers of rights, "rather than the recipients of [state or] corporate kindness" (Martin-Ortega and Wallace, 2013, p. 117; p. 126). Both instruments also pay explicit attention to the impact of business activities that affect children's natural environment (Martin-Ortega and Wallace, 2013, p. 127). Although they don't create new human rights obligations, and they could have been more progressive in interpreting existing human rights law, both GC 16 and the CRB Principles may be useful instruments to guide and inspire "willing" states and enterprises. As a General Comment, GC 16 constitutes an authoritative source to interpret the CRC in relation to business activities. As a voluntary instrument, the CRB principles suffer from the same lack of enforcement possibilities as the general human rights initiatives discussed above, depending for their impact on the goodwill of enterprises.

4.1.3. The Inter-American human rights system

Article 19 of the 1969 American Convention on Human Rights (ACHR) guarantees the right of every child "to the measures of *protection* required by his condition as a minor on the part of his family, society, and the State" (emphasis added). This protective focus is reflective of the spirit of that age (20 years before the adoption of the CRC), and is also manifested in the Inter-American case-law, which has mainly dealt with issues relating to the protection of, among others, children living on the streets, children deprived of their liberty by the state, and children in the context of (internal) armed conflict (see Feria Tinta, 2008).

Human rights conventions are living instruments and should be interpreted in the light of evolving circumstances. In relation to children's rights, the Court considered in the *Street Children* case that "[b]oth the American Convention and the Convention on the Rights of the Child form part of a very comprehensive international *corpus juris* for the protection of the child that should help this Court establish the content and scope of the general provision established in article 19 of the American Convention" (IACtHR, 1999, §194).[5] This does not imply, however, "that any given provision of the CRC automatically amounts to a 'measure of protection required'" by Art. 19 ACHR (Neuman, 2008, p. 114, n. 68). In light of the current interpretation of children's rights at the international level, it could be expected from the Court, however, to also give effect to the provision and participation rights of children.

Various cases have been brought before the Inter-American human rights system, in which natural resource exploitation by corporations played a role, by leading to or aggravating human rights violations – especially in relation to indigenous peoples.[6] In *Case 12.010 – Children and*

---

5 The Court's comprehensive understanding of the right to life in the *Street Children* case, including not only the right not to be arbitrarily deprived of one's life, but also the right to access conditions guaranteeing a dignified existence (IACtHR, 1999, §144) may be relevant for resource exploitation cases.
6 At the African level, the most important case on natural resource exploitation is the *Ogoni* case. In 2001, the African Commission on Human and Peoples' Rights held that the Nigerian government, by participating in environmentally destructive oil production within Ogoniland, had violated the collective rights of the Ogoni people, among which their right to a general satisfactory environment (ACHPR, 2001). Children were not mentioned in the decision.

Youth of the Paynemil Community of the Mapuche People, Neuquén, Argentina, hydrocarbon exploitation had exposed Mapuche children and youth to mercury and lead contamination. A national court decision ordering the Argentinean state to provide drinking water, carry out health and environmental studies and provide medical assistance had not been adequately complied with. Therefore, the Official Defender of Minors of the Neuquén Province filed a complaint with the Inter-American Commission in 1999, alleging violations of, among others, children's right to receive protection measures as required by their status as minors, as well as their right to health and a healthy environment (Falaschi and Osés, 2012). Although the case was discussed in various hearings and the Inter-American Commission visited the country, no full implementation has yet been achieved (ESCR-Net, n.d.). In contrast to the cases discussed hereinafter, where children and young people have been implicitly or explicitly included in a broader group of victims, here children and young people were interestingly the main focus of analysis.

In the landmark case on indigenous land rights, *Mayagna (Sumo) Awas Tingni Community v. Nicaragua* of 2001, the Inter-American Court found that Nicaragua had violated the right to property by awarding a logging concession to a Korean corporation on the lands of the Awas Tingni community without their consent (IACtHR, 2001). Although it can be supposed that this judgment will also benefit the children of the Awas Tingni community, children were not explicitly mentioned as stakeholders, neither by the petitioners nor by the Court. The latter grounded its interpretation of the right to property in a way that reflected the collective, multi-dimensional relationship of indigenous peoples to their territories, on, among other things, testimonies of various anthropologists.

Sawhoyamaxa Indigenous Community v. Paraguay was the first case where a violation of Art. 19 ACHR in relation to *indigenous* children was found (IACtHR, 2006). The Court considered the death of 18 children of the Sawhoyamaxa community attributable to the Paraguayan state because the latter had not adopted the necessary positive measures to prevent the loss of their lives, constituting a violation of the right to life (Art. 4 ACHR) as regards to Art. 1(1) ACHR, and additionally of the rights of the child (Art. 19 ACHR). Among other things, the case presented a conflict between the territorial claims of an indigenous people and the livestock industry. The Sawhoyamaxa community had been dispossessed of their ancestral territories, which had been partly deforested by cattle farmers – the present owners – as pasture land for grazing.

In the past decade, two cases against the Peruvian state were declared admissible by the Inter-American Commission, in which, among others, a violation of the rights of children as a consequence of extractive activities by business actors is alleged. In the case of *Community of San Mateo de Huanchor and its Members*, the petitioners claimed that the Peruvian state is responsible for violating the human rights of the community concerned, because of the effects suffered by its members from the environmental pollution caused by toxic waste of a mining company (IACHR, 2004b, §5). According to the petitioners, "those who are most severely affected are the children, who show high indices of lead, arsenic, and mercury in their organism, which if not treated will have severe consequences for their integral development" (IACHR, 2004b, §26). Most of the about 5,600 inhabitants of the Community of San Mateo de Huanchor identify themselves as indigenous (IACHR, 2004b, §§15–16). On 17 August 2004, the Commission adopted precautionary measures, requesting the Peruvian government, among others, to establish a "health assistance and care program for the population of San Mateo de Huanchor, especially its children", to draw up an environmental impact assessment study required for removing the toxic waste sludge, and, after completion of and in accordance with the said study, to start with the transfer of the sludge to a safe site (IACHR, 2004b, §12). On 15 October 2004, the Commission declared the petition admissible.

In the second case, *Community La Oroya*, a smelter located in the Peruvian Andes owned by US capital has for a long time affected children living in the area. According to a 1999 survey of the Peruvian Ministry of Health, 99.1 percent of the children had blood lead levels that considerably exceeded acceptable limits. A study of Saint-Louis University, requested by the Archdiocese of the region, confirmed these high blood lead levels and moreover found elevated levels of arsenic, cadmium and other toxic metals in the residents of La Oroya, which were associated with the mining and smelting activities and which led to health problems (Serrano, 2005; Fraser, 2009). This scientific study was used in the case filed before the Inter-American Commission, where the petitioners emphasized the particularly harmful effects of the contamination on children: "[B]ecause children are undergoing physical and cognitive development, they are more sensitive than adults to the adverse neurological effects of lead poisoning" (IACHR, 2009, n. 6). In 2009, the Commission declared the case admissible, finding, among other things, that the illnesses and deaths allegedly resulting from the severe pollution produced by the smelter constitute a potential violation of the rights to life and integrity, including the rights of children (IACHR, 2009, §77).[7] If the Inter-American Court will find a violation, "[t]he case would be the first time that the Court has assessed the responsibility of a state for the violation of human rights of a *non-indigenous* community caused by contamination of the environment" (Spieler, 2010, p. 19, emphasis added).

In the case of the *Kichwa Indigenous People of Sarayaku v. Ecuador*, the state had allowed a private oil company to operate in the ancestral territory of the Kichwa people of Sarayaku, without prior consultation. Whereas both the claim of the petitioners and the admissibility decision of the Inter-American Commission explicitly mentioned article 19 ACHR on the rights of the child (IACHR, 2004a, §§2 and 74), the article was not included anymore in the application submitted by the Commission to the Court (IACHR, 2010). In June 2012, the Court found that the state of Ecuador was responsible for violating the rights to consultation, indigenous communal property and cultural identity, the right to life and to personal integrity, and the right to judicial guarantees and judicial protection (IACtHR, 2012). This judgment should also benefit the children and young people of the Sarayaku community. Here, it is interesting that for the first time a delegation of judges visited the site of the events and that during this visit, the delegation heard various statements from members of the Sarayaku people, "including young people ... and children from the community" (IACtHR, 2012, §21).

Recapitulating, the relationship between children's rights and natural resource exploitation has entered the Inter-American jurisprudence in various, albeit still relatively modest, ways. In the *Sawhoyamaxa* case, the impact of resource exploitation by third parties on the state's human rights violations was rather indirect. In the two cases declared admissible by the Inter-American Commission, *San Mateo de Huanchor* and *La Oroya*, on the other hand, the alleged responsibility of the state for violations of children's rights is directly connected with resource exploitation activities by third parties. These cases have not been decided on the merits though. From a procedural perspective, a positive evolution in the *Sarayaku* case is that children and young people were listened to during a field visit by a Court's delegation. The attention on children may be on the rise, at least indirectly, because the Inter-American Court is increasingly dealing with rights of entire groups through petitions filed on behalf of various victims, in which the rights of children are then also included (Feria Tinta, 2008, p. 11).

---

7   On 31 August 2007, precautionary measures had been granted in favour of 65 residents of La Oroya, including children.

4.2. The UN Committee on the Rights of the Child on natural resource exploitation in Latin America

Assessing the CRC Committee's approach to natural resource exploitation in Latin America is not straightforward, since "resource exploitation" is not a distinct unit of analysis of the Committee. Reviewing its latest concluding observations (March 2003 (Haiti) until June 2013 (Guyana)) on all Latin American countries shows that in various cases, natural resource exploitation activities are explicitly mentioned. They pop up in different sections, mostly those on "economic exploitation, including child labour" and "environmental health". More recently, resource exploitation is often also addressed under the new heading "child rights and business", which appeared regarding Latin America for the first time in the concluding observations on Bolivia (UN Committee CRC, 2009b).

In other instances, natural resource exploitation activities are not named as such, but problems are identified that may be connected to or caused by such exploitation, for instance in the section "indigenous children". In the case of Chile, the Committee expressed its concern over "reports that indigenous youth have been victims of police brutality" and recommended the Chilean state to "take both preventive and corrective action when abuse is suspected" (UN Committee CRC, 2007c, §73; §74). There is sufficient evidence that police brutality in the case here referred to by the Committee is closely linked to natural resource exploitation, namely the forest companies against which Mapuche youth have been protesting, as discussed above (Aylwin, 2010).

Other cases where resource exploitation *may* be one of the underlying root causes, include, among others, the "pollution of soils and water traditionally used by the indigenous communities" (UN Committee CRC, 2009b, §85) and the "very high number of working children among indigenous children" (UN Committee CRC, 2010b, §79). To be able to link these children's rights issues to natural resource exploitation requires a study of the country's situation (including its periodic and alternative reports), since such a connection cannot be derived from the concluding observations – the latter document being however the most widely disseminated. Although one can submit that a country's nationals will probably "know" whether resource exploitation lies behind a certain children's rights issue, it can still be identified as a shortcoming that the Committee does not always seem to pin-point this. In this way, the Committee risks obscuring the seriousness and vastness of challenges related to resource exploitation.

The remainder of the analysis concentrates on those instances where the concluding observations explicitly refer to natural resource exploitation activities, reviewing the types of resource exploitation most commonly cited, the effects on children's rights identified, and the recommendations made by the Committee. The objective is to give an overall impression of how the Committee approaches resource exploitation, not to present an exhaustive overview.

Mining is the most frequently mentioned activity, occurring in about 45 percent of the concluding observations reviewed. Attention is extended towards the oil sector in Peru (UN Committee CRC, 2006b, §50) and Ecuador (UN Committee CRC, 2010a, §30). The Committee also considers more country-specific exploitation activities, such as the coca plantations in Colombia (UN Committee CRC, 2006a, §72; §82), deep-sea fishing in Honduras (UN Committee CRC, 2007a, §72), the forest, soya, sugarcane and brazil nut sectors in Bolivia (UN Committee CRC, 2009b, §17; §74), banana plantations in Ecuador (UN Committee CRC, 2010a, §70), and tobacco, "mate" herb and soya plantations in Argentina (UN Committee CRC, 2010c, §29; §73).

The children's rights issues most recurrently linked with resource exploitation are economic exploitation and child labour, especially dangerous and/or degrading work in mines, and (negative impacts on) the right to health, for instance because of the use of toxic substances. Other effects explicitly related to resource exploitation include sexual exploitation, such as the rape of indigenous girls in mining and forestry regions in Suriname (UN Committee CRC, 2007b, §67), lack of school attendance (e.g., UN Committee CRC, 2010a, §70), and negative impact on property rights and family life (UN Committee CRC, 2011a, §25).

An evolution can be observed in the Committee's recommendations. State Parties have been suggested to carry out rights-based environmental and social impact assessments in relation to resource exploitation activities (e.g., UN Committee CRC, 2006a, §73; UN Committee CRC, 2006b, §51). More recently, recommendations have included enacting an appropriate regulatory framework for the business sector to protect and respect children's rights (e.g., UN Committee CRC, 2010a, §31; UN Committee CRC, 2010c, §30), considering experiences from abroad in applying the UN "Protect, Respect and Remedy" Framework (UN Committee CRC, 2011a, §26; UN Committee CRC, 2011b, §21) and complying with the Guiding Principles (UN Committee CRC, 2013b, §23(c)). The impact of the norm-setting on human rights and business is thus clearly noticeable, leading to a greater emphasis on the State's duty to protect. With the adoption of GC 16, the Committee should be able in future concluding observations to formulate more precise recommendations as to, among others, what an "appropriate regulatory framework for the business sector" entails.

The impact of free trade and investment agreements on children's enjoyment of their human rights, documented above, has also been addressed by the Committee, which has recommended studying the adoption of children's rights clauses when negotiating investment agreements with multinational corporations and foreign governments (UN Committee CRC, 2010c, §31) as well as conducting "human rights assessments, including on child rights" prior to negotiating and concluding free trade agreements and adopting "measures to prevent and prosecute violations, including by ensuring appropriate remedies" (UN Committee CRC, 2013b, §23(b)).

The predominant child image emerging from these analyses and recommendations seems to be one of a vulnerable child, which above all must be protected in the context of natural resource exploitation. Some concluding observations on economic exploitation confirm this "protective reflex" of the Committee and moreover show its limited openness towards the diversity of realities existing on the ground – going against the context-specific approach argued for in this Handbook. The Committee has recommended the states of Argentina and Ecuador "to respect the right of the child to be heard" in policy debates on child labour (UN Committee CRC, 2010a, §71(d); UN Committee CRC, 2010c, §73(d)). While laudable at first sight, the potential to really listen and give due weight to children's opinions is seriously undermined by the addition that this right to be heard concerns the development and application of measures "to eliminate child labour in all its forms" (UN Committee CRC, 2010c). The Committee's alignment with the ILO's abolitionist approach towards child labour does not correspond to the reality of working children who claim a right to work in dignity (see Hanson, Volonakis and Al-Rozzi, Chapter 18 in this Handbook; Saadi, 2012).

In conclusion, natural resource exploitation issues are not addressed by the Committee in a systematic way: at worst, they are not mentioned whereas they are at least sometimes presumably a root cause of children's rights topics that are explicitly discussed; at best, they are taken up in various and changing places throughout the concluding observations. Although not necessarily problematic, one could nonetheless argue that such a scattered approach downplays the extent of problems caused by resource extraction and does not adequately account for the interconnections between different rights issues, as was illustrated by the case studies.[8] Moreover, the Committee seems to focus mostly on protection (against economic exploitation, against negative health impacts), considering children thus primordially to be "in danger" in the context of resource exploitation. Only exceptionally, the Committee makes allusion to the resilience and agency of children in a resource extraction context, such as in the case of Chile (where however the link with resource exploitation is not explicitly made by the Committee, see above).

5. Fields of tension

This section discusses two fields of tension emerging from the analysis of children's rights in the context of natural resource exploitation: the child-specificity of issues and rights, and the integration of insights from other disciplines in legal analyses and proceedings.

5.1. Child-specificity of needs and norms

The first bundle of reflections concerns the relationship between children and young people, specific children's rights standards and general human rights standards. An initial question here is whether particular consideration of children and young people is actually required or desirable, when undertaking a human rights analysis in the context of natural resource exploitation. This question implies taking a step back, to critically review the *raison d'être* of this chapter.

Two types of arguments justify a specific focus on (the rights of) children and young people in relation to exploitation-related challenges. First, due to their physiology, children and young people are more sensitive than adults to environmental degradation and pollution caused by natural resource industries, leading to more serious health hazards. Children and young people may also be more susceptible to suffering (more seriously) from other problems than adults, ranging from economic exploitation to lack of access to quality education. On the basis of these and similar considerations, it can be argued that children and young people need more protection than adults in resource extraction contexts. Whereas it is thus recognized that children are often more sensitive to negative health, environmental and social impacts of resource exploitation, this recognition should not lead to a conceptualization of children as *inherently and exclusively* vulnerable. This goes against seeing children as independent bearers of rights and reduces their agency (see also Vandenhole and Ryngaert 2013, pp. 70–73).

Second, children may easily be overlooked in consultation and participation processes in relation to natural resource exploitation. From an intergenerational equity perspective, it is however submitted that precisely they should be privileged conversation partners. As Liebel (2012, p. 103) has noted: "One example [of generational discrimination] is the lack of consideration for children as a social group in political decisions, which have negative consequences on the later lives of children and even for following generations, such as … the impact of fossil energy production on the environment and the climate". From both a protection and a participation perspective, one can thus adduce arguments in support of a "privileged" consideration of (the rights of) children and young people in exploitation-related matters.

On the other hand, many of the challenges that arise in relation to resource exploitation are not unique to children, but relevant for all human beings involved in or impacted by the

---

8   The argument that natural resource exploitation is a recent phenomenon and therefore has not received a separate heading within the concluding observations, is not valid given the explicit inclusion of other new themes such as "child rights and business" – the latter one not to be equated with resource exploitation (see above).

exploitation concerned – and should thus be tackled at a general level. This is illustrated by a 2003 report of Save the Children, entitled "Extractive industry, children and governance". Whereas the title indicates a focus on children, children are actually explicitly mentioned very little throughout the text. The recommended measures, such as enhanced revenue transparency and good resource management, are not child-specific, but will benefit citizens in general, and – consequently – also children. This shows the close interconnectedness between the interests of adults and children in the context of resource exploitation, also observed when reviewing the Inter-American human rights jurisprudence.

The potential for tensions between (the rights of) children and adults thus seems less high in the context of natural resource exploitation, than in other domains of life (such as alternative care, as mentioned in this Handbook's introduction). On the contrary, guaranteeing the rights of parents may be a prerequisite for guaranteeing the rights of their children in a resource exploitation context. In relation to the DRC, for example, it has been argued that keeping children out of mining activities implies "ensuring that conditions for *adult* artisanal miners significantly improve so that they receive proper remuneration for their labour and that the mine sites operate according to the highest possible safety standards" (Feeney, 2013, p. 92, emphasis added). Exclusively or predominantly focusing on the rights of children and young people, without appropriately considering the rights of their parents and other adults (such as extended family members or other caretakers), may thus actually turn out detrimental for them. Hence, *even from a children's rights perspective*, arguments can be advanced for considering the rights of children and young people together with the rights of other human beings. From an integrated human rights perspective, this would naturally be the case, as this requires "taking into account the human rights of all rights holders whose rights are affected by a particular situation" (Brems, 2014).

Reflecting upon the child-specificity of interests and needs in relation to resource exploitation thus leads to a nuanced assessment. A second question concerns the relevance of the children's rights framework and its relationship with the human rights framework. Regarding business-related standards, it was noted that in general human rights initiatives, children were overlooked or only mentioned in relation to child labour. This gave rise to specific norm-setting initiatives on children's rights and business (GC 16 and the CRB Principles). Moreover, in the general human rights documents, the predominant child image was one of a vulnerable child, whereas in the children's rights instruments, the child image of the autonomous child was more present, recognizing children as rights-bearers. In this sense, there is an added value in the specific children's rights instruments, compared to the general human rights documents. In the Committee's concluding observations on Latin America, however, the prevalence of a protective approach was noted. Another illustration of a contribution of the children's rights framework concerns the recognition of the right of the child to be heard and his views to be given due weight (Art. 12 CRC), and the guidelines that have been developed in this respect (see, e.g., UN Committee CRC, 2009a). Also in the context of natural resource exploitation, children and young people have gradually become more involved in normative developments: they were consulted during the drafting processes of both GC 16 and the CRB Principles, and were listened to during a field visit in the *Sarayaku* case. The actual impact of these contributions remains sometimes difficult to assess, however.

Other challenges appear common to the children's and broader human rights framework. An example constitutes the current state-centred focus of international human rights law, whereas the most adverse consequences of resource exploitation have been observed in the context of investments and activities by corporate actors. Re-thinking and extending the notion of duty-bearers thus emerges as an urgent task for children's and human rights scholarship alike (see Vandenhole *et al.*, 2014).

The attention for "children's rights and business" followed upon a shift in general human rights law towards considering its relation with business. Looking to the future, there seems potential for children's rights to take the lead and play an avant-garde role, as was illustrated by the inclusion of mandatory language in GC 16 regarding the obligations of home states in the context of businesses' extraterritorial operations. It may be politically more feasible to achieve considerable breakthroughs on the legal obligations of business actors in the realm of children's rights first. This could then pave the way for similar developments in the general human rights framework.

5.2. The (dis)empowering effect of incorporating insights from other disciplines in legal approaches

This chapter analysed the interaction between children's rights and natural resource exploitation from a predominantly legal perspective. Some insights were drawn from other disciplines such as political economy (on trade agreements) and (legal) anthropology (on indigenous peoples' relationship with their lands, territories and resources). It was also observed that in cases before the Inter-American Court of Human Rights, findings from other disciplines have been invoked by the applicants and/or built on by the judges, both from the social sciences (e.g. anthropologists' testimonies in the *Awas Tingni* case) and the exact sciences (e.g. the public health study in the *La Oroya* case).

Natural resource exploitation seems indeed an area where the contribution of other disciplines may be pertinent for an appropriate legal approach to children's rights. The way knowledge is used, and the power relations in which this use is embedded, will however determine its empowering or disempowering impact on persons affected by resource exploitation in general and children and young people in particular (cf. Foucault). Exact sciences could for example substantiate with "hard" data that certain rights (e.g., to health) are threatened or violated, and in this way give disadvantaged groups, including children and young people, more leverage to claim respect for their rights (e.g., *La Oroya*). Findings from exact sciences can also be "misused", however, for instance when they are opaquely presented in rights-based environmental and social impact assessments, in a way incomprehensible for lay people, so disguising the impact of envisaged exploitation and thus limiting potential reactions.

Similarly, insights provided by anthropological scholarship on the meaning and use of natural resources for and by certain (indigenous) groups, could be used to sustain resistance to natural resource exploitation with the objective of safeguarding the rights of (indigenous) children and young people. A disturbing trend though is the fact that anthropologists are increasingly being recruited by oil and mining companies, or are working for them as consultants, to gather knowledge about the way of living and resource management practices of local, particularly indigenous, populations and to foster community relations, for instance in Peru (Mujica Bermúdez and Piccoli, 2014) and Ecuador (IACtHR 2012, §75). This knowledge could then be (ab)used by companies when trying to acquire lands or to obtain the communities' consent to exploitation or relocation. This evolution entails an inappropriate diversion and instrumentalization of anthropological methods and knowledge, given that one of the original objectives of the anthropological discipline is to disentangle unequal power relationships (Mujica Bermúdez and Piccoli, 2014). Integrating insights from other disciplines in legal assessments and judicial proceedings may thus be both empowering and disempowering, and sufficient caution must be displayed in and towards such endeavours. Given the huge financial interests permeating resource exploitation, the potential for abusing knowledge seems higher here than in other domains impacting on children's rights.

6. Some concluding and future-oriented reflections

This chapter has analysed the relevance of children's rights in the context of natural resource exploitation. Legal instruments and research addressing this matter as a whole and in its complexity appear to be in their early development. Both the attention for children('s rights) in resource exploitation cases (as exemplified by the case law of the Inter-American human rights system) and the attention for resource exploitation in children's rights (as evident from the concluding observations of the CRC Committee) have been limited at best, non-existent at worst. Looking at natural resource exploitation also raises questions on child-specificity and on the relationship between children's rights and human rights law. This final section discusses three overarching and/or future-oriented themes: (i) the need for effective remedies and change at the domestic level, (ii) the importance of an intercultural and context-specific approach, and (iii) the proposal to shift focus in future research.

First, although natural resource exploitation does not necessarily have negative implications for children and young people, there are many instances in which it has affected them adversely. When actual violations occur, "businesses and States are failing children who in reality have very limited options to obtain remedy for corporate violations of their rights" (Sheahan, 2011, p. 33). Accessible and effective paths for children to obtain remedy should be further developed. Lambooy et al. (2013, p. 377) suggest that in the case of oil companies, effective remedies not only include compensation for the past, but also "safer plans for future operations". Although the authors do not focus on children, such a future-oriented approach appears particularly relevant for them. In Latin America, children and young people seem to have played quite a limited role in judicial proceedings, at least before the Inter-American human rights system. Moreover, even when a case reaches the regional or international level, states far from always comply with decisions and recommendations of these organs. This points to the importance of change at the domestic (legal and policy) level, in addition to and beyond the international level.[9]

Second, this chapter supports an intercultural and localized (De Feyter, 2007, 2011; Vandenhole, 2012b) approach to (children's) human rights. Case studies of Latin America made the human rights intricacies for children and young people in a resource exploitation context tangible, and showed the need for a tailored approach. That human rights concerns are triggered by resource exploitation seems to be a reality shared by most Latin American states, including those who promote a neoliberal extractivist model, as well as those who have started questioning neoliberal paradigms and are promoting social transformation based on resource extraction, such as Bolivia and Ecuador. As a way to confront these extractivist models, indigenous peoples in the region have called for alternative models of development to be considered, based for instance on the notion of *"buen vivir"* or good living. According to Gudynas (2011, p. 442), the concept of *buen vivir* comes from the Kichwa wording *sumak kawsay*, which is used to refer to "a fullness life in a community, together with other persons and Nature". Such notion has been acknowledged in recent years in the Constitutions of Ecuador (2008) and Bolivia (2009), and has inspired alternative development policies and initiatives throughout the region. Notwithstanding its potential, the notion of *buen vivir* is quite vague and open. Ideas on

---

9 Here, inspiration could be drawn from other regions. In the Philippines, for instance, several children, represented by their parents, succeeded in filing a class action to obtain the annulment and non-issuance of timber license agreements, alleging a violation of their right to a balanced and healthful ecology. The Supreme Court of the Philippines moreover accepted that the minors represented both others of their generations and future generations (Supreme Court of the Philippines, 1993).

how to effectively realize such a way of living may diverge or clash, depending on the vantage point one takes (compare with the openness of the umbrella concept of "the best interests of the child"). Moreover, in the relevant literature on *buen vivir*, children and their rights are not often explicitly considered – indicating potential for future development.

Finally, this article focused on natural resource *exploitation* as the problem calling most urgently for our attention. In line with a holistic perspective, it is suggested that research and policy move towards a more inclusive approach on how we engage with our natural resources, i.e. not (only) by exploiting them, but (most importantly) by conserving and sustainably using them. In this way, a shift in future research towards "natural resources and children's rights" is proposed.

Questions for debate and discussion

- How could the responsibility of corporations involved in resource extraction for children's rights violations be enforced? Which steps should be taken by states and by the international community to ensure the extraterritorial responsibility of corporations for children's rights violations?
- How would you address children's rights in a case of natural resource exploitation, as a member of (i) the Inter-American Court of Human Rights, (ii) the UN Committee on the Rights of the Child?
- In what ways can disciplines such as law, anthropology or political economy facilitate a better understanding of the connections between children's rights and resource extraction?
- How could the normative processes taking place in international fora concerning children's rights and resource exploitation be localized in contexts where resource extraction takes place, and how could experiences of children and young people be considered in future normative developments?

Acknowledgement

This research has been funded by the Interuniversity Attraction Poles Programme (IAP) initiated by the Belgian Science Policy Office, more specifically the IAP "The Global Challenge of Human Rights Integration: Towards a Users' Perspective" (www.hrintegration.be).

References

ACHPR (African Court on Human and Peoples' Rights) (2001). *The Social and Economic Rights Action Center for Economic and Social Rights v. Nigeria*, Comm. No 155/96.

Anaya, J. (2009). Promotion and Protection of all Human Rights, Civil, Political, Economic, Social and Cultural Rights, Including the Right to Development: Report of the Special Rapporteur on the Situation of Human Rights and Fundamental Freedoms of Indigenous People. [James Anaya. Addendum]. *Report on the Situation of Human Rights of Indigenous Peoples in Brazil*. A/HRC/12/34: United Nations. Available at http://unsr.jamesanaya.org/docs/countries/2009_report_brazil_en.pdf

ANIDE (Fundación de Apoyo a la Niñez y sus Derechos) (2012). *Informe sobre violencia institucional mapuche en Chile. Resumen ejecutivo*. Santiago, Chile. Unpublished report presented at a Hearing to the Inter-American Commission on Human Rights, 25 March 2012.

Auty, R. (1993). *Sustaining Development in Mineral Economies: The Resource Curse Thesis*. London and New York: Routledge.

Aylwin, J. (2009). *Os dereitos dos povos indígenas em Mato Grosso do sul, Brasil; Confinamento e tutela no século XXI*. Copenhague: IWGIA.

Aylwin, J. (2010). The TTPA and Indigenous Peoples: Lessons from Latin America. In J. Kelsey (ed.). *No

Ordinary Deal. Unmasking the Trans-Pacific Partnership Free Trade Agreement (pp. 70–81). Auckland: Bridget Williams.

Bass, L. (2008). Working Children in Bolivia: Mining. In IREWOC Foundation (International Research on Working Children). *The Worst Forms of Child Labour in Latin America: Main Findings from Guatemala, Bolivia and Peru* (pp. 17–22). Amsterdam: IREWOC.

Bebbington, A. (2011). *Learning from the Impact of the Extractive Industries in Latin America*. Procasur-Ford Foundation. Available at http://procasur.org/extractive-industries/wp-content/uploads/2011/05/Extractive-Industries-in-the-Andean-Region-Bebbington.pdf.

Bilchitz, D. (2010). The Ruggie Framework: An Adequate Rubric for Corporate Human Rights Obligations? *SUR – International Journal on Human Rights*, 7(12), 199–229.

Brems, E. (2014). Should Pluriform Human Rights Become One? Exploring the Benefits of Human Rights Integration, *European Journal of Human Rights*, 4, 447–470.

Buhmann, K. and Ryngaert, C. (2012). Human Rights Challenges for Multinational Corporations Working and Investing in Conflict Zones. *Human Rights & International Legal Discourse*, 6(1), 3–14.

Clapham, A. (2006). *Human Rights Obligations of Non-State Actors*. Oxford: Oxford University Press.

CEPAL (Comisión Económica para América Latina y el Caribe) (2012a). *La Sostenibilidad del Desarrollo a 20 Años de la Cumbre de Río. Avances, Brechas y Lineamientos Estratégicos para América Latina y el Caribe*. Naciones Unidas.

CEPAL (Comisión Económica para América Latina y el Caribe) – Alianza Territorial Mapuche (2012b). *Desigualdades territoriales y exclusion social del pueblo mapuche en Chile. Situación en la comuna de Ercilla desde un enfoque de derechos*. Santiago: NU CEPAL.

Cultural Survival (n.d.). *The Guarani*. Available at www.survivalinternational.org/tribes/guarani/despair.

De Feyter, K. (2007). Localising Human Rights. In W. Benedek, K. De Feyter and F. Marrella (eds), *Economic Globalisation and Human Rights* (pp. 11–40). Cambridge: Cambridge University Press.

De Feyter, K. (2011). Sites of Rights Resistance. In K. De Feyter, S. Parmentier, C. Timmerman and G. Ulrich (eds), *The Local Relevance of Human Rights* (pp. 11–39). Cambridge: Cambridge University Press.

Del Popolo, F. (2012). El derecho a bienestar para la infancia indígena: Situación y avances en América Latina. *Desafíos*, 14, 4–9.

De Schutter, O. (ed.) (2006). *Transnational Corporations and Human Rights*. Oxford: Hart.

Desmet, E. (2011). *Indigenous Rights Entwined with Nature Conservation*. Cambridge: Intersentia.

Deva, S. and Bilchitz, D. (eds) (2013). *Human Rights Obligations of Businesses: Beyond the Corporate Responsibility to Respect?* Cambridge: Cambridge University Press.

Ensing, A. (2008). Working Children in Mining in Peru. In IREWOC Foundation (International Research on Working Children). *The Worst Forms of Child Labour in Latin America: Main Findings from Guatemala, Bolivia and Peru* (pp. 31–36). Amsterdam: IREWOC.

ESCR-Net (n.d.), Mapuche Paynemil and Kaxipayiñ Communities, Case N° 12.010. Available at www.escr-net.org/docs/i/405939.

Falaschi, C. O. and Osés, N. (2012). *CIDH: La causa N° 12.010. Comunidades Mapuche Paynemil y Kaxipayiñ, Neuquén, Argentina*. Available at www.escr-net.org/docs/i/400620.

Feeney, P. (2013). Children's Rights and Mining: Democratic Republic of Congo. In *Droits de l'enfant et secteur privé: amener les Etats et les entreprises à remplir leurs obligations* (pp. 83–92). Sion, Switzerland: Institut international des Droits de l'Enfant.

Feria Tinta, M. (2008). *The Landmark Rulings of the Inter-American Court of Human Rights on the Rights of the Child: Protecting the Most Vulnerable at the Edge*. Leiden: Martinus Nijhoff.

Fraser, B. (2009). La Oroya's Legacy of Lead. *Environmental Science and Technology*, 43, 5555–5557.

Gerber, P., Kyriakakis, J., and O'Byrne, K. (2013). General Comment 16 on State Obligations Regarding the Impact of the Business Sector on Children's Rights: What is its Standing, Meaning and Effect? *Melbourne Journal of International Law*, 14, 1–36.

Gudynas, E. (2011). Buen Vivir: Today's Tomorrow. *Development*, 54(4), 441–447.

IACHR (2004a). Report N° 64/04, Admissibility, The Kichwa Peoples of the Sarayaku Community and its Members, Ecuador, 13 October 2004.

IACHR (2004b). Report N° 69/04, Admissibility, Community of San Mateo de Huanchor and its Members, Peru, 15 October 2004.

IACHR (2009). Report N° 76/09, Admissibility, Community of La Oroya, Peru, 5 August 2009.

IACHR (2010). Application to the Inter-American Court of Human Rights in the case of Kichwa People of Sarayaku and its members (Case 12.465) against Ecuador, 26 April 2010.

IACtHR (1999). *"Street Children" (Villagran-Morales et al.) v. Guatemala*, 19 November 1999 (Merits).

IACtHR (2001). *Mayagna (Sumo) Awas Tingni Community v. Nicaragua*, 31 August 2001 (Merits, Reparations and Costs).
IACtHR (2006). *Sawhoyamaxa Indigenous Community v. Paraguay*, 29 March 2006 (Merits, Reparations and Costs).
IACtHR (2007). *Saramaka People v. Suriname*, 28 November 2007 (Preliminary Objections, Merits, Reparations, and Costs).
IACtHR (2012). *Kichwa Indigenous People of Sarayaku v. Ecuador*, 27 June 2012 (Merits and Reparations).
ICJ and OHCHR (International Commission of Jurists (IJC) and Office of the High Commissioner for Human Rights) (2011). *Expert meeting on child rights and the business sector: Exploring the content of the general comment by the Committee on the Rights of the Child*. Geneva, 16 September 2011.
IFHR (International Federation for Human Rights) (2012). *Lima Declaration on Human Rights and Business*. Available at www.fidh.org/Lima-Declaration-on-Human-Rights
INDH (Instituto Nacional de Derechos Humanos) (2013). *Informe anual 2012*. Programa de Derechos Humanos y Función Policial. Santiago, Chile: INDH.
Jägers, N. (2011). UN Guiding Principles on Business and Human Rights: Making Headway Towards Real Corporate Accountability? *Netherlands Quarterly of Human Rights, 29*(2), 159–164.
Lambooy, T., Argyrou, A. and Varner, M. (2013). An Analysis and Practical Application of the Guiding Principles on Providing Remedies with Special Reference to Case Studies Related to Oil Companies. In Deva, S. and Bilchitz, D. (eds), *Human Rights Obligations of Businesses: Beyond the Corporate Responsibility to Respect?* (pp. 329–377). Cambridge: Cambridge University Press.
Leiva, F. (2011). Development and Change in Latin America and the Caribbean. In H. Veltmeyer (ed.), *The Critical Development Studies Handbook: Tools for Change* (pp. 230–233). Black Point, Nova Scotia: Fernwood Publishing.
Liebel, M. (2012). Discriminated against Being Children: A Blind Spot in the Human Rights Arena. In M. Liebel (ed.). *Children's Rights from Below: Cross-Cultural Perspectives* (pp. 94–107). New York: Palgrave Macmillan.
Mares, R. (ed.) (2012). *The UN Guiding Principles on Business and Human Rights: Foundations and Implementation*. Leiden: Martinus Nijhoff.
Martin-Ortega, O. and Wallace, R. (2013). Business, Human Rights and Children: The Developing International Agenda. *The Denning Law Journal, 25*, 105–127.
Mena, S., De Leede, M., Baumann, D., Black, N., Lindeman, S., and McShane, L. (2010). Advancing the Business and Human Rights Agenda: Dialogue, Empowerment, and Constructive Engagement. *Journal of Business Ethics, 93*, 161–188.
Miranda, L. (2012). Biofuel Industry Exterminating Guarani Kaiowá People on South Brazil. *The Real Agenda*. Available at http://real-agenda.com/2012/10/16/biofuel-industry-exterminating-guarani-kaiowa-people-in-south-brazil/.
Mujica Bermúdez, L. and Piccoli, E. (2014). L'anthropologie en terrain minier. Réflexions sur les pratiques professionnelles des anthropologues au Pérou en contexte d'exploitation des ressources naturelles. In C. Bréda, M. Chaplier, J. Hermesse and E. Piccoli, *Terres (dés)humanisées: ressources et climat* (pp. 79–104). Louvain-la-Neuve: Academia.
Neuman, G.L. (2008). Import, Export and Regional Consent in the Inter-American Court of Human Rights. *The European Journal of International Law, 19*(1), 101–123.
OECD (Organisation for Economic Cooperation and Development) (2011). *OECD Guidelines for Multinational Enterprises*. Paris: OECD Publishing.
Pahis, S. (2011). *Bilateral Investment Treaties and International Human Rights Law: Harmonization through Interpretation*. Geneva: International Commission of Jurists.
PUINAMUDT (2014). *Niños y niñas Kukamas del Marañón envían mensaje a Ollanta Humala y Nadine Heredia*. [Pueblos Indígenas Amazónicos Unidos en Defensa de sus Territorios]. Available at http://observatoriopetrolero.org/ninos-y-ninas-kukamas-del-maranon-envian-mensaje-a-ollanta-humala-y-nadine-heredia/.
RRI (Rights and Resources Initiative) (2012). *Impact of the Extractive Industry on the Collective Land and Forest Rights of Peoples and Communities: A Summary*. Available at www.rightsandresources.org/documents/files/doc_5915.pdf.
Ross, M. (2001). *Extractive Sectors and the Poor*. Washington, DC: Oxfam America.
Ruggie, J. (2010). *Business and Human Rights: Further Steps toward the Operationalization of the "Protect, Respect and Remedy" Framework*. [UN Special Representative of the Secretary-General on the issue of human rights and transnational corporations and other business enterprises]. UN Doc. A/HRC/14/27.

Saadi, I. (2012). Children's Rights as "Work in Progress": The Conceptual and Practical Contributions of Working Children's Movements. In M. Liebel (ed.). *Children's Rights from Below: Cross-Cultural Perspectives* (pp. 143–161). New York: Palgrave Macmillan.

Save the Children (2003). *Lifting the Resource Curse: Extractive Industry, Children and Governance*. London: Save the Children.

Save the Children (2012). *Doing Good Work for Us Children: Children's and Adolescent's Contributions to the Draft General Comment on Child Rights and Business Sector*. Stockholm: Save the Children.

Serrano, F. (2005). *Environmental Contamination in the Homes of La Oroya and Concepción and Its Effects in the Health of Community Residents: Executive Summary*. School of Public Health, Saint Louis University. Available at http://lib.ohchr.org/HRBodies/UPR/Documents/Session2/PE/EJ-AIDA_PER_UPR_S2_2008anx_StudyofcontaminationinLaOroya.pdf.

Sheahan, F. (2011). *Effective Remedy and Corporate Violations of Children's Rights*. Geneva: UNICEF.

Shier, H. (2009). "Pathways to Participation" Revisited: Learning from Nicaragua's Child Coffee Workers. In N. Thomas and B. Percy-Smith (eds), *A Handbook of Children and Young People's Participation: Perspectives from Theory and Practice* (pp. 215–229). Abingdon, UK: Routledge.

Simons, P. (2012). International Law's Invisible Hand and the Future of Corporate Accountability for Violations of Human Rights. *Journal of Human Rights and the Environment*, 3(1), 5–43.

Spieler, P. (2010). The La Oroya Case: the Relationship Between Environmental Degradation and Human Rights Violations. *Human Rights Brief*, 18(1), 19–23.

Supreme Court of the Philippines (1993). *Oposa et al. v. Fulgencio S. Factoran, Jr. et al.* (G.R. No. 101083), 30 July 1993.

Tranter, P. and Sharpe, S. (2007). Children and Peak Oil: An Opportunity in Crisis. *International Journal of Children's Rights*, 15(1), 181–198.

UN CERD (UN Committee on the Elimination of Racial Discrimination) (2010). *Concluding Observations: Australia*. UN Doc. CERD/C/AUS/CO/15–17.

UN CERD (UN Committee on the Elimination of Racial Discrimination) (2011a). *Concluding Observations: Norway*. UN Doc. CERD/C/NOR/CO/19-20.

UN CERD (UN Committee on the Elimination of Racial Discrimination) (2011b). *Concluding Observations: United Kingdom*. UN Doc. CERD/C/GBR/CO/18-20.

UN CERD (UN Committee on the Elimination of Racial Discrimination) (2012). *Concluding Observations: Canada*. UN Doc. CERD/C/CAN/CO/19-20.

UN Committee on the Rights of the Child (2006a). *Concluding Observations: Colombia*. UN Doc. CRC/C/COL/CO/3.

UN Committee on the Rights of the Child (2006b). *Concluding Observations: Peru*. UN Doc. CRC/C/PER/CO/3 § 50.

UN Committee on the Rights of the Child (2007a). *Concluding Observations: Honduras*. UN Doc. CRC/C/HND/CO/3.

UN Committee on the Rights of the Child (2007b). *Concluding Observations: Suriname*. UN Doc. CRC/C/SUR/CO/2.

UN Committee on the Rights of the Child (2007c). *Concluding Observations: Chile*. UN Doc. CRC/C/CHL/CO/3.

UN Committee on the Rights of the Child (2009a). *General Comment No. 12. The Right of the Child to Be Heard*. UN Doc. CRC/C/GC/12.

UN Committee on the Rights of the Child (2009b). *Concluding Observations: Bolivia*. UN Doc. CRC/C/BOL/CO/4.

UN Committee on the Rights of the Child (2010a). *Concluding Observations: Ecuador*. UN Doc. CRC/C/ECU/CO/4

UN Committee on the Rights of the Child (2010b). *Concluding Observations: Paraguay*. UN Doc. CRC/C/PRY/CO/3.

UN Committee on the Rights of the Child (2010c). *Concluding Observations: Nicaragua*. UN Doc. CRC/C/NIC/CO/4.

UN Committee on the Rights of the Child (2011a). *Concluding Observations: Costa Rica*. UN Doc. CRC/C/CRI/CO/4.

UN Committee on the Rights of the Child (2011b). *Concluding Observations: Cuba*. UN Doc. CRC/C/CUB/CO/2.

UN Committee on the Rights of the Child (2013a). *General Comment No. 16. On State Obligations Regarding the Impact of the Business Sector on Children's Rights*. UN Doc. CRC/C/GC/16.

UN Committee on the Rights of the Child (2013b). *Concluding Observations: Guyana.* UN Doc. CRC/C/GUY/CO/2-4.
UNEP (UN Environment Programme) (2012). *Keeping Track of Our Changing Environment. From Rio to Rio+20 (1992–2012).* Nairobi, Kenya: UNEP.
UN General Assembly (2013). *Report of the Working Group on the Issue of Human Rights and Transnational Corporations and Other Business Enterprises.* UN Doc. A/68/279.
UN Human Rights Council (2008). *Protect, Respect and Remedy: A Framework for Business and Human Rights. Report of the Special Representative of the Secretary-General on the Issue of Human Rights and Transnational Corporations and Other Business Enterprises, John Ruggie.* UN Doc. A/HRC/8/5.
UN Human Rights Council (2011a). *Report of the Special Representative of the Secretary-General on the Issue of Human Rights and Transnational Corporations and Other Business Enterprises, John Ruggie. Guiding Principles on Business and Human Rights: Implementing the United Nations "Protect, Respect and Remedy" Framework.* UN Doc. A/HRC/17/31.
UN Human Rights Council (2011b). *Human Rights and Transnational Corporations and Other Business Enterprises.* UN Doc. A/HRC/RES/17/4.
UN Human Rights Council (2014). *Elaboration of an International Legally Binding Instrument on Transnational Corporations and Other Business Enterprises with Respect to Human Rights.* UN Doc. A/HRC/26/L.22/Rev.1.
UNICEF, Save the Children and the UN Global Compact (2012). *Children's Rights and Business Principles.* Geneva: UNICEF, Save the Children and the UN Global Compact.
UN Sub-Commission on the Promotion and Protection of Human Rights (2003). *Norms on the Responsibilities of Transnational Corporations and Other Business Enterprises with Regard to Human Rights.* UN Doc. E/CN.4/Sub.2/2003/12/Rev.2.
Vandenhole, W. (2012a). Contextualising the State Duty to Protect Human Rights as Defined in the UN Guiding Principles on Business and Human Rights. *Revista de estudios jurídicos / Universidad de Jaén. Facultad de Ciencias Sociales y Jurídicas, 12,* 1–10.
Vandenhole, W. (2012b). Localising the Human Rights of Children. In M. Liebel (ed.), *Children's Rights from Below: Cross-cultural Perspectives* (pp. 80–93). New York: Palgrave Macmillan.
Vandenhole, W. and Ryngaert, J. (2013). Mainstreaming Children's Rights in Migration Litigation: Muskhadzhiyeva and others v. Belgium. In E. Brems (ed.), *Diversity and European Human Rights. Rewriting Judgments of the ECHR* (pp. 68–92). Cambridge: Cambridge University Press.
Vandenhole, W., Erdem Türkelli, G., and Hammonds, R. (2014). Reconceptualizing Human Rights Duty-Bearers. In A. Mihr and M. Gibney (eds), *The Sage Handbook of Human Rights* (pp. 1031–1046). Los Angeles: Sage.

23
Conclusions
Towards a field of critical children's rights studies

Ellen Desmet, Sara Lembrechts, Didier Reynaert and Wouter Vandenhole

This volume takes a critical approach to children's rights. We have identified the key components of such an approach in the introduction. Here, we illustrate, refine or revisit some of these components in light of the contributions to this Handbook. After a fresh look at notions of childhood, we address a context-specific approach, interdisciplinary dialogue and critiques of children's rights. At the very end of this conclusion, we explore how a field of critical children's rights *studies* may evolve.

Without any doubt, at the core of a critical approach to children's rights are (i) a context-specific approach, (ii) an interdisciplinary dialogue, and (iii) an approach of critique. Whether each of them is *indispensable* for what we call critical children's rights studies, is probably too early to tell, and may smack of a kind of dogmatic thinking that we do not want to impose. Nonetheless, we do shed some light on the way we believe these three components intersect.

1. Dynamic childhoods

This Handbook started with the recognition that universally accepted definitions of childhood are nonexistent. As several layers of social, economic, political and cultural realities coexist in multidimensional experiences of children and adults alike, there is a diversity of 'childhoods' (and 'adulthoods'). Also, and related to this, the capacity of children to meaningfully participate in society varies and is shaped not only by children's agency, but also by social structures and power relations that may limit or enhance the autonomy of children. These differences among children – as well as in the ways we look at them – are an important and recurrent theme throughout the various contributions.[1]

---

1 This focus on difference does not intend to do away with the recognition of similarities between children. For example, as Mayall (Chapter 5) points out, the way children experience a lack of respect for their membership of human society did not change much in the course of the twentieth century.

We will first identify three dimensions in which differences in childhood may arise, i.e. over time, across space and place, and as a consequence of socio-political identity markers. Then we will reflect on the relations between (images of) children and adults – in line with our argument below that a field of critical children's rights studies should not only focus on children, but also research their relations with other societal groups, especially adults. Finally, it is shown how dynamic childhoods impact on perceptions of (the nature of) children's rights.

1.1. Dimensions of difference in childhood

To start with, differences in the way we look at children are clearly visible *over time* (Verhellen, Chapter 3; Vanobbergen, Chapter 4; Reynaert and Roose, Chapter 6, in this Handbook). This process of changing images of childhood is not necessarily historical or linear, but at least dynamic. Multiple authors refer to the way that in the global North, an image of children as active participants in society is gradually gaining ground next to an image of passive, vulnerable children, who were isolated from society, lived outside of moral agency, were not accountable and had to be protected by adults. Romantic images of innocent, needy, sacralized, obedient, playful children, subject to care and mere recipients of parental culture and upbringing, increasingly compete with images of children as autonomous human beings, as bearers of human rights with a legal status that questions existing power relations (Verhellen, Chapter 3; Vanobbergen, Chapter 4; Mayall, Chapter 5; Reynaert and Roose, Chapter 6; Aitken, Chapter 8; De Graeve, Chapter 9).[2] Beyond the image of children as rights holders, some chapters also refer to a growing tendency of seeing children as social and political agents, citizens, active meaning-makers, for whom e.g. participation becomes an expression of agency[3] and not an expression of rights[4] (Moosa-Mitha, 2005, p. 380; Vanobbergen, Chapter 4; Aitken, Chapter 8; De Graeve, Chapter 9; Mitchell, Chapter 10).

Second, differences in childhood images, as well as in children's capacity for action, are apparent *across social and geographical space* (André, Chapter 7; and Aitken, Chapter 8). The

---

[2] Irrespective of whether one tends to embrace the CRC standards (e.g. Verhellen, Chapter 3; Ceriani, Chapter 19; Lenzer, Chapter 16; Liefaard, Chapter 14; Kilkelly, Chapter 13) or put them to discussion (e.g. André, Chapter 7; Aitken, Chapter 8; Vandenhole, Chapter 2; Reynaert and Roose, Chapter 6), the adoption of the Convention in 1989 remains a convenient common point of reference to explain that turn. Authors seem to agree that the Convention was both a response to and an impulse for a changing childhood image. It enhanced a shift in the definition of rights from the focus of protection and provision to also include participation and agency rights. Consequently, the CRC also boosted an increased visibility of children in terms of their capacity for individuated autonomous decision-making (Moosa-Mitha, 2005, p. 379).

[3] As Morrow (2005, p. 11) explains, '"agency" is a concept that is understood differently by different disciplines, and indeed by different theorists within the same discipline.' Here, agency is used as referring to its sociological meaning as developed by Giddens (1984). He explained agency as a person's capacity or capability to act and 'to make a difference to a pre-existing state of affairs or course of events' (Giddens, 1984, p. 14).

[4] Understood as a right, participation implies that 'as soon as children are able to express a preference about a matter affecting them, they have the right to form an opinion, make it known to others and have it considered' (Melton, 2006, p. 7). This right in itself does not say anything about the person's capacity or capability to act so as to realize that right. Freeman (2007, p. 8) further explains the difference between agency and rights as follows: 'Rights are important because those who have them can exercise agency. Agents are decision-makers. They are people who can negotiate with others, who are capable of altering relationships or decisions, who can shift social assumptions and constraints. And there is now clear evidence that even the youngest can do this. ... As agents, rights-bearers can participate. They can make their own lives, rather than having their lives made for them.'

dominant image of the child that underpins social policies in the West since the beginning of the twentieth century, for example, tends to focus on children's future role in a knowledge-based economy (see e.g. Verhellen, Chapter 3, on children as *human becomings* in compulsory education policies, and Reynaert and Roose, Chapter 6, on the institutionalized youth land in which to-be-protected children were, and still are today, isolated from the rest of society). The living conditions of many children in developing societies, however, require them to take up quite some responsibilities in childhood, often much earlier than children whose families do not face economic hardship in the same way (see e.g. Hanson, Volonakis and Al-Rozzi, Chapter 18, on the importance of child labour to contribute to the family economy, or Cantwell, Chapter 15, on child-headed households).

Third, different 'childhoods' also occur between the lived realities of individuals within a single temporal or spatial frame of reference, for example because children differ in *socio-political identity markers* such as age, gender, class, ethnicity or religious background (Aitken, Chapter 8; De Graeve, Chapter 9), or because the circumstances in which they find themselves can vary endlessly. Taken together, these 'fault lines' lead children to experience different 'capabilities' (i.e. children's real opportunities for functioning and choice; see Reynaert and Roose, Chapter 6), different 'priorities', as well as different 'boundaries of what is possible, appropriate and expected' in the given circumstances (Morrow, 2011, pp. 5–6). These differences, which may entail both potentials and limitations for children, may result from personal identity, structural relations or a combination of both (Vanobbergen, Chapter 4; Reynaert and Roose, Chapter 6).

In light of the above, it is important to note that different and even competing childhood images can *coexist in one single person*. As is illustrated by Desmet and Aylwin (Chapter 22) in relation to natural resource exploitation, children can simultaneously be victims and beneficiaries. Children – just like adults – are never inherently vulnerable (Desmet and Aylwin, Chapter 22), nor are they ever fully-fledged (Aitken, Chapter 8). Even in situations of extreme violence against children (Lenzer, Chapter 16), such as FGM (Leye and Middelburg, Chapter 17), where the vulnerable child may seem stripped of all agency and where their capacity to act would seem nonexistent, this does not *need* to be the case. With her concept of 'tactical agency', Honwana (2005) for example explains that even persons in a subordinate social situation, such as child soldiers, may still find strategies and ways to cope with, or even take advantage of, the weak position they are in. Similarly, Cheney (2013) has described how aids orphans may still possess a certain degree of discretion and influence to exercise autonomy, even if their realm of choice is severely constrained.

1.2. Generational dynamics in defining childhood

Difference between childhood and adulthood is found in every society (Mayall, Chapter 5). As Mayall explains, '*generation*' remains a fundamental concept structuring how we think about childhood as distinct from adulthood (see also Mestrum, Chapter 20, on inter-generational solidarity). Usually, child–adult relations are characterized by an adult understanding of childhood, often confusing biological realities with socially constructed ones (Mayall, Chapter 5; Vanobbergen, Chapter 4). Some authors see generations as a cognitive boundary (Mayall, Chapter 5, referring among others to Bourdieu),[5] but for others (e.g. Blanchet-Cohen,

---

5   This is thematized e.g. by Hanson, Volonakis and Al-Rozzi, Chapter 18, in their rejection of an adult-driven abolitionist perspective on child labour, seeing child labour as a moral category to be abolished no matter what the real impact on children's lives is, just because children *should not work*.

Chapter 21, on intergenerational conflict in indigenous societies) it remains (also) a tangible reality. In both camps, the binary category of −18 and +18 is seen as hampering the realization of children's rights.

As regards *differences between adults and children*, in a number of thematic chapters, it becomes clear that the image of the passive, vulnerable or exploited child is used as a primary way to explain why children, at least in certain situations, have to be considered different from adults. The need of children for special protection is discussed e.g. by Ceriani (Chapter 19) when describing the wrongful impact of detention as a mechanism of border control. Desmet and Aylwin (Chapter 22) refer to children's sensitivity for the consequences of natural resource exploitation, e.g. in terms of environmental impact, which has more detrimental consequences for children than for adults. Mestrum (Chapter 20), in turn, holds that the question of child poverty cannot be seen separately from poverty in the family or in society, but still acknowledges that poverty has a stronger impact on children – who are 'not responsible' for poverty – than on adults. Also to Liefaard (Chapter 14 on juvenile justice), it is clear that a punitive response aiming at retribution and deterrence used for adults is unfit for children. At the same time, however, he warns that too much focus on separation runs the risk of disregarding the fact that children, like adults, are entitled to a fair and equal treatment in Court. Finally, Reynaert and Roose (Chapter 6) are taking an atypical position with regard to the difference between adults and children by turning the reasoning around. Children are indeed considered as vulnerable human beings. However, this vulnerability is not typically for children. Vulnerability characterizes both childhood and adulthood. Therefore, they argue that 'we are all children' (Mortier, 2002).

It is important to note here that the image of childhood may vary *across generations*. Children's own understanding, for example of what constitutes their childhood or what constitutes a good life, may be different from what adults presuppose are the standards against which such assessment should be made (see e.g. Liebel, 2013; Hunner-Kreisel and Kuhn, 2010). Vanobbergen (Chapter 4) and Aitken (Chapter 8; also Mayall, Chapter 5) make a similar point, ascertaining that concepts such as agency put the autonomously thinking adult at centre stage; as such turning it into an adult ideal that a child may not necessarily wish to live up to. Both authors not only warn against making children fit into an adult model rather than questioning the model itself, but also underline that rights are to be shaped in a participative way, a process during which both adults and children participate in the definition of the context. In retrospect, this issue may have remained underexposed in this Handbook. With the exception of Mayall (Chapter 5) and Mitchell (Chapter 10), who address children and young people as main informants of the data presented, and – to a lesser extent – Tisdall (Chapter 11) and Blanchet-Cohen (Chapter 21) who respectively incorporate quotes from a pupil councillor and indigenous youths, children's own views have not been explicitly incorporated in the methodology of the different chapters.[6]

1.3. Implications of 'dynamic childhoods' for children's rights

A final theme concerns the relation between understandings of childhood and (the nature of) children's rights. Various contributions have shown how society's understanding of childhood is inextricably related with the way in which it defines children's rights. Two examples are illustrative cases in point. On the one hand, Hanson, Volonakis and Al-Rozzi (Chapter 18) explain

---

6   Nevertheless, André (Chapter 7) recognizes the implications of an image of children as active agents for certain methodological choices in anthropological research, most notably placing children at the centre of research questions and problem-solving strategies.

how the changing image of working children – i.e. no longer, or not only, as subject to brutal treatment and exploitation, but also as social agents – implied a move away from a purely abolitionist perspective to a claim to a right to work in dignity. On the other, Quennerstedt (Chapter 12) shows that the position of children's rights in teacher training is weakened by the predominant image of children as human *becomings*.

Whether children should have special rights, different from those of adults, or rights equal to adults' human rights is subject to debate. For Verhellen (Chapter 3), a separate human rights instrument (the CRC) is needed, as children would otherwise not be able to enjoy their rights on an equal basis with other human beings. Ceriani (Chapter 19) argues along the same lines that the absence of a child-specific focus in migration policy leads to denying specific needs and rights of migrant children (as different from the adult male, who tends to be at the heart of migration policy). In the debate on child poverty, Mestrum (Chapter 20) nuances this view by arguing that child-specific actions to counter child poverty are welcome, but should not be de-linked from poverty of other people and from society as a whole. Instead, a child-approach should preferably be mainstreamed into a broader context of general poverty/environmental/health policies addressing all groups. Desmet and Aylwin (Chapter 22) concur in that a more comprehensive approach to natural resource exploitation is needed beyond focusing only on children, even though a separate children's rights document has added value as it puts more emphasis on children as active participants of society, a perspective that is often missing in the general human rights discourse.

For Vanobbergen (Chapter 4) and Mitchell (Chapter 10), the issue is not whether children should have special or equal rights, but how children can contribute to shaping adults' understanding of human rights and citizenship respectively, in order to move away from adult-centric ideas on these concepts. Aitken (Chapter 8; on the right of children to become 'other' than what adults imagined for them) and Tisdall (Chapter 11; on not judging children's agency on the basis of their degree of 'participation' in adult structures) take up this point as well.

Overall, it is clear that children do not exist in a vacuum (Morrow, 2011, p. 11). They are in constant interaction with the world around them, including with adults, in a relational and interdependent way. Nevertheless, it remains important to realize that being 'subjects of rights' or 'agents' still leaves society to recognize children as such, and, more importantly, to act upon that: participating in society requires much more than merely possessing participation rights. Similarly, an image of children as rights holders or social agents does not in itself grant children a real capacity for action. The main challenges to be identified here are for adults to recognize children as co-actors in the dialogue about their childhood, rights, choices and interests (Vanobbergen, Chapter 4; Mayall, Chapter 5; Aitken, Chapter 8), to critically address the expectations and assumptions society has towards different social groups including children (Mayall, Chapter 5), and the need to incorporate children's own views – or even involve them actively as researchers in their own right (Dedding *et al.*, 2013). Addressing these challenges will help to realize that children have the right to be and become something different from what adults imagine for them (Aitken, Chapter 8).

2. A context-specific approach to children's rights

The key importance of a context-specific approach to children's rights, proposed in the introduction of this Handbook, has been confirmed and elaborated on by many contributions, across disciplines and themes. Recognition of the diversity existing both among children and in the contexts in which they grow up – which leads to a need for contextualization – is prevalent in most disciplinary perspectives. It seems inscribed in the DNA of some disciplinary approaches that they are inclined to pay more attention to one particular 'type' of diversity, such as cultural diversity in anthropology, socio-economic and political contexts in sociology, geographical diversity in geography, and gender in gender studies. Other disciplinary perspectives include a general 'attention for diversities' in their approach. 'Respect for diversities', for instance, is a central principle of the definition of social work (see Reynaert and Roose, Chapter 6). Furthermore, from the beginning of childhood studies, more emphasis was put on the diversity among children (see Vanobbergen, Chapter 4). For the legal discipline, on the other hand, taking local diversity into account was, at least traditionally, not so evident, as 'norm-setting ... tends to be top-down and adult-driven' (see Vandenhole, Chapter 2, p. 39). As elaborated below, recent scholarship on 'children's rights from below' and 'living rights' is challenging such a view on norm-creation, and probably also aims to influence the development of children's rights *law* (Vandenhole, Chapter 2).

In various thematic chapters, a lack of attention to context has been denounced, as hampering an effective realization of children's rights. With regard to participation, for instance, the lack of 'recognising and addressing wider contextual issues ... may well be one reason for the criticisms of children and young people's participation as being culturally inappropriate in some contexts and ineffectual in influencing decision-making in others'[7] (Tisdall, Chapter 11, p. 188). In other chapters, it is shown how a context-sensitive approach to children's rights is being developed and experimented with. Blanchet-Cohen demonstrates how indigenous peoples have appropriated and transformed the CRC upon implementation, for instance in relation to the definition of the concept of 'indigenous'. In the domain of alternative care, the CRC already incorporated a certain degree of openness towards other (cultural) contexts, by including references to the extended family and *kafala*. More recently, the 2009 Guidelines for Alternative Care of Children 'have arguably set the stage for a more nuanced view of how efforts might be oriented toward [a] context-specific viewpoint' (Cantwell, Chapter 15, p. 272).

On the basis of both the disciplinary and the thematic part, it can be observed that the interest for a context-sensitive approach to children's rights is informed by at least two interrelated tendencies. A first tendency links up with a 'traditional' debate in the field of human and children's rights, one that mainly emerged from the discipline of anthropology. Here, the call for a contextual orientation could be considered as a counter-movement against strong universalist appeals in children's rights thinking. It is argued that the idea of children's rights originates out of a particular understanding and vision of society and humanity, one that is grounded in a Western liberal tradition. This debate, on universalism versus relativism, developed during the past few decades to a point where it is generally recognized that children's rights are relevant in a non-Western context where they can achieve a certain ground of legitimacy, on the condition that they are the object of a particular way of contextual translation and/or reinterpretation. This is in line with for instance the 'cultural legitimacy thesis' as developed by An-Na'im, where the existence of universal (human rights) standards is accepted, '...while seeking to enhance their cultural legitimacy within the major traditions of the world through internal dialogue and struggle to establish enlightened perceptions and interpretations of cultural values and norms' (An-Na'im, 1992, p. 21). What An-Na'im seeks for is an internal reinterpretation of human rights (of children) based on a contextual orientation, in order to broaden and deepen universal consensus.

In a second tendency, and partly linked with the first one, a context-sensitive orientation could be considered as a shift away from a strong trend towards individualization, mainly in Western conceptions of children's rights. Individualization highlights a person's independency

---

7   References omitted.

and autonomy as the core values of human existence. A strong focus on individual entitlements in understanding children's rights stems from the tradition of Western liberal individualism, considering people, including children, as individual rights bearers or citizens, equal and autonomous individuals with inalienable personal rights. Critiques to this strong egalitarian doctrine came from gender studies, postcolonial studies and Marxist theory, amongst others. One central claim that was made, for instance from the feminist ethics of care, is that rights should not be considered as individual entitlements but rather as an interpersonal or interrelational practice. Interdependency, rather than autonomy is highlighted within this school of thought. Children's rights should then not be understood as individual entitlements but as an experience embedded within relations of care (see e.g. De Graeve, Chapter 9 on gender studies). Context here is understood rather on a *relational level*, as something that exists in between people (e.g. in families, communities, etc.). Others, such as Aitken (Chapter 8), emphasize context on a *structural level*, referring to power relations in the broader society. With his focus on space and place, Aitken explains that: 'The idea of place that I focus on in this chapter is less about a phenomenological sense-of-place and belonging wherein people emotionally experience their place in the world (although it is that too), and more about the political use of places to define those who have access and rights and those who are excluded' (Aitken, Chapter 8, p. 133).

The context-specific approach to children's rights, developed throughout the chapters of this Handbook, links up with an emerging 'new' paradigm in the study of children's rights as envisaged by, for instance, Liebel (2012) in his idea of 'children's rights from below', Hanson and Nieuwenhuys (2013) in their concept of 'living rights', Vandenhole (2012) using the notion of 'localizing children's rights' or Reynaert et al. (2010a), starting from a 'lifeworld orientation in children's rights'. This new approach starts from a critique on current understandings of children's rights 'from above'. As Liebel argues: '…little attention is given to [children's rights'] broader meaning and implications, the social and political contexts and conditions of their creation and exercise…' (Liebel, 2012, p. 1). On the basis of the thematic chapters of this Handbook, two ways in which context matters can be analytically distinguished.

First, contextual circumstances may lead to a *different appreciation of a similar phenomenon*. As illustrated by Hanson, Volonakis and Al-Rozzi (Chapter 18), depending on the circumstances, child labour has been either condemned and rejected (today, especially by the Global North and international organizations) or officially recognized and valued (during the industrialization period, and regarding the involvement of British schoolchildren in agricultural production during the Second World War).

Second, the different contexts in which children live have led to *widely divergent approaches on the ground to tackle children's (rights) issues*, both at the regional, national and local level. This is obvious in the large variety of practices existing in the domains of juvenile justice (Liefaard, Chapter 14) and alternative care (Cantwell, Chapter 15), as well as in the tailored approaches developed for and by indigenous peoples (Blanchet-Cohen, Chapter 21). From a geographical perspective, Aitken proposes that rights should encompass 'spatial variability and personal flexibility' (Chapter 8, p. 138). According to Cantwell, a relevant context-sensitive approach to children's rights requires 'a constructively critical review of global conventional wisdom on children's rights' (Chapter 15, p. 258). A context-sensitive approach to children's rights allows for regional and local variation, and eschews any dogmatic approaches.

It is proposed that contextualization in relation to children's rights (and probably human rights more generally) should be analysed and realized along two axes: one content-related and one scale-related. The first axis concerns the analysis of a context-sensitive approach to children's rights across the different 'substantive' determinants of a certain context, ranging from, but not limited to, the cultural, the socio-economic, the geographical, the socio-political and the historical. The second axis suggests not to limit attention for contextualization to specific cases ('the local'), but also pay attention to context when looking at the development and interpretation of children's rights at a transnational, 'global' level. Both axes should be viewed as a continuum.

Of the various 'factors' that influence and constitute a context-sensitive approach to children's rights, *culture* is arguably one of the most discussed and – at least for some decades – contested. The relation between human rights and cultural diversity has been abundantly debated in scholarship, from both a legal/political science (e.g. Brems, 2001; Donnelly, 2013) as well as an anthropological point of view (e.g. Cowan, Dembour and Wilson 2001; Goodale, 2009). The particular relationship between children's rights and cultural diversity has equally received quite some scholarly attention (see, e.g. Alston, 1994; André, Chapter 7; Brems, 2002, 2013; Desmet, 2011; Harris-Short, 2003). Culture should not be seen in opposition to human rights, nor 'demonized' (Merry, 2003). Although the human rights project often envisages cultural change, human rights realization may also build on cultural practices (Brems, 2001, 2013). For anthropological scholarship has demonstrated that culture should be understood as fluid, hybrid, contested and dynamic, rather than static (Merry, 2003). Moreover, the pursuit of human/children's rights must itself be considered as a cultural process (Cowan *et al.*, 2001). The risk remains however that a cultural contextualization approach is considered as condoning or even legitimizing certain practices. This concern has been voiced for instance with regard to FGM (Leye and Middelburg, Chapter 17). However, paying attention to culture does not mean to justify or condone certain practices. Such an approach rather invites a better understanding of the dynamics and context, so as to possibly mobilize children's rights differently. For instance, since FGM is often an essential prerequisite in the transition to womanhood, there may be a certain degree of ambiguity towards the practice at the local level (Vandenhole, 2012, p. 88). Vandenhole relates how, based on an in-depth understanding of these predicaments, a women's organization in Kenya chose not to support criminalization of FGM, but to focus on awareness raising and alternative initiation rites. Such rites uphold the social and cultural meaning of FGM, but abolish the practice itself. This is an example of how children's rights can be used differently, when there is a 'thick' understanding of the local context – even though questions regarding the girls' participation in these evolutions and power relations within the community may remain (Vandenhole, 2012).

The relation between the human rights (of children) and the *socio-economic dimension* of a context was probably nowhere as intensively debated as in the field of development (see e.g. Mestrum, Chapter 20). Especially, resourcist approaches and theoretical frameworks such as the capability approach focused on the question as to which social and economic means are necessary in a particular context (of a country or a region) and what are the opportunities of a person to use these resources to realize social justice and human dignity (Brighouse and Robeyns, 2010; Nussbaum, 2011). These approaches were considered as complementing human rights-based approaches, as the insight progressively grew that being entitled to (social and economic) rights does not guarantee the realization of social justice and human dignity (Nussbaum, 2007). It brought the discussion on human rights (of children) in relation to the socio-economic dimension of a context to the recognition of the importance of *opportunities* in implementing human rights (of children). So, children can have a right to health care, and health care institutions may be in place in a certain neighbourhood/context, but still, children will make use of these health care institutions in a different way or will not use them at all. This can be due to lack of means to pay for health care services or more generally the socioeconomic status (SES) of an individual child. This shows that the socio-economic dimension of a context influences in a decisive way the realization of children's rights. These insights have been highlighted, inter alia, in the field of social policy and social work. Reynaert and Roose for instance, in Chapter 6, point at social processes such as the Matthew effect to argue that children's rights are determined by the social and economic dimensions of a context. So, just like the cultural dimension, the socio-economic dimension of a context asks for a profound analysis and understanding of the way socio-economic means are mobilized and whether this mobilization contributes to the realization of the human dignity of children.

Finally, still in relation to the content-related axis, it is important to point out the *socio-political dimension* of a context-specific approach. This dimension can be illustrated by referring to more 'identity-related' characteristics that impact a contextual orientation of children's rights. Scholarly work on personal categories such as gender, ethnicity, sexual orientation, religion etc. do not just point towards these characteristics as personal traits of children. It emphasizes the socio-political dimension of these categories, as these categories only acquire meaning within complex power relations in a particular context. Children often experience discrimination and violations of their rights based on labels such as gender or religion for instance (see e.g. Taefi, 2009). Moreover, these labels may reinforce one another and result in further violations of children's rights. These simultaneously existing and mutually reinforcing forms of discrimination, generally known as intersectionality, show how power operates in a very complex but subtle way resulting in violations of children's rights (see on intersectionality also De Graeve, Chapter 9). So, as Wilson (2013) argues, intersectionality offers an analytical frame that focuses on the structural and political dynamics of power. The analysis of power dimensions in a particular context opens up possibilities for critical engagement with children's rights (see Section 4, below, for more on critique).

The second axis of a context-sensitive approach concerns the relation between the local and the global. A contextual approach to children's rights is often associated with a 'local', 'case-specific' approach. Although this is certainly one dimension of a context-specific approach, children's rights practices generally cannot be understood without reference to their global dimension. Globalization is often considered as the root cause of violations of children's rights. Globalization is then equated with economic globalization and the spread of a neo-liberal model of society, ignoring social concerns like for instance the realization of children's rights. However, viewing globalization as the ultimate root cause of children's rights violations ignores local children's rights practices that are not de facto in the interest of children. Also at the local level, children's rights can be impeded from full realization due to, for instance, misinterpretation, lack of resources or imbalanced power relations. Furthermore, such a consideration assumes that global processes related to children's rights cannot be in the interest of children. However, globalization just as localization can be the motor of emancipating tendencies. Globalization is not merely an economic process but became just as well the carrier of the endeavour to realize global social justice (Widdows and Smith, 2013; compare Mestrum, Chapter 20, and her plea for alter-globalization). The global campaign for education that was set up in the early 1990s is a good example of global efforts to realize the right to education for all (Verger and Novelli, 2012).

Furthermore, for a good understanding of how children's rights are constructed in a particular setting, it is vital to analyse local children's rights practices in relation to global processes. As André argues in Chapter 7, 'previously more remote societies have been progressively penetrated by external dimensions and global systems of values and monitored by global institutions that have integrated them into global power relations' (André, Chapter 7, p. 113). So, we cannot understand local interpretations of children's rights without linking them to the global social and political context. This is obvious in the context of migration, as Ceriani in Chapter 19 explains, where some of the root causes of child migration lie exactly in the current context of

Conclusions: critical children's rights studies

globalization. However, this is not to say that local practices just undergo these global processes or that local communities can have no influence on globalization. Ife describes how for instance the use of social media can be used as part of a process of 'globalisation from below' (Ife, 2001), where local practices can have an impact on the global level by using the opportunities offered by globalization.

Finally, it is suggested that attention should also be paid to (the impact of contextual factors on) the diverging, and at times contrasting, interpretations and approaches to children's rights in the transnational/global arena. Children's rights are not unidimensional in their origin, significance and interpretation. The context in which children's rights 'emerge' transnationally is equally important to enhance a better understanding of children's rights. For instance, with regard to child labour, Hanson, Volonakis and Al-Rozzi note that '[t]he global character of [the worldwide movement against child labour] does not however mean that there is one single global perspective on child labour, in fact quite the contrary' (Chapter 18, p. 321). They plead for attention to these 'multifaceted realities of child labour' (Chapter 18, p. 322). In the field of human rights, such a research effort has been undertaken by Merry (2006) in relation to gender violence and the Convention on the Elimination of All Forms of Discrimination against Women.

To conclude, there appears to be a broad consensus, across disciplinary and thematic contributions, that a context-sensitive interpretation and realization of children's rights is necessary and feasible. Nevertheless, children's rights, with their universal dimension and their necessity for a contextual understanding, are discursive in nature. Therefore, children's rights practices need on-going reflection on different characteristics of a context. We identified two of these characteristics in particular, which we defined as two distinguishable axes: one content-related and one scale-related.

3. Interdisciplinary dialogue and a critical approach to children's rights

In the introduction, the concepts of multidisciplinarity, interdisciplinarity and transdisciplinarity were understood as referring to different degrees of interaction between disciplinary perspectives that can be situated on a continuum, ranging from juxtaposition (*multi*) over interaction (*inter*) to integration (*trans*). At the level of chapters, this Handbook can be qualified to a large extent as multidisciplinary. The first part offers a critical analysis of how various (inter-) disciplines approach children's rights, whereas various authors in the second, thematic part take one disciplinary perspective as point of departure. However, delving into the particularities of each chapter, the boundaries between disciplinary perspectives are often transgressed to a greater or lesser extent. In most chapters, insights from other disciplines are drawn upon to critically reflect upon the approach of one's own discipline to children's rights – in general or in relation to a thematic issue.

Some chapters seek to adopt a more robust interdisciplinary or transdisciplinary approach. For instance, Hanson, Volonakis and Al-Rozzi demonstrate how looking at child labour and working children by combining insights from 'history, anthropology, childhood sociology, international labour law, human rights law and children's rights studies' provides a more in-depth understanding of the complexities and ambiguities of the topic (Hanson, Volonakis and Al-Rozzi, Chapter 18, p. 317). In Chapter 10 on citizenship studies, Mitchell pleads for a problem-oriented rather than a discipline-centred approach. In his view, such transdisciplinary research establishes its own standards, and implies a 'greater legitimisation of knowledge creation by Indigenous stakeholders and other marginalised groups located in non-elite spaces outside the political confines of the increasingly corporate-industrial-academic complex' (Mitchell, Chapter 10, p. 175).

The notion of 'interdisciplinary interaction' that we use here, following Klein (1990), may play out in different ways, such as: (i) borrowing, i.e. where analytical tools, methods or concepts from another discipline are used (see André, Chapter 7, on the use of ethnographic tools by other disciplines; most if not all thematic chapters engage in this type of interdisciplinary interaction); (ii) the interaction between disciplines to solve a specific problem, but without aiming for a conceptual unification of knowledge (e.g. Lenzer, Chapter 16; Leye and Middelburg, Chapter 17); (iii) the 'increased consistency of subject matters and methods', leading to an 'overlapping area' between disciplines; and (iv) the development of a new interdiscipline (see e.g. Vanobbergen, Chapter 4 on childhood studies; De Graeve, Chapter 9 on gender studies).

For the purposes of this Handbook, an important question is how the relationship between a critical approach to children's rights and interdisciplinarity should be conceptualized. Phrased as an, admittedly normative, question: does a critical approach to children's rights *require* an engagement with other disciplines, and thus a certain degree of 'interdisciplinary interaction'? In the tentative answer provided hereinafter, nuance is vital. Also, the reflections deal with a critical approach *to children's rights*, as a critical stance towards a certain discipline may be adopted, yet from a 'mainstream' understanding of children's rights.

There seems to be a strong positive correlation between an interdisciplinary approach – in the sense of seriously engaging with other disciplines – and a critical approach to children's rights. Transgressing disciplinary boundaries, both methodologically and conceptually, enhances a multidimensional understanding of children's rights and leads to questioning, often disciplinary-specific, assumptions and constructions – the latter being a key element of an attitude of critique (see the introduction and Section 4 on critique, below). There does not appear to be an indispensable connection, however, between an interdisciplinary and a critical approach. On the one hand, not every interdisciplinary endeavour implies an attitude of critique. Interdisciplinary collaborations may be oriented towards addressing practical problems on the ground, and thus be governed by an implementation logic rather than a critical approach. On the other, it may be possible to adopt a critical perspective *within* the contours of a particular disciplinary approach. André, for instance, recounts how anthropologists were and are very critical of children's rights, both as a concept and as an object of research (André, Chapter 7). Different schools within a certain discipline may also challenge each other in their understanding of and approach to children's rights. Reynaert and Roose point out the distinction between relational social work and structural social work (Chapter 6), and Aitken references the importance of Marxist and feminist geographers (Chapter 8). In order not to overlook the expertise and particular knowledge interest of each discipline, Quennerstedt even proposes to ground research on children's rights again more firmly in specific disciplines (Chapter 12).

The potential of critical reflection on children's rights within the boundaries of a discipline seems to vary, however, with the nature of the discipline concerned. Doctrinal legal scholarship, for instance, is characterized by an 'internal approach' whereby legal rules and principles are analysed from 'the perspective of an insider in the system' (McCrudden, 2006, p. 632). Judicial decisions and legislation are evaluated on the basis of a closed system of legal reasoning, referring to (other) authoritative texts and concentrating on issues of legal coherence. Legal systems are conceived as more or less autonomous (McCrudden, 2006). In the words of Vick (2004, pp. 178–179), '[t]he law, in essence, is treated as a sealed system which can be studied through methods unique to the 'science of law', and legal developments can be interpreted ... by reference to the internal logic of this sealed system.' Remaining within the system's logic, such doctrinal legal analysis or 'black-letter' research does not call into question the foundations or ways of functioning of the legal system as such, nor does it look at the impact of law and legal institutions on society. These particular characteristics of doctrinal legal scholarship thus seem to complicate the possibility of adopting a critical approach to children's rights by remaining within the contours of the legal discipline. For a critical legal perspective on children's rights, it seems necessary to draw upon insights and methodologies developed in other disciplines. Such an 'external' approach' has materialized in the development of socio-legal studies, critical legal studies and law-and-economics, among others (McCrudden, 2006).

Engaging in (a certain degree of) interdisciplinarity may entail various pitfalls and challenges though. A first prerequisite, in order to be able to adequately engage with other disciplinary perspectives, is a firm and profound understanding of the technicalities of one's own discipline. Without a sound knowledge of the 'home' discipline, a dialogue with other disciplines may result in a slippery slope. Second, there is a danger of underestimating the complexities of other disciplinary approaches, leading to a superficial or unidimensional view. For instance, when non-lawyers engage with the legal discipline, risks seem to include adopting a dogmatic approach and taking legal provisions at face value, without a proper understanding of the nature of legal qualifications. Similarly, children's rights may be equated with children's rights *law*. Another scenario is that only the dominant school of a certain discipline is considered, whereas other, smaller, counterhegemonic schools remain under the radar. Additional hazards of interacting with another discipline include a lack of understanding of the limitations and biases of this discipline's research methods, as well as misinterpreting research results (Vick, 2004, p. 185). Moreover, there is a potential of abuse of knowledge when integrating insights from other disciplines (Desmet and Aylwin, Chapter 22). Finally, studies that claim interdisciplinarity or transdisciplinarity run the risk of 'lacking body', as it may not be clear anymore which methods or frameworks of reference are employed, and how the research is to be situated within a broader body of knowledge.

Recapitulating, it is suggested that a critical approach to children's rights hugely benefits from being infused with theories, concepts, methods and research findings from other disciplines, even though it may be possible to critically reflect on children's rights within the confines of a certain discipline. Whereas in legal scholarship the need for interdisciplinary dialogue seems even greater because of the particular way of knowledge building, also in other disciplines certain issues may remain unaddressed when there is no engagement with other disciplinary perspectives. Every disciplinary approach sheds light on certain aspects of a research problem while obscuring others (e.g. a focus on individual (psychology) versus societal (sociology) factors), since every discipline is characterized by its own paradigms, research interests and methodologies. Therefore, entering into dialogue with other disciplinary perspectives seems to greatly enhance the potential for critical reflection on the human rights of children and young people.

4. Critiques of children's rights

What we present under this heading are those components of what we consider a critical approach that have not been covered under the previous headings. In the introduction, we coined this as critique, i.e. an on-going process of questioning assumptions, knowledge and acts as well as the associated norms and values that shape the social, educational or legal practices that rely on the children's rights framework. Analytically, we distinguish critique from the other key components of a critical approach to children's rights, i.e. context-specificity and disciplinary interaction. However, it has become clear that some of these key characteristics of a critical approach certainly intersect and possibly even overlap to some extent. Contextualization is a case in point. Leaving space for diverse framings and interpretations – as a key feature of critique – is directly connected to openness for local contextualization, as diverse framings and interpretations often originate from specific local contexts.

In the introduction, we tentatively conceptualized critique along four lines. First, critique does not take for granted that children's rights or children's rights law offer fully-fledged solutions for social problems. Put more positively, critique builds on children's rights to detect underlying social problems and to analyse how such problems are constructed and defined. Second, a critical approach implies that the understanding of children's rights is an interactive process between all involved rather than a technical process of establishing objective knowledge. This implies that different interpretations may co-exist. How children themselves shape their rights and thus produce a certain knowledge and interpretation of their contexts and society is of crucial importance in critique and in a critical approach more generally. Third, the broader societal structures cannot be disregarded, since children's rights and the lifeworlds of children are embedded in them. Fourth and finally, critique creates space for alternative ideas on children's rights, and hence potential for transformation and emancipation.[8]

A key question in further elucidating the nature of critique is whether cherry-picking is possible, or whether the four elements outlined above all need to be in place in order to qualify as critique. On the one hand, it is important to note that an approach of critique is not a school of thought with a doctrinal rigour or a certain orthodoxy that has to be subscribed to. On the other hand, some elements of the approach of critique may be essential in order not to dilute the approach completely.

As Figure 23.1 illustrates, we propose here to slightly re-phrase critique as being characterized ideal-typically by three elements. One reflects the diagnostic dimension, i.e. the use of children's rights to deconstruct the way in which social problems are defined (for example Lenzer, Chapter 16; Mestrum, Chapter 20; Reynaert and Roose, Chapter 6). The deliberative dimension refers to the way in which children's rights scholarship is undertaken, i.e. as on-going reflection that leaves space for diverse interpretations (André, Chapter 7; Blanchet-Cohen, Chapter 21; Cantwell, Chapter 15; De Graeve, Chapter 9; Leye and Middelburg, Chapter 17), thereby avoiding closure or blackboxing (Stenner, 2011, p. 3). Children's rights are given meaning in interactive processes that also include children (André, Chapter 7; Mayall, Chapter 5; Reynaert and Roose, Chapter 6; Tisdall, Chapter 11; Vanobbergen, Chapter 4); (compare Aitken, Chapter 8, who also argues in support of more open notions of development and progress). Third, the finality of children's rights scholarship is said to be social transformation and emancipation; this is the emancipatory dimension. Whereas all three dimensions interrelate, the first (diagnostic dimension) and third one (emancipatory dimension) may be less explicitly present without rendering an approach of critique to children's rights hollow or emptied of substance. On the other hand, an approach of critique seems very unlikely without on-going reflection and openness for diverse interpretations, including those of children themselves.

In the multidisciplinary setting of this Handbook, the question arises whether the ideal-typical picture of critique strikes a chord within each discipline, or to the contrary, whether our characterization of critique holds a disciplinary bias. Yet another way of framing the issue is whether there is a need to diversify the understanding of critique along disciplinary lines. The origin of the ideal-typical approach of critique to children's rights as presented here, lies partly in social work/educational sciences, which in turn is indebted to the critical theory in the

8   This analytical framework builds mainly on the work of D. Reynaert et al. (2012).

Conclusions: critical children's rights studies

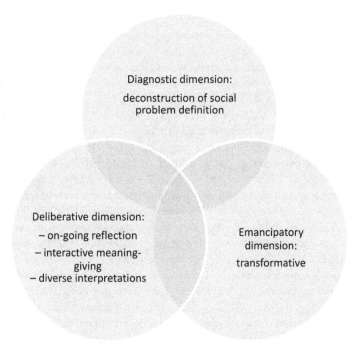

Figure 23.1 Key dimensions of a critique of children's rights

tradition of the Frankfurt school, but also in anthropology and childhood studies. These disciplines may be primarily interested in the deconstruction of social problems definition, hence their understanding of children's rights in their diagnostic dimension, i.e. as analytical tools for deconstructing the ways in which social problems are defined. Other disciplines may not share that basic orientation. The legal discipline, for instance, primarily seeks to regulate behaviour (through legal norm creation and interpretation). Whereas it may be interested in the deconstruction of social problems definition, it will be more interested to see whether and how legal regulation is needed. Likewise, not all disciplines may include an explicit transformative and emancipatory finality in their self-definition, although one may wonder whether that element characterizes disciplines or rather approaches within disciplines (e.g., socio-legal studies or critical legal studies do seem to embrace the emancipatory dimension). It goes without saying that not every discipline may be expected (or be equipped) to undertake, for instance, a diagnostic exercise or to capture children's interpretations of children's rights, but it can draw on other disciplines to do so (see above on disciplinary interaction). In that respect, the key elements of critique should not too easily be categorized as discipline-specific.

At the same time, the emancipatory dimension in particular cannot be assumed at face value, and is in need of further clarification. A core concept in the emancipatory dimension is human dignity, as the end goal of emancipation or social transformation. Human dignity has become closely connected to human rights, but its meaning and relationship with human rights remains unclear (Düwell, 2014, pp. 28–31). The emancipatory dimension of an approach of critique to children's rights therefore needs to clarify the relationship between children's rights and human dignity. Human dignity is for example sometimes mobilized to support individual choice, and sometimes works as a break on individual choice (Brownsword, 2014, p. 1; a way-out may be offered by the notion of relational autonomy, see De Graeve, Chapter 9). When turning to children's rights as vehicles for emancipation and transformation, a key determinant is power and power relations. Power analysis within children's rights studies therefore needs to receive more attention than it has received so far (De Graeve, Chapter 9; Mayall, Chapter 5). Some work has already been done on child participation and power (Gallagher 2008; Hart 2008; Hinton 2008; Morrow and Pells 2012; Tisdall, Chapter 11). Approaches to power analysis in development work and the concepts used may be instructive for children's rights too. The power cube, for example, distinguishes levels, forms and spaces of power. Power may be visible, hidden or invisible; it may work at global, national or local level; and spaces for engagement may be closed, invited or claimed/created (Gaventa 2006; on space, see Aitken, Chapter 8).

Another question is how the emancipatory dimension coincides with or differs from activist scholarship. For sure, contributors to this Handbook take different positions. For some, children's rights scholarship should carve out its own place next to activism; they may question the emancipatory dimension. Others strongly favour an emancipatory objective, and see that realized, by and large, to its full potential by current children's rights (law) (Ceriani, Chapter 19; Kilkelly, Chapter 13; Lenzer, Chapter 16; Leye and Middelburg, Chapter 17; Verhellen, Chapter 3). Yet others endorse the finality, but point out the limitations of children's rights (law) to deliver on that prospect (Hanson, Volonakis and Al-Rozzi, Chapter 18; Vandenhole, Chapter 2; Desmet and Aylwin, Chapter 22) or emphasize the need for appropriation and transformation by stakeholders as an intermediate step (Blanchet-Cohen, Chapter 21).

In sum, the approach of critique may be somewhere in between the radical school, which defines itself mainly in terms of deconstruction, and a technical approach, in which neutral, pre-defined, final solutions are claimed to be possible. The approach of critique includes but does not stop with deconstruction (diagnostic dimension). It is also characterized by openness for diverse interpretations that continue to evolve, and that engage with one another in dialogue or confrontation (deliberative dimension). Finally, the approach of critique to children's right explicitly gives up any claim to neutrality. To the contrary, it defines itself in terms of a finality of transformation and emancipation (emancipatory dimension).

5. Towards critical children's rights studies

Based on the findings set forth in the previous sections of this conclusion, we end here by suggesting further directions in children's rights research. Given the critical approach of this Handbook, we call this children's rights research agenda 'critical children's rights studies'. In recent years, the notion of 'children's rights studies' has emerged in several publications (see e.g. Vandenhole *et al.*, 2010; Reynaert *et al.*, 2010b; Stalford, 2012; Hanson and Nieuwenhuys, 2013), emphasizing exactly the need to deepen the theoretical foundations of children's rights. As we stated in the preface, there is hardly a tradition in the (academic) field of children's rights that critically analyses children's rights without at the same time forswearing the framework of children's rights (Reynaert *et al.*, 2012). Much more insight is needed in the underlying norms, values and logics that shape children's rights practices today and the way in which these are understood. Making these norms, values and logics explicit is the fundamental mission of what can be considered as a 'new' academic field of 'children's rights studies'.

The notion of 'children's rights studies', although already in use for a number of years with various scholars, was only recently given real substance. Hanson (2014) for instance locates children's rights studies at the intersection of childhood studies and human rights studies. In his view, the field of children's rights studies is in essence an interdisciplinary field. Recently the

European Network of Masters in Children's Rights, a network of universities offering higher education in children's rights, has used the notion of children's rights studies to emphasize 'an understanding of children's rights as socially and culturally contextualised subjective rights'.[9] In an article published in the *International Journal of Children's Rights* in 2012, Reynaert et al. argued in favour of developing a new field of 'critical children's rights studies'. Based on these ideas, we propose a research agenda for 'critical children's rights studies' to be developed grounded in the following fundamental starting points:

1. Children's rights are universal principles and entitlements embodying children's human dignity. However, these principles need to be understood and interpreted as social constructs in a particular social, cultural, economic, political and historical context. Critical children's rights studies should therefore conduct research on the interplay – and possible tension – between universal and particular understandings of children's rights and on how these understandings are moving between the global and the local.
2. Children's rights are the human rights of children, i.e. they refer to an idea of human dignity and social justice that is common to humankind, not just to children. Critical children's rights studies should therefore not exclusively focus on the interests of children, but should understand the rights of children in relation to the rights of other groups in society, in particular adults in general. This also means that the institutionalized distinction between children and adults is a permanent object of theoretical reflection.
3. How children's rights are shaped by children themselves and through the interaction of children with other groups in society, in this way producing a certain knowledge, is a central focus of critical children's rights studies. Therefore, critical children's rights studies should use methods of inquiry tailored to children and consider the possibility to involve children as researchers.
4. A critical perspective is a fundamental starting point in critical children's rights studies: meaning that the way children's rights are shaped is an object of constant analysis; mainstream paradigms are perpetually deconstructed; the different meanings and interpretations of children's rights are confronted with each other; and their goal is emancipation and social transformation. Children's rights also need to be studied in disciplinary interaction and in a contextualized way.

Of course, this is only a preliminary agenda of an emergent field of critical children's rights studies. We hope that this Handbook will further trigger and mature the discussion on constructions and understandings of children's rights in the years to come, and on how to research children's rights. We are convinced that contextuality, disciplinary interaction and critique (in its threefold dimension: diagnostic, deliberative and emancipatory) will be pivotal in elaborating the critical children's rights studies' research agenda. The substance of it is open to further discussion and debate.

Acknowledgement

This research has been funded by the Interuniversity Attraction Poles Programme (IAP) initiated by the Belgian Science Policy Office, more specifically the IAP 'The Global Challenge of Human Rights Integration: Towards a Users' Perspective' (www.hrintegration.be)

---

9   Available at www.enmcr.net/ (last accessed 15 September 2014).

References

Alston, P. (ed.) (1994). *The Best Interests of the Child: Reconciling Culture and Human Rights*. Oxford: Clarendon, 1–25.

An-Na'im, A. A. (ed.). (1992). *Human Rights in Cross-Cultural Perspectives: A quest for Consensus*. Philadelphia, PA: University of Pennsylvania Press.

Brems, E. (2001). *Human rights: Universality and Diversity*. Leiden: Martinus Nijhoff.

Brems, E. (2002). Children's rights and universality. In J. C. M. Willems (ed.), *Developmental and Autonomy Rights of Children. Empowering Children, Caregivers and Communities* (pp. 21–45). Antwerp: Intersentia.

Brems, E. (2013). Inclusive universality and the child-caretaker dynamic. In Hanson, K., and Nieuwenhuys, O. (eds). (2013). *Reconceptualizing Children's Rights in International Development: Living Rights, Social Justice, Translations*. Cambridge: Cambridge University Press.

Brighouse, H., and Robeyns, I. (eds) (2010). *Measuring Justice: Primary Goods and Capabilities*. Cambridge: Cambridge University Press.

Brownsword, R. (2014). Human dignity from a legal perspective. In M. Düwell, J. Braarvig, R. Brownsword and D. Mieth (eds), *The Cambridge Handbook of Human Dignity: Interdisciplinary Perspectives*. Cambridge: Cambridge University Press, 1–22.

Cheney, K. (2013), Malik and his three mothers: AIDS orphans' survival strategies and how children's rights hinder them. In K. Hanson and O. Nieuwenhuys (eds), *Reconceptualising Children's Rights in International Development: Living Rights, Social Justice, Translations*, Cambridge: Cambridge University Press.

Cowan, J. K., Dembour, M. B., and Wilson, R. A. (eds) (2001). *Culture and Rights: Anthropological Perspectives*. Cambridge: Cambridge University Press.

Dedding, C., Jurrius, K., Moonen, X., and Rutjes, L. (eds) (2013). *Kinderen en jongeren actief in wetenschappelijk onderzoek. Ethiek, methoden en resultaten van onderzoek met en door jeugd* [Children and young people active in scientific research: Ethics, methods and results of research with and by young people]. Houten: Uitgeverij Lannoo Campus.

Desmet, E. (2011). Is het glas halfvol of halfleeg? Kinderrechten en culturele diversiteit [Is the glass half full or half empty? Children's rights and cultural diversity]. In D. Reynaert, R. Roose, W. Vandenhole and K. Vlieghe (eds), *Kinderrechten: springplank of struikelblok? Naar een kritische benadering van kinderrechten* [Children's rights: Steppingstone or stumbling block? Towards a critical approach of children's rights]. Antwerp: Intersentia, 79–93.

Donnelly, J. (2013). *Universal Human Rights in Theory and Practice*. Ithaca, NY: Cornell University Press.

Düwell, M. (2014). Human dignity: Concepts, discussions, philosophical perspectives. In M. Düwell, J. Braarvig, R. Brownsword and D. Mieth (eds), *The Cambridge Handbook of Human Dignity: Interdisciplinary Perspectives*. Cambridge: Cambridge University Press, 23–49.

Freeman, M. (2007). Why it remains important to take children's rights seriously. *International Journal of Children's Rights*, 15, 5–23.

Gallagher, M. (2008). Foucault, power and participation. *International Journal of Children's Rights*, 16(3), 395–406.

Gaventa, J. (2006). Finding the spaces for change: A power analysis. *IDS Bulletin*, 37(6), 23–33.

Giddens, A. (1984), *The constitution of society: Outline of the Theory of Structuration*. Cambridge: Polity Press.

Goodale, M. (2009). *Surrendering to Utopia: An Anthropology of Human Rights*. Stanford, CA: Stanford University Press.

Hanson, K. (2014). Children's rights studies. An interdisciplinary study field at the intersection of childhood studies and human rights studies, presentation given at the ESA RN 4 Mid-term symposium – Sociology of childhood. *Theorizing Childhood: Citizenship, Rights, Participation*. University of Modena and Reggio Emilia, Italy, 21–23 May 2014.

Hanson, K., and Nieuwenhuys, O. (eds) (2013). *Reconceptualizing Children's Rights in International Development: Living Rights, Social Justice, Translations*. Cambridge: Cambridge University Press.

Harris-Short, S. (2003). International human rights law: Imperialist, inept and ineffective? Cultural relativism and the UN Convention on the Rights of the Child. *Human Rights Quarterly*, 25, 130–181.

Hart, J. (2008). Children's participation and international development: Attending to the political. *International Journal of Children's Rights*, 16(3), 407–418.

Hinton, R. (2008). Children's participation and good governance: Limitations of the theoretical literature. *International Journal of Children's Rights*, 16(3), 285–300.

Honwana, A. (2005). *Child Soldiers in Africa*. Philadelphia, PA: University of Pennsylvania Press.

Hunner-Kreisel, C. and Kuhn, M. (2010). Children's perspectives: Methodological critiques and empirical studies. In S. Andresen, I. Diehm, U. Sander and H. Ziegler (eds), *Children and the Good Life: New Challenges for Research on Children*. New York: Springer.

Ife, J. (2001). Local and global practice: Relocating social work as a human rights profession in the new global order. *European Journal of Social Work*, 4(1), 5–15.

Klein, J. T. (1990). *Interdisciplinarity: History, Theory, and Practice*. Detroit, MI: Wayne State University Press.

Liebel, M. (2012). *Children's Rights from Below: Cross-Cultural Perspectives*. Basingstoke, UK: Palgrave Macmillan.

Liebel, M. (2013). *Kinder und Gerechtigkeit: Über Kinderrechte neu nachdenken* [Children and justice – A new way of thinking on children's rights]. Landsberg, Germany: Beltz Juventa.

McCrudden, C. (2006). Legal research and the social sciences. *Law Quarterly Review*, 122, 632–650.

Melton, G. (2006). *Background for a general comment on the right to participate: Article 12 and related provisions of the Conventions on the Rights of the Child*. Prepared for use by the UN Committee on the Rights of the Child.

Merry, S. E. (2003). Human rights law and the demonization of culture (and anthropology along the way). *Political and Legal Anthropology Review*, 26(1), 55–85.

Merry, S. E. (2006). *Human Rights and Gender Violence: Translating International Law into Local Justice*. Chicago, IL: University of Chicago Press.

Moosa-Mitha, M. (2005). A difference-centred alternative to theorization of children's citizenship rights. *Citizenship Studies*, 9(4), 369–388.

Morrow, V. (2011). *Understanding Children and Childhood* [Centre for Children and Young People Background Briefing Series, no. 1] (2nd ed.). Lismore, Australia: Centre for Children and Young People, Southern Cross University.

Morrow, V., and Pells, K. (2012). Integrating children's human rights and child poverty debates: Examples from young lives in Ethiopia and India. *Sociology*, 46(5), 906–920.

Mortier, F. (2002). We zijn allemaal kinderen: bruggen tussen rechten voor kinderen en rechten voor volwassenen [We are all children: bridges between rights for children and rights for adults]. *Tijdschrift voor Jeugdrecht en Kinderrechten [Journal for Youth Law and Children's Rights]*, 3 (extra edition): 10–17.

Nussbaum, M. C. (1997). Capabilities and human rights. *Fordham Law Review*, 66, 273–300.

Nussbaum, M. C. (2011). *Creating Capabilities: The Human Development Approach*. Cammbridge, MA: Harvard University Press.

Reynaert, D., Bouverne-De Bie, M., and Vandevelde, S. (2010a). Children, rights and social work: Rethinking children's rights education. *Social Work and Society*, 8(1), 60–69.

Reynaert, D., Bouverne-De Bie, M., and Vandevelde, S. (2010b). *The Children's Rights Movement: A Social Movement?* Paper presented at the 8th annual TiSSA Conference 'Social work in times of crisis. What can social work deliver – and who benefits?' Tallinn, Estonia, 25–27 August 2010.

Reynaert, D., De Bie, M., and Vandevelde, S. (2012). Between 'believers' and 'opponents': critical discussions on children's rights. *The International Journal of Children's Rights*, 20(1), 1–15.

Stalford, H. (2012). *Children and the European Union: Rights, Welfare and Accountability*. Oxford: Hart.

Stenner, P. (2011). Subjective dimensions of human rights: What do ordinary people understand by 'human rights'? *The International Journal of Human Rights*, 15(8), 1215–1233.

Taefi, N. (2009). The synthesis of age and gender: Intersectionality, international human rights law and the marginalisation of the girl-child. *International Journal of Children's Rights*, 17(3), 345–376.

Vandenhole, W. (2012). Localising the human rights of children. In M. Liebel (ed.), *Children's Rights from Below: Cross-cultural Perspectives*. New York: Palgrave Macmillan, pp. 80–93.

Vandenhole, W., Vranken, J., and De Boyser, K. (2010). *Why Care? Children's Rights and Child Poverty*. Antwerp: Intersentia.

Verger, A., and Novelli, M. (eds) (2012). *Campaigning for 'Education for All': Histories, Strategies and Outcomes of Transnational Social Movements in Education*. Rotterdam: Sense.

Vick, D. W. (2004). Interdisciplinarity and the discipline of law. *Journal of Law and Society*, 31(2), 163–193.

Widdows, H., and Smith, N. J. (eds) (2013). *Global Social Justice* (Vol. 31). Abingdon, UK: Taylor and Francis.

Wilson, A. R. (ed.) (2013). *Situating Intersectionality: Politics, Policy, and Power*. Basingstoke, UK: Palgrave Macmillan.

Index

abuse *see* violence against children
adults *see also* parents: adult–child relationship, rethinking of 61; adult citizenship re-theorised through child citizenship 167–8
African Union (AU), children's rights framework 30
age limits *see* juvenile justice
agency: autonomy and 3, 69, 72, 151, 194; child-images and 4, 72, 150, 158, 413; children as participatory subjects 73–5; children as social actors 70, 72–3, 79, 83, 98, 112, 114, 141, 150–1, 326, 389, 412, 413, 415, 415–16; in children's lifeworlds 10; children's rights as agency rights 287–8; competence and 88; control of 88; CRC's approach to 71; denial of children's agency 244; economic agency 320; establishment of 290; exercise of 88, 104–5, 153, 154, 192, 225, 322; institutional structures and 78, 79; interdependency and 121; opportunities for 87; parents and 158, 170–1, 210; participation and 196, 413, 416; promotion of 272; recognition of 389, 395, 403, 414; recognition of children's agency 85, 89, 97, 99, 119, 133, 137, 138, 159, 173, 190, 259, 264, 291; 'resourcist view' of 105; self-determination and 5; social work and 98; socialisation and 68; vulnerability and 12
alternative care of children: applicable rights 258–60, 273; author's analytical approach 17–18, 258; bottom-up approach to 271–2; child-headed households 264–5; child-images 258, 259, 270; deinstitutionalisation 268–9, 269, 270–1; foreign financing of 269; formal arrangements 257, 262, 265–6, 266–7, 267; Guidelines (2009) 260, 272–3; 'human rights inflation' 273; informal kinship care 257, 262–3; institutional care 269–70, 270, 287; localisation factors 258; necessity principle 260–2; participation rights and 264; private control of 269; 'right to a family' 268–9, 273; scope of 257; state control of 270; suitability principle 260–2
American Convention on Human Rights 1969 (ACHR) 29–30
anthropology: author's analytical approach 14–15; bottom-up approaches to rights 113, 119–22, 126; capitalism and rights 123–4; child-images 113, 115, 118; child protection and and international development in relation 124–5; citizenship studies and 164–5; CRC and 113, 114; critique of children's rights 115–18, 125–6; cultural relativism 113, 116–17, 119; globalisation and rights 113, 122; miserabilism 113; populism 113; renewed interest in childhood 112, 113, 114–15; top-down approaches to rights 113, 126
Apollonian child 64
asylum-seekers *see* migration
autonomy *see also* competence; self-determination: agency and 3, 69, 72, 151, 194; 'autonomous child' concept 3, 98–102; and best interests of the child 32; child-images 101; children as participatory subjects 72–3; competence and 51, 72; CRC and 71; dependency and 50, 74; participation rights and 72; right to 45

best interests of the child, principle of 31, 32
bottom-up approaches to rights: anthropology 113, 119–22, 126; children's rights law 39; citizenship studies 165; CRC 56; gender

studies 148, 159; generally 1–2, 7, 417, 418; 'globalisation from below' 421; natural resource exploitation 392; social work 95, 106; violence against children 287, 288, 289, 290
Bunge, Bill, 'geographical expeditions' 135–6
business *see* natural resource exploitation

capacity *see* competence
care: alternative *see* alternative care of children; ethics of *see* gender studies
child citizenship *see* citizenship studies
child development: feminist critiques of 151–2; new theoretical approaches 66, 79; theories 63–6, 79
child-friendly information 249
child-friendly justice *see* juvenile justice
'child-friendly' provision 71
child-headed households 264–5
child-images: agency and 4, 72, 150, 158; anthropology and 113, 115, 118; Apollonian image 64; autonomous child 101; changes in 44–5, 55, 95, 97, 413–16; child labour 320, 322; childhood and 3–6; childhood studies 61; children in care 258, 259, 270; coexistent images 414; in CRC 48, 50–2, 244; cross-generational variation 415; Dionysian image 64; gender studies and 149–52, 153–4; as human 'becomings' 416; incompetent child 101; long-term sick children 61; in media 115; 'minority group child' 68; natural resource exploitation 388, 389; normal child 63, 64; 'Other' than the adult 65, 415; rights holders 416; social work and children's rights movement in relation 98–101; 'socially constructed child' 69; 'socially developing child' 68; 'tribal child' 69; vulnerable child 402, 404
child labour: abolitionist arguments 316–17, 323, 325–6; attitudes to 325–7; author's analytical approach 19, 317; 'child employment', concept of 323, 327; child-images 320, 322; 'child labour' and 'child work' distinguished 317, 323–4, 327; as children's rights violation 316–17; contextual diversity 322–5; contrasting viewpoints 316; definition of 322–5; division with adult labour 80, 84–5; drafting of CRC provisions 317–18; empowerment perspective 326; historical overview 319–21; laissez-faire attitude 325; participation rights and 318, 326; and poverty 357, 364–5; recognition of children's rights as workers 316, 317, 325, 326, 327; regulation approach 326
child law: children's rights law distinguished 27; development of separate legal regime for children 45; 'not-yet' status of children 45, 55, 61

child protection: indigenous children's rights 382–3; introduction of laws 45; protection principle in CRC 50; and respect for family life 34–6
child soldiers, citizenship issues 164, 167
childhood: child-images and 3–6; coexisting social constructions of 4–5; definitions of key concepts 2–5; dimensions of difference in 413–14; dynamic childhoods 412–13, 415–16; generational dynamics in defining 414–15; as preparation for adulthood 61
Childhood Matters, publication of 133
childhood studies *see also* sociology of childhood: author's analytical approach 13, 62–3; child-images 61; children's rights in relation to 62, 71–4; definition of 61, 148; interdisciplinary approach 276–7; key themes 61, 74; 'new childhood paradigm' 150; origin of 62, 276; sociology of childhood distinguished from 61–2
children: adult–child relationship, rethinking of 61; coexisting images of 4–5; competence 55; definitions of key concepts 2–4; plurality of identity 148, 152, 154, 156; respect for 77–8; as separate social beings 71; tension between dependence and autonomy 50; threefold domination of 112–13
children at risk, growth of 72–3
children in care *see* alternative care of children
children with disabilities, right to education 36–7
children's agency *see* agency
children's rights: bottom-up approach to 7; categorisation of 6; children as bearers of rights 45–6; children's competence to exercise rights 55, 84; critical approach to *see* critical approach to children's rights; definitions of key concepts 2–7; dimensions to rights 81; disciplinary perspectives summarised 12–16; historical background to 44–6; as human rights 5–7, 45, 202; image of child as rights holder 416; inter-disciplinary approach to 8–9; new conceptualisations of 1–2; pragmatic trend 55; respect for 81, 85; scope of 5; structure of book 11–12; thematic perspectives summarised 16–21
children's rights law: author's analytical approach 12; bottom-up approaches to rights 39; child law distinguished from 27; children's rights distinguished from 27; definition of 27; domestic state as duty-bearer 39; education *see* right to education; family life *see* family life; general obligations and principles 31–2; global framework 28–9; human rights treaties 28–9; implementation gap 27, 38–9; juvenile justice *see* juvenile justice; monitoring bodies 28–9; regional frameworks 29–30; social

431

change through 38–9; sources of 28; standards 27, 27–8, 39; substantive themes 32; top-down approaches to rights 39
Children's Rights Movement: aim of 45; 'autonomous child' concept 98–101; concept of children's rights 117; social work and 98; view of children 45–6
children's rights studies, emergence of 11
citizenship studies: adult citizenship re-theorised through child citizenship 167–8; author's analytical approach 15–16, 164–5; bottom-up approaches to rights 165; child citizenship 166–7, 167–8, 173–4, 174–6; child soldiers 164, 167; children as active citizens 73; CRC implementation 164, 165, 166–7, 168, 169, 170, 171, 173, 174, 176–7; ethnographic studies and 164–5; global citizenship 166–7, 171–3; human rights 164, 169–71, 171–3; indigenous peoples 164; transdisciplinary approach to 174–6
Committee on the Rights of the Child: complaints handling 29; composition of 28; general comments 29, 186–7, 282–4, 303; general principles 31; guidance by 217; Reporting Guidelines 31; reporting procedure 28–9
competence: agency and 88; autonomy and 51; child-images 101; of children to exercise rights 55, 84, 98; gender and 150
consent to medical treatment 221–2
context-specific approach to rights 416–21
Convention see United Nations' Convention on the Rights of the Child 1989 (CRC)
corporal punishment: Committee on the Rights of the Child, General Comment 8 282–4; CRC provisions 35; ECtHR case-law 35–6; in schools 286
corporations see natural resource exploitation
Corsaro, William A, 'interpretive reproduction' theory 70–1
Council of Europe, children's rights framework 30
countries of origin, migration duties 351–2
criminal law see juvenile justice
critical approach to children's rights see also specific topics at 'author's analytical approach': context-specific approach 416–21; critical children's rights studies 426–7; 'critique' and 'criticism' distinguished 10; critiques of children's rights 423–6; dialectic process 10; dimensions of difference in childhood 413–14; dynamic childhoods 412–13, 415–16; elements of 412; ethical stance 10; generational dynamics in defining childhood 414–15; identification of social problems 9–10; interdisciplinary approach 421–3; wider social perspective 10

cultural perspectives see anthropology
cultural relativism: concept of 113, 116; critiques of 116–17; universalism and 119

deaths from violence 286
decision making see participation
deinstitutionalisation see alternative care of children
dependency: autonomy and 50, 74; child development and 66; childhood 82, 83, 88; gender and 150; juvenile justice and 33
deportation see migration
detention of minors, ECtHR case-law 33
development: of children see child development; global see global social development
difference, gender studies of 149, 152, 153, 154, 155, 156, 157, 158, 159
Dionysian child 64
disability see children with disabilities
discrimination, feminist perspectives of 152, 153, 159
due process of law guarantees as to migration 347

education: author's analytical approach 16–17, 201–2; children's experience and ideas of school 77–8; children's rights perspective on 202–3, 210–11; CRC and 202, 208, 211–12; educational research into children's rights issues 211–12; experience-based learning 208; globalisation and 124; human rights perspective on 201–2; indigenous children's rights 380–2; participation in school councils 194–5; participatory processes in 208–9; right to education 36, 36–7, 36–8, 37, 37–8, 38, 201, 203–4, 204–5, 205, 205–6, 206; rights in education 206–7, 207–9, 209–11; student protests against neoliberal reform of 132, 142–3; violence against school children 286
employment see child labour
'erased' children 131–2, 143
ethics of care see gender studies
ethnography see anthropology
European Court of Human Rights (ECtHR): children's rights case-law 30; juvenile justice 33–4
exclusion from school 205–6
expulsion of foreign juvenile offenders, ECtHR case-law 34

fair trial see juvenile justice
family law proceedings, participation in 194–5
family life: corporal punishment 35–6; CRC provisions 34–6; ECtHR case-law 34–6; intergenerational responsibility 89–90; parent-orientation in family law 194; respect for 34–6, 238; right to 348–9; 'right to a family' 268–9, 273; right to protection of 6

family reunification *see* migration
female genital mutilation: abolition 295–6, 312–13; age when performed 296–7; author's analytical approach 18–19, 295–6; categories of 296; as children's rights violation 298–300; CRC and 298–301; cross-cultural best interests argument 299; data on 295; health consequences 297; human rights practice 304–5, 305–6, 306–7, 307, 307–9, 308, 309–11, 311–12; as human rights violation 297–300; 'light' forms as harm-reduction strategy 310–11; participation rights and 311–12; psychological consequences 297; reasons for 296; 'respect for other cultures' argument 306–7; state duties as to regulation 300–4; as violence against children 299
feminist geography 136–7
foreign juvenile offender expulsion, ECtHR case-law 34
'from below', rights *see* bottom-up approaches to rights

gender studies: author's analytical approach 15, 148–9; bottom-up approaches to rights 148, 159; child-images 149–52, 153–4; childhood studies and 150–1; definition of 148; dependency of children 150; developmental theories critiqued 151–2; of difference 149, 152, 153, 154, 155, 156, 157, 158, 159; of discrimination 152, 153, 159; ethics of care 155–9, 160; feminist geography 136–7; 'feminist studies' defined 148; further development of feminist theories 152; gender-biased inequality 147; 'gender-constituting' nature of child/adult relationships 149–50; 'gender' defined 149; incompetence of children 150; of interdependence 156, 159; intersectional theory 148, 152–5, 159; and 'new childhood paradigm' 150; plurality of children's identity 148, 152, 154, 156; socialisation theory critiqued 151; of subordination 147, 148, 149, 152–3, 156, 157; universalist approach to rights critiqued 148, 155–6
'generationing' theory 70–1
geography: author's analytical approach 15, 132–3; *Childhood Matters*, publication of 133; CRC and 135, 139–40, 141, 142; critical rights-based approach to children's geographies 134–5; examples of geographic variability of child rights 131–2, 142–3; feminist perspectives 136–7; global and local perspectives in relation 138–9; heterotopias 138–9; 'maps of consciousness' 135–6; Marxist perspectives 135–6; neoliberal approach to rights critiqued 138–9, 142–3; post-structural relationality 134; 'sites of reproduction' 136–7; top-down approaches to rights 139–40; universalist approach to rights critiqued 139–42; universalist misunderstandings of spatiality 134–5
global social development: child poverty reduction 361–5; children's rights linked with human rights 358; conditions for successful poverty reduction 367–9; deprivation statistics 357; extremely poor people, tables of data 361; ideology of poverty 365–7; intra-generational solidarity 357; poverty and globalisation 358–60; poverty reduction policies 360–1; wider context for poverty reduction 357–8
globalisation: challenges of 89; of childhood 113, 115; of citizenship *see* child citizenship; education and 124; local contexts in relation to 7, 138–9; neoliberalism and 137, 139

health: author's analytical approach 17, 217; barriers to exercising rights 216; children's views on healthcare services 226–7; consent to medical treatment 221–2; CRC and 216–17, 218–21, 229–30; diversity of children's needs 217, 220; feminist study of health care workers 78; health promotion 222–3; home-based health care 137; implementation of children's rights 223, 228–9; participation in decision-making 223–6, 228–9; participation in policy making and service design 226; right to health in international law 217; sexual and reproductive health 222; transdisciplinary approach to 176
heterotopias 138–9
human 'becomings', images of children as 416
human rights: children as bearers of 45–6, 55; children as participatory subjects 73–5; children's rights as 5–7, 45, 202; divergence from children's rights 164; generations of 46; historical background to 46–8; internationalisation of 46–7; regionalisation of 47–8
'human rights inflation' 273
human rights treaties *see also* United Nations' Convention on the Rights of the Child 1989 (CRC): domestic implementation of 30; historical background to 46–8; previous instruments incorporated in CRC 43, 60, 97; relevance to children 28, 29

images *see* child-images
indigenous children: author's analytical approach 20, 371–2; child protection rights 382–3; citizenship issues 164; CRC 371, 371–3, 372, 373–4, 376, 379–80, 383–4; education rights 380–2; 'indigenous peoples' defined 376–7;

Index

international law developments 374–5; participation rights and 372, 378, 380; right to enjoy his or her own culture 377–9; rights appropriation 380
individualism, neoliberalism and 118, 123, 138, 142, 143
institutional care *see* alternative care of children
interdependence: agency and 121; feminist perspectives of 156, 159
interdisciplinary approach to rights 421–3
'interpretive reproduction' theory 67–8
intersectional theory *see* gender studies
intra-generational solidarity and global social development 357

juvenile justice: age limits 242–3; author's analytical approach 17, 236; child-friendly information 249; child-friendly justice 33, 238, 249; complexity of implementation issues 235–6; CRC provisions 33, 254–5; deprivation of liberty 252–4; disposition of cases 250; diversion from judicial proceedings 250–1; ECtHR case-law 33–4; expulsion of foreign offenders 34; extreme sentences 251–2; gap between international and national human rights standards 234–5; guidance from international organisations and NGOs 238–9; international standards 236–7; minimum age of criminal responsibility (MACR) 33–4, 243–4; minors in pre-trial detention 33; non-custodial sentences 251–2; objectives of 240–2; participation rights and 235, 236, 238, 246, 248–50; protection of society as objective of 235; public concerns about crime 235; regional standards 237–8; rehabilitation as objective of 235; restorative justice 250–1; right to fair trial 246, 247–8, 248–50; sentencing 251–2; separation, specificity and specialisation 239–40; standard-setting 33; upper age limit 244–6

labour *see* child labour
law *see* children's rights law; family law proceedings; juvenile justice
Lenzer, Gertrud, origin of childhood studies 62, 276
lifeworlds: coexisting interpretations of 10; 'lifeworld orientation' and social work 104–6
'living rights' *see* bottom-up approaches to rights
long-term sick children, image of 61

'maps of consciousness' 135–6
Marxist geography 135–6
medical treatment *see* health
migration: asylum-seekers 86; author's analytical approach 19–20, 332; categories of children 333; child rights-based perspective 332, 353; children born to migrant parents in host countries 334–5; children left behind by migrant parents 334; children migrating with their families 334; children's invisibility 331; children's rights implementation challenges summarised 352–3; CRC and 331–2, 339–41; deported children 335–6; due process of law guarantees 347; duties of countries of origin 351–2; family reunification 334, 336, 339, 340, 345, 348, 349, 351; growth of 331; irregular migration status 333, 334, 335, 336, 337, 338, 339, 343–4, 345, 346, 347, 348, 349, 350; migration control policies and 341–2; non-deportation principle 342–5; non-detention principle 345–7; parents' detention and deportation 347–8; participation right 340, 342, 347; repatriated/returned children 335–6; right to education 37–8, 206; right to family life 348–9; root causes of, and rights-based policy approaches 336–9; separated children 333–4; social rights of migrants 349–51; unaccompanied children 333–4
minimum age of criminal responsibility: CRC provisions 33; ECtHR case-law 33–4
'minority group child', image of 68
minors in pre-trial detention, ECtHR case-law 33

natural resource exploitation: author's analytical approach 20–1, 387; business-related standards 393; case studies 390–2; challenge of 387, 406–7; child-images 388, 389; child-specificity of issues and rights 403–5; children's rights 396–8; Committee on the Rights of the Child 401–3; context-specific approach to rights 406–7; diversity of children and young people 388; diversity of exploitation activities 388; future research priorities 407; human rights cases 398–400; human rights standards 393–6; impacts of 388–9; insights from non-legal disciplines 405; legal standards 392–3; need for national responses 406; participation rights and 391, 396, 397, 398, 403; policies 389–90
neoliberalism *see also* top-down approaches to rights: alternatives to 74; CRC and 140; dominance of 123; education reform 132, 137, 142–3; 'erased' children and 143; exclusion of the young by 121; globalisation and 137, 139; individualism and 118, 123, 138, 142, 143; larger neoliberal agenda 139; origin of 142; universal autonomous child 141
normal child, image of 63, 64
'not-yet' status of children 45, 55

Organization of American States (OAS), children's rights framework 29
'Other' than the adult, image of child as 65, 415

parents: advice from childcare experts 79; and alternative care of children 257–64, 266, 267, 270; and 'autonomous child' 98, 100–1; and child labour 317–18, 326, 357, 364–5; and children's agency 158, 170–1, 210; children's rights in relation to 6, 72, 206, 211, 212; and corporal punishment 35–6; and 'critical perspective' on children's rights 10; death of 86; detention and deportation 347–8; and education 36, 121, 204–5; family law proceedings 189–92, 194; and female genital mutilation 297, 299, 300, 305, 306, 307, 308, 312; gendering by 151; and health 216, 218, 220, 221, 222, 223, 224, 228; indigenous children 381, 388; interdependency with 121; and juvenile justice 241, 245, 247, 249, 251; migration see migration; and natural resource exploitation 392, 404; negotiations with 83, 100; parental risks 72; parenting support 100; participation in rights making 73, 105, 106; and poverty 363, 368; representations of 113, 114, 115, 118, 149–50; responsibility of 80–1, 88–9, 125, 150; separation from 34–5, 288, 382; and violence against children 279, 280, 281, 290
participation: agency and 196, 413, 416; author's analytical approach 16, 186; autonomy and 72; children's participatory self-determination 72–5; context-specific approach 417, 419; critiques of 194–6; definition of participation 186–7; emerging themes as to 196; mainstreaming of 194–7; national implementation of CRC 189–94; origins of 185; participation principle in CRC 50, 84, 185–7, 196–7; principle of 31, 32, 194; in specific areas see specific topics; transformative projects for 195–6; typologies of participation 187–9
policy making see participation
post-structural relationality 134
poverty: and global social development see global social development; as violence against children 287
pragmatic trend in children's rights 55
pre-trial detention of minors, ECtHR case-law 33
pregnancy, healthcare provision 222
protection of children see child protection
provision principle in CRC 50
'purist' approaches see top-down approaches to rights

Qvortrup, Jens, *Childhood Matters* 133

refugees see migration
relationality, post-structural 134
repatriation see migration
reproductive healthcare provision 222
'resourcist view' of agency 105
respect for family life see family life
respect for the views of the child, principle of 31
returned children see migration
'right to a family' 268–9, 273
right to education see education
right 'to enjoy his or her own culture' 377–9
right to equality, principle of 31
right to fair trial see juvenile justice
right to family life see family life
right to health see health
right to life, survival and development 31, 32
right to non-discrimination, principle of 31–2
right to participation see participation
risk see children at risk
Roma children, right to education 37

school see education
school councils, participation in 194–5
segregation issues in education 205
self-determination: agency and 5; children as participatory subjects 72–3
separated children see migration
sexual and reproductive health 222
sexual healthcare provision 222
'sites of reproduction' 136–7
social actors, children as 70, 72–3, 79, 83, 98, 112, 114, 141, 150–1
social change through children's rights law 38–9
social constructs of children and childhood, changes in 44–5
social development see global social development
social work: as academic discipline 94–5; author's analytical approach 14, 95; child-images 98–101; and children's agency 98; children's rights 105–6; children's rights movement and 98–101; fragmented identity of 95–8; and institutionalisation of childhood 101–4; international definition of 94–5; learning process as to children's rights 106; and 'lifeworld orientation' 104–6; limitations for children's rights research 107; relational social work 97–8; relational tradition 97–8; 'resourcist view' of children's rights 105; structural tradition 98
socialisation theory, critiques of 151
'socially constructed child', image of 69
'socially developing child', image of 68
'sociological child' theory 68–9
sociology of childhood: author's analytical approach 13–14, 78; childhood studies

435

distinguished from 61–2; childhood studies in relation to 66; children and division of labour 80, 84–5; children as distinct social group 79–81; children's dependency on family 88–9; children's rights and 84–5; critical approach to 78; dimensions to rights 81; emergence of 133; 'generationing' theory 70–1; globalisation, challenges of 89; insights from from research studies 85–8; intergenerational responsibility in families 89–90; 'interpretive reproduction' theory (Corsaro) 67–8; local understandings of childhood, importance of 88; relational approaches 78, 79; relationship between childhood and adulthood 82–4; respect for children's rights 81, 85; 'sociological child' theory 68–9; sociological perspectives, value of 78; structural approaches 78–81

space *see* geography

student protests against neoliberal education reform 132, 142–3

subordination, feminist perspectives of 147, 148, 149, 152–3, 156, 157

suspension from school 205–6

teachers *see* education

top-down approaches to rights: alternative care of children 273; anthropology 113, 119–22, 126; children's rights law 39; education 212; female genital mutilation 311; generally 1–2, 417; geography 139–40; participation 192, 196

'tribal child', image of 69

unaccompanied children *see* migration

undocumented migrants, right to education 37–8

United Nations' Convention on the Rights of the Child 1989 (CRC): adoption of 1, 43, 47, 60, 117, 234, 276; age related definitions in 82; ambiguity towards children's agency 71; anthropological perspectives on 113, 115, 117; application of 2; binding force of 52; bottom-up approaches to rights 56; characteristics of 48; child-images 48, 50–2, 244; as children's human rights 202; children's participation *see* participation; children's status under 118; citizenship perspectives on 164, 165, 166–7, 168, 169, 170, 171, 173, 174, 176–7; compliance with *see* Committee on the Rights of the Child; comprehensiveness of 49; cultural sensitiveness of 117, 123–4; diverse perspectives incorporated in 5; drafting of 6, 79, 85, 89; education

perspectives on 208, 211–12; as framework for children's rights debate 43, 55–6; general principles 5, 31–2, 49–50; geographical perspectives on 135, 139–40, 141, 142; globalisation of childhood 113, 115; health perspectives *see* health; historical background to 12–13, 44, 60–1; holistic childhood image in 50–2; as human rights convention 77; in human rights framework 5–6; implementation and interpretation principles 49; implementation in national laws 86–7, 164, 174, 189–94; implementation in specific topics *see specific topics*; implementation monitoring 2, 52, 52–4, 54–5; as instrument for change 60, 234; legal perspectives *see* children's rights law; juvenile justice; minimum standards 5, 52; neoliberalism and 140; optional protocols 5, 28, 43; participation *see* participation; parties to 5, 28, 43–4; preamble 48; previous instruments incorporated in CRC 43, 60, 97; protection principle 50; provision principle 50; ratification of 5, 28, 43–4, 78, 124, 173, 234; as reference point in children's rights development 2, 276; scope of 31; as separate Convention for children 47–8; sociological perspectives on 81, 83, 85, 86; structure of 28, 48; young people's participation *see* participation

universal autonomous child 141

universalism: and cultural relativism 119; feminist critiques of 148, 155–6; geography and 139–42; spatiality and 134–5

violence against children *see also* corporal punishment; female genital mutilation: author's analytical approach 18; bottom-up approach to rights 287–9; case study 284–5, 286, 287; child protection emphasis of CRC 277; Committee on the Rights of the Child, general comments 282–3, 291; emergence of concept of 278; female genital mutilation as 299; *Hidden in Plain Sight: A Statistical Analysis* (2014) 291–2; participation rights and 280, 287–9, 290–1; progress on abolition 291; research on effects of 289–90; Special Representative of the Secretary General 281–2; *World Report* (2006) 277, 278–9, 279–80, 280–1

vulnerability: agency and 12; child-images 402, 404

women *see* feminist geography

work *see* child labour

CPSIA information can be obtained
at www.ICGtesting.com
Printed in the USA
LVHW060215210421
685093LV00008B/262